New York City

written and researched by

Martin Dunford and **Jack Holland**

revised and updated by

Nicky Agate, **Todd Obolsky** and **Nelson Taylor**

www.roughguides.com

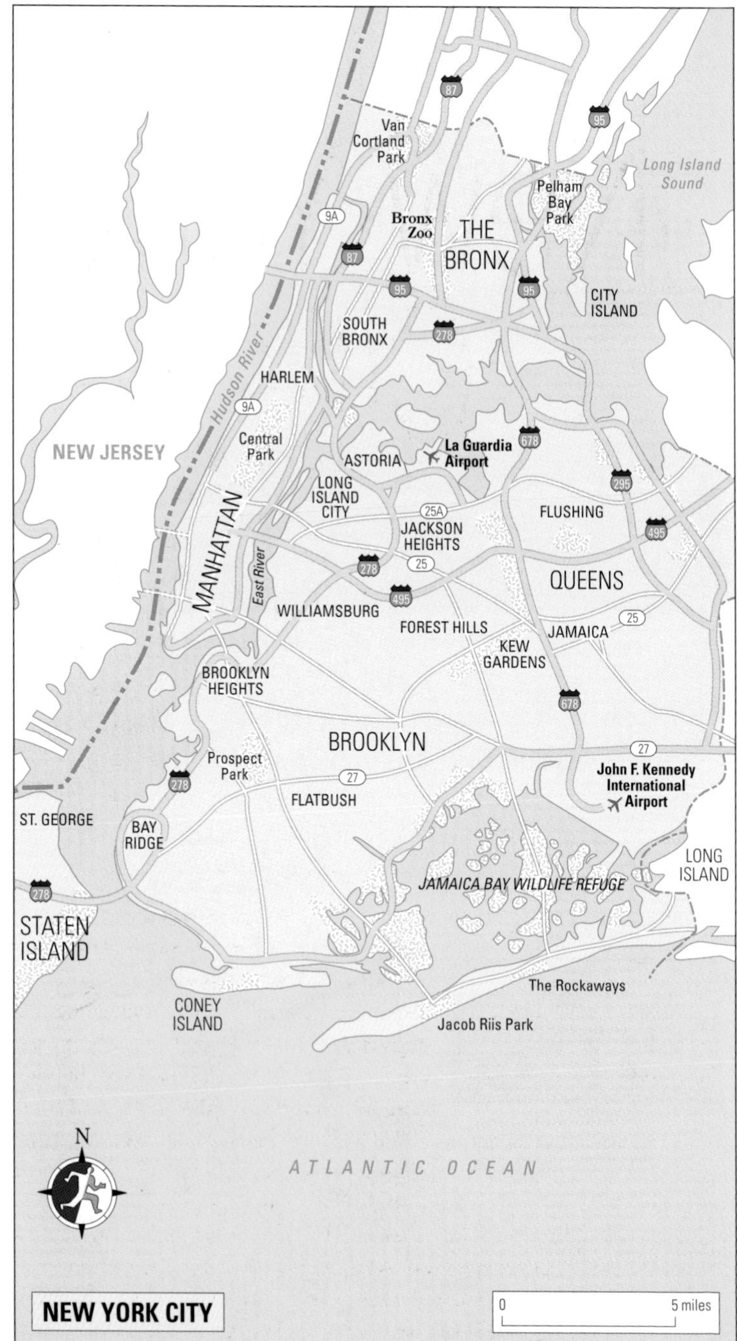

Van Cortland Park
Long Island Sound
Pelham Bay Park
Bronx Zoo
THE BRONX
CITY ISLAND
SOUTH BRONX
Hudson River
HARLEM
NEW JERSEY
Central Park
ASTORIA
La Guardia Airport
LONG ISLAND CITY
FLUSHING
JACKSON HEIGHTS
MANHATTAN
East River
QUEENS
WILLIAMSBURG
FOREST HILLS
JAMAICA
KEW GARDENS
BROOKLYN HEIGHTS
BROOKLYN
Prospect Park
John F. Kennedy International Airport
FLATBUSH
ST. GEORGE
BAY RIDGE
LONG ISLAND
JAMAICA BAY WILDLIFE REFUGE
STATEN ISLAND
The Rockaways
CONEY ISLAND
Jacob Riis Park
N
ATLANTIC OCEAN
NEW YORK CITY
0
5 miles

Introduction to

New York City

The most beguiling city in the world, New York is an adrenaline-charged, history-laden place that holds immense romantic appeal for visitors. Wandering the streets here, you'll cut between buildings that are icons to the modern age – and whether gazing at the flickering lights of the midtown skyscrapers as you speed across the Queensboro Bridge, experiencing the 4am half-life downtown, or just wasting the morning on the Staten Island ferry, you really would have to be made of stone not to be moved by it all. There's no place quite like it.

While the events of September 11, 2001, which demolished the World Trade Center, shook New York to its core, the populace responded resiliently under the composed aegis of then-Mayor Rudy Giuliani. Until the attacks, many New Yorkers loved to hate Giuliani, partly because they saw him as committed to making their city too much like everyone else's. To some extent he succeeded, and during the late Nineties New York seemed cleaner, safer and more liveable, as the city took on a truly international allure and shook off the more notorious aspects of its reputation. However, the maverick quality of New York and its people still shines as brightly as it ever did. Even in the aftermath of the World Trade Center's collapse, New York remains a unique and fascinating city – and one you'll want to return to again and again.

What to see

You could spend weeks in New York and still barely scratch the surface, but there are some key attractions – and some pleasures – that you won't want to miss. There are the different **ethnic neighborhoods**, like lower Manhattan's Chinatown; and the more artsy concentrations of SoHo, TriBeCa, and the East and West Villages. Of course, there is the celebrated **architecture** of corporate Manhattan; and there are the **museums**, not just the Metropolitan and MoMA, but countless other smaller collections that afford weeks of happy wandering. In between sights, you can **eat** just about anything, at any time, cooked in any style; you can **drink** in any kind of company; and sit through any number of obscure **movies**. The more established arts – **dance**, **theater**, **music** – are superbly catered for; and New York's **clubs** are as varied and exciting as you might expect. For the avid consumer, the choice of **shops** is vast, almost numbingly exhaustive in this heartland of the great capitalist dream.

Some orientation and highlights

New York City comprises the central island of Manhattan along with four outer boroughs – Brooklyn, Queens, the Bronx and Staten Island. Manhattan, to many, *is* New York. Certainly, whatever your interest in the city it's here that you'll spend the most time, and, unless you have friends elsewhere, are likely to stay. Understanding the intricacies of Manhattan's layout, and above all getting some grasp on its subway and bus system, should be your first priority. Most importantly, you should realize that New York is very much a city of neighborhoods, and one that is best explored on foot – a fact reflected in the chapters of this guide, which we've divided to reflect the best walking tours. For an overview of each neighborhood, and what to see and do there, turn to the introduction of each chapter.

Downtown, Uptown: The layout of Manhattan

Despite its **grid-pattern** arrangement, Manhattan can seem a wearyingly complicated place to get around – blocks of streets and avenues, apparently straightforward on the map, can be uniquely confusing on foot, and too many subway lines just don't meet up where you would expect them to (and are sometimes poorly marked underground). Don't be daunted by subways and buses, though, since with a little know-how you'll find them efficient and fast. And if you're at all unsure, just ask – New Yorkers are accurate direction-givers and take a surprising interest in initiating visitors into the great mysteries of their city. You should also bear in mind that you'll hear the terms "lower Manhattan," "midtown" and "upper Manhattan." Roughly speaking, **lower Manhattan** runs from the southern tip of the island to around 14th Street; **midtown Manhattan** stretches from about 34th Street to the southern tip of Central Park; and **upper Manhattan** contains the park itself, the neighborhoods on either side of it, and the whole area to the north. From north to south the island of Manhattan is about thirteen miles long and from east to west around two miles wide. Whatever is north of where you're standing is **uptown**; whatever south, **downtown**. East or west is **crosstown** (hence "crosstown buses"). The southern – downtown – part of Manhattan was first to be settled, which means that its streets have names and that they're somewhat randomly arranged; similarly, the tangle of West Village is difficult to navigate, and you can waste much time wondering how W 4th and W 11th streets could possibly intersect. Above Houston Street on the East Side, 14th Street on the West, the streets are numbered and follow a strict grid pattern. The numbers of these streets increase as you move north. Up as far as 59th Street, **Fifth Avenue**, the greatest of the big north–south avenues, cuts through the center of Manhattan and serves as a dividing line between the **East Side** and the **West Side**. Above here, Central Park, does Fifth's job for about fifty blocks, separating the Upper West and Upper East Sides. **House numbers** increase as you walk away from either side of Fifth Avenue; numbers on avenues increase as you move north.

Skyscrapers

Along with Chicago, Kuala Lumpur and Hong Kong, Manhattan is one of the best places in the world in which to view **skyscrapers**, its puckered, almost medieval skyline of towers the city's most familiar and striking image. In fact there are only two main clusters of skyscrapers, but they set the tone for the city – the Financial District, where the combination of narrow streets and tall buildings forms slender, lightless canyons, and midtown Manhattan, where the big skyscrapers have long competed for height and prestige. The first generally recognized skyscraper in New York was the Flatiron Building on Madison Square (see p.130), designed in 1902, not least for the obvious way its triangular shape made the most of the new iron-frame technique of construction that had made such structures possible. A few years later, in 1913, New York clinched the title of the world's tallest building with the sixty-story Woolworth Building on lower Broadway, and went on to produce such landmarks as the Chrysler and Empire State buildings, and, more recently, the World Trade Center, whose destruction the city witnessed on September 11, 2001.

Styles have changed over the years, perhaps most influenced by the stringency of the city's zoning laws, which, early in the century, placed restrictions on the types of building permitted. At first skyscrapers were sheer vertical monsters, maximizing the floor space possible from any given site with no regard to how this affected neighboring buildings. City authorities later invented the concept of "air rights," limiting how high a building could be before it had to be set back from its base. This forced skyscrapers to be designed in a series of steps – a law most elegantly adhered to by the Empire State Building (see p.132), which has no less than ten steps in all – and is a pattern you will see repeated all over the city.

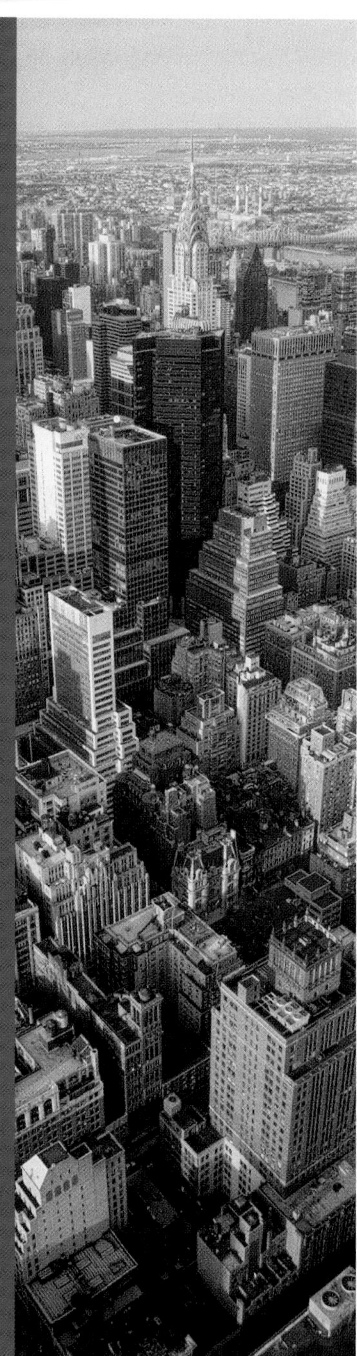

The guide starts at the southern tip of the island and moves north: **The Harbor Islands** comprises the first section of New York (and America) that most nineteenth-century immigrants would have seen – the Statue of Liberty and Ellis Island, the latter recalling its history in its excellent Museum of Immigration. The **Financial District** takes in the skyscrapers and historic buildings of Manhattan's southern reaches, although the most famous aspect of the skyline down here, the World Trade Center, sadly no longer exists, and the area immediately around was still off-limits at the time of writing. Just east is the area around **City Hall**, New York's well-appointed municipal center. North of here, **Chinatown** is Manhattan's most populous ethnic neighborhood, a vibrant locale that's great for Chinese food and shopping. Nearby, **Little Italy** bears few traces of the once-strong immigrant presence, while the **Lower East Side** is the city's traditional gateway neighborhood for new immigrants – originally German, then Jewish, now Hispanic and increasingly Chinese – and is nowadays scattered with some interesting and often trendy bars and clubs. To the west, **SoHo** is one of the premiere districts for galleries and the commercial art scene, not to mention designer shopping – much like its even swankier neighbor **TriBeCa**, just to the south, on the edge of the Financial District. North, the **West** and **East Villages** form a focus of bars, restaurants and shops catering to students and would-be bohemians – and of course tourists. **Chelsea** is a largely residential neighborhood that is now mostly known for its gay scene and art galleries and borders on Manhattan's old **Garment District**. **Murray Hill** contains the city's largest skyscraper and most enduring symbol, the Empire State Building.

New York is very much a city of neighborhoods, and one that is best explored on foot

Beyond **42nd Street**, the main east-west artery of midtown, the character of the city changes quite radically, and the skyline becomes more high-rise and home to some of New York's most awe-inspiring, neck-cricking architecture. There are also some superb museums and the city's best shopping as you work your way north up **Fifth Avenue** as far as 59th Street, where the classic Manhattan vistas are broken by the broad expanse of **Central Park**, a supreme piece of nineteenth-century landscaping, without which life in

Can I eat that?

One thing you're going to be doing a lot of in New York is eating. There's really no better place to sample all the cuisines of the world, and you should try to experiment if you can. There are, however, some things the city does particularly well. Jewish-American deli fare is great – overstuffed brisket and pastrami sandwiches, great smoked fish and bagels, latkes, and chopped liver; there's excellent Chinese food all over the city, but particularly in Chinatown; you can't move for Japanese food and sushi bars; Brazilian, Ethiopian and Korean cuisines all have their loyal partisans and there are always the great, classic New York steakhouses, if you're feeling especially ravenous. Slick establishments abound that ape provincial France, bring together the regional cuisines of Italy, or simply follow the trends of electic, modern American cooking. Check these out if you can afford them, even if you have no idea what you're eating because it's so covered in withered greens or shards of truffle. Our extensive restaurant recommendations begin on p.313.

Manhattan would be unthinkable. Flanking the park, the mostly residential and fairly affluent **Upper West Side** boasts Lincoln Center, Manhattan's temple to the performing arts, the American Museum of Natural History and Riverside Park along the Hudson River. On the other side of the park, the **Upper East Side** is wealthier and more grandiose, with its nineteenth-century millionaires' mansions now transformed into a string of magnificent museums known as the "Museum Mile," the most prominent being the vast **Metropolitan Museum of Art**. Alongside is a patrician residential neighborhood that boasts some of the swankiest addresses in Manhattan, and a nest of designer shops along Madison Avenue in the seventies. Immediately above Central Park, **Harlem**, the historic black city-within-a-city whose name was for a long time synonymous with racial tension and urban deprivation, has today a healthy sense of an improving go-ahead community – a trend not hindered at all by former President Clinton deciding to set up his offices on 125th Street, Harlem's main drag. Further north still, **Washington Heights**, a largely Hispanic neighborhood that few visitors ever venture to visit, features the unusual Cloisters, a nineteenth-century mock-up of a medieval monastery, packed with great

European Romanesque and Gothic art and (transplanted) architecture – in short, one of Manhattan's must-sees.

It's a fact that few visitors, especially those with limited time, bother to venture off Manhattan Island and out to the outer boroughs, which is a pity, because each of them – **Brooklyn, the Bronx**, **Queens** and **Staten Island** – has points of great interest, both from an historical and a contemporary point of view. Some of the city's best ethnic neighborhoods, and consequently best food, is to be found in the outer boroughs. The more frequented destinations include the picturesque streets of Brooklyn Heights, just across the Brooklyn Bridge from Manhattan, and the old-world charm of Coney Island and the nearby Russian enclave of Brighton Beach. But get out too, if you can, to sample the Greek seafood restaurants of Astoria in Queens, the Italian restaurants of the Bronx's Belmont section or the hip nightlife of increasingly trendy Williamsburg in Brooklyn – to name just a few options.

When to go

New York's **climate** ranges from the stickily hot and humid in midsummer to well below freezing in January and February: deep midwinter and high summer (many people find the city unbearable in July and August) are much the worst time you could come. Spring is gentle, if unpredictable, and usually wet, while fall is perhaps the best season: come at either time and you'll find it easier to get things done and the people more welcoming. Whatever time of year you come, dress in layers: buildings tend to be overheated during winter months and air-conditioned to the point of iciness in summer. Also bring comfortable and sturdy shoes – you're going to be doing a lot of walking.

Average New York monthly temperatures and rainfall

	Temp °F		Temp °C		Rainfall	
	max	min	max	min	inches	mm
January	**38**	**26**	**3**	**-3**	**3.5**	**89**
February	40	27	4	-3	3.1	79
March	**50**	**35**	**10**	**2**	**4.0**	**102**
April	61	44	16	7	3.8	97
May	**72**	**54**	**22**	**12**	**4.4**	**112**
June	80	63	27	17	3.6	91
July	**85**	**69**	**29**	**21**	**4.4**	**112**
August	84	67	29	19	4.1	104
September	**76**	**60**	**24**	**16**	**4.0**	**102**
October	65	50	18	10	3.4	86
November	**54**	**41**	**12**	**5**	**4.4**	**112**
December	43	31	6	-1	3.8	97

31

things not to miss

It's not possible to see everything that New York City has to offer in one trip – and we don't suggest you try. What follows is a selective taste of the city's highlights: its best museums, most memorable restaurants, greatest architecture and most vibrant neighborhoods. They're arranged in five color-coded categories, which you can browse through to find the very best things to see and experience. All highlights have a page reference to take you straight into the guide, where you can find out more.

01 Grand Central Station tours Page **138** • Take a free Wednesday lunchtime tour of this magnificent building, featuring the station's majestic concourse.

02 Gotham Bar & Grill Page **326** • One of the city's priciest dining experiences, but the service, environment and, of course, the food are all impeccable.

03 Unicorn tapestries Page **232** • There's plenty at the Cloisters Museum to tempt you this far up Manhattan, most notably the recently restored fifteenth- and sixteenth-century unicorn tapestries.

04 Coney Island Page **252** • Eat a hot dog at *Nathan's* and take a ride on the Cyclone rollercoaster – not necessarily in that order.

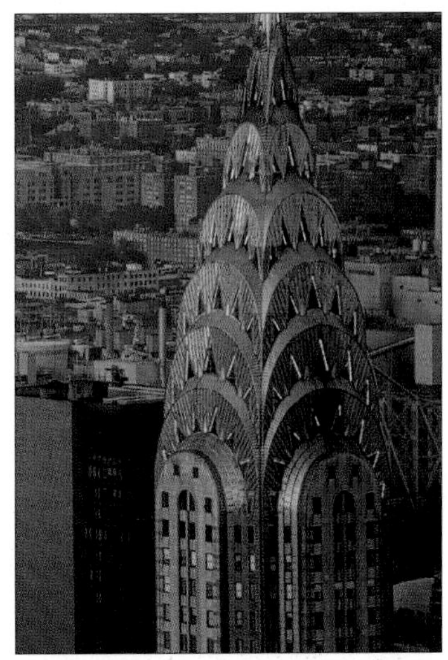

05 Chrysler Building Page **139** • Inside, you may not be able to view much more than the lobby, but this building perhaps defines New York's skyline more than any other.

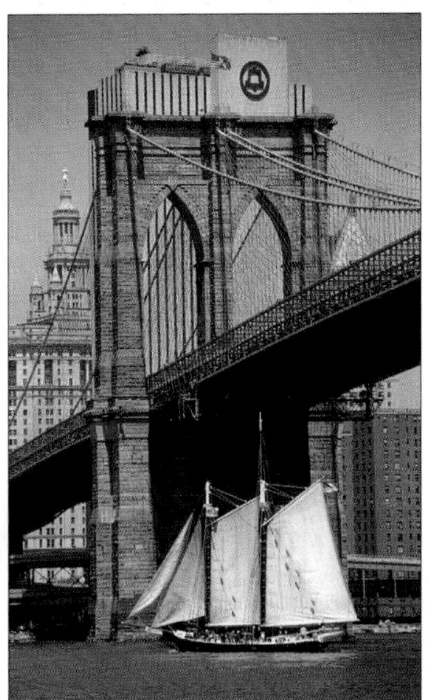

06 Brooklyn Bridge Page **77** • Take the less-than-a-mile walk across the bridge, taking in the skyline of the Financial District as well as the Harbor Islands.

07 St John the Divine Page **216** • Admire the splendor of the largest cathedral in North America.

08 Katz's Deli Page **319** • A slice of the old Lower East Side, with overstuffed sandwiches served to you by the wisecracking guys behind the counter.

09 Radio City Music Hall tours Page **145** • The tours of this Art Deco gem are a midtown must.

10 New York Stock Exchange tour Page **61** • Turn up early to see where the purse strings of the western world are pulled.

11 The Knitting Factory Page **369** • Head downtown to hear one of the *Knitting Factory*'s eclectic jazz, rock or klezmer shows.

12 Central Park Page **165** • Whether taking a boat ride, watching Shakespeare in the Park or picnicking in the Conservatory Garden after going to a museum, you'll find everything about Central Park fantastic.

13 Chinatown Page **83** • Manhattan's bustling, most densely packed neighborhood – come here to eat, shop for Asian delicacies or just to wander around.

14 New York Public Library Page **136** • This Beaux Arts masterpiece contains one of the largest circulating libraries in the world.

15 The Frick Collection Page **190** • He may have been a ruthless coal baron, but Henry Frick's discerning eye for art and the easy elegance of his collection's setting make this perhaps the city's best gallery.

16 Zabar's Page **209** • This classic New York deli features gourmet food and Jewish "appetizing."

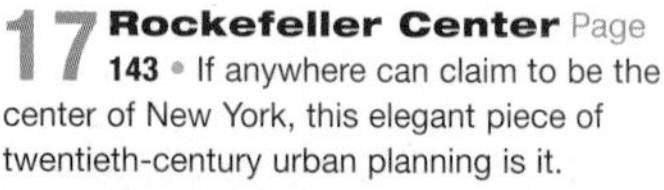

17 Rockefeller Center Page **143** • If anywhere can claim to be the center of New York, this elegant piece of twentieth-century urban planning is it.

18 Baseball at Yankee Stadium Page **266** • If you're here between April and October, it would be a shame not to take in a ballgame, and there's no better place than the Bronx location they call, simply, "The Stadium."

19 Macy's Page **123** • Quite simply the largest department store in the world, it still retains something of an old-fashioned charm.

20 Ellis Island Page **57** • America is a country established by immigrants, and for many this building was where it all began.

21 The Metropolitan Museum of Art Page **174** • You can easily spend a whole day at the Met, exploring everything from Egyptian artifacts to modern masters.

22 The Fulton Fish Market Page **72** • Catch the smells and the frenzy of the Fulton Fish Market at 5am.

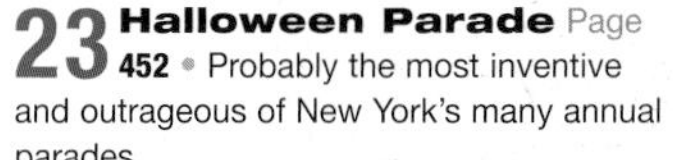

23 Halloween Parade Page **452** • Probably the most inventive and outrageous of New York's many annual parades.

24 Bronx Zoo Page **268** • There are lots of reasons to make a trip to the Bronx, but this long-established yet innovative and humane zoo is perhaps the best.

25 Sylvia's Restaurant in Harlem Page **346** • Sample the celebrated soulfood at *Sylvia's*, a Harlem institution for forty years.

26 Empire State Building Page **132** • Probably the most original and elegant skyscraper of them all.

30 Lower East Side Tenement Museum Page **92** • The excellent guided tours of preserved nineteenth-century tenements make this one of New York's most informative and moving museums.

27 Strand Bookstore Page **422** • With around eight miles of used books, this is the secondhand bookstore *par excellence*.

28 The Esplanade at Brooklyn Heights Page **239** • This boardwalk-cum-park serves as the backyard to some of Brooklyn's finest apartment buildings – and has views of downtown Manhattan to match.

29 The Nuyorican Cafe Page **107** • Check out a poetry slam at the *Nuyorican Café*, an East Village standby.

31 A Night at the Opera Page **208** • Put on your gladrags for a night out at the Met – New York's spectacular opera house.

contents

Using the Rough Guide

We've tried to make this Rough Guide a good read and easy to use. The book is divided into six main sections, and you should be able to find whatever you want in one of them.

front section

The front color section offers a quick tour of New York. The **introduction** aims to give you a feel for the city, with suggestions on where to go and information on what the weather is like. Our authors then round up their favorite aspects of New York in the **things not to miss** section – whether it's great food, amazing sights or a special museum. Right after this, comes the Rough Guide's full **contents** list.

basics

You've decided to go and the basics section covers all the **pre-departure** information to help you plan your trip. This is where to find out which airlines fly to your destination, what to do about money and insurance, about internet access, food, security, public transport, car rental – in fact just about every piece of **general practical information** you might need.

guide

This is the heart of the Rough Guide, divided into user-friendly chapters, each of which covers a specific neighborhood. Every chapter contains an **introduction** that helps you to decide where to go, depending on your time and interests. Similarly, accounts of the various smaller areas within each chapter should help you plan your itinerary and tour the individual sights.

listings

This section offers critical **reviews** of the city's hotels, restaurants, bars, shops, and theaters, as well as detailed information on festivals, galleries and kids' New York.

contexts

Read Contexts to get a deeper understanding of how New York City ticks. We include a brief **history**, an article about **modern American art** together with a detailed section that reviews numerous **books** and **films** relating to the city.

index and small print

Apart from a **full index**, which includes maps as well as places, this section covers publishing information, credits and acknowledgments, and also has our contact details in case you want to send in updates and corrections to the book – or suggestions as to how we might improve it.

contents ▸

basics ▸

guide ▸

listings ▸

contexts ▸

index ▸

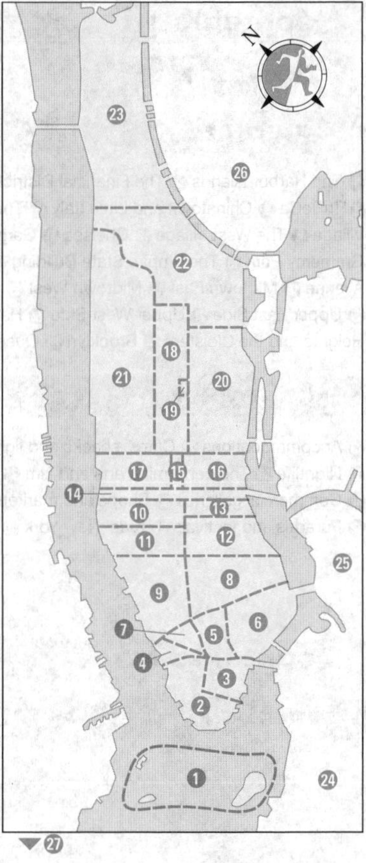

contents

front section i–xvi

basics 9–51

guide 52–277

listings 278–464

contexts 465–510

index and small print 511–522

color maps at back of book

map symbols

maps are listed in the full index using colored text

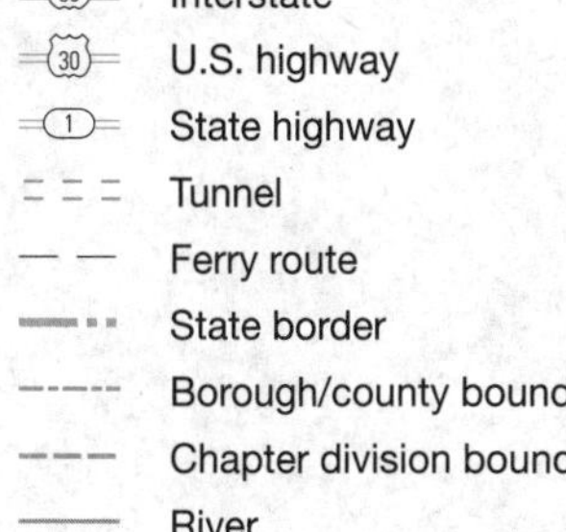

- Interstate
- U.S. highway
- State highway
- Tunnel
- Ferry route
- State border
- Borough/county boundary
- Chapter division boundary
- River
- Airport
- Subway station
- Information center
- Post office
- Synagogue
- Buddhist temple
- Building
- Church
- Cemetery
- Park/wildlife refuge

basics

basics

Getting there

Unless you are coming from close by on the east coast, the quickest and easiest way of getting to New York is by flying into one of its three major airports, John F. Kennedy, Newark or La Guardia (see "Arrival" on p.19 for specific details on each). Your cost will depend on where you're coming from and when, but New York is going to be on every major airline's itinerary, so you shouldn't want for choice. The highest fares will be May through September and mid-December through early January, though if you're traveling within the US there will be a lot less seasonal variance.

You can often cut costs by going through a specialist flight agent – either a consolidator, who buys up blocks of tickets from the airlines and sells them at a discount, or a discount agent, who in addition to dealing with discounted flights may also offer special student and youth fares and a range of other travel-related services such as travel

Online booking agents and general travel sites

ⓦ **travel.yahoo.com** Incorporates a lot of Rough Guide material in its coverage of destination countries and cities across the world, with information about places to eat, sleep and other practicalities.
ⓦ **www.cheapflights.com** Flight deals, travel agents, plus links to other travel sites.
ⓦ **www.cheaptickets.com** Discount flight specialists.
ⓦ **www.deckchair.com** Bob Geldof's online venture, drawing on a wide range of airlines.
ⓦ **www.etn.nl/discount.htm** A hub of consolidator and discount agent web links, maintained by the nonprofit European Travel Network.
ⓦ **www.expedia.com** Discount airfares, all-airline search engine and daily deals.
ⓦ **www.flyaow.com** Online air travel info and reservations site.
ⓦ **www.gaytravel.com** Gay online travel agent, concentrating mostly on accommodation.
ⓦ **www.hotwire.com** Bookings from the US only. Last-minute savings of up to forty percent on regular published fares. Travelers must be at least 18 and there are no refunds, transfers or changes allowed. Log-in required.
ⓦ **www.lastminute.com** Offers good last-minute holiday packages and flight-only deals.
ⓦ **www.priceline.com** Bookings from the US only. Name-your-own-price website that has deals at around forty percent off standard fares. You cannot specify flight times (although you do specify dates) and the tickets are non-refundable, non-transferable and non-changeable.
ⓦ **www.princeton.edu/Main/air800.html** Has an extensive list of airline toll-free numbers and websites.
ⓦ **www.skyauction.com** Bookings from within the US only. Auctions tickets and travel packages using a "second bid" scheme. The best strategy is to bid the maximum you're willing to pay, since if you win you'll pay just enough to beat the runner-up regardless of your maximum bid.
ⓦ **www.smilinjack.com/airlines.htm** Lists an up-to-date compilation of airline website addresses.
ⓦ **www.travelocity.com** Destination guides, hot web fares and best deals for car hire, accommodation and lodging as well as fares. Provides access to the travel agent system SABRE, the most comprehensive central reservations system in the US.
ⓦ **www.travel.priceline.co.uk** British version of priceline.com.
ⓦ **www.travelshop.com.au** Australian website offering discounted flights, packages, insurance, online bookings.
ⓦ **www.uniquetravel.com.au** Australian site with a good range of packages and good value flights.

insurance, rail passes, car rentals, tours and the like. Some agents specialize in charter flights, which may be cheaper than anything available on a scheduled flight, but again departure dates are fixed and withdrawal penalties are high. Package trips, in which accommodation, sometimes even Broadway tickets, is included along with the flight, can also work out to be less expensive.

Another option if traveling from the US or Canada is to go by **train, bus or car**, though these inevitably take much longer than a plane and sometimes work out no cheaper.

Booking flights online

Many airlines and discount travel **websites** offer you the opportunity to book your tickets online, which may cut out the costs of agents and middlemen. Good deals can often be found through discount or auction sites, as well as through the airlines' own websites.

Flights and other approaches from the US and Canada

From most places in North America, **flying** is the fastest and easiest way to reach New York. It can also be the cheapest – but finding that cheap fare won't always be easy. Fares fluctuate wildly, and it doesn't make sense to try to quote them here. Even the shuttles – flights used mainly by business people during the week – from nearby Boston and Washington, DC, can vary from month to month.

Regardless, New York is a **major hub** for North American traffic. Prices depend more on passenger volume than anything else, so you'll do better (if you have a choice) flying from a large city. Call the major airlines as early as possible – even earlier if you're traveling at Thanksgiving or Christmas – because cheap fares usually account for only a portion of the seats available on a given flight. It's not impossible to get a last-minute deal, but on the major airlines cheapest fares usually require you to purchase your ticket 14 or 21 days in advance and stay a Saturday night. Keep an eye open for any special promotional fares. The smaller airlines often pitch in with cheaper deals. Travel agents won't necessarily find you a better fare so much as save you the trouble of phoning yourself. Round-trip fares from the West Coast tend to average around $425, though can be as little as $325; from Chicago it's about $250 and roughly $200 from Miami. From Canada, reckon on paying CAN$340 or so from Toronto or Montréal and about CAN$840 from Vancouver. Change fees on most major airlines have risen to $100, so be sure of your schedule before the ticket is issued.

Look for details on specialist flight agents in small ads in the backs of newspapers – they can be the best place to find last-minute options and one-way tickets, which can be ridiculously expensive on the big airlines. Penalties for changing your plans can be stiff, and these companies make their money by dealing in bulk – so don't expect them to answer lots of questions. These agents often book flights on small, no-name airlines; that's how they get them so cheap.

Inclusive tours

Many operators run **all-inclusive vacations**, combining plane tickets and accommodation with (for example) sightseeing, dining or admission to Broadway shows. Even if the "package" aspect doesn't thrill you, these deals can be more convenient and more economical than arranging the same thing yourself, providing you don't mind losing a little flexibility. With so many packages available, it's impossible to give an overview – major travel agents have brochures detailing what is being offered.

Airlines

Air Canada ⓣ1-888/247-2262, ⓦwww.aircanada.ca
America West Airlines ⓣ1-800/235-9292, ⓦwww.americawest.com
American Airlines ⓣ1-800/433-7300, ⓦwww.aa.com
Continental Airlines ⓣ1-800/525-0280, ⓦwww.flycontinental.com
Delta Airlines ⓣ1-800/221-1212, ⓦwww.delta.com
Hawaiian Airlines ⓣ1-800/367-5320, ⓦwww.hawaiianair.com
JetBlue ⓣ1-800/538-2583, ⓦwww.jetblue.com
Northwest Airlines ⓣ1-800/225-2525, ⓦwww.nwa.com
Southwest Airlines ⓣ1-800/435-9792, ⓦwww.iflyswa.com

TWA ⓣ1-800/221-2000, ⓦwww.twa.com
United Airlines ⓣ1-800/241-6522, ⓦwww.ual.com
US Airways ⓣ1-800/428-4322, ⓦwww.usairways.com

Discount flight agents

Council Travel 205 E 42nd St, New York, NY 10017, two others in NYC and branches in many other US cities. ⓣ1-800/COUNCIL or 212/822-2700, ⓦwww.counciltravel.com. Student/budget travel agency.
Now Voyager 74 Varick St, Suite 307, New York, NY 10016 ⓣ212/431-1616, ⓦwww.nowvoyagertravel.com. Lesbian and gay-friendly consolidator.
STA Travel 5900 Wilshire Blvd, Suite 2110, Los Angeles, CA 90036, and other branches in the Los Angeles, San Francisco, Boston, Miami, Chicago, Seattle and Washington DC areas. ⓣ1-800/777-0112 or 212/627-3111, ⓦwww.sta-travel.com. Worldwide discount travel firm specializing in student/youth fares; also student Ids,travel insurance, car rental, rail passes, etc.
Travel Avenue 10 S Riverside, Suite 1404, Chicago, IL 60606 ⓣ1-800/333-3335, ⓦwww.travelavenue.com. Full-service travel agent that offers discounts in the form of rebates.
Travel Cuts 187 College St, Toronto, ON M5T 1P7 ⓣ1-800/667-2887 or 416/979-2406, ⓦwww.travelcuts.com. Branches in Montréal, Vancouver, Calgary, Winnipeg, etc. Canadian discount travel organization.
UniTravel 11737 Administration Drive, Suite 120, St Louis, MO 63146 ⓣ1-800/325-2222 or 314/569-2501. Consolidator. Worth calling for last-minute bookings or to avoid such restrictions as Saturday night stay requirements.

Tour operators

American Airlines Vacations ⓣ1-800/321-2121, ⓦwww.aavacations.com
American Express Vacations ⓣ1-800/346-3607, ⓦwww.americanexpress.com/travel
Amtrak Vacations ⓣ1-800/654-5748, ⓦwww.amtrakvacations.com
Broadway Theatours 1350 Broadway, Suite 1203, New York, NY 10018 ⓣ1-800/NYSHOWS, ⓦwww.manhattanconcierge.com
Delta Vacations ⓣ1-800/654-6559, ⓦwww.deltavacations.com
Globus and Cosmos 5301 S Federal Circle, Littleton, CO 80123, ⓦwww.globusandcosmos.com
International Gay and Lesbian Travel Association ⓣ1-800/448-8550, ⓦwww.iglta.org. Trade group with lists of gay-owned or gay-friendly travel agents, accommodations and other travel businesses.
Smithsonian Study Tours & Seminars 1100 Jefferson Drive SW, Room 3077, Washington, DC 20560 ⓣ202/357-4700, ⓦwww.si.edu/tsa/sst

By train

For those heading to New York from within the same radius as the shuttle flights, travel **by train** is an alternative, though not likely to be much cheaper. The most frequent services are along the Boston-to-Washington corridor. Fares from Boston are about $120 round-trip, or $220 for the Acela Express, which can save half an hour. DC trains run about $145, considerably more on the Metroliner and Acela Express (which gets you a reserved seat, but is not significantly faster). One daily train links Montréal and Toronto with New York. Round-trip fares on these services start at around CAN$195. Train fares are often based on availability; book as early as possible to get the cheapest rates.

Although it's possible to haul yourself **long-distance** from the West Coast, the Midwest or the South, it's an exhausting trip (three days plus from California) and fares are expensive. A much better deal, allowing you to stagger the journey over up to 45 days with up to three stopoffs, is Amtrak's "Explore America Pass"; for $499 in the high season (June through mid-September) or $429 in the low season, you can travel throughout the country. If you travel in only one of their "zones," the price is reduced. A "North America Rail Pass" is sold by the Canadian Rail network but can be booked through Amtrak (ⓣ1-800/722-6137). This allows thirty days' travel in Canada and the US with three stopovers for $674, CAN$1004 (high season, June 1 to Oct 16) or $471, CAN$702 (low season). A National USA Rail Pass allows non-US citizens only unlimited fifteen-day travel for $440 (high season) or $295 (low) or thirty days for $550 (high) or $385 (low). Ask your travel agent for information, call Amtrak's info and reservations number (ⓣ1-800/USA-RAIL) or go to ⓦwww.amtrak.com.

All Amtrak services arrive at Penn Station at 32nd St and 7th and 8th aves; only local Metro-North commuter trains use Grand Central Station.

By bus

Going **by bus** is the most time-consuming and least comfortable mode of travel; because of the time factor, it's never the most economical. On the other hand, buses generally run more frequently than trains and serve a much larger portion of the country – so if New York is just one stop on an eclectic backcountry tour, check out Greyhound's Ameripass, though it is (like Amtrak's USA Railpass) open to foreign citizens only and can only be bought overseas or in New York. It offers unlimited travel on the network for four days ($135), seven days ($155), fifteen days ($235), thirty days ($335) or sixty days ($449). Greyhound has a similar pass available to all, offering seven days unlimited travel ($185), fifteen days ($285), thirty days ($385) or sixty days ($509). Greyhound's regular maximum fare for any distance with no advance booking is $136 (one-way) or $209 (round-trip). Buy your ticket seven days in advance and the price drops to $95/$189. Call ☎1-800/231-2222 for more information or ☎1-888/454-7277 for the passes.

In the busy **northeast corridor**, bus competition can be fierce, sending prices up and down within hours. One-way from either DC or Boston to New York can go for as little as $30. Bonanza (☎1-800/556-3815) has a $65 Boston–New York round-trip fare.

The famous, slightly alternative **Green Tortoise** bus connects San Francisco with New York every couple of weeks, May to October. Gregarious types can look forward to a laid-back journey with generally like-minded souls through some of America's most beautiful spots. There are plenty of stops for hiking, river-rafting, hot springs and more, and the buses are comfortable, with tape-deck systems and ample mattresses. The 10-day northern route (via Reno, Wyoming, Minnesota, Chicago and Pennsylvania) runs mostly in the hottest part of the summer and costs about $469 plus $121 for food; the 14-day southern route (generally via Los Angeles, Arizona, Texas, New Orleans and Appalachia) costs $499 plus $131 for food. From outside the San Francisco area call ☎1-800/TORTOIS (415/956-7500 if you're local), or write to 494 Broadway, San Francisco, CA 94133.

Buses arrive in New York at the Port Authority Bus Terminal, 8th Ave and 42nd St.

By car

If you're coming from the east coast (or if you don't mind long journeys), **driving** is an option, but note that you probably won't need (or want) a car once you're in the city. Major highways come in from most directions (I-84 or 95 from the north; I-95 from the south; I-80 from the west), and you'll pay a toll over any number of bridges or tunnels to get into the city.

Potentially the cheapest way to get to New York is to arrange for a **driveaway**, in which you deliver a car cross-country for its owner. Look in the Yellow Pages under "Automobile Transporters." It helps if you are flexible.

The usual requirements: You must be 21 and have a valid driver's license (and sometimes a clean record from your DMV) plus around $300 as a deposit. Theoretically there's nothing to pay on the way except gas and motel bills. While it's accepted that you may want to see a bit of the country on the way, there are generally tight delivery deadlines. Try to hit the company up for extra days and mileage when you take the job.

Flights from Britain and Ireland

Flying to New York from the UK takes about seven hours; flights tend to **leave Britain** in the morning or afternoon and arrive in New York in the afternoon or evening, though the odd flight does leave as late as 8pm. Coming back, most flights depart in the evening and arrive in Britain early next morning; flying time, due to the prevailing winds, is shorter – six to seven hours.

As far as **scheduled flights** go, British Airways offers the most direct services each day from London Heathrow to JFK, and also flies from Heathrow to Newark, and to JFK from London Gatwick and Manchester. American Airlines, Virgin, Continental and United also fly direct on a daily basis; there is not tons of difference in the prices on the different airlines, and you'll need to really shop around to get the best deals.

The only nonstop scheduled services to New York **from Ireland** are provided by Aer Lingus.

Fares and courier flights

Ask an airline about cut-price deals (particularly in winter), but they're more likely to offer an **Apex** ticket. The conditions are pretty standard whoever you fly with: seats must be booked 21 days or more in advance, and you must stay at least seven nights, a maximum of one month; they're usually non-refundable and can't be changed without penalty. Prices are about the same: low-season midweek rates start at around £250 return, rising to around £350 in spring and over £400 in high season. A tax of £58.10 is added to all fares, and flying at the weekend costs extra. A fully flexible economy fare may cost £900 or more. An Apex ticket from Ireland (Shannon) to JFK can cost up to IR£500.

If on a really tight budget, consider flying as a courier, although during the off season it may not be worth the hassle given the low fares available. Courier flights can be arranged with Flight Masters, 83 Mortimer St, London W1 (⊕020/7462 0022) or Bridges Worldwide, Old Mill Road House, West Drayton, Middlesex TW3 (⊕01895/465065). The flights involve a package being checked through with your luggage, in return for a cheaper flight; return times and luggage are restricted. Or, join the International Association of Air Travel Couriers, c/o International Features, 1 Kings Rd, Dorchester, Dorset DT1 (⊕0800/746481, ⊛www.courier.org or ⊛www.aircourier.co.uk).

Inclusive tours

All-in deals – flights plus accommodation in New York City – can be a good idea for a short stay. Low-season prices per person for a return flight plus three nights in a mid-range midtown hotel start at £400–500 and rise to more like £600–700 at peak periods; seven nights would cost £600–900 per person, depending on the time of year. Most High Street travel agents can advise on the best deals.

Airlines

Aer Lingus Ireland ⊕01/886 8844, ⊛www.aerlingus.ie
American Airlines UK ⊕0845/778 9789, ⊛www.aa.com
British Airways UK ⊕0345/222111, Ireland ⊕1-800/626747, ⊛www.british-airways.com
Continental Airlines UK ⊕0800/776464
Delta Airlines UK ⊕0800/414767, Ireland ⊕1-800/768080
United Airlines UK ⊕0845/8444777, ⊛www.ual.com
Virgin Atlantic UK ⊕01293/747747, Ireland ⊕01/873 3388, ⊛www.fly.virgin.com

Travel agents

Joe Walsh Tours Dublin ⊕01/872 2555 or ⊕01/676 3053, Cork ⊕021/277959, ⊛www.joewalshtours.ie. General budget fares agent.
STA Travel UK ⊕0870/160 6070, www.statravel.co.uk. Worldwide specialists in low-cost flights and tours for students and under-26s, though other customers welcome.
Trailfinders UK ⊕020/7628 7628, Ireland ⊕01/677 7888, ⊛www.trailfinders.com. One of the best-informed and most efficient agents for independent travelers.
Travel Bag UK ⊕0870/900 1350, ⊛www.travelbag.co.uk. Discount flights.
Travel Cuts UK ⊕020/7255 2082. Canadian company specializing in budget, student and youth travel and round-the-world tickets.
Usit Campus UK ⊕0870/240 1010, ⊛www.usitcampus.co.uk. Student/youth travel specialists, offering discount flights. Specialists in North America travel.
USIT Now Belfast ⊕028/9032 7111, Dublin ⊕01/602 1777 or 677 8117, Cork ⊕021/270 900, Derry ⊕028/7137 1888, ⊛www.usitnow.ie. Student and youth specialists.

Tour operators

American Holidays Lombard House, Lombard St, Belfast 1 ⊕028/9023 8762, 38/39 Pearse St, Dublin 2 ⊕01/679 8800 or 679 6611
British Airways Holidays Worldwide ⊕0870/242 4245, ⊛www.baholidays.co.uk
Destination USA London ⊕020/7400 7000, ⊛www.destination-group.com
Thomas Cook Holidays ⊕01733/563200, ⊛www.thomascook.com
Trans Atlantic Vacations Horley ⊕01293/774441
United Vacations Heathrow Airport ⊕020/8313 0999
Virgin Holidays Crawley ⊕01293/617181

Flights from Australia and New Zealand

There are no direct flights to New York **from Australia or New Zealand**, no surprise considering the great distance between the two end points. Most people reach the eastern United States by way of the West Coast gateway cities of Los Angeles and San Francisco (flying time is approximately ten hours to the West Coast, with another six-hour flight to New York). You can buy an all-in ticket via LA or San Francisco or simply fly to LA and use one of the **domestic flight coupons**, or **air passes,** you can buy with your international ticket (these must be bought before you leave your home country). These flight coupons cost around A$800 for three, which is the minimum you can purchase.

Fares from eastern Australian capitals are generally the same (airlines offer a free connecting service between these cities); fares from Perth and Darwin are about A$400 more. Return flights in low season (which is mid-January to February and October through November) start at around A$2000/NZ$2900 and go up from there; you might do better just by purchasing a direct ticket to either San Francisco or LA, then using the air passes to get to New York. The best connections through San Francisco and LA tend to be with United, Air New Zealand and Qantas.

Round-the-world and air passes

If you intend to take in New York as part of a world trip, a **round-the-world ticket** offers the best value for money, working out just a little more than an all-in ticket. Check with the airlines listed below for the best options; it's quite possible you'd only spend an extra few hundred dollars than on a normal return ticket.

Airlines

Air New Zealand Australia ⓣ13 2476, NZ ⓣ0800/737 000 or ⓣ09/357 3000, ⓦwww.airnz.com
American Airlines Australia ⓣ1300/650 747, NZ ⓣ09/309 0735 or ⓣ0800/887 997, ⓦwww.aa.com
Korean Air Australia ⓣ02/9262 6000; NZ ⓣ09/307 3687, ⓦwww.koreanair.com
Qantas Australia Australia ⓣ13/13 13, NZ ⓣ09/357 8900 or ⓣ0800/808 767, ⓦwww.qantas.com.au
United Airlines Australia ⓣ13/1777, NZ ⓣ09/379 3800, ⓦwww.ual.com

Travel agents

Anywhere travel Australia ⓣ02/9663 0411 or ⓣ018 401 014, ⓔanywhere@ozemail.com.au
Budget travel NZ ⓣ09/366 0061 or ⓣ0800/808 040
Destinations Unlimited NZ ⓣ09/373 4033
Flight Centres Australia ⓣ02/9235 3522 or for nearest branch ⓣ13 1600, NZ ⓣ09/358 4310, ⓦwww.flightcentre.com.au
Northern Gateway Australia ⓣ08/8941 1394, ⓔoztravel@norgate.com.au
STA travel Australia ⓣ13 1776 or ⓣ1300/360 960, NZ ⓣ09/309 0458 or ⓣ09/366 6673, ⓦwww.statravel.com.au
Student Uni travel Australia ⓣ02/9232 8444, ⓔAustralia@backpackers.net
Thomas Cook Australia ⓣ13 1771 or ⓣ1800/801 002, NZ ⓣ09/379 3920, ⓦwww.thomascook.com.au
Trailfinders Australia ⓣ02/9247 7666
Usit Beyond NZ ⓣ09/379 4224 or ⓣ0800/788 336, ⓦwww.usitbeyond.co.nz

Entry requirements

Citizens of Britain and Ireland do not require visas for US visits of less than ninety days. You must have a full passport (valid for at least ninety days from the date on which you enter the US), and your ticket must be a return ticket (or onward ticket, but not to a US neighbor, including Caribbean countries). For further details, contact the American embassies in Britain (24–31 Grosvenor Square, London W1A 1AE, ⓣ020/7499 9000 or 0891/200290, recorded information) or Ireland (42 Elgin Rd, Ballsbridge, Dublin, ⓣ01/668 7122). The best way to get

information is through the embassy (@www.usembassy.org.uk). British and Irish consulates in New York are listed on p.462.

Australian and New Zealand passport holders staying fewer than ninety days do not require a visa, providing they arrive on a commercial flight with an onward or return ticket. For longer stays a US multiple-entry visa costs AUS$78. You need an application form from the US visa information service (☎1902/262 682), one signed passport photo and your passport. You must either mail it or personally lodge it at one of the American embassy or consulate addresses – in Australia, 21 Moonah Place, Canberra, ACT 2600 (☎02/6214 5600), and in New Zealand, 29 Fitzherbert Terrace, Thorndon, Wellington (☎04/472 2068). For postal applications in Australia, payment can be made at any post office; include the receipt of payment and an SAE. Processing takes about ten working days for postal applications; personal lodgements take two days – but check details with the consulate first.

For a brief excursion, **Canadian citizens** need only proof of their citizenship (such as a passport or a birth certificate in conjunction with a photo ID) to enter the US. If you have any questions, the US embassy in Canada is at 100 Wellington St, Ottawa, ON K1P 5A1 (☎613/238-5335). Other US consulates are in Calgary (☎403/266-8962), Halifax (☎902/429-2485), Montréal (☎514/398-9695), Quebec City (☎418/692-2095), Toronto (☎416/595-1700) and Vancouver (☎604/685-4311). For visits of longer than 90 days, a visa is required. If you plan to work or study in the US, check with your embassy about additional requirements.

Health

Coming from Europe, you don't require any inoculations to enter the States. You do need insurance (see p.18), because medical bills for the most minor accident can be astronomical.

Doctors and pharmacies

If you need a **doctor**, see the Yellow Pages under "Clinics" or "Physicians and Surgeons." A basic consultation fee can be upwards of $250, and medicines – prescribed or over-the-counter – don't come cheap. **Minor ailments** can be remedied at a drugstore. These sell a fabulous array of lotions and potions, but many pills available over the counter in other countries (for example, codeine-based painkillers) are by prescription only here and brand names can be confusing. Many brand-name drugs distributed under generic names can be much cheaper. When in doubt, ask at a pharmacy, where prescription drugs are dispensed (for addresses, see pp.426–427).

Should you be in an **accident**, a medical service will pick you up and charge later. For minor accidents, emergency rooms are open 24 hours at these Manhattan hospitals: Bellevue, 1st Ave and E 27th St (☎562-4141); St Vincent's, 7th Ave and W 11th St (☎604-7996); New York, Cornell Medical Center E 70th St at York Ave (☎746-5050); and Mount Sinai, Madison Ave at 100th St (☎241-7171). The Dental Referral Service (☎1-800/577-7317) will recommend a dentist in your area.

Alternative and natural medicine

You'll find plenty of **alternatives to conventional medicine**, but they won't be any cheaper than the standard kind. C.O.

Bigelow Apothecaries at 414 6th Ave between 8th and 9th sts (☎212/473-7324) has the largest selection of homeopathic products in the city; a knowledgeable staff can assist you or recommend a naturopathic doctor. The New York Open Center, 83 Spring St, east of Broadway (☎212/219-2527), has a bookstore and free publications on (among other things) health and natural living; you can find acupuncture, massage therapy, Chinese herbology, Bach flower remedies and other options through them. Check listings in the Yellow Pages and on the bulletin boards of health-food stores and natural-food restaurants. Many insurers, however, are reluctant to recognize alternative treatments.

Insurance

Travel insurance is definitely recommended before setting out on your trip, and one that includes medical coverage (if you're coming from abroad) is essential, considering the high costs of health care in the US. A typical travel insurance policy provides cover for the loss of baggage, tickets and, to an extent, cash or checks, and cancellation of your trip. Read the small print of any insurance policy you take out.

Many policies can be chopped and changed to exclude coverage you don't need – for example, sickness and accident benefits can often be excluded or included at will. If you do take medical coverage, ascertain whether benefits will be paid as treatment proceeds or only after return home, and whether there is a 24-hour medical emergency number. When securing baggage cover, make sure that the per-article limit will cover your most valuable possession. If you need to make a claim, you should keep receipts for medicines and medical treatment, and in the event you have anything stolen, you must obtain an official statement from the police.

Before spending on a new policy, however, it's worth checking whether you are **already covered**: some all-risks home insurance policies, for example, may cover your

Rough Guide travel insurance

Rough Guides offers its own travel insurance, customized for our readers by a leading UK broker and backed by a Lloyds underwriter. It's available for anyone, of any nationality, traveling anywhere in the world.

There are two main Rough Guide insurance plans: Essential, for basic, no-frills cover; and Premier – with more generous and extensive benefits. Alternatively, you can take out annual multi-trip insurance, which covers you for any number of trips throughout the year (with a maximum of 60 days for any one trip). Unlike many policies, the Rough Guides plans are calculated by the day, so if you're traveling for 27 days rather than a month, that's all you pay for. If you intend to be away for the whole year, the Adventurer policy will cover you for 365 days. Each plan can be supplemented with a "Hazardous Activities Premium" if you plan to indulge in sports considered dangerous, such as skiing, scuba-diving or trekking. Rough Guides also does good deals for older travelers, and will insure you up to any age.

For a policy quote, call the Rough Guide Insurance Line on US toll-free ☎1-866/220 5588 or UK freefone ☎0800/015 0906 or, if you're calling from elsewhere ☎+44 1243/621046. Alternatively, get an online quote at www.roughguides.com/insurance

possessions against loss or theft when overseas, and many private medical plans include cover when abroad, including baggage loss, cancellation or curtailment and cash replacement as well as sickness or accident.

Americans should find that their health insurance covers any unforeseen medical costs they may have while visiting New York. In **Canada**, provincial health plans usually provide partial cover for medical mishaps overseas, while holders of official student/teacher/youth cards in Canada and the US are entitled to meager accident coverage and hospital in-patient benefits. Students will often find that their student health coverage extends during the vacations and for one term beyond the date of last enrollment. Some bank and credit cards include certain levels of medical or other insurance and you may automatically get travel insurance if you use a major credit card to pay for your trip.

Arrival

Three major airports serve New York. International and domestic flights are handled at John F Kennedy (JFK) (☎718/244-4444), in the borough of Queens, and Newark (☎973/961-6000), in northern New Jersey; La Guardia (☎718/533-3400), also in Queens, handles domestic flights only.

Wherever you arrive, the cheapest way into Manhattan is by **bus**. In the following sections we've outlined the bus connections from each airport, along with their public transit alternatives. The two Manhattan bus terminals, used by all airport buses, are Grand Central Station and the Port Authority Bus Terminal. Grand Central (at Park Ave and 42nd St) is more convenient, in the heart of midtown and a short walk or taxi ride to many hotels; its subway station leads to eastern city locales. Some large midtown hotels – the *Marriott Marquis*, *Hilton*, etc – operate a free shuttle service to and from Grand Central. The **Port Authority Terminal** at 8th Ave at 42nd St (☎212/564-8484) isn't as good a bet for Manhattan (you must carry luggage from bus to street level), though you'll find it handy if you're heading for the West Side of the city or out to New Jersey (by bus). Some airport buses stop at Penn Station at 34th St between 7th and 8th aves where you can catch Amtrak long-distance trains to other parts of America.

Taxis are the easiest option if you are in a group or are arriving at an antisocial hour. Reckon on paying $16–22 from La Guardia, a flat rate of $30 from JFK and $35–55 from Newark; you'll be responsible for the turnpike and tunnel tolls – an extra $5 or so. And don't forget a tip of fifteen to twenty percent. Ignore the individual drivers vying for attention as you exit the baggage claim; these "gypsy cab" operators are notorious for ripping off tourists. Any airport official can direct you to the taxi stand, where you can get an official New York City yellow taxi. A few car services have direct phones near the exits; they're competitive in price with taxis (they charge set rates).

The **Gray Line Air Shuttle** is a minibus you can pick up at the three airports (check with the ground transportation desk or the courtesy phone in the baggage area) or arrange by phone (☎1-800/451-0455 or 212/315-3006). These shuttles give the older airport buses (see below) a run for their money; for a few dollars more they take you to your hotel – if you're staying in midtown. The shuttles operate from the airport between 7am and 11.30pm, and from the hotels between 6am and 7pm; the cost (one-way) if you buy your ticket at the airport is $13 per person to La Guardia, $14 to JFK or Newark; otherwise it's $16 to JFK, $19 to La Guardia or Newark. Round-trip fares are double those for one way. Super Shuttle (☎1-800/BLUEVAN or 212/258-3826) operates to and from Manhattan only, 24 hours daily. Representatives are in the baggage claim areas, and courtesy phones are available. One-way fares are $15 from La Guardia, $19 from JFK and Newark. Reserve from Manhattan to the airport at least one or two days ahead of time; they may pick up other departees along the way, adding to your travel time.

For general information on getting to and from the airports, call ⓣ1-800/AIR-RIDE.

JFK

New York Airport Service. Buses leave JFK for Grand Central Station, Port Authority Bus Terminal, Penn Station and midtown hotels every 15 to 20 minutes between 6am and midnight. In the other direction, they run from the same locations every 15 to 30 minutes between 5am and 10pm. Journeys take 45 to 60 minutes, depending on time of day and traffic conditions; the fare is $13 (students $6) one-way; discounts are available to senior citizens, the disabled and children when you travel from (not to) Grand Central Station. For details on services, discounts, etc, call ⓣ212/875-8200.

Public transit. Free shuttle buses run from all terminals at JFK to the Howard Beach subway stop on the #A train; from there, one subway token ($1.50) takes you anywhere in the city. Late at night, this isn't your best choice – trains run infrequently and can be rather deserted – but in the daytime or early evening it's a viable, if tedious, option. Travel time is at least an hour from Howard Beach. Or, take the #Q10 green bus (subway token or $1.50, exact change and no paper money) to its last stop, right by the subway in Kew Gardens, Queens, and pick up the #E or #F train (for an additional token) to Manhattan. Travel time is about the same, but at rush hour avoid this route – the most overcrowded line in the transit system. See the subway map (color map at back) to determine the most convenient route to your destination. For more info on subway and bus options, call ⓣ718/330-1234, 24 hours any day.

When you come to catch your flight home, remember that JFK is large and very spread out: if your terminal is last on the bus route (like British Airways) allow an additional fifteen minutes or so to get there.

Newark

Olympia Airport Express. Buses leave for Manhattan every 20 to 30 minutes (5am to 3.30am), stopping at Port Authority Grand Central and Penn stations; going the other way, they run just as frequently (4.15am to 2.45am); service to and from the Port Authority runs 24 hours a day. In either direction, the journey takes 30 to 45 minutes depending on the traffic, and the fare is $11. A connecting service to certain midtown hotels costs an extra $5. Buses go from Newark to JFK for $23 and to La Guardia for $20, with a connection at Port Authority or Grand Central Station. Buses for these airports run from 6am to midnight every 20 minutes. Details on ⓣ212/964-6233 or 908/354-3330.

PATH Rapid Transit. Take a shuttle bus (AIRLINK #302) to Newark's Penn Station, where PATH trains run to stations in Manhattan; the fare is $4 for the bus, $1.50 for the train. Airlink buses run from about 6.15am to 1.40am. (The PATH train runs 24 hours a day, but between midnight and 6am service is limited.) The bus service runs every 20 to 30 minutes Mon–Fri and every 30 minutes Sat–Sun. Buy tickets at the bus's point of departure. Call New Jersey Transit at ⓣ1-800/626-7433.

Airline offices in New York City

Many of these airlines have additional offices throughout the city.

Air Canada ⓣ1-800/776-3000
125 Park Ave (at 42nd St)

Air India ⓣ751-6200 or 407-1460
570 Lexington Ave (at 51st St), 15th Floor

American ⓣ1-800/433-7300
125 Park Ave (at 42nd St), 2nd Floor

Delta ⓣ1-800/221-1212
100 E 42nd St (at Park Ave)

El Al ⓣ852-0600
120 W 45th St (between 6th and 7th aves)

Kuwait ⓣ659-4200
350 Park Ave

Northwest/KLM ⓣ1-800/225-2525
100 E 42nd St (at Park Ave)

United ⓣ1-800/241-6522
1 E 59th St (at 5th Ave)

Virgin Atlantic ⓣ1-800/862-8621
100 E 42nd St (at Park Ave)

La Guardia

New York Airport Service buses run between Manhattan (Grand Central Station and Port Authority Bus Terminal) and La Guardia every 15 to 30 minutes either way. The service operates 6am to midnight (to Grand Central and Port Authority), 5am to 10pm (from Grand Central), 6.40am to 9pm (from Port Authority). Buses also run to Penn Station from 6.40am to 11.40pm every 30 minutes, 10 and 40 after the hour; from Penn Station, 7.40am to 8.10pm, same time-scale as above. Journey time is 45 to 60 minutes, depending on traffic, and the fare is $10 (students $6) each way. For details on services, discounts, etc, call ⓣ212/875-8200.

Public transit. The best (and least-known) bargain in New York airport transit is the #M60 bus, which for $1.50 takes you into Manhattan, across 125th St and down Broadway to 106th Street. Ask for a transfer when you get on the bus and you can get almost anywhere (for an explanation of transfers, see p.24). *Hosteling International* (p.284) is four blocks from the #M60's last stop. Journey time ranges from 20 minutes late at night to an hour in rush-hour traffic.

If the Upper West Side is not your destination, consider the #Q33 or #Q47 bus ($1.50/$1 off-peak and weekends) from La Guardia to the Roosevelt Avenue subway stop in Jackson Heights, Queens, where for another $1.50 you can get the #7, #E, #F or #R, minutes to midtown.

La Guardia to JFK

Manhattan Airport Service links JFK and La Guardia airports between 5.40am and 11pm. Buses leave, on average, every 30 minutes (though it varies depending on your direction and the time of day) and take 45 minutes to 60 minutes; at select times they stop once along the way. The fare is $11 one way. Call ⓣ212/875-8200.

Arriving by bus or train

If you come by Greyhound, Trailways, Bonanza or any other long-distance **bus line**, you arrive at the Port Authority Bus Terminal at 42nd St and 8th Ave. By Amtrak **train**, you arrive at Penn Station, 32nd St and 7th and 8th aves. (See p.19 for details on both terminals.)

City transportation

Getting around the city is likely to take some getting used to; public transit here is on the whole quite good, extremely cheap, and covers most conceivable corners of the city, whether by bus or subway. Don't be afraid to ask someone for help if you're confused. You'll no doubt find the need for a taxi from time to time, especially if you feel uncomfortable in an area at night; you shouldn't ever have trouble tracking one down – the ubiquitous yellow cabs are always on the prowl for passengers.

The subway

The New York **subway** is dirty, noisy, intimidating and initially incomprehensible. It's also the fastest and most efficient way to get from A to B in Manhattan and the outer boroughs, and it is safer and more user-friendly than it once was. Put aside your qualms: Six million people ride the subway every day, quite a few for the first time.

Learn about the system when you arrive. Study the map at the back of this book, or get a free map at any station (or at the information booth on the Grand Central concourse, the New York Convention and Visitors Bureau, or any tourist info center listed on p.26). The following guidelines make more sense when combined with visual information.

The basics

- Most Manhattan train routes run uptown or downtown, following the great avenues and converging, as the island itself does, in the downtown financial district. Crosstown routes are few.
- Trains and their routes are generally identified by a number or letter. Though the subway is open 24 hours a day, some routes operate at certain times of day only; read your map carefully. Also, in the interest of safety, some entrances to stations are open only during certain hours. The green globe outside the subway entrance identifies an open station.
- There are two types of train. The **express** stops only at major stations. The **local** stops at every station. If your destination is an express stop, the quickest way to get there is to change from local to express at the first express station – walk across the platform or take the stairs to another level.
- Any subway journey costs **$1.50**. You may pay your fare with a **subway token**, available from any token booth. To avoid waiting in line, buy extra tokens; they may also be used for buses.
- The **MetroCard**, a multi-trip card with an electronic strip that allows you to transfer (for free) from subway to bus, bus to subway or bus to bus within a period of 2 hours, is the most convenient and economical way to pay for your trip. It's available from token booths and vending machines, in several forms: cards can be bought for $3 to $80; $15 purchases allow 11 rides for the cost of 10, and $30 purchases allow 22 rides for the cost of 20. Unlimited-ride cards allow unlimited travel for a certain period of time: a 7-day pass for $17, a 30-day pass for $63 and a daily "Fun Pass" for $4. Unfortunately, the "Fun Pass," valid for 24 hours, is not available from token booths, but can be found at most major hotels and grocery stores (look for "fun pass" stickers on the door) such as Gristedes or call ⓣ212/638-7622 to find out the closest location to purchase one.
- **Service changes** due to track repairs and other maintenance work are frequent (especially after midnight and on weekends) and confusing even to longtime subway riders. Read the red-and-white Service Notice posters on bulletin boards throughout the system. Don't be afraid to ask other passengers what's going on. Listen closely to all

Main lines in Manhattan

- The local **#1** and **#9** and express **#2** and **#3** trains run north and south along Broadway and 7th Ave. They are also known as the Broadway line or the 7th Ave line. Pay close attention north of 96th St and south of Chambers St, where the local and express trains diverge. At the time of writing, service below Chambers St on the #1 and #9 has been suspended owing to the collapse of the World Trade Center.
- The local **#6** and express **#4** and **#5** trains run north and south along Lexington and Park aves, diverging north of 125th St and south of Brooklyn Bridge. This is also called the Lexington Avenue line.
- The **#7** train runs east and west along 42nd St from Times Square (Broadway/7th Ave) to Grand Central (Park Ave) and then out to Queens.
- Often known as the 8th Ave line, the express **#A** and local **#C** and **#E** trains run north and south along 8th Ave in midtown Manhattan. The #E branches off south of Canal St (terminating at the site of the former World Trade Center) and north of 50th St (where it heads crosstown out to Queens). The #C terminates at Washington Heights while the #A continues on to Inwood at the northern tip of Manhattan.
- The local **#F** and express **#B**, **#D** and **#Q** trains run north and south along 6th Ave in midtown, turning east at W 4th St. Traveling uptown, north of the 47th–50th St stop (Rockefeller Center), the #F, the #Q, and the #B branch off to go crosstown to Queens; owing to service changes, the #B becomes a #W before crossing into Brooklyn, while the #D becomes a #Q train. Check map for details.
- The **#N** and **#R** trains run along Broadway from lower Manhattan to 57th St. Traveling south, they head to Brooklyn after the Whitehall Street/South Ferry stop; in the other direction, they ride east and to Queens via the Queensboro Bridge after hitting 57th St.
- The Grand Central–Times Square Shuttle, running under 42nd St, connects the east and west sides of the IRT. It's marked on maps as the **#S** train.
- The **#L** runs east and west along 14th St between 8th and 1st aves. East of 1st Ave, the #L runs out to Williamsburg and points further east in Brooklyn.

announcements (though to be sure they can be hard to understand); occasionally, express trains run on local tracks.

- Don't hesitate to **ask directions** or **look at a map** on the train or in the station. If you travel late at night, know your route before you set out. Follow common sense safety rules (see "Crime and personal safety," p.43).
- If you are **lost**, phone ☎718/330-1234. State your location and destination; the operator will tell you the most direct route by subway or bus.

Lines and train names

Perhaps the main source of confusion for visitors is the multiplicity of **line and train names**. You might hear them called by anything from their number or letters to the general route they travel. Thus, the Broadway Local, 7th Avenue Local and Number 1 train are all the same thing. New Yorkers generally do *not* refer to trains by color: if you're looking for the #2 or #3 and ask for the red line, you'll probably be met with blank stares.

The main lines and directions in Manhattan are outlined below. To acclimate yourself to the transit system, see the Subway map at the back of the book.

Safety on the subway

At night, always try to use the center cars, because they are more crowded. Yellow signs on the platform saying "During off hours train stops here" indicate where the conductor's car will stop. While you wait, keep to the "Off-Hour Waiting Area" (marked in yellow), where the token booth attendants can see you; when this area is on a different level, a flashing sign (accompanied by a high electronic beep) will let you know a train is arriving, so don't worry about missing your train.

By day the whole train is safe, but don't go into empty cars if you can help it. Some trains have doors that connect between cars, but do not use them other than in an emergency, because this is dangerous and illegal.

Keep an eye on bags at all times, especially when sitting or standing near the doors. With all the jostling in the crowds near the doors, this is a favorite snatching spot.

For more information on safety, see "Crime and personal safety," p.43.

Buses

The **bus system** is simpler than the subway, and you can see where you're going and hop off at anything interesting. It also features many more crosstown routes. The major disadvantage of buses is that they can be extremely slow – in peak hours almost down to walking pace, and extremely full to boot. In response to cries of overcrowding along several routes, the MTA recently introduced "accordion buses" – two buses attached with a flexible rubber accordion, which helps the big vehicle turn corners. However, because these run slightly less frequently than the ones they replaced, they still get crowded.

Bus maps, like subway maps, can be obtained at the main concourse of Grand Central or the Convention and Visitors Bureau at 53rd St and 7th Ave. A glance at the routes reveals that they run on almost all the avenues and across major streets. Most buses with an M designation before the route number travel exclusively in Manhattan; others may show a B for Brooklyn, Q for Queens, or Bx for the Bronx. The most useful routes are the crosstown ones, especially the ones through Central Park. In addition, they can take you to areas of the Lower East Side (or, really, any location east of the park) where subway coverage is sparse. Most crosstown buses take their route number from the street they traverse, so the M14 will travel along 14th St. The main lines and directions in Manhattan are outlined below.

- The M8, M23, M34, M42, M50, M57, M72, M79, M86 and M96 all travel east/west. The M8 travels on Christopher, West 10th, East 9th and East 10th sts. The M50 goes westbound on West 49th St and eastbound on 50th St.
- The M14 is good for getting to the Lower East Side and Alphabet City (avenues A, B, C and D).
- The M9 from Lower Manhattan also travels through the Lower East Side, and terminates at 14th St and Broadway.
- For most of its route, the M15 rides north on 1st Ave and south on 2nd Ave.
- The M1, M2, M3 and M4 travel south on 5th Ave and north on Madison Ave from 34th St to 110th, where they diverge. There is part-time M1 service as far south as Battery Park.

There are three types of bus: regular, which stop every two or three blocks at five- to ten-minute intervals; limited stop, which travel the same routes but stop at only about a quarter of the regular stops; and express, which cost extra and stop hardly anywhere, shuttling commuters in and out of the outer boroughs and suburbs. Buses display their number, origin and destination up front.

Bus stops are marked by yellow curbstones and a blue, white and red sign that often (but not always) indicates which buses stop there. In addition, a sign may show routes and times (rarely accurate). To signal that you want to get off a bus, press the yellow strip on the wall. The "Stop Requested" sign at the front of the bus will come on, and the driver will stop at the next official bus stop. After midnight, you can ask to get off on any block along the route, whether or not it's a regular stop.

Fares and transfers

Anywhere in Manhattan the **fare is $1.50,** payable on entry with either a subway token, a **MetroCard** (the most convenient way) or with the correct change – no bills.

If you're going to use buses a lot, it pays to understand the transfer system. A transfer allows a single fare to take you, one way, anywhere in Manhattan. Because few buses go up and down *and* across, you can transfer from any bus to almost any other that continues your trip. (You can't use transfers for return trips.) They're given free on request when you pay your fare. The top of the transfer tells you how much time you have in which to use it – usually around two hours. If unsure where to get off to transfer, consult the map on the panel behind the driver, or ask the driver for help. If you use a MetroCard, you can automatically transfer for free within two hours from swiping the card.

> **Bus and subway information**
> ☎718/330-1234 (24 hours daily)
> **Lost and found** ☎212/712-4500

Taxis

Taxis are always worth considering, especially if you're in a hurry or in a group or late at night.

In Manhattan, there are two types: medallion cabs, immediately recognizable by their yellow paintwork and medallion up top, and gypsy cabs, unlicensed, uninsured operators who tout for business wherever tourists arrive. Avoid gypsy cabs like the plague – they're rip-off merchants. Their main hunting grounds are outside tourist arrival points like Grand Central.

Up to four people can travel in an ordinary medallion cab or, if you're lucky enough to find it, the last-remaining, old-fashioned Checker cab. Fares are $2 for the first fifth of a mile and 30¢ for each fifth of a mile thereafter or for each 90 seconds in stopped or slow traffic. The basic charge rises by 50¢ from 8pm to 6am, and by 100 percent if you take a cab outside the city limits (eg, to Newark airport). Trips outside Manhattan can incur toll fees; not all of the crossings cost money, however, and the driver should ask you which route you wish to take.

The tip should be fifteen to twenty percent of the fare; you'll get a dirty look if you offer less. Drivers don't like splitting anything bigger than a $10 bill, and are in their rights to refuse a bill over $20.

Before you hail a cab, work out exactly where you're going and if possible the quickest route there – a surprising number of cabbies are new to the job and some speak little English. If you feel the driver doesn't seem to know your destination, point it out on a map. An illuminated sign atop the taxi indicates its availability. If the words "Off Duty" are lit, the driver won't pick you up.

Certain regulations govern taxi operators. A driver can ask your destination only when you're seated – and must transport you (within the five boroughs), however undesirable your destination may be. You may face some problems, though, if it's late and you want to go to an outer borough. Also, if you request it, a driver must pick up or drop off other passengers, open or close the windows, and stop smoking (drivers can also ask you to stop). If you have a problem with a driver, get the license number from the right-hand side of the dashboard, or medallion number from the rooftop sign or from the print-out receipt for the fare, and phone the NYC Taxis and Limousine Commission, ☎212/302-8294. Also call this number if you've left something in a cab.

Driving

Don't. Even if you're brave enough to try dodging demolition-derby cab drivers and jaywalking pedestrians, car rental is expensive, parking lots almost laughably so, and street parking hard to find. There's not much else to compare it to in the States.

If you must drive, bear in mind a number of rules. Seatbelts are compulsory for everyone in front and for children in back. The city speed limit is 35mph, and you can be pulled over and given a breathalyzer test at a police officer's discretion. (You may refuse, but you must then go to police headquarters.) Unlike most of the country, it's illegal to make a right turn at a red light.

Read signs carefully to figure out where to park – if the sign says "No Standing," "No Stopping" or "Don't Even THINK of Parking Here" (yes, really), that's a no. Watch for street-cleaning hours (when an entire side of a street will be off-limits for parking), and don't park in a bus stop or in front of a fire hydrant. Private parking is expensive, extremely so at peak periods, but it makes sense to leave your car somewhere legitimate: if it's towed away you must liberate it from the car pound (☎212/971-0770) – expect to pay around $150 in cash ($15 for each additional day they store it for you) and waste the better part of a day.

Car theft and vandalism are more of a problem in less-traveled parts of the city where vandals won't be seen working on your car. If you're going to have a car in the city for a while, utilize a deterrent to would-be thieves – the long yellow bar that locks between steering wheel and windshield is popular, as is the "Club." Never leave valuables in your car.

In some counties surrounding the city (but not the city itself – yet) the use of hand-held cell phones is illegal while driving. As noted above, driving, especially here, is an activity that demands your undivided attention.

Cycling

Cycling can be a viable, if somewhat dangerous, form of transportation. Do as the locals do and go for all possible rentable safety equipment: pads, a helmet (required by law), goggles and a whistle to move straying pedestrians. When you park, double-chain and lock your bike to an immovable object if you'd like it to be there when you return.

Bike rental starts at about $7 an hour or $35 a day – which means opening to closing (9.30am to 6.30pm for instance), so ask about 24-hour rates. You need one or two pieces of ID (passport and credit card will be sufficient) and, in some cases, a deposit (around $200), though most firms will be satisfied with a credit card imprint. Rates and deposits are generally more for racing models and mountain bikes.

The Yellow Pages has full listings of bike rental firms. Good-value and central suppliers include:

Bikes in the Park Loeb Boathouse, Central Park (☎212/861-4137). The best place to rent bikes to tour the park. You can rent a tandem for $14 an hour.

Metro Bicycles 1311 Lexington Ave at 88th St (☎212/427-4450); 546 6th Ave at 15th St (☎212/255-5100) and other branches in Manhattan. One of the city's largest bike stores.

Midtown Bicycles 360 W 47th St at 9th Ave (☎212/581-4500). Standard at $7 an hour and $35 a day, or $45 if you return the bike by the next day's closing.

West Side Bikes 231 W 96th St between Broadway and Amsterdam (☎212/663-7531). Upper West Side store, again handy for Central Park.

Walking

Few cities equal New York for street-level stimulation. Getting around **on foot** is often the most exciting – and tiring – method of exploring. Figure fifteen minutes to walk ten north–south blocks – rather more at rush hour. However you plan your wanderings you're still going to spend much of your time walking. Footwear is important (sneakers are good for spring/summer; winter needs something waterproof). So is safety: a lot more people are injured in New York carelessly crossing the street than are mugged. The city has a law against jaywalking, and some midtown intersections have cattle gates to prevent crossing at certain corners. Tickets are sometimes handed out for jaywalking, but usually only during the Christmas season or when the police have little else to do. Pedestrian crossings don't give you automatic right of way unless the WALK sign is on – and, even then, cars may be turning, so be prudent. A good rule of thumb is to make eye contact with the driver, giving him or her your best "don't mess with me" New York look.

In-line skating

Although **in-line skating** is still popular as recreation, plenty use it as a speedy way to get around the city. If you're not proficient, the streets of Manhattan aren't really the place to learn; get some practice in Central Park or one of the other traffic-free blading spots (see "Sports and outdoor activities," p.432), though, and you're away. You'll find rentals in the Yellow Pages, or try one of the popular Blades stores (120 W 72nd St between Central Park W and Columbus Ave, ☎212/787-3911 or 1414 2nd Ave between 73rd and 74th sts, ☎212/249-3178). A credit card should be deposit enough, and prices run the gamut, ranging from $16 for 2 hours or $27 for 24 hours on weekends to $16 for 24 hours during the week.

Information, maps and websites

Information

The best place for **information** is the New York Convention and Visitors Bureau at 810 7th Ave at 53rd St (Mon–Fri 8.30am–6pm, weekends and holidays 9am–5pm, or call one of their counselors at ☎212/484-1222, ⓦwww.nycvisit.com). They have up-to-date leaflets on what's going on in the arts and elsewhere plus bus and subway maps and information on hotels and accommodation – though they can't actually book anything for you. Their quarterly *Official NYC Guide* is good too, though the kind of information it gives – on restaurants, hotels, shopping and sights – is also available in the various free tourist magazines and brochures in hotels and elsewhere. These include complete (if superficial) rundowns on what's on in the more mainstream arts, eating out, shops, etc.

The state-run I Love New York organization has free booklets and maps available from 1 Empire State Plaza, Albany, NY 12223 (☎518/474-4116). Much of their information concentrates on New York State, though; before exploring beyond the five boroughs, get their statewide map and regional guides. They do also have info on New York City, including maps and restaurant and hotel lists.

You'll find other small tourist information centers and kiosks all over the city, starting with the airports, Grand Central and Penn stations and Port Authority Bus Terminal. You'll probably come across others without trying, but the following list should help:

Visitors bureaus

Bloomingdale's International Visitors' Center Lexington Ave (at 59th St) ☎212/705-2098.

Harlem Visitors' Bureau 219 W 135th St (between 7th and 8th aves). Call first. ☎212/283-3315.

NYU Information Center Shimkin Hall, 50 W 4th St (at Greene St/Washington Square) ☎212/998-4636.

Saks Fifth Avenue Ambassador Concierge Desk, 611 5th Ave (at 49th St) ☎212/940-4141.

Times Square Visitor and Transit Information Center 1560 Broadway (between 46th and 47th sts); open every day 8am–8pm. ☎212/869-1890.

Websites

Countless **internet websites** contain travel information about New York; you may want to do some extra research before (or during) your trip. What follows is a short list of fun and informative sites for travelers. Here you'll find what's on around town, a sampling of local media and significant Jerry Seinfeld locations. Be sure, too, to check out our own website at ⓦwww.roughguides.com.

CitySearch NY ⓦwww.newyork.citysearch.com
A solid search engine, weekly updated listings and tame features on this comprehensive site.

Data Lounge ⓦwww.datalounge.com
Where gay travelers can peruse community news, glance at the city's social calendar, or simply test the matchmaking skills of Edwina.

NYC Beer Guide ⓦwww.nycbeer.org/
The Beer Guide serves up the suds, from microbreweries to well-stocked bodegas.

NYC Transit Authority ⓦwww.mta.nyc.ny.us
Official subway/bus/Metro-North and LIRR website – schedules, fare info, reroutings, history and fun facts (more than 1.3 billion people ride the subway each year!).

NYC Visitors Bureau ⓦwww.nycvisit.com
Official website of the New York Convention and Visitors Bureau.

PaperMag ⓦwww.papermag.com
Updated daily and covering the cultural gamut, this hip guide has been on the cutting edge of every trend to hit the streets.

Parks Department ⓦwww.nycparks.org
The official word on all of the events in the city's parks.

Seinfeld's Real New York
home.earthlink.net/~asena/srny
Everything you ever wanted to know about Jerry: where he lived, ate and got into trouble with George, Elaine and Kramer.

Time Out New York ⓦwww.timeoutny.com
What's on this week in music, clubs, book readings, museums, movies, and other features from the publication.

Total NY ⓦwww.totalny.com
One of the few guides sporting real New York attitude, Total's quirky features and eclectic listings tell you where to go and what to do.

The Village Voice ⓦwww.villagevoice.com
The best thing here, from the elder (some say out-of-touch) alternative weekly, is the paper's witty listings section, "Choices."

Webtunes ⓦwww.webtunes.com
Loaded with RealAudio samples and venue listings, this site has the lowdown on the city's music scene.

Maps

Our maps should be fine for most purposes; commercial maps, like the Rand McNally *Plan of the City and all Five Boroughs* ($3.95), fill in the gaps. Others include the laminated Streetwise maps – neatly laid out and not expensive at around $7 from most bookstores. Street atlases of all five boroughs cost around $10-13; if you're after a map of one of the individual outer boroughs, try those produced by Geographia or Hagstrom at about $4, on sale in bookstores. For fun, the *New York Popout Map* covers Manhattan and costs $5.95. CrimeSmart Manhattan ($6) provides crime data by street and neighborhood. The Complete Traveler is a good map and guide shop; see p.422.

Tours

There are many different ways to take in the city: exploring streets and neighborhoods on your own; heading up to the tops of buildings, like the Empire State (see p.132) to get a good perspective on the lay of the land, or going on any number of city tours, which might let you experience New York from angles never before thought of.

Bus tours

Apart from equipping yourself with a decent map, perhaps the most obvious way to orient yourself to the city is to take a **bus tour**. These are extremely popular, though frankly you're swept around so quickly as to scarcely see anything. Still, the tops of double deckers are a great place to figure out what's where for later explorations. The

Big Apple Greeter

If you're nervous about exploring New York, or overwhelmed by the possibilities the city offers, look into **Big Apple Greeter**, one of the best – and certainly cheapest – ways to see the city from a native's viewpoint. This not-for-profit organization matches visitors with their corps of 500 trained volunteer "greeters." Specify the part of the city you'd like to see, indicate an aspect of New York life you'd like to explore or plead for general orientation – whatever your interests, chances are they will find someone to take you around. Visits have a friendly, informal feel, and generally last a few hours (although some have gone on all day). The service is free. You can call once you're in New York, but it's better to contact the organization as far in advance as possible to ensure greeter availability. Write to: Big Apple Greeter, 1 Centre St, 19th floor, NY 10007 (Ⓣ212/380-8159, Ⓕ380-3685, Ⓔinformation@bigapplegreeter.org, Ⓦwww.bigapplegreeter.org).

basics are the same: you purchase a ticket from any number of locations including the bus terminal, your hotel, or the bus itself at one of its many stops, and you can hop on and off the bus anywhere along its route. The more you spend, the more of the city you're entitled to see, and the longer time you have for seeing it – in general, an all-city tour over two days will cost $30–45, although you can also have half-day or limited-area tours for around $25. Both tours have discounts for children under 12. Buses run seven days a week, from (approximately) 9am to 6pm, with special rates and times for evening tours.

Tour companies

City Sightseeing (Coach) 1040 6th Ave, NY 10018 Ⓣ1-800/876-9868 for tickets and locations. Terminal: 8th Ave and 53rd St
Gray Line Sightseeing Terminal Port Authority at 42nd St and 8th Ave, NY 10019 Ⓣ1-800/669-0051 for tickets and locations

Helicopter tours

A more exciting option is to look at the city from the air, by **helicopter**. This is expensive, but you won't easily forget the experience. Liberty Helicopter Tours, at the western end of 30th St or from the Wall St heliport at Pier 6 (Ⓣ212/967-4550, closed on weekends), offers flights ranging from $59 (for four-and-a-half minutes) to $187 (15 minutes). If you leave from 30th St, the best seat for photos is on the right in the back. Helicopters take off regularly between 9am and 9pm every day unless winds and visibility are bad; you don't need a reservation, but in high season (and nice weather) you may have quite a wait if you just show up. Should you go by day or night? After doing one, you'll probably want to do the other.

Tours on water

A great way to see the island of Manhattan is a voyage on the **Circle Line ferry** (Ⓣ212/563-3200, Ⓦwww.circleline.com). Departing from Pier 83 at West 42nd St and 12th Ave, it circumnavigates Manhattan, taking in everything from the tall buildings of downtown Manhattan to the subdued stretches of Harlem and the Bronx – complete with a live wisecracking commentary; the three-hour tour is $24 ($12 for children under 12). The evening Harbor Lights Cruise offers dramatic views of the skyline. The Harlem Spirituals Gospel Cruise will make a believer out of you. These two-hour tours are $25. Boats departing from Pier 16 at South Street Seaport feature a one-hour downtown skyline cruise ($13, $7 for children) plus two-hour live music tours (offering a choice of Blues, Jazz or Gospel), with prices ranging from $30 to $40. If you're feeling really sporty, try *The Beast*, a bright red speedboat that will throw you around for thirty minutes at a dashing 45 miles an hour. Boats run between late March and mid-December, roughly twice a day in low season, almost hourly in midsummer.

Alternatively, check out tours offered by **NY Waterway** (Ⓣ1-800/533-3779, Ⓦwww.nywaterway.com). Its 90-minute tours leave the west end of 38th St four times daily: $18, children 3–12 $9, seniors $16. For a small additional fee they will provide audio in your choice of six languages. NY Waterway also offers Hudson Valley tours to historic spots up the river.

The bargain that still can't be beaten, even more so now that the fare has been eliminated, is the free Staten Island Ferry (Ⓣ718/390-

5253), which leaves from its own terminal in Lower Manhattan's Battery Park. It's a commuter boat, so avoid crowded rush hours if you can; at other times, grab a spot at the back (going out) and watch the skyline shrink away. Departures are every 15–20 minutes at rush hours, every 30 minutes mid-day and evenings, and every hour late at night – weekend services are less frequent. (Few visitors spend much time on Staten Island; it's easy to just turn around and get back on the ferry. For info on what's on Staten Island, see p.273.)

Walking tours

Options for walking tours of Manhattan or the outer boroughs are many and varied. Usually led by experts, they offer fact-filled wanders through neighborhoods or focus on particular subjects. You'll find fliers for some of them at the various Visitor Centers; for what's happening in the current week, check the *New York Times* (Friday or Sunday), the weekly *Village Voice* or *New York Press* (both out on Wednesday), or any of the free weekly papers around town. Detailed below are some of the more interesting tours: they don't all operate year-round, the more esoteric only setting up for a couple of outings at specific times of the year. Phone ahead for the full schedules. Most go rain or shine.

Tour companies

Art Tours of Manhattan ⓣ609/921-2647 Much the best people to go with if you want first-hand accounts of the city's art scene, establishment and fringe. The custom-designed tours include the galleries of SoHo, Chelsea, 57th St and Madison Ave, as well as a "hospitality" visit to an artist's studio, all guided by qualified – and entertaining – art historians. This individual attention doesn't come cheap. Tours for up to four people cost around $225.

Big Onion Walking Tours ⓣ212/439-1090, ⓦwww.bigonion.com Founded by two Columbia University graduate students, Big Onion specializes in tours with an ethnic and historical focus: pick one particular group, or take the "Immigrant New York" tour and learn about everyone. Cost is $10 or $8 for students and seniors; the food-included "Multi-Ethnic Eating Tour" costs $13 or $11. These last about two hours.

Braggin' About Brooklyn ⓣ718/297-5107 African-American themed Brooklyn tours are $15. Tour times change daily; call for details.

Bronx County Historical Society 3309 Bainbridge Ave, Bronx ⓣ718/881-8900, ⓦwww.bronxhistoricalsociety.org Neighborhood tours range from strolls through suburban Riverdale to hikes across the South Bronx. Excellent value at $10 per person ($5 for society members), though tours are given the least frequently of any company listed here.

Brooklyn Center for the Urban Environment Tennis House, Prospect Park, Brooklyn ⓣ718/788-8500, ⓦwww.bcue.com Focusing on the architectural as well as the natural environment, this organization specializes in summertime neighborhood "noshing" tours that give you a flavor – literally – of Brooklyn's distinct ethnic neighborhoods. Other frequent tours focus on historic Green-Wood Cemetery (see p.247); all walking tours cost $8, students and seniors $5. Ask about the $35 ($30 for members, students and seniors) ecology boat tours around the oddly fluorescent Gowanus Canal.

Greenwich Village Literary Pub Crawl ⓣ212/613-5796 A two-and-a-half-hour tour guided by actors from the New Ensemble Theater Company, who lead you to several of the most prominent bars in literary history and read from associated works. Tours meet at the *White Horse Tavern*, 567 Hudson St, at 2pm every Saturday. Reservations are highly recommended: $12, students and seniors $9.

Harlem Heritage Tours 230 W 116th St, Suite #5C ⓣ212/280-7888, ⓦwww.harlemheritage.com Cultural tours of Harlem, general and specific (such as "Harlem Jazz Clubs"), are led mid-day and evening. Walking tours are $15–20, with the Evening Jazz Experience from $30–65. Reservations are recommended. Call for details. Very helpful tour guides.

Harlem Spirituals Gospel and Jazz Tours 690 8th Ave, 2nd floor ⓣ212/757-0425, ⓦwww.harlemspiritual.com Various tours of Harlem, the Bronx, and Brooklyn, ranging from Sunday-morning church visits to night-time Soul Food and Jazz affairs taking in dinner and a club. Professionally run and excellent value, with prices in the range of $25–75 per person (discounts for children). Reservations necessary.

Hassidic Discovery Welcome Center 305 Kingston Ave, Brooklyn ⓣ1-800/838-TOUR, ⓦwww.jewishtours.com Three-hour tours on Sundays of Hassidic Crown Heights conducted by Rabbi Beryl Epstein. Transport from midtown Manhattan available. Reservations required.

Lower East Side Tenement Museum 90 Orchard St ⓣ212/431-0233, ⓦwww.tenement.org This museum organizes weekend walking tours of the Lower East Side, April–Dec, focusing on the heritage of the various ethnic groups present, community rebuilding and relations among different groups; $9, students and seniors $7. And tickets are available for museum admission and a tour combined at a reduced price.

Municipal Arts Society 457 Madison Ave, between 50th and 51st sts ☎212/439-1049 or 935-3960, ⓦwww.mas.org Opinionated tours looking at neighborhoods from an architectural, cultural, historical and often political perspective. They may visit spots not otherwise open to the public – look out for "hard hat" jaunts around construction sites; call for a schedule. Free (donations requested) Wednesday lunchtime tours of Grand Central Station start at 12.30pm from the information booth. Most other tours also start at 12.30pm, last for 90 minutes, and cost $10–$15, with discounts for students and seniors. Weekend and day-long tours cost more.

The 92nd Street Y 1395 Lexington Ave, between 91st and 92nd sts ☎212/996-1100, ⓦwww.92ndsty.org None better, offering a mixed bag of walking tours ranging from straight explorations of specific New York neighborhoods to art tours, walking tours of political New York or a pre-dawn visit to the city's wholesale meat and fish markets. Average costs are $20–55 per person; specific tours can be organized to accommodate groups with special interests. Consider, too, day excursions by bus to accessible parts of the Tri-State area. The commentary is almost always erudite and informative, and the organization, which sponsors concerts, readings and other events, is well worth checking out in any case.

Queens Historical Society 143-35 37th Ave, Flushing, Queens ☎718/939-0647, ⓦwww.preserve.org/queens No actual guided walking tours, but if you visit their Kingsland Homestead headquarters (see p.263), they'll give you a free do-it-yourself walking tour of the Flushing Freedom Mile.

Radical Walking Tours ☎718/492-0069 Fifteen different $10 tours of "alternative" Manhattan from a distinctly left-wing perspective. Tours focus on political and social history, such as "Central Park – Trees, Grass and the Working Class"; no reservations required; call for schedule.

River to River Downtown Tours 375 South End Ave ☎212/321-2823 Individual and small group tours of Lower Manhattan by New York aficionado Ruth Alscher-Green. Individual prices are $35, or $50 for two people, for a unique two-hour tour spiced with gossip and anecdotal tidbits.

Street Smarts NY ☎212/969-8262 Lively weekend tours, with favorites such as "SoHo Ghosts," "Pubs and Poltergeists" and "Manhattan Murder Mysteries." All tours are $10 and generally begin around 2pm; no reservations needed. Call for meeting place and info.

The Urban Park Rangers A varied selection of free educational walks in all five boroughs throughout the year, focusing on nature and sometimes history in the city's parks. (For walks and information on other events in the parks ☎1-888/NY-PARKS, ⓦwww.nyparks.org).

The media

Newspapers and magazines

The 1990s were not good to the print media, and the days are gone when New York could support twenty daily newspapers. Today, only **three remain**: the broadsheet the *New York Times* and the tabloids the *Daily News* and the *New York Post*. The demise of a fourth, the semi-tabloid *Newsday* (still available in the city, but only in Queens and Long Island editions), reminded both readers and publishers of the precarious standing of the rest. The tabloids, especially, seem to take turns battling for survival.

The *New York Times* (75¢), an American institution, prides itself on being the "paper of record" – the closest thing America has to a quality national paper. It has solid, sometimes stolid, international coverage, and places much emphasis on its news analysis. Each weekday there are "Metro," "Business Day," "Sports" and "Arts" sections in addition to the main paper plus rotating special sections – "Dining In," "House and Home," "Science Times", etc – and separate Weekend sections devoted to "Movies and Performing Arts" and "Fine Arts and Leisure" on Fridays. The Sunday edition ($3) is a thumping bundle of newsprint divided into a number of supplements that take days to read. The legendary crossword puzzles, which increase in difficulty throughout the week, culminate in Sunday's *New York Times Magazine* puzzle, which should keep you occupied all day.

It takes serious coordination to read the *Times* on the subway, one reason (but a minor one) why many turn to the *Post* and the *Daily News*. Tabloids in format and style, these arch rivals concentrate on local news, usually screamed out in banner headlines. The *Daily News* (50¢) is renowned as a picture newspaper but with intelligent features and many racy headlines.

The *New York Post* (25¢), the city's oldest newspaper, started in 1801 by Alexander Hamilton, has been in decline for many years. Known for its solid city news reporting, not to mention consistent conservative-slanted sermonizing, it's perhaps renowned most for its sensational approach to stories.

The other New York-based daily newspaper is the *Wall Street Journal* ($1), in fact a national financial paper that also has strong national and international news coverage (with a decidedly conservative bent) – despite an old-fashioned design that eschews the use of photographs.

The weeklies and monthlies

Of the **weekly papers**, the *Village Voice* (Wednesdays, free in Manhattan, $1.25 elsewhere) is the most widely read, mainly for its comprehensive arts coverage and investigative features. Originating in Greenwich Village, it made its name as an intelligent, vaguely left-leaning journal – the nearest the city ever got to "alternative" journalism. It offers vocal and opinionated news stories with sharp focus on the media, gay issues and civil rights. It's also one of the best pointers to what's on around town. Catch it early enough on Wednesday morning (or late Tuesday night at select locations around the city) and grab a free pass to a new movie the following week; look for the full-page ad that tells you where to wait in line. Its main competitor, the *New York Press*, is an edgier alternative, angrier and not afraid to offend just about everyone. The listings are quite good and look for its "Best of Manhattan" special edition, published each September.

Other leading weeklies include glossy *New York* magazine ($3.99), which has reasonably comprehensive listings and is more of an entertainment journal than the harder-hitting *Voice*, and *Time Out New York* ($2.99) – a clone of its London original, combining the city's most comprehensive what's on listings with New York-slanted news stories and entertainment and lifestyle features. The long-established *New Yorker* ($3.95) still features poetry and short fiction alongside its much-loved cartoons. The late Andy Warhol's *Interview* ($2.95) is mainly given over to interviews and fashion. *Soho Style* ($5) claims to define the Downtown Experience. Perhaps the best, certainly the wackiest, most downtown-oriented alternative to the *Voice* is *Paper* magazine ($3.50), a monthly that carries witty and well-written rundowns on New York City nightlife and restaurants and all the current news and gossip. Finally, if you want a weekly with more of a political edge, there's the ironic, pink *New York Observer* ($1) and the earnest, black *Amsterdam News* (75¢).

International publications

British and European newspapers are widely available, usually a day after publication – except for the *Financial Times*, which is printed (via satellite) in the US and sold on most newsstands. If you want a specific paper or magazine, try these outlets: Universal Magazines, 1586 Broadway between 47th and 48th streets (☎212/586-7205), where you can pick up more than 7000 titles; Magazine Store, at 20 Park Ave S between 17th and 18th sts (☎212/598-9406); Hotalings, 142 W 42nd between Broadway and 6th Ave (☎212/840-1868); Hudson News, 753 Broadway at 8th St; Dina News Corp., 2077 Broadway between 71st and 72nd sts (☎212/875-8824) or Nico's, at 6th Ave and 11th St (☎212/255-

9175) – one of the best sources for general and specialist magazines. The Barnes & Noble Superstores and Borders (see p.421) stock magazines and international newspapers, which you can peruse for free over coffee.

Television

Any American will find **on TV** in New York mostly what they find at home, with the addition of some wacky public access shows featuring all manner of oddball, and plenty of multilingual stations. For foreign travelers, the 70-plus stations available on cable may be a bit more of a fascination: home shopping networks, psychic hotlines, Spanish soap operas, and tabloid talk shows. You may even forget to see the New York sights altogether.

Here's a brief guide to help you sort through some of what's available: for more complete listings, grab a copy of *TV Guide* ($1.99) or check the newspaper listings.

Broadcast TV

Broadcast TV is what you automatically get when you plug a TV into the wall; on most hotel TV sets, you'll get some or all of the channels listed below.

A major trend in American broadcast TV in the 1990s was the explosion of **daytime talk shows**, which all but obliterated the game shows that once dominated the mornings. Generally devoted to exploiting bizarre weaknesses of everyday people, these shows feature confrontational or sympathetic hosts who interrogate guests with the help of a vocal audience. Competition has seen the topics become more and more sensational; it's common practice to tell guests they're on stage for one reason and then spring the real topic on them. Another recent trend is the proliferation of **court and trial shows**. The more factually based exposés and discussions are found most easily on the cable channel CourtTV (which also shows crime series and movies). The alternative is played anything but straight – you can collapse into laughter as clueless dupes bring their small-claims cases to the likes of Judge Judy Sheindlin, who berates plaintiff and defendant alike for their lack of common sense.

Broadcast TV channels

2	WCBS (CBS)
4	WNBC (NBC)
5	WNYW (Fox)
7	WABC (ABC)
9	WWOR (Independent)
11	WPIX/WB11 (Independent)
13	WNET (PBS)
21	WLIW (PBS)
25	WNYE (Educational)
31	WPXN (Independent)
41	WXTV (Spanish language)
47	WNJU (Spanish language)
55	WLNY (Independent)

Something else you'll notice if you're from abroad is the amount of scheduled **news** shown every evening. Despite all the offerings, you can still find yourself uninformed: most of the news is local, much time is devoted to sports and weather, and sensational stories dominate as the various networks battle for the limited attention span of the public. The only truly national news coverage is at 6.30pm on ABC, CBS and NBC. International news is generally limited to spots in these programs and on CNN, and the BBC World News on WLIW (21) at 7pm and 11pm weeknights. *Sixty Minutes* (CBS, Sunday at 7pm) is probably the best news analysis show, and an American institution, with top-quality investigative reporting. *Nightline* (ABC, 11.30pm Monday to Friday), anchored by leading journalist Ted Koppel, is also worth catching for debate on the major stories that day.

"Reality television" is the latest wave in entertainment, ranging from involving (*Survivor*) to embarrassing. Game shows, both new and imported, are also resurging. While the networks scramble to attract ever younger – and whiter – audiences (the target groups most valuable to advertisers), they've been unable to stop the mass defection of viewers to cable – witness the success of the quirky Mafia series *The Sopranos* on HBO.

Channels 13 and 21 are given over to PBS (Public Broadcasting Service), which earned the nickname "Purely British Station" for its fondness for BBC drama series. Where it excels, however, is with its wonderfully evocative historical documentaries.

TV show tapings

If you want to experience the excitement, horror, boredom and surprise of American TV up close, there are **free tickets** for various shows. While some of the more popular require written requests months in advance, almost all have standby lines where you can try your luck on a particular day. Not all shows tape year-round. For most shows you must be 16 and sometimes 18 to be in the audience; if you're underage or traveling with children, call ahead. Here are some of the more popular shows:

Morning shows

The Early Show Waking up with Bryant Gumbel would seem to be enough to dampen anyone's day, but some people watch the standard mix of news, weather, human interest stories and network stars plugging their shows. Due to its smaller fan base, you should be okay if you show up when the show starts at 7am, at 59th St and 5th Ave.

Good Morning America Because Disney has taken over much of Times Square, it seems fitting that this show on Disney-affiliated ABC broadcasts from Broadway and 44th St. To reserve a standing-room place, call ☎212/580-5176 and leave your name, number of people in your party, phone number and preferred date (if within two months of your call), and a staff member will call back. If it is longer than that, they ask you to reserve via their website, ⓦgma.abcnews.com. Show up at the Broadway entrance for a shot at a stand-by ticket. Be there around 6am in either case.

Today The original, and arguably the best, of the three broadcast early morning get-out-of-bed shows. Katie Couric and the equally popular Matt Lauer enhance the distinguished history of the show that debuted in 1952. It also has the least complicated way to participate: just show up. Of course, hundreds more will have the same idea. Fans start arriving at around 6am; for the two-or-three song concerts given by pop stars in the summer, some have been known to wait out all night. Arrive at 49th St, between 5th and 6th aves; unlike the rest of the morning shows, which run until 9am, Today ends at 10am.

Daytime shows

Judge Mills Lane The Nevada District Judge and boxing referee whose "Let's get it on!" inspired Mike Tyson to bite off Evander Holyfield's ear holds court on WB11/WPIX. For tickets call ☎212/691-3129 a month in advance.

Live with Regis and Kelly The show is a throwback to early days of talk TV, with topics for a family audience. Regis Philbin, Hollywood veteran and also emcee of the popular *Who Wants to be a Millionaire*, hosts with soap-opera graduate Kelly Ripa. You face a year's wait, but if you want to try, send a postcard with your name, address and telephone number to Live Tickets, PO Box 230777 Ansonia Station, New York, NY 10023-0777. Include your preferred date(s) and number of tickets (limit 4). Or stop by ABC at 67th St and Columbus Ave as early as 7am for a standby number that might get you in. Information: ☎212/456-1000.

Montel Williams His show, aimed at young and old, focuses on resolving problems – particularly interracial obstacles. Call the Montel Williams Show ☎212/989-8101 for information on getting into a taping.

Ricki Lake The shows of this younger, fresh face of talk are fun and unlikely to make you feel like you're spying on people less fortunate than you. Information: ☎212/352-3322.

Rosie O'Donnell. Rising above the morning sludge, Rosie's show is immensely popular; guests are Hollywood stars. Expect a year's wait. As with *Saturday Night Live*, tickets are awarded in a postcard lottery (send 'em from March to June). Write to: NBC Tickets, "The Rosie O'Donnell Show," 30 Rockefeller Plaza, New York, NY 10112. Tapings are Monday to Thursday at 10am with an additional show on Wednesday at 2pm. Standby tickets (which do not guarantee admission) are available at the Page Desk at 30 Rockefeller Plaza. Information: ☎212/664-4000.

Sally Jessy Raphael She tackles the trashy, though her shows are more sedate than some. Tapings are Monday to Wednesday; reserve up to a day in advance by calling ☎1-800/411-7941 ext 7470. For same-day standby tickets, go to the *Hotel Pennsylvania* at 33rd St (between 7th Ave and Broadway) by 9am.

Total Request Live (TRL) On MTV's most popular show our baby-faced hero, Carson Daly, plays videos and interviews teen-pop favorites, to the delight of screaming teenagers. Call ☎212/398-8549 and leave your name and number; a staff member will call back. However, only those who get a confirmation call will be in the audience. Alternatively, stand outside the

continued overleaf

continued from overleaf

studio at 1515 Broadway with the throngs and hope to be brought inside. Live Monday to Thursday 4–5pm, Friday to 5.30pm.

Late-night shows

David Letterman Still everyone's top choice. Send a postcard (two-ticket limit per card) as far ahead as possible to Letterman Tickets, 1697 Broadway, New York, NY 10019. Shoots Monday through Thursday at 5.30pm, with an additional show Thursday at 8pm; you must be there one hour and fifteen minutes before taping starts. Information: ☏212/975-1003.

Late Night with Conan O'Brien Letterman's replacement on NBC is fun in a harmless sort of way. Write to NBC Tickets, "Late Night with Conan O'Brien," 30 Rockefeller Plaza, New York, NY 10112. Pickup is at 4pm on the day of the show from the Page Desk at the same address. For standby tickets go to the same place before 9am, Tuesday to Friday. Information: ☏212/664-4000.

Saturday Night Live Audiences keep coming to a legendary show, despite constant cries that it's not as funny as it once was. The policy of an annual ticket lottery still stands – not very convenient unless you're willing to plan your trip around the date they give you. Send a postcard – which must arrive in August – with your name, address and phone number to NBC Tickets, "Saturday Night Live," 30 Rockefeller Plaza, New York, NY 10112, and see what happens. Tickets are issued to either the dress rehearsal or the actual show. They hand out standbys (one per person, admission not guaranteed) at the 49th St side of the GE Building at 30 Rockefeller Plaza at 9.15am any Saturday that there's a show (call ☏212/664-4000 to make sure; some Saturdays are reruns).

Cable TV

Cable TV is available in many hotels. Viewing a recently released film on a pay-per-view channel usually adds about $5 to your bill. Cable nets appear on different channels in different parts of New York; if the back of the remote (a fixture no cable box is without) doesn't list them, ask the hotel desk or just surf.

Cable highlights include HBO (Home Box Office), which produces its own programming and shows movies; sports channels (ESPN, ESPN2) showcasing international and American games (look for British Premier League soccer on Sunday nights on Fox Sports Network); and plenty of news. CNN (Cable News Network), well-known in Europe, offers around-the-clock news; C-SPAN does much the same but concentrates on news from Congress and the Supreme Court, as well as the British House of Commons. NBC and Fox news channels provide fast-paced, fast-talk saturation coverage of sensational news stories.

A&E (Arts and Entertainment) and Bravo offer intelligent coverage of the arts, while the Independent Film Channel presents some of the strangest films recently released. Looking for something more idiosyncratic? Check out the public access channels. You may find colorfully garbed psychics, sex-phone numbers, a satanic mass, alternative lifestyle programming, or live demonstrations of piercing.

Radio

The FM dial is crammed with local stations of varying quality and content. Bring your Walkman and skip through the channels. Stations constantly change formats and open up and close down, but here is a list of some of what's on. Whereas you'll find mostly music on FM, AM stations tend to be talk-oriented. The *New York Times* lists highlights daily; explore on your own, and you're sure to come across something interesting.

Incidentally, it's possible to tune in to the BBC World Service on the 49-meter shortwave band, or just the World Service news, broadcast on a number of the public radio stations.

FM radio stations

88.3 (WBGO) Jazz*
89.9 (WKCR) Columbia University
90.7 (WFUV) Contemporary folk/Celtic/international*
91.5 (WNYE) Educational/community/children
92.3 (WXRK) "K Rock" Classic rock/Howard Stern in the morning
92.7 (WLIR) "Modern" rock (alternative/80s new wave)
93.1 (WPAT) Spanish
93.9 (WNYC) Classical*
95.5 (WPLJ) Top 40
96.3 (WQXR) Classical
97.1 (WQHT) "Hot 97" Hip-hop, R&B
97.5 (WALK) Adult contemporary
97.9 (WSKQ) Spanish
98.7 (WRKS) "Kiss" Urban classics
99.5 (WBAI) Varied/ethnic
99.9 (WEZN) Adult contemporary
100.3 (WHTZ) "Z100" Top 40
101.1 (WCBS) Oldies
101.9 (WQCD) Smooth Jazz
102.7 (WNEW) Talk/personality
103.5 (WKTU) Pop/Disco
104.3 (WAXQ) Classic rock
105.1 (WTJM) R&B oldies
105.9 (WCAA) Multiethnic
106.7 (WLTW) Adult contemporary
107.5 (WBLS) Urban contemporary

AM radio stations

570 (WMCA) Christian/talk
620 (WSNR) Sports
660 (WFAN) Sports/Imus in the Morning
710 (WWOR) News/talk/sportscasts
770 (WABC) Talk/news/Rush Limbaugh/sportscasts
820 (WNYC) News/talk*
880 (WCBS) News
930 (WPAT) Spanish
970 (WWDJ) Christian music
1010 (WINS) News
1050 (WEVD) News/talk
1130 (WBBR) News
1190 (WLIB) Afro-Caribbean news/talk
1280 (WADO) Spanish
1380 (WNNY) Multiethnic
1560 (WQEW) Children's programming/Radio Disney
1600 (WWRL) Gospel/soul

**Indicates national public radio (NPR), often with syndicated programs*

Costs, money and banks

New York is an expensive place to visit any way you slice it. Though there's plenty to do and see that's fairly inexpensive, or even free, inevitably the costs catch up to you – most likely in the form of accommodation and food and drink. It's hard to find much less for $100 a day on the former, and $35 a day is probably minimum for just getting by on the essentials; sky's the limit as far as the maximum you might spend. There are budget options; see Chapter 28 "Accommodation," Chapter 29 "Restaurants" and Chapter 31 "Drinking" for details on our recommendations across the spectrum.

Taking and getting money

Expect to pay most major expenses by credit card; hotels and car-rental agencies usually require a credit card imprint as security, even if you intend to settle the bill in cash.

You'll also need to carry cash. If you have a MasterCard or Visa, or a cash-dispensing card linked to an international network such as Cirrus or Plus – check with your home bank before you set off – you can withdraw cash from appropriate automatic teller machines (ATMs), which usually dispense $20 bills.

For both American and foreign visitors, travelers' checks are a better way to carry money than ordinary bills; they offer the great security of knowing that lost or stolen checks will be replaced. Checks such as American Express, Visa and Thomas Cook are universally accepted as cash in stores, restaurants and gas stations. Order a good number of checks in lower denominations: few places like to hand over all their spare cash and change in return for a check. Foreign travelers should bring travelers' checks issued in US dollars.

Emergencies

All else has failed. You're broke and 3500 miles from home. Before you jump off the Brooklyn Bridge, weigh the alternatives.

Assuming you know someone who is prepared to send you money in a crisis, have them take the cash to the nearest Travelers Express Moneygram (☎1-800/543-4080) office and have it wired to the office nearest you. This should take five to ten minutes. They charge according to the country involved and the amount sent: From the US the rate for wiring $100 is $12 while $1000 will incur a fee of $66; from Canada the rates for the equivalent amounts are CAN$18/CAN$85; from Europe $20/$60; from Australia or New Zealand $12/$50. The option of using a credit card is available only when wiring money in the US. There's a maximum of $500 and an additional fee of $12. Western Union offers a similar service, at slightly higher rates (US ☎1-800/325-6000; UK ☎0800/833833).

If you have enough leeway, consider a postal money order, which is exchangeable at any post office. Whether this works out cheaper will depend on the type of mail service you use – priority, express, etc. The equivalent for foreign travelers is the international money order, for which you need to allow up to seven days in the mail before arrival. Estimates as to how long an ordinary check sent from overseas takes to clear range from 4 to 8 weeks.

Banks and exchange

Banking hours are usually (with some variation) Monday–Friday 9am–3pm: some banks stay open later on Thursdays or Fridays, and a few have limited Saturday hours. Major banks – such as Citibank and Chase – will exchange travelers' checks and currency at a standard rate. Outside banking hours, you're dependent on a limited number of private exchange offices in Manhattan (listed *WHERE*), as well as offices at the airports. All change travelers' checks and currency, although they may have disadvantageous rates and commission charges, the cost of which it's wise to ask about first.

Exchange offices

The following offices are all open outside banking hours, and handle wire transfers and money orders as well as straightforward transactions.

Avis Currency Exchange 200 Park Ave at 45th St (Met Life Building), Third Floor East, Room 332 (Mon–Fri 8am–5pm ☎1-800/258-0456 or 212/661-0826). Also on the main concourse at Grand Central (Mon–Fri 7am–9pm, Sat & Sun 10am–6pm ☎212/661-7600) and at 401 West Broadway (at Spring), operating as Eurochange (daily 10am–6pm ☎212/966-7080).

Thomas Cook 317 Madison Ave at 42nd St (Mon–Sat 9am–7pm, Sun 9am–5pm; ☎212/883-0401). Also 511 Madison Ave at 53rd St (Mon–Fri 9am–7pm, Sat–Sun 9am-5pm ☎753-0117), 1590 Broadway at 48th St (Mon–Sat 9am–7pm, Sun 9am–5pm; ☎212/265-6063), 1271 Broadway at 32nd St (Mon–Sat 9am–6.30pm, Sun 9am–5pm ☎679-4877) and at 29 Broadway at Morris St (Mon–Fri 9am–5pm ☎212/363-6206).

Lost credit cards or travelers' checks

American Express checks ☎1-800/221-7282
American Express cards ☎1-800/528-4800
Citicorp/Citibank ☎1-800/645-6556
Diners Club ☎1-800/234-6377
MasterCard cards ☎1-800/826-2181
Thomas Cook/MasterCard checks ☎1-800/223-9920
Visa cards ☎1-800/336-8472
Visa checks ☎1-800/227-6811

Money: a note for foreign travelers

US currency comes in bills of $1, $2, $5, $10, $20, $50 and $100, plus various larger (and rarer) denominations. All are the same size and same green color, making it necessary to check each bill carefully. The dollar is made up of 100 cents (¢) in coins of 1 cent (usually called a penny), 5 cents (a nickel), 10 cents (a dime), 25 cents (a quarter), 50 cents (a half dollar) and one dollar. The $2 bill and the half-dollar and dollar coins are seldom seen. Change – especially quarters – is needed for buses, vending machines and telephones, so always carry plenty.

In approximate terms, one pound sterling will buy $1.45; one Canadian dollar is worth 65¢; one Australian dollar is worth 50¢; and one New Zealand dollar will get you 40¢.

Phones, mail and email

Phone calls

Public telephones are easily found – on street corners and in hotel lobbies, bars and restaurants, and some actually work. Most New Yorkers will tell you to look for the more reliable Verizon phones; the others don't usually give the same value. The cost of a local call – one within the 212 and 718 area codes covering the five boroughs – is 25¢ (slightly more to or from remote parts of 718). If your pay phone won't accept your quarter, the change box is full. Verizon's local rate is 25¢ for 3 minutes. When your time is up, a voice will instruct you to put in more money: 5¢ for each extra 2 minutes. If you don't, you'll be cut off.

Calling from your hotel room may cost more than from a pay phone – the hotel may charge as much as $2 per call. (You'll usually find pay phones in the lobby.) Some budget hotels offer free local calls from rooms – ask when you check in.

Long-distance and international calls

All **long-distance** and **international calls** can be dialed direct from any private or public phone. If it's the latter, just dial the number and an operator will tell you the rate for the first 3 minutes; a problem is coming up with the copious amounts of change necessary to call anywhere for any length of time. Solution: a **prepaid phone card**, which you can buy at most grocery stores and newsstands. They are issued by phone companies and countless others (who may charge exorbitant rates – so beware!) and give you a prepaid dollar amount of long-distance time, which you access by punching in numbers – shown on the card – at any public phone.

All phones accept **credit cards** – an operator or recorded message will tell you to either read out or punch in the number; international rates are usually competitive. Beware of using your BT or Mercury charge cards – their international rates can be staggeringly expensive. Reverse-charge calls (or "collect calls") can also prove costly: use a collect call to give your number to the people you are calling – and then get them to call you back. However, many public phones do not accept incoming calls. To make a collect call you can dial ⓣ0 followed by the number you wish to call and an operator will take it from there. Otherwise, dial ⓣ1-800/COLLECT or 1-800/CALLATT – these both claim to be the cheapest options.

Within the US, **rates** are generally cheapest between 11pm and 8am weekdays, all day on weekends; the next cheapest time is between 6pm and 11pm weekdays. For overseas, the best times vary depending on the time difference. The three big long-distance companies – AT&T, Sprint and MCI – are constantly warring to offer the best deal to customers. Their rates are generally within a cent of each other. But before you call using any option listed above, dial the operator to check the rate.

Area codes around New York

Bronx, Brooklyn, Queens and Staten Island (1) **718, 347**
Long Island (1) **516**
Other nearby areas of New York State (1) **914**
New Jersey (1) **201**, **973**, **908**, **609** or **732**
To phone into Manhattan from these areas or anywhere else (1) **212** (and sometimes **646**)

Service numbers

Emergencies **911** for police, ambulance and fire
Operator **0**
Directory assistance **411** (New York City); 1 + **(area code) + 555-1212** (numbers in other area codes)

Useful telephone codes

The telephone code to dial **to the US** from the outside world is **1**.
To make international calls **from the US**, dial **011** followed by the country code:
Australia 61
Denmark 45
Germany 49
Ireland 353
Netherlands 31
New Zealand 64
Sweden 46
United Kingdom 44
For codes not listed here, dial the operator or check the front of the local White Pages.

Overseas operator numbers

To call an operator in your own country in order to make a collect call from the US, dial the following numbers:
Australia ☎1-800/682-2878, 1-800/937-6822 or 1-800/676-0061 (☎008/032 032 in Australia for information).
Ireland ☎1-800/562-6262 (☎1800/250 250 in Ireland for information).
New Zealand ☎1-800/248-0064 (☎123 or 126 in New Zealand for information).
United Kingdom ☎1-800/445-5667 (☎0800/345144 in the UK for information).

Telephone services and helplines

AIDS Hotline ☎212/447-8200; for counseling and information ☎1-800/590-2437
Al-Anon (for families of alcoholics) ☎212/254-7230
Alateen (for teenage drinkers) ☎212/254-7230
Alcoholics Anonymous ☎212/647-1680
Crime Victims Hotline ☎212/577-7777 (24 hours)
Herpes Advice Line ☎212/213-6150; 24hr recorded info ☎212/540-0540
Missing Persons Bureau – New York City Police Department ☎212/374-0319
Movies ☎212/777-FILM
Narcotics Anonymous ☎212/929-6262
New York City On Stage ☎212/768-1818
New York Council on Problem Gambling ☎1-800/437-1611
NYC Gay and Lesbian Anti-Violence Project ☎212/807-0197
Pills Anonymous ☎212/874-0700
Sex Crimes Report Hotline (N.Y.C.P.D.) ☎212/267-7273
Sex Crimes Victim Services Agency ☎212/577-7777 (24 hours)
Suicide Hotline (24 hours) ☎1-800/543-3638, ☎673-3000 (The Samaritans)
Suicide Prevention Hotline ☎718/389-9608

Area codes

Normally, **telephone numbers** are in the form of ☎123/456-7890. The first three digits are the **area code**. In New York City, the **212** code covers Manhattan, with newer phone numbers assigned **646**. The outer boroughs of Brooklyn, the Bronx, Queens, and Staten Island use **718**, or less commonly, **347**. Cell phones have their own area code: **917**. To phone within any area code, simply dial the last seven digits of the number. Outside the area, dial 1 first, then the area code and number.

Any number with 800, 888 or 877 in place of the area code is toll-free. Many national firms, government agencies, inquiry numbers, hotels and car-rental firms have a central toll-free number. To find it, look in the Yellow Pages or dial ☎1-800/555-1212 for toll-free directory inquiries. Dial ☎411 at any NY area pay phone for free directory assistance to find phone numbers, addresses or even just a cross street.

A so-far purely American phenomenon is using letters as part of a phone number – the idea is that it'll be easier for you to remember that way. Whether it's a toll-free information number (such as ☎1-800/AIR RIDE for airport transport) or a chicken delivery service (in Brooklyn's Cobble Hill, a sign says simply "DIAL HOT BIRD"), it seems to work. Use the keypad of any phone.

Phone books

The **Verizon White Pages** list private numbers and businesses (blue-edged pages sandwiched between the two sections contain listings for New York City, state and federal government agencies); the **Yellow Pages** details consumer-oriented businesses and services; restaurants are listed by cuisine.

Letters and poste restante

The New York (and American) postal service ranks a poor second to the phone system. New Yorkers tell of postcards arriving thirty years after they were sent – legends, mostly, but with a basis in truth. Even within Manhattan, mail can take a few days to arrive, and a letter to LA might take a week. Overseas airmail takes five to fourteen days; surface mail? – four to eight weeks.

The General Post Office at 8th Ave between 31st and 33rd sts is open 24/7 for important services; go at 11.30pm on April 15 (tax day in the US), when television news crews capture the procrastinators' frantic last-minute rush. Letters posted from this or other large post offices seem to arrive soonest, whereas the blue mailboxes on street corners tend to take a couple of days more.

Letters

Ordinary mail **within the US** costs 34¢ (at press time) for letters weighing up to an ounce, 20¢ for postcards. Letters to Canada and Mexico are 60¢ for up to an ounce. Postcards to either country are 50¢.

Airmail service is the same price for anywhere else in the world. Postcards and aerograms are 70¢; letters are 80¢ for the first ounce and rise steeply after that.

Envelopes in the US must include the sender's address and the recipient's zip code: without the code, letters can end up terminally lost, and certainly delayed. If you're unsure of a Manhattan zip, phone ☎212/967-8585, or ask for the relevant zip code directory at the post office.

You can buy stamps in shops, some supermarkets and delis, though these may cost considerably more than the face value. The best place is a post office: although the hours vary (you're unlikely to find the Wall St branch open on Saturdays), they are, roughly, Monday–Friday 9am–5pm, Saturday 9am–noon; some branches have limited evening hours during the week. You may wait on line or buy stamps at vending machines. Put enough postage on – the US Postal Service doesn't like being shortchanged.

Packages

The price of a **package** increases in proportion to the weight of the package, the distance of the location, and the speed of the service. The post office sells boxes in different sizes. Seal your box well with tape, but don't tie it with string – a disaster in automated postal equipment. Before buying a box or using a tape, verify with a postal official that they are acceptable for the contents and for the service you want. Mark both the address it's going to and your return address (General Delivery is OK) on the same side of the package, clearly indicating ("TO" and

"FROM") which is which. If the package is headed overseas, the clerk will have you fill out a Customs Declaration form, which is straightforward – if all you're sending home is old clothes, put NCV (No Commercial Value) instead of a dollar amount on the form.

Telegrams

To send a **telegram**, go to a telegraph company office, addresses of which can be found in the Yellow Pages. With a credit card, phone (Western Union ☎1-800/325-6000 or Globalcomm ☎1-800/835-4723) and dictate. Prices for international telegrams are around $15 for the first 7 words, then about $1 for each extra word. Assuming the cooperation of the postal service in the country to which they are sent, they should take 2–3 days. For domestic service, send a telegram (delivered by hand the same day) or a mailgram (delivered by mail, taking 12 to 48 hours but costing less).

Poste restante

You can receive international mail poste restante by having it addressed to you c/o Poste Restante, General Post Office, 421 8th Ave, NY 10001. To collect letters, go to the window (☎212/330-3099) between 10am and 1pm Monday–Saturday; show your passport or some other photo ID. Check regularly, as mail is kept for only thirty days before being returned to sender – so tell your correspondents to make sure there's a return address on the envelope. The post office will not forward mail to a new address once you leave. For domestic mail the routine is slightly different: The correct address is c/o General Delivery, the window hours are 10am–1pm Monday–Saturday and the mail is held for only ten days. To receive mail at someone else's address, be sure your correspondent puts "c/o" before that person's name on the envelope.

Manhattan post offices

Ansonia 178 Columbus Ave off 68th St, NY 10023

Bowling Green 25 Broadway between State and Morris sts, NY 10004

Canal Street 350 Canal St between Broadway and Church St, NY 10013

Cathedral 215 W 104th St between Broadway and Amsterdam Ave, NY 10025

Church 90 Church St between Vesey and Barkley sts, NY 10007

Cooper 93 4th Ave at 11th St, NY 10003

Franklin D Roosevelt 909 3rd Ave between 54th and 55th sts, NY 10022

Gracie 229 E 85th St between 2nd and 3rd aves, NY 10028

Grand Central 450 Lexington Ave at 45th St, NY 10017

JAF Building 421 8th Ave at 33rd St, NY 10001

Knickerbocker 128 E Broadway between Pike and Essex sts, NY 10002

Lenox Hill 217 E 70th St between 2nd and 3rd aves, NY 10021

Madison Square 149 E 23rd St between Lexington and 3rd aves, NY 10010

Manhattanville 365 W 125th St between St Nicholas and Morningside aves, NY 10027

Midtown 223 W 38th St between 7th and 8th aves, NY 10018

Morningside 232 W 116th St between 7th and 8th aves, NY 10026

Murray Hill, 115 E 34th St between Park and Lexington aves, NY 10016

Old Chelsea, 217 W 18th St between 7th and 8th aves, NY 10011

Peck Slip 1 Peck Slip between Pearl and Water sts, NY 10038

Peter Stuyvesant,432 E 14th St between Ave A and 1st Ave, NY 10009

Planetarium 127 W 83rd St between Columbus and Amsterdam aves, NY 10024

Prince 103 Prince St between Greene and Mercer sts, NY 10012

Radio City 322 W 52nd St between 8th and 9th aves, NY 10019

Rockefeller Center 610 5th Ave at 49th St, NY 10020

Times Square 340 W 42nd St between 8th and 9th aves, NY 10036

Village 201 Varick St at W Houston St, NY 10014

Wall Street 73 Pine St between Williams and Pearl sts, NY 10005

Yorkville 1619 3rd Ave between 90th and 91st sts, NY 10128

The internet

If you're traveling without your own computer and modem, accessing the **internet** is possible at a couple of locations. Try the Cybercafe, 273A Lafayette St at Prince St (☎212/334-5140) and 250 W 49th St between Broadway and 8th Ave (☎212/333-

4109), Ⓦwww.cyber-cafe.com; and alt.coffee, 139 Ave A between 9th St and St Marks (Ⓣ212/529-2233, Ⓦwww.altdotcoffee.com). You can also visit Easy Everything, 234 W 42nd St between 7th and 8th aves (Ⓣ212/398-0775, Ⓦwww.easyeverything.com), with 800 terminals. These places charge about $10 an hour; you can access your email account back home and pick up and send mail. You can surf the net to your heart's content, fiddle around with CD-ROMs, scan, print, or just drink coffee; if you're new at this, the staff (at the smaller places, at least) will gladly help you figure things out. An alternative is to stop by a branch of the New York City Public Library, where free internet use is available. Each branch has its own rules; ask a librarian how to get online.

You can also send your findings about New York to us: our email address is newyork@roughguides.co.uk. Visit our website at Ⓦwww.roughguides.com as a starting point for travel information (and many other resources).

Sights and museums

There's no doubt you'll be spending lots of time in New York amazed at what you see; its collection of modern architecture, old churches and art museums is largely unparalleled. Below are a few practicalities that might help organize your wanderings before you set off.

Museums

As a city, New York does not lack visual stimulation, and you may find there's enough on the streets to look at without walking inside a museum. But you should be aware of what you're missing. New York offers an extraordinary array of museums, large and small, dedicated to showcasing art and design, history, nature, film and television, ethnic themes and more. In the big two Manhattan museums alone – the **Metropolitan** and the **Museum of Modern Art** (see p.147) – there are few aspects of Western art left untapped. The Metropolitan, in particular, is exhaustive (mercilessly so, if you try to take in too much too quickly), with arguably the world's finest collection of European and American art as well as superlative displays of everything from ancient Egyptian to Chinese art. The Museum of Modern Art (MoMA) takes over where the Met leaves off, emphasizing exactly why (and how) New York became the art capital of the world.

Among the other **major museums**, there are exciting collections of contemporary art and invariably excellent temporary shows at the **Whitney** (see p.196) and **Guggenheim** (see p.191); a wide array of seventeenth- and eighteenth-century paintings at the **Frick** (see p.190); and – amid an unexpectedly pastoral setting – a glorious display of medieval art at **The Cloisters** (see p.232). **The American Museum of Natural History** (see p.212) offers the largest exhibition in the world of items related to evolution, biology and the natural world. All things, time permitting, are worth seeing. So also are many of the **smaller museums**, often quirkily devoted to otherwise obscure subjects and perfectly sized for a quick visit.

The quarterly *Museums New York* ($4.95) has short features on traditional and modern artists and detailed listings of exhibitions at museums and galleries. *Gallery Guide* ($3) does the same thing with less flair. *Stubs* ($12.95) provides floor plans of all the major Broadway houses and sporting arenas (so you can see just how bad those tickets really are).

Opening hours and admission fees

Opening hours don't fall into any fixed patterns; many museums are closed on

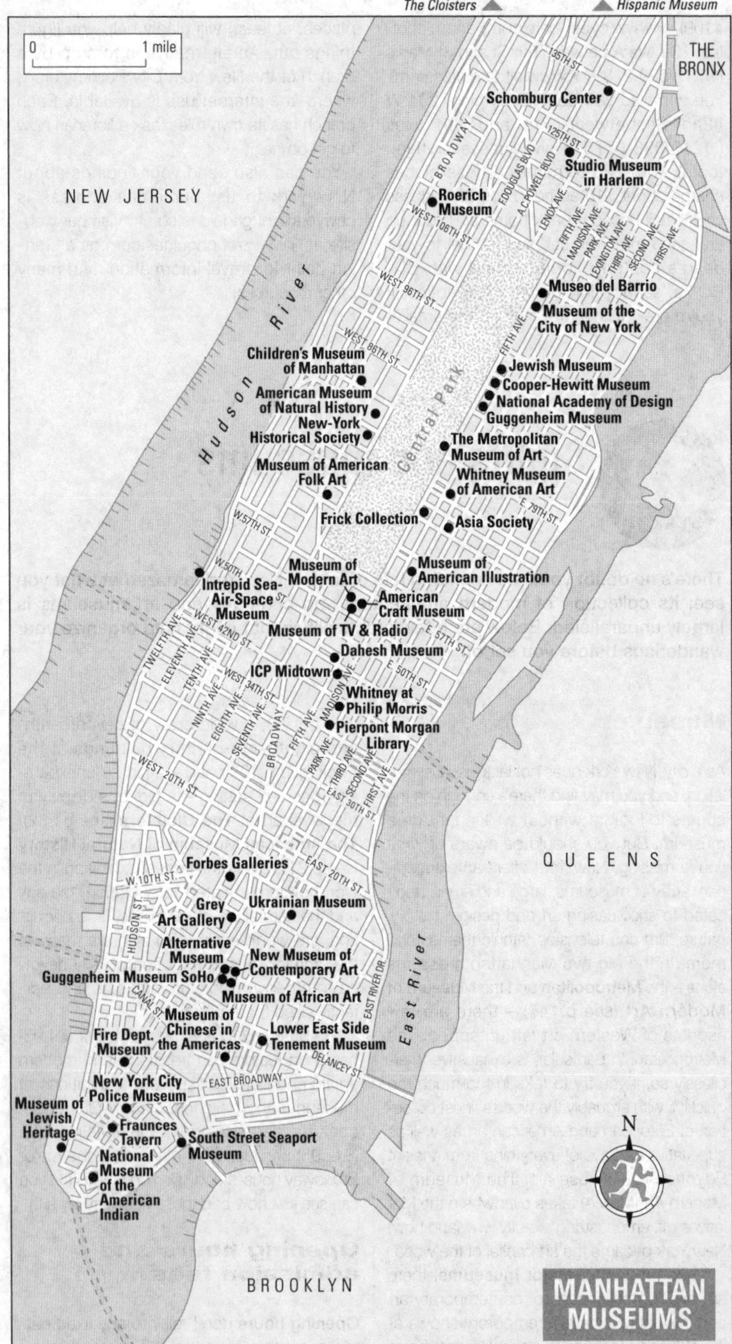
MANHATTAN MUSEUMS
0 1 mile
The Cloisters
Hispanic Museum
THE BRONX
NEW JERSEY
QUEENS
BROOKLYN
Hudson River
East River
Central Park
Schomburg Center
Studio Museum in Harlem
Roerich Museum
Museo del Barrio
Museum of the City of New York
Children's Museum of Manhattan
American Museum of Natural History
New-York Historical Society
Jewish Museum
Cooper-Hewitt Museum
National Academy of Design
Guggenheim Museum
The Metropolitan Museum of Art
Whitney Museum of American Art
Museum of American Folk Art
Frick Collection
Asia Society
Museum of Modern Art
Museum of American Illustration
Intrepid Sea-Air-Space Museum
American Craft Museum
Museum of TV & Radio
Dahesh Museum
ICP Midtown
Whitney at Philip Morris
Pierpont Morgan Library
Forbes Galleries
Grey Art Gallery
Ukrainian Museum
Alternative Museum
New Museum of Contemporary Art
Guggenheim Museum SoHo
Museum of African Art
Museum of Chinese in the Americas
Fire Dept. Museum
Lower East Side Tenement Museum
New York City Police Museum
Museum of Jewish Heritage
Fraunces Tavern
South Street Seaport Museum
National Museum of the American Indian
135TH ST.
125TH ST.
BROADWAY
F.DOUGLAS BLVD
A.C.POWELL BLVD
LENOX AVE.
FIFTH AVE.
MADISON AVE.
PARK AVE.
LEXINGTON AVE.
THIRD AVE.
SECOND AVE.
FIRST AVE.
WEST 106TH ST.
WEST 96TH ST.
WEST 86TH ST.
E. 79TH ST.
W.57TH ST.
W.50TH ST.
WEST 42ND ST.
E. 57TH ST.
E. 50TH ST.
WEST 34TH ST.
TWELFTH AVE.
ELEVENTH AVE.
TENTH AVE.
NINTH AVE.
EIGHTH AVE.
SEVENTH AVE.
WEST 20TH ST.
EAST 30TH ST.
EAST 20TH ST.
W. 10TH ST.
HUDSON ST.
CANAL ST.
EAST RIVER DR.
DELANCEY ST.
EAST BROADWAY
N

Mondays (and national holidays) and are open into the early evening one or two nights a week. Admission charges are high, with a slight discount for those with student ID cards; to offset the prices, some major museums are free (or offer a much-reduced entrance charge) one evening a week. Some museums also utilize the "suggested donation" system. In theory, this means you're allowed to give as little or as much as you'd like for an entry fee (hence enabling museums to keep their charitable status). A few (like the American Museum of Natural History) are quite amenable to taking an amount lower than the suggested one, others (like the Met) are less open-minded – so it really all depends on how brazen you are feeling.

Crime and personal safety

Police

The New York City Police – the **NYPD**, aka "New York's Finest" – are for the most part approachable, helpful and overworked. This means that asking directions gets a friendly response, while reporting a theft may bring a weary "Whaddya want me to do about it?" – and any smile is greatly appreciated. In this realm of New York life as in others, race can play a part in the response you get. Wary of strained relations between police and minority communities, officers – even those from minority communities themselves – may be a little more reserved if your skin is any color but white. This is not to say that they'll refrain from helping you if you're in trouble, however.

Each area of New York has its own **police precinct**; to find the nearest station to you, call ⓣ212/374-5000 (during business hours only) or check the phone book or call ⓣ411. In emergencies phone ⓣ911 or use one of the outdoor posts that give you a direct line to the emergency services. Out of the city you may have to tangle with the State Police, who operate the Highway Patrol.

Staying out of trouble

Irrespective of how dangerous New York is – it is much safer than it was, say, in 1990 – it can sometimes *feel* dangerous. Perhaps more than in any other city, a sense of nervy self-preservation is rife here: people make studied efforts to avoid eye contact, and any unusual behavior clears a space immediately: the atmosphere of impending violence is sometimes sniffable.

The reality is somewhat different. There is a great deal of crime in New York, some of it violent. But keep in mind that more than eight million people live in the city, and, as far as per capita crime rates go, Boston is more dangerous, as are New Orleans, Dallas, Washington, DC and, believe it or not, more than one hundred other US cities. Even considering New York on its own, it's pleasing (and not misleading) to note that in the late 1990s the city boasted its lowest crime rate – violent crimes included – since 1968. And it's still on its way down. This is due in part to a crackdown, led by Mayor Rudy Giuliani, on so-called "quality of life" crimes (minor offenses like jaywalking, fare evasion, shoplifting, even public urination), which gets potential criminals' stats on record (and makes them easier to catch on their next offense), periodic gun amnesties and increased gun confiscation. A less inspiring contributing factor is the shift in focus of the criminal drug culture; where crack, a stimulant that inspired violence in addicts, once ruled, heroin, a depressant that causes more sluggish behavior, is now more prevalent.

Which is not to say you should discount the possibility of danger altogether. Just do as the locals do and keep it in the back of your consciousness, not at the forefront. As with any big city, walk with confidence and remember the few places and/or times that you really should avoid. This guide outlines places where you should be careful and those few best skirted altogether, but really it's a case of using common sense; it doesn't take long to figure out that you're somewhere unsavory.

The rule that will best enable you to travel safely and confidently is this: **be aware of your surroundings at all times**. Contrary to popular belief, it's OK to let on you're a visitor – if you follow rules of paranoia and never look up, you'll miss a lot of what's striking about New York. Looking up and around, reading this guidebook, and pulling out your camera may make you more of a target, but only if you look like a careless tourist. While looking at your map, you are much more likely to have your pocket picked than you are to encounter something more violent. So carry bags closed and across your body, don't let cameras dangle, keep wallets in front – not back – pockets, and don't flash money or your Oyster Rolex around. Avoid crowds, especially around rip-off merchants like street gamblers, where half the con is played on the participants and the other half on the spectators. Move away if you feel someone is standing too close to you.

Murders make the big headlines: ninety percent of the victims are known to their killers, which is to say most killings are personal disputes rather than random attacks. Mugging, on the other hand, can and does happen. It's impossible to give hard and fast rules on what to do should you meet up with a mugger: whether to run or scream or fight depends on you and the situation. Most New Yorkers would hand over the money every time, and that's probably what you should do – in fact, some people carry a spare $20 or so as "mug money," lest their attacker turn nasty at finding empty pockets. Having a spare $20 should be your common practice anyway; if you find yourself somewhere you'd rather not be, you want to be able to jump in a cab.

Of course the best tactics involve following the "awareness" rules outlined above. Some good late-night points are worth adding to that: even if you are terrified or drunk (or both), don't appear so; never walk down a dark side street, especially one you can't see the end of, or through a deserted park; stick to the streetside edge of the sidewalk or where it's easy for you to run into the street if necessary and attract the attention that muggers hate.

If the worst happens and your assailant is toting a gun or a knife, play it calmly. Keep still, don't make any sudden movements – and do what he says. When he has run off, hail a cab and ask to be taken to the nearest police station: taxis rarely charge for this, but if they do the police are supposed to pay. Standing around on the street in a shocked condition is inviting more trouble, though you'd be pleasantly surprised at the number of people who would sincerely come to your aid. At the station, you'll get sympathy and little else; file the theft and take the incident report to claim your insurance back home.

Victim services

If you are unlucky enough to be mugged, the city's Victim Services 24-hour hotline (☎212/577-7777) offers telephone advice and will direct anyone who has suffered a crime against their person to where they can receive one-to-one counseling.

Note too that possession of any "**controlled substance**" is absolutely illegal. Should you be found in possession of a small amount of marijuana, you probably won't go to jail – but can expect a hefty fine and, for foreigners, the possibility of deportation.

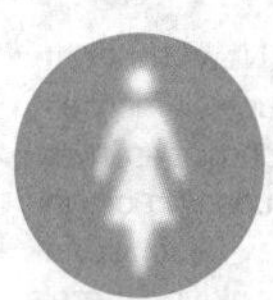

Women's New York

Newcomers, male or female, face the fact that New York is huge, overwhelming and – going by movie and television legend at least – a potentially violent place. On a first visit, you will probably need a few days to mentally adjust to the city and its culture, and this is the time when you'll feel (and appear) your most vulnerable. Affecting an attitude of knowing where you're going (even if you don't) and, like the most seasoned New Yorker, looking like nothing will stop you getting there tends to protect you from trouble, as will some basic tips in survival psychology.

The first – and fundamental – step is to avoid being seen as an easy target: female New Yorkers project a tough, streetwise image through their body language and dress, even when they're all glammed up and ready to party. There's nothing unusual in **women traveling in the city** alone or with other women, at pretty much any time of day or night, so you won't be the focus of attention that you might be in other parts of the world. People gravitate to New York from the rest of America whether to study, further their careers or just hang out – so it's easy to move around, make friends and plug into New York's networks. Also on the positive side, the women's movement has had a much more dynamic effect in New York (indeed throughout East and West Coast America) than in Europe. Women are much more visible in business, politics and the professions than you may be used to.

All this progress has had a somewhat paradoxical effect, however, with successful mainstreaming eliminating the impetus, if not the need, for a strong women's community. Until recently, most if not all feminist activism centered on reproductive rights, which – since the Supreme Court's 1973 decision in *Roe v Wade* – has been one of the most volatile issues in American politics. Now, with George W. Bush as a pro-life president, the matter is more contentious than ever.

The last few years, though, have seen a resurgence of interest in a more psychological feminism, with the launch of the so-called "third wave." The correspondences with this movement are beginning to show on New York's streets, with pro-woman sex shops, an excellent new feminist and lesbian bookstore and high-profile events such as Eve Ensler's *The Vagina Monologues*, played to a packed crowd at Madison Square Garden. For more information, check out the lesbian listings in "Gay and lesbian New York," on p.388.

Feeling safe

It must be safe to travel around New York; American women do it all the time. So runs the thinking, but New York does throw up unique and definite problems for women – and especially for women traveling alone and just getting to know the city. If you feel and look like a visitor, not quite knowing which direction to ride the subway, for instance, it's little comfort to know that New York women routinely use it on their own and late in the evening. Here are a few points to bear in mind when you begin to explore the city.

You're much more likely to feel unsafe than be unsafe – a mindset that can lead to problems in itself, for part of the technique in surviving (and enjoying) New York is to look as if you know what you're doing and where you're going. Maintain the facade and you should find that a lot of the aggravation fades away, though bear in mind that for Americans subtle hints aren't the order of the day: If someone's bugging you, either turn away, leave, or let him know your feelings loudly and firmly. These tactics, while not much good in the event of real trouble, can lend you confidence, which in turn wards off creeps. Much more powerful are chemical repellents such as pepper sprays, available from sporting goods stores. If you do carry one of these, make sure you know how and when to use it, and what its effects will be. Properly used they are extremely effective at disabling your attacker long enough for you to make good your escape, and they do not cause any lasting injury to the attacker.

You're far, far less likely to be raped than mugged. For a few ground rules on lessening chances of mugging, see p.44, but above all be wary about any display of wealth in the wrong place – if you wear jewelry or an expensive watch, think about where you're walking before setting out for the day; tuck necklaces inside your clothing and turn rings so the stones don't show, at least when you're on the street or riding the subway at night. If you are being followed, turn around and look at the person following you, and step off the sidewalk and into the street; attackers hate the open, and they'll lose confidence knowing you've seen them. Never let yourself be pushed into a building or alley and never turn off down an unlit, empty-looking street. If you're unsure about the area where you're staying, ask other women's advice. They'll tell you when they walk and when they take a bus so as to avoid walking more than a block; which bars and parks they feel free to walk in with confidence; and what times they don't go anywhere without a cab. However, don't avoid parts of the city just through hearsay – you might miss out on what's most of interest – and learn to expect New Yorkers (Manhattanites in particular) to sound alarmist; it's part of the culture.

If you don't have much money, accommodation is important: it can be unnerving to stay in a hotel with a bottom-of-the-heap clientele. Make sure that your hotel lobby is well-lit, the door locks on your room are secure and the night porters seem reliable. If you feel uneasy, move. If you're staying for a couple of weeks or more, you might try one of the city's women-only long-term residences; for addresses of these, see "Staying on," p.49.

Crisis/support centers

There are competent and solid support systems for women in crisis, or in need of medical or emotional support. At the following you can be assured of finding skilled, compassionate staff.

Sex Crimes Hotline ☎212/267-7273 or 267-RAPE. Staffed by specially trained female detectives of the New York City Police Dept who will take your statement any time of day and night and conduct an investigation, referring you to counseling organizations if you wish. They also speak Spanish. If you are in Brooklyn, there's another 24-hour number to call: ☎718/250-2000. If you don't want to go to the police, then the **Bellevue Hospital Rape Crisis Program**, on the 4th floor at 1st Ave and 27th St (☎212/562-4730 or ☎212/562-3435) provides free and confidential counseling, medical treatment and follow-up counseling and referral as necessary. The entrance to the Emergency Room is at 462 First Avenue. See also Safe Horizon ☎212/227 3000.

Women's Healthline ☎212/230-1111, ⓦwww.ci.nyc.ny.us/html. Provides a broad range of information on women's health problems (such as birth control, abortion, sexually transmitted diseases) and can refer callers to state licensed clinics and hospitals.

Other hotline numbers to call for advice are the **Coney Island Hospital Rape Crisis Program** ☎1-800/TEL-RAPE, the NYC Gay and Lesbian Anti–Violence Project ☎212/714-1141 and the Rape, Abuse and Incest National Network ☎1-800/656-HOPE.

Other contacts

Barnard Center for Research on Women **Barnard College, 117th St and Broadway ☎212/854-2067, ⓦwww.barnard.edu/crow.** A friendly but primarily academic resource that maintains an extensive research library collection of books, articles and periodicals.

Bluestockings Women's Book Store **172 Allen St (between Stanton and Rivington sts) ☎212/777-6028.** An excellent source of lesbian and feminist literature, this charming Lower East Side store also serves as an information resource and a space for readings and community events.

Ceres **584 Broadway (between Prince and Houston sts), Suite 306 ☎212/226-4725.** Art gallery run by an all-women cooperative. Exhibits mainly – though not exclusively – women's work.

Enchantments **341 E 9th St ☎212/228-4394.** Lesbian-friendly center for spiritual enlightenment. Useful bulletin board.

Eve's Garden **119 W 57th St (between 6th and 7th aves), Suite 1201 ☎212/757-8651 or ☎1-800/848-3837.** This "sexuality boutique for women and their partners" stocks erotic accessories, books and videos. Mon–Sat 11am–7pm.

NARAL (New York affiliate of the National Abortion & Reproductive Rights Action League), 462 Broadway (between Grand and Broome sts), Suite 540 ⓣ212/343-0114, ⓦwww.naralny.org. A good source of information on current legal issues; they'll also refer you to reliable providers of reproductive services.

National Council of Jewish Women 820 2nd Ave (at 43rd St) ⓣ212/687 5030 or ⓣ1-800-829-6259, ⓦwww.ncjwny.org. Organization focused primarily on community service. Occasionally sponsors lectures, discussion groups and other events.

National Organization for Women 150 W 28th St (at 7th Ave), Room 304 ⓣ212/627-9895, ⓦwww.nownyc.org. The largest feminist organization in the US.

Planned Parenthood of New York City Inc Margaret Sanger Center, 26 Bleecker St (at Mott St) ⓣ212/274-7200, or for a clinic appointment ⓣ212/965 7000, ⓦwww.ppnyc.org. Sexual and reproductive health services.

Refuse and Resist 305 Madison Ave, Suite 1166 ⓣ212/713-5657, ⓦwww.refuseandresist.org. Activist group defending reproductive rights and fighting against hate crimes.

Toys in Babeland 94 Rivington St (at Ludlow) ⓣ212/375 1701, ⓦwww.toysinbabeland.com. Excellent sex toy store with well-educated staff, free sex tip sheets and a very relaxed vibe. Workshops on topics such as G-spot stimulation, dyke sex and female ejaculation. Mon–Sat noon–10pm, Sun noon–8pm.

WOW Cafe (Women's One World Theater) 59 E 4th St (between 2nd and 3rd aves) ⓣ212/777-4280. Feminist/lesbian theater collective with meetings open to all women on Tuesdays at 6.45pm (ring the buzzer). Call for information on upcoming events.

See also the lesbian listings and women's/lesbian bars and clubs listed in "Gay and lesbian New York" on pp.392.

Disabled travelers

For disabled travelers, New York presents challenges, to be sure, but the rewards almost always outweigh the difficulties.

New York City has had wide-ranging disabled access regulations imposed on an aggressively disabled-unfriendly system. The Americans with Disabilities Act, a landmark achievement essentially guaranteeing the rights of the disabled in the US, stipulated that public buildings (and this includes hotels) built after 1993 must be accessible. Buildings built before that time must be modified – to the extent that this is possible – although this is open to some interpretation. The reality in New York is that there are wide variations in accessibility, making navigation a tricky business. At the same time, you'll find New Yorkers surprisingly willing to go out of their way to help you. If you're having trouble and you feel that passersby are ignoring you, it's most likely out of respect for your privacy – if you need assistance, never hesitate to ask.

In an effort to make up for the limitations to the city's accessibility, city agencies offer a considerable amount of information and advice. New York is also home to many of the country's largest disabled services and advocacy groups, so you can be almost certain to find the support you need to overcome initial obstacles. The key is to be informed before you arrive. To that end, we've listed the most useful contacts below.

Getting around

For wheelchair users, getting around on the subway is next to impossible without someone to help you, and extremely difficult at most stations even then. Some stations are equipped with elevators, but these enhancements are few and do not occur on all lines, and thus don't make much of a difference. The New York City Mass Transit Authority is working to make the majority of stations accessible, but at the rate they're going (and the state the subway is in), it won't happen soon. Buses are another story, and are the first choice of many disabled New Yorkers. (For a detailed explanation of the bus system, see "Buses," p.23.) All MTA buses are equipped with wheelchair lifts and locks. To get on a bus, wait at the bus stop to signal the driver you need to board; when he or she has seen you, move to the back door, where he or she will assist you. For travelers with other mobility difficulties, the driver will "kneel" the bus to allow you easier access. Wheelchair users may also be eligible for the MTA's Access-a-Ride bus service, though probably not if you're staying a very short time. For more information, including a Braille subway map, contact the MTA by calling the Accessible Line ⓣ718/596-8585, ⓣ718/596-8273 or by writing to 370 Jay St, Brooklyn, NY 11201.

Taxis are a viable option for visitors with visual and hearing impairments and minor mobility difficulties; for wheelchair users, however, the disappearance of all but one of the big Checker cabs has made taxi travel pretty impossible. If you have a collapsible wheelchair, drivers are required to store it and assist you; the unfortunate reality is that most drivers won't stop if they see you waiting. If you're refused, try to get the cab's medallion number and report the driver to the Taxi and Limousine Commission at ⓣ212/221-8294.

Aside from the bus, the best way to travel New York by wheelchair is still the sidewalk. Watch out for uneven curbs and cobblestones, especially on smaller streets, but overall you shouldn't have a problem.

General advice and information

Big Apple Greeter 1 Center St, NY 10007 Accessibility info on ⓣ212/380-8159, ⓕ380-3685, ⓦwww.bigapplegreeter.org. Big Apple Greeter, which employs a full-time access coordinator, is accepted by many as the main authority on New York accessibility. The free service matches you with a volunteer (they have 50 disabled volunteers in addition to 500 others) who spends a few hours showing you the city. Big Apple Greeter has also compiled a resource list especially for travelers with disabilities, and they'll be happy to supply you with this on request. See also p.28.

The Lighthouse 111 E 59th St, NY 10022 ⓣ212/821-9200. General services for the visually impaired. They also have Braille and large-print guides to New York.

The Mayor's Office for People with Disabilities 100 Gold St, 2nd floor, NY 10038 (between Frankfort and Spruce sts) ⓣ212/788-2830, TTY 788-2838. General information.

New York Society for the Deaf 817 Broadway, 7th floor, NY 10003 ⓣ and TTY 212/777-3900. A good source of information on interpreter services.

The New York State Travel Information Center 1 Commercial Plaza, Albany, NY 12245 ⓣ1-800/225-5697. Write or call for the *I Love New York Travel Guide*, a general booklet to the state and city that includes accessibility ratings.

Upward Mobility ⓣ718/645-7774. Lift-equipped, wheelchair accessible limousine service.

Finally, **Access for All** is a comprehensive guide to cultural resources for the disabled. A copy is available for $5; write to Hospital Audiences, Inc, 548 Broadway, 3rd Floor, NY 10012 ⓣ212/575-7663, TDD 575-7673).

Staying on

Few people say it's easy to live and work in New York City. New Yorkers talk obsessively about their jobs and salaries (assuming they have them), and where they live, or will live, or won't be living any more. Finding a place to live that's safe, clean and affordable is a challenge at best and torture at worst. And once you've got that, you still must get a job to pay for it. Then you are eligible to join the legions of Manhattanites who gather for a Sunday brunch and complain about high rent, water pressure, unrepaired elevators, heat (or the lack thereof) in winter and air conditioning (or the lack thereof) in summer.

Some basic rules

If you're a **foreigner**, you start at a disadvantage, at least as far as contacts go. The British Consulate says that each year an alarming number of Britons wind up in New York City in need of shelter, sustenance and sympathy. Both work and rooms, however, are there, if you've got the energy, imagination or plain foolhardiness to pursue them. Below are the basic ground rules and those matters of bureaucracy that, even if you choose to ignore them, you should certainly know about.

For visitors granted admission to the US under the **visa waiver scheme** (see p.17), the date stamped in your passport is the latest you're legally entitled to stay. Leaving a few days after may not matter, especially if you're heading home, but more than a week or so can result in a protracted – and generally unpleasant – interrogation from officials: it's been known for immigration control to question overstayers deliberately long enough to cause them to miss their flights. These people will make you squirm – your interrogation will likely be of a proportionate length to the amount of time you overstayed, and it will be assumed that you were working illegally. Also, you may find that you are denied entry to the US in the future and that your American hosts and employers face legal proceedings. Exceeding your time limit by more than 180 days can subject you to a ban of up to 10 years!

If you want to stay on, the best option is to get an **extension** before your time is up. Apply to the US Immigration and Naturalization Service for an Issuance or Extension of Permit to Re-Enter the USA. The New York office at 26 Federal Plaza (at Worth St between Lafayette and Centre sts) is open Monday–Friday, 7.30am–3.30pm. You can also speak to an officer by phone 8am–5.30pm (ⓣ1-800/375-5283) or request that forms be mailed to you (ⓣ1-800/870-3676) or download them from the internet (ⓦwww.ins.usdoj.gov). Brace yourself – you're plunging, voluntarily, into a side of American bureaucracy known for being frustrating, unpleasant and, above all, suspicious. Your application (on form I-539) must be submitted before your I-94 (the card you are issued at the point of entry) expires or no fewer than 15 and not more than 90 days before your visa expires, and it costs a non-refundable $120. Think about how you'll answer any questions, as it will be assumed you are working illegally; you must prove that you can support yourself financially. Bring an upstanding US citizen to vouch for you. Think up a good reason why you didn't allow the extra time initially: well-worn but effective excuses include saying that your money lasted longer than you planned, or that your parents/husband/wife have decided to come over for a while.

Your other option, by no means infallible, is to leave the country and return. From New York, Montréal is a short flight or a long train/bus ride away, Mexico somewhat farther; neither requires that you have a visa to get in. You can apply for a new visa there or, if you came in on a visa waiver, just turn around and come back – but preferably not the next day! This method is not as easy as it was in years gone by; the longer you spend out of the country, the less obvious your return to New York will be.

Legal (and illegal) work

For extended legal stays in the US it helps if you have relatives (parents, or children over

21) who can sponsor you. Alternatively, a firm offer of work from a US company or, less promisingly, an individual, will do. Armed with a letter stating this offer, you can apply for a **special working visa** from any American embassy or consulate abroad before you set off for the States.

There are a whole range of these visas, depending on your skills, projected length of stay, etc – but with a couple of exceptions they're extremely hard to get. The **easiest tend** to be for academic posts or other jobs (in the computer field, for instance) that the US feels it particularly needs to fill. For students (and occasionally non-students) there are a limited number of Exchange Visitor Programs (EVPs). Participants get a J-1 visa that entitles them to accept paid summer employment and to apply for a social security number (an identification for tax purposes that virtually no American citizen is without). Most J-1 visas are issued for positions in American summer camps through schemes like BUNAC: information is available from their office at 16 Bowling Green Lane, London EC1R 0BD (Ⓣ020/7251 3472, Ⓦwww.bunac.co.uk).

Each year thousands of visitors forget regulations and hunt out work on their own. They pound the streets, check bulletin boards (see the "Directory" on p.462) and the media, and often make up a social security number (or borrow one from a friend) to satisfy a prospective boss. It usually takes about six months for the tax man to catch up with them, so many not planning to stay much longer than half a year see it as their best choice, perhaps their only one: employment visas can't realistically be obtained in the city. Be advised, though, that for anyone with only a standard tourist visa, any kind of work is totally illegal. If you're caught, you could be deported and your employer fined substantially – a tough approach that has severely hampered the market for casual labor (except in the case of the hospitality industry, which would fall apart without its underpaid and often unpaid foreign workers).

Would-be workers must first find out what people do in New York – and how they can fit in. For ideas (and positions) check the employment ads in the *New York Times*, *New York Press*, *Village Voice* and the free neighborhood tabloids available throughout the city. Also check the ethnic weeklies that crowd newsstands: the *Irish Voice* and *Irish Echo* are useful for Irish travelers who want to connect with the large immigrant population that came first.

Possibilities obviously depend on one's personal skills and inventiveness. Here are some of the better opportunities.

- **Restaurant and bar work.** With thousands of restaurants in the city, this is perhaps the best bet. Mind you, many illegal workers find tips are their only pay, as restaurateurs pay them a minimal hourly sum. For the reasons mentioned above, however, restaurateurs in the more upmarket establishments are also much more wary than they were about taking on someone who doesn't have (or who has obviously made up) a social security number, and jobs are no longer assured in this field. Experience helps, as does dropping by in person, because most restaurants won't deal with you over the phone.
- **Childcare, house-cleaning, dog-walking, cat-sitting.** New Yorkers frequently advertise these tasks on notices posted in supermarkets, corner drugstores, health food shops, pet stores and bus shelters and on college bulletin boards, and workers will get paid in cash. Again, references are a plus.
- **Telemarketing/market research.** They're often not too choosy about whom they employ – and are sometimes impressed (especially the market research people) with accented speakers.
- **Music teacher.** If a visitor can teach guitar, saxophone or keyboards, opportunities abound among wannabe band members in the East Village.
- **Painting and decorating.** The work is hard but the pay is good. Some agencies offer this kind of work – or visitors can hunt privately through friends.
- **Foreign language lessons.** Someone with a language or two can advertise on a bulletin board or in the weeklies. Rates can be good.
- **Artist's model.** Visitors can pass their name and a contact number around to the various independent studios or artist hangouts in SoHo or TriBeCa, or try to reach the model-booking directors at the art schools themselves.
- **Blood donation.** A final, if slightly desperate, option for quick emergency cash. The Yellow Pages list agencies and hospitals.

An internship, basically offering services for free in return for contacts, experience or possible sponsorship is a great way to get one's foot in the door.

Finding a place to stay

A studio apartment – one room with bathroom and kitchenette – in a reasonably safe Manhattan neighborhood can rent for upwards of $1200 a month. Many newcomers share studios and one-bedrooms among far too many people; the alternative is to look in the outer boroughs or the nearby New Jersey towns of Jersey City or Hoboken. However, even those neighborhoods are becoming expensive, and to find a real deal you must hunt hard and check out even the most unlikely possibilities.

The best source for actually hearing about an apartment or room is, as anywhere, word of mouth. Watch the ads in the *Village Voice*, the *New York Times* and the ethnic papers mentioned above; and if you're reading this before setting out for New York, consider advertising yourself, particularly if you have a flat in a popular foreign city to exchange. Try commercial and campus bulletin boards too, where you might secure a temporary apartment or sublet while the regular tenant is away.

Some of the city's many colleges also provide vacancies, especially in the summer. Barnard College (write to Summer Housing at Barnard, Columbia University, 3009 Broadway, NY 10027 ⓣ212/854-8021, ⓦwww.barnard.columbia.edu/sumprog/main) offers dormitory facilities from the end of May to early August for $550 to $850 a month with a 7-night minimum stay. Write well in advance, as they're "selective" about who gets a room, and be prepared to show that you have a temporary job, internship, or course of study that requires you to be in the city. New York University Summer Housing (14A Washington Place, NY 10003 ⓣ212/998-4621, ⓦwww.nyu.edu/housing/summer/) charges a weekly rate that varies according to the room's amenities and your enrollment status (if you are not a student, plan to pay $190 to $260 per week, with mandatory and optional meal plans). There's a three-week minimum stay, and priority goes to students in NYU programs; write well in advance.

Less satisfactory perhaps, but still a fall-back option are long-stay hotels. A few cater specifically to single women on long stays: Webster Apartments, 419 W 34th St, NY 10001 (ⓣ212/967-9000); Parkside Evangeline Residence, 18 Gramercy Park S, NY 10003 (ⓣ212/677-6200); and Catherine House, 118 W 13th St, NY 10011 (ⓣ212/242-6566). The last two are in a much nicer part of the city, though each usually has a long waiting list – call ahead. It's even harder to find a cheap, long-stay accommodation open to both women and men; most hostel-style establishments have strict limits on the number of days they will allow you to stay. One exception is International House, 500 Riverside Drive, NY 10027 (ⓣ212/316-8400, ⓦwww.ihouse-nyc.org); open to students only, it can be expensive – up to $1565 for a one-bedroom apartment – once you upgrade from a basic dorm room (from $582/month). Most cheaper hotels offer reduced weekly rates. Contact the respective reservations managers for full details.

The New York Convention and Visitors Bureau, 810 7th Ave between 52nd and 53rd streets (ⓣ212/484-1222, ⓦwww.nycvisit.com), can also be worth a call. They have a leaflet listing hotel rates. As a last resort, call Safe Horizon (ⓣ212/577-7700, ⓦwww.safehorizon.org). Although they've officially assumed the duties of the "Traveler's Aid" booth formerly in Times Square, their concern is more with crime, rape and domestic violence victims and US teens stranded without funds. Don't expect much sympathy unless you fall into one of those categories; however, they may be able to refer you to low-budget (or even free) temporary accommodation. One piece of advice – city shelters are notoriously dangerous and unsavory, so don't end up there if you can at all avoid it.

Just possibly (and only if you can afford the fee), you might resort to one of the several roommate-finding agencies. Oldest and most reliable is Roommate Finders, off Broadway at 250 W 57th St (ⓣ212/489-6862, ⓦwww.roommatefinders.com), a nondiscriminatory but discriminating company that charges a flat all-inclusive rate of $300. If you use another agency – the *Voice* carries all their names, numbers and descriptions – make sure you read the contract before money changes hands or papers are signed.

Finding a place to stay

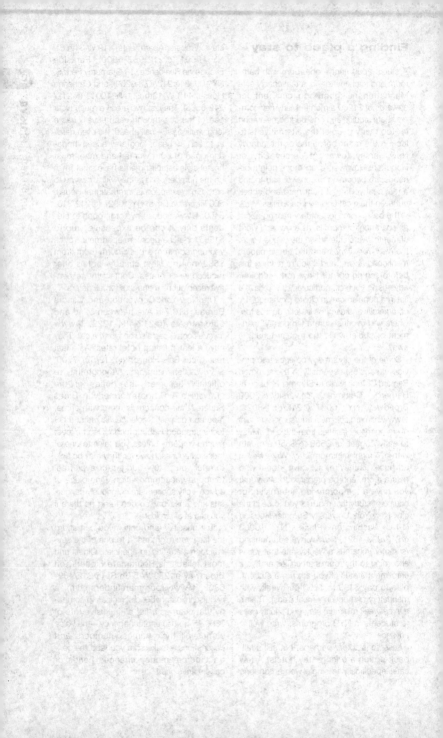

the city

the city

The Harbor Islands

The tip of Manhattan Island and the enclosing shores of New Jersey, Staten Island and Brooklyn form the broad expanse of New York Harbor, one of the finest natural harbors in the world. The first immigrants to settle here several centuries ago were impressed by this almost landlocked body of water, divided into the Upper and Lower Bay, some hundred miles square in total and stretching as far as the Verrazano Narrows – the thin neck of land between Staten Island and Long Island. While it's possible to appreciate Manhattan by simply gazing out from the promenade in Battery Park, to get a proper sense of New York's uniqueness and to get the best views of the celebrated skyline, you should really take to the water. You can do this either by taking a ride on the Staten Island ferry, or by taking the Circle Line ferry out to the **Statue of Liberty** and **Ellis Island** – two highly compelling targets for a trip.

At the time of writing, service on the #1 and #9 trains to South Ferry, the closest stop to the ferries, has been discontinued owing to the cleanup following the World Trade Center's collapse. The best way to reach the ferries is to take the #4 or #5 trains to Bowling Green.

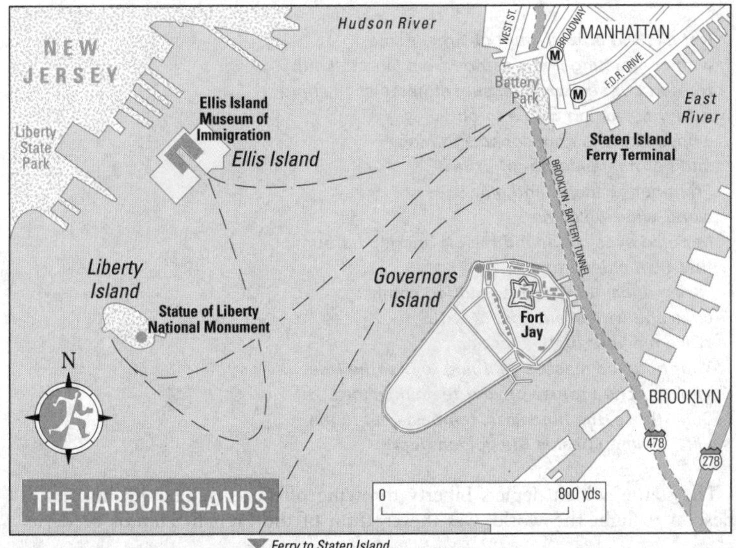

Ferries to the Islands

Ferries, run by Circle Line, go to both the Statue of Liberty and Ellis Island and leave from the pier in Battery Park in lower Manhattan, every twenty minutes from 8.30am to 4.30pm seven days a week all year round. Round-trip tickets are $8 (senior citizens $6, children 3–17 $3) that can be purchased inside Castle Clinton in Battery Park (ⓣ212/269-5755, ⓦwww.statueoflibertyferry.com). If you take the last ferry, it won't be possible to see both islands, so it's best to try and leave as early as possible, thereby avoiding the lines (which can be very long, especially on summer weekends) and giving yourself enough time to explore both islands thoroughly. Liberty Island needs a good couple of hours, especially if the weather's nice and there aren't too many people; Ellis Island, too, demands at least two hours if you want to see the Museum of Immigration.

The Statue of Liberty

Of all America's symbols, none has proved more enduring than the 151-foot tall (from base to torch) **Statue of Liberty** (9.30am–5pm; free; ⓣ212/363-7770, ⓦwww.nps.gov/stli). This giant figure, torch in hand and clutching a stone tablet, has acted for more than a century as a figurehead of the American Dream; indeed there is probably no more immediately recognizable profile in existence. For Americans at least, the statue is a potent reminder that the USA is a land of immigrants. It was in New York Harbor where the first big waves of European immigrants arrived, their ships entering through the Verrazano Narrows to round the bend of the bay and catch a first glimpse of "Liberty Enlightening the World" – an end of their journey into the unknown, and the symbolic beginning of a new life.

These days, although a would-be immigrant's first view of the US is more likely to be the customs check at JFK Airport, the statue remains a stirring sight. Emma Lazarus's poem, *The New Colossus*, written originally to raise funds for the statue's base, is no less quotable now than when it was written:

Not like the brazen giant of Greek fame,
with conquering limbs astride from land to land;
Here at our sea-washed, sunset gates shall stand
a mighty woman with a torch
whose flame is imprisoned lightning,
and her name Mother of Exiles.
From her beacon-hand glows
world-wide welcome;
her mild eyes command the air-bridged harbor
that twin cities frame.
"Keep ancient lands your storied pomp!"
cries she with silent lips.
"Give me your tired, your poor,
Your huddled masses yearning to breathe free,
The wretched refuse of your teeming shore.
Send these, the homeless, tempest-tost to me,
I lift my lamp beside the golden door!

The statue, which depicts Liberty throwing off her shackles and holding a beacon to light the world, was the creation of the French sculptor Frederic

Auguste Bartholdi, who crafted it a hundred years after the American Revolution to commemorate the solidarity between the French and American people. (Actually, he originally intended the statue for Alexandria in Egypt.) Bartholdi built Liberty in Paris between 1874 and 1884, starting with a terra-cotta model and enlarging it through four successive versions to its present size, a construction of thin copper sheets bolted together and supported by an iron framework designed by Gustave Eiffel. The arm carrying the torch was exhibited in Madison Square Park for seven years, but the whole statue wasn't officially accepted on behalf of the American people until 1884, after which it was taken apart, crated up and shipped to New York.

It was to be another two years before it could be properly unveiled: money had to be collected to fund the construction of the base, and for some reason Americans were unwilling – or unable – to dip into their pockets. Only through the campaigning efforts of newspaper magnate Joseph Pulitzer, a keen supporter of the statue, did it all come together in the end. Richard Morris Hunt built a pedestal around the existing star-shaped Fort Wood, and Liberty was formally dedicated by President Cleveland on October 28, 1886, in a flag-waving shindig that has never really stopped. Indeed, fifteen million people descended on Manhattan for the statue's centennial celebrations, and six million people make the pilgrimage each year.

Today you can climb 192 steps to the top of the pedestal or the entire 354 steps up to the crown, but the cramped stairway up through the torch is sadly closed to the public. The best time to visit is as early in the morning as possible, otherwise, don't be surprised if there's an hour-long wait to ascend, especially if the weather's nice. Even if there is, Liberty Park's views of the lower Manhattan skyline are spectacular enough.

Ellis Island

Just across the water from Liberty Island, fifteen minutes further by ferry, sits **Ellis Island**, the first stop for over twelve million immigrants hoping to settle in the USA. The island, originally known as Gibbet Island by the English (who used it for punishing unfortunate pirates), became an immigration station in 1892, a necessary processing point for the massive influx of mostly southern and eastern European immigrants. It remained open until 1954, when it was abandoned and left to fall into atmospheric ruin.

The immigration process

Up until the 1850s, there was no official **immigration process** in New York. Then, the surge of Irish, German and Scandinavian immigrants escaping the great famines of 1846 and failed revolutions of 1848 forced authorities to open an immigration center at Castle Clinton in Battery Park. By the 1880s, widespread hardship in eastern and southern Europe, the pogroms in Russia and the massive economic failure in southern Italy forced thousands to flee the Continent. At the same time, America was experiencing the first successes of its industrial revolution, and more and more people started to move to the cities from the country. Ellis Island opened in 1892, just as America came out of a depression and began to assert itself as a world power. News spread through Europe of the opportunities in the New World, and immigrants were soon leaving their homelands by the millions.

The immigrants who arrived at Ellis Island were all steerage-class passengers; richer immigrants were processed at their leisure on-board ship. The scenes on the island were horribly confused: most families arrived hungry, filthy and penniless, rarely speaking English and invariably awed by the beckoning metropolis across the water. Immigrants were numbered and forced to wait for up to a day while Ellis Island officials frantically tried to process them. Though the center had been designed to accommodate 500,000 immigrants a year, double that number arrived during the early part of the century – as many as 11,747 passed through on a single day in 1907. Con men preyed on all sides, stealing immigrants' baggage as it was checked and offering rip-off exchange rates for whatever money they had managed to bring. Each family was split up – men sent to one area, women and children to another – while a series of checks took place to weed out the undesirables and the infirm. The latter were taken to the second floor, where doctors would check for "loathsome and contagious diseases" as well as signs of insanity. Those who failed medical tests were marked with a white cross on their backs and either sent to the hospital or put back on the boat. Steamship carriers had an obligation to return any immigrants not accepted to their original port, though according to official records, only two percent were ever rejected, and many of those jumped into the sea and tried to swim to Manhattan, or committed suicide, rather than face going home.

There was also a legal test, which checked nationality and, very important, political affiliations. The majority of the immigrants were processed in a matter of hours and then headed either to New Jersey and trains to the West, or into New York City to settle in one of the rapidly expanding ethnic neighborhoods.

Ellis Island Museum of Immigration

By the time of its closing in 1954, Ellis Island was a formidable complex. The first building burned down in 1897, the present one was built in 1903, and there were various additions built in the ensuing years – hospitals, outhouses and the like, usually on bits of landfill that were added to the island in an attempt to contend with the swelling numbers passing through. The buildings were derelict until the mid-1980s; since then, the main, four-turreted central building has been completely renovated, reopening in 1990 as the **Ellis Island Museum of Immigration** (Ellis Island; daily 9.30am–5pm; free; ⓣ212/363-3200, ⓦwww.ellisisland.org). This is an ambitious museum that eloquently recaptures the spirit of the place with artifacts, photographs, maps and personal accounts that tell the story of the immigrants who passed through Ellis Island on their way to a new life in America. The museum is surprisingly well done and not commercial, considering how easy it would be to pull at heartstrings and make the place a sugary tourist trap. All the same, you can't help but feel that it might have been more memorable before the authorities got their hands on the place.

Some 100 million Americans can trace their roots back through Ellis Island, and, for them especially, the museum is an engaging display. On the first floor, located in the old railroad ticket office, is the excellent permanent exhibit "Peopling of America," which chronicles four centuries of American immigration, offering a statistical portrait of those who arrived – who they were, where they came from and why they came.

The huge, vaulted **Registry Room** on the second floor, scene of so much immigrant trepidation, elation and despair, has been left bare, with just a couple of inspectors' desks and American flags. In the side hall, a series of interview rooms re-create step by step the process that immigrants passed through on their way to being naturalized; the white-tiled rooms are soberingly bureaucratic. Each room is augmented by the recorded voices of those who passed through Ellis Island, recalling their experiences, along with photographs, thoughtful and informative explanatory text and small artifacts – train timetables and familiar items brought from home. Descriptions of arrival and the subsequent interviews are presented, as well as examples of questions asked and medical tests given. One of the dormitories, used by those kept overnight for further examination, has been left almost intact. On the top floor, there are evocative photographs of the building before it was restored, along with items rescued from the building and rooms devoted to the peak years of immigration. In the museum's theater, the Hypothetical Theater Company puts on "Ellis Island Stories," stirring re-enactments of immigrant experiences based on oral histories from the museum archive, several times daily.

The museum's **American Family Immigration History Center** (Ⓦ www.ellisislandrecords.org) offers an interactive research database that contains information from ship manifests and passenger lists concerning over 22 million immigrants who passed through the Port of New York between 1892 and 1924. The center furnishes visitors with advanced computer and multimedia equipment, invaluable printed materials and professional assistance for searching genealogical exploration.

Outside, the museum has an eerie, unfinished feel, heightened by the empty shell of what was once the center's hospital. On the fortified spurs of the island, names of immigrant families who passed through the building over the years are engraved in copper, paid for by a minimum donation of $100 from their descendants. This "American Immigrant Wall of Honor," launched in 1990, helped fund the restoration and, at the time of writing, features the names of over 600,000 individuals and families. The museum, which is always accepting new submissions (see Ⓦ www.wallofhonor.com for details), intends to release new editions of the wall every couple of years and is currently accepting submissions for the "New Millennium Edition" of the wall.

Governors Island

"Nowhere in New York is more pastoral," wrote travel writer Jan Morris of **Governors Island**, a 172-acre tract of land with unobstructed views of lower Manhattan and New York Harbor and a handful of colonial and nineteenth-century houses, Fort Jay (1794) and Castle Williams, erected in 1811 to complement the near-identical Castle Clinton. Until the mid-Nineties, the last of the three small islands just south of Manhattan was the largest and most expensively run Coast Guard installation in the world, housing some 3800 service personnel and their families. Active since 1637, it was also the oldest military installation in continuous service in the US. The annual upkeep was too much to justify in light of budget cuts and the end of the Cold War, so in 1995 Governors Island was handed over to the General Services Administration of the Federal Government. The Coast Guard was moved to Homeport, Staten Island, and for the last several years rumors have abounded about the picturesque spot's uncertain future. In his second term President Clinton even made an offer to sell it to the city for $1, provided New York came up with an acceptable land-use plan. Some haggling and last-ditch efforts proved fruitless, and at the time of writing, the island remains closed to the public except via monthly tours by Big Onion Walking Tours (see p.29).

2

The Financial District

The **Financial District** has been synonymous with the Manhattan of the popular imagination for some time – its tall buildings and skyline, its busy streets, its symbols of economic strength and financial wheeling and dealing. So when the September 11, 2001, attacks on the World Trade Center resulted in the collapse of the Twin Towers and the death of thousands of New Yorkers (see box on p.64), the impact it had was not just on the neighborhood, but on the city and country as well. The district will be recovering for some time: blocks, buildings and subway lines were put in various states of disrepair; the celebrated skyline you've seen in movies was radically altered. There is still plenty to see in the area, however, and many visitors might find a pilgrimage to the site of the former Twin Towers – or as near as you can get – hard to resist.

The heart of the nation's – and the world's – business trade, the southern tip of the island is where Manhattan began, reflected in the twisting streets and dense development. Many of the early colonial buildings that once lined these streets were either burned down during the Revolutionary War or in the Great Fire of 1835, or demolished by big businesses eager to boost their corporate image with headquarters around **Wall Street**. The commercial development of **South Street Seaport**, an increase in local cultural events, and the conversion of old office space to residential units all helped the Financial District begin to shed its nine-to-five aura in the past decade or so; it's hard to predict if this will continue in light of recent developments.

At the time of writing, some of the subway lines that were running below the World Trade Center have not reopened; the best way to reach the Financial District is by taking the #1, #2, #4 or #5 to Wall Street and starting your wanderings there.

Wall Street and the Stock Exchange

The Dutch arrived here first, building a wooden wall at the edge of New Amsterdam in 1635 to protect themselves from British settlers to the north and giving the narrow canyon of today's **Wall Street** its name. Even in the eighteenth century, Wall Street was associated with money: not only did the city's

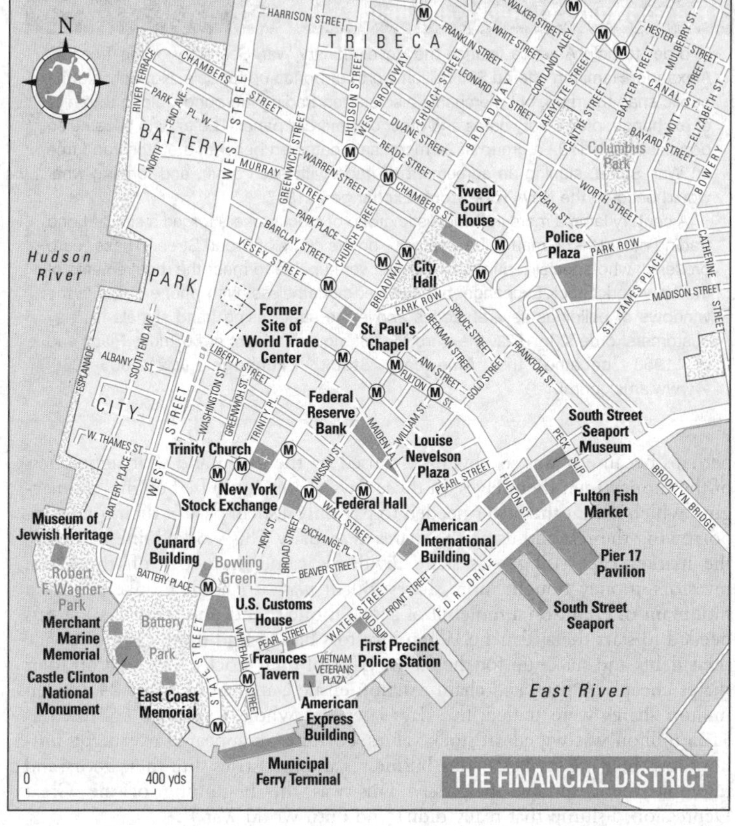

wealthiest live on Wall Street, but it was here that the first banks and insurance companies established their offices. And still today, from behind the Neoclassical facade of the **New York Stock Exchange** at 8 Wall St, the purse strings of the capitalist world are pulled. Take a long look at the mythological figures on the building's pediment. They represent Progress overseeing Agriculture and Industry. When the original stone figures began deteriorating in the Manhattan air, the Exchange clandestinely replaced them with these virtually indestructible sheet-metal copies, for under no circumstances was any aspect of vulnerability to be associated with the Exchange.

Come before noon for the best chance of getting into the **NYSE Interactive Education Center**, 20 Wall St (Mon–Fri 8.45am–4.30pm; free; ⓣ212/656-3000, ⓦwww.nyse.com), where the Exchange floor appears like a melee of brokers and buyers, scrambling for the elusive fractional cent on which to make a megabuck. Sit through the glib introductory film, though, and the hectic scurrying and constantly moving hieroglyphs of the stock prices make more sense. Along with the film, there's a small exhibition on the history of the Exchange – notably quiet are the more spectacular screw-ups. The most disastrous, "Black Tuesday" of 1929, is mentioned almost in passing,

The early days of stocks and bonds

In order to help America finance the Revolutionary War, Secretary of the Treasury Alexander Hamilton offered $80 million worth of bonds up for sale. Not only did the public snap them up, but merchants also started trading the bonds, along with bills of exchange, promissory notes and other commercial paper. The trading became so popular that in 1792 a group of 24 merchants gathered beneath a buttonwood tree on Wall Street, signing an agreement to trade with each other, and forming what would become the **New York Stock Exchange** in 1817.

A century later, a more individualistic group of stockbrokers forged a similar bond trading outside – no matter the weather – on the curbs of Broad Street. These "curb brokers," who specialized in risky stocks, were unable to meet the requirements of the New York Stock Exchange, but survived nonetheless, with phone clerks in the windows of buildings several stories above the street using hand signals to relay customers' orders. In 1921, the Curb Market moved indoors at 86 Trinity Place and in 1953 became the **American Stock Exchange** (Ⓣ212/306-1000, Ⓦwww.amex.com).

perhaps because it was so obviously caused by the greed and shortsightedness of the money men themselves. In those days, shares could be bought "on margin," which meant the buyer needed to pay only a small part of their total cost, borrowing the rest and using the shares as security. This worked fine as long as the market kept rising – as share dividends came in to pay off the loans, investors' money bought more shares. But it was, as Alistair Cooke put it, "a mountain of credit on a molehill of actual money," and only a small scare was needed to start the avalanche. When investors had to find more cash to service their debts and make up for the fall in value of their stocks, they sold off their shares cheaply. A panicked chain reaction ensued, and on October 24, sixteen million shares were traded; five days later, the whole Exchange collapsed as $125 million was wiped off stock values. Fortunes disappeared overnight: millions lost their life savings; banks, businesses and industries shut their doors; and unemployment spiraled helplessly. This was the beginning of the Great Depression, a slump that really didn't end until World War II.

It said much for America's safety nets that the tumultuous crash of October 1987 caused comparatively negligible reverberations. Some thirteen years later the country felt a bit more impact when the bottom fell out of the new economy; mavens like Microsoft's Bill Gates and Amazon's Jeff Bezos were estimated to lose billions, alongside many others caught in the frenzy of profitless dot-coms and failed IPOs.

Federal Hall

The **Federal Hall National Memorial**, 26 Wall St (Mon–Fri 9am–5pm; free; Ⓣ212/825-6888, Ⓦwww.nps.gov/feha), at the street's canyon-like head, can't help but look like an Ionic temple that woke up one morning and found itself surrounded by skyscrapers. The building was built by Town and Davis as the Customs House in the 1830s and served briefly as the first capitol of the United States. An exhibition inside relates the heady days of 1789 when George Washington was sworn in as America's first president from a balcony on this site. It was a showy affair for a great, if rather pompous, man: "I fear we may have exchanged George III for George I," commented one senator after observing Washington's affectations. Washington's pretensions notwithstanding, democracy got its start here some sixty years earlier when printer John Peter

The Trial of John Peter Zenger

German immigrant **John Peter Zenger** (1697–1746) rapidly established a reputation as a printer and journalist for the *New York Weekly Journal*, which took an anti-British stance and published inflammatory writings in an age when British law maintained that truth was no defense in cases of libel. The *Journal*'s views made him unpopular with the royal authorities in New York, and in 1734 Zenger was arrested for articles considered slanderous against the Crown. Philadelphia attorney **Andrew Hamilton** (see p.230) took Zenger's case *pro bono,* ensuring that his libel trial became a fight for freedom of the press. Urging the jury to find in Zenger's favor, the fiery Hamilton declaimed that "the laws of our country have given us a right: the liberty of both exposing and opposing arbitrary power by speaking and writing the truth." It took only minutes before the jury reached a verdict of not guilty.

Zenger was acquitted of libel in 1735, setting an important precedent for freedom of the press in America (see box above). The documents and models inside repay a wander, as does the hall with its elegant rotunda and Cretan maidens worked into the decorative railings. Washington's statue stands, very properly, on the steps.

Trinity Church and around

At Wall Street's western end, **Trinity Church** (Mon–Sat free guided tours daily at 2pm) waits darkly in the wings, an ironic and stoic onlooker to the street's dealings. King William III of England granted the church a charter and some land in 1697, and while there's been a church here ever since, this knobby neo-Gothic structure – the third model – went up in 1846. For fifty years it was the city's tallest building, a reminder of just how relatively recent high-rise Manhattan sprung up. Trinity has the air of an English church (Richard Upjohn, its architect, was English), especially in the sheltered graveyard, resting place of early Manhattanites and lunching office workers. A search around the old tombstones rewards with such luminaries as the first secretary of the Treasury, Alexander Hamilton, steamboat king Robert Fulton, signer of the Declaration of Independence Francis Lewis and many others.

Trinity Church is an oddity amid its office-building neighbors, several of which are worth nosing into. **One Wall Street**, immediately opposite the church, is among the best, with an Art Deco lobby in red and gold that suggests a bankers' bordello. East down Wall Street, the **Morgan Guaranty Trust Building**, at no. 23, bears the scars of a weird happening on September 16, 1920: a horse-drawn cart pulled up outside and its driver jumped off and disappeared down a side street. A few seconds later, the cart blew up in a devastating explosion, knocking out windows half a mile away. Thirty-three people were killed and hundreds injured, but the explosion remains unexplained. One theory holds that it was a premeditated attack on Morgan and his vast financial empire; another claims that the cart belonged to an explosives company and was illegally traveling through the city. Recent research indicates that the blast was the doing of an Italian anarchist in retribution for the executions of Sacco and Vanzetti. Curiously, or perhaps deliberately, the pockmark scars on the building's wall have never been repaired.

Just down Wall Street, at the corner of Nassau Street, stands the **Skyscraper Museum**, at no. 16 (Mon–Fri noon–6pm; suggested donation $2; ⓣ212/968-1961, ⓦwww.skyscraper.org), though it won't be here for long. Founded in

1996, the museum is slated in mid-2002 to move to the ground floor of the new *Ritz-Carlton Downtown Hotel* at 39 Battery Place.

The Federal Reserve Plaza and around

North of Wall Street lies Fulton Street, which arcs right across lower Manhattan with Maiden Lane as its southern parallel, forming an area composed of small finance houses, discount goods stores and fast-food restaurants. Where Nassau and Maiden Lane meet, Johnson and Burgee's **Federal Reserve Plaza** is a Lego fortress and cavernous arched hall, which complements the original 1924 Federal Reserve Bank. The Federal Reserve Plaza proved to be one of Philip Johnson's last projects with John Burgee: he split with the architect soon after, leaving Burgee broke and in the architectural wilderness.

There's good reason for the Reserve Bank's iron-barred exterior: stashed eighty feet below the somber neo-Gothic interior are most of the "free"

The World Trade Center 1972–2001

On **September 11th, 2001**, a hijacked airline slammed into the north tower of the **World Trade Center** at 8.45am; eighteen minutes later another hijacked plane struck the south tower. As thousands looked on in horror – in addition to millions more viewing on TV – the south tower collapsed at 9.50am, its twin about half an hour later. That afternoon, a smaller building in the World Trade Center complex also crumbled, and the Center was reduced to a monument of steel, concrete and glass rubble. As black clouds billowed above, the whole area was covered in a blanket of concrete dust several inches thick; mountains of other debris reached up several hundred feet in the air.

The devastation was staggering. While most of the 50,000 working in the towers had been evacuated before the towers fell, many never made it out; hundreds of firemen, policemen and rescue workers who arrived on the scene when the planes struck were crushed when the buildings collapsed. In all, around 4000 perished in what was easily the largest attack on America in history.

In the days after the attack, downtown was basically shut down, and the seven-square-block vicinity immediately around the WTC – soon to be known as **Ground Zero** – was the obvious focus of the rescue effort. New Yorkers lined up to give blood and volunteer to help the rescue workers; vigils were held throughout the city, most notably in Union Square, which became peppered with all manner of candles and makeshift shrines; and all city hospitals were on red alert to receive injured victims. Precious few came, and as weeks passed, reality began to sink in. Through it all Mayor Giuliani cut a highly composed and reassuring figure as New Yorkers struggled to come to terms with the physical and emotional assault on their city. It was more than just sheer numbers – the lives lost, the expected $60 billion cost of insurance payouts, property value loss, cleanup (expected to take a full year) – life was irrevocably changed.

The chief **suspect** in the attacks was Osama bin Laden's terrorist network that he operated from the mountains of Afghanistan. In October 2001, the US government began launching military strikes against Afghanistan's ruling Taliban, known to harbor and support bin Laden.

world's gold reserves – 9000 tons of them, occasionally shifted from vault to vault as wars break out or international debts are settled. It is possible – but tricky – to tour the piles of gleaming bricks; contact the Public Information Department, Federal Reserve Bank, 33 Liberty St, NY 10045 (Ⓣ212/720-6130, Ⓦwww.ny.frb.org) several weeks ahead, as tickets have to be mailed. Upstairs, in the Bank, dirty money and counterfeit currency are weeded out of circulation by automated checkers that shuffle dollar bills like endless packs of cards.

When you've adjusted to the sight of high finance's gold, you can see more of its glitter at **1 Chase Manhattan Plaza**, immediately to the south between Pine and Liberty streets. This, the prestigious New York headquarters of the bank, boasts a boxy tower that was the first of its kind in lower Manhattan, and which brought to downtown the concept of the plaza entrance. Unfortunately, Chase Manhattan's plaza has all the charm of a parking lot, and even Dubuffet's *Four Trees* sculpture can't get things going. Continue to the end of Cedar Street, where the **Marine Midland Bank Building**, 140 Broadway, is a smaller, more successful tower by the same design team, decorated with a sculpture by Noguchi. More sculpture worth catching lies behind Chase Manhattan Plaza on Louise Nevelson Plaza, which divides Maiden Lane and Liberty Street. Here, a clutch of Nevelson's works perch like a mass of shrapnel on an island

A brief history of the towers

Dominating lower Manhattan's landscape from nearly any angle, the 110-story **Twin Towers** always appeared a little incongruous amid their surroundings; harsher critics charged that, spirited down to a tenth of their size, the towers wouldn't get a second glance. In any event, the first tower went up in 1972 and the second a year later, only to be quickly surpassed as the world's tallest buildings by the Sears Tower in Chicago (itself exceeded by Kuala Lumpur's Petronas Towers). The towers were the most celebrated examples of tube buildings – constructions that used exterior columns and beams to form steel tubes that withstood the mighty wind pressures encountered by buildings of such heights. At 1368 and 1362 feet – over a quarter of a mile – the towers afforded mind-blowing views; on a clear day, visitors to the observation deck could see 55 miles into the distance.

While the Twin Towers became integral parts of the New York skyline, they also evolved into emblems of American power in the eyes of various Islamic extremists. On February 26, 1993, the World Trade Center complex was rocked by an explosive device left in one of the underground parking lots; six people were killed and over a thousand injured. Blame for the bomb fell upon a terrorist group led by the radical Muslim cleric Sheikh Omar Abdel-Rahman, who was found guilty, with nine co-defendants, of involvement by a NYC court in summer 1995. It's hard to believe how inconsequential this attack would seem in the light of future events.

The future of the site

After the rubble is cleared, it will likely be years before anything is constructed in the towers' former site. That hasn't stopped all manner of architects, city planners and officials from putting forth their ideas: proposals range from some form of memorial to the dead to a reconstruction of the towers as they stood, to erecting four buildings at half their size. The current lease-holding group, which swung a 99-year deal with the Port Authority ownership just before the attacks, has promised to rebuild. Whatever winds up happening, it's sure to stoke emotions and memories – not that you need look further than the altered skyline for that.

of land: a striking ploy of sculpture that works well in the urban environment. The mural painting of Seurat's *A Sunday Afternoon on the Grande Jatte* to one side of the plaza served as a backdrop in the film *Die Hard With a Vengeance*, a film that played on urban fears of terrorism that now seem quite dated.

Go back down Liberty Street to Church Street, and at 1 Liberty Plaza you'll find the **US Steel Building**, a black mass that has justly been called a "gloomy, cadaverous hulk." To make way for it, the famed Singer Building, Ernest Flagg's 1908 construction, one of the most delicate on the New York skyline, was demolished in 1968. When the World Trade Center collapsed, many of the US Steel Building's windows popped out, and it was feared that the building itself would tumble.

Before you conclude that modern monoliths seem to be all size and no style, double back down John Street to **no. 127**, where you'll see a most playful creation, a bit cutesy but cheekily out of synch with its surroundings. Designed by Emery Roth and Sons, the building struts a blue and red neon exterior that is the antithesis of the Financial District's staid and streamlined facades; its interior, featuring brightly colored ducts and pipes wrapped in twinkling Christmas lights, is enough to induce heart attacks in the area's conservative populace. The restaurant adjacent to the property refused to sell to the developer, so architects made its side wall a giant-size digital clock, which keeps accurate time, even down to the second.

St Paul's Chapel and south on Broadway

The oldest church in Manhattan, **St Paul's Chapel** dates from 1766 – eighty years earlier than Trinity Church, almost prehistoric by New York standards. Though the building seems quite American in feel, its English architect used St Martin-in-the-Fields in London as his model for this unfussy eighteenth-century space of soap-bar blues and pinks. George Washington worshipped here and his pew, zealously treasured, is on show.

Heading south along Broadway, a most impressive leftover of the confident days before the Wall Street Crash is the old **Cunard Building** at no. 25. Its marble walls and high dome once housed a steamship's booking office – hence the elaborate, whimsical murals of variegated ships and nautical mythology splashed around the ceiling. As the large liners gave way to jet travel, Cunard could no longer afford such an extravagant shop window. Today, it houses a post office – one that's been fitted with little feeling for the exuberant space it occupies – while on the second floor is the **New York City Police Museum** (Tues–Sat 10am–6pm; free; ⓣ212/301-4440, ⓦwww.nycpolicemuseum.org). A collection of 250 years' worth of memorabilia of the New York Police Department, the largest and oldest in the country. Staffed by cops from the force's community affairs department, it showcases the history and personal effects of New York's Finest: night sticks, guns, uniforms, photos and the like – over 10,000 items in all. There's a copper badge from 1845 that was worn by the sergeants of the day, earning them the nickname of "coppers," and a pristine-looking Tommy gun – in its original gangster-issue violin case – that was used to rub out Al Capone's gang leader, Frankie Yale.

In front of the Cunard Building, rearing on the street partition, is a sculpture of a **Charging Bull** – not, as one might imagine, the symbol of an eternally bullish market, but a sculpture the artist didn't know what to do with. As the story goes, on December 15, 1989, Arturo Di Modica installed his sculpture in the middle of Broad Street. The sculpture was removed by the city the next day, but the public outcry forced the city to find it a home here. Across the street at 26 Broadway, located in the former headquarters of **John D. Rockefeller's Standard Oil Company**, is the **Museum of American Financial History**, 28 Broadway (Tues–Sat 10am–4pm; $2; ⓣ212/908-4110, ⓦwww.financialhistory.org). This is the largest public archive of financial documents and artifacts in the world, featuring such finance-related objects as the bond signed by Washington bearing the first dollar sign ever used on a Federal document, and a stretch of ticker tape from the opening moments of 1929's Great Crash. Also on view are early photographs of Wall Street and furnishings from *Delmonico's* restaurant, where the Robber Barons held court. Fortunately, this isn't just a self-congratulatory temple to big business: changing educational exhibits concentrate on such themes as the colonies' emergence from debt in the wake of the Revolutionary War to the process by which companies raise capital. On Fridays, the museum also offers a "World of Finance" walking tour ($15).

Bowling Green

Broadway comes to a gentle end at **Bowling Green Park**, originally the city's meat market, but in 1733 turned into an oval of turf used for the game by colonial Brits on a lease of "one peppercorn per year." The encircling iron fence is an original from 1771, though the crowns that once topped the stakes were removed by later revolutionary fervor, as was a statue of George III, which was melted into musket balls – little bits of the monarch that were fired at his troops during the Revolutionary War. In 1783, the green was one of the last areas to be evacuated by the British, and it was the site of celebration when New York ratified the Constitution in 1788.

Earlier, the green was the location of one of Manhattan's more memorable business deals, when Peter Minuit, first director general of the Dutch colony of New Amsterdam, bought the whole island from the Indians in 1626 for a bucket of trade goods worth sixty guilders (about $24). The other side of the story (and the part you never hear) was that these particular Indians didn't actually own the island; no doubt both parties went home smiling.

The US Customs House and the Museum of the American Indian

The green sees plenty of office folk picnicking in the shadow of Cass Gilbert's **US Customs House**, a heroic monument to the Port of New York and home of the **Smithsonian National Museum of the American Indian**, 1 Bowling Green (daily 10am–5pm; free; ⓣ212/514-3700, ⓦwww.si.edu/nmai). This excellent collection of artifacts from almost every tribe native to the Americas was largely assembled by one man, George Gustav Heye (1874–1957), who traveled throughout the Americas picking up such works for over fifty years. Only a small portion of the collection is on view here – more will be displayed in the new museum built on the Mall in Washington DC. In addition to several temporary shows a year, there are two large permanent exhibitions: "Creation's Journey: Masterworks of Native American Identity and Belief," consisting of 165 items chosen by the museum's curators, and "All Roads are Good: Native Voices on Life and Culture," with over 300 artifacts chosen by different Native American groups to represent their world views and beliefs. A rather extraordinary facet of the museum is its repatriation policy, adopted in 1991, which mandates that it give back to Indian tribes, upon request, any human remains, funerary objects, and ceremonial and religious items it may have illegally acquired. If the major museums of the world followed suit, they would surely all be virtually empty.

Built in 1907, the Customs House itself was intended to pay homage to the booming maritime market. The four **statues** (sculpted by Daniel Chester French, who also created the Lincoln Memorial in Washington, DC) at the front of the building represent the four continents; the twelve scenes on the facade personify the world's commercial centers; and the head of Mercury – Roman god of commerce – adorns the top of each exterior column for good measure. As if French foresaw the House's current use, the sculptor blatantly comments on the mistreatment of Indians in his statues: most striking is the work on the left side of the front main staircase, which depicts a Native American in full headdress timidly peering over the shoulder of "America," who sits grandly on her throne and holds an oversized sheaf of corn on her lap – a symbol of Indian prosperity and contribution to world culture. Equally telling is the sculpture on the opposite side of the stairs, in which "America," this time her throne decorated with Mayan glyphs, has her foot on the head of Quetzalcoatl, the plumed serpent god worshiped by the Aztecs. Inside the House, on the rotunda, are blue, gray and brown murals of bustling ships, painted by Reginald Marsh.

Battery Park and Castle Clinton

Due west, lower Manhattan lets out its breath in **Battery Park**, a bright and breezy space with tall trees, green grass, lots of flowers and views overlooking the panorama of the Statue of Liberty, Ellis Island and Governors Island, all dotting America's largest harbor. Various monuments and statues ranging from Jewish immigrants to Celtic settlers to the city's first wireless telegraph operators adorn the park.

Before a landfill closed the gap, **Castle Clinton**, the 1811 fort on the west side of the park, was on an island, one of several forts defending New York Harbor, with its battery of cannons – hence its name. Yet not a shot was ever fired from this fort, and in 1823 it was ceded to the city, which leased it to a group that created the Castle Garden resort. Later, it found new life as a prestigious concert venue – in 1850, the enterprising P.T. Barnum threw a hugely hyped concert by soprano Jenny Lind, the "Swedish Nightingale," with tickets at $225 a pop – before doing service (pre-Ellis Island) as the dropoff point for arriving immigrants. From 1855 to 1890 eight million immigrants passed through these walls. Today, the squat castle is open daily 8.30am–5pm and is the place to buy tickets for and board ferries to the Statue of Liberty and Ellis Island (see "The Harbor Islands," p.55).

South of Castle Clinton stands the **East Coast Memorial**, a series of granite slabs inscribed with the names of all the American seamen who were killed in World War II. To the castle's north, perched ten feet into the harbor, is the **American Merchant Mariners' Memorial**, an eerie depiction of a marine futilely reaching for the hand of a man sinking underneath the waves. Fittingly, both these memorials look out across New York Harbor. They also offer tremendous views of the Statue of Liberty and Ellis Island.

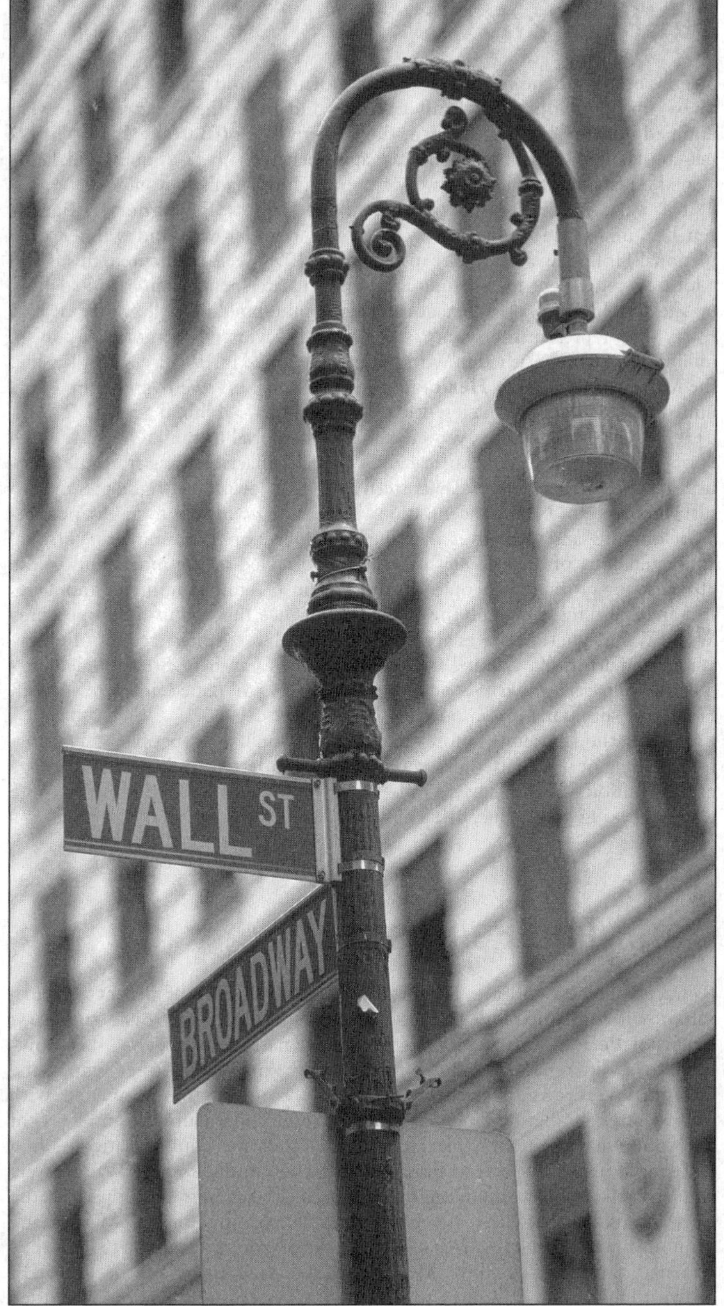

△ Wall Street stands at the center of international finance

Battery Park City

The hole dug for the foundations of the former World Trade Center's towers threw up a million cubic yards of earth and rock; these excavations were dumped into the Hudson to form the 23-acre base of **Battery Park City**, a self-sufficient island of office blocks, apartments, chain boutiques, and landscaped esplanade that feels a far cry from much of Manhattan indeed.

At its very southern end is the entrance to **Robert F. Wagner Jr. Park** – zen-like in its peacefulness away from the ferry crowds and winner of a National Honor Award for Urban Design in 1998. Well-manicured, this is still a local secret, where many summer afternoons are spent reading and soaking up the sun. In the park, a hexagonal, pale granite building will grab your eye. Its six sides represent the points of the Star of David and memorialize the six million Jews who perished in World War II. Designed in 1997 by Kevin Roche, the **Museum of Jewish Heritage**, 18 First Place (Sun–Wed 9am–5pm, Thurs until 8pm, Fri 9am–5pm, closed Jewish holidays; $7, children $5; ⓣ212/509-6130, ⓦwww.mjhnyc.org), was created as a memorial to the Holocaust. Three floors of exhibits feature historical and cultural artifacts ranging from the practical accoutrements of everyday Eastern European Jewish life to the prison garb survivors wore in Nazi concentration camps, along with photographs, personal belongings and narratives. Among the collection is Himmler's personal annotated copy of *Mein Kampf* and a notebook filled by the inhabitants of the "barrack for prominent people" in the Terazin Ghetto. Multimedia montages and archival films catalogue the Jewish experience this century: Europe's pre-World War II ghettos, the establishment of Israel, even the successes of entertainers and artists like Samuel Goldwyn and Allen Ginsberg. Steven Spielberg's moving *Survivors of the Shoah Visual History Project* (taped interviews with Holocaust survivors) is also on view here.

Outside the museum, more than likely you'll see people exercising, rollerblading or just lazily walking on the **esplanade**, a path that skirts the edge of the Hudson River for over a mile, ending at the edge of TriBeCa. The route is very relaxing and scenic, best enjoyed at night.

Water and Pearl streets

Retrace your steps through Robert F. Wagner Park to **Water Street** and turn east down Old Slip. The pocket-size palazzo, which was once the **First Precinct Police Station**, slots easily into the narrow strip, a cheerful throwback to a different era. A little to the south, off Water Street, stands the **Vietnam Veterans' Memorial**, an assembly of glass blocks etched with troops' letters home. The mementos are sad and often haunting, and a recent renovation has made the place a peaceful spot for contemplation – and enjoying a nice view of the East River. If you continue along Water Street you'll reach an attenuated agglomeration of skyscrapers developed in the early 1960s. At that time, the powers-that-were thought that Manhattan's economy was stagnating because of lack of room for growth, so they widened throughways like Water Street by razing many of the Victorian brownstones and warehouses that lined the waterfront. By doing so, they missed a vital chance to allow the old to give context to the new; ironically, a decent chunk of the office buildings they ambitiously built have since been converted to condos.

For perspective of Manhattan's eighteenth-century heart, the **Fraunces Tavern Museum**, 54 Pearl St at Broad St (Mon–Fri 9am–5pm; $3, children, seniors, students $2; ⓣ212/425-1778, ⓦwww.frauncestavernmuseum.org), which escaped the 1835 fire, retains eleven 1830s-era buildings. The ochre-and-red-brick Fraunces Tavern claims to be a colonial inn, although in truth it is more of an expert fake. Having survived extensive modification, several fires and nineteenth-century use as a hotel, the three-story Georgian brick house was almost totally reconstructed by the Sons of the Revolution in the early part of the century to mimic its appearance on December 4, 1783 – complete with period interiors and furnishings. It was then, after the British had been conclusively beaten, that a weeping George Washington took leave of his assembled officers, intent on returning to rural life in Virginia: "I am not only retiring from all public employments," he wrote, "but am retiring within myself." With hindsight, it was a hasty statement – six years later he was to return as the new nation's president. The Tavern's second floor re-creates the site's history with a series of illustrated panels.

At 6 Pearl St, you'll find **New York Unearthed** (Mon–Fri noon–6pm; free; ⓣ212/748-8628), the South Street Seaport Museum's tiny, hands-on annex devoted to the city's archeology. Built on the site of Herman Melville's 1819 birthplace, the building's upper floor consists of artifacts excavated from different periods of New York's history. There's a "Pitt and Liberty" plate commemorating William Pitt's opposition to the Stamp Act, Britain's first attempt to tax the colonies; a selection of personal items from Brooklyn's Weeksville, the first free African-American community in New York State after the 1827 abolition of slavery; and even 1950s-era luncheonette ware. In the basement, relics from an 1835 fire that ravaged Lower Manhattan are also on display. Along the curve of State Street, just across from Battery Park, a rounded dark, red-brick Georgian facade, no. 7, identifies the **Shrine of Elizabeth Ann Seton**, 7-8 State St (Mon–Fri 6.30am–5.30pm, Sat & Sun 8am–6pm; ⓣ212/269-6865), the first native-born American to be canonized. St Elizabeth lived here briefly before moving to found a religious community in Maryland. The shrine – small, hushed and illustrated by pious and tearful pictures of the saint's life – is one of a few old houses that have survived the modern onslaught.

South Street Seaport

At the eastern end of Fulton Street, the **South Street Seaport** comes girded with the sort of praise and publicity that generally augur commercial blandness. In reality, the Seaport is a mixed bag: a fair slice of commercial gentrification was necessary to woo developers and tourists, but the presence of a centuries-old working fish market has kept things real in a way that should be a lesson. Unfortunately, like so much of bona fide New York, the market is under threat from city officials, while rumor has it that fish truckers find the Hunt's Point wholesale market in the Bronx more convenient.

The Seaport dates back to the 1600s, when this stretch of the waterside was New York's sailship port: it began when Robert Fulton started a ferry service from here to Brooklyn, leaving his name on the street and then its market. In fact, New York owes most of what it has become to its access to the sea. The harbor lapped up the trade brought by the opening of the Erie Canal (1825) and by the end of the nineteenth century was sending cargo ships on regular runs to California, Japan and Liverpool. When the FDR Drive was constructed in the 1950s, the Seaport's decline was rapid. A private initiative beginning in 1967 rescued the remaining warehouses and saved the historic seaport just in time. Regular guided tours of the Seaport run from the **Visitors' Center**, an immaculate brick-terraced house located at 12–14 Fulton St.

The Seaport Museum and Paris Café

Housed in a series of painstakingly restored 1830s warehouses, the **South Street Seaport Museum**, 207 Water St (daily: April–Sept 10am–6pm, Oct–March 10am–5pm; $5, includes all tours, films, galleries and museum-owned ships, as well as New York Unearthed; Ⓣ212/748-8600, Ⓦwww.southstseaport.org), offers a collection of refitted ships and chubby tugboats (the largest collection of sailing vessels – by tonnage – in the US), plus a handful of maritime art and trades exhibits, a museum store and info about the Fulton Fish Market. In the summer, the 1885 schooner *Pioneer*, the 1893 fishing schooner *Lettie G. Howard* and the tug *W.O. Decker* will coast you around the harbor for an additional consideration; call the museum for schedules.

Next door is **Bowne & Co., Stationers**, 211 Water St (Mon–Sat 10am–5pm; Ⓣ212/748-8651), a gas-lit nineteenth-century shop that produces examples of authentic letterpress printing. You can order a set of business cards made by hand with antique handpresses. A set of 100 will cost you $85, and unless you are planning to be in New York City for three to four weeks, you will need to have them shipped home. At 213 Water St, the **Mellville Library** (open by appointment only; Ⓣ212/748-8648) serves as a reference facility for the public researching any aspect of shipping, the Port of New York or the South Street Seaport District.

If it's afternoon and you wish to take a load off, back track one block to Beekman Street and head toward the water. You couldn't ask for a better spot than the **Paris Café**, at 119 South St, located in *Meyer's Hotel* at the end of Peck Slip, one of the last and most important harbor slips. The café played host in the late 1880s to a panoply of luminaries. Thomas Edison used the café as a second office while designing the first electric power station in the world on Pearl Street; the opening of the Brooklyn Bridge was celebrated on the roof with Annie Oakley and Buffalo Bill Cody as guests; Teddy Roosevelt broke bread here; and journalist John Reed and other members of the Communist Labor Party of America met secretly here in the early twenties. These days, without presidents or communists, the elegant square bar, tempting seafood specials and outdoor seating still pull in a lively crowd. For a stellar **view of the Brooklyn Bridge**, walk out to the small waterfront park and have a seat on the benches or have your photo taken in front of one the most beautiful backdrops New York City has to offer.

The Fulton Fish Market

Follow your nose south. The elevated East Side Highway forms a suitably grimy gateway to the **Fulton Fish Market**, the city's oldest and largest wholesale outlet. Business has been done on this site since 1835 and now generates over a billion dollars in revenues annually. This is a place where word of honor still seals business dealings. If you can manage it, the time to be here is around 5am when buyers' trucks park up beneath the highway to collect the catches;

the air reeks of dead fish and salt and there's lots of nasty things to step in. It's invigorating stuff, a twilight world that probably won't be around much longer – the city's regulation of the area, along with the adjacent Pier 17 Pavilion, a hypercomplex of restaurants and shops, may be nails in its coffin. Tours can be arranged through the South Street Seaport Museum the first and third Wednesday of the month, April–Oct (Ⓣ212/748-8786). The market will be moving to Hunts Point in the Bronx in 2003.

Pier 17 and the rest of the seaport

To many, **Pier 17**, right next to the Fish Market, has become the focal point of the district, created from the old fish market pier demolished and then restored in 1982. A three-story glass-and-steel **pavilion** houses all kinds of restaurants and shops; a bit more interesting is the outdoor promenade, always crowded in the summer, when you can listen to free music, tour historic moored ships like the *Peking* (1911), the *Ambrose Lightship* (1908) or the *Wavetree* (1855), or book cruises with the New York Waterway (two-hour cruises $12; Ⓣ1-800/533-3779, Ⓦwww.nywaterway.com), though you don't have to spend a dime to take in the fantastic views of the Brooklyn and Manhattan bridges from the promenade.

Just across South Street, there's an assemblage of upmarket chain shops like Ann Taylor, Abercrombie & Fitch and the Body Shop that line Fulton and the adjacent Front Street. Keep your eyes peeled for some unusual buildings preserved here, like at **203 Front St**; this giant J. Crew store was an 1880s hotel that catered to unmarried laborers on the dock. Not far away, cleaned-up **Schermerhorn Row** is a unique ensemble of Georgian-Federal-style early warehouses, dating to about 1811. Here, at the corner of South and Fulton streets is the "English" *North Star Pub*, which boasts a large inventory of single-malt scotches.

If you want to end the day by sampling some fresh ocean catch, wander down Front Street past the formerly derelict residences, to *Carmine's Italian Seafood* at 140 Beekman St, a crusty old joint located here since 1903, or walk a little farther to *Jeremy's Ale House* at 254 Front St (at Dover Street), a silver-painted brick warehouse that serves tasty, inexpensive fried clams, calamari and oysters.

3

City Hall Park and the Brooklyn Bridge

Since the early days of the city, the seats of New York's federal, state and city government have been located around **City Hall Park**, and though many of the original civic buildings no longer stand, there remain great examples of some of the city's finest architecture here. The **Woolworth Building** stands by as a venerable onlooker; the **Brooklyn**

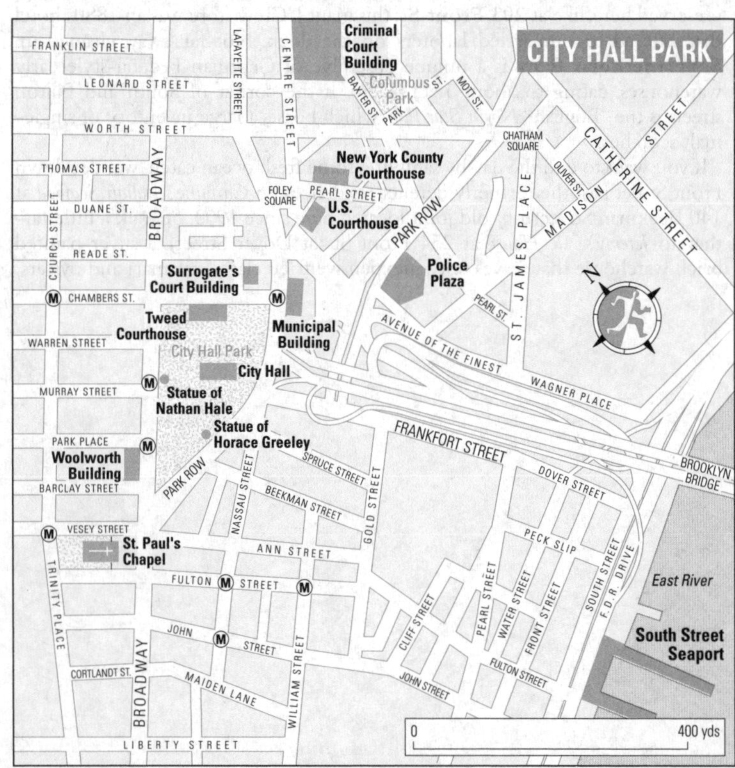

Bridge zooms eastward over the river; the park itself contains **City Hall** and the **Tweed Courthouse**, and the **Municipal Building** stands sentry to Police Plaza and the courthouses that form the center of New York's judicial system. The best way to approach the park is by taking the subway to Fulton Street, the cross street for #A, #C, #E, #M, #4, #5, #2 and #3 trains, or the #N or #R to City Hall.

City Hall Park

Landscaped in 1730, verdant **City Hall Park** is formed by the merging of Broadway and Park Row to the south and by Chambers Street to the north. This triangular wedge is dotted with statues, not least of which is of Horace Greeley, founder of the *New York Tribune* newspaper, and in front of whose bronzed countenance a **farmer's market** is held each Tuesday and Friday (April–Dec 8am–6pm). Prize position among the patriotic statues here goes to Nathan Hale who, in 1776, was captured by the British and hanged for spying, but not before he'd spat out his gloriously and memorably famous last words: "I regret that I only have but one life to lose for my country." Three months earlier, George Washington ordered the first reading in the city of the Declaration of Independence here. Thomas Jefferson's eloquent, stirring statement of the new nation's rights had just been adopted by the Second Continental Congress in Philadelphia, and it no doubt fired the hearts and minds of the troops and people assembled.

> ***We hold these truths to be self-evident, that all men are created equal, that they are endowed by their creator with certain unalienable rights, that among these are Life, Liberty and the pursuit of Happiness; that to secure these rights Governments are instituted among Men, deriving their just powers from the consent of the governed; that whenever any form of Government becomes destructive of these ends, it is the Right of the People to alter or abolish it, and to institute new Government.***

City Hall

At the top of the park is **City Hall** (Mon–Fri free tours at 10am, 11 and 2pm; ⓣ212/788-6865), finished in 1812 to a good-looking design that's a marriage of French Chateau and American Georgian stands at the top of the park. Its first moment of fame came in 1865 when Abraham Lincoln's body lay in state for 120,000 sorrowful New Yorkers to file past. Later, after the city's 1927 fêting of the returned aviator Charles Lindbergh, it became the traditional finishing point for Broadway tickertape parades given for astronauts, returned hostages and World Series winners. Inside, it's an elegant meeting of arrogance and authority, with the sweeping spiral staircase delivering you to the precise geometry of the Governor's Room and the self-important rooms that formerly contained the Board of Estimates Chamber.

The Woolworth Building

The world's tallest skyscraper until it was surpassed in 1930 by the Chrysler Building (see p.139), the **Woolworth Building** exudes money, ornament and prestige. The soaring, graceful lines of Cass Gilbert's 1913 "Cathedral of Commerce" are fringed with Gothic-style gargoyles and decorations that are more for fun than for any portentous allusion. Frank Woolworth made his fortune from his "five and dime" stores – everything cost either 5¢ or 10¢, strictly no credit. True to his philosophy, he paid cash for the building of his skyscraper, and the whimsical reliefs at each corner of the lobby, open during office hours, show him doing just that: counting out the money in nickels and dimes. Facing him in caricature are Gilbert (clutching a model of his building), the renting agent and the builder. Within, vaulted ceilings ooze honey-gold mosaics and even the brass mailboxes are magnificent. The whole building has a well-humored panache absent in the more modern buildings, such as next door's Citibank tower.

The Tweed Courthouse

If City Hall is the acceptable face of New York's municipal bureaucracy, the **Tweed Courthouse** (where the Museum of the City of New York, p.194, will move in late 2003) is a reminder of its infamous nineteenth-century corruption. Located directly behind City Hall and bordering Chambers Street, William Marcy "Boss" Tweed's monument to greed looks more like a genteel mansion than a municipal building: its long windows and sparse ornamentation are, ironically, far less grandiose or ostentatious than those of many of its peers. The man behind its construction, Tweed, had worked his way from nowhere to become chairman of the Democratic Central Committee at Tammany Hall in 1856 and, by a series of adroit and illegal moves, had manipulated the city's revenues into both his own and his supporters' pockets. He consolidated his position by registering thousands of immigrants as Democrats, offering them a low-level welfare system in return, and by paying off the legion of critics.

For a while Tweed's grip strangled all dissent (even over the courthouse's budget, which rolled up from $3 million to $12 million) until a political cartoonist, Thomas Nast, and the editor of the *New York Times* (who'd refused a $500,000 bribe to keep quiet) turned public opinion against him in the late 1860s. With suitable irony Tweed died in 1878 in Ludlow Street Jail – a prison he'd had built when Commissioner of Public Works.

The Municipal Building and around

Straddling Chambers Street, the **Municipal Building** stands like an oversized chest of drawers across Centre Street, as though attempting to engulf City Hall. Built between 1907 and 1914, the building was architects McKim, Mead and White's first skyscraper. Atop it, an extravagant pile of columns and pinnacles signals a frivolous conclusion to a no-nonsense building that houses public records; below, though not apparent, subway cars travel through its foundation. Walk through the building's arch (on Chambers Street) – towards the bright red Bernard Rosenthal sculpture – and you'll reach **Police Plaza** and the **NYC Police Headquarters**, one of New York's most urbane civic buildings. The left side of the plaza runs down past the anachronistic neo-Georgian Church of St Andrew's to the pompous-looking United States Courthouse, and stops at the glum-gray **Foley Square**, named after the sheriff and saloon-keeper Thomas "Big Tom" Foley. On the northeast edge of the square resides the **New York County Courthouse**, a grand though underwhelming building whose rotunda is decorated with storybook Works Progress Association

The African burial ground

In 1991, construction of a Federal office building at 290 Broadway uncovered an African burial ground, where as many as an estimated 20,000 free and enslaved African Americans were buried in the 1700s – before Chambers Street was laid over it. For over a decade since, heated discussions have taken place over how best to preserve this archeological and historical find – while of course proceeding with construction of the building – with a few tangible results. An outdoor garden next to the building is dedicated to the burial ground and an internment of the remains already excavated is in the works. Commissioned sculptures and paintings commemorate the ground inside the lobby of the building, where construction of an African Burial Ground interpretative center is planned.

murals illustrating the history of justice. The 1950s courtroom drama *Twelve Angry Men* was filmed here.

At 100 Centre St, the 1939 Art Deco **Criminal Courts Building**, reminiscent of a Babylonian temple, houses the **Manhattan Detention Center of Men**, which is nicknamed "The Tombs," after the funereal Egyptian-style building that once stood across the street. The nearby fortress-like **Family Court** (60 Lafayette St) building resembles a Rubik's Cube that's been partially twisted and spit-shined. All courts are open to the public (Mon–Fri 9am–5pm); the Criminal Courts are your best bet for viewing the New York City justice system in action.

By and large, civic dignity begins to fade north of here, as ramshackle electrical stores and signs offering "Immigrant fingerprinting and photo ID" mark the edge of Chinatown (see p.83). Circle back through the arch of the Municipal Building to Centre Street, in the center of which you can catch the footpath that runs over the Brooklyn Bridge.

The Brooklyn Bridge

One of several spans across the East River (the Manhattan and Williamsburg bridges, respectively, are in sight behind it), the **Brooklyn Bridge**'s Gothic gateways are dwarfed by lower Manhattan's skyscrapers. But in its day, the Brooklyn Bridge was a technological quantum leap: it towered over the brick structures around it and, for twenty years, was the world's largest and longest suspension bridge, the first to use steel cables and – for many more – the longest single span. To New Yorkers, it was an object of awe, the massively concrete symbol of the Great American Dream, and the painter Joseph Stella called it "a shrine containing all the efforts of the new civilization of America." Indeed, the bridge's meeting of art and function, of romantic Gothic and daring practicality, became a sort of spiritual model for the next generation's skyscrapers.

The bridge didn't go up without difficulties. John Augustus Roebling, its architect and engineer, crushed his foot taking measurements for the piers and died of gangrene three weeks later; his son, Washington, took over only to be crippled by the bends from working in an insecure underwater caisson, and subsequently directed the work from his sickbed overlooking the site. Twenty workers died during the construction and, a week after the opening day in 1883, twelve people were crushed to death in a panicked rush on the bridge's footpath. Despite this (and innumerable suicides), New Yorkers still look to the bridge with affection: for the 1983 centennial it was festooned with decorations – "Happy Birthday Brooklyn Bridge" ran the signs – and the city organized a party, replete with shiploads of fireworks.

Whether or not you find the bridge similarly inspiring or not, the **view** from below as well as on top is undeniably spectacular. You can walk across its wooden planks from City Hall Park, but it's best not to look back till you're midway: the Financial District's giants clutter shoulder to shoulder through the spidery latticework of the cables; the East River pulses below as cars hum to and from Brooklyn. It's a glimpse of the twenty-first-century metropolis, and on no account to be missed, though you may want to wait until a day when you have time to tour Brooklyn.

TriBeCa

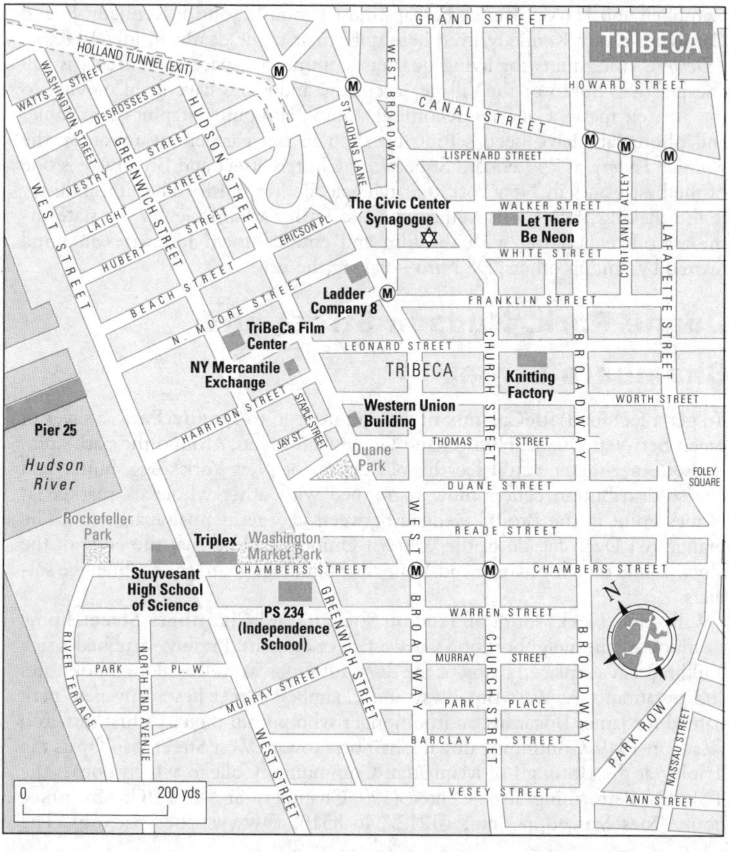

Thanks to savvy real estate developers, **TriBeCa** (Try-beck-a), the *Tri*angle *Be*low *Ca*nal Street, has been transformed from a wholesale garment district to an upscale community that mixes commercial establishments with loft residences, studios, galleries and chic eateries. Less a triangle than a crumpled rectangle – the neighborhood is bounded by Canal and Murray streets, Broadway and the Hudson River – it takes in spacious industrial buildings whose upper layers sprout plants and cats behind tidy glazing: the apartments of TriBeCa's new gentry.

As little as ten years ago, the sound of footsteps would echo off the cobbled streets and against the cast-iron buildings come nightfall. TriBeCa used to shut down when the Wall Street crowd went home, but the growth of Battery Park City (see p.70) and the continued influx of residents has brought smart restaurants into the neighborhood, many of which can be found along Hudson and Greenwich streets (see "Restaurants," p.319).

Some history

As with "SoHo," the name TriBeCa was a semiotic construct better suited to the neighborhood's increasing trendiness than its former moniker, Washington Market – the mid-Seventies invention of an entrepreneurial realtor. The late Seventies saw the first residential renovation of previously industrial buildings, encouraged by tax abatements. In the late 1980s, as the East Village became gentrified and SoHo properties skyrocketed in value, there was a scramble for TriBeCa's warehouses. Today, however, living space in TriBeCa has reached SoHo's in status and price, and a zoning loophole allowing for the addition of penthouses has been fully exploited. For the past decade, the neighborhood has attracted the media elite, including the likes of Robert De Niro, Naomi Campbell and Harvey Keitel. Perhaps most famously, John F. Kennedy, Jr. and Carolyn Bessette Kennedy, lived here until their tragic deaths in July 1999.

Despite rising rents for living quarters, commercial space in TriBeCa is still cheaper than SoHo or the Village, so creative industries have been moving to the area en masse. Galleries, recording studios, computer graphics companies and photo labs have been setting up shop in old garment warehouses; the *Knitting Factory*, at 74 Leonard St between Church Street and Broadway, is one of the best places in New York to catch eclectic live music. The film industry is also making TriBeCa its home, with the TriBeCa Film Center – a state-of-the-art office building with the film and entertainment industries in mind owned by, among others, De Niro – paving the way.

Duane Park, Hudson Street and Chambers Street

To get a feel for TriBeCa's mix of old and new, go to **Duane Park**, a sliver of green between Duane, Hudson and Greenwich streets. Around the park's picturesque perimeter you'll see the old depots of New York's egg, butter and cheese distribution center (now regrouped with other wholesale markets at Hunt's Point in the Bronx) wedged between new residential apartments. The orange Art Deco facade of the Western Union Building is at the edge of the block, while the Woolworth and Municipal buildings guard the skyline like soldiers.

Walk a few blocks south on Hudson Street toward **Chambers Street**, home to much of the neighborhood's newest development. Freshly scrubbed brick buildings have replaced many of the discount shops, as well as along bookstores and restaurants. At West Broadway and Chambers Street lies a tiny new park named for James Bogardus, an ironmonger who put up the city's first cast-iron facade in 1849. Continuing down Chambers toward West Street, you'll pass the Triplex at the Borough of Manhattan Community College, which houses the TriBeCa Performing Arts Center (199 Chambers St #S11OC; box office hours Tues–Sat noon–6pm; ⓣ212/346-8510, ⓦwww.tribecapac.org). The

TriBeCa Galleries

Below are a few of the more prominent or interesting mixed-media galleries in the neighborhood, along with a very brief description of what you might find; more reviews and details can be found in Chapter 35, "Commercial galleries". Try to visit on a weekday, when all the galleries tend to be less crowded.

123 Watts 123 Watts St; by appointment only; ⓣ212/219-1482. Contemporary art work in a variety of media.

Apex Art 291 Church St; Tues–Sat 11am–6pm; ⓣ212/431-5270, ⓦwww.apexart.org. Thematic multimedia exhibits.

Art in General 79 Walker St; Tues–Sat noon–6pm, closed June–Aug; ⓣ212/219-0473, ⓦwww.artingeneral.org. Contemporary art in all media.

Art Projects International 429 Greenwich St; by appointment only; ⓣ212/343-2599, ⓦwww.artproject.com. Contemporary Asian art.

Cheryl Pelavin Fine Art 13 Jay St; Tues–Sat 11am–6pm; ⓣ212/925-9424, ⓦwww.cherylpelavin.com. International works on paper.

Moving Image Gallery 414 Broadway; Tues–Fri 10am–2pm; ⓣ212/966-4741, ⓦwww.movingimagegallery.com. New art technologies.

largest performing arts center in lower Manhattan, it stages over 200 (somewhat poorly advertised) events a year, all going for about $10–15 a ticket.

TriBeCa Bridge and Rockefeller Park

A few blocks further along Chambers Street leads to the **TriBeCa Bridge**, a futuristic walkway across West Street made of silver steel tubes, white girders and glass; the bridge crosses to the orange-brick Stuyvesant High School of Science, one of the city's most prestigious public schools. Along the river uptown, a jogging and cycling promenade begins wending its way up to 59th Street, passing by Pier 25, a public recreation center boasting three beach volleyball courts – built atop 540 cubic yards of sand trucked in from New Jersey – and a miniature golf course. West from TriBeCa Bridge toward the river, you'll find yourself in **Rockefeller Park**, a promenade jutting into the Hudson. Don't miss the bronze dog, attached to the water fountain at the far end of the park, straining his leash to get at a bronze cat, which is about to pounce on a bronze bird. Follow the park along the Hudson toward Battery Park City, or turn back to TriBeCa.

Celebrity Dining Haunts

TriBeCa has become home to some of the city's best-known – and priciest restaurants. Actors and actresses working at one of TriBeCa's production companies or screening rooms can often be found frequenting the following spots, though best to keep your adulation under wraps. Tops for this are *TriBeCa Grill*, at 375 Greenwich St (ⓣ212/941-3900), co-owned by Robert De Niro and celebrity restaurateur Drew Nieporent; *Church Lounge*, in the *TriBeCa Grand Hotel*, at 6th Ave (ⓣ212/519-650), for martinis at $15 a pop; *Montrachet*, 239 W Broadway (ⓣ212/219-2777), whose justifiably high prices practically demand VIP status, and *Nobu*, at 105 Hudson St (ⓣ212/219-0500), which offers Japanese-Peruvian delicacies that draws folks from near and far. Hint: If you can't get into *Nobu*, don't forget to inquire about *Next Door Nobu*, a lower-priced (yet still pricey) option right next door. For more detailed reviews, see Chapter 30, "Restaurants," and Chapter 31, "Drinking."

West Broadway and White Street

West Broadway is one of TriBeCa's main thoroughfares; on its northeast corner with **White Street** stands one of the rare remaining Federal-era stores, in continuous use since 1809, now home to the stylish yet wholly unpretentious bar called *The Liquor Store*. Walk east along White Street; at no. 49 is the **Civic Center Synagogue**, a 1967 temple whose curving, wave-like facade, covered in marble tiles, is quite striking; at no. 38, Rudi Stern's Let There Be Neon, a gallery boasting signs, chairs, household goods and stage sets all in – you guessed it – neon. Back across West Broadway, at the intersection of Varick and North Moore, **Ladder Company 8**, a turn-of-the-nineteenth-century brick-and-stone firehouse dotted with white stars, served as headquarters in the movie *Ghostbusters*.

Chinatown and Little Italy

With more than 200,000 residents (125,000 of them Chinese and the rest other Asian ethnicities), seven Chinese newspapers, twelve Buddhist temples, around 150 restaurants and over 300 garment factories, **Chinatown** is Manhattan's most highly populated ethnic neighborhood. Since the Eighties, it has pushed its boundaries north across Canal Street into **Little Italy** and sprawls east across Division Street and East Broadway into the nether fringes of the Lower East Side. Chinatown and Little Italy can both best be reached by taking the #J, #M, #N, #Q, #R, #W, #Z or #6 lines to the Canal Street station.

Chinatown

On the surface, Chinatown is prosperous – a "model slum," some have called it – with the lowest crime rate, highest employment and least juvenile delinquency of any city district. Walk through its crowded streets at any time of day, and every shop is doing a brisk and businesslike trade. Restaurant after restaurant is booming; there are storefront displays of shiny squids, clawing crabs and clambering lobsters; and street markets offer overflowing piles of exotic green vegetables, garlic and ginger root. Chinatown has the feel of a land of plenty, and the Chinese themselves – even here, in downtown Manhattan – have been careful to preserve their own way of dealing with things, preferring to keep affairs close to the bond of the family and allowing few intrusions into a still-insular culture. There are several concessions to Westerners and tourists – storefront signs offer English translations, and the area around lower Mott Street smacks of McChinese opportunism – there's even a Häagen Dazs ice-cream store here that seems less incongruous by the day. Explore the narrow side streets around, though, and you will be rewarded with a taste – and a glimpse – of the real Chinatown.

Beneath the neighborhood's blithely prosperous facade, however, there is a darker, ruthless underbelly. Sharp practices, such as extortion and protection rackets, continue to flourish, while non-union sweatshops – their assembly lines grinding from early morning to late into the evening as workers are paid below minimum wage for seventy-plus-hour workweeks – are still investigated by the US Department of Labor. Living conditions are abysmal for the poorer Chinese – mostly recent immigrants and the elderly – who reside in small rooms in overcrowded tenements ill-kept by landlords. Visitors won't detect much hint of difficulties, however, unless they reside in Chinatown for a considerable length of time.

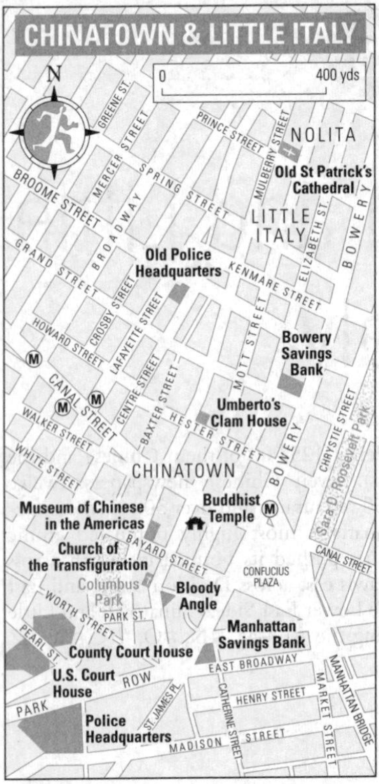

Some history

The Chinese began to arrive in the mid-nineteenth century, following in the wake of a trickle of Irish and Italian immigrants. Most of these Chinese had previously worked out West, building railways and digging gold mines, and few intended to stay: their idea was simply to make a nest egg and retire to a life of leisure with their families (99 percent were men) back in China. Some, a few hundred perhaps, did go back, but on the whole the big money took rather longer to accumulate than expected, and so Chinatown became a permanent settlement. The residences were not particularly welcomed by the authorities: the Mafia-like Tongs' protection rackets, which doubled as municipal aid societies and dabbled in prostitution, gambling and opium dens on the side, gave the neighborhood a bad rap. By the end of the nineteenth century, the quarter's violence was notorious, as far as white observers were concerned. As a result, in 1882, the US government passed the Exclusion Act completely forbidding entry to any further Chinese workers for ten years. The immigration quotas of the early twentieth century, particularly the 1924 National Origins Provision, severely restricted the entry of Asians – as well as southern and eastern Europeans – into America.

After the 1965 Immigration Act did away with the National Origins Provision, a large number of new immigrants, many of whom were women, began arriving in Chinatown; within a few years, the area's massive male majority had been displaced. Local businessmen took advantage of the declining midtown garment business and made use of the new, large and unskilled female workforce: they opened garment factories and paid their workers low wages. Entrepreneurial activity suited Chinese immigrant labor: opening a hand (or, as they came to be known, "Chinese") laundry, for example, required neither a high level of English nor winning the respect of a white employer. At the same time, many small restaurants opened up, spurred by the early 1970s Western interest in Chinese food and by the plight of working Chinese women, who, no longer having time to cook, took food from these restaurants home to feed their families. When the Wall Street crowd became interested in the area, fancier restaurants, more money and greater investment flowed into the quarter; that capital soon attracted more Asian money from overseas. In little time, Chinatown had an internal economy unlike any other new immigrant neighborhood in New York.

In the early 1990s, waves of illegal immigrants from the Fujian province of China began to arrive in New York, upsetting the power structure in Chinatown. Unlike the established Cantonese, who had dominated Chinatown's politics for a century or so, these were largely uneducated laborers who spoke Mandarin. The cultural and linguistic differences made it difficult for the Fujianese to find work in Chinatown, and a large number turned to more desperate means. Fujianese-on-Fujianese violence comprised the majority of Chinatown's crime in 1994, prompting local Fujianese leaders to break Chinatown's traditional bond of silence and call in city officials for help. They also began to construct a network of social agencies and political groups to improve the immigrants' plight. Aided by this, and by the fact that many well-off Cantonese have moved to the outer boroughs and the suburbs, the Fujianese have now become the controlling force here. While Chinatown is, perhaps inevitably, the central Chinese community in New York City, there are major Chinese neighborhoods in Flushing, Queens, as well as Sunset Park, Brooklyn, which between them are home to a further 150,000 Chinese-Americans.

Along Mott Street

Most New Yorkers come to Chinatown not to get the lowdown on Chinese politics but to eat. Nowhere in this city can you eat so well, and so much, for so little. **Mott Street** is the area's most obvious tourist restaurant row, although the streets around – Canal, Pell, Bayard, Doyers and Bowery – host a glut of restaurants, tea and rice shops and grocers that are much more local and fun. The food is dotted all over; Cantonese cuisine predominates, but there are also many restaurants that specialize in the spicier Szechuan and Hunan cuisines, along with Fukien, Soochow and the spicy Chowchou dishes. Anywhere you walk into is likely to be good, but remember that most Chinese restaurants start closing up around 9.30pm – best to go early if you want friendly service and atmosphere. If you're looking for specific recommendations (especially for BYOB lunchtime *dim sum*), some of the best are detailed in Chapter 30, "Restaurants."

Besides scoffing down Asian delights, the lure of Chinatown lies in wandering amid the exotica of the shops and absorbing the neighborhood's vigorous street life. Be forewarned: population density and congestion make this area among New York's hottest on a summer's day. Meandering comes highly recommended, though, and provided you arm yourself with a bottle of water,

Chinese New Year

During the **Chinese New Year festival** (see p.447), held annually on the first new moon of the first lunar month of the year (generally late January or early February), Chinatown bursts open to watch a giant red, green and gold dragon made of wood, cloth and papier-mâché run down Mott Street. The firecrackers that traditionally accompanied the festival are now banned by the city as a fire hazard (much to local chagrin), yet the gutters still run with ceremonial dyes.

there are several interesting, vaguely structured routes to take. Mott Street is the obvious starting point: follow it north from Worth Street and the site of the old Chinatown Museum at the southern end. The museum is now little more than a bizarre and very popular video arcade called **Chinatown Fair**, where a predominantly male crowd gathers to smoke, prowl and play anything from pinball to 1950s Test Your Own Strength machines and the most modern interactive video phenomena.

Further north along Mott Street, a rare edifice predating the Chinese arrival dominates the corner of Mott and Mosco streets. It's the early nineteenth-century green-domed Catholic school and **Church of the Transfiguration**, an elegant building that has been undergoing massive renovations since 1999. Masses are held here daily in Cantonese and English, with additional services in Mandarin on Sunday. Just across from the church is picturesquely crooked Doyers Street, once known as "Bloody Angle" for its reputation as a dumping ground for dead bodies – the underside of relations between the Tongs. Around the Angle there is a lattice of streets and alleys where you'll find a cornucopia of Asian trinkets and plastic tourist goods.

Columbus Park, Canal and Grand streets

Once you've exhausted your spending power, return to Mott and take a left down Bayard Street to **Columbus Park**, a shady haunt away from all the hectic consumerism of the streets, and favored for this very reason by the neighborhood's elderly. At the park's northernmost tip is an open-air concert hall, topped by a pagoda roof and decorated with fading pictures of a bird and a dragon. Continue north along Baxter Street and you'll arrive at **Canal Street**, at all hours a crowded thoroughfare crammed with jewelry shops and kiosks hawking sunglasses, T-shirts and fake Rolexes. Two shopping institutions on Canal are not to be missed: one, the **Pearl River Department Store**, at no. 277 (the corner of Canal and the Bowery), is the closest you'll ever get to a Shanghai bazaar without going to China. Specialties here include all sorts of embroidered slippers and silk clothing, rice cookers, pottery and beautiful lacquered paper umbrellas – much sought by interior decorators working on the cheap. Across the street at no. 308, housed in an imposing red-and-white-painted turn-of-the-nineteenth-century warehouse, are the many floors of **Pearl Paint**, which claims to be the largest art supply store in the world. Take Mott or Mulberry Street north toward **Grand Street**, which used to be the city's Main Street in the mid-1800s, and you will find outdoor fruit, vegetable and live seafood stands lining the curbs, offering snow peas, bean curd, fungi, oriental cabbage and dried sea cucumbers to the passersby. Ribs, whole chickens and Peking ducks glisten in the storefront windows: the sight of them can put more than a vegetarian off his food. Perhaps even more fascinating are the Chinese herbalists. The roots and powders in their boxes, drawers and glass bottles are century-old remedies, but, to those accustomed to Western medicine, may seem like voodoo potions.

Museum of Chinese in the Americas

Cross Bayard Street at Mulberry Street and look for the double red doors of the community center right on the corner. Two floors up lies the tiny but fascinating **Museum of Chinese in the Americas**, 70 Mulberry St (Tues–Sat noon–5pm; $3, children $1; (ⓣ212/619-4785, ⓦwww.moca-nyc.org), dedicated to documenting the experiences of Chinese immigrants in the Americas as well as reclaiming and preserving Chinese history in the West. The displays include Chinese photographs and cultural memorabilia, temporary exhibits of Asian-American art, and a CD-ROM slideshow on the history of Chinatown. The museum also offers guided historical group tours of Chinatown ($10, call three weeks ahead to book).

The Bowery, Chatham Square and the Manhattan Bridge

Once you've traveled this circuit (or at least a rough approximation of it), you've seen the heart and history of Chinatown. Moving east from Mulberry Street, stroll over to **the Bowery** and wander the streets leading down to the housing projects that flank the East River, most of which are nowadays inhabited by Fujianese Chinese. On your way, you'll pass Confucius Plaza at the intersection of Bowery and Division streets; guarded by a statue of Confucius, this housing complex, built in the 1970s, was and still is considered the best living quarters in Chinatown. Fronting the plaza is the gilded and gloriously tacky **Mahayana Buddhist Temple**, at 133 Canal St (daily 8am–6pm). This brash religious retreat is certainly worth a peek, at least for the fairy lights, the neon circlets and the gaudy gold Buddha that dominates the main room, if not the 32 plates telling the story of Buddha himself. Despite the assault of red and gold, though, it's actually a surprisingly peaceful place.

Leaving the temple, make a point as well of crossing **Chatham Square**, where proud Fujianese civic organizations recently erected a statue of Lin Zexu, a Fujian Province official who helped start the Opium Wars of the nineteenth century by banning the drug. Lin used opium as an excuse to fight the British, but the Fujianese, often stereotyped as Chinatown's drug lords, have cast their hero a staunch foe of drugs: inscribed in English and Chinese at the statue's base are the words Say No to Drugs. Opposite Chatham Square and slightly to the south, on Park Row between James and Oliver streets, is the anomalous first cemetery of the Spanish and Portuguese Synagogue, Congregation Shearith Israel, the oldest Jewish congregation in New York (now located in a synagogue at 70th Street and Central Park West). It was in use from 1656 to 1833, and the pleasure of the rare sight of eroded seventeenth-century headstones in Manhattan is only dampened by the fact that the site cannot be visited.

Double back by way of East Broadway or Henry Street to where the **Manhattan Bridge**, with its grand Beaux Arts entrance out of place amid the neon signs and Chinese movie theaters, crosses the East River to Brooklyn. From here you could head north up Chrystie Street, which forms the nominal border between Chinatown and the Lower East Side (see p.90), or west down Canal Street, past the hubbub and into the area known as Little Italy, traditionally the center of the city's considerable Italian community.

Little Italy

Signs made out of red, green and white tinsel effusively welcome visitors here, a signal perhaps that today's **Little Italy** is light years away from the solid ethnic enclave of old. The neighborhood is a lot smaller and more commercial than it was, and the area settled by New York's huge nineteenth-century influx of Italian immigrants – who (like their Jewish and Chinese counterparts) cut themselves clannishly off to re-create the Old Country – is encroached upon a little more each year by Chinatown. In fact, if you walk north from Canal Street to get here, the transition from the cultural heart of Chinatown to Little Italy's Big Tomato tourist schmaltz can be a little difficult to stomach. Few Italians still live here and the surfeit of restaurants – some of which pipe the music of NY's favorite Italian son, Frank Sinatra, onto the street – tend to have valet-parking and high prices. In fact, it is this quantity of restaurants, more than anything else, that gives Little Italy away: go to the city's true Italian areas, Belmont in the Bronx or Carroll Gardens in Brooklyn, and you'll find very few genuine Italian eateries, since Italian Americans prefer to consume their native food at home. It's significant that when Martin Scorsese made *Mean Streets* in 1973 he decided to shoot many scenes in Belmont and LA, even though the film was about Little Italy.

But that's not to advise missing out on Little Italy altogether. Some original bakeries and *salumerias* (Italian specialty food stores) do survive, and there, amid the imported cheeses, sausages and salamis hanging from the ceiling, you can buy sandwiches made with slabs of mozzarella or eat slices of homemade focaccia. In addition, there still are plenty of places to indulge yourself with a cappuccino and pricey pastry, not least of which is *Ferrara's*, 195 Grand St, the oldest and most popular. Also of note is the belt-defying *Lombardi's*, at 32 Spring St, which happens to serve some of the best pizza – and the very best clam pie – in New York.

Along Mulberry Street

If you're here in mid-September, the ten-day Festa di San Gennaro (see p.451) is a wild and tacky celebration of the day of the patron saint of Naples. Italians from all over the city converge on **Mulberry Street**, Little Italy's main strip, and the area is transformed by street stalls and numerous Italian fast-food and snack outlets. The festivities center around the **Church of the Most Precious Blood**, just off Canal at 109 Mulberry St, and provide a rare chance to see this quaint, small church, normally closed up and protected from the public gaze.

None of the restaurants around here really stands out, but the former site of **Umberto's Clam House**, on the corner of Mulberry and Hester streets, was quite notorious in its time: it was the scene of a vicious gangland murder in 1972, when Joe "Crazy Joey" Gallo was shot dead while celebrating his birthday with his wife and daughter. Gallo, a big talker and ruthless businessman, was keen to protect his business interests in Brooklyn; he was alleged to have offended a rival family and so paid the price. *Umberto's Clam House* has since relocated to 386 Broome St, between Mott and Mulberry, but that hasn't stopped its celebrity clientele – ranging from Michael Douglas to Bette Midler and Martin Scorsese to Robert De Niro – from popping in for a bite.

Old St Patrick's Cathedral and the Old Police Headquarters

In striking counterpoint to the lawlessness of the Italian underworld, the **Old St Patrick's Cathedral**, 263 Mulberry St, was the first Catholic cathedral in the city and the parent church to its much more famous offspring on Fifth

Avenue and 50th Street (see p.145). The walled cemetery behind, which is unfortunately almost always locked – houses the remains of Pierre Toussaint, a Haitian man born into slavery who moved in the 1770s with his wife to New York, where they dedicated their lives to charity. In 2000, he became the first black American candidate for sainthood. Nearby at 210 Elizabeth St lies the Elizabeth Street Garden, a random patch of greenery replete with enormous pieces of statuary and maintained by the art gallery opposite (Mon–Thurs 10am–6pm, Fri 10am–5pm; ⓣ212/644 6969).

Reaction to Little Italy's illicit past is to be found at the corner of Centre and Broome streets, where you'll find the **Old Police Headquarters**, a palatial 1909 Neoclassical confection meant to cow would-be criminals into obedience with its high-rise dome and lavish ornamentation. The police headquarters moved to a bland modern building around City Hall in 1973, and the overbearing palace was converted in the late Eighties into upmarket condominiums, some of which have been called home by Steffi Graf, Winona Ryder and Christy Turlington. Walk west beyond Broadway and you're already in SoHo (see p.96), which, like Chinatown, is a booming district bursting its borders from the further side of Broadway.

NoLita

Just east of Broadway and south of Houston, fashion, style and nonchalant living have found fertile new breeding ground. Lining the streets are fresh, creative and independent designer boutiques, coffeehouses and cafés, such as the posh vintage store Resurrection, at 217 Mott St, the smoke-and-shades-friendly café *Gitane* at 242 Mott and the hipper-than-thou *Habana* at 17 Prince St, establishing this area as the latest in chic. Referred to (by realtors and editors determined to label every block in the city) as **NoLita**, this section north of Little Italy, which extends east from Lafayette, Mott and Elizabeth streets between Prince and Houston, is great for only-in-New York, hip accessory shopping. Among the browse-worthy boutiques are Mixona, 262 Mott St, for racy underwear, Minette at 238 Mott St for bags, and Push at 240 Mulberry St for jewelry. NoLita is not cheap by any means, but the young, artsy and restless hanging outside the area's proliferation of über-trendy stores, bars and restaurants make it an excellent place for a late-afternoon drink and a spot of beautiful-people watching.

The Lower East Side

I don't wanna be buried in Puerto Rico
I don't wanna rest in Long Island cemetery
I wanna be near the stabbing shooting
gambling fighting and unnatural dying
and new birth crying
So please when I die . . .
Keep me nearby
Take my ashes and scatter them thru out
the Lower East Side . . .

Miguel Piñero, *A Lower East Side Poem*

Historically the epitome of the American ethnic melting pot, the **Lower East Side** is one of Manhattan's and enthralling downtown neighborhoods. While a fair proportion of its inhabitants are working-class Puerto Rican or Chinese, today you are just as likely to find students, moneyed artsy types and other refugees from the overly gentrified areas of SoHo and the nearby East Village. The Lower East Side of today is still pretty seedy in its most southeastern reaches, but in the past decade the area has become considerably depopulated and better maintained, and one of the hippest areas around for shopping, drinking, dancing and (what else?) food.

Some history

The neighborhood began to attract international humanitarian attention toward the end of the nineteenth century, when it became an insular slum for over half a million Jewish immigrants – and the most densely populated spot in the world. Coming here from Eastern Europe via Ellis Island, these refugees were in search of a better life, scratching out a living in a free-for-all of crowded competition centered around sweatshops, piecework and pushcarts. The area's lank brick tenements (a term which comes from the Latin *tenare*, to hold, and literally denotes a human holding-tank), ribbed with blackened fire escapes, must have seemed a bleak destiny for those who arrived to be crammed into a district that became daily more densely populated. Low standards of hygiene and abysmal housing made disease rife and life expectancy low: in 1875, there was 40 percent infant mortality, mainly due to cholera. It was conditions like these that spurred local residents like Jacob Riis and, later, Stephen Crane to record the plight of the city's immigrants in their writings and photographs, thereby spawning not only a whole school of realistic writing but also some notable social reforms. Not for nothing – and not without some degree of success – did the Lower East Side become known as a neighborhood where political battles were fought, from the 1904 and 1908 rent strikes against the appalling housing conditions to the protests in the late Eighties against the neighborhood's increased yuppification.

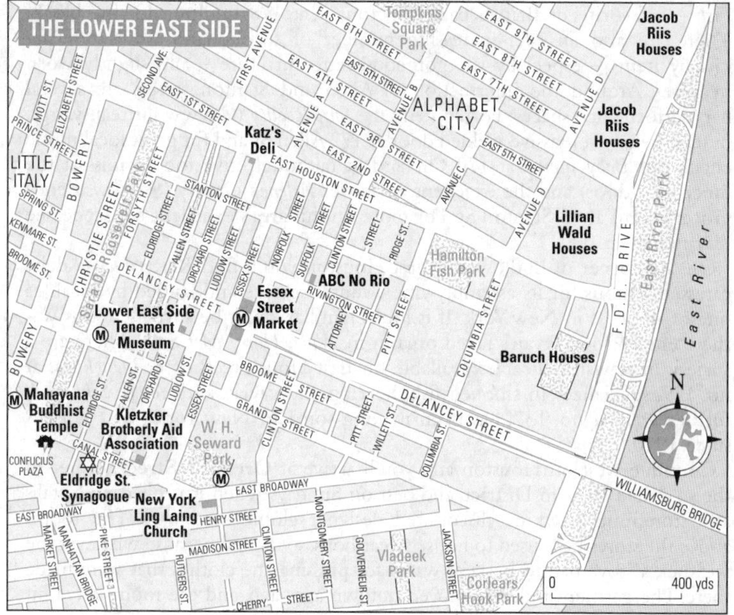

Houston Street to Grand Street

The most readily explored – and the most rewarding – part of the Lower East Side was known as *Kleine Deutschland* (Little Germany) in the first half of the nineteenth century, when it was home to relatively well-off German and Jewish merchants. However, as these early immigrants moved onward and upward, a more desperate group of Jewish immigrants, fleeing poverty and pogroms in Eastern Europe, flooded in. On the streets south of **Houston**, between Orchard and Essex streets, Jewish immigrants indelibly stamped their character with their own shops, delis, restaurants, synagogues and, later, community centers. Even now, with the overflow of immigrants from Chinatown having settled in the neighborhood, it still holds remnants of its Jewish past, such as the area's homemade kosher cuisine and its ritual bathhouse for women who are "unclean" (see p.94).

Some outsiders are drawn to the area for the **bargain shopping**. You can get just about anything at cut-price in the stores: clothes on Orchard Street, lamps and shades and kitchen equipment on the Bowery, ties and shirts on Allen Street, underwear and hosiery on Grand Street and textiles on Eldridge Street. And, whatever you're buying, people will if necessary haggle down to the last cent.

Ludlow and Orchard streets

Ludlow Street sparked the hipster migration south of the East Village where a half-dozen or so bars, such as the popular *Local 138* at 138 Ludlow and *Max*

Fish – a favorite of British bands on tour – at 178 Ludlow, dot the block. There are also an ever-increasing number of secondhand stores offering kitschy items – especially the gorgeous, retro furniture – and slightly worn treasures. Around the intersection of Allen and Stanton streets are several bar/performance spaces. For comedy try *Surf Reality* (Ⓦwww.surfreality.org), hidden behind a massive welded door at 172 Allen St and for great local music check out *Baby Jupiter* at 170 Orchard St (although give food a miss at the diner next door) and the excellent, no-cover *Arlene's Grocery* (Ⓦwww.arlene-grocery.com) at 95 Stanton St. For more on this area's excellent bar scene, see "Drinking," p. 000.

On the corner of Ludlow and East Houston you'll find *Katz's Deli*, a delicatessen famous for its assembly-line counter service and lauded by locals as one of the best in New York. If it looks familiar, don't be surprised: this was the scene of Meg Ryan's faked orgasm in *When Harry Met Sally*. There are a variety of Jewish delicacies available on East Houston: *Russ & Daughters*, at no. 179, specializes in smoked fish, herring and caviar, and *Yonah Schimmel*, further west at no. 137, has been making some of New York's best knishes since 1910.

Continue west on Houston and you'll arrive at **Orchard Street**, center of the so-called Bargain District, and best on Sundays when it is filled with stalls and storefronts hawking discounted designer clothes and bags. The rooms above the stores here used to house sweatshops, so named because whatever the weather, a stove had to be kept warm for pressing the clothes that were made there. The garment industry moved uptown ages ago, and the rooms are a bit more salubrious now – often home to pricey apartments.

Lower East Side Tenement Museum

If you haven't got the time to tour the Lower East Side extensively, make sure to visit the **Lower East Side Tenement Museum** at 90 Orchard St (Tues–Fri 1–5pm, Thurs 1–8pm, Sat & Sun 11am–4.30pm; Ⓣ212/431-0233, Ⓦwww.tenement.org). This excellent local museum does a brilliantly imaginative job of bringing to life the neighborhood's immigrant past and present. This will probably be your only chance to see the crumbling, claustrophobic interior of an 1863 tenement (purchased by the museum in 1992 and the first tenement ever to be designated as a landmark), with its deceptively elegant, though ghostly, entry hall and two communal toilets for every four families. Guided tours available include the Tenants' Rights Tour (Thurs 6.30pm; $9); the Tenement House Tour (Tues–Fri 1, 1.30, 2, 2.30, 3 & 4pm, Sat & Sun every half-hour; $9) and the Confino Family Apartment Tour (Sat & Sun hourly noon–3pm; $8). The museum also offers an hour-long Sunday walking tour of ethnic neighborhoods (April–Dec, 1 & 2.30pm; $9). The displays show photographs and community-based displays that concentrate on the multiple ethnic heritages in the area, and the whole affair is an earnest and sympathetic attempt to document the immigrant experience. Come early on weekends, as tours often sell out.

Delancey and Essex streets

Orchard Street bisects **Delancey Street**, the horizontal axis of the Jewish Lower East Side, now a tacky boulevard, and to the **Williamsburg Bridge**, the building of which in 1903 greatly altered the social demographic of both the Lower East Side and Williamsburg. After the bridge opened an influx of Jewish settlers crossed the "Jews' Bridge" into Williamsburg, inducing its longtime Irish and German residents to migrate to Queens. On either side of Delancey sprawls the **Essex Street Market**, erected under the aegis of Mayor LaGuardia in the 1930s, when pushcarts were made illegal (ostensibly because they clogged the streets, but mainly because they competed with established businesses). Here you'll find all sorts of fresh fruit, fish and vegetables, along with random clothing bargains and the occasional trinket or piece of tat. A bit further south of Delancey, at 35 Essex, you'll find the Essex Street (Guss') Pickle Products, where people line up outside the storefront to buy fresh homemade pickles, olives and other yummy picnic staples from huge barrels of garlicky brine.

East of Essex Street, the atmosphere generally changes from a smorgasbord of ethnic treats to an edgy melting pot of local Latinos and young whites, though a holdout is *Ratner's Dairy Restaurant*, one of the Lower East Side's most famous dairy restaurants, at 138 Delancey. Incongruously, the back room of *Ratner's* has been converted into *Lansky Lounge*, a somewhat hidden nightspot (the alley entrance is at 104 Norfolk St; look for murals of various desserts on the building's walls), which is allegedly owned by the local mafia and doubles as a restaurant. Still, much of the area has lost the traditional Sunday bustle of Jewish market shopping, replaced instead by the Saturday afternoon Spanish chatter of the new residents – Puerto Ricans, Dominicans, and many others – shopping for records, inexpensive clothes and electrical goods. **Clinton Street**, a mass of cheap Latino retailers, restaurants and travel agents, is in many ways the central thoroughfare of the Puerto Rican Lower East Side. This area is still bargain territory although upscale restaurants such as the hugely popular (book weeks in advance) *Clinton Fresh Food*, at no. 71, mean that there are always several lost SoHo souls in suits, hugging their briefcases close as they wait for the clients they're here to impress.

At 156 Rivington St, a welded gate composed of old gears and scrap metal identifies **ABC No Rio**, (Ⓣ212/254-3697,Ⓦwww.abcnorio.org), a downtrodden community arts center struggling between a squalid past and upmarket future. In 1980, the space was given to a group of artists who had put on a notable exhibit concerning skyrocketing rents; since then it has hosted gallery shows, loud concerts, a zine library, installations and the like. After trying to reclaim the space in June 1995, the Housing and Preservation Department agreed to sell the building to ABC for one dollar, provided they raise the capital (at least $100,000) to renovate and put the space to community use. Though ABC has reached that target, it still does not own the building, and renovations, not surprisingly, look far more expensive than anticipated.

The Bowery

The western edge of the Lower East Side is marked by **the Bowery**, which spears north out of Little Italy, running a mile from Chatham Square up to Cooper Square on the edge of the East Village. This wide thoroughfare has gone through many changes over the years: it took its name from *bouwerij*, the Dutch word for farm, when it was the city's main agricultural supplier. Toward the closing decades of the nineteenth century, it was flanked by music halls, theaters, hotels and middle-market restaurants, drawing people from all parts of Manhattan. The city's only thoroughfare never to have housed a church, it is still somewhat of a skid row for the city's drunk and derelict.

The Bowery's notoriety made it a suitable subject to be immortalized in literature, and many writers made use of its reputation as a home for those without one. Theodore Dreiser closed his turn-of-the-nineteenth-century tragedy *Sister Carrie* with a suicide in a Bowery flophouse, while fifty years later one-time resident William S. Burroughs alluded to the area in a story that complained of bums waiting to "waylay one in the Bowery."

Canal Street and East Broadway

Though the southern half of **East Broadway** is now almost exclusively Chinese, the street used to be the hub of the Jewish Lower East Side. For the old feel of the quarter – where the synagogues remain active (many in the area have become churches for largely Puerto Rican congregations) – start on Canal Street and wind your way north along Eldridge Street, two blocks west of Orchard. Built in 1886, the **Eldridge Street Synagogue**, at 12 Eldridge St, was the first constructed by Eastern European Orthodox Jews, as a testament to their faith in the New World. In its day it was one of the neighborhood jewels: a brick and terra-cotta hybrid of Moorish arches and Gothic windows, including the west wing rose window – a spectacular Star of David roundel. Tours of the majestic interior are offered (Tues & Thurs at 11.30am and 2.30pm; Sun hourly 11am–4pm; $4; ⓣ212/219-0888). Across Eldridge, the dingy tenement at no. 19 was home to vaudeville and film star Eddie Cantor.

Carry on east down Canal Street and, at nos. 54–58, look above the row of food and electrical stores and you'll see the stately facade of **Sender Jarmulowsky's Bank**, dwarfing the buildings around it. Founded in 1873 by a peddler who made his fortune reselling ship tickets, the bank catered to the financial needs of the influx of non-English-speaking immigrants. Around the turn of the century, as the bank's assets accrued, rumors began circulating about its insolvency. As World War I became imminent, the bank was plagued by runs and riots when panicked patrons tried to withdraw their money to send to relatives back in Europe. Finally, in 1914, the bank collapsed; with its closure, thousands lost what little savings they had.

Further east along Canal, at the corner of Ludlow Street and prominently marked with a Star of David and the year 1892, the **Kletzker Brotherly Aid Association** building stands at no. 5. The building is a vestige of a time when Jewish towns set up their own lodges (in this case, the town was Kletzk in modern-day Belarus) to provide community health care and Jewish burials, assistance for widows, and the like. The tradition has been schizophrenically preserved by an Italian funeral parlor at the front of the building and a Chinese funeral home at the side.

Continue on east, past the junction of Canal Street and East Broadway to the latter's intersection with Grand Street. Here, adjacent to the bodegas and the concrete and glass eyesore Public School 134, proudly stands a cultural anachronism: an operating *mikveh*, or ritual bathhouse, where Orthodox Jewish women must bathe prior to marriage and monthly thereafter.

East Broadway, Essex and Grand streets frame the pie-slice-shaped complex that comprises **Seward Park** and its neighboring apartment blocks. Constructed in 1899 by the city to provide a bit of green space in the overburdened precincts of the Lower East Side, the park boasted the first public playground in New York and is still surrounded by benevolent institutions set up for the benefit of ambitious immigrants.

Grand Street heads east through housing projects to the messy East River Park – not one of the city's most attractive open spaces. It's better to skip that area and double back up Grand, toward Essex Street, where you'll find more stores and activity. A few blocks on your way, you'll pass the **Church of St Mary**, at 440 Grand St, the third-oldest Catholic church (1832) in the city. It's now a favorite resting spot of elderly Jewish couples, who sit on the benches outside and watch the world go by.

7

SoHo

The grid of streets that lies between Houston and Canal streets and roughly between Sixth Avenue and Lafayette Street, **SoHo** – short for *So*uth of *Ho*uston – has come to mean fashion chic, urbane shopping, cosmopolitan galleries and cast-iron facades. High-end chains attract hordes of tourists, making it difficult on weekends to navigate the neighborhood; nevertheless, SoHo is a grand place to brunch at an outside café or for poking in and out of chichi antique, art and clothes shops. Because SoHo is the place to see and be seen, people are decked out to the nines, and some of the best people watching in the city is here. Houston Street (pronounced *How*ston rather than *Hew*ston) marks the top of SoHo's trellis of streets, any exploration of which necessarily means crisscrossing and doubling back. Greene Street is as good a place to start as any, highlighted all along by the nineteenth-century cast-iron facades that, in part if not in whole, saved SoHo from the bulldozers. Prince Street, Spring Street and West Broadway hold the best selection of shops and galleries in the area. The #W, #Q and #F trains all go to the Broadway-Lafayette stop, the #6 stops

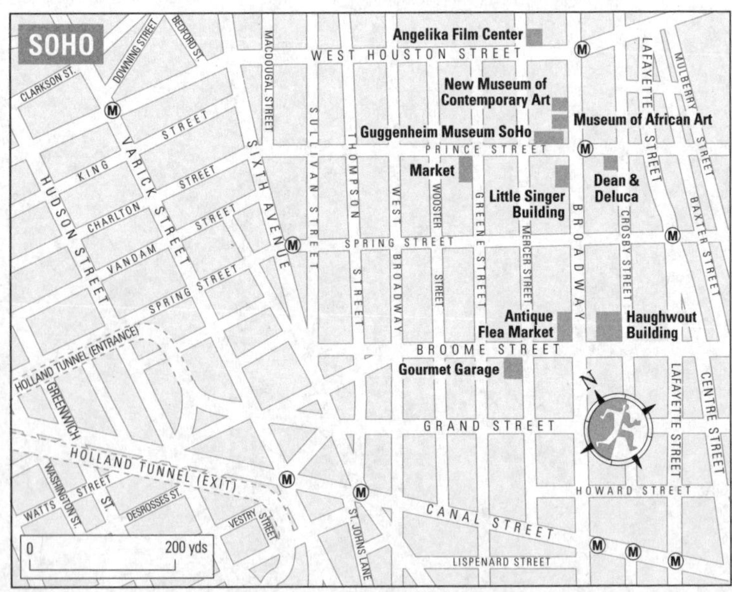

at Spring Street, the #N and #R stop at Prince Street and the #1 and #9 stop at Houston.

Some history

For most of the twentieth century, SoHo has been a raggedy, gray wasteland of manufacturers and wholesalers and, even up to the late 1960s, was considered a slum. Though it experienced a bit of a vogue in the mid-nineteenth century when it fringed Broadway, New York's then-liveliest and most fashionable street, when 14th Street replaced Broadway during the mid-nineteenth century as New York's commercial and entertainment center, SoHo became a seamy backdrop to industrial and red-light areas – cheerfully known as Hell's Hundred Acres.

In the 1940s, rising rents drove artists from Greenwich Village, and they began moving into SoHo, converting the large, cheap and light-filled factories into lofts and workspaces. One hindrance faced them, however: the buildings were zoned exclusively for small industry, shipping and warehouses; residence in them was illegal. Pestered by these lawbreakers (common in a city where living expenses are so high), the city government attempted to raze parts of SoHo in the early 1960s. Joining forces with the conservationist movement, wily artists trumpeted SoHo's formidable cast-iron architecture – indeed, possibly the most impressive in America – and saved the quarter (and their accommodations) by having the area declared an historic district. In the late 1960s, the mayor of New York revised the building codes to allow industrial spaces to be open to "artists in residence." Three thousand artists moved in the first year, and contemporary New York's full-scale intertwining of industry and art began.

In 1970, several major uptown galleries (Leo Castelli, Andre Emmerich and John Weber) moved to SoHo and injected money into the scene. Castelli's 420 W Broadway served as the focal point of contemporary art for the next thirty years, and the Guggenheim Museum opened its SoHo branch on Broadway at Prince Street in 1992. Nowadays, few artists or experimental galleries are left in the area. The late-1980s art boom led by Ross Bleckner, David Salle, Eric Fischl and Julian Schnabel drove up rents, and only the more established or consciously "commercial" galleries can afford to stay. In more recent years SoHo has become a playground for the rich, with moderately sized living space going for between $3000 and $15,000 per month. While there's still some great gallery hopping to be done, the risk-takers have moved elsewhere – to TriBeCa, Chelsea, or, more recently, to the fringes of the island and the outer boroughs.

Broadway and Lafayette

The wide streets of **Broadway** and **Lafayette** in essence mark the eastern boundary of SoHo, though in the first few blocks south of Houston neither feels especially like the neighborhood proper – save for Broadway's profusion of relatively major downtown museums (see below) and Lafayette's pricey furniture stores.

Continue down Broadway and you'll spot some of SoHo's distinctive **cast-iron architecture**. At the northeast corner of Broome and Broadway stands the magnificent 1857 **Haughwout Building**, 88–92 Broadway, perhaps the ultimate in the cast-iron genre. Rhythmically repeated motifs of colonnaded arches are framed behind taller columns in a thin sliver of a Venetian palace –

the first building ever to boast a steam-powered Otis elevator. In 1904, Ernest Flagg took the possibilities of cast iron to their conclusion in his **Little Singer Building** – office and warehouse for the sewing machine company – at 561 Broadway, a twelve-story terra-cotta design whose use of wide window frames points the way to the glass curtain wall of the 1950s.

New Museum of Contemporary Art

For a view of recent art from outside SoHo's geographic and stylistic confines, drop in on the **New Museum of Contemporary Art**, 583 Broadway (Wed & Sun noon–6pm, Thurs–Sat noon–8pm; $6, students and seniors $3, under 18s free, Thurs 6–8pm free; ⓣ212/219–1222, ⓦwww.newmuseum.org), which hosts rotating offbeat and often risky exhibitions by contemporary American and international artists. Housed within the museum itself is the city's only commercial space devoted to digital art, experimental video and sound. Originally this address was the Astor Building, built in 1896 on the site of the wealthy family's estate office. The building's interiors were renovated in 1998 by the celebrated architect Arata Isozaki.

Guggenheim SoHo

On the same block, the **Guggenheim Museum SoHo,** 575 Broadway (Thurs–Mon 11am–6pm; free; ⓣ212/423-3500, ⓦwww.guggenheim.org), occupies two floors of a loft building in the heart of SoHo. The Guggenheim was the first major museum to move downtown to the then-nucleus of New York's contemporary art scene. After a brief period of closure, the foundation reopened the museum's doors in mid-1999 with a show of **Andy Warhol**'s last works, known as *The Last Supper* series. An impressive store downstairs stocks an excellent range of art books, jewelry and contemporary design. (At the time of writing, Prada was due to open a store in the museum's basement in conjunction with the Guggenheim. Designed by the Dutch architect Rem Koolhaas, the store will serve as a retail space by day and performance space by night.)

Museum for African Art

At the **Museum for African Art**, 593 Broadway (Tues–Fri 10.30am–5.30pm, Sat & Sun noon–6pm; $5, students & kids $2.50, free Sun and every third Thurs from 5.30–8.30pm; ⓣ212/966-1313, ⓦwww.africanart.org), two floors of changing exhibitions feature the best of modern and traditional African art: paintings, sculpture, masks, sacred objects and more. The understated museum interior was designed in 1993 by Maya Lin, designer of the Vietnam War Memorial in Washington, DC. Temporary exhibits focus on regional art, cultural and political themes and contemporary African painting and sculpture – an eye-opener compared with the token ethnic collections usually seen. Film screenings, lectures and weekend family workshops are held regularly; call ahead for schedules.

Greene Street

While SoHo's sidestreets lend themselves to aimless strolls with random stops at galleries, **Greene Street**, two blocks west of Broadway, is a great place to start a brief walking tour. Greene Street lies within the SoHo **Cast-Iron Historic District**, which contains one of the largest collection of cast-iron buildings in the world – erected on these cobblestone streets between 1869 and 1895. Cast-iron architecture was used simply as a way of assembling buildings quickly and cheaply, with iron beams rather than heavy walls carrying the weight of the floors. The result was the removal of load-bearing walls, greater space for windows and, most noticeably, remarkably decorative facades. Almost any style or whim could be cast in iron and pinned to a building, and architects indulged themselves in Baroque balustrades, forests of Renaissance columns and all the effusion of the French Second Empire to glorify SoHo's sweatshops.

At **72–76 Greene St** stands an extravagance whose Corinthian portico stretches the whole five stories, all in painted metal, and at the strongly composed elaborations at **no. 28–30**; together these are known as the King and Queen of Greene Street. These are the best examples of cast-iron buildings, but from Broome to Canal streets, most of the fronts on Greene Street's west side are either real (or mock) cast iron. Ironically, what began as an engineering trait turned into a purely decorative one, as stone copies of cast iron (you'd need a magnet to tell the real from the replicas) came into fashion.

Prince, Spring and West Broadway

Shopping addicts should head to the blocks of **Prince Street, Spring Street** and **West Broadway**, for the high – and pricey – concentration of funky shoe stores, antique shops and fashionable clothes and jewelry designers. Many galleries are here too, though plenty more can be found by just glimpsing down Mercer, Wooster, or any other SoHo block. What you'll find makes for fascinating browsing, with just about every variety of contemporary artistic expression on view. For listings of galleries (and details of gallery tours) see the box

SoHo galleries

Galleries of all kinds can be found in SoHo, though they are best known these days for offering pieces by more established artists working in traditional media. More reviews and details can be found in Chapter 35, "Commercial galleries." Try to visit on a weekday, when all the galleries tend to be less crowded.

Artists Space 38 Greene St; Tues–Sat 11am–6pm; ⓣ212/226-3970, ⓦwww.artistsspace.org. Video, performance art, architecture and design.

David Zwirner 43 Greene St; Sept–May Tues–Sat 10am–6pm, June–Aug Mon–Fri10am–6pm; ⓣ212/966-9074, ⓦwww.davidzwirner.com. Emerging international artists in a variety of media.

Deitch Project 18 Wooster St; Tues–Sat noon–6pm; ⓣ212/343-7300. Contemporary art in all media.

The Drawing Center 35 Wooster St; Tues–Sat 11am–6pm; ⓣ212/219-2166, ⓦwww.drawingcenter.com. Nonprofit organization devoted to drawing exhibits.

Ronald Feldman Fine Arts 31 Mercer St; Tues–Sat 10.30am–6pm; ⓣ212/226-3232; ⓦwww.feldmangallery.com. Contemporary work, particularly graphic design.

Woodward Gallery 476 Broome St; Tues–Sat 11am–6pm; ⓣ212/966-3411. Painting and sculpture.

on p.99 or pick up a copy of the *Gallery Guide* (available free at galleries on request) for more information on current shows and exhibitions.

Break up your poking about with brunch, lunch or dinner at one of SoHo's many fine restaurants, such as star-filled *Balthazar* at 80 Spring St (and don't forget its bakeshop next door, which serves flaky pastries and rich coffee). For something light, the *Soup Kiosk* serves soup to go from a shack at Mercer and Prince. Grab some soup, sit where you can, and take in the scene. For more on eating in SoHo, see "Restaurants," p.321.

South to Canal Street

Loosely speaking, SoHo's diversions get grittier as you drop south. Still, Broome and Grand streets, formerly full of dilapidated storefronts and dusty windows, have recently become home to a small band of boutiques, galleries, cafés and eclectic restaurants. The ultra-chic (and ultra-expensive) *SoHo Grand Hotel* occupies the corner of Canal and West Broadway. If you don't want to fork out the dough for a room, at least look around the lobby, designed by Larry Bogdanow, or have a cocktail at the bar. Canal Street links the **Holland Tunnel** with the Manhattan Bridge and marks SoHo's southern entrance, though in truth the street is in look and feel more Chinatown than any other area.

The East Village

Like the Lower East Side, which it abuts, the **East Village**, east of Broadway between Houston and 14th streets, was once a refuge of immigrants and solidly working class. It became home to New York's nonconformist intelligentsia in the earlier part of the twentieth century when, disenchanted and impoverished by rising rents, they left the city's traditional Bohemia in Greenwich Village and set up house here.

During the Nineties, escalating rents forced many people out, and the East Village is no longer the hotbed of dissidence and creativity it once was. Nevertheless, the area remains one of downtown Manhattan's most vibrant neighborhoods, with boutiques, thrift stores, record shops, bars and restaurants, populated by a mix of old-world Ukrainians, students, punks, artists, skaters and burn-outs. Despite the vaudevillian circus of St Mark's Place and corporate attempts to turn the whole neighborhood into a Starbucks, thoughtful resistance to the status quo can still be found. That said, the area's high standard of living and panoply of restaurants, nightlife, theaters and bars, never mind its proximity to NYU, ensure that rents here are almost – although not quite – as insane as those in the West Village. To reach the East Village, take the #6 train to Astor Place or the #N or the #R to 8th Street and Broadway.

The Village's cultural heritage

Over the years, the East Village has hosted its share of famous artists, politicos and literati. W.H. Auden lived at **77 St Mark's Place**; from the same building the Communist journal *Novy Mir* was run, numbering among its more historic contributors Leon Trotsky, who lived for a brief time in New York. The East Village also became the New York haunt of the Beats – Kerouac, Burroughs, Ginsberg et al – who, when not jumping trains across the rest of the country, would get together at Ginsberg's house on **E 7th Street** for declamatory poetry readings. Later, Andy Warhol debuted the Velvet Underground at the Fillmore East, which played host to just about every band you've ever heard of – and forgotten about – then became The Saint (also now defunct), a gay disco known for its three-day parties.

St Mark's Place and Cooper Square

To explore the East Village, it's best to use **St Mark's Place** as a base and branch out from there. On its block between Second and Third avenues, independent book and discount record stores compete for space with hippy-chic clothiers and head shops in a somewhat contrived atmosphere of MTV cool.

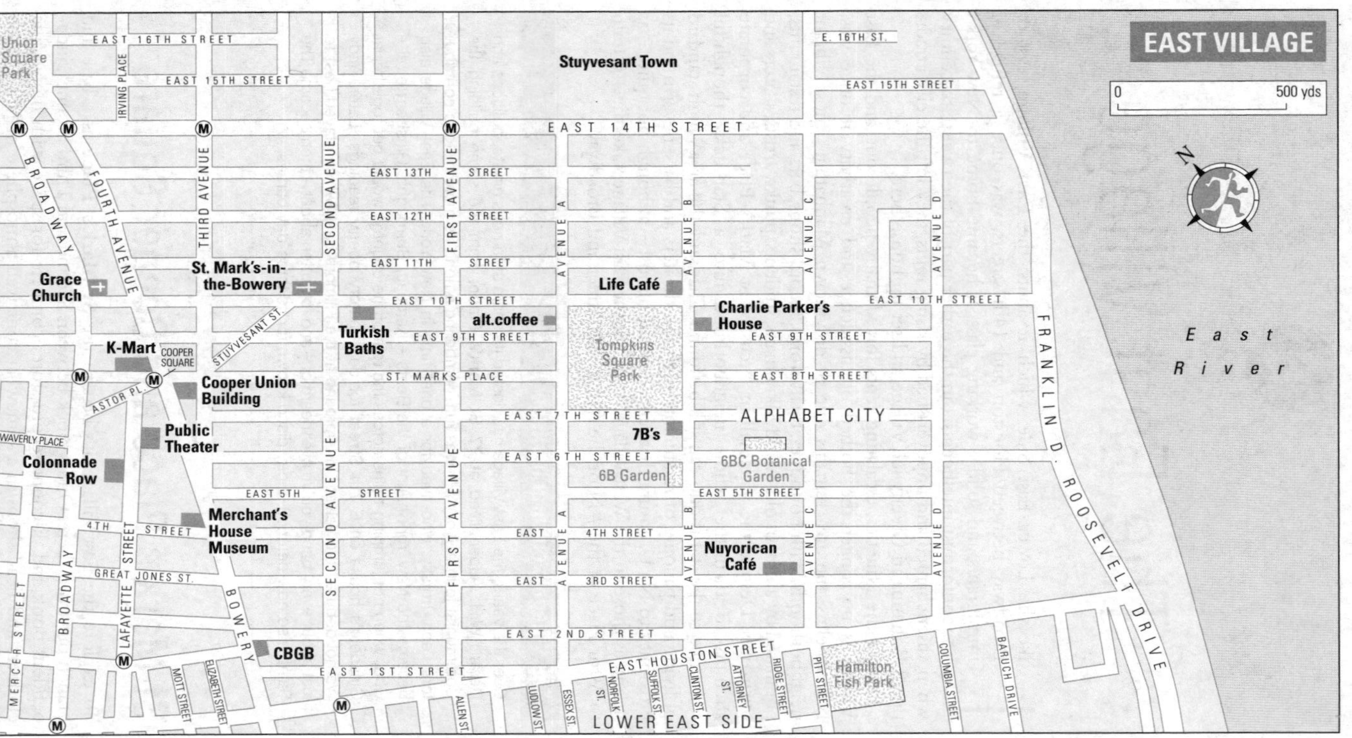
EAST VILLAGE
0
500 yds
N
East River
FRANKLIN D. ROOSEVELT DRIVE
Union Square Park
Stuyvesant Town
ALPHABET CITY
LOWER EAST SIDE
EAST 16TH STREET
E. 16TH ST.
EAST 15TH STREET
EAST 14TH STREET
EAST 13TH STREET
EAST 12TH STREET
EAST 11TH STREET
EAST 10TH STREET
EAST 9TH STREET
ST. MARKS PLACE
EAST 8TH STREET
EAST 7TH STREET
EAST 6TH STREET
EAST 5TH STREET
EAST 4TH STREET
EAST 3RD STREET
EAST 2ND STREET
EAST 1ST STREET
EAST HOUSTON STREET
IRVING PLACE
BROADWAY
FOURTH AVENUE
THIRD AVENUE
SECOND AVENUE
FIRST AVENUE
AVENUE A
AVENUE B
AVENUE C
AVENUE D
STUYVESANT ST.
COOPER SQUARE
ASTOR PL.
WAVERLY PLACE
GREAT JONES ST.
LAFAYETTE STREET
MERCER STREET
BOWERY
MOTT STREET
ELIZABETH STREET
ALLEN ST.
LUDLOW ST.
ESSEX ST.
NORFOLK ST.
SUFFOLK ST.
CLINTON ST.
ATTORNEY ST.
RIDGE STREET
PITT STREET
COLUMBIA STREET
BARUCH DRIVE
Washington Square Park
Grace Church
St. Mark's-in-the-Bowery
K-Mart
Cooper Union Building
Public Theater
Colonnade Row
Merchant's House Museum
CBGB
Turkish Baths
alt.coffee
Life Café
Tompkins Square Park
Charlie Parker's House
7B's
6B Garden
6BC Botanical Garden
Nuyorican Café
Hamilton Fish Park
M

CBGB (This Ain't No Party)

The New York punk rock scene began at CBGB, 315 Bowery, in the 1970s when, despite its initial intentions (CBGB stands for country bluegrass blues), this legendary club forged a reputation as a leading venue for the sounds of the underground. Television was one of the first bands to play here, back in 1973, when admission was a dollar and the crowd had no spare cash for drinks. Also closely associated with the club are bands like the Ramones, Blondie, Patti Smith and Talking Heads, all of whom frequented the joint throughout the 1970s and beyond. Little has changed since then – the place is still ratty, plastered with posters and decrepit tables and chairs. The music remains loud, proud and angry, but if punk rock and bondage pants just aren't your thing, you can also catch some of the city's best slam poetry in the downstairs club OMFUG or gentle acoustic sounds at CB's 313 Gallery next door.

Seventh Street boasts used-clothing stores as well as several original boutiques, while **6th Street** between First and Second avenues, also known as "Indian Row," offers endless choices of all things curry.

Countless teenagestyle-gods and hipsters from out of town mill around, wolfing down pizza, drinking cheap beer or eyeing the mildewed wares at the unofficial flea market on **Cooper Square**, a busy crossroads formed by the intersection of the Bowery, Third Avenue and Lafayette Street. This is dominated by the seven-story brownstone mass of **Cooper Union**, erected in 1859 by the wealthy industrialist Peter Cooper as a college for the poor, and the first New York structure to be hung on a frame of iron girders. It's best known as the place where, in 1860, Abraham Lincoln wowed an audience of top New Yorkers with his so-called "might makes right" speech, in which he boldly criticized the pro-slavery policies of the Southern states and helped propel himself to the White House later that year. Today, Cooper Union remains a working and prestigious art and architecture school, whose nineteenth-century glory is evoked with a statue of the benevolent Cooper just in front.

Astor Place and around

Just west of Cooper Square lies **Astor Place**, named after John Jacob Astor and, for a very brief few years, just before high society moved west to Washington Square, one of the city's most desirable neighborhoods. In the 1830s Lafayette Street in particular was home to the city's wealthiest names, not least of whom was John Jacob, one of New York's most hideously greedy tycoons, notorious for having won his enormous fortune by deceiving everybody right up to the president. It's said that when he was old and sick in his house here – no mean affair by all accounts yet long since destroyed – although so weak he could accept no nourishment except a mother's milk and so fat he had to be tossed up and down in a blanket for exercise, his greed for money was such that he lay and dispatched servants daily to collect his rents. The old-fashioned kiosk of the Astor Place subway station, bang in the middle of the junction, discreetly remembers Astor on the platforms, its colored mosaic reliefs depicting beavers recalling Astor's first big killings – in the fur trade. The orange-brick Astor Building (housing one of the city's ubiquitous *Starbucks* on its lower level) with arched windows, is where John Jacob Astor III conducted

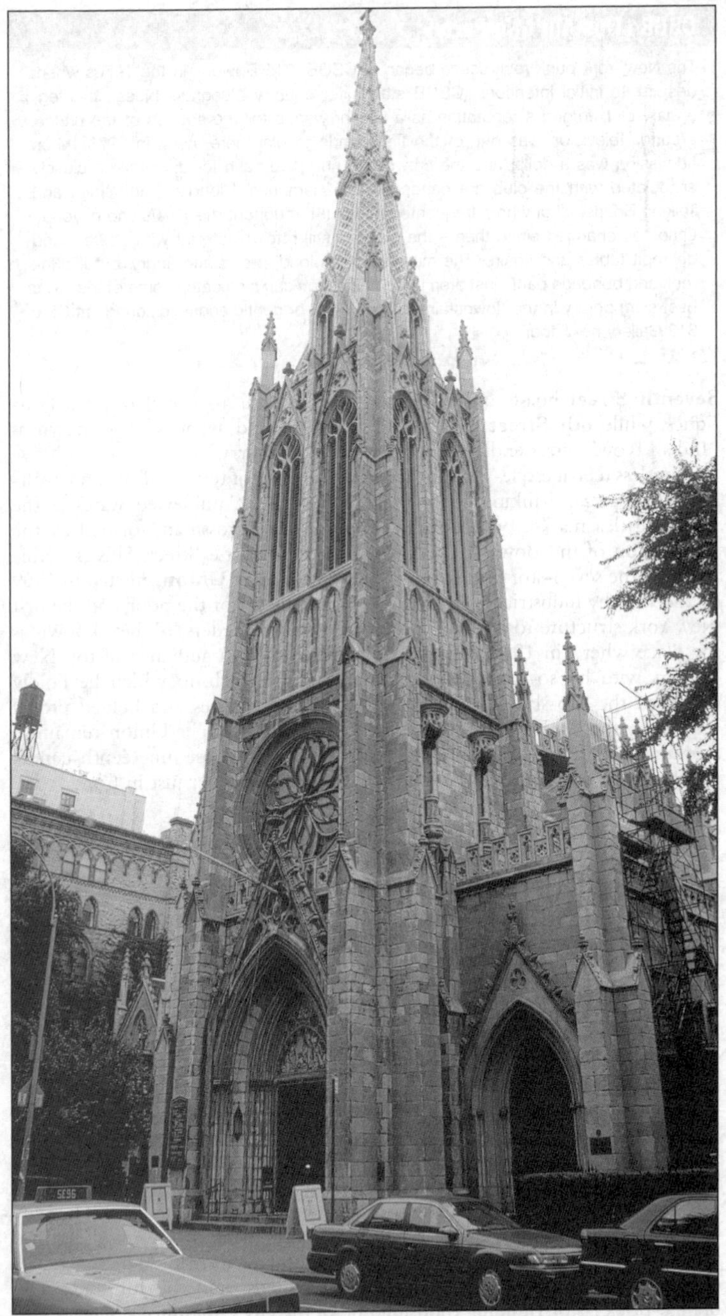

△ Grace Church provides a refuge from the bustle of the East Village business. It's now being converted into $1 million loft apartments, despite intense neighborhood resistance – one indication of the speed of East Village gentrification. Another is the discount retail store K-Mart on the northwest corner, which opened its doors in 1997 to the general horror of locals. If the weekend lines are to be believed, however, they've become happily accustomed to it now.

Today it's hard to believe that Astor Place was once home to wealth and influence. **Lafayette Street** cuts a grimy trail along the edge of the East Village and down into SoHo – all that's left to hint that this might once have been more than a down-at-heel gathering of industrial buildings is Colonnade Row, just south of Astor Place. This strip of four 1832 Greek Revival houses with a Corinthian colonnade is now home to the Colonnade Theater. Opposite, the stocky brownstone and brick building was the Astor Library, built with a bequest from John Jacob Astor starting in the 1850s and the first public library in New York. In 1965, Joseph Papp established his Public Theater here, something of a legend as forerunner of Off-Broadway theater as well as the original venue of hit musicals like *Hair* and *A Chorus Line* and for years run by the man who pioneered Shakespeare in the Park (see p.172). On the ground floor, the hip performance space/restaurant/bar, *Joe's Pub*, plays host to concerts, readings and celebrity-studded private parties. The strip is also home to a number of expensive furniture shops, a fashion designer or two, and the *Village Voice* (see p.31).

Take a quick detour on to 4th Street between Lafayette and Bowery, where the **Merchant's House Museum** (Thurs–Mon 1–5pm with guided tours available at the weekend; $5, $3 students and seniors; ⓣ212/777-1089, ⓦwww.merchantshouse.com) stands at no. 29. The building is the only nineteenth–century family home preserved, both inside and out, as a museum. It cost a bank-breaking $18,000 to build back in 1832, a small fortune at the time, but its neighbors are reputedly selling for around $12 million today. The magnificent interior contains the genuine property, including furniture fashioned by nineteenth-century New York's best cabinetmakers and the personal possessions of the house's original inhabitants. Weekend tours are led by extremely enthusiastic volunteers, yet you can amble through the five floors of sumptuous surroundings alone – just don't miss the perfectly manicured garden behind.

Five minutes west of 4th Street, on the **corner of Washington Place and Greene Street**, one of the city's most notorious sweatshops burned to the ground in 1911, killing 125 female workers and spurring the state to institute laws forcing employers to take account of their employees' safety. Even now, though, there are sweatshops in New York in which safety conditions are probably little better. Back on Broadway, look north: filling a bend in the street is the lacy marble of **Grace Church**, built and designed in 1846 by James Renwick (of St Patrick's Cathedral fame) in a delicate neo-Gothic style. Dark and aisled, with a flattened, web-vaulted ceiling, it's one of the city's most successful churches – and, in many ways, one of its most secretive escapes.

East toward Tompkins Square

Walk east of Broadway, cross back over Third Avenue and you come to another, quite different church – **St Mark's-in-the-Bowery**, a box-like structure originally built in 1799 but with a Neoclassical portico added half a century later. In the 1950s, the Beat poets gave readings here, and it remains an important literary rendezvous, with regular readings, dance performances and music recitals, where you can often catch the likes of Lou Reed, Patti Smith and Lee Ranaldo do their thing, as well as a traditional gathering point for the city's weary down-and-outs. Further north, at 203 2nd Ave, you'll find the **Ukrainian Museum** (Wed–Sun 1–5pm; ⓣ212/228-0110, ⓦwww.ukrainianmuseum.org), dedicated to chronicling the history of this area's main immigrant community. The small collection contains little to attract or enlighten outsiders, although the collection of ethnic items and Ukrainian costumes might hold interest for some.

Back down Second Avenue, on this stretch lined with Polish and Ukrainian restaurants, head to 10th Street, formerly the heart of the East Village art scene and now home to local designers and antique shops. Follow this street east, past the old red-brick **Tenth Street Russian and Turkish Baths** (see p.444 for details), its steam and massage services active back into the last century. Make sure to wander through these streets where new shops and old treasures meld without effort. Just north at 11th Street and First Avenue is *Veniero's*, a beloved village institution tempting the neighborhood with heavenly pastries since 1894. Venture further east and you'll catch up with Avenue A, which borders the once-sketchy, now-safe Tompkins Square Park and buzzes with thrift stores and trendy bars.

Tompkins Square Park

Long a focus for the Lower East Side/East Village community, **Tompkins Square Park** has acquired a reputation as the city's center for political demonstrations and home of radical thought. It was here in 1874 that the police massacred a crowd of workers protesting against unemployment and here in the 1960s that a myriad of protests were organized. The late Yippie leader Abbie Hoffman lived nearby, and residents like him, along with many incidents in the square and on St Mark's Place (which joins the square on its western side), have given the East Village its maverick reputation.

In the Eighties, Tompkins Square Park became the focus of dissent against the gentrification of the East Village and Lower East Side. Large chunks of real estate were bought up, renovated and turned into condominiums, co-ops or high-rent apartments for the new professional classes, much to the fury of the old squatters and new activists. Until the early 1990s, the park was more or less a shantytown (known locally as "**Tent City**") for the homeless, who slept on benches or under makeshift shelters on the patches of green between the paths. In the winter, only the really hardy or truly desperate lived here, but when the weather got warmer the numbers swelled, as activists, anarchists and all manner of statement-makers descended upon the former army barracks from around the country, hoping to rekindle the spirit of 1988. That was the year of the Tompkins Square **riots**, when in August massive demonstrations led to the police, badge numbers covered up and nightsticks drawn, attempting to clear the park of people. In the ensuing battle, many demonstrators were hurt, including a large number of bystanders, and in the investigation that followed the police were heavily criticized for the violence that had occurred. In the summer of 1995 another riot erupted as police tried to evict a group of squatters that had set up house in an empty apartment building nearby. This time, protesters were armed with video cameras and, though heated, the riot never reached the proportions of the 1988 violence.

Despite this resistance, the park was overhauled, its winding pathways and playground restored: an 11pm lock-up and police surveillance have secured the changes, and while a mix of homeless people still congregate on the benches and around the chessboards, they are joined by locals and visitors from nearby streets. One of the few things to see on the square is a small relief just inside the brick enclosure on the northern side, which shows a woman and child gazing forlornly out to sea. It's a commemoration of a disaster of 1904, when the local community, then mostly made up of German immigrants, was devastated by the sinking of a cruise ship, the *General Slocum*, in Long Island Sound, with the death of around a thousand people. At 151 Avenue B, on the eastern side of the park, is **Charlie Parker's house**, a simple whitewashed 1849 structure with a Gothic doorway. The Bird lived here from 1950 until 1954, when he died of a pneumonia-related hemorrhage.

Alphabet City

East Houston Street divides the Lower East Side from the East Village and **Alphabet City**, one of the most dramatically revitalized areas of Manhattan. Here the island bulges out beyond the city's grid structure, the extra avenues being named A to D, and is known to its primarily Puerto Rican residents as *Loisaida*. Like Tompkins Square Park, this was not long ago a notoriously unsafe corner of town, run by drug pushers and gangsters, with cars lining up for fixes in the street, shoes hanging from lampposts to mark the spot where a body had been shot and the burned-out buildings were well-known safe-houses for the brisk heroin trade. Most of this was brought to a halt in 1983 with "Operation Pressure Point," a massive police campaign to clean up the area and make it a place where people would want to live. This has certainly been achieved: crime is way down, the old buildings have been renovated and (unfortunately) supplemented by ugly new ones and today the streets have become the haunt of moneyed twenty-somethings and daring tourist youth. Only Avenue D might still give you some pause; avenues A, B and C have some of the coolest bars, cafés and stores in the city. The profusion of sushi bars and French boites are easy indicators of the neighborhood's increasingly upmarket image. See chapters 30, "Restaurants," and 31, "Drinking," for listings of the best in the area.

Comestibles and consumerism aside, it's worth a wander around this part of town just to see some of the murals and public art, like the **Iglesia San Isidiro y San Leandro**, on 345 E 4th St, which is decorated with mosaics and mirrors, and the numerous community gardens (see box below). As on the Lower East Side, Hispanic residents have recycled their predecessors' institutions: have a look at 638 E 6th St (between avenues C and B), where a former synagogue has been converted into a colorful community center and Catholic church. Also of note is the *NuYorican Poets Café* at 236 E 3rd St; open sporadically, it plays host to some of the biggest stars of the **spoken word scene** (call ⓣ212/505-8183 for events).

Community Gardens

In the 1970s, huge parts of the East Village burned to the ground after cuts in the city's fire-fighting budget closed many of the local firehouses. Since then, East Village residents have reclaimed these neglected and empty lots, turning their rubble-filled mess into some of the prettiest and most verdant spaces in lower Manhattan. Not being able to leave well enough alone, the city decided that these spaces could be used for something much more valuable than grass – more real estate. Despite an agreement in 1999 ensuring the safety of around 100 of its over 600 gardens, the battle reached a pitch in February 2000, when El Jardin de la Esperanza on 7th Street between B and C was bulldozed to make way for market-priced housing. Around thirty local residents were arrested while protesting the action; and the city began to bulldoze the garden while the last resister was still being removed – a mere forty minutes before an injunction was issued to prevent the city from destroying any community gardens.

The fight seems well worth it. In summertime there is no nicer way to while away an evening or a Sunday afternoon than to grab some picnic ingredients and relax among the lush trees and carefully planted foliage of any number of such spaces. Of particular note is the 6th Street and Avenue B affair, overgrown with wildflowers, vegetables, trees and roses, and home to a spectacular four-story-high sculpture maintained by a grumpy local fanatic. The garden also provides a space for summer yoga classes in the morning and evening performance art, as well as numerous bake sales, singalongs and other community events. Other gardens nearby include the very serene 6BC Botanical Garden, on 6th Street between B and C; Miracle Garden on 3rd Street between A and B; El Sol Brillante on 12th Street between A and B; and the Liz Christie Garden on Houston Street and Second Avenue.

9

West Village

When the *Village Voice*, NYC's most venerable listings/comment/investigative magazine, began life as a chronicler of Greenwich Village nightlife in the 1960s, "the Village" really had a dissident, artistic, vibrant voice. While the nonconformist image of Greenwich Village, more commonly known today as the **West Village**, survives to an extent, the tag is no longer truly accurate. And though still one of the more progressive neighborhoods in the city, the West Village has attained a moneyed status over the last four decades and is firmly for those who have Arrived.

Not that the Village doesn't have appeal: to a great extent the neighborhood sports the attractions that brought individuals here in the first place, and people still clamor for a Village address: quaint side streets and stunning historic brownstones and brick townhouses unrivaled elsewhere in Manhattan. It's quiet, residential, but with a busy streetlife that stays up later than many other parts of the city; there are more restaurants per head here than anywhere; bars, while seldom cheap, clutter every corner; and Washington Square Park is a hub of aimless activity throughout the year. The West Village is easily reached by taking the #1 or #9 to Christopher Street or the #A, #C, #E, or #F/S to West 4th Street.

Some history

Greenwich Village grew up as a rural retreat from the early and frenetic nucleus of New York City, sought after during the yellow fever epidemic of 1822 as a refuge from the infected streets downtown. When the fever was at its height, the idea was mooted of moving the entire city center here. It was spared that dubious fate, though, and left to grow into a wealthy residential neighborhood that sprouted elegant Federal and Greek Revival terraces and lured some of the city's highest society names. Later, once the rich had moved further uptown and built themselves a palace or two on Fifth Avenue, these large houses were to prove a fertile hunting ground for struggling artists and intellectuals on the lookout for cheap rents. By the turn of the nineteenth century, Greenwich Village was well on its way to becoming New York's Left Bank. Gentrification set in rather quickly with the conversion of decrepit rowhouses into bohemian-style apartments and the construction in 1926 of a luxury apartment block at the northern edge of Washington Square.

Of early Village characters, one Mabel Dodge was perhaps most influential. Wealthy and radical, she threw parties for the literary and political cognoscenti – parties to which everyone hoped, sooner or later, to be invited. Just about all of the well-known names who lived here during the first two decades of the century spent some time at her house at 23 Fifth Ave, just north of Washington Square. Emma Goldman discussed anarchism with Gertrude Stein and Margaret Sanger; Conrad Aiken and T.S. Eliot dropped in from time to time;

and John Reed – who went on to write *Ten Days That Shook the World*, the celebrated firsthand account of the Russian Revolution – was a frequent guest. The 1930s saw further investment in the arts, most notably with Gertrude Vanderbilt opening a museum dedicated to modern American art. After the war, the Beat movement flourished here, laying the path for further rebellious and countercultural groups and activities in the 1960s.

Washington Square

The best way to see the Village is to walk, and by far the best place to start is its natural center, **Washington Square**, commemorated in the 1880 novel of that title by Henry James and haunted by most of the Village's illustrious past names. It is not an elegant-looking place – too large to be a square, too small to be a park, but it does retain its northern edge of red-brick row houses – the "solid, honorable dwellings" of Henry James's novel and, now home to mostly administrative offices for New York University (NYU) – and, more imposingly, Stanford White's famous Triumphal Arch, built in 1892 to commemorate the centenary of George Washington's inauguration as president. Marcel Duchamp, along with an agitator going by the name of "Woe," climbed to the top of the arch in 1913 to declare the Free Republic of Greenwich Village. Don't plan on repeating that stunt; the arch has been cordoned off around its perimeter in an effort to ward off graffiti. Unfortunately, James wouldn't recognize the south side of the square now: only the fussy Judson Memorial Church stands out amid a messy blend of modern architecture, its interior given over these days to a mixture of theater and a wide array of community-based programs.

Most importantly, though, Washington Square remains the symbolic heart of the Village and its radicalism – so much so that when Robert Moses, the tarmacker of great chunks of New York City (see p.509), wanted to plow a four-lane roadway through the center of the square there was a storm of protest that resulted not only in the stopping of the road but also the banning of all traffic from the park, then used as a turnaround point by buses. And that's how it has stayed ever since, notwithstanding some battles in the 1960s, when the authorities decided to purge the park of folk singers and nearly had a riot on their hands.

Nowadays, the square is rife with undercover police officers, part of a fairly recent and (mildly) successful effort to clear drug dealers. More effective than the cops, perhaps, is the fact that the park itself is closed after 11pm, a curfew that is strictly enforced. Not that you should be worried about your safety here; frankly, little is likely to happen to you in this part of town, and if things look at all hazardous it's just as easy to walk around the square than through it. As soon as the weather gets warm, the square becomes running track, performance venue, chess tournament and social club, boiling over with life as skateboards flip, dogs run, and acoustic guitar notes crash through the urgent cries of performers calling for the crowd's attention. Of particular note are Guerrilla Rep's outdoor performances of Shakespeare plays (for more details see p.377) around sunset; at times like this, there's no better square in the city.

Around Washington Square

Eugene O'Neill, one of the Village's most acclaimed residents, lived (and in 1939 completed *The Iceman Cometh*) at **38 Washington Square S** and consumed vast quantities of ale at The Golden Swan Bar, which once stood on the corner of Sixth Avenue and W 4th Street. The Golden Swan (variously called The Hell Hole, Bucket of Blood and other enticing nicknames) was best known in O'Neill's day for the dubious morals of its clientele – a gang of Irish hoodlums known as the Hudson Dusters – and for the pig in the basement that ate the customers' trash. O'Neill was great pals with this crowd and drew many of his characters from the bar's personalities. It was nearby, also, that he got his first dramatic break, with the **Provincetown Players** who, on the advice of John Reed, had moved down here from Massachusetts and set up shop on MacDougal Street, in a theater which still stands at no. 177. On the basketball court that now fronts the block joining W 4th and W 3rd streets on Sixth Avenue, some of the best and toughest street basketball you'll see is played in the summer to an ever-present crowd of spectators, scouts and the occasional

TV crew. Next door, on other side of the W 4th Street subway entrance, lies a case of urban renewal at its best: a newly planted garden growing over what was once one of the most notorious drug-dealing spots in the city.

Back on Washington Square, don't miss the university's innovative art space at the **Grey Art Gallery**, 100 Washington Square E (Tues, Thurs & Fri 11am–6pm, Wed 11am–8pm, Sat 11am–5pm; suggested donation $2.50; ⓣ212/998-6780). The gallery hosts top dollar traveling art exhibitions as well as a wide range of its own media – sculpture, painting, photography and video shows. Their excellent permanent collection is only shown when pieces are included in special exhibits – a shame when you consider that the gallery is famous for its New York University Art Collection, which includes a strong group of American paintings from the 1940s onwards and prints by Picasso, Miró and Matisse, as well as the Abbey Weed Grey Collection of Contemporary Asian and Middle Eastern Art.

In the NYU Student Center at Washington Square South and La Guardia Place lies the site of Madame Katherine Blanchard's House of Genius, a former boarding house that Willa Cather, Theodore Dreiser and O'Henry called home. From the southwest corner of the park, follow MacDougal Street south, pausing for a detour down pretty Minetta Lane (once the site of one of the city's most prodigious slums) until you reach Bleecker Street, with its touristy concentration of shops, bars, people and restaurants. Here you'll find the European-style sidewalk cafés that have been literary hangouts since Modernist times. The **Café Figaro**, made famous by the Beat writers in the 1950s, is always thronged throughout the day: it's still worth the price of a cappuccino to people-watch for an hour or so. Afterwards, you can follow Bleecker Street east toward the solid towers of Washington Square Village, built with typical disregard for history by NYU in 1958, or west right through the hubbub of West Village life.

West of Sixth Avenue

Sixth Avenue itself is mainly tawdry stores and plastic eating houses, but on the other side, across Father Demo Square and up Bleecker Street (until the 1970s there was an Italian open marketplace on this stretch, and it's still lined by a few Italian stores), are some of the Village's prettiest residential streets. Turn left on Leroy Street and cross over Seventh Avenue where, confusingly, Leroy Street becomes St Luke's Place for a block. The houses here, dating from the 1850s, are among the city's most graceful. One of them (recognizable by the two lamps of honor at the bottom of the steps) is the ex-residence of **Jimmy Walker**, mayor of New York in the 1920s. Walker was for a time the most popular of mayors, a big-spending wisecracker who gave up his work as a songwriter for the world of politics and lived an extravagant lifestyle that rarely kept him out of the gossip columns. Nothing if not shrewd, at a time when America had never been so prosperous, he for a time reflected people's most glamorous, big-living aspirations. He was, however, no match for the hard times to come, and once the 1930s Depression took hold he lost touch and – with it – office.

South of Leroy Street, the Village fades slowly into SoHo and TriBeCa's warehouse districts – an architecturally bleak area where the buildings are an odd mixture of Federal facades juxtaposed against grubby-gray rolldown-entranced packing houses, but one which houses many designer boutiques, galleries and eating places nonetheless. For a more aesthetically pleasing facade, there's a neatly preserved row from the 1820s on Charlton Street between Sixth Avenue and Varick. In the area just to its north, **Richmond Hill**, was the site of the estate that was George Washington's headquarters during the Revolution, later the home of Aaron Burr and John Jacob Astor. But those apart, you should continue on Hudson Street up to **St Luke's in the Fields Church** at Barrow Street. The church dates back to 1821 and one of its founding wardens was none other than Clement Clarke Moore, scholar and author of "Twas the night before Christmas." The row of Federal-style brick houses next door, housing for school and church administrators, went up a few years later. These days the church is very active in AIDS-outreach work, hosts a festive gay pride evensong celebration for the local community and has entered a sizeable parish contingent in the annual Pride parade. Look behind the church for the beautiful **St Luke's Gardens**, a labyrinthine patchwork of garden, grass and benches open to the public during the day and accessible through the gate between church and school. There's an excellent thrift store here too, housed in the basement by the school.

Hudson Street north of the church and up to Abingdon Square (where Hudson bends to become Eighth Avenue and heads for Chelsea) is a good avenue for meandering, with a bevy of unique stores, coffee bars and restaurants catering to its upwardly mobile and moneyed residential community. The excellent *White Horse Tavern*, 567 Hudson St, is where Dylan Thomas had his last drink; see p.357 for details.

Grove and Bedford streets

Directly opposite St Luke's, **Grove Street** runs east into **Bedford Street**, where you will find Grove Court, one of the neighborhood's most typical and secluded little mews. Along with Barrow and Commerce streets nearby, Bedford Street is one of the quietest and most desirable Village addresses – Edna St Vincent Millay, the young poet and playwright who did much work with the Provincetown Playhouse, lived at no. 75½ – said to be the narrowest house in the city, nine feet wide and topped with a tiny gable. Built in 1799, the clapboard structure next door claims to be the oldest house in the Village, but much renovated since and probably worth a considerable fortune now.

Further down Bedford at no. 86, the former speakeasy *Chumley's* (see "Drinking," p.357) is recognizable only by the metal grille on its door – a low profile useful in Prohibition years that makes it hard to find today. Enter through the unmarked speakeasy door on Bedford or through the patio garden on Barrow Street. Follow Bedford back onto Grove Street, following it toward Seventh Avenue and looking out for *Marie's Crisis Café* at 59 Grove St. Now a gay bar, it was once home to Thomas Paine, English by birth but perhaps the most important and radical thinker of the American Revolutionary era, and from whose *Crisis Papers* the café takes its name. Though significantly involved in the Revolution, Paine was regarded with suspicion by the government afterwards, especially after his active support for the French Revolution. By the time of his death here, in 1809, he had been condemned as an atheist and stripped of citizenship of the country he helped to found. Seventh Avenue meets Grove Street at one of the Village's busiest junctions, Sheridan Square – not in fact a square at all unless you count Christopher Park's slim strip of green, but simply a wide and hazardous meeting of several busy streets.

Christopher Street

Christopher Street, the main artery of the West Village, leads off from here – traditional heartland of the city's gay community. The square was named after General Sheridan, cavalry commander in the Civil War, and holds a pompous-looking statue to his memory. It is better known, however, as the scene of one of the worst and bloodiest of New York's Draft Riots (see History in "Contexts," p.471), when a marauding mob assembled here in 1863 and attacked members of the black community, several of whom were lynched.

Scenes of violence also erupted in 1969, when the **gay community** wasn't as readily accepted as it is now. The violence on this occasion was provoked by the police, who raided the Stonewall gay bar, and started arresting its occupants – for the local gay community the latest in a long line of harassment from the police. Spontaneously, word went around to other bars in the area, and before long the Stonewall was surrounded, resulting in a siege that lasted the better part of the night and sparked up again the next two nights. The riot ended with several arrests and a number of injured policemen. Though hardly a victory for their rights, it was the first time that gay men had stood up en masse to the persecutions of the city police and, as such, formally inaugurated the gay rights movement. The event is honored by the annual **Gay Pride march** (held on the last Sunday in June).

Nowadays the gay community is fairly synonomous with West Village life. From Sheridan Square down to the Hudson is a tight-knit enclave – focusing on Christopher Street – of bars, restaurants and bookstores used specifically, but not exclusively, by gay men. The scene along the Hudson River – around West Street and the river piers – is considerably raunchier at night. By day, an attractive pedestrian walkway links Battery Park City up to the top of the Village and is bustling with bikers, runners and bladers who come for the river breezes and the view. Once the sun goes down, though, only the really committed or curious should venture (native New Yorkers, gay ones included, warn against going there at all). But on the far east stretch of Christopher, things crack off with the accent less on sex and more on excessive, fun camp. Among the more accessible gay bars here are *The Monster* on Sheridan Square itself and *Marie's Crisis Café* on Grove Street (see p.113); for more complete listings of gay bars and clubs, see p.390.

North of Washington Square

At the eastern end of Christopher Street is another of those car-buzzing, life-risking West Village junctions where Sixth Avenue is met by Greenwich Avenue, one of the neighborhood's major shopping streets. Hover for a while at the romantic Victorian bulk of the **Jefferson Market Courthouse**, voted fifth most beautiful building in America in 1885, and built with all the vigor of the age. It hasn't actually served as a courthouse since 1946; indeed, at one time – like so many buildings in this city – it was branded for demolition and was saved thanks to the efforts of a few determined Villagers, including e. e. cummings, and now lives out its days as the local library. Walk around behind for a better look, perhaps pondering for a moment on the fact that the adjacent well-tended garden was, until 1971, the Women's House of Detention, a prison known for its abysmal conditions and numbering Angela Davis among its inmates. Look out, also, for **Patchin Place**, a tiny mews opening onto West 10th Street, whose neat, gray rowhouses are yet another Village literary landmark, home to the reclusive Djuna Barnes for more than forty years. Barnes's longtime neighbor cummings used to call her "just to see if she was still alive." Patchin Place was at various times also home to Marlon Brando, John Masefield, Dreiser, O'Neill and Reed.

Across the road, *Balducci's* forms a pricey downtown alternative to its Upper West Side rival, *Zabar's*, and its stomach-tingling smells are hard to resist. Nearby, Bigelow's Pharmacy, 414 6th Ave is possibly the city's oldest drugstore; and south a block to the east, W 8th Street is an occasionally rewarding strip of brash shoe stores, tattoo parlors and cut-price clothes stores. Up W 10th and 11th streets are some of the best-preserved early nineteenth-century townhouses in the Village, with the exception of the rebuilt facade of **18 W 11th St** (see box, below).

A couple of imposing churches are to be found by following 10th Street over to Fifth Avenue, where the neighborhood's low-slung residential streets lead to some eminently desirable apartment buildings. On the corner stands the nineteenth-century **Church of the Ascension**, a small structure built by Richard Upjohn (the Trinity Church architect), later redecorated by Stanford White and restored outside and in, where a gracefully toned La Farge altarpiece and some fine stained glass are on view. A block north at 11th Street, Joseph Wells's bulky, chocolate-brown Gothic revival **First Presbyterian Church** is decidedly more sober, with a tower said to have been modeled on the one at Magdalen College Oxford, England. To look inside, you need to enter through the discreetly added Church House (ring the bell for attention if the door's locked). Nearby is one of the city's best small museums, **Forbes Galleries**, at Fifth Avenue and 12th Street (Tues, Wed, Fri & Sat 10am–4pm; free; ⓣ212/206-5549), which contains a treasure trove of tiny delights, from the world's largest collection of Fabergé eggs, delicate and intricate in their beauty, to over 500 model boats and a ten-thousand-strong host of tin soldiers from various eras and armies. Also on view are early Monopoly boards and plenty of historical documents, including past papers of presidents. Afterwards, you're just five blocks north of the pin-neat prettiness of **Washington Mews**, a small cobbled street of old pastel-colored buildings that seem out of place amid the grand mansions of Washington Square, just a block further south.

The Weathermen

In the late 1960s, five members of the **Weather Underground**, a domestic terrorist organization dedicated to halting the Vietnam War, set up a bomb factory in the basement of the Henry Brevoort-designed house at 18 W 11th St, with the ultimate aim of blowing up the Columbia University Library. The plan, however, backfired and on March 6, 1970, the arsenal exploded in the house, killing three of the group. The other two Weathermen escaped, and managed to evade capture for more than a decade. Incidentally, the terrorists' neighbor at the time was none other than actor Dustin Hoffman, whose home at no. 16 suffered extensive damage from the blast.

Chelsea

A low-built, occasionally seedy grid of tenements, rowhouses and warehouses, **Chelsea**'s heart lies west of Broadway between 14th and 23rd streets. For years, these dreary facades and neglected buildings gave Chelsea an atmosphere of neglect, with the grid plan too wide and the streets too bare to encourage visitors to linger. It's in this main area now, though, that Chelsea has become a commercial player, mostly shaped by the arrival, in the late Seventies and early Eighties, of a large new gay community. Today, its districts are filled with affluent townhouses whose dwellers relish the luxury of a few extra square feet of space. Stores, restaurants and a few tourist attractions pepper the scene, along with excellent cutting-edge art galleries and increasingly upmarket real estate. Despite the encroachment of these moneyed forces, some of the long-entrenched Hispanic community has managed to stay put in their rent-controlled apartments. Chelsea can be reached by taking the #1 or #9 to 23rd or 18th in Broadway or by taking the #C or #E to 23rd and Eighth Avenue.

Some history

Chelsea began to take shape in 1830 thanks to Clement Clarke Moore, more famous as the author of the surprise poetic hit *A Visit from St Nick* (popularly known as *The Night Before Christmas*). Anticipating Manhattan's movement

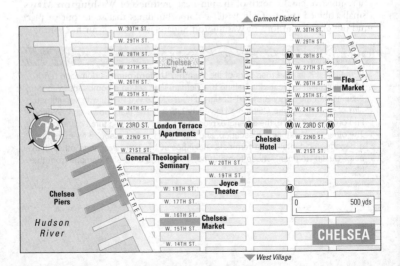

Garment District
W. 30TH ST.
W. 29TH ST.
W. 28TH ST.
W. 27TH ST.
W. 26TH ST.
W. 25TH ST.
W. 24TH ST.
W. 23RD ST.
W. 22ND ST.
W. 21ST ST.
W. 20TH ST.
W. 19TH ST.
W. 18TH ST.
W. 17TH ST.
W. 16TH ST.
W. 15TH ST.
W. 14TH ST.
ELEVENTH AVENUE
TENTH AVENUE
NINTH AVENUE
EIGHTH AVENUE
SEVENTH AVENUE
SIXTH AVENUE
BROADWAY
WEST STREET
Chelsea Park
Flea Market
London Terrace Apartments
Chelsea Hotel
General Theological Seminary
Joyce Theater
Chelsea Piers
Chelsea Market
Hudson River
N
0 500 yds
CHELSEA
West Village

uptown, Moore laid out his land for sale in broad lots. Stuck as it was between the ritziness of Fifth Avenue, the hipness of Greenwich Village and the poverty of Hell's Kitchen, the area never quite made it onto the short list of desirable places to live. Manhattan's chic residential focus leapfrogged Chelsea, to the East 40s and 50s, and the arrival of the slaughterhouses, an elevated railroad and working-class poor sealed Chelsea's fate as a rough-and-tumble no-go area for decades. The area enjoyed a brief respite from the dank and gloom in the 1870s and 1880s when its proximity to glitzy Gramercy Park and Murray Hill made it a center for Manhattan's theatrical activity. Bohemians flocked here, lured by the novelty of down-and-out charm, only to abscond to the West Village at the turn of the century.

The last few decades have seen a totally new Chelsea emerge and, with it, good reason to visit. New York's peripatetic art scene has been extremely influential in the neighborhood's transformation. In the late 1980s and early 1990s, a number of respected galleries began making use of the large spaces available in the low-rise warehouses of Chelsea's western reaches, bringing a new cultural edge to the once down-and-out neighborhood. This has been complemented by an explosion in superstore retail, especially along Sixth and Seventh avenues, and the building of the Chelsea Piers, making the area as crowded as any with shoppers, restaurant-goers and the like.

Eighth, Ninth and Tenth avenues

If Chelsea has a main drag it's **Eighth Avenue**, where the transformation of the neighborhood is most pronounced. The West Village glides up here into a stretch of vibrant retail energy to rival the fast-moving traffic in the street. A spate of bars, restaurants, health food stores, gyms, bookstores and clothes shops has opened in the last five years in response to the new population – not exactly a picturesque route, though a few minor diversions down the side streets balance things out. Meanwhile, Eighth Avenue at 19th Street is home to one of the more important dance theaters in New York, the **Joyce**. The accomplished Feld Ballet is in residence here and a host of other touring companies keep this Art Deco-style theater (complete with garish pink and purple neon signs) in brisk business (see p.379) – it's also one of the best places in the city to see modern dance.

Back down at **319 W 14th St**, between Eighth and Ninth avenues, Orson Welles resided at the tender age of twenty. Just around the corner on **Ninth Avenue**, the red-brick **Chelsea Market** fills an entire block between 15th and 16th streets. This high-class food temple is housed in the old Nabisco factory, where the Oreo cookie is rumored to have been created. Many of the factory features remain, including pieces of rail track used to transport supplies. The handpicked retailers inside supply most of Manhattan's upscale restaurant trade, and their wares include fresh fruit, fish, bread, wine, brownies and flowers. Also here, the **Chelsea Wine Vault** lets you store your (store-bought) collection on site – perfect if your wine cellar encroaches on valuable closet space.

Further north, the cross streets between Ninth and Tenth avenues, specifically 20th, 21st and 22nd streets, constitute the **Chelsea Historic District** (although the label "district" is a bit grand for an area of three blocks), and boast a great variety of predominantly Italianate and Greek Revival rowhouses in brick and various shades of brownstone. Dating from the 1830s to the 1890s, they demonstrate the faith some early developers had in Chelsea as an up-and-coming New York neighborhood. Of particular historic note is 41 W 22nd St, where the area's first real estate developer, James Wells, resided. At **404 W 20th St**, the oldest house in the neighborhood stands out with its 1829 wooden-sided structure, predating Wells' all-brick constructions. The ornate iron fencing along this block heading west is original and spectacular. However, the nineteenth century meets the modern era at the corner of West 22nd Street and Tenth Avenue in the Flash Gordonesque aluminum-sided *Empire Diner*, built in the 1930s.

Between Ninth and Tenth avenues, the block bounded by 20th and 21st streets contains one of Chelsea's secrets, the **General Theological Seminary** on Chelsea Square. Clement Clarke Moore donated an island of land to the institute in which he formerly taught, and today the harmonious assembly of ivy-clad Gothicisms surrounding a restive green feels like part of an Ivy League college campus. Though the buildings still house a working seminary, it's possible to explore the park on weekdays and Saturday at lunchtime, as long as you sign in and keep quiet (the entrance is via the modern building on Ninth Avenue). And if you're at all interested in theological history, you should check out their collection of Latin bibles while you are here – it's one of the largest in the world.

London Terrace

Well west along 23rd Street is one of New York's premier residences for those who believe in understated opulence. The **London Terrace Apartments**, two rows of apartment buildings a full city block long between Ninth and Tenth avenues surrounding a private interior garden, had the misfortune of being completed in 1930 at the height of the Great Depression. Despite a swimming pool and doormen dolled out in London police uniforms, many of the 1670 London Terrace apartments stood empty for several years. Today, though, it's home to some of New York's trendier names, especially those from the fashion, art and music worlds. It was nicknamed "The Fashion Projects" by the *New York Times*, as much for its retinue of big-time designer, photographer and model residents (including Isaac Mizrahi, Annie Leibovitz and Deborah Harry) as for its ironic proximity to Chelsea's real housing projects just to the south and east.

The Chelsea piers and galleries

Continue west along 23rd Street and brave crossing the West Side Highway, and you'll reach one of Manhattan's most ambitious waterfront projects, **Chelsea Piers** (Ⓦwww.chelseapiers.com), a $100 million, 1.7-million-square-foot development along the historic 59th, 60th, 61st and 62nd piers on the Hudson River. Opened in 1910 and designed by Warren and Whetmore (who were also at work on Grand Central Terminal at the time), this was the place where the great transatlantic liners would disembark their passengers (it was en route to the Chelsea Piers in 1912 that the *Titanic* sank). By the 1950s, however, the newer passenger ships were docking uptown at larger terminals, and the Piers were only used for freight. In the 1960s, the Piers fell into disuse and decay, and as late as the mid-1980s an official report condemned them as "shabby, pathetic reminders of a glorious past." Since then, money and effort has been poured into the revival of this once-illustrious land. The heart of the development is a huge sports complex, with two enclosed ice rinks and two open-air roller rinks, and a landscaped golf driving range, all open to the public (see "Sports and outdoor activities," p.443). There is also an impressive (though membership-only) indoor sports center, with basketball courts, batting cages, a rock-climbing wall and more. Perhaps the best part of the development, though, is its emphasis on **public spaces**, including a waterfront walkway of over a mile and a pleasant water's edge park at the end of Pier 62. Should you walk up a thirst, there's also the *Chelsea Brewing Company* on Pier 59, along with a few outdoor restaurants along the water. These all feel somewhat contrived, but they still offer an away-from-the-city atmosphere and put you as close to the Hudson River as you can (or would want to) get.

For entertainment in this part of town, the *Frying Pan* is an unusual and very cool venue for a different kind of night out. This old lightship was operational between 1929 and 1964 on the North Carolina coast, before it was submerged and abandoned, and then brought to New York in the 1980s. These days, it acts as a performance space, playing host to dance parties (including the excellent, outdoor Turntables on the Hudson), theater and live bands. It's often hired out for private parties, though, so call (☎212/989-6363) to check the journey west is worth your while.

The Chelsea art scene

Back over the West Side Highway and along 22nd Street are the galleries and warehouse spaces that house one of New York's most vibrant art scenes. The New York commercial art scene is in constant motion, always in search of better rents and the ultimate "cool" place to be and be seen. Galleries and exhibition spaces are already here, and more are on the way: nearly a dozen galleries have opened recently with an especially strong presence along West 22nd Street between Tenth and Eleventh avenues. The **Dia Center for the Arts**, a Chelsea pioneer, with space here since 1987, has its main exhibition gallery at 548 W 22nd St, featuring a dramatic **open-air space** on top where the Rooftop Urban Park opened in 1991. The effect of the two-way glass mirror pavilion is remarkable, its impact in constant flux as it works with the changing light and visual effects of the sky. Nearby, Sonnabend at no. 536 and Matthew Marks at no. 522 are just two more of the many galleries in this neighborhood. (See "Commercial Galleries," p.395, for more details on Chelsea's galleries.) Also masquerading as art on this stretch is the space-age ovular entrance way to *Comme des Garçons* – the store is just west of Tenth Avenue, at no. 518.

The Chelsea Hotel

Double back east along 23rd Street, past Eighth Avenue over to its intersection with Seventh to find one of the neighborhood's major claims to fame – the **Chelsea Hotel.** Chelsea has had several incarnations since its early nineteenth century development, the most colorful of which was arguably its heyday as Manhattan's Theater District in the 1870s and 1880s, before the scene moved uptown. Little remains of the theaters now, but the hotel that put up all the actors, writers and bohemian hangers-on was the first building in New York to be declared a landmark for both architectural and historical interest, in 1966. Originally built as a luxury cooperative apartment building, with New York's first penthouses and duplexes, in 1882, the building never attracted many affluent tenants, who then scorned cooperative living: but its soundproofed walls would eventually make it ideal for rock bands. Despite its official status as a hotel, more than half the guests here are permanent residents, paying for personally decorated rooms at a reduced monthly rate.

Since its conversion in 1905, the *Chelsea Hotel* has been the undisputed watering hole of the city's harder-up literati. Mark Twain and Tennessee Williams lived here and Brendan Behan and Dylan Thomas staggered in and out during their New York visits. Actresses Sarah Bernhardt and Lilly Langtry resided here around the turn of the nineteenth century. Thomas Wolfe assembled *You Can't Go Home Again* from thousands of pages of manuscript he had stacked in his room, and in 1951 Jack Kerouac, armed with a specially adapted typewriter (and a lot of Benzedrine), typed the first draft of *On the Road* non-stop onto a 120-foot roll of paper. William Burroughs (in a presumably more relaxed state) completed *Naked Lunch* here, and Arthur C. Clarke wrote *2001: A Space Odyssey* while in residence. Arthur Miller (who was sick of having to put on a tie just to pick up his mail at the stylish *Plaza*) and Paul Bowles have also been guests.

In the 1960s, the *Chelsea* entered a wilder phase. Andy Warhol and his doomed protégés Edie Sedgwick and Candy Darling walled up here and made the film *Chelsea Girls* in a (sort of) homage. Recently deceased artist Robert Mapplethorpe and NY veteran singer Patti Smith also lived here in the late 1960s and early Seventies. Nico, Hendrix, Zappa, Pink Floyd, Patti Smith and various members of the Grateful Dead passed through; Bob Dylan wrote songs in and about the hotel and Sid Vicious stabbed Nancy Spungen to death in 1978 in their suite, a few months before his own colorfully tragic life ended with an overdose of heroin. The owner of the hotel, in fact, had to divide their room into several smaller ones because visitors began to leave wreaths and candles outside the door. On a more cheerful note, the hotel inspired Joni Mitchell to write her song *Chelsea Morning* – a song that twanged the heartstrings of the young Bill and Hillary Clinton, who named their daughter after it (though there's no record of Chelsea ever having stayed in her eponymous hotel).

With a pedigree like this it's easy to forget the hotel itself, which has a down-at-heel Edwardian grandeur all of its own and, incidentally, is also an affordable place to stay. (Don't be surprised if you find yourself sharing the elevator with Dee Dee Ramone.) See "Accommodation," p.290.

East Chelsea

The eastern edge of Chelsea has become a busy strip of commerce, concentrated mostly along **Sixth Avenue**, where a crush of moderately priced clothing stores, such as Old Navy and Today's Man, have driven the likes of local institution Barney's to bankruptcy. A little **literary history** took place here too, before all the commercialism: Stephen Crane lived at 165 W 23rd St as an impoverished twenty-something, while further east, at 14 W 23rd St, Edith Wharton was born.

Heading north above 23rd Street, away from Chelsea's heart, the city's largest **antiques market** (and surrounding junk sales) takes place on weekends in a few open-air parking lots centered around Sixth Avenue and 26th Street (see "Shops and Markets," p.401). The area around 28th Street is Manhattan's **Flower Market** – not really a market as such, more the warehouses where potted plants and cut flowers are stored before brightening offices and atriums across the city. Nothing marks the strip, and you come across it by chance, the greenery bursting out of drab blocks, blooms spangling storefronts and providing a welcome touch of life to a decidedly industrial neighborhood. For the record, West 28th Street was the original **Tin Pan Alley**, where music publishers would peddle songs to artists and producers from the nearby theaters. When the theaters moved away, so did the publishers and the area's creative light seemed to fade away.

The Garment District

Muscling in between Sixth and Eighth avenues from 34th to 42nd streets, the **Garment District**, which takes in the twin modern monsters of Penn Station and Madison Square Garden, offers little of interest to the casual tourist. The majority of people who cross the Garment District do so for a specific reason – to catch a train or bus, to watch wrestling or basketball, or to work – and it's only a wedge of stores between Herald and Greeley squares that attracts visitors.

It is in this patch of land that three-quarters of all the women's and children's clothes in America are made, though you'd never believe it from walking around. Outlets are strictly wholesale, with no need to woo customers, and the only evidence of the industry inside are the racks of clothes shunted around on the street and occasional bins of offcuts that give the area its look of an open-air rummage sale. Every imaginable button, bow, boa and bangle is on display, including trimmings and trinkets you'd have thought were long obsolete.

One of the benefits of walking through this part of town is to take advantage of the designer's **sample sales**, where floor samples and models' used castoffs are sold to the public at cheap prices, though if you can't afford a $750 Donna Karan dress, you probably still can't afford it at $450 (see p.411 for more on sample sales). And a warning for any squeamish anti-fur zealots – steer clear of W 30th Street and its surroundings, where peeking from industrial-sized barrels in cooled storefronts are the heads and tails of whole minks and foxes, waiting their turn to become winter coats.

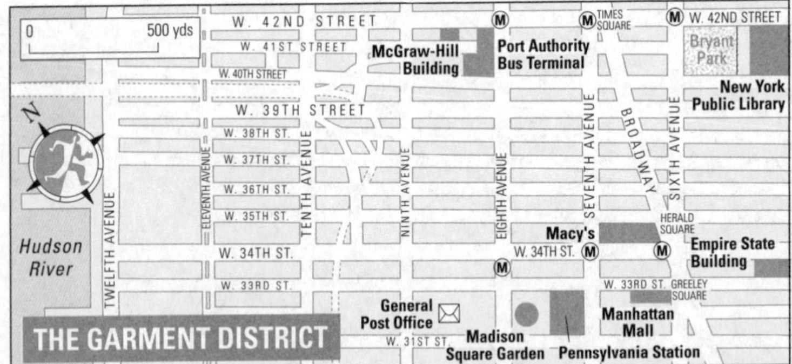

Greeley and Herald squares

Sixth Avenue collides with Broadway at **Greeley Square**, an overblown name for what is a trashy triangle celebrating Horace Greeley, founder of the *Tribune* newspaper. Perhaps he deserves better: known for his rallying call to the youth of the nineteenth century to explore the continent ("Go West, young man!"), he also supported the rights of women and trade unions, denounced slavery and capital punishment and commissioned a weekly column from Karl Marx. His paper no longer exists and the square named after him is one of those bits of Manhattan that looks ready to disintegrate at any moment.

Herald Square faces Greeley Square in a headlong stone replay of the battles between the *Herald* newspaper and its archrival, Horace Greeley's *Tribune*. During the 1890s this was the Tenderloin area, with dance halls, brothels and rough bars like Satan's Circus and the Burnt Rag thriving beside the elevated railway that ran up Sixth Avenue. When the Herald arrived in 1895 it gave the square a new name and dignity, but it's perhaps best recognized as the square singer George M. Cohan asked to be remembered to in 1904. These days its grimy mediocrity wouldn't fire anyone to sing about it, the area's unkempt and unglamorously seedy nature is tempered only by Macy's on the corner below.

Macy's

Macy's is the all-American superstore. Until the mid-1970s it contented itself with being the world's largest store (which it remains); then, in response to the needs of the high-rolling 1980s yuppie lifestyle it went fashionably and safely upmarket. When the economy went into a tailspin in 1990, Macy's fortunes declined dramatically, burdened by overexpansion and debt. New Yorkers were stunned when word went around that it was near closure, and the ensuing media coverage was about as intense as if the mayor had sold the Statue of Liberty to Iraq. Fortunately Macy's scrambled out of bankruptcy by the skin of its teeth, with a debt-restructuring plan that allowed it to continue financing its famed annual Thanksgiving Day Parade, one of the most famous and best-attended Manhattan processions, marked by its giant cartoon-character balloons and the arrival of Santa (see "Parades and Festivals," p.453). Like all great stores, Macy's is worth exploring – there's an amazing food emporium plus a reconstruction of *P.J. Clarke's* bar in the basement – though it may be wise to leave all forms of spending power at home. Next door, the tacky Manhattan Mall can't hold a candle to Macy's.

Madison Square Garden and around

The most prominent landmark in the Garment District is the **Pennsylvania Station and Madison Square Garden complex**, a combined box and drum structure that swallows up millions of commuters into its train station belly while housing Knicks basketball and Rangers hockey games (for ticket details, see p.440). There's nothing memorable about the railway station: its subterranean levels seem to have all the grime and just about everything else that's wrong with the subway and, to add insult to injury, the original Penn Station, demolished in 1963 to make way for this, is now hailed as a lost masterpiece,

Old Penn Station and the Landmarks Preservation Law

When, in 1963, the old Penn Station was demolished in order to expand the Madison Square Garden sports complex, the notion of conservation was about ten years away from crystallizing into the broad-based middle-class power group that was to wield so much force in New York through the 1970s and 1980s. Despite the vocal complaints of a few, the forces of "modernization" were then all-powerful – so much so that hardly anything was saved of the original building: even a number of its carefully crafted statues and interiors became landfill for New Jersey's Meadowlands complex just across the Hudson River.

It was public disgust with the destruction of the station – along with the demolition of the Singer Building, an early, graceful skyscraper in the Financial District around the same time – that brought about the passing of the Landmarks Preservation Law. It ensures that buildings granted landmark status – for their aesthetic value, historical importance or associations – cannot be destroyed or even altered.

one that brought an air of dignity to the neighborhood and created the stage for the ornate General Post Office and other elaborate Belle Epoque structures that followed. One of McKim, Mead and White's greatest designs, the station's original edifice reworked the ideas of the Roman Baths of Caracalla to awesome effect, its grand arcade lavishly covered with floors of pink marble and walls of pink granite. Glass tiles in its main waiting room allowed the light from the glass roof to flow through to the trains and platforms below: "Through it one entered the city like a god . . . One scuttles in now like a rat," mourned architectural historian Vincent Scully in the 1960s.

Photos of the older station can be seen in the Amtrak waiting area of the new Penn Station. And you can walk back in time at the new entryway to the Long Island Railroad ticket area on 34th Street at Seventh Avenue: one of the old station's four-faced time pieces now hangs from the tall steel-framed glass structure which is itself reminiscent of the original building. Andrew Leicester's *Ghost Series* was commissioned in 1994 and lines the walls of the new corridor: terracotta wall murals saluting the Corinthian and Ionic columns of the old Penn Station, as well as a rendering of *Day & Night*, an ornate statue surrounding a clock that once welcomed passengers at the old station's entrance. Also of note in the Long Island Railroad ticket area: look above your head for Maya Lin's *Eclipsed Time*, a sculpture of glass, aluminum and fiber optics that alludes to the immeasurability of time in a subtly crafted ellipsis with random number patterns.

One further, more whimsical reminder of the old days is the **Hotel Pennsylvania** on the corner of Seventh Avenue and 33rd Street. A main venue for Glenn Miller and other big swing bands of the 1940s, it keeps the phone number that made it famous – ⓣ212/736-5000 (under the old system, "PENNsylvania 6-5000") the title of Miller's affectionate hit. It has recently been refurbished, and now bravely claims to offer "New York's newest rooms"; look round the corner, though, onto 33rd Street, for a glimpse of the old hotel sign, a true taste of times gone by.

The General Post Office

Immediately behind Penn Station, the **General Post Office** is a 1913 McKim, Mead and White structure that survived, a relic from an era when municipal pride was all about making statements – though to say that the Post Office is monumental in the grandest manner still seems to underplay it. The old joke is that it had to be this big to fit in the sonorous inscription above the columns ("Neither snow nor rain nor heat nor gloom of night stays these couriers from the swift completion of their appointed rounds"), a claim about as believable as the official one that the Manhattan postal district handles more mail than Britain, France and Belgium combined. There's still a working post office branch here, though the main sorting stations have moved into more modern space further west. In early 2001, Fraport AG, a German architectural firm, won the highly contested and much-delayed contract to create a new Penn Station for Amtrak in the General Post Office building, an edifice that will aim to expiate the destruction of the original structure.

The Port Authority Terminal Building at 40th Street and Eighth Avenue (for practical details see p.19) is another grimy gathering place, though its poor reputation as a haven for down-and-outs is belied by its appearance these days as a spruced-up and efficiently run modern bus station. Greyhound leaves from here, as do regional services out to the boroughs, and (should you arrive in the early hours) it's a remarkably safe place, station staff keeping the winos and weirdos in check. Harder to believe is that the station holds an exceptional bowling alley, should you immediately have the urge upon arrival (see p.442 for more details). To the west of Port Authority, at 330 42nd St, is the McGraw-Hill Building, a greeny-blue radiator built in 1972 that architects raved over: "proto-jukebox modern," the critic Scully called it. The lobby should definitely be seen.

12

Union Square and Gramercy Park

Broadway forms a dividing line between Chelsea to the west and the area that comprises **Union Square** and **Gramercy Park**. It is here, between the great avenues – Third, Park and Fifth – that midtown Manhattan's skyscrapers begin to rise from the low-lying buildings. Before heading on to those jaw-droppers, like the Empire State Building (see p.132), it's certainly worth at least a jaunt around the more genteel parts of these two neighborhoods, which offer some decent architecture themselves, like the Flatiron building. The #N, #R, #Q, #L, #W, #4, #5 and #6 trains all stop at Union Square.

Union Square

Once the elegant center of the city's theatrical and shopping scene, **Union Square**, where Broadway, Fourth and Park avenues meet between 14th and 18th streets, invites you to stroll its paths, feed the squirrels and gaze at its array of statuary. Unfortunately, the proliferation of chain cafés and superstores around makes it impossible to forget you are on the fringes of the most commercial part of New York, but the park is still a welcome respite from the crazed taxi drivers and rushed pedestrians on 14th Street. Among the park's statues are an equestrian figure of George Washington, a Lafayette by Bartholdi (more famous for the Statue of Liberty) and, at the center of the green, a

The Farmers' Market

On Mondays, Wednesdays, Fridays and Saturdays from 7am until 6pm, the park plays host to the city's best and most popular **Farmers' Market** on its northern edge. Farmers and other food producers from upstate New York, Long Island, New Jersey and as far as Pennsylvania Dutch country sell fresh fruit and vegetables, baked goods, cheeses, eggs, meats, fish, plants and flowers. The quality of the produce is generally very high (an advisory committee sets up and enforces stringent rules on the growers and keeps out wholesalers and brokers). Buying picnic fodder from the market and concocting a feast is one of the finest things you can do here on a summer or spring day.

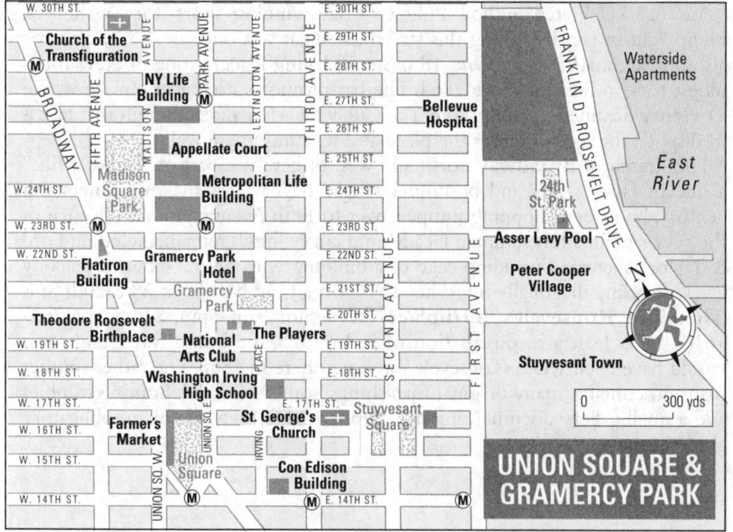

massive flagstaff base whose bas-reliefs symbolize the forces of Good and Evil in the American Revolution.

The square is flanked by several good cafés and restaurants, serving everything from macrobiotic Japanese to swanky bistro cuisine to overpriced diner fare. It's also surrounded by a mismatched hodgepodge of architecture, not least of which is the old **American Savings Bank** building on the eastern edge – now the Daryl Roth Theatre – of which only the grandiose columned exterior survives. The pedimented Union Square Theater just south of here is the former **Tammany Hall** (see p.471), once notorious headquarters of the Democratic Party, a fine example of Colonial Revival architecture, while the narrow building almost opposite was Andy Warhol's original Factory. The **Consolidated Edison** (or ConEd) building, off the southeast corner, the headquarters of the company responsible for providing the city with energy and those famous steaming sewer access holes, is, with its campanile, an odd premonition of the Metropolitan Life Building on Madison Square (see p.130). Opposite the greenmarket is yet another Barnes & Noble store, albeit a particularly good one, noteworthy for the excellent series of author's readings it hosts two or three times a week.

Irving Place and around

East of Union Square, walk the six graceful blocks of **Irving Place** north toward Gramercy Park. Irving Place was named for Washington Irving, the early-nineteenth-century American writer whose creepy tale of the Headless Horseman, *The Legend of Sleepy Hollow*, has itself now passed into literary and celluloid legend. Although he never actually lived here, this seven-block strip bears his name and a bust of Irving, the first American writer to earn a living from his craft, stands in front of the turn-of-the-nineteenth-century Washington Irving High School.

Another celebrated author, Pulitzer Prize-winning short-story writer O. Henry, did in fact live along this stretch, at what was once no. 55, and there's also the landmark *Pete's Tavern* (18th St and Irving Place) – one of New York's oldest bars, in business since 1864. The bar promotes itself as the place where O. Henry dreamed up and wrote *The Gift of the Magi* and, although that fact is in dispute, the legend serves the place and its atmosphere well.

The stretch of **Broadway** north and west of here was part of "Ladies' Mile," a line of fancy stores and boutiques whose heyday was the mid-nineteenth century. High-end shopping jumped over to Fifth Avenue around the turn of the century, but a few sculpted facades and curvy lintels remain, including Lord & Taylor's Victorian wedding cake of a building with several exterior balcony levels, standing diagonally opposite at 901 Broadway. Nearby at 28 E 20th St is **Theodore Roosevelt's birthplace** (Wed–Sun 9am–5pm; $2; ⓣ212/260-1616), or at least a reconstruction of it. In 1923, the house was rebuilt as it would have been when Roosevelt was born there in 1858. The rather somber mansion contains many original furnishings, some of Teddy's hunting trophies and a small gallery documenting the president's life, viewable on an obligatory guided tour.

Gramercy Park

Once you've left the click of high heels and the swish of power suits behind on Park Avenue South, Manhattan's clutter suddenly breaks into the ordered open space of **Gramercy Park**. This former swamp between 21st and 22nd streets divides Irving Place and Lexington Avenue and is one of the city's prettiest squares. Its center is beautifully planted and, most noticeably, completely empty for much of the day – principally because it is the city's last private park and the only people who can gain access are those rich or fortunate enough to live here. Famous past key holders have included Mark Twain, Julia Roberts and Winona Ryder, never mind all those Kennedys and Roosevelts. Despite its exclusivity, though, it's well worth a stroll around the edge to catch a feeling of an area that was once the center of New York's theater scene. Inside the gates is a statue of the actor Edwin Booth (brother of Lincoln's assassin, John Wilkes Booth) in the guise of Hamlet, one of his most famous roles. (Ironically, Edwin rescued Lincoln's son, Robert, from a train accident years before John's fatal action.) In 1888, Booth turned his parkside home – 16 Gramercy Park S – into **The Players**, a private club with additions by architect (and Gramercy Park resident) Stanford White. Back then, actors and theater types were not accepted into regular society, so Booth created the club for play and socializing – neglecting, however, to admit women, who were only allowed in at the shockingly late date of 1989. At the same time, Booth established a Theater Library in the club to chronicle the history of the American stage. Later members included the Barrymores, Irving Berlin, Frank Sinatra, and (oddly) Sir Winston Churchill. These days it seems to be the club that is trying to keep regular society out – rather than vice versa – and you can see the inside of this beautiful place only by making an appointment for a group tour (minimum 10 guests) in advance ($5, $3.50 students and seniors; ⓣ212/228-7610).

Next door to The Players is the equally patrician **National Arts Club**, which moved in 1906 to this location, Victorianized in the 1870s by Central Park co-designer Calvert Vaux at the request of owner Governor Samuel

Tilden, and studded with terra-cotta busts of Shakespeare, Milton and Franklin, among others. Collectors Henry Frick, J.P. Morgan and Teddy Roosevelt were prominent members of this institution, which was founded to support American artists at home. Unfortunately, the priceless members' dining room, with its vaulted glass dome and stained-glass window panels, is off-limits to the public, but rotating exhibitions can be viewed. The club also hosts a year-round program of lunch-hour theater called Food for Thought, featuring one-act plays by writers as diverse as Anton Chekhov and Tony Kushner, executed by an alternating repertory of guest stars and supplemented by a light lunch. The program, which often feels more like an exclusive salon, is often performed by important theatrical types, making advance booking highly recommended (Mon–Thurs 1–2pm; $29, $27 students; ⓣ212/362-2560).

Have a walk around the square to get a look at the many early-nineteenth-century townhouses and later buildings which housed celebrated figures too numerous to mention here. The **School of Visual Arts**, 17 Gramercy Park S, occupies the former home of Joseph Pulitzer; while at the northeast corner of the square, no. 38, is the mock Tudor building in which John Steinbeck, then a struggling reporter for the now-defunct *New York World*, lived from 1925 to 1926 (it took getting fired from that job to plunge him into fiction). At 52 Gramercy Park N, the starting point of Lexington Avenue, is the imposing 1920s bulk of the old-fashioned **Gramercy Park Hotel** (see "Accommodation," p.292), whose early elite residents included Mary McCarthy, a very young John F. Kennedy and Humphrey Bogart with first wife, Mayo Methot. Lining Gramercy Park West is a splendid row of brick Greek Revival townhouses from the 1840s with ornate wrought-iron work; James Harper, of the publishing house Harper & Row, lived at no. 4.

East of Gramercy Park

Perhaps the city's most successful examples of densely packed urban housing, **Peter Cooper Village** and **Stuyvesant Town**'s tall, angled apartment buildings are aligned by peaceful, tree-lined walkways. This is private not public housing, and the owners, Metropolitan Life, were accused of discriminating against non-whites when the projects first opened around 1947 for returning soldiers from World War II. Certainly, the contrast with the immigrant slums a little way downtown isn't hard to detect. At the northeast corner of Peter Cooper Village, at E 23rd Street and Avenue A, stands the Asser Levy Recreation Center, named after the country's first Jewish citizen and kosher butcher, who arrived in America in 1654. The most notable of the many city-run athletic centers, the Asser Levy building was originally constructed in 1908 as a bathhouse – modeled on the Roman public baths – for the huddled, unwashed masses (the tenements of the East Side supposedly had but one bath for every 79 families). Abandoned in the 1970s, it was reopened as a city gym in 1990; the indoor sky-lit pool is anchored by a marble dolphin statue that doubles as a fountain. As with all city gyms, membership costs $25 a year (see p.442).

The land that makes up **Stuyvesant Square**, bisected by Second Avenue between 15th and 17th streets, was a gift to the city from Peter Stuyvesant, the last governor of New Netherland. As with Gramercy Park, the park later landscaped in the middle of the square was modeled on the squares of London's Bloomsbury. Though partially framed by the buildings of Beth Israel Medical Center and cut down the middle by the bustle of Second Avenue, it still retains something of its secluded quality, especially on the western side. Here there's a smatter of elegant terraces and the Friends' Meeting House, whose austere Greek Revivalist structure contrasts with the weighty Romanesque brownstone of St George's Episcopal Church next door. Built on old farmland donated by the Stuyvesants in 1846, the church is best known as the place where financier J.P. Morgan worshiped and today houses not only a playground but also an antique furniture and thrift store in the basement.

Madison Square, the Flatiron and Met Life buildings

Northwest of Gramercy Park, where Broadway and Fifth Avenue meet, lies Madison Square. Though a maelstrom of cars and cabs, buses and dodging pedestrians, because of the stateliness of its buildings and the park-space in the middle, it possesses a grandiosity and neat seclusion that Union Square has long since lost. The lofty, elegant and decidedly anorexic **Flatiron Building** (originally the Fuller Construction Company, later renamed in honor of its distinctive shape), set on a triangular plot of land on the square's southern side, is one of the city's most famous buildings, evoking images of Edwardian New York. Its uncommonly thin, tapered structure creates unusual wind currents at ground level, and years ago policemen were posted to prevent men gathering to watch the wind raise the skirts of women passing on 23rd Street. The cry they gave to warn off voyeurs – "23 Skidoo!" – has passed into the language. It's hard to believe that this was the city's first true skyscraper (although this is hotly debated), hung on a steel frame in 1902 with its full twenty stories dwarfing all the other structures around. Not for long though: the **Metropolitan Life Company** soon erected its clock tower, in 1902, on the eastern side of the square which, at least in terms of height, put the Flatiron Building to shame.

Next door to the Metropolitan Life Building is the Corinthian-columned marble facade of the **Appellate Division** of the New York State Supreme Court, resolutely righteous with its statues of Justice, Wisdom and Peace turning their weary backs on the ugly, black-glass New York Life Annex behind. The grand structure behind that, the **New York Life Building** proper, was the work of Cass Gilbert, creator of the Woolworth Building downtown. It went up in 1928 on the site of the original Madison Square Garden, renowned scene of drunken and debauched revels of high and Broadway society and former heart of the theater district.

Madison Square Garden has moved twice since then, first to a site on Eighth Avenue and 50th Street, finally to its present location in a hideous drum-shaped eyesore on the corner of 32nd Street and Seventh Avenue (see p. 000). There is, however, one reminder of the time when this was New York's theaterland: the **Church of the Transfiguration** just off Fifth Avenue on East 29th Street (chapel open daily 8am–6pm). Built in 1849, this dinky rusticated church set back from the street, brown brick and topped with copper roofs, has long been a traditional place of worship for showbiz people and other such outcasts. Its first rector, Rev George Hendric Houghton, served for 49 years, during which time he maintained a breadline for the unemployed and sheltered escaped slaves during the draft riots of the Civil War. It was not until 1870, though, that members of the theater profession began to come. That year, the place was tagged with the name "The Little Church Around the Corner" after a devout priest from a rather more stuffy church nearby had refused to officiate at the funeral of an actor named George Holland, but sent his friends

The murder of Stanford White

Madison Square Garden was the site where one of its architects, Stanford White, was murdered by Harry Thaw. A partner in the illustrious architectural team of McKim, Mead and White, which designed many of the city's great Beaux-Arts buildings, such as the General Post Office, the old Penn Station and Columbia University, White was something of a rake by all accounts. His former romance with Thaw's future wife Evelyn Nesbit, a Broadway showgirl (who was still unattached at the time), had been well publicized – even to the extent that the naked statue of the goddess Diana on the top of the building was said to have been modeled on her. Millionaire Thaw was so infuriated by this, that one night in 1906 he burst into the roof garden of White's tower apartment in Madison Square Garden, found the architect surrounded as usual by doting women and admirers, and shot him through the head. Thaw was carted away to spend most of his life in mental institutions, and his wife's show business career took a tumble: she resorted to drugs and prostitution, dying in 1966 in Los Angeles.

here instead. Since then, the church has been a haven for actors, and there is even an Episcopal Actors' Guild, the members of which perform regular poetry readings and the like in the Guild Hall (call ⓣ212/685–2342 for program information). The chapel itself is an intimate wee building set in a gloriously leafy garden, providing comfort and solace away from the rapidly ascendant skyscrapers on Fifth Avenue. Its interior is furnished throughout in warm wood, soft candlelight, and the figures of famous actors (most notably Edwin Booth as Hamlet) memorialized in the stained glass.

North of Madison Square

Lexington Avenue, which begins its long journey north at Gramercy Park, heads uptown, past the lumbering **69th Regiment Armory** at 25th Street. The site of the famous Armory Show of 1913, which brought modern art to New York (see "Twentieth-century American art" in Contexts), it is now a venue for antiques shows and art fairs. One of Manhattan's most condensed ethnic enclaves, **Little India**, aligns Lexington Avenue, between 27th and 30th streets – blink, and you might miss it altogether. Most of New York's 175,000 Indians live in Queens, yet there's still a sizeable handful of restaurants and fast-food places – slightly outnumbered by those down on East 6th Street – and a pocket of sweet and spice shops.

13

The Empire State Building and Murray Hill

Straggling east from Fifth Avenue down 34th Street lies **Murray Hill**, a tenuously tagged residential area of statuesque canopy-fronted apartment buildings, but with little apart from its WASPish anonymity – and the presence of the **Empire State Building** and the **Morgan Library** – to mark it out from the rest of midtown Manhattan. Built on one of the few remaining actual hills in the lower part of Manhattan island, Murray Hill is residential by design – no commercial building was allowed until the 1920s, when greedy real estate interests successfully challenged the rule in court. It lacks any real center, sense of community and, unless you work, live or are staying in Murray Hill, there's little reason to go there at all; indeed, you're more likely to pass through without even realizing it. Its boundaries are indistinct, but lie somewhere between Fifth and Third avenues and, very roughly, 32nd to 40th streets, where begins the rather brasher commercialism of midtown.

The Empire State Building

With the destruction of the World Trade Center, the **Empire State Building** is again the city's tallest skyscraper. The building occupies what has always been a prime site in this neighborhood of lavish department stores: nearby, filling the space between 38th and 39th streets, is the extravagant headquarters of Lord & Taylor (see p.405), and Macy's is just a short stroll away on Herald Square. Before it appeared, this was home to the first Waldorf Astoria Hotel, built by William Waldorf Astor to convince his formidable aunt, Caroline Schermerhorn, into moving uptown. The hotel opened in 1893 and immediately became a focus for the city's rich –"Meet me at the Waldorf" was the catchphrase *du jour*. Though the reputation of the Waldorf – at least for its prices – endures to this day, it didn't remain in its initial premises for very long, moving in 1929 to its current Art Deco home on Park Avenue.

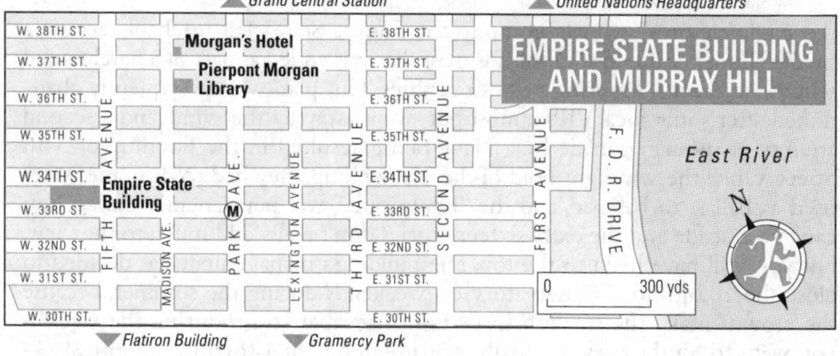

Since its completion in 1931, the Empire State Building has easily remained the most potent and evocative symbol of New York, despite being surpassed in height by the former Twin Towers (see p.64). John Jacob Raskob, a Wall Street visionary, and his partner Alfred E. Smith, a former governor, began compiling funds just three weeks before the stock market crash in October 1929, but despite the Depression, the building proceeded full steam ahead and came in well under budget after just fourteen months of construction. Soon after, King Kong clung to it and distressed squealing damsels while grabbing at passing planes; in 1945, a plane negotiating its way through heavy fog crashed into the building's 79th story, killing thirteen people; while in 1979, two Englishmen parachuted from its summit to the ground, only to be carted off by the NY Police Department for disturbing the peace. The darkest moment in the building's history came in February 1997, when a man opened fire on the observation deck, killing one tourist and injuring seven others; as a result there is tighter security upon entrance, with metal detectors, package scanners and the like. This vigilance has only been tightened after September 11th, 2001.

Its 103 stories and 1454 feet – toe to TV mast – rank the Empire State Building behind only the Sears Tower in Chicago and the Petronas Towers in Kuala Lumpur, Malaysia, but its height is deceptive, rising in stately tiers with steady panache. Standing on Fifth Avenue below, it's easy to walk right by without even realizing that it's there; only the crowds serve as an indicator of what stretches above. Inside, its basement serves as an underground marbled shopping mall, lined with newsstands, beauty parlors, cafés, even a post office, and is finished everywhere with delicate Art Deco touches. Shopping, though, is not what most people are here for, and also worth missing is the **New York Skyride** on the second floor. The eight-minute simulated flight (daily 10am–10pm; $13.50, $10.50 kids and seniors; Ⓣ212/299-4922 or Ⓣ1-888/SKY-RIDE, Ⓦwww.skyride.com) soars above the skyscrapers, through Times Square, down Coney Island's Cyclone, and among other New York landmarks, but will leave the weak-hearted merely dizzy and the strong-willed wondering why they spent their money on this.

Getting to the top

The first elevators take you to the 86th floor, summit of the building before the radio and TV mast was added. The views from the outside walkways here are as stunning as you'd expect; on a clear day visibility is up to eighty miles, but, given the city's pollution, on most it's more likely to be between ten and twenty. If you're feeling brave, and can stand the wait for the tight squeeze into the single elevator, you can go up to the Empire State's last reachable zenith, a small cylinder at the foot of the TV mast that was added as part of a harebrained scheme to erect a mooring post for airships. This plan was subsequently abandoned after some local VIPs almost got swept away by the wind, and a second attempt at mooring, made by a Navy blimp, resulted in the flooding of 34th Street. Once the wind got hold of the Navy blimp, they had to drop the water used as ballast to balance, and the "blimp port" was permanently closed. You can't go outside and the extra sixteen stories don't really add much to the view, but you will have been to the top. The building's management has decided to close the 102nd floor Observatory on weekends during the summer, because the crowds make the smallish space unmanageable, so go during the week if you want to hit the very top (daily 9.30am–midnight, last trip 11.30pm; $9, $4 for under 12s, $7 for seniors, free for children under 5; combined tickets for New York Skyride and the Observatory $17, $10 for under 12s; ⓣ212/736-3100, ⓦwww.esbnyc.com).

Murray Hill and the Morgan Library

When Madison Avenue was on a par with Fifth as the place to live, **Murray Hill** came to be dominated by the Morgan family, the crusty old financier J.P. and his offspring, who at one time owned a clutch of property here. Morgan Junior lived in the brownstone on the corner of 37th Street and Madison (now headquarters of the American Lutheran Church), his father in a house that was later pulled down to make way for an extension to his library at no. 36 next door, the mock but tastefully simple Roman villa that still stands and is commonly mistaken for the old man's house. In fact, Morgan would simply come here to luxuriate among the art treasures he had bought up wholesale on his trips to Europe: manuscripts, paintings, prints and furniture. Here, during a crisis of confidence in the city's banking system in 1907, he entertained New York's richest and most influential men night after night until they agreed to put up the money to save what could have been the entire country from bankruptcy. Morgan gave up $30 million himself as an act of good faith. Visitors to the **Morgan Library**, 29 E 36th St (Tues–Thurs 10.30am–5pm, Fri 10.30am–8pm, Sat 10.30am–6pm, Sun noon–6pm; suggested donation $8, $6 students and seniors, under 12 free; ⓣ212/685-0610, ⓦwww.morganlibrary.org), will be richly rewarded. Its splendid interior and priceless collection of nearly 10,000 drawings and prints, including works by Da Vinci, Degas and Dürer, make it one of the city's finest small museums. A garden café, serving light fare, coffees and Sunday brunch, makes the library a truly grand place to while away a lazy afternoon.

Exploring the library

The focal points of the museum are the two **Historic Rooms** located off a corridor often lined with some excellent prints by Rembrandt. The **West Room** served as the great man's study, and has been left much as it was when he worked here. Particularly of note is a carved sixteenth-century Italian ceiling and, in a more contemporary vein, a desk custom-carved to a design by Charles McKim of the firm McKim, Mead and White, the architects of this palace. A domed and pillared hallway leads through to the library proper, or the

East Room, a sumptuous three-tiered cocoon of rare books, autographed musical manuscripts and various trinkets culled from Morgan's European travels, all exuding that glorious, musty, old-book smell that evokes past opulence.

The exhibits change so frequently that it's impossible to catalogue what visitors will see – but a copy of the 1455 Gutenberg Bible (the museum owns a magnificent three out of the eleven surviving manuscripts) is always on display. Other works from the permanent collection, displayed on a rotating basis, include the world's largest collection of original scores by Mahler, as well as those of Beethoven, Schubert, and Gilbert and Sullivan; the only complete copy of Thomas Malory's *Morte d'Arthur*; letters from the likes of Vasari, Mozart and George Washington, and the literary manuscripts of Dickens, Jane Austen and Thoreau.

The rest of Murray Hill

Most of the rest of the neighborhood is fairly nondescript, and nowhere that's especially worth wandering, either day or night. Perhaps the most worthwhile idea is to continue north up Madison Avenue, where the influence of the Morgans rears its head again in the shape (or at least the name) of *Morgan's Hotel* between 37th and 38th streets – the last word in ostentatious discretion, not even bothering to proclaim its presence with the vulgarity of a sign. Stop in at its elegant bar for a drink if you've got the cash, and for details on how much it costs to sleep here, see p.292.

14

42nd Street

Home to some of the city's most distinctive buildings, from great Beaux-Arts palaces like the New York Public Library to credit-card traps like the *Grand Hyatt Hotel*, **42nd Street** offers the visitor just about anything, highbrow or low. Lined with superb architecture while providing breathtaking views northward up the great avenues, this legendary street, one of the few boulevards in the world to have a musical named after it, is a marvel in itself and an access route to many of the city's wonders. Indeed, 42nd Street often forms the first impressions of New York for visitors arriving at majestic **Grand Central Station** or relatively seedy Port Authority Bus Terminal (see p.19). Most of what you'll want to see sightwise occurs from the Public Library on the east; to the west are somewhat grungier blocks, running into the borders of Times Square and the Garment District.

The New York Public Library

The New York Public Library – Center for the Humanities (Mon & Thurs–Sat 10am–6pm, Wed 11am–7.30pm; ⓣ212/870-1630, ⓦwww.nypl.org), on the corner of 42nd Street and Fifth Avenue, is the first notable building on 42nd Street's eastern reaches. Beaux Arts in style and faced with white marble, it is the headquarters of what is the largest branch public library system in the world. Its steps, framed by two majestic reclining lions, the symbols of the NYPL, are a meeting point and general hangout for pockets of people throughout the year. To explore the library, either walk around yourself or take one of the tours, which last an hour and give a good all-round picture of the building. The traditional highlight of such a tour, also accessible by just poking around by yourself, is the large coffered Reading Room on the third floor. Leon Trotsky worked here on and off during his brief sojourn in New York just prior to the 1917 Russian Revolution, introduced to the place by his

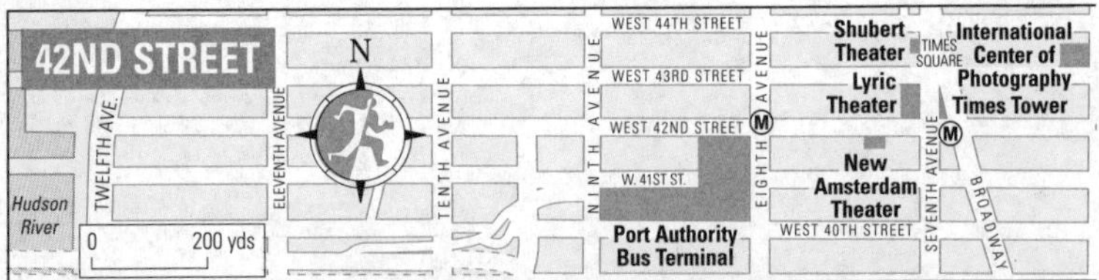

Bolshevik comrade Nikolai Bukharin, who was bowled over by a library you could then use so late in the evening. The opening times are considerably less impressive now, but the library still contains the largest research library with a circulating system in the world. Its 88 miles of books are stored on eight levels of stacks beneath the reading room and running the length of Bryant Park (behind the library), which alone covers half an acre. The library also features impressive displays that run the gamut from Charles Addams cartoons to the original toys belonging to Christopher Robin Milne, on which his father based the Winnie the Pooh stories.

Bryant Park

The restoration of **Bryant Park**, on Sixth between 40th and 42nd streets, is one of the new 42nd Street's resounding success stories: until 1992 a seedy spot, it is now a beautiful, grassy, square block filled with slender trees, flower beds and inviting green chairs (the fact that they aren't chained to the ground is proof enough of revitalization). Forming the backyard of the New York Public Library on Fifth Avenue, Bryant Park is, like Greeley Square to its south, named after a newspaper editor – William Cullen Bryant of the *New York Post*, also famed as a poet and instigator of Central Park. Bryant Park has a rich history – it was the site of the first American World's Fair in 1853, with a Crystal Palace, modeled on the famed London Crystal Palace, on its grounds. Sitting here in the warmer months, you can imagine yourself in Paris's Jardins de Luxembourg, while the corporate lunch crowd is just grateful for a pleasant place to eat.

Grab an espresso or even a quick meal at one of the park's small, reasonably priced eateries – *Pasta to Go* and *Focaccia Fiorentina*. There's also a rather aggressive singles' scene at the outdoor *Bryant Park Cafe* (which becomes the indoor *Bryant Park Grill* for the remaining seasons). Summertime brings a lively scene to the park – free jazz and various performers throughout the week, and free outdoor movies on Monday evenings. Games, lectures and rallies also take place in the park, and you can even rent a portion of it for your own event. (Call ⓣ212/768-4242 or visit the park's website at ⓦwww.bryantpark.org.)

Just across from the park at 40 W 40th St is the recently opened *Bryant Park Hotel*, a swanky, boutique getaway for people wanting to be near the action but out of the limelight of Times Square. Designed by Raymond Hood for the American Radiator Company and constructed in 1924, the building claims attention for its Gothic tower, polished black granite facade and gold terracotta detail. Georgia O'Keeffe's painting *Radiator Building – Night, New York* captured its somber beauty. To the north of the park, the **Grace Building**

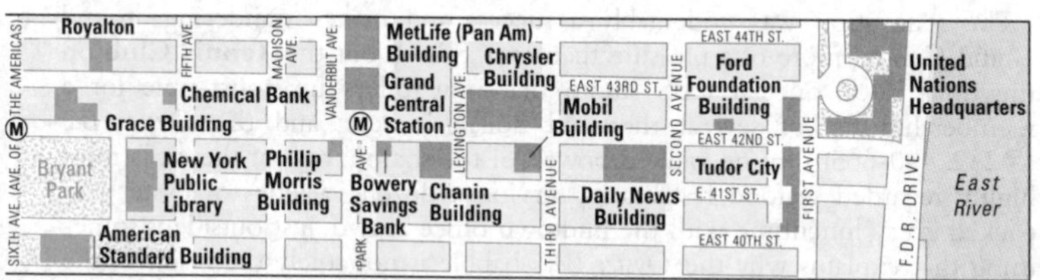

swoops down on 42nd Street, breaking the rules by stepping out of line with its neighbors.

Grand Central Station

Returning east to the library, push through the crush crossing Fifth Avenue and walk east on 42nd Street to where Park Avenue lifts off the ground at Pershing Square to weave its way around the solid bulk of **Grand Central Station**. This, for its day, was a masterly piece of urban planning. After the electrification of the railways made it possible to reroute trains underground, the rail lines behind the existing station were sold off to developers and the profits went toward the building of a new terminal – constructed in 1913 around a basic iron frame but clothed with a Beaux-Arts skin. Since then Grand Central has taken on an almost mythical significance. Although, today, its major traffic consists mainly of commuters speeding out no farther than Connecticut or Westchester County, Grand Central remains in essence what it was in the nineteenth century – a symbolic gateway to an undiscovered continent.

You can explore Grand Central on your own or take an excellent **free tour** run by the Municipal Arts Society (see p.30). But for the efforts of a few dedicated New Yorkers (including the late Jacqueline Onassis, whose voice was no doubt a godsend), Grand Central wouldn't be here at all, or at least it wouldn't be in such good shape. It was deemed a National Landmark only in 1978, after Grand Central's owners', the Penn Central Railroad, plan to cap the whole thing with an office building was quashed. The most spectacular aspect of the building is its size, though it is now dwarfed by the Met Life Building (formerly known as the Pan Am building, headquarters of the now-defunct airline). The station's main concourse is one of the world's finest and most imposing open spaces, 470 feet long and 150 feet high. The **barrel-vaulted ceiling** is speckled like a Baroque church with a painted representation of the winter night sky, its 2500 stars shown back to front – "as God would have seen them," the painter reputedly remarked. Stand in the middle and you realize that Grand Central represents a time when stations were seen as "a city within a city," as this edifice has been called. Walking around the resounding marble corridors is an elegant experience.

In 1995, the Metropolitan Transit Association (MTA) embarked on a massive renovation of Grand Central, cleaning the ceiling and restoring faded treasures such as the massive chandeliers. The plans were not without commercial thrust – they included four new restaurants overlooking the main concourse – but the terminal's more esoteric reaches remain (thankfully) intact, and the main concourse has even been improved with the addition of a second sweeping staircase to counterbalance the first (both staircases were in the original plans but only one was built because of a lack of funds).

The renovation was undeniably a success and makes wandering around Grand Central more of a pleasure than ever. Search out the **Tennis Club** on the third floor, once a CBS studio that now offers up court-time for a membership fee of several thousand dollars a year; and the *Oyster Bar* (Ⓣ212/490-6650) in the vaulted bowels of the station, one of the city's most highly regarded seafood restaurants, serving a dozen varieties of oyster and packed every lunchtime with the midtown office crowd. Just outside is something that explains why the *Oyster Bar*'s babble is not solely the result of the big-mouthed business people who eat there: you can stand on opposite sides of any of the vaulted spaces and hold a conversation just by whispering, an acoustic fluke that makes this the loudest eatery in town.

The Chrysler Building and around

Across 42nd Street, the former **Bowery Savings Bank**, now *Cipriani's 42nd Street*, echoes Grand Central's grandeur. Like its sister branch downtown, it extravagantly lauds the virtues of sound investment and savings. The Roman-style basilica has a floor paved with mosaics; the columns are each fashioned from a different kind of marble and, if you look at the elevator doors (through a door on the right), you'll see bronze bas-reliefs of bank employees hard at various tasks. This kind of lavish expenditure is typical of the buildings on this stretch of 42nd Street, which is full of lobbies worth popping inside for a glimpse. Start with the **Philip Morris Building**, at 120 Park Ave right across from Grand Central, which contains a small offshoot of the Whitney Museum of American Art. Situated in the atrium of the Philip Morris Building, the **Whitney at Philip Morris**, a Whitney Museum satellite, has two sections: a small **Picture Gallery** (Mon–Fri 11am–6pm, Thurs 11am–7.30pm; free) with commissioned site-specific works by mid-career or emerging artists, on just about any modern theme that you can think of; and a **Sculpture Court** (Mon–Sat 7.30am–9.30pm, Sun 11am–7pm; free). About six times a year, contemporary performances (anything from string quartets to dance recitals) are held here, too.

The Grand Hyatt Hotel, further east on the north side of 42nd Street, is another notable instance of excess, perhaps the best example in the city, of all that is truly vulgar about contemporary American interior design. The slushing waterfalls, lurking palms and gliding escalators represent plush-carpeted bad taste at its most meretricious.

The Chrysler Building, across Lexington Avenue, is a different story, dating from a time (1930, though renovated in 2000 by Philip Johnson) when architects carried off prestige with grace and style. This was for a fleeting moment the world's tallest building – until it was surpassed by the Empire State Building in 1931 – and, since the rediscovery of Art Deco, has become easily Manhattan's best loved. Its car-motif friezes, a spire resembling a car radiator grill, and hood-ornament gargoyles jutting from the setbacks and almost completely made of stainless steel all link this amazing building with the golden age of motoring and bring the Manhattan skyline as close as it comes to Fritz Lang's 1926 futuristic thriller, *Metropolis*. Its designer, William Van Alen, indulged in a feud with an erstwhile partner, H. Craig Severance, who was designing a building at 40 Wall St at the same time. Each was determined to have the higher skyscraper: Van Alen secretly built the stainless steel spire inside the Chrysler's crown; when 40 Wall Street was finally topped out a few feet higher than the Chrysler, Van Alen popped the 185-foot spire out through the top of the building, and won the day. But Van Alen was hardly rewarded for his achievement as Walter Chrysler accused him of taking bribes from contractors and refused to pay him. While he could get over not being paid, he never recovered from the slur and practiced architecture for the rest of his life in obscurity.

The Chrysler Corporation moved out some time ago, and for a while the building was allowed to decline by a company that didn't wholly appreciate its spirit. But the current owner has pledged to keep it lovingly intact. The lobby, once a car showroom, is for the moment all you can see (there's no observation deck), but that's enough in itself, with opulently inlaid elevators, walls covered in African marble and on the ceiling a realistic, if rather faded, study of work and endeavor, showing airplanes, machines and brawny builders who worked on the tower.

Beyond the Chrysler Building

Two more buildings worthy of study flank each side of Lexington Avenue on the south side of 42nd Street. The **Chanin Building**, 122 E 42nd St, on the right, is another Art Deco monument, cut with terra-cotta carvings of leaves, tendrils and sea creatures. More interestingly is the design on the outside of the weighty **Mobil Building** across the street. Built in 1956, it was the largest metal-clad office building in the world at the time.

The stone facade of the somber yet elegant former **Daily News Building**, 20 E 42nd St – with a backlit mural over the entrance – fronts a surprising Deco interior. The interior was bastardized somewhat in the 1950s: white marble replaced the original golden marble, an annex was added to the building and stainless steel elevator doors replaced the original bronze ones. The most impressive remnant of the original 1923 decor is a large globe encased in a lighted circular frame (with updated geography), made famous by Superman, in which the Daily News Building appropriately housed the Daily Planet. Various bronze meteorological devices, displayed on the walls, were once connected to a weather station on the roof. The marble floor is inlaid with intersecting bronze lines that detail the distances between New York and other major cities. The tabloid paper after which the building is named has moved to West 33rd Street. Note that the building is not open on weekends.

On the left (north side), between Second and First avenues, is one of the city's most peaceful (if surreal) spaces of all – the **Ford Foundation Building**, 320 E 43rd St. Built in 1967, the building was the first of the atriums that are now commonplace across Manhattan and certainly the most lush. Structurally, it's a giant greenhouse, gracefully supported by soaring granite columns and edged with two walls of offices visible through the windows. Workers, in turn, can look down on the subtropical garden, which changes naturally with the seasons. This was one of the first attempts to create a "natural" environment, and it's astonishingly quiet. Forty-second Street is no more than a murmur outside, and all you can hear is the burble of water, the echo of voices and the clipped crack of feet on the brick walkways, mingled with the ripe smell of the atrium's considerable vegetation. The indoor/outdoor experience here is one of New York City's great architectural coups.

At the east end of 42nd Street, steps lead up to the 1925 ensemble of **Tudor City**, which rises behind a tree-filled parklet. With its coats of arms, leaded glass and neat neighborhood shops, it is the very picture of self-contained residential respectability, and an official historic district. Trip down the steps from here and you're plum opposite the **United Nations** (see p.156).

15

Fifth Avenue

For the last two centuries, a **Fifth Avenue** address has signified social position, prosperity and respectability. Whether around its lower reaches on Washington Square or far uptown around the Harlem River, Fifth Avenue has been the home to Manhattan's finest mansions, hotels, churches and stores. Between 42nd and 59th streets, Fifth Avenue has always drawn crowds – particularly during Christmas, when department store windows are filled with elaborate displays – to gaze at what has become the automatic image of wealth and opulence, or to visit Rockefeller Center, Radio City Music Hall or the Museum of Modern Art. As though not content with its usual crush of pedestrians, Fifth Avenue is also home to most of the city's many parades and processions (see Chapter 38, "Parades and festivals," for more details).

42nd Street to Rockefeller Center

In its lower midtown reaches, Fifth Avenue isn't really as alluring as the streets to either side. The only eye-catcher is the **Chemical Bank** on the southwest corner of 43rd, an early glass 'n' gloss box that teasingly displays its vault (no longer used) to passersby, a reaction against the fortress palaces of earlier banks. Around the next corner, West 44th Street contains several old guard New York institutions. The Georgian-style **Harvard Club** (Ⓣ212/840-6600, Ⓦwww.hcny.com) at no. 27, easily identified in the evening by the paparazzi hanging around outside, has interiors so lavish that lesser mortals aren't allowed to enter (you must be a Harvard alumnus). The Harvard Club, built in 1894, was the first of several elite clubs such as the Yale Club, the Century Club and others that moved to the neighborhood. Over the years, the building has gone through a series of expansions to match a growing membership. Another is scheduled for completion in December 2002.

Down West 44th Street: the Royalton and Algonquin

The New York Yacht Club, at 37 W 44th St (Ⓣ212/382-1000, Ⓦwww.nyyc.org), chartered in 1844, is just down the block. In its current location since 1901, this playfully eccentric exterior of bay windows is molded as ships' sterns; waves and dolphins complete the effect of tipsy Beaux-Arts fun. For

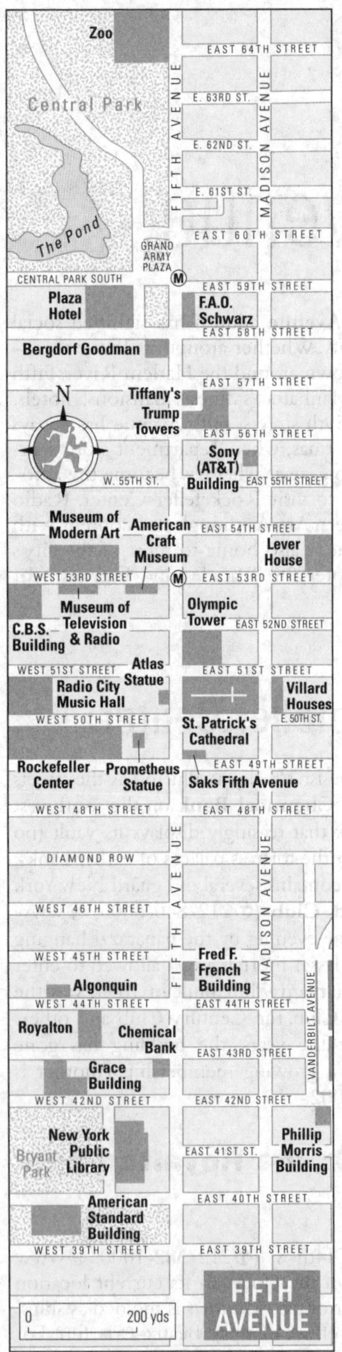

years this has been the home of the America's Cup, a yachting trophy first won by the schooner *America* in 1851.

"Dammit, it was the twenties and we had to be smarty." So said Dorothy Parker of the literary group known as the Round Table, whose members hung out at the **Algonquin Hotel** at 59 W 44th St (Ⓣ212/840-6800) and gave it a name as the place for literary visitors to New York – a name that to some extent still endures. The offices of the *New Yorker* magazine are around the corner. The Round Table, comprised of some the city's sharpest-tongued wits, lunched and drank here regularly. The group, which featured Dorothy Parker, Robert Benchley, Robert Sherwood and George S Kaufman, among others, had a reputation for being as egotistical as it was exclusive. Other regulars were Noel Coward (ask nicely and someone will point out his table), George Bernard Shaw, Irving Berlin and Boris Karloff. Times have changed considerably, but over the years the Algonquin has continued to attract a steady stream of famous guests, many with some kind of literary bent. The bar, the *Oak Room*, is one of the most civilized in town and hosts an acclaimed cabaret series.

Taking over from the Algonquin as the lunch and supper spot for the literary set since the 1990s is the **Royalton**, at 44 W 44th St (Ⓣ212/869-4400), one of many of the hotelier Ian Schrager's unique boutique hotels. Designed by Philippe Starck (their first collaboration), the lush, velvety style and Deco atmosphere bring the word "trendy" to new heights. Step into the nearly unmarked hotel for a peek at the elongated lobby cum lounge – keeping an eye out for Armani-clad doormen, whose snappy appearance belies the fact that behind the padded doors is a hotel, not a private club. This rectangular room is a great place to relax and drink with friends – or dine toward the rear. With the type of clientele this place attracts, you never know who might sit down next to you.

Heading north: the Dahesh Museum

West 47th Street, or **Diamond Row** (described on p.162), is another surprise off Fifth Avenue but, before hitting that, duck into the **Fred F. French Building** at 551 Fifth Ave. The colorfully tiled mosaics on its outside are a mere prelude to the combination of Art Deco and Near Eastern imagery ranged on the vaulted ceiling and bronze doors of the lobby. Also striking (and indicative of another era on Fifth) is the facade of what was once **Charles Scribner's Sons bookstore** at 597 Fifth Ave. The black-and-gold iron-and-glass storefront that seems to have fallen from an Edwardian engraving has been given historic landmark status. All the more anachronistic, then, that the building now houses a United Colors of Benetton store; the lone remnant of its literary history is a basement café-cum-salon that hosts frequent readings.

Before you duck into Rockefeller Plaza, there's the **Dahesh Museum of Art**, 601 Fifth Ave at 48th Street (Tues–Sat 11am–6pm; free; Ⓣ212/759-0606, Ⓦwww.daheshmuseum.org). The small museum features nineteenth- and early-twentieth-century European artwork collected by Dr. Dahesh, a Lebanese writer and philosopher passionate about European academic art. The Dahesh is the only American museum collecting academic art from this period. The history of academic art recounts the elevation of the artist from the status of a craftsperson or artisan, as in Medieval times, to that of a recognized creatively trained personality. The permanent collection contains more than 3000 works.

Rockefeller Center and around

Central to this stretch of Fifth is a complex of buildings that, more than any other in the city, succeeds in being utterly self-contained and at the same time in complete agreement with its surroundings. Built between 1932 and 1940 by John D. Rockefeller, Jr., son of the oil magnate, **Rockefeller Center** (Ⓣ212/332-6868, Ⓦwww.rockefellercenter.com) is one of the finest pieces of urban planning anywhere. Office space with cafés, a theater, underground concourses and rooftop gardens work together with an intelligence and grace rare in any building then or now. It was a combination that shows every other city-center shopping mall the way, leaving you thinking that Cyril Connolly's snide description – "that sinister Stonehenge of Economic Man" – was way off the mark.

You're lured into the center from Fifth Avenue down the gentle slope of the **Channel Gardens** (whimsically named because they divide La Maison Française and the British Empire Building) to the **GE Building** (formerly the RCA Building, but renamed when General Electric took it over), focus of the Center. Rising 850ft, its monumental lines match the scale of Manhattan itself, though softened by symmetrical setbacks to prevent an overpowering expanse of wall. At its foot the **Lower Plaza** holds a sunken restaurant in the summer months – a great place for afternoon cocktails – linked

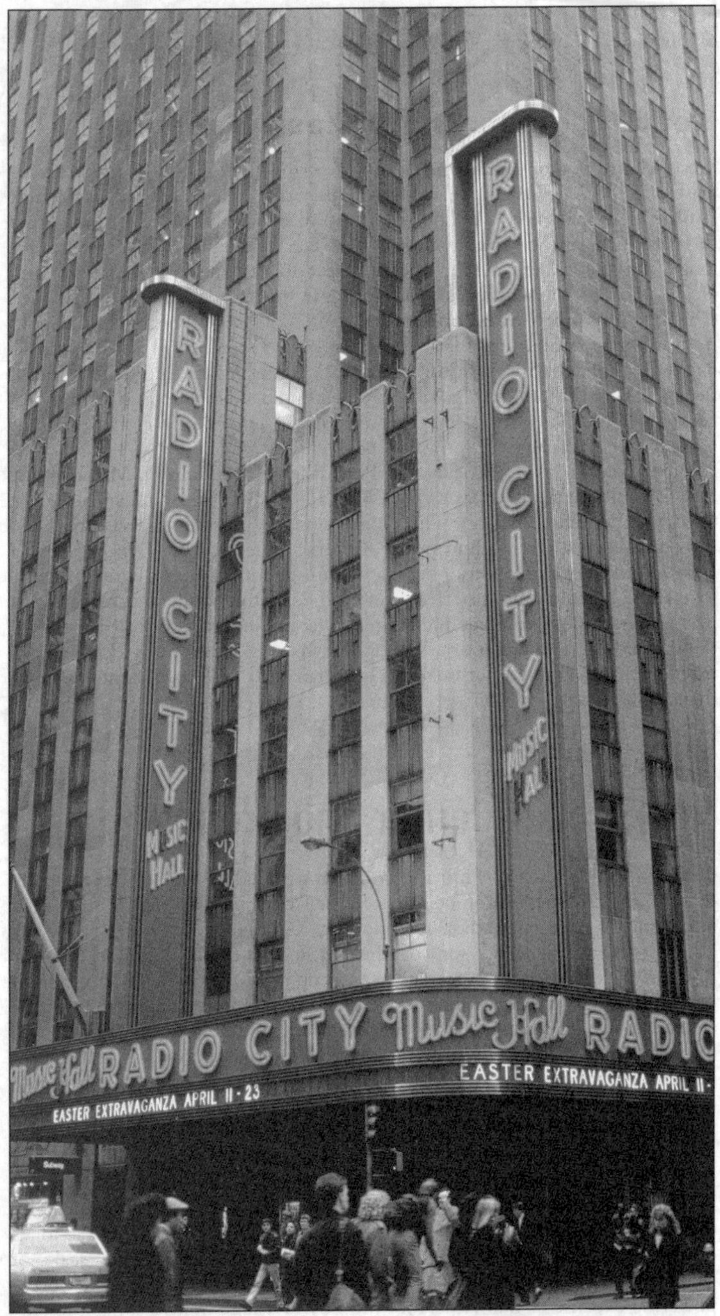

△ Radio City Music Hall is the last word in 1930s luxury

visually to the downward flow of the building by **Paul Manship**'s sparkling sculpture *Prometheus*. In winter this sunken area becomes an **ice rink**; skaters show off their skills to passing shoppers. Many events take place throughout the year at the plaza, Christmas being one of the biggest. Since 1931 a huge lighted tree has been on display, becoming over the years a New York tradition. The lighting of the tree, with accompanying musical entertainment, on a night in early December, draws throngs of locals and tourists in the city for the holidays.

Inside, the GE Building is no less impressive. In the lobby **José Maria Sert**'s murals, *American Progress* and *Time*, are faded but eagerly in tune with the 1930s Deco ambience – presumably more so than the original paintings by Diego Rivera, which were removed by John D.'s son Nelson Rockefeller when the artist refused to scrap a panel glorifying Lenin. A leaflet available from the lobby desk details a self-guided tour of the Center (also available online).

NBC Studios, one of the many office ensembles in the GE Building, is home for the network's long-established comedy show *Saturday Night Live*, as well as *Late Night with Conan O'Brien* and *The Rosie O'Donnell Show*. Get a backstage look at NBC's studios on the **NBC Experience Tour** (Mon–Sat 8.30am–5.30pm, Sun 9.30am–4.30pm; $17.50, seniors and children $15, under 6 not allowed on tour; ⓣ212/664-3700). Tours leave from The NBC Experience Store on 49th Street between Fifth and Sixth avenues. For an early-morning TV thrill, gawk at NBC's *Today Show*, which broadcasts live from 7am to 9am weekday mornings from glass-enclosed studios in the new NBC News Building on the southwest corner of 49th and Rockefeller Plaza. But come early if you plan to wave to mom, because space fills up fast. (During the summer the *Today Show* hosts concerts every Friday morning from the likes of Sting, Willie Nelson, Ricky Martin and many other popular performers.)

Radio City Music Hall

Just northwest of Rockefeller Center, at Sixth Avenue and 50th Street, is **Radio City Music Hall**, an Art Deco jewel box that represents the last word in 1930s luxury. The staircase is regally resplendent with the world's largest chandeliers, the Stuart Davis murals from the men's toilets are now in the Museum of Modern Art, and the huge auditorium looks like an extravagant scalloped shell or a vast sunset: "Art Deco's true shrine," as Paul Goldberger (former architecture critic of the *New York Times*) rightly called it. Believe it or not, Radio City was nearly demolished in 1970: the outcry this proposal caused resulted in its being designated a national landmark. To explore, take a tour (daily 10am–6pm; $15, under 12 $9; ⓣ212/631-4345, ⓦwww.radiocity.com) from the lobby. You will be ushered backstage, tour the private suite, get a glimpse of the costume room and meet one of the famous Rockettes.

North to the MoMA

Return to Fifth Avenue and you'll see another sumptuous Deco component of Rockefeller Center, the **International Building**, whose black marble and gold leaf give the lobby a sleek, classy feel dramatized by the ritziness of escalators and the view across **Lee Lawrie**'s bronze *Atlas* out to **St Patrick's Cathedral**. Designed by James Renwick and completed in 1888, St Patrick's sits bone-white amid the glitz like a misplaced bit of moral imperative, and seems the result of a painstaking academic tour of the Gothic cathedrals of Europe: perfect in detail, lifeless in spirit. A spirituality can be found, however, in the peaceful **Lady Chapel** at the back of the Cathedral; here the graceful, simple altar captures the mysticism that its big sister lacks. Nevertheless, St Patrick's is an essential part of the midtown landscape, a rich counterfoil to Rockefeller Center and one of the most important churches (perhaps the most important Catholic church) in America. In all, the Gothic details of the compound are striking and the Cathedral's twin towers are certainly a work of art – and made all the more so by the backing of the sunglass-black Olympic Tower. Across the street, at 611 Fifth Ave (the corner of 50th Street), are the striped awnings of **Saks Fifth Avenue**, one of the last of New York's premier department stores to relocate in midtown (from Herald Square). With its columns on the ground floor and yellow brick road-like pathways through fashion collections, Saks is every bit as glamorous as it was when it opened in 1922.

Museum of Television and Radio

If your body needs the kind of rejuvenation only an hour in front of a television can offer, visit the **Museum of Television & Radio**, at 25 W 52nd St between Fifth and Sixth avenues (Tues, Wed, Fri–Sun noon–6pm, Thurs noon–8pm; $6, students $4, under 13 $3; ⓣ212/621-6600, ⓦwww.mtr.org). In a building designed by Philip Johnson, the MTR preserves an archive of 100,000 mostly American TV shows, radio broadcasts and commercials. The museum's excellent computerized reference system allows you to research news, public affairs, documentaries, sporting events, comedies, advertisements and other aural and visual selections. To appease wary pop culture critics, the museum also conducts educational seminars and screenings in its four theaters. The MTR becomes unbearably crowded on weekends and holidays, so plan to visit at other times.

The 21 Club and the American Craft Museum

If you need some food and drink after a long afternoon in the museum, right next door, the place with all the colorful iron jockey statues in front. **The 21 Club**, at 21 W 52nd St (ⓣ212/582-2000), has been around since the early days of Prohibition. Founded by Jack Kriendler and Charlie Berns, the club quickly became one of the most exclusive establishments in town, a place where the young socialites of the Roaring Twenties could spend wild nights dancing the Charleston and enjoying wines and spirits of the finest quality. Although *21* was raided more than once, federal agents were never able to pin anything on Jack and Charlie. At the first sign of a raid, they would activate an ingenious system of pulleys and levers, which would sweep bottles from the bar shelves and hurl the smashed remains down a chute into the New York sewer system. Today this bar and restaurant still attracts New York's upper crust, and anybody who is anybody frequents *21*.

On the next block north, look for the **American Craft Museum**, at 40 W 53rd St (Tues–Sun 10am–6pm, Thurs 10am–8pm; $5, students $2.50; ⓣ212/956-3535, ⓦwww.americancraftmuseum.org), which consists of three floors of contemporary crafts presented by the American Craft Council. Changing exhibits cover a wide array of materials (from paper to porcelain to metal to glass) and styles, and are accompanied by lectures and workshops.

The Museum of Modern Art (MoMA)

Of the many museums and galleries along and near this stretch of Fifth Avenue, one ranks above all others as measured by its size, the reach of its ambition, and its influence in the world of art. This is the **Museum of Modern Art**, at 11 W 53rd St (Sat–Tues & Thurs 10.30am–6pm, Fri 10.30am–8.30pm; $9.50, students $6.50, Fri 4.30–8.15pm pay what you wish; recorded audio tour $4; ⓣ212/708-9480, ⓦwww.moma.org).

Founded in 1929 by three wealthy women, including Abby Aldrich Rockefeller (the wife of John D., Jr.), as the very first museum dedicated entirely to modern art, the Museum of Modern Art moved to its present home ten years later. Philip Johnson designed expansions in the Fifties and Sixties, and in the mid-1980s Cesar Pelli designed a steel pipe and glass renovation that doubled its gallery space. MoMA, as it is affectionately called, offers the finest and most complete account of late nineteenth- and twentieth-century art you're likely to find, with a permanent collection of more than 100,000 paintings, sculptures, drawings, prints, photographs, architectural models and design objects, as well as a world-class film archive.

Yet another renovation is in the works, and the current is to be demolished in the summer of 2002 and rebuilt by summer 2005, the museum's 75th anniversary. After a bitterly contested, multi-year design competition that involved many of the world's top architects, the design contract was awarded to Yoshio Taniguchi, architect of several prominent museum buildings in Japan, including a wing of the Tokyo National Museum. Plans call for creating new galleries and updating existing space – expanding the central sculpture garden, restoring the famous Bauhaus staircase in the main building, building a research and education facility and adding a building connected to the Pelli Museum Tower, among other things. The expansion will allow MoMA to display more of its permanent collection, as well as mount even larger temporary exhibits.

As this book goes to press, the sculpture garden and several galleries are already closed. But during the reconstruction, the museum will move to Long Island City in the borough of Queens. This temporary space is referred to as **MoMAQNS**, 45-20 33rd St at Queens Blvd, subway #7 to 33rd St stop (ⓣ212/708-9400), and it's in a reinvention of the Swingline Factory. Along with the permanent collection, most of which will be moved to this location, there will be special Picasso and Matisse exhibits. Call ahead for the schedule.

Because all of the galleries will be continuously reshuffled for several years, it is impossible to predict what will be on display, much less where. Instead, here are some highlights of each of the three major sections of the permanent collection (early-modern painting and sculpture, late-modern and contemporary painting and sculpture, and architecture and design) and two minor sections: photography and film.

Early-modern painting and sculpture

This collection includes an impressive array of **Post-Impressionist** masterworks such as **Cézanne**'s *Bather* (1885) and paintings by **Gauguin**, **Seurat** and **Van Gogh**, including *Starry Night*, not to mention **Monet**'s *Water Lilies*. These are enormous, stirring attempts to abstract color and form, and their swirling jades, pinks and purples create the feeling of sitting in a giant aquarium.

Cubism is represented by **Picasso, Derain** and **Braque**, among others. Most notable is Picasso's *Demoiselles d'Avignon* (1907), a jagged, sharp and, for its time, revolutionary clash of tones and planes that some hold to be the embodiment of Cubist principles. Picasso's later works include the *Charnel House*, which, like *Guernica*, is an angry protest against the horrors of war.

There are paintings by **Chagall** and **Mondrian**, including the latter's *Broadway Boogie Woogie*, painted in 1940 after he had moved to New York and reflecting his love of jazz music; its short, sharp stabs of color convey an almost physical rhythm. MoMA's **Matisse** collection centers on *The Dancers* (1909), *The Red Studio*, a depiction of Matisse's studio in France in which all perspective is resolved in shades of rusty red, and *Le Bateau*. When this last painting was first exhibited, MoMA hung it upside down for 47 days before noticing the mistake. Other highlights include swirling canvases by **Kandinsky**, the brooding skies of **de Chirico**, works by **Miró**, notably his hilarious *Dutch Interior*, and a handful of dreamlike paintings by **Dalí** (*Persistence of Memory*) and **Magritte** (*The Menaced Assassin*).

Late-modern and contemporary painting and sculpture

As the collection moves toward the present, it has more of an American slant. It features paintings such as **Wyeth**'s *Christina's World*, one of the best known of modern American paintings, and works by **Hopper**, including *House by the Railroad* and *New York Movie*, potent and atmospheric pieces that give a bleak account of modern American life. The more abstract pieces include **Gorky**'s Miró-like doodles and the anguished scream of **Bacon**'s *No. 7 from 8 Studies for a Portrait*.

Some of the biggest draws are the paintings from the **New York School** – large-scale canvases meant to be viewed from a distance, perfect for MoMA's large, airy rooms. The best examples are the paintings of **Pollack** and **de Kooning** – wild, and in Pollack's case, textured patterns with no clear beginning or end – and the more ordered **Color Field** works. In **Barnett Newman**'s words, their paintings are "drained of impediments of memory, association, nostalgia, legend, myth, and what have you" – in other words, pure color, as in the radiating, almost humming blocks of color by **Rothko** and perhaps, most palpably, in the black canvases of **Reinhardt**.

And who could overlook the famous examples of **Pop Art**, including **Johns**'s *Flag*, a well-known piece in which a cloth Stars and Stripes is painted onto newsprint, transforming America's most potent symbol into little more than an arrangement of shapes and hues, and **Warhol**'s *Gold Marilyn Monroe* and the familiar *Campbell Soup Cans* canvas.

Architecture and design

After painting and sculpture, architecture and design are MoMA's most important concern. Models and original drawings by the architects of key modern buildings include **Frank Lloyd Wright**'s *Fallingwater* and projects by **Le Corbusier** and **Mies van der Rohe**. Further aspects of modern design are traced through the overdone glasswork of **Tiffany** and **furniture** designed by van der Rohe, **Charles Rennie Mackintosh**, **Alvar Aalto** and **Henry van de Velde**, to name a few. Some more than others represent successful examples of applied design. Oversized items include an E-type 1963 Jaguar roadster and a green Bell helicopter from 1945.

Photography and film

The museum also has an extraordinary collection of **photographs**, **prints** and **drawings**. The photographs, in particular, are marvelous – one of the finest, most eclectic collections around, and a vivid evocation of twentieth-century America, from the dramatic landscapes of **Ansel Adams** to **Alfred Stieglitz**'s dynamic views of New York to the revealing portraits of **Man Ray**. MoMA's **film and video collection** is also justly famous, with 14,000 films and four million film stills. It includes silent works by **D.W. Griffith**, **Sergei Eisenstein**, **Charlie Chaplin** and **Buster Keaton**, as well as films by later directors including **John Ford**, **Orson Welles**, **Akira Kurasawa** and **Ingmar Bergman**, to name a few.

North toward Central Park

As you walk north, Fifth Avenue's ground floors quickly shift from airline offices to all-out glamour, with **Cartier**, **Gucci**, and **Tiffany and Co** among many gilt-edged names. If you're keen to do more than merely window-shop, Tiffany's is worth a perusal, its soothing green marble and weathered wood interior best described by Truman Capote's fictional Holly Golightly: "It calms me down right away . . . nothing very bad could happen to you there." Equally notable is a branch of Japan's largest department store chain, **Takashimaya**, at no. 693, where East meets West, expensively (try the authentic Japanese tea room). Further along, the famed rich people's department store **Bergdorf Goodman**, at no. 754, offers a wedding-cake interior, all glossy pastels, chandeliers, pink curtains and the like. Just next door are the glittering (and virtually priceless) window displays of **Harry Winston Jewelers**, beloved by Princess Di and countless others. More recent arrivals in this prestigious area are the hardly-needed-but-here-anyway NBA store at no. 666 and the Coca-Cola Store at no. 711.

Just when you thought the glitter had gone about as far as it could, you arrive at **Trump Tower** below 57th Street. Its outrageously overdone atrium is just short of repellent to many – though perhaps not to those who frequent the glamorous designer boutiques here. Perfumed air, polished marble paneling and a five-story waterfall are calculated to knock you senseless with expensive "good taste": it's all very entertaining. The building is clever, a neat little outdoor garden is squeezed high in a corner, and each of the 230 apartments above the atrium provides views in three directions. Donald Trump, the property developer all New York traditionalists love to hate, lives here, along with other worthies of the hyper-rich crowd.

Topping all this off is **F.A.O. Schwarz**, a block north at 767 Fifth Ave at 58th Street, a colossal emporium of children's toys that welcomes visitors with an animatronics-like clock endlessly repeating the frustratingly catchy jingle "Welcome to our world of toys." Fight the kids off and there's some great stuff to play with – once again, the best (and biggest, including gas-powered cars, life-sized stuffed animals, Lego creations and sophisticated electronics that money can buy. If you are in New York over the Christmas holidays, don't miss the store's window installations, which are some of the most inventive in the city. Across 58th Street, Fifth Avenue broadens to **Grand Army Plaza** and the fringes of Central Park with a golden statue of William Tecumseh Sherman standing guard.

Looming impressively on the plaza is, aptly enough, the copper-edged **Plaza Hotel**, familiar from its many film appearances. Take time to soak in the (slightly faded) gilt-and-brocade grandeur; the inside, including the snazzy *Oak Room* bar, is worth a snoop, too. The hotel's reputation was built not just on looks, but on lore: it boasts its own historian, keeper of such tidbits as when legendary tenor Enrico Caruso, enraged with the loud ticking of the hotel's clocks, stopped them all by throwing a shoe at one (they were calibrated to function together). The Plaza apologized with a magnum of champagne.

To continue with the rest of Midtown, return to 57th Street and head east toward Madison Avenue – going northward, it's an elegant stretch of exclusive shops and art galleries, albeit with the odd superstore. One dubious, though impossible to miss, attraction, at 6 E 57th St, is **Nike Town**, an unrestrained celebration of the sneaker that needs to be seen to be believed. The overly earnest attempt at a museum, laden with sound effects, space-age visuals and exhibits inlaid into the floor, walls and special display cases – including one that holds a custom-designed gold-plated athletic shoe worn by Michael Jordan – can't mask the commercialism.

Midtown East

If there is a stretch that is immediately and unmistakably New York, it is the area that runs east of Fifth Avenue in the 40s and 50s. The great avenues of **Madison**, **Park**, **Lexington** and **Third** reach their richest heights as the skyscrapers line up in neck-cricking vistas, the streets choke with yellow cabs and office workers, and Con Edison vents belch steam from old heating systems. More than anything else, buildings define this part of town. Many house anonymous corporations and supply excitement to a skyline that was largely formed during the 1960s build-'em-high glass-box bonanza. Others, like the **Sony Building** and the **Citicorp Center**, don't play that game; and enough remains from the pre-box days to maintain variety. The commercial properties largely disappear as midtown slinks toward the East River, giving way to the quietly affluent residential **Beekman and Sutton places** as well as the unappealing mass of the **United Nations complex**, which anchors itself like a barnacle to the eastern edge of the city.

Madison Avenue

Madison Avenue parallels Fifth with some of its sweep but less of the excitement. It is a little removed from its 1960s and Seventies prime, when it was internationally recognized as the epicenter of the advertising industry. Nevertheless, it remains a major upscale shopping boulevard. Several good stores – notably several specializing in men's haberdashery, shoes and cigars – sit behind the scenes here. Brooks Brothers, traditional clothier to the Ivy League and inventor of the button-down collar, occupies a corner of East 44th Street. Between 50th and 51st streets the **Villard Houses**, a replay of an Italian palazzo (one that didn't quite make it to Fifth Avenue) by McKim, Mead and White merit more than a passing glance. The houses have been surgically incorporated into the *Helmsley Palace Hotel* and the interiors polished up to their original splendor.

Madison's most interesting sites come in a four-block strip above 53rd Street: **Paley Park**, on the north side of East 53rd between Madison and Fifth, is a tiny vest-pocket park. The soothing mini-waterfall and a transparent water tunnel are juxtaposed with a haunting five-panel section of the former Berlin Wall. Around the corner the **Continental Illinois Center** looks like a cross between a space rocket and a grain silo. However, the **Sony Building** (formerly the AT&T Building), between 55th and 56th streets, grabbed more headlines. A Johnson-Burgee collaboration, it followed the postmodernist

theory of eclectic borrowing from historical styles: a modernist skyscraper sandwiched between a Chippendale top and a Renaissance base – the idea being to quote from great public buildings and simultaneously return to the fantasy of the early part of the twentieth century. The building has its fans, but in popular opinion the tower doesn't work, and it's unlikely to stand the test of time. Perhaps Johnson should have followed the advice of his teacher, Mies van der Rohe: "It's better to build a good building than an original one." The first floor is well worth ducking into to soak in the brute grandeur. It now houses a music store and a spate of interactive exhibits on record production and video-game production (ceremoniously named the Sony Wonder Technology Lab). The requisite coffee bar and deli abut a rather somber public seating area.

The **IBM Building**, next door at 590 Madison Ave, has a far more user-friendly plaza. In the calm glass-enclosed atrium, tinkling music, tropical foliage, yet another coffee bar and comfortable seating area make for a far less ponderous experience. Across 57th Street, as the first of Madison's boutiques appear, the **Fuller Building** is worth catching – black-and-white Art Deco, with a fine entrance and tiled floor. Cut east down 57th Street to find the **Four Seasons Hotel**, notable for its I.M. Pei-designed foyer and lobby, ostentatious in its sweeping marble.

Park Avenue

"Where wealth is so swollen that it almost bursts," wrote Collinson Owen of **Park Avenue** in 1929, and things aren't much changed: corporate headquarters jostle for prominence, pushed apart by Park's broad avenue that was built to accommodate elevated rail tracks. Whatever your feelings about conspicuous wealth, Park Avenue in the 40s and 50s and farther north is one of the city's most awesome sights. Looking south from the 50s, everything progresses to the high altar of the New York Central Building (rechristened the **Helmsley Building**), a delicate, energetic construction with a lewdly excessive Rococo lobby that rises in the middle of the avenue. In its day it formed a skilled punctuation mark to the avenue, but had its thunder stolen in 1963 by the **Met Life Building**, then called the Pan Am Building, which looms behind and above (with Grand Central Terminal on the other side). Bauhaus guru Walter Gropius had a hand in designing Pan Am, and the critical consensus is that he could have done better. As the headquarters of the now-defunct international airline, the building, in profile, was meant to suggest an aircraft wing, and the blue-gray mass certainly adds drama to the cityscape. Whatever success the Met Life scores, though, it robs Park Avenue of the views south it deserves and needs, sealing 44th Street and sapping much of the vigor of the surrounding buildings. Another black mark was the building's rooftop helipad. It was closed in the 1970s after a helicopter undercarriage collapsed shortly after a landing, causing a rotor to sheer off and kill four disembarking passengers and injure several people on the ground.

Despite Park Avenue's power, an individual look at most of the skyscrapers reveals the familiar glass box, and the first few buildings to stand out do so exactly because that's what they are not. Wherever you placed the solid mass of the **Waldorf Astoria Hotel** (between 49th and 50th streets) it would hold its own, a resplendent statement of Art Deco elegance. Duck inside to stroll through a block of vintage Deco grandeur, sweeping marble and hushed plushness. If you're tempted, it's a smidgen cheaper than the comparable competition, with double rooms between $250 and $350. Crouching across the street, **St Bartholomew's Church** is a low-slung Byzantine hybrid that adds immeasurably to the street, giving the lumbering skyscrapers a much-needed sense of scale. That hasn't stopped the church fathers from wanting to sell the valuable air rights to real estate developers; so far landmark preservationists have prevented them from wrecking one of the few remaining bits of individuality in this part of the city. Directly behind it, the spiky-topped **General Electric Building** seems like a wild extension of the church, its slender shaft rising to a meshed crown of abstract sparks and lightning strokes that symbolizes the radio waves used by its original owner, RCA. A New York designated landmark, the building is another Art Deco delight, with nickel-silver ornamentation, carved red marble, and a lobby with a vaulted ceiling (entrance at 570 Lexington).

Among all this it's difficult at first to see the originality of the **Seagram Building** between 52nd and 53rd streets. Designed by Mies van der Rohe with Philip Johnson, and built in 1958, this was the seminal curtain-wall skyscraper, the floors supported internally rather than by the building's walls, allowing a skin of smoky glass and whiskey-bronze metal (the colors of a late-night watering hole, the domain of Seagram's distilled products). Sadly, it's now weathered to a dull black. In keeping with the era's vision, every interior detail down to the fixtures and lettering on the mailboxes was specially designed. It was the supreme example of modernist reason, deceptively simple and cleverly detailed, and its opening was met with a wave of approval. The **plaza**, an open forecourt designed to set the building apart from its neighbors and display it to advantage, was such a success as a public space that the city revised the zoning laws to encourage other high-rise builders to supply plazas. Forty-five years later, the city is revamping its regulations to forestall the construction of any more of these buildings, and the idea of allowing architects to build higher in exchange for public plazas may soon be a thing of the past.

Across Park Avenue, McKim, Mead and White's **Racquet and Squash Club** seems like a classical continuation of the Seagram Plaza. More interesting is **Lever House**, rising across the avenue between 53rd and 54th, the building that set the modernist ball rolling on Park Avenue in 1952. Then, the two right-angled slabs that form a steel and glass bookend seemed revolutionary when compared with the traditional buildings that surrounded it. As of writing, the Lever House is undergoing renovations that are due for completion in mid-2002.

Lexington Avenue and Citicorp Center

Lexington Avenue is always active, especially around the mid-40s, where commuters swarm around Grand Central and a well-placed **post office** on the corner of 50th Street. Just as the Chrysler Building dominates these lower stretches, the chisel-topped **Citicorp Center** (between 53rd and 54th streets) anchors and dominates the northern midtown section. Finished in 1979, the building, now one of New York's most conspicuous landmarks, looks as if it is sheathed in shiny graph paper, while the slope of tower resembles a linear representation of a mathematical equation. A story goes that a student of the building's engineer was playing with some of the equations of the just-finished tower's design when he discovered a flaw that placed it, as built, in danger from very strong winds. Though the force of wind required to topple the building was an unlikely occurrence, a secretive mission to reinforce the structure was undertaken. Before the project was completed, the drama of a hurricane warning was played out with not a few architects, engineers and lawyers having a sleepless night. The slanted roof was designed to house solar panels and provide power, but the idea was ahead of the technology and Citicorp had to content itself with adopting the distinctive top as a corporate logo. The atrium of stores known as **The Market** is pleasant enough, with some food options.

Hiding under the Center's skirts is **St Peter's**, known as "the Jazz Church" for being the venue of many a jazz musician's funeral. The tiny church was built to replace the one demolished to make way for Citicorp, and part of the deal was that the church had to stand out from the Center – which explains the granite material. Explore the thoroughly modern interior, including sculptor **Louise Nevelson**'s **Erol Beaker Chapel**, venue for

Wednesday lunchtime jazz concerts (and evening concerts as well). More black angular Nevelson sculpture can be seen on the partition running down Park Avenue.

In direct contrast to the simple, contemporary St Peters is the **Central Synagogue**, at 652 Lexington Ave. Striking because of its Moorish appearance, it was built in 1872 by German immigrant Henry Fernbach. The oldest continually used Jewish house of worship in the city, it was heavily damaged in a blaze in 1998, and the repairs – though complete – were unable to fully restore all the site's features.

Third, Second and First avenues

Citicorp provided a spur for the development of **Third Avenue**, though things really took off when the old elevated railway that ran here was dismantled in 1955. Until then, Third had been a strip of earthy bars and run-down tenements, in effect a border to the more salubrious midtown district. After Citicorp gave it an "official" stamp of approval, office buildings sprouted, revitalizing the flagging fortunes of midtown Manhattan in the late 1970s. The best section is between 44th and 50th streets – look out for the sheer marble monument of the **Wang Building** (between 48th and 49th), whose cross-patterns reveal the structure within.

All this office space hasn't totally removed interest from the street (there are a few good bars here, notably *P.J. Clarke's* at 55th, a New York institution – see p.361), but most life, especially at night, seems to have shifted east to **Second Avenue** – less corporate and more residential, with any number of bars to crawl between. The area from Third to the East River in the upper 40s is known as **Turtle Bay** (though most New Yorkers would be hard pressed to tell you just where this area is), and there's a scattering of brownstones alongside chirpier shops and restaurants that disappear as you head north. Of course, the UN Secretariat Building (see below) has had a copycat effect, producing buildings like 1 UN Plaza at 44th and First, a futuristic chess piece of a hotel that takes its design hints from the UN Building itself. Inside, its marbled, chrome lobby is about as uninviting as any other modern American luxury hotel. Should this be your cup of tea, a double room will set you back a few hundred dollars; if not, just pray that all New York hotels don't end up like this.

First Avenue has a certain raggy looseness that's a relief after the concrete claustrophobia of midtown. **Beekman Place** (49th to 51st streets between First Avenue and the East River) is quieter still, a beguiling enclave of garbled styles. Similar, though not quite as intimate, is **Sutton Place**, a long stretch running from 53rd to 59th between First and the river. Originally built for the lordly Morgans and Vanderbilts in 1875, Sutton Place increases in elegance as you move north and, for today's crème de la crème, **Riverview Terrace** (off 58th St at the river) is a (very) private enclave of five brownstones. The UN Secretary-General has an official residence on Sutton Place. The locals are choosy about whom they let in: the disgraced ex-President Richard Nixon was refused on the grounds he would be a security risk. Two small public parks here afford fine views of the river and Queens' industrial waterfront, which awaits its own development boom.

Trump World Tower

For a few hundred million dollars, financier Donald Trump erected the latest monument to himself, the **Trump World Tower**, at 845 UN Plaza (E 47th Street at First Avenue). The tallest (72 stories) residential building in the world attracted controversy from the start, as famous (such as Walter Cronkite) and regular-guy area residents objected to a structure that would destroy the cozy vibe of the neighborhood and obliterate the view for some. However, since the blueprints were in compliance with regulations, the Tower went up as planned. As part of a large-scale overhaul of city building policy, the loopholes in the zoning codes that allowed the developers to build here have been closed, preventing another Trump-scale building from appearing outside of central midtown or the Financial District.

The United Nations

Some see the **United Nations complex** – which rose up after World War II, when John D. Rockefeller donated $8.5 million to buy the 18-acre East River complex – as one of the major sights of New York; others, usually those who've been there, are not so complimentary. For, whatever the symbolism of the UN, few buildings are quite so dull to walk around. What's more, as if to rationalize the years of UN impotence in war and hunger zones worldwide, the (obligatory) guided tours emphasize that the UN's main purpose is to promote dialogue and awareness rather than enforcement. So the organization itself moves at a snail's pace – bogged down by regulations and a lack of funds – which is the general feel of the tour as well.

For the determined, the complex consists of three main buildings – the thin glass-curtained slab of the **Secretariat**, the sweeping curve of the **General Assembly Building** and, just between, the low-rise connecting **Conference Wing**. The buildings went up after World War II and were finished in 1963, the product of a suitably international team of architects that included Le Corbusier – though he pulled out before the construction was completed. Hour-long daily tours leave from the monumental General Assembly lobby at First Avenue and 46th Street (Mar–Dec daily 9.30am–4.45pm, Jan–Feb Mon–Fri 9.30am–4.45pm; $7.50, seniors $6, students $5, children 5–14 $4; ⓣ212/963-TOUR). The tours take in the main conference chambers of the UN, the foremost of which is the **General Assembly Chamber** itself, expanded a few years back to accommodate up to 179 national delegations (though there are at present only 159). It's certainly impressive, even given (or perhaps because of) its 1960s feel. Other council chambers in the Conference Building include the **Security Council**, the **Economic and Social Council** and the **Trusteeship Council** – all similarly retro (note the clunky machinery of the journalists' areas) and sporting some intriguing Marxist murals.

Once you've been whisked around all these sites and seen examples of the many artifacts that have been donated to the UN by its various member states (among them rugs, sculptures, and a garishly colored mosaic based on a Norman Rockwell painting courtesy of Nancy Reagan), the tour is more or less over and will leave you in the basement of the General Assembly Building. Here, a couple of shops sell ethnic items from around the world. A **post office** will make you a UN postage stamp to prove that you've been here – though bear in mind it's only valid on mail posted from the UN. A **restaurant** serves a daily lunch buffet with dishes from different UN member countries, but the food, like the tour, is fairly taste-free. Where the UN has real class is in its beautiful **gardens**, with their modern sculpture and a view of the East River. Carpets of daffodils and flowering cherry trees in spring and an extensive rose garden in summer make them worth a visit. The many statues outside the complex include *Reclining Figure* (1982) by **Henry Moore**.

Midtown West

The area west of Fifth Avenue in midtown Manhattan takes **Times Square** as its center, an exploded version of the East Side's more tight-lipped monuments to capitalism. Though in some ways it cannot compete with the richer avenues and enclaves to the east, the area north of the once "naughty, bawdy 42nd Street" is well worth exploring. Most of Times Square's pornography and crime is gone, replaced in part by products of Disney imagination, modern high-rise office buildings and hotels that threaten to spoil the square's historic greasy appeal. For vintage seediness, keep heading west to

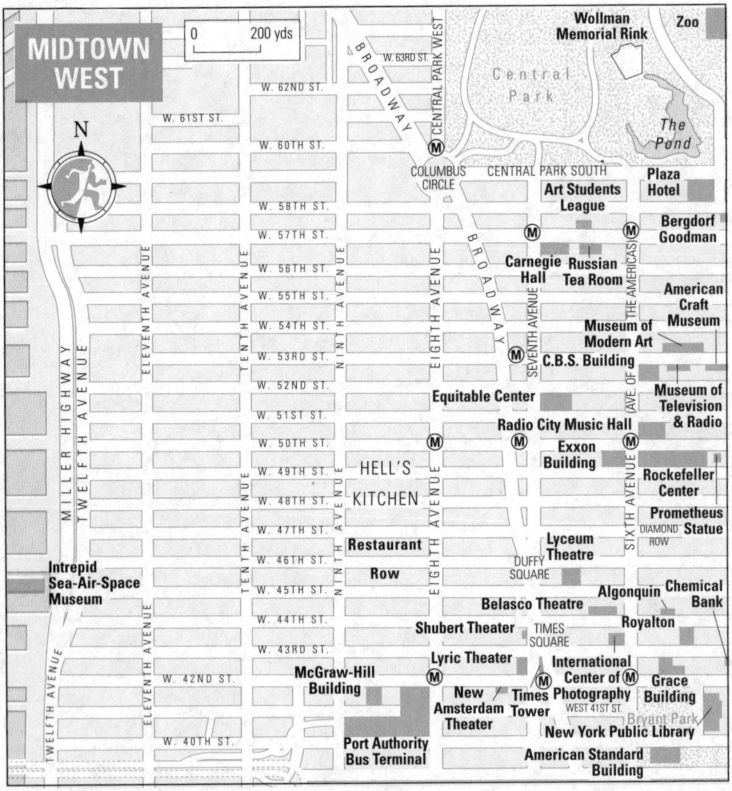

Eighth Avenue and beyond – but hurry: gentrification is fast approaching. There aren't many tourist attractions in this direction, which may be reason enough to go, though all the way over at the Hudson River, a retired US aircraft carrier encompasses the massive **Intrepid Sea-Air-Space Museum**.

Times Square

Forty-second Street meets Broadway at the southern margin of **Times Square**, the center of the theater district, where the pulsating neon suggests a heart for the city itself. Because of the major cleanup launched by the city and by business interests, the ambience along 42nd Street and north has changed dramatically. Traditionally a melting pot of debauch, depravity and fun, the area became increasingly edgy, a place where out-of-towners provided easy pickings for petty criminals, drug dealers and prostitutes (always, seemingly, a companion to theater districts). Most of the peep shows and sex shops have been pushed out, and Times Square is now a largely sanitized universe of popular consumption. If you have never seen Times Square, plan a visit at night. Without passing through it, take a taxi to 57th and Broadway and start walking south. Slowly at first and then with a rush, the spectacle opens out before your blinking eyes.

Like Greeley and Herald squares, Times Square took its name from a newspaper connection when the *New York Times* built offices here in 1904. While the *Herald* and *Tribune* fought each other in ever more vicious circulation battles, the *Times* stood on more restrained ground under the banner "All the news that's fit to print," a policy that enabled the paper to survive and become one of the country's most respected voices. At the southernmost end of the square was the newspaper's headquarters, **Times Tower**, originally an elegant building modeled on Giotto's Campanile in Florence. In 1928, the famous zipper sign displaying the news of the world was added; the building was "skinned" in 1965 and covered with the lifeless marble slabs visible today. The paper itself has long since moved off around a corner to a handsome building with globe lamps on 43rd Street, and today most of the printing is done in New Jersey.

Not an actual square at all, Times Square was created by the intersection between straight-arrow Seventh Avenue and left-leaning Broadway; the latter more or less follows true north through much of the island, which tilts to the northeast. So narrow is the angle between these two thoroughfares that Broadway, which meets Seventh Avenue at 43rd Street, does not begin to strike off on its own until 48th Street. Here, in the intervening blocks and in the immediate side streets at midnight every December 31, hundreds of thousands of deliriously happy people, many of them running on alcohol, shrink-wrap themselves into this pickpocket's paradise to witness a giant sparkling ball drop from the top of Times Tower. The bash for the faux centennial/millennium on the last night of 1999 capped the world's celebration.

The theaters and Duffy Square

Dotted around here are most of New York's great **theaters** (see "The Performing Arts and Film"), though many have been destroyed (like the vaudeville palaces that preceded *them*) to make way for office buildings. Thus, the original Paramount Theater made way for the majestic 1927 clock-and-globe-topped **Paramount Building** at 1501 Broadway, between 43rd and 44th streets. The **New Amsterdam** and the **New Victory**, both on 42nd Street between Seventh and Eighth avenues, have been refurbished by Disney to their original splendor (see p.377), one of the truly welcome results of the massive changes here. The **Lyceum**, at 149 W 45th St, has its original facade, while the **Shubert Theater**, at 225 W 44th St, which hosted *A Chorus Line* during its twenty-odd year run, still occupies its own small space and walkway. Among the oldest is the **Belasco**, at 111 W 44th St, which was also the first of Broadway's theaters to incorporate machinery into its stagings. At 432 W 44th St is the former Presbyterian Church that in 1947 became **The Actors Studio**, where Lee Strasberg, America's leading proponent of Stanislavski's method-acting technique, taught his students. The neon, so much a signature of the square, was initially confined to the theaters and spawned the term "the Great White Way." In 1922, the lights moved G.K. Chesterton to remark, "What a glorious garden of wonder this would be, to anyone who was lucky enough to be unable to read."

The illumination is not limited to theaters, of course. Myriad ads, forming one of the world's most garish nocturnal displays, promote hundreds of products and services. Today, businesses that rent offices here are actually required to allow signage on their walls – the city's attempt to retain the square's traditional feel. The displays, of course, have been modernized and even the **Port Authority Bus Terminal** on 42nd and Eighth (see p.19), a former sink of decadence, is to be covered with a skin of metal for ad displays.

Duffy Square is the northernmost island in the heart of Times Square and offers an excellent panoramic view of the square's lights, megahotels, theme stores and theme restaurants. The nifty canvas-and-frame stand of the **TKTS booth**, modest in comparison, sells half-price, same-day tickets for Broadway shows (whose exorbitant prices these days make a visit to TKTS a near necessity). A lifelike statue of Broadway's doyen **George M. Cohan** looks on – though if you've ever seen the film *Yankee Doodle Dandy* it's impossible to think of him as other than a swaggering Jimmy Cagney. At eye level, you can find enough gifts in the souvenir shops for your 500 best friends.

The last word on the scene belongs to Henry Miller from *Tropic of Capricorn*:

> ***It's only a stretch of a few blocks from Times Square to Fiftieth Street, and when one says Broadway . . .it's really nothing, just a chicken run and a lousy one at that, but even at seven in the evening when everyone's rushing for a table there's a sort of electric crackle in the air and your hair stands on end like an antenna and if you're receptive you not only get every bash and flicker but you get the statistical itch, the quid pro quo of the interactive, interstitial, ectoplasmic quantum of bodies jostling in space like the stars which compose the Milky Way, only this is the Gay White Way, the top of the world with no roof and not even a crack or a hole under your feet to fall through and say it's a lie. The absolute impersonality of it brings you to a pitch of warm human delirium which makes you run forward like a blind nag and wag your delirious ears.***

Heading north from Times Square, the **West 50s** between Sixth and Eighth avenues scream to tourists at every opportunity. Edged by Central Park in the north and the Theater District to the south, and with Fifth Avenue and

Rockefeller Center within easy striking distance, the area has been invaded by overpriced restaurants and more cheapo souvenir stores: should you wish to stock up on "I Love New York" underwear, this is the place. One sight worth searching out, however, is the **Equitable Center**, 757 Seventh Ave. The building itself is dapper if not a little self-important, and Roy Lichtenstein's 68-foot *Mural with Blue Brush Stroke* pokes you in the eye as you enter.

Hell's Kitchen

To the west of Times Square lies **Clinton** (named for nineteenth-century Governor Dewitt Clinton), more famously known as **Hell's Kitchen**, an area centered on the engaging slash of restaurants, bars and ethnic delis of **Ninth Avenue**. Extending down to the Garment District and up to the low 50s, this was once one of New York's most violent and lurid neighborhoods.

Hell's Kitchen was once rumored to be named after a tenement at 54th Street and Tenth Avenue. More commonly, the name has been attributed to Dutch Fred the Cop, a veteran policeman. In response to his young partner's comment – while watching a riot – that the place was hell, Fred reportedly replied, "Hell's a mild climate. This is Hell's kitchen." The area originally contained soap and glue factories, slaughterhouses and the like, with sections named "Misery Lane" and "Poverty Row." Irish immigrants were the first inhabitants, soon joined by Greeks, Latinos, Italians and blacks; amid the overcrowding, tensions rapidly developed between (and within) ethnic groups. Gangs with names like The Gophers and Dead Rabbits roamed the streets, but their rule largely ended in 1910 after a major police counteroffensive. The neighborhood was renamed Clinton in 1959 to hide its notorious past, but the name hasn't really stuck. A violent Irish gang, the Westies, claimed the streets in the 1970s and early 1980s, but the area has been cleaned up and is far less dangerous than it was (but still keep your wits about you). Currently, the district is moving up in a way the East Village did in the late 1990s; it's attracted a new population, mostly musicians and Broadway types, and renovation and construction of apartment buildings has never moved faster.

Head to it from Eighth Avenue (which now houses the porn businesses expelled from the square) by walking west on 46th Street along the so-called **Restaurant Row** – the area's preferred haunt for pre- and post-theater dining. Here you can begin to detect a more laid-back feel which only increases on many of the side streets around Ninth and Tenth avenues, whose cramped apartment buildings frequently hide small garden oases. Also check out the unstuffy **St Clements' Episcopal Church** at 423 W 46th St. It doubles as a community theater and in its foyer is a picture of Elvis Presley and Jesus, with the caption, "There seems to be a little confusion as to which one of them actually rose from the dead."

Intrepid Sea-Air-Space Museum

Continuing west to the river, you reach the **Intrepid Sea–Air–Space Museum**, 46th St and 12th Ave at Pier 86 (April–Sept Mon–Fri 10am–5pm, Sat–Sun 10am–7pm; Oct–March Tue–Sun 10am–5pm; $12, 12–17 $9, 6–11 $6, 2–5 $2, 2 years and under free; ⓣ212/245-0072, ⓦwww.intrepidmuseum.org). This impressive, huge (900-foot long) old aircraft carrier has a distinguished history; it picked up capsules from the Mercury and Gemini space missions and made several trips to Vietnam. Today it holds an array of modern and vintage air- and seacraft, including the A-12 Blackbird, the world's fastest spy plane, and the *USS Growler*, the only guided missile submarine open to the public. It also has interactive CD-ROM exhibits and an on-board restaurant. If you're visiting at the end of May, **Fleet Week** (the week leading up to Memorial Day) is a big deal here, and deservedly so, with ships visiting from all corners of the globe, and military demonstrations and competitions.

Otherwise, there's not too much to see this far west. Ragged Eleventh Avenue is home to the automobile warehouses that once spiced up Times Square's Automobile Row. Past that is the sleazy West Side Highway. These streets are undistinguished, highlighted only by two well-preserved, old-time restaurants on Eleventh, the *Landmark Tavern* (46th Street) and the *Market Diner* (44th Street).

Sixth Avenue

Sixth Avenue is properly named **Avenue of the Americas**, though no New Yorker ever calls it this: guidebooks and maps labor the convention, but the only manifestations of the tag are lamppost flags of Central and South American countries that serve as useful landmarks. Sixth is distinguished by its width, a result of the elevated railway that once ran along here (now, the Sixth Avenue line runs underground). In its day the Sixth Avenue "El" marked the border between respectability to the east and dodgier areas to the west, and in a way it's still a dividing line separating the glamorous strips of Fifth, Madison and Park avenues from the brasher western districts. Today, looking south from the vantage point of the mid-50s, the buildings on either side of the avenue look like two large sets of dominoes set on end.

At the base of Sixth Avenue in this neighborhood is the **International Center of Photography** at 1133 Sixth Ave at 43rd Street (Tues–Thurs 10am–5pm, Fri 10am–8pm, Sat–Sun 10am–6pm; $8, students $6, voluntary contribution Fri 5–8pm; ⓣ212/768-4682, ⓦwww.icp.org), an unassuming building that contains all manner of photos and theme exhibits on a rotating basis. Founded by Cornell Capa (brother of war photographer Robert Capa), the permanent archived collection contains most of the greats, and often shows more avant-garde and experimental work, from photographers based around the world.The Center also conducts classes and educational trips.

One of the best things about New York City are the small hidden pockets abruptly discovered when you least expect them. West 47th Street between Fifth and Sixth avenues is a perfect example: **Diamond Row** (you'll know it by the diamond-shaped lamps mounted on pylons at either end) is a strip of shops chock-full of gems and jewelry, largely managed by Hasidic Jews. The Hasidim are Orthodox Jews, and traditionally they wear beards, sidelocks and dark, old-fashioned suits. Maybe they are what gives the street its workaday feel; Diamond Row seems more like the Garment District than the vicinity of Fifth Avenue, and the conversations you overhear on the street or in the nearby delicatessens seem to transport you to the Middle East. Come here to get jewelry fixed at reasonable prices.

Another one-street neighborhood can be found one block south. **Little Brazil Street** (46th between Fifth and Sixth avenues) holds many of the city's (few) Brazilian restaurants and, during lunchtime on weekdays, you'll hear more Portuguese than English.

By the time Sixth Avenue reaches midtown Manhattan from TriBeCa, it has become a dazzling showcase of corporate wealth. True, there's little of the ground-floor glitter of Fifth or the razzmatazz of Broadway, but what *is* here, and in a way what defines the stretch from 47th to 51st streets, is the **Rockefeller Center Extension**. Following the **Time & Life Building** at 50th Street, three near-identical buildings went up in the 1970s, and if they don't have the romance of their predecessor they at least possess some of its monumentality. Backing onto Rockefeller Center proper, the repeated statement of each building – by day and especially by night – comes over with some power, giving the wide path of Sixth Avenue much of its visual excitement. At street level things can be just as interesting: the broad sidewalks allow peddlers of food and handbills, street musicians, mimics and actors to do their thing.

Across the avenue at 50th Street **Radio City Music Hall** has far greater rewards, since being restored to its original 1932 majesty in 1999 for a cost of $70 million. Catch the large painted medallions on the side, representing song, drama and dance.(For a complete description, see p.145.) Keep an eye open too for the **CBS Building** on the corner of 52nd Street: dark and inscrutable, this has been compared to the monolith from the film *2001: A Space Odyssey* and, like it or not, it certainly forces a mysterious presence on this segment of Sixth Avenue.

A block farther north, enjoy the company of Venus, in the form of three 25-foot green copper statues, anchoring the fountains in front of the **Credit Lyonnais Building** at no. 1301. But best of all, look out for the **AXA Financial Building** at 1290 Sixth, which hosts Thomas Hart Benton's *America Today* murals. This creation (1931), which dynamically and magnificently portrays ordinary life in the days before the Depression, was celebrated for its representation of Americans from a variety of classes, shown both at work and at leisure. It spurred an interest in murals as public art, and lent momentum to the Federal Arts Project (helping to provide both employment for artists suffering through the decade, and a morale boost for the rest of the public) in the 1930s. It is sweeping, dramatic and priceless.

57th Street

Fifty-seventh Street between Fifth and Sixth avenues competes with SoHo and Chelsea as the center for upmarket art sales. Galleries here are noticeably snootier than their downtown relations, often requiring an appointment for viewing. A couple that usually don't are the **Marlborough Gallery** (2nd floor, 40 W 57th), specializing in famous names both American and European, and the **Kennedy Gallery**, at 730 5th Ave, which deals in nineteenth- and twentieth-century American painting. Also noteworthy is the **Art Students League** at 215 W 57th, built in 1892 by Henry J. Hardenbergh (who later built the *Plaza Hotel*) to mimic Francis I's hunting lodge at Fontainebleau. Today this art school provides inexpensive art classes to the public.

At 154 W 57th St is stately **Carnegie Hall**, one of the world's greatest concert venues, revered by musicians and audiences alike. The Renaissance-inspired structure was built in the 1890s by steel magnate and self-styled "improver of mankind" Andrew Carnegie, and the superb acoustics ensure full houses most of the year. Tchaikovsky conducted the program on opening night and Mahler, Rachmaninov, Toscanini, Frank Sinatra and Judy Garland all played here (as well as Duke Ellington, Billie Holiday, the Beatles and Spinal Tap). If you don't want, or can't afford, to attend a performance, sneak in through the stage door on 56th Street for a look – no one minds as long as there's not a rehearsal in progress. Alternatively, catch one of the tours (Mon–Tues, Thurs–Fri, except summer, 11.30am, 2pm & 3pm; $6, students $5; ⓣ212/247-7800).

A few doors down at no. 150, the *Russian Tea Room* (see p.337) reigns as one of those places to see and be seen at, ever popular with "in" names from the entertainment business. Its revolving doors continue to usher in a well-heeled crowd, as would be expected in this posh part of town.

18

Central Park

"All radiant in the magic atmosphere of art and taste," raved *Harper's* magazine on the opening of **Central Park** in 1876, and though that was a slight overstatement, today few New Yorkers could imagine life without it. The park is devotedly used by the locals, and serves purposes as varied as the New Yorkers (and visitors) who take advantage of it. At various times and places, the park functions as a beach, theater for all things cultural, environmental haven, singles scene, athletic activity center, and animal behavior lab, both human and canine. Over the years the park has occasionally fallen on hard times, from official neglect to some truly horrible crime waves, but recently it has benefited from a major renovation project and is cleaner, safer and more user-friendly than ever. In bad times and good, New Yorkers still treasure it more than any other city institution. Certainly life in New York would be a lot poorer without it.

Some history

Central Park came close to never happening at all. It was the poet and newspaper editor **William Cullen Bryant** who had the idea for an open public space back in 1844. He spent seven years trying to persuade City Hall to carry it out, while developers leaned heavily on the authorities not to give up any valuable land. Eventually the city agreed, paying $5 million for 840 acres north of the (then) city limits at 38th Street, a desolate swampy area occupied at the time by a shantytown of 1500 squatters who were duly relocated. The two architects commissioned to design the landscape, **Frederick Law Olmsted** and **Calvert Vaux**, planned to create a rural paradise called "Greensward," an illusion of the countryside smack in the heart of Manhattan. Greensward was to bring nature to an increasingly congested city thought to be badly in need of its edifying virtues.

The sparseness of the terrain provided Olmsted and Vaux with the perfect opportunity to design the park according to the precepts of classic English landscape gardening. They designed 36 elegant bridges, each unique, and planned a revolutionary system of four sunken transverse roads to segregate different kinds of traffic. Finally, after the nearly twenty years required for its construction, Central Park opened to the public in 1876 to such acclaim that Olmsted and Vaux were soon in demand as park architects all over the States. Locally, they went on to design Riverside and Morningside parks in Manhattan, and Prospect Park in Brooklyn. Working alone, Olmsted laid out the campuses of Berkeley and Stanford Universities in California, and had a major hand in that most televised of American sights, Capitol Hill in Washington, DC.

At its opening, Central Park was declared a "people's park" – though most of the impoverished masses it was allegedly built to serve had neither the time nor the carfare to come up from their downtown slums to 59th Street and enjoy

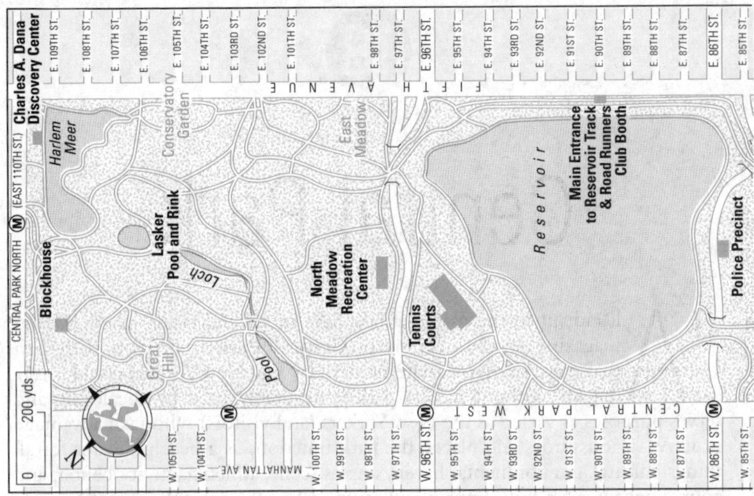

it. But as New York grew and workers' leisure time increased, people started flooding in, and the park began to live up to its mission, sometimes in ways that might have scandalized its original builders.

Robert Moses, a relentless urban planner and parks commissioner from 1935 to 1960 who was for decades the power behind the city's largest building projects, tried hard to put his imprint on Central Park. Thankfully, public opinion kept damage to a minimum; he only managed to pave over a small portion of the park, mostly in the form of unnecessary parking lots

Visiting the park

Central Park is so enormous that it's almost impossible to miss and nearly as impossible to cover in one visit. Nevertheless, the intricate **footpaths** that meander with no discernible organization through the park are one of its greatest successes; after all, the point here is to lose yourself . . . or at least to feel as if you can. That said, you can never stray too far from the footpaths, landmarks, or the more route-savvy regulars that blanket the park. **To figure out exactly where you are**, find the nearest **lamppost**: the first two digits on the post signify the number of the nearest cross street. It is also helpful to stop by one of the four Visitor Centers to pick up a free park map (see the box on p.173).

If you're traveling via one of the park drives during the weekend or when closed to vehicular traffic, you'll still need to keep a watchful eye. Crossing the road amid the serious hordes of goggled and walkmanned rollerbladers, cyclers and joggers may pose a problem. Just be patient.

As for **safety**, you should be fine during the day, though always be alert to your surroundings and try to avoid being alone in an isolated part of the park. After dark, it's safer than it used to be but still not advisable to walk around. If you want to look at the buildings of Central Park West lit up, as they were in Woody Allen's film *Manhattan*, the best option is to fork out for a buggy ride (see below). The exception to the rule is in the case of a public evening event such as a concert or a summertime Shakespeare in the Park performance; these events are very safe, just make sure you leave when the crowds do.

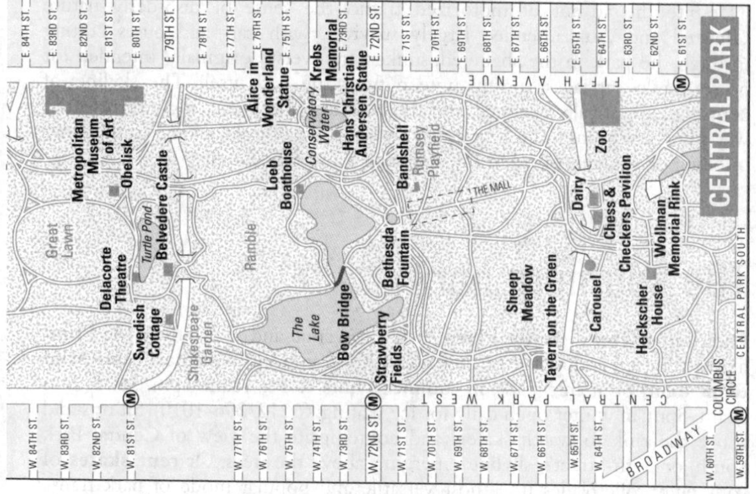

(since reconverted to green space). When he tried to tear down a park playground in 1956 to build a parking lot for *Tavern on the Green*, Moses was thwarted by outraged citizens – mothers and their young children stood in the way of the bulldozers, and the city sheepishly backed down. Today, a non-profit group called the Central Park Conservancy looks out for the park, and the city government has earmarked large funds to maintain it, increase its policing, and restore large areas, such as the Great Lawn, where renovations were completed in 1998.

The **Reservoir** divides Central Park in two. The larger **southern part** holds most of the attractions (and people), but the **northern part** (above 86th St) is well worth a visit for its wilder natural setting and dramatically quieter ambience. Organized walking tours are available from a number of sources including the Urban Park Rangers and the Visitors Centers (see the box on p.173), but almost any stroll, formal or informal, will invariably lead to something interesting. To visit Central Park is to begin to understand New York City and its residents – not to mention the fact that the park offers some of the city's most enjoyable and most reasonably priced (or even free!) activities.

Bicycle rental and buggy rides

One of the best ways to see the park is to **rent a bicycle** from either the Loeb Boathouse (see p.169), Metro Bicycles, West Side Bikes or Midtown Bicycles (see p.25 for details). Bikes from the Boathouse are $9 for the first hour ($5 each additional half hour) and from Metro $7 an hour (or $35 for the day); both require a credit card or refundable cash deposit ($250). That's a much better deal than the famed romantic buggy rides ($34 for a 20min trot and $10 for every additional 15min after that; ⓣ212/246-0520 for more information). Bear in mind that there has been longstanding vocal opposition to these rides being allowed at all, fueled by claims that the incompetence and greed of the buggy drivers lead to great cruelty to the horses used. Care has been improved though; according to a law enacted in 1994, the horses must get fifteen-minute rest breaks every two hours and cannot work more than nine hours a day. They're also not supposed to work at all when the temperature goes above 90ºF. Buggy drivers can get their licenses suspended or revoked for disobedience.

Despite the advent of motorized traffic, the sense of disorderly nature Olmsted and Vaux intended largely survives, with cars and buses cutting through the park in the sheltered, sunken transverses originally intended for horse-drawn carriages, mostly unseen from the park itself. The skyline, of course, has drastically changed, and the buildings that menacingly thrust their way into view seem to be kept at bay by a fortress of trees, adding to the sense of being on a green island in the center of a magnificent city.

The southern park

Entering at **Grand Army Plaza**, at Fifth Avenue and 59th Street, the **Pond** lies to your left and a little further north you'll find the **Wollman Memorial Rink** (63rd St at mid-park; in summer Thurs & Fri 11am–6pm, Sat & Sun 11am–8pm; in winter open daily for ice skating; ⓣ212/396-1010). Sit or stand above the rink to watch skaters and contemplate the view of Central Park South, or 59th Street's, skyline emerging above the trees. Or **rent skates** of your own: rollerblades (the most versatile and popular mode of park transportation) and ice skates are both available here.

East of the skating rink, at 64th Street and Fifth Avenue, lies the small **Central Park Wildlife Center** (Mon–Fri 10am–5pm, Sat, Sun & holidays 10am–5.30pm; $3.50, 50¢ children aged 3–12, free for children under 3; ⓣ212/439-6500), a zoo whose collection is based on three climatic regions – the Tropic Zone, the Temperate Territory and the Polar Circle. Remodeled in 1988 at a cost of over $35 million, the zoo has over a hundred species on view in mostly natural-looking homes with the animals as close to the viewer as possible: the penguins, for example, swim around at eye-level in Plexiglas pools. Other top attractions include polar bears, monkeys, a nocturnal exhibit, and sea lions cavorting in a pool right by the zoo entrance. This complex also boasts the **Tisch Children's Zoo**, with a petting zoo, interactive displays and a musical clock just outside the entrance that draws rapt children at the top of each hour. However, if you've got the time or want a more extensive look at wildlife, you're better off heading to the **Bronx Zoo** (p.268).

Unless you're attracted to a game of chess at the **Chess and Checkers Pavilion** (playing pieces are available at the Dairy Visitor Center), the next point to head for is the **Dairy** (65th Street at mid-park), a kind of Gothic toy ranch building built in 1870 and originally stocked with cows (and milkmaids) for the purpose of selling milk and other dairy products to mothers with young children. It now houses one of the Park's **Visitor Centers** (Tues–Sun 10am–5pm; ⓣ212/794-6564), a worthwhile rest stop that distributes free leaflets and maps (and sells better ones), sells books on the history and development of the park and puts on sporadic exhibitions. Weekend walking tours often leave from here; call for times.

Just west of the Dairy, you will see the octagonal brick building that houses the **Carousel**. Built in 1903 and moved to the park from Coney Island in 1951, this is one of the park's little gems (64th Street at mid-park; open Mon–Fri 10am–6pm, Sat & Sun 10am–7pm, weather permitting; ⓣ212/879-0244). One of fewer than 150 left in the country (one of the others is at Coney Island), the Carousel offers a ride on still-magical, hand-carved, colorfully painted jumping horses accompanied by the music of a military band organ for only $1 a pop or six tickets for $5. (You can also book it for birthday parties; Wollman Rink handles its special events, call ⓣ 212/396-1010, ext 13).

If the weather's nice and you continue straight ahead and north past the Dairy and through the **Mall**, you will witness every manner of street performer. Flanked by statues of the ecstatic-looking Scottish poet Robert Burns and a pensive Sir Walter Scott, with Shakespeare, Giuseppe Mazzini and Ludwig van Beethoven nearby, the Mall is the park's most formal but by no means quiet stretch. At the base of the Mall is the only acknowledgment to park architect Olmsted, in the guise of a small colorful flowerbed. To the west lies the **Sheep Meadow** (between 66th–69th streets), fifteen acres of commons where sheep grazed until 1934; today the area is usually crowded in the summer with picnic blankets, sunbathers and Frisbee players. Two lawn-bowling and croquet grass courts are maintained on a hill near the Sheep Meadow's northwest corner; to the southeast are a number of very popular volleyball courts (call ⓣ212/360-8133 for information on lawn bowling; call ⓣ212/408-0226 for volleyball and other ball field permit information). On warm weekends, an area between the Sheep Meadow and the north end of the Mall is filled with colorfully attired rollerbladers dancing to loud funk, disco and hip-hop music – one of the best free shows around town. Just west of the Sheep Meadow is the once-exclusive, still-expensive, but now tacky landmark restaurant, **Tavern on the Green** (67th Street and Central Park West). If nothing else, take a look at the exterior (the original 1870 building used to be a sheepfold) and the huge fake topiary trees in front of the Crystal Room (you'll know it when you see it). If you're not in the mood for pretension, grab a hot dog instead at the **Ballplayer's House** near the southern end of the Sheep Meadow.

East of *Tavern on the Green*, at the northernmost point of the Mall lie the **Bandshell**, **Rumsey Playfield**, site of the free SummerStage performance series (see box, p.172), and the **Bethesda Terrace and Fountain** (72nd Street at mid-park). Bethesda Terrace, the only formal element of the original Olmsted and Vaux plan, overlooks the lake; beneath it is an **Arcade** whose tiled floors and elaborate decoration are currently being restored. The crowning centerpiece of the **Bethesda Fountain** is the nineteenth-century *Angel of the Waters* sculpture; its earnest puritanical angels (Purity, Health, Peace and Temperance) continue to watch disappointedly over their wicked city. (Theater fans may remember that the last scene of Tony Kushner's Pulitzer Prize–winning play *Angels in America* is set at this fountain.) You can go for a Venetian-style gondola ride or rent a rowboat from the **Loeb Boathouse** on the lake's eastern bank (March–Nov daily 10am–6pm, weather permitting; rowboats are $10 for the first hour, $2.50 each 15min after, with a $30 refundable deposit; gondola rides are available 5–10pm for $30 per 30min per group and require reservations; ⓣ212/517-2233).

Across the water, at the narrowest point on the lake, is the elegant cast-iron and wood **Bow Bridge**, designed by park architect Calvert Vaux. Directly over the bridge you will find yourself in the unruly woods of **The Ramble**, a 37-acre area filled with narrow winding paths, rock outcroppings, streams and an array of native plant life. Once a favorite address for drug dealing and anonymous sex (a police crackdown and the AIDS epidemic lessened both), it is now a great place to watch for one of the park's 54 species of birds, or take a quiet stroll (though still not advisable at night).

Picnicking in the park

As large as it is, Central Park has ample **picnicking opportunities**, the most obvious in the hectic expanse of the Sheep Meadow. Other fine locations: the west shore of the Lake, near Hernshead; the rock at Belvedere Castle; Conservatory Garden; the somewhat sloped lawn of the Ramble; Strawberry Fields; the Arthur Ross Pinetum or the areas around the Delacorte Theater. For your provisions, it's very easy to "take-in" from any number of shops, and one vendor (*It's a Wrap*, p.310) will even deliver your lunch to selected locations inside the park.

To the west of Bethesda Terrace, along the 72nd Street Drive, is the **Cherry Hill Fountain**, originally a turnaround point for carriages that was designed to have excellent views of the Lake, the Mall and the Ramble. One of the pretty areas paved over by Parks Commissioner Moses in the Thirties for use as a parking lot, it was restored to its natural state in the early 1980s.

West of here, across the Park Drive, is **Strawberry Fields** (72nd Street and Central Park West), a peaceful region of the park dedicated to the memory of John Lennon, who was murdered in 1980 in front of his home at the **Dakota Building**, across the street on Central Park West. (See box on page p.211 for more on the death of John Lennon.) Strawberry Fields is invariably crowded with those here to remember Lennon, as well as picnickers and seniors resting on the park benches. Near the West 72nd Street entrance to the area is a round Italian mosaic with the word "Imagine" at its center, donated by Lennon's widow, Yoko Ono, and invariably covered with flowers. Every year without fail on December 8th, the anniversary of Lennon's murder, Strawberry Fields is packed with his fans, singing Beatles songs and sharing their grief, even after all these years.

Back to the east of Bethesda Terrace is the **Boat Pond** (72nd St and Fifth Ave), officially named the **Conservatory Water** (though New Yorkers never call it that), a small manmade pond where you can watch model boat races and regattas every Saturday in the summer (or participate by renting a craft from the cart in front of the **Krebs Memorial Boathouse**, just east of the water; $10 per hour). The fanciful *Alice in Wonderland* statue at the northern end of the pond was donated by publisher George Delacorte and is a favorite climbing spot for kids. During the summer the New York Public Library sponsors Wednesday morning (11am) storytelling sessions for children at the *Hans Christian Andersen* statue on the west side of the pond (☎212/340-0906 for more information). A storyteller from the Central Park Conservancy also appears here at 11am on Saturdays throughout the summer.

If you continue north you will reach the backyard of the **Metropolitan Museum of Art** to the east at 81st Street (see Chapter 19) and the **Obelisk** (nicknamed Cleopatra's Needle by locals) to the west, an 1881 gift from Egypt that dates back to 1450 BC. A twin obelisk lies along the Thames River in London. Also nearby is the **Great Lawn** (81st St at mid-park), reopened in 1998 after a massive two-year, $18.5 million reconstruction. Originally the site of a reservoir from 1842 until 1931, it was drained and made into a playing field in the Thirties. It became a popular site for free concerts (Simon and Garfunkel, Elton John, Garth Brooks, Sting and others often attract half a million people or more, as did the Pope who celebrated mass here in 1995) and political rallies, but was badly overused and had serious drainage problems. Now rebuilt, reseeded and renewed, it will try to stay that way by only hosting the more sedate free New York Philharmonic and Metropolitan Opera concerts (see box overleaf). The lawn features eight softball fields and, at its northern end, new basketball and volleyball courts, and a 1/8-mile running track. The refurbished **Turtle Pond** is at the southern end of the Lawn, with a new wooden dock and nature blind for better viewing of the aquatic wildlife (yes, there actually is wildlife here, including ducks, fish and frogs). What's not new, on the southeast corner of the pond, is a massive statue of fourteenth-century Polish king **Wladyslaw Jagiello**, which appeared at the New York World's Fair in 1939 and was a subsequent gift of the Polish government to the park. It is the occasional site of Polish folk dancing displays.

Southwest of the Lawn is the **Delacorte Theater** which, as the venue of the annual free Shakespeare in the Park festivals, is appropriately anchored by Milton Hebald's sculptures of Romeo & Juliet and Prospero (from *The Tempest*). Next door, the tranquil **Shakespeare Garden** claims to hold every species of plant or flower mentioned in the Bard's plays. East of the garden is **Belvedere Castle**, a mock medieval citadel first erected atop **Vista Rock** in 1869 as a lookout, but now the home of the Urban Park Rangers and a **Visitor Center** (Tues–Sun 10am–5pm; ⓣ212/772-0210; walking tours, bird-watching excursions and educational programs). The highest point in the park (and therefore a splendid viewpoint), the Castle also houses the New York Meteorological Observatory's weather center, responsible for providing the official daily Central Park temperature readings, and makes a lovely background prop for the Delacorte's Shakespeare performances. The **Swedish Cottage Marionette Theater** (mid-park at 79th St) at the base ofVista Rock holds puppet shows such as *The True Story of Rumpelstiltskin* or *Gulliver's Travels* for children (ⓣ212/988-9093 for reservations and information).

The northern park

There are fewer attractions, but more open space, above the Great Lawn. Much of it is taken up by the **Reservoir** (86th–97th streets at mid-park, main entrance at 90th St and Fifth Ave), a 107-acre, billion-gallon reservoir that was originally designed in 1862 as part of the Croton Water System. No longer an active reservoir, but still referred to as one, it's unofficially called the Jacqueline Bouvier Kennedy Onassis Memorial Reservoir, after the area's most famous resident (Onassis lived nearby on Fifth Avenue and was frequently seen in the park). The reservoir is encircled by a running track, around which disciplined New Yorkers faithfully jog (the New York Road Runners' Club has a booth at the main entrance). The raised 1.58 mile track is a great place to get breathtaking 360-degree views of the skyline; just don't block any jogger's path or there will be hell to pay. Just north of the reservoir are a tennis court complex and the newly refurbished soccer fields of the **North Meadow Recreation Center** (97th St at mid-park; ⓣ212/348-4867). Continuing on, you'll feel more as if you are in Upstate New York than New York City if you meander through the North Woods. This 90-acre wild area contains manmade but natural-looking stone arches, the Loch (which is now actually more of a stream), and the stream valley of the Ravine (concealing five small waterfalls).

If you see nothing else above 86th Street in the park, don't miss the **Conservatory Garden**, between East 103rd and 106th streets, along Fifth Avenue, a pleasing, six-acre space filled with flowering trees and shrubs, planted flower beds, fanciful fountains, and shaded benches, and frequented by

Seasonal events and activities

• SummerStage and Shakespeare in the Park are two of the most popular urban summertime programs. Both activities are free and help to take the sting out of New York's infamous hazy, hot and humid summers. In 1986 **SummerStage** presented its inaugural Central Park concert with Sun Ra performing to an audience of fifty people, but by the time he returned with Sonic Youth six years later, the audience had grown to ten thousand. Musical acts are of consistently good quality, and have ranged from Cowboy Junkies to Basement Jaxx and Craig David. Located at the Rumsey Playing Field near 72nd St and Fifth Ave, a concert here is an invariably crowded, sticky but somehow bonding experience; in other words, well worth the free admission. Dance performances, spoken word, DJ sets and (paid admission) benefits are also put on. Call the SummerStage hotline (ⓣ212/360-2777) for more information, or see ⓦwww.summerstage.org.

Shakespeare in the Park takes place at the open-air Delacorte Theater, located near the W 81st St entrance to the park, where tickets are distributed daily at 1pm for that evening's performance, but you'll have to get in line well before. If you are downtown, tickets are also distributed at the Public Theater (425 Lafayette Street) between 1pm and 3pm the day of the performance. Two plays are performed each summer (mid-June through early Sept, Tues–Sun at 8pm; free); Shakespeare is the Festival's meat, but having just completed the entire cycle of his plays over the course of more than twenty years, other works are produced here as well. Call the Shakespeare Festival (ⓣ212/539-8750) for more information.

• **New York Philharmonic in the Park** (ⓣ212/875-5709) and **Metropolitan Opera in the Park** (ⓣ212/362-6000) hold several evenings of classical music in the summer, often with a booming fireworks display to usher the crowds home.

• **Claremont Riding Academy** 175 W 89th St (ⓣ212/724-5100) Open Mon–Fri, 6.30am–10pm, Sat & Sun 6.30am–5pm. Horseback riding lessons are available, as are rentals for riders experienced in the English saddle. $42 for 30min lesson, $35 for a ride on Central Park's bridlepaths.

• **The Harlem Meer Festival** 110th St between Fifth and Lenox aves (ⓣ 212/860-1370) Fairly intimate and enjoyable free performances of jazz and salsa music outside the Charles A. Dana Discovery Center on Sundays from 4–6pm throughout the summer.

families, lovers, painters and sketch artists. It's a great place to stop for a break while navigating the Museum Mile just east on Fifth Avenue. The iron-gated entrance at 105th Street and Fifth Avenue is known as the Vanderbilt Gate; it was the main entry to the Vanderbilt Mansion, previously situated at Fifth Avenue and 58th Street, and is now a favorite spot for weekend wedding party photographs. The garden itself is actually three gardens, each landscaped in a distinct style (English, French and Italian). The Italian garden is the first one encountered, and the most reserved, with verdant lawns and trimmed hedges. To the south is the English, enhanced by the Burnett Fountain, which depicts the two children from the classic book *The Secret Garden*. The French garden, the northernmost of the three, hosts the Untermyer Fountain (*Three Dancing Maidens*, by sculptor Walter Schott) and an exceedingly vivid cast of 20,000 tulips (spring) or, in the fall, over 2,000 chrysanthemums. Just south of the garden is the **Robert Bendleim Playground** for disabled children, at 108th Street near Fifth Avenue. Here physically challenged youngsters play in "accessible" sandboxes and swings, or work out their upper bodies on balance beams, all very much in keeping with the inclusive nature of Central Park.

At the top of the park is the **Charles A. Dana Discovery Center**, an environmental education center and Visitor Center, with free literature, changing

General information

• **General Park Information** ⓣ212/360-3444, ⓦwww.centralparknyc.org. Also ⓣ1-888/NYPARKS for special events information.

• Founded in 1980, the Central Park Conservancy is a nonprofit organization dedicated to preserving and managing the park. The Conservancy runs four Visitor Centers, with free maps and other helpful literature, as well as special events. All are open Tues–Sun, 10am–5pm: The Dairy (mid-park at 65th St; ⓣ212/794-6564); Belvedere Castle (mid-park at 79th St; ⓣ212/772-0210); North Meadow Recreation Center (mid-park at 97th St; ⓣ212/348-4867; also open Monday); and the Charles A. Dana Discovery Center (110th St off Fifth Ave; ⓣ212/860-1370).

• **Manhattan Urban Park Rangers** ⓣ212/628-2345 (activities information). The rangers are there to help; they lead walking tours, give directions and provide first aid in emergencies.

• The new **Parks Library collection** (in the Arsenal, 830 Fifth Ave at 64th Street, Room 240; Mon–Fri 9am–6pm; ⓣ212/360-8240), contains materials on the history of New York and the Parks system, wildlife and ecological concerns. The **photo archive** (ⓣ212/360-8110) documents park events and improvements from the 1930s onward, but you must make an appointment (and state your interest and intent) to use the collection.

• **Restrooms** are available at Hecksher Playground, the Boat Pond (Conservatory Water), Mineral Springs House (northwest end of Sheep's Meadow), Loeb Boathouse, the Delacorte Theater, the North Meadow Recreation Center, The Conservatory Garden and the Charles A. Dana Discovery Center.

• **Traffic**: the East and West drives run just inside the periphery of the park and are closed to automobile traffic on weekdays, 10am–3pm and 7–10pm; weekends, 7pm Friday to 6am Monday; and holidays, 7pm the night before until 6am the day after.

• In case of emergency, use the **emergency call boxes** located throughout the park and along the Park Drives (they provide a direct connection to the Central Park Precinct), or dial 911 at any pay phone.

visual exhibits, bird walks every Saturday at 11am in July and August, and multicultural performances (see box overleaf). Crowds of locals fish in the adjacent **Harlem Meer**, an eleven-acre pond created in 1864 and restored to its original, natural state (once again undoing the determined cement work of Parks Commissioner Robert Moses) and stocked with more than 50,000 fish. The Discovery Center provides bamboo poles and bait free of charge, though you'll have to release your catch of the day. In the extreme corner of the park at 110th Street and Fifth Avenue is a monument to Duke Ellington, the esteemed musician and composer of such favorites as "Take the A Train" and "Mood Indigo." Dedicated in July of 1997, it was the first memorial to an African American in the city. Atop three columns that summon the nine muses, the Duke stands before his grand piano, looking toward Harlem for the next generation of musical vanguards.

19

The Metropolitan Museum of Art

The **Metropolitan Museum of Art**, or the Met, as it's usually called, is the foremost art museum in America. It was first unveiled in 1880 as a Gothic Revival-style brick building, contrasting with the prevailing notion of the day that a museum should be a magnificent, daunting structure. For architects Jacob Wrey Mould and Calvert Vaux, however, it was important that the features of Central Park were not diminished by the building. Much of the museum's familiar multi-columned, wide-stepped facade on Fifth Avenue was added later by McKim, Mead and White in 1906, while other architects contributed to the renovations completed in 1926.

The collection takes in over two million works of art and spans the cultures of America, Europe, Africa, the Far East, and the classical and Islamic worlds. A quick stroll through the museum is out of the question: the Met demands many and specific visits or, at least, self-imposed limits. Broadly, the museum breaks down into **seven major collections**: European Arts – Painting and Sculpture; Asian Art; American Painting and Decorative Arts; Egyptian Antiquities; Medieval Art; Ancient Greek and Roman Art; and the Art of Africa, the Pacific and the Americas. You'll find the highlights of these and the Modern Art collection detailed below. Keep in mind, however, that there is much, much more of which space forbids anything other than a passing mention. Among the **less famous Met collections** are Islamic Art (possibly the largest display anywhere in the world with 12,000 objects); European Decorative Arts; Arms and Armor Galleries (the largest and most important in the Western Hemisphere); a Musical Instrument Collection (containing the world's oldest piano); and the Costume Institute. All this material sometimes

The Met's location, hours, and prices

The Met is located on Fifth Avenue at 82nd Street, set into Central Park. Take subway #4, #5 or #6 to 86th St–Lexington Ave. Hours are Tues–Thur & Sun 9.30am–5.15pm, Fri & Sat 9.30am–8.45pm; suggested donation $10, students $5 (includes admission to the Cloisters on the same day, see p.232); recorded "acoustiguide" tours of the major collections $5; free conducted tours, "Highlights of the Met," daily; also highly detailed tours of specific galleries, call for details; several restaurants and excellent book and gift shops; ⓣ212/879-5500 or 535-7710 for recorded information.

METROPOLITAN MUSEUM OF ART

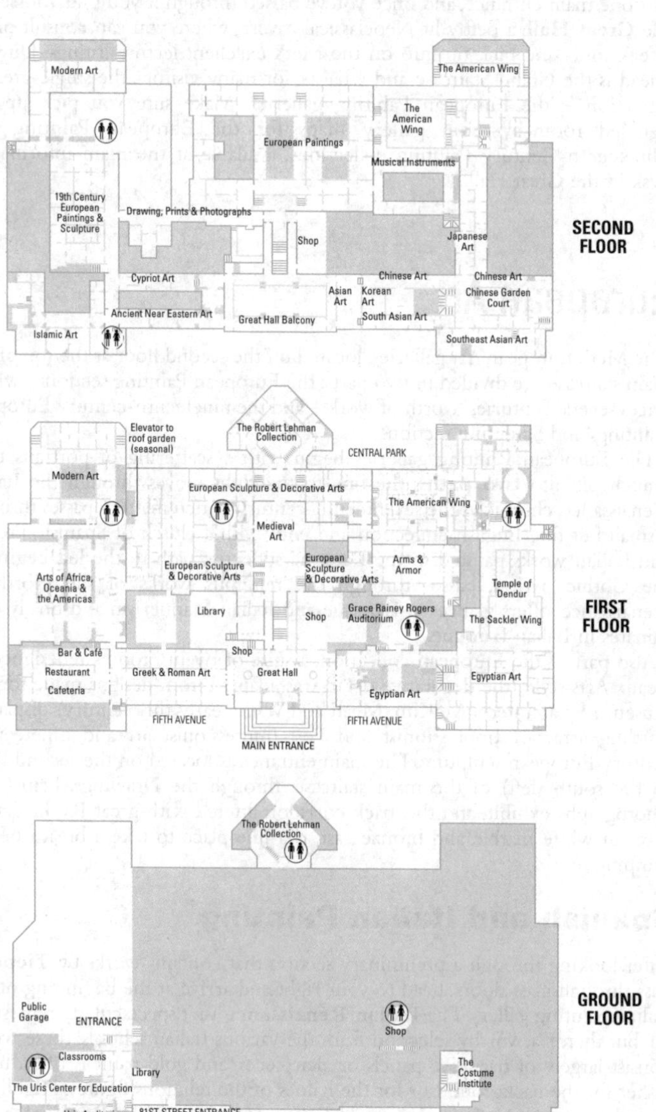

SECOND FLOOR
Modern Art
The American Wing
The American Wing
European Paintings
Musical Instruments
19th Century European Paintings & Sculpture
Drawing, Prints & Photographs
Shop
Japanese Art
Cypriot Art
Chinese Art
Chinese Art
Asian Art
Korean Art
Chinese Garden Court
Ancient Near Eastern Art
South Asian Art
Great Hall Balcony
Islamic Art
Southeast Asian Art
FIRST FLOOR
Elevator to roof garden (seasonal)
The Robert Lehman Collection
CENTRAL PARK
Modern Art
European Sculpture & Decorative Arts
The American Wing
Medieval Art
European Sculpture & Decorative Arts
European Sculpture & Decorative Arts
Arms & Armor
Arts of Africa, Oceania & the Americas
Temple of Dendur
Library
Shop
Grace Rainey Rogers Auditorium
The Sackler Wing
Shop
Bar & Café
Restaurant
Greek & Roman Art
Great Hall
Egyptian Art
Cafeteria
Egyptian Art
FIFTH AVENUE
FIFTH AVENUE
MAIN ENTRANCE
GROUND FLOOR
The Robert Lehman Collection
Public Garage
ENTRANCE
Shop
Classrooms
The Costume Institute
Library
The Uris Center for Education
Uris Auditorium
81ST STREET ENTRANCE

overshadows the museum's temporary exhibits, culled from both the Metropolitan's collection and loans from other galleries, which can supplement any of the major collections.

Despite the museum's size, **initial orientation** is not too difficult. There is just one main entrance, and once you've passed through it you find yourself in the **Great Hall**, a deftly lit Neoclassical cavern where you can consult plans, check tours and pick up info on the Met's excellent lecture listings. Directly ahead is the Grand Staircase and what is, for many visitors, the single greatest attraction – the European Painting galleries. Make sure you pick up the detailed room-by-room gallery maps for the European Painting and Nineteenth-Century Painting collections, available at the main information desk in the Great Hall.

European Art

The Met's European Art galleries, located on the second floor at the top of the main staircase, are divided in two parts: the European Painting section – which traces several centuries' worth of work – and the nineteenth-century European Paintings and Sculpture section.

The European Painting galleries begin with a scattering of portraits then branch off into **two paths**: the one to the right moves through the Italian Renaissance, chronicles the seventeenth-century Dutch masters, passes through a small but fine English collection and ends with a clutch of Spanish, French and Italian works painted in the Baroque style; the path to the left begins in the Gothic period, passes through the religious works of the Northern Renaissance, offers glances at Baroque and Italian Mannerism and finally culminates in Italian Baroque.

Also part of the European collection, a suite of twenty rooms redesigned in Beaux Arts style (the decorative detail was adapted from designs made for the museum by architects McKim, Mead and White early this century) displays a startling array of Impressionist and Post-Impressionist art and nineteenth-century European sculpture. The main entrance is located on the second floor to the south (left) of the main staircase, through the Drawings, Prints and Photographs exhibit, and this back corridor, littered with great Rodin sculptures in white marble and bronze cast, is a fine place to take a breath before jumping in.

Spanish and Italian Painting

After looking through a preliminary section that contains works by **Tiepolo**, pass through glass doors, head to your right and arrive at the beginning of the Italian painting gallery. The **Italian Renaissance** isn't spectacularly represented, but there's a worthy selection from the various Italian schools; these works consist largely of narrative panels or altarpieces, and gold paint is often used, either for the background or for the haloes of the religious figures. Highlights include an early *Madonna and Child Enthroned with Saints* by **Raphael**, a late **Botticelli** (the crisply linear *Three Miracles of Saint Zenobius*), **Filippo Lippi**'s *Madonna and Child Enthroned with Two Angels*, and **Michele de Verona**'s handsome *Madonna and Child with the Infant John the Baptist*, in which the characters are almost sculpturally rendered. Also look out for the roaring dragon in

Problems in visiting the Met

There are a couple of **difficulties** in visiting, other than the obvious frustrations of the crowds, the size of the collection and the time necessary to do the Met justice: **Layout**. The Met has developed in a piecemeal way, for its nineteenth-century multimillionaire benefactors were often as intent on advertising their own tastes as setting America on the cultural high road. Their bequests, therefore, often stipulated that their donations be housed in distinct galleries. If you're interested in one particular period or movement of art, you won't necessarily find all of its examples in the same place.

Reorganization. The museum is constantly reorganizing its galleries: rotating the works, creating space for special exhibits, loaning out pieces for retrospectives, and refurbishing rooms. This means that although the master works stay pretty much in the same locations, the order in which we've listed various standouts may not be that in which they appear and some might be away on loan.

One tactic to deal with the often-crushing mob – go during the early evening hours 5 to 8.45pm on Fridays and Saturdays. You won't fully avoid the crowds, but many tourists will have other activities planned during these times, and in addition to some clearer pathways, you'll have the benefit of a classical string quartet in the Great Hall Balcony, and a piano or guitar soloist to accompany your meal in the restaurant.

Crivelli's *St George* and the fly (representing sin) in his beautiful *Madonna and Child*. **Mantegna**'s rigid and sculptural *Adoration of the Shepherds* is also worth your time. At the end of the Italian section is a room filled with luminous works by **Titian** and **Tintoretto**.

There are surprisingly few **Spanish** painters here. Near the end of the English and Dutch masters, as you loop back to the entrance to the painting galleries you'll pass through a smattering of works by Spanish, French and Italian painters, most notably **Goya** and **Velázquez**. The latter's piercing and somber *Portrait of Juan de Pareja* shouldn't be missed; when it was first exhibited in 1650, a critic dramatically remarked, "All the rest are art, this alone is truth." An appealing portrait of a toddler in a red jumpsuit, the familiar *Don Manuel Osorio Manrique de Zuniga* by Goya, seems more sinister on second glance, as the caged birds on the floor are about to be confronted by three wide-eyed cats. There is also a room with a few masterful **El Greco**'s at the end of the Italian section. His extraordinary *View of Toledo* – all brooding intensity as the skies seem about to swallow up the ghost-like town – is perhaps the best of his works anywhere in the world, and a satisfying conclusion to the gallery.

Dutch Painting

This collection, dominated by the major works of **Rembrandt, Vermeer** and **Hals**, is the culmination of the main European galleries – and arguably the finest single group of paintings in the museum.

Vermeer, genius of the domestic interior, is represented by some of his best works. His *Young Woman with a Water Jug*, with its themes of purity and temperance, is a perfect example of his skill in composition and tonal gradation, combined with an uncannily naturalistic sense of lighting. *A Girl Asleep* is deeper in its composition, or at least appears to be, the rich fabric separating the foreground from the rooms beyond. Vermeer often used this trick, and you'll see it again in *Allegory of the Faith*, where the drawn curtain presents the tableau and separates the viewer from the lesson presented. Most haunting of all is the great *Portrait of a Young Woman*, displaying Vermeer at his most complex – and the Met collection at its most fortunate.

As Vermeer's pictures depict the domestic harmony of seventeenth-century Holland, Hals's early paintings reveal its exuberance. In *Merrymakers at Shrovetide*, the figures explode out from the canvas in an abundance of gesture and richness. *Young Man and a Woman at an Inn*, painted in 1623, shows a more subdued use of color (without expense of vitality).

The best of Rembrandt's works here are also portraits, marked by their subject's rosy cheeks and the mostly dark grounds. There is a beautiful painting of his common-law wife, *Hendrike Stoffjels*, finished three years before her early death – a blow that marked a further decline in the artist's fortunes. In 1660, he went bankrupt, and the superb *Self-Portrait* of that year shows the self-examination he brought to later works.

In addition to these three famous artists, the Dutch rooms also display a good scattering of works by their contemporaries. Most memorable is **Pieter de Hooch**'s *Two Men and a Woman in a Courtyard of a House*, his acknowledged masterpiece, with its perfect arrangement of line, form and color. While de Hooch was painting peaceful courtyards and Vermeer lacemakers and lute players, **Adriaen Brouwer** was turning his eye to the seamier side of Dutch life. When he wasn't drunk or in prison he came up with works like *The Smokers*, a portrait of Brouwer and his drinking pals – he's the one in the foreground, in case you hadn't guessed.

English Painting

Though the Met's **English gallery** is essentially a prelude to the other major collections here, it's an unusually brilliant and elegant collection of paintings. At its heart are a group of portraits by **Sir Joshua Reynolds**, **Thomas Gainsborough** and **Sir Thomas Lawrence**, the trio of great eighteenth-century English portraitists. Gainsborough's *Mrs Grace Dalrymple Elliott* is typical of his portrait style – an almost feathery lightness softening the monumental pose. Lawrence is best represented by *The Calmady Children*, a much-engraved portrait that was the artist's favorite among his works, and by his likeable and quite large virtuoso study of *Elizabeth Farren*, which he painted at the precocious age of 21. Upon seeing the picture, Sir Joshua Reynolds remarked, "This young man begins where I leave off," a rather modest comment considering the number of portraits by Reynolds that are included here.

Early Flemish and Netherlandish Painting

Follow the **left-hand fork** from the preliminary rooms and you'll arrive at Early Flemish and Netherlandish Painting from the fifteenth and sixteenth centuries, precursors of both the Northern and Italian Renaissances. Inevitably, the first paintings are by **van Eyck**, who is generally attributed with beginning the tradition of North European realism. *The Crucifixion* and *The Last Judgement* – painted early in his career and much like the miniatures he painted for the Turin-Milan Hours – are bright, realistic and full of expressive (even horrific) detail. In *Judgement*'s three-level world, the heavenly figures at the top project light and purity, while below earth, under a grinning skeleton's outstretched legs, the denizens of a dark hell share their world with hungry, sharp-toothed animals.

There's more allusion to things Gothic in **Rogier van der Weyden**'s *Christ Appearing to His Mother*, the apocryphal visit surrounded by tiny statuary depicting Christ's earlier and Mary's later life; its warmth of design and feeling contrast well with Van Eyck's hard draughtsman's clarity. Another great Northern Gothic painter, **Gerard David**, used local settings for his religious scenes; the background of his exquisite *Virgin and Child with Four Angels* is medieval Bruges and *The Rest on the Flight to Egypt* features a forest glade (with the turrets of Bruges visible down below). **Pieter Bruegel the Elder**'s *Harvesters*, one of the Met's most reproduced pictures and part of the series of six paintings that included his (Christmas-card familiar) *Hunters in the Snow*, shows how these innovations were assimilated.

Impressionist Painting

Establishment artists and precursors of the Impressionists such as **Ingres** and **Delacroix**, as well as artists from the **Barbizon School**, are located to the far left of the gallery. Straight ahead are exhibits centering around **Manet**, the Impressionist movement's most influential precursor, whose early style of contrasting light and shadow with modulated shades of black can be firmly linked to the tradition of Hals, Velázquez and Goya. *The Spanish Dancer*, an accomplished example of this tradition, was well received on Manet's debut at the Paris Salon in 1861. Within a few years, though, he was shocking the same establishment with the striking *Young Lady in 1866* – the same woman, incidentally, modeled for all three paintings.

Courbet and **Degas**, too, are well represented – Courbet with examples of each phase and period of his career, including *Woman with a Parrot*, a superbly erotic and exotic work that gave Manet the idea for his work of the same name. As for Degas, there are studies here in just about every medium, from pastels to sculpture. Many examine the theme he returned to again and again – dancers, a lovely example of which is *Dancers Practicing at the Bar.* In addition to showing the grace and beauty of the dancers, the painting is about structure, alluded to in the way the lines of the watering can mimic the position of the dancers' legs. Also here is a casting of his *Little Dancer*, complete with real tutu, hair ribbon and slippers.

Monet was one of the Impressionist movement's most prolific painters, returning again and again to a single subject to produce a series of images capturing different nuances of light and atmosphere. There are a number of his works here, including three superb examples – *Rouen Cathedral, The Houses of Parliament (Effect of Fog)* and *The Doge's Palace Seen from San Giorgio Maggiore* – which show the beginnings of his final phase of near-abstract Impressionism.

Cézanne's technique was very different. He labored long to achieve a painstaking analysis of form and color, an effect clear in the *Landscape of Marseilles*. Of his few portraits, the jarring, almost Cubist angles and spaces of *Mme Cézanne in a Red Dress* seems years ahead of its time. Take a look, too, at *The Card Players*, whose dynamic triangular structure thrusts out, yet retains the quiet concentration of the moment. **Renoir** is perhaps the best represented among the remaining Impressionists, though his most important work here dates from 1878, when he began to move away from the mainstream techniques he'd learned while working with Monet. *Mme Charpentier and her Children* is a likeable enough piece, one whose affectionate tone manages to sidestep the sentimentality of Renoir's later work.

Post-Impressionist Painting

The Post-Impressionists, logically enough, follow Monet and Cézanne, with one of the highlights of the collection being **Gauguin**'s masterly *La Orana*

Maria. The scene was a staple of the Renaissance, transferred here to a different culture in an attempt to unfold the symbolic meaning, and perhaps voice the artist's feeling for the native South Sea islanders. *Two Tahitian Women* hangs adjacent – skillful, studied simplicity.

Toulouse-Lautrec delighted in painting the world Gauguin went to Tahiti to escape. *The Sofa* is one of a series of sketches he made in Paris brothels. The artist's deformity (he broke both his legs at a young age, and his bones subsequently failed to grow) distanced him from society, and he identified with the marginalized life of the prostitutes in his sketches. He also hated posed modeling, which made the bored women awaiting clients an ideal subject.

All of this scratches little more than the surface of the galleries. There are also major works by **Van Gogh** (including *Irises* and *Self Portrait with Straw Hat*), **Rousseau**, **Pissarro** and **Seurat** (*Circus Sideshow*).

Asian Art

The second floor's **Asian Art galleries** gather an impressive and vast array of Chinese, Japanese, Indian and Southeast Asian sculpture, painting, ceramics and metalwork, as well as an indoor replica of a Chinese garden. Approach from the Great Hall balcony: lining the corridor's back wall is an exhibit of fifth- to eighth-century Kuran pottery, which includes some fancifully glazed and decorated ceremonial pieces among the everyday jugs and bowls. First up is **Chinese Sculpture**, a collection of stone works arranged around two twenty-foot-high buddhas. The focal point, however, is the enormous (and exquisite) fourteenth-century mural, *The Pure Land of Bhaishajyaguru*. This piece, masterfully reconstructed after being severely damaged in an earthquake, is a study in calm reflection.

Take the right fork from this gallery to arrive at **South Asian Art**. Note the ancient pair of golden earrings from India as you enter – actually quite rare, for it was custom there to melt down and recast jewelry after the owner died to avoid inheriting that person's karma. **Statues** of Hindu and Buddhist deities form the bulk of the works, alongside numerous pieces of **friezes**, many of which still possess exceptional detail despite years of exposure. *The Great Departure and the Temptation of the Buddha*, carved in the third century, is a particularly lively example: Siddhartha setting out on his spiritual journey being chased by a harem of dancing girls and grasping cherubs.

Past a set of stairs that leads to a small third-floor gallery (for temporary exhibits) lies **Chinese Art**. There is so much here – painting, jewelry, jade carvings – that the works tend to run into one another. In this section, *Stele with Paired Bodhisattvas and Thousand Buddha Motif*, dating from the early eighth century AD, is especially noteworthy for its use of dramatic black marble and for the painstaking effort in the carving of all those tiny buddhas.

The highlight in this area is the **Chinese Garden Court**, a serene, minimalist retreat enclosed by the galleries, and the adjacent **Ming Room**, a typical salon decorated in period style with wooden lattice doors. The naturally lit garden is representative of one found in Chinese homes, assembled by experts from the People's Republic: a pagoda, small waterfall and stocked goldfish pond landscaped with limestone rocks, trees and shrubs conjure up a sense of peace.

The Sackler Wing

After your meditation, forge right to the Sackler Wing, part of a cluster of rooms dedicated to **Japanese Art**. Less structured than the other galleries, this section holds objects from the prehistoric era to the present, divided into thematic sections: "Gods and Ancestors," "Spirits and Teachers," "Characters in a Story" and "The Moral and Immoral." Complementing this core are rotating exhibits of textiles, paintings and prints. Earliest of Japanese **religious art** are the *dogu,* female figurines dating from 10,500 BC up to 400 BC. The coming of Buddhism in the sixth century AD changed the strategy of Japanese art, and the results – greatly exaggerated depictions of physical perfection – can be seen in the **Japanese Buddhist painting and sculpture** collection. All of which is a prelude to the exhibit's crown jewel – the several galleries of seventeenth- and eighteenth-century **hand-painted Kano screens**. The screens range from the elegantly mundane (books on a shelf) to elaborate scenes of historical allusion and divine fervor, and owing to the Japanese admiration of the Chinese aesthetic at this time, reflect a Chinese sensibility. Also make sure to see the recreated *shoin* (study) room, which projects serenity and scholarly virtue. Since all the exhibited paintings, calligraphy and scrolls of Asian art are rotated every six months or so, the scenes change, but their beauty remains constant.

The Cantor Roof Garden

From May through October, you can ascend to the **Cantor Roof Garden** (accessible by elevator from the first floor) located on top of the Wallace Wing, which displays **contemporary sculpture** against the dramatic backdrop of New York's midtown skyline. In October this also happens to be a great place to see the colorful fall foliage in Central Park. Drinks and snacks are served, perhaps on the expensive side – though the breathtaking views make up for it.

The American Wing

Close to being a museum in its own right, **the American Wing** is a thorough introduction to the development of fine art in America. Galleries lead off from the **Charles Engelhard Court**, a shrub-filled sculpture garden enclosed at the far end by the *Facade of the United States Bank,* lifted in its entirety straight from Wall Street. Step through this facade and you'll be standing in the **Federal period** rooms, surrounded by the restrained Neoclassical elegance of the late eighteenth century – the first of twenty-five **furnished historical rooms** that lie adjacent to the American painting galleries on three floors. If this is your first visit to this section of the Met, go up to the third floor and work your way down so that you'll see the rooms in (roughly) chronological order. The **early Colonial period**, represented most evocatively in the Hart Room of around 1674, begins the tour; **Frank Lloyd Wright**'s *Room from the Little House, Minneapolis*, with its windowed walls demonstrating Wright's concept of minimizing interior–exterior division, ends it. On the second floor balcony, don't miss the iridescent Favrile glass of **Louis Comfort Tiffany**: an elegant Art Nouveau accompaniment to the decor.

The American painting collection

The **American painting collection** begins in a maze of rooms on the second floor with **eighteenth-century** portraits, but really get going with the works of **Benjamin West**, an artist who worked in London and taught or influenced many of the American painters of his day – *The Triumph of Love* is typical of his Neoclassical, allegorical works. More heroics come with **John Trumbull**, one of West's pupils, in *Sortie Made by the Garrison of Gibraltar* and the fully blown Romanticism of *Washington Crossing the Delaware* by **Emanuel Leutzes**. This last enormous canvas shows Washington escaping across the river in the winter of 1776; although historically and geographically inaccurate – the American flag, shown dramatically flowing in the background, hadn't yet been created – the picture is nonetheless a national icon.

Early in the nineteenth century, American painters embraced landscape painting and nature. **William Sidney Mount** depicted scenes of his native Long Island, often with a sly political angle as with *Cider Makers* and *The Bet*, and the painters of the **Hudson Valley School** glorified the landscape in their vast lyrical canvases. **Thomas Cole**, the school's doyen, is represented by *The Oxbow*, his pupil **Frederick Church** by an immense *Heart of the Andes* – combining the grand sweep of the mountains with minutely depicted flora. **Albert Bierstadt** and **S.R. Gifford** continued to concentrate on the American West – their respective works *The Rocky Mountains*, *Lander's Peak* and *Kauterskill Falls* have a near-visionary idealism, bound to a belief that the westward development of the country was a manifestation of divine will.

Winslow Homer is allowed most of a gallery to himself – fittingly for a painter who so greatly influenced the late-nineteenth-century artistic scene in America. Homer began his career illustrating the day-to-day realities of the Civil War – there's a good selection here that shows the tedium and sadness of that era. His talent in recording detail carried over into his late, quasi-Impressionistic studies of seascapes of which *Northeaster* is one of the finest.

The mezzanine below takes American art into the late nineteenth and early **twentieth century**. Some of the initial portraiture here tends to the sugary, but **J.W. Alexander**'s *Repose* deftly hits the mark – a simple, striking use of line and light with a sumptuous feel and more than a hint of eroticism. By way of contrast, there's **Thomas Eakin**'s subdued, almost ghostly *Max Schmitt in a Single Scull*, **Childe Hassam**'s *Avenue of the Allies: Great Britain 1918*, patriotic art filled with light and color, and **William Merritt Chase**'s *For the Little One*, an Impressionist study of his wife sewing. Chase studied in Europe and it was there that he painted his *Portrait of Whistler*. Whistler in turn painted his own portrait of Chase but destroyed the work on seeing Chase's (quite truthful) depiction of himself as a dandified fop, done in a teasing style that mimicked his own. Whatever Whistler's conceits, though, his portraits are adept: witness the *Arrangement in Flesh Color and Black: Portrait of Theodore Duret* nearby.

The reputation of **Sargent** has suffered its ups and downs over the years, but he seems to be coming back into fashion. There is certainly a virtuosity in his large portraits, like that of *Mr and Mrs I.N. Phelps Stokes*, the couple purposefully elongated as if to emphasize their aristocratic characters. The *Portrait of Madam X* (Mme Pierre Gautreau, a celebrated Parisian beauty) was one of the most famous pictures of its day: exhibited at the 1884 Paris Salon, it was considered so improper that Sargent had to leave Paris for London. "I suppose it's the best thing I've done," he said wearily on selling it to the Met a few years later.

The Egyptian collection

"A chronological panorama of ancient Egypt's art, history and culture," boasts the blurb to the **Egyptian collection**, and it is no exaggeration, as nearly all of the 35,000 objects in the collection are on lavish display. Brightly efficient corridors steer you through the treasures of the museum's own digs during the 1920s and 1930s, as well as other art and artifacts from 3000 BC to the Byzantine period of Egyptian culture.

Enter from the Great Hall on the first floor and be prepared to be awed: the large **statuary** are the most immediately striking of the exhibits, such as those from Queen Hatshepsut's Temple, along with numerous **tombs** and **sarcophagi** in the first few rooms. Ultimately, it's the smaller sculptural pieces that hold the attention longest. Figures like *Merti and his Wife* were modeled as portraits, but often carvings were made in the belief that a person's *Ka,* or life force, would continue to exist in an idealized model after his or her death. A beautifully crafted example is the *Carving of Senbi* in gallery nine; what was probably **Senbi's tomb** is displayed nearby along with other funerary objects like Canopic jars. In the room next door is the dazzling collection of **Princess Sit-Hathor-yunet jewelry**, a pinnacle in Egyptian decorative art from around 1830 BC. In nearby rooms you will find models of Mekutra's House from around 1198 BC gallery four, and in gallery seventeen, the radiant *Fragmentary Face of a Queen*, possibly Nefertiti sensuously carved in polished yellow jasper.

The Temple of Dendur

At the end of the collection sits the **Temple of Dendur**, housed in a vast airy gallery with photographs and information about the temple's history and its original site on the banks of the Nile. Built by the Emperor Augustus in 15 BC for the Goddess Isis of Philae, the temple was moved here as a gift of the Egyptian government during the construction of the Aswan High Dam in 1965 – otherwise it would have drowned. Though you can't walk all the way inside, you can go in just enough to get a glimpse of the interior rooms, their walls filled with hieroglyphs. The temple itself is on a raised platform, surrounded by a narrow moat which in the front widens to become a rather pretty reflecting pool, no doubt designed to make visitors think of the Nile – it doesn't, but it's a nice touch anyway. The entire high-ceilinged gallery is glassed-in on one side, and looks out onto Central Park. Illuminated at night, the gallery seems to glow, lending the temple an air of mystery that is missing during the day.

Medieval art

Although you could move straight to the **medieval art** from the American Wing, you'd miss out on the museum's carefully planned approach. Instead, enter these galleries via the **corridor** from the back of the Great Hall, to the left of the main staircase; there you'll see displays of the sumptuous **Byzantine metalwork and jewelry** that financier J.P. Morgan donated to the museum in its early days. At the end of the corridor is the main **sculpture hall**, piled high with religious statuary and carvings (a tremendous *St Nicholas Saving Three*

Boys in the Brine Tub) and divided by a massive *reja* (a decorative open-work, iron altar screen) from Valladolid Cathedral. If you're here in December, you'll see a highlight of New York's Christmas season: a beautifully decorated, twenty-foot-high **Christmas tree** lit up in the center of the sculpture hall.

The **medieval treasury** to the right of the hall has an all-embracing – and magnificent – display of objects religious, liturgical and secular. And beyond are the **Jack and Belle Linski Galleries**: Flemish, Florentine and Venetian painting, porcelain and bronzes.

Scattered throughout the medieval galleries are later **period rooms**: paneled Tudor bedrooms and Robert Adam fineries from England, florid Rococo boudoirs and salons from France, and an entire Renaissance patio from Velez Blanco in Spain. It's all fascinating, but a bit much, leaving you with the feeling that Morgan and his robber baron friends would probably have shipped over Versailles if they could have laid their hands on it.

Greek and Roman art

This is one of the largest collections of ancient art in the world, its display of classical Greek art second only to Athens. The collection is exhibited in eight galleries on the first floor, re-created according to original McKim, Mead and White designs. Enter from the museum's Great Hall, and you'll soon find yourself in the **Belfer Court**, a sort of preamble to the exhibit. The court displays prehistoric and early Greek art – characterized by simpler, more geometric shapes and patterns, such as a fanciful **Minoan vase** in the shape of a bull's head from around 1400 BC and a charming sculpture of a seated man playing the harp from around 3000 BC. The central hall, which displays sixth- to fourth-century BC marble sculpture including several large sphinxes, is flanked by three rooms on either side, each fully renovated, with exhibits arranged by theme, medium and chronology. You'll find everything from large **funerary monuments** to tiny **terra-cotta figures** to intricately carved **gold jewelry** in the same room, with artfully arranged display cases that you can circle to get views from all angles. Standing in the center of the first gallery to the left of the central hall is a marble sculpture of a nude boy – known as the **New York Kouros** – one of the earliest *kouros*, or funerary statue, to have survived intact. Dating from 580 BC and originally from Attica, it marked the grave of the son of a wealthy family, created according to tradition as a memorial to ensure he would be remembered.

Art of Africa, the Pacific and the Americas

Son of Governor Nelson Rockefeller, Michael C. Rockefeller disappeared during a trip to West New Guinea in 1961. In 1969, Nelson Rockefeller donated the entire collection of his Museum of Primitive Art, over 3300 works, plus library and photographic material to the Met, and this wing, on the first floor past the Greek and Roman galleries, stands as a memorial to his son. It includes many of his finds of Asmat objects, such as carved *mbis* (memorial) poles, figures and a canoe, from Irian Jaya, alongside the Met's comprehensive collection of art from **Africa, the Pacific and the Americas**. It's a superb set of galleries, the muted, understated decor throwing the exhibits into sharp and often dramatic focus. The **African exhibit** has recently been completely renovated, expanded and reinstalled, offering an overview of the major geographic regions and their cultures, though West Africa is better represented than the rest of the continent. Particularly awe-inspiring is the new display of art from the Court of Benin (present-day Nigeria) – tiny **carved ivory statues and vessels**, created with astonishing detail. The **Pacific collection** covers the islands of Melanesia, Micronesia, Polynesia and Australia, and contains a wide array of objects such as wild, somewhat frightening, **wooden masks** with piercing all-too-realistic eyes. Sadly **Mexico, Central and South America** get somewhat short shrift here, though there is a nice collection of **pre-Columbian jade**, Mayan and Aztec pottery, and Mexican ceramic sculpture. But the best part by far is the entire room filled with **gold jewelry and ornaments** – particularly the exquisite hammered gold nose ornaments and earrings from Peru and the richly carved, jeweled ornaments from Colombia.

Modern art

Housed over two floors in the Lila Acheson Wallace Wing, directly to the rear of the Rockefeller Wing, the Met's **modern art** collection is a fascinating and relatively compact group of paintings. The first floor begins with the collection's most recent acquisitions and proceeds with a chronological installation of American and European art **from 1905 to 1940**. Such paintings as **Charles Demuth**'s *The Figure Five in Gold* and **di Chirico**'s *Ariadne* are here, alongside works by **Klee**, **Modigliani**, **Braque** and **Klimt**. There is also a room devoted largely to **Picasso**, ranging from his *Portrait of Gertrude Stein* and provocative, blue-period *The Blind Man's Meal*, through his Cubist period to his more familiar skewed-perspective portraits. Other highlights include **Hopper**'s *Views From Williamsburg Bridge*, a visually stunning if somewhat idealized take on brick tenements in Brooklyn, a wall of **O'Keeffe**'s, including the sumptuous, erotic *Black Iris*, and **Soutine**'s *Houses at Cagnes*, a Cézanne-like townscape in a funhouse mirror – off-kilter and vaguely sinister. In addition there is a small design collection, featuring rotating pieces of furniture, ceramics and almost anything else from the museum's holdings.

The top floor contains European and American painting **from 1945 to the present**, opening with a room filled with the gigantic, emotional canvases of Abstract Expressionist **Clyfford Still**. Highlights on this floor include **Pollock**'s masterly *Autumn Rhythm (Number 30)*, **R.B. Kitaj**'s *John Ford on his Deathbed*, a dreamlike painting of the director of western movies, Pop Artist **James Rosenquist**'s vibrant *House of Fire*, an **Ellsworth Kelly** thirteen-panel color-block installation called *Spectrum V* (resembling a child's xylophone) and **Andy Warhol**'s *Last Self-Portrait* from 1986. There are also works by **Beckmann**, **Lichtenstein**, **Rothko**, **Johns** and **de Kooning**.

The Lehman Pavilion

The two-floor **Lehman Pavilion** was tacked on to the rear of the Met in 1975 to house the collection of Robert Lehman, millionaire banker and art collector. This section in the rear of the building breaks from the Met's usual sober arrangement of rectangular floor plans: Rooms are laid out beside a brilliantly lit atrium, with some rooms re-created from Lehman's own home.

Lehman's enthusiasms fill important gaps in the Met's account of **Italian Renaissance** painting. This period was his passion, and his personal collection is shown on the first floor of the pavilion, centering around **Botticelli's** *Annunciation*, a small but exquisite celebration of the Florentine perspective. From the Venetian School comes a sculptural *Madonna and Child* by **Bellini** and, following **Bartolomeo Vivarini**'s exquisitely detailed altarpiece *Death of the Virgin*, a quartet of works by the Sienese **Giovanni di Paolo**; most notable are *The Creation of the World* and the *Expulsion from Paradise*, in which an angel gently ushers Adam and Eve from Eden, while white-bearded God, surrounded by feathered blue angels, points to their place of banishment.

Continuing on, there is a small but strong group of sixteenth-century portraits by **El Greco**, **Ingres** (the luminescent *Princesse de Broglie*), **Ter Borch** and **Velázquez**. One painting stands out from them all, though: **Rembrandt**'s *Portrait of Gerard de Lairesse*. Although de Lairesse was supposedly disliked for his luxurious tastes and unpleasant character, his most apparent flaw was his disfigured face – ravaged by congenital syphilis.

In the gallery to the left of this collection are works from the **Northern Renaissance**, highlighted by a trio of paintings by **Hans Memling**, **Hans Holbein the Younger** and **Petrus Christus**. On the ground floor, there is also a small collection of **nineteenth- and twentieth-century art,** mostly minor works by major artists – Renoir, Van Gogh, Gauguin, Cézanne and Matisse – along with some lesser-known painters.

20

The Upper East Side

The defining characteristic of Manhattan's Upper East Side, a two-square-mile grid that includes the great **avenues of Fifth, Madison and Park**, is wealth – and wealth does have its privileges. While other neighborhoods are affected by incursions of immigrant groups, artistic trends and the like, this remains primarily an enclave of the well-off, with upscale shops, clean and relatively safe streets, well-preserved buildings and landmarks, and most of the city's finest museums. Until recent decades, the avenues and streets east of **Lexington Avenue** primarily contained past-their-prime walk-up multi-unit brownstones and low-density apartment buildings. However, the demand for housing has produced a still-growing forest of giant metal and stone stumps closer to the East River as well as the restoration of many old brownstones on the side streets. In the East River itself, **Roosevelt Island** is less salubrious still, if an intriguing dose of un-Manhattan-like city life.

Fifth Avenue

Fifth Avenue has been the haughty patrician face of Manhattan since the opening of Central Park in 1876 lured the Carnegies, Astors, Vanderbilts, Whitneys and other capitalists north from lower Fifth Avenue and Gramercy Park to build their fashionable residences on the strip alongside. Upper Fifth Avenue addresses became not only acceptable but stylish. To this day the address remains so prestigious that buildings with no Fifth Avenue entrance to speak of call themselves by their would-be Fifth Avenue addresses instead of the more accurate side-street addresses. The parkside buildings on Fifth Avenue went up when Neoclassicism was the rage, hence the surviving originals are cluttered with columns and classical statues. A great deal of what you see, though, is third- or fourth-generation construction: through the latter part of the nineteenth century, fanciful mansions were built at vast expense, but then lasted only ten or fifteen years before being demolished for even wilder extravagances or, more commonly, grand apartment buildings. Rocketing land values made the opportunity to sell at a vast profit irresistible.

As Fifth Avenue progresses north, it turns into the so-called Museum Mile, New York's greatest concentration of art and exhibitions – several of them housed in a few remaining mansions. Henry Clay Frick's house at 70th Street is marginally less ostentatious than its neighbors and is now the deliciously intimate and tranquil home of the **Frick Collection**, one of the city's musts. The modern structure of the **Guggenheim** is further up this way.

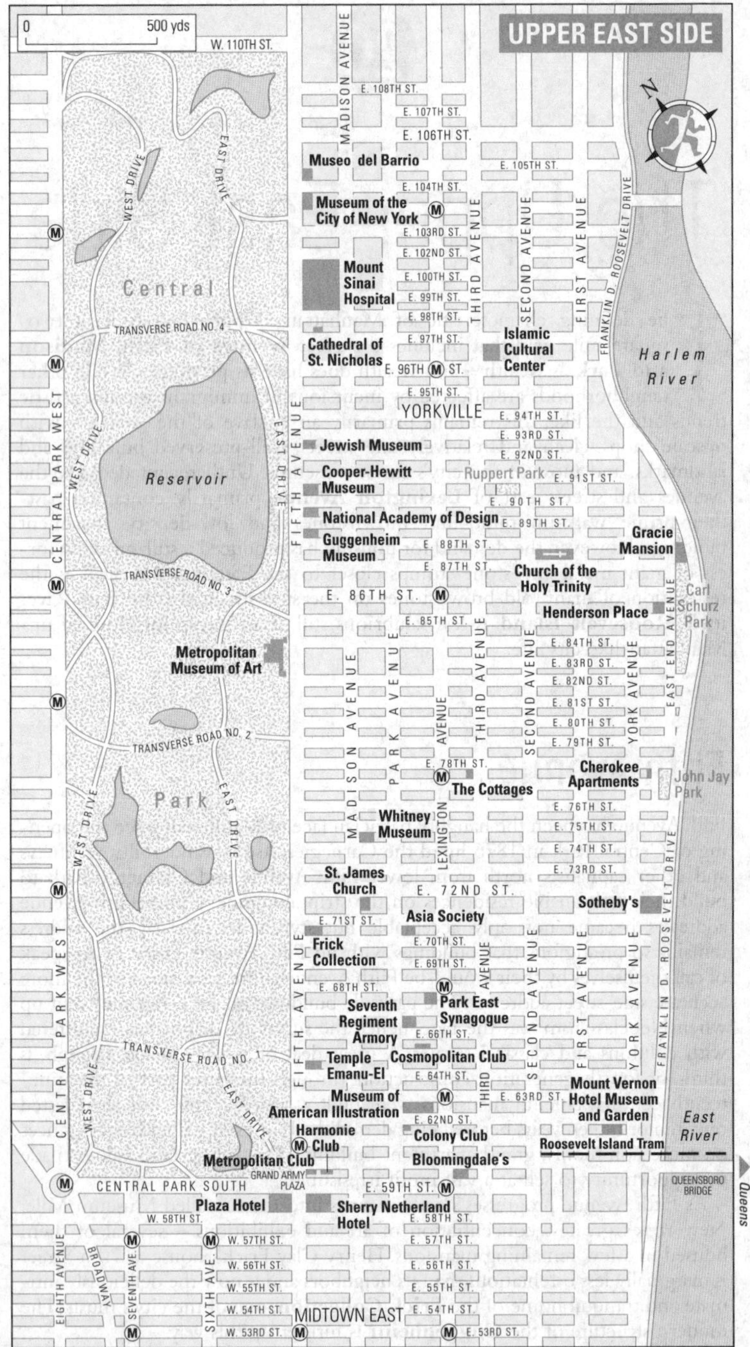
UPPER EAST SIDE
0 500 yds
N
Central
Park
Reservoir
Harlem River
East River
YORKVILLE
MIDTOWN EAST
Museo del Barrio
Museum of the City of New York
Mount Sinai Hospital
Cathedral of St. Nicholas
Islamic Cultural Center
Jewish Museum
Cooper-Hewitt Museum
National Academy of Design
Guggenheim Museum
Ruppert Park
Gracie Mansion
Church of the Holy Trinity
Henderson Place
Carl Schurz Park
Metropolitan Museum of Art
Cherokee Apartments
John Jay Park
The Cottages
Whitney Museum
St. James Church
Sotheby's
Asia Society
Frick Collection
Park East Synagogue
Seventh Regiment Armory
Temple Emanu-El
Cosmopolitan Club
Mount Vernon Hotel Museum and Garden
Museum of American Illustration
Harmonie Club
Colony Club
Roosevelt Island Tram
Metropolitan Club
Bloomingdale's
GRAND ARMY PLAZA
QUEENSBORO BRIDGE
Queens
Plaza Hotel
Sherry Netherland Hotel
W. 110TH ST.
MADISON AVENUE
FIFTH AVENUE
PARK AVENUE
LEXINGTON AVENUE
THIRD AVENUE
SECOND AVENUE
FIRST AVENUE
YORK AVENUE
EAST END AVENUE
FRANKLIN D. ROOSEVELT DRIVE
CENTRAL PARK WEST
CENTRAL PARK SOUTH
WEST DRIVE
EAST DRIVE
TRANSVERSE ROAD NO. 4
TRANSVERSE ROAD NO. 3
TRANSVERSE ROAD NO. 2
TRANSVERSE ROAD NO. 1
E. 108TH ST.
E. 107TH ST.
E. 106TH ST.
E. 105TH ST.
E. 104TH ST.
E. 103RD ST.
E. 102ND ST.
E. 100TH ST.
E. 99TH ST.
E. 98TH ST.
E. 97TH ST.
E. 96TH ST.
E. 95TH ST.
E. 94TH ST.
E. 93RD ST.
E. 92ND ST.
E. 91ST ST.
E. 90TH ST.
E. 89TH ST.
E. 88TH ST.
E. 87TH ST.
E. 86TH ST.
E. 85TH ST.
E. 84TH ST.
E. 83RD ST.
E. 82ND ST.
E. 81ST ST.
E. 80TH ST.
E. 79TH ST.
E. 78TH ST.
E. 76TH ST.
E. 75TH ST.
E. 74TH ST.
E. 73RD ST.
E. 72ND ST.
E. 71ST ST.
E. 70TH ST.
E. 69TH ST.
E. 68TH ST.
E. 66TH ST.
E. 64TH ST.
E. 63RD ST.
E. 62ND ST.
E. 59TH ST.
W. 58TH ST.
E. 58TH ST.
W. 57TH ST.
E. 57TH ST.
W. 56TH ST.
E. 56TH ST.
W. 55TH ST.
E. 55TH ST.
W. 54TH ST.
E. 54TH ST.
W. 53RD ST.
E. 53RD ST.
EIGHTH AVENUE
BROADWAY
SEVENTH AVE.
SIXTH AVE.

Grand Army Plaza to the Frick

Grand Army Plaza, an oval at the junction of Central Park South (59th Street east of the park) and Fifth Avenue, marks the division between Fifth as a shopping district to the south and a residential boulevard to the north. One of the city's most dramatic public spaces, it boasts a fountain and a recently replated gold statue of Civil War General William Tecumseh Sherman. (The replating resulted in complaints that the yellow color was too dazzling, but now the statue has become somewhat more subdued in appearance.) To the south stands the extended copper-lined chateau of the **Plaza Hotel** (see p.150), with the darkened, swooping television screen facade of the **Solow Building** behind. Across the plaza to the east, the imposing marble-faced lines of the **General Motors Building** surround six stories of toys inside at **F.A.O. Schwarz** (see p.149), the building's main commercial tenant. Two more hotels, the high-necked **Sherry Netherland** and the **Pierre**, luxuriate nearby. Many of the rooms here have permanent guests; needless to say, they're not on welfare.

Continuing the show of wealth, Fifth Avenue and its environs are dotted with clubs that serviced, and still cater to, the upper crust. When J.P. Morgan, William and Cornelius Vanderbilt, and their pals arrived on the social scene in the 1890s, established society still looked askance at bankers and financiers, and its downtown clubs were closed to Morgan and anyone else it considered less than up to snuff. Never to be slighted or outdone, Morgan commissioned Stanford White to design his own club, bigger, better and grander than all the rest – and so the **Metropolitan Club** at 1 E 60th St was born, an exuberant confection with a marvelously outrageous gateway. Just the thing for arriving robber barons.

Another unwelcome group, affluent Jews, founded the elegant **Harmonie Club** in the 1850s and erected its home at 4 E 60th St around the same time. So many *parvenus* caused alarm, and in 1915 the **Knickerbocker Club**, a handsome brick Federal-style building on the corner of Fifth Avenue and 62nd Street, was put up in response to the "relaxed standards" of the **Union Club** (101 E 69th St), which had admitted several friends of Morgan and the Vanderbilts. Before even the thought of admitting women to these bastions of old guard maleness occurred, there was the **Colony Club** on 564 Park Ave at 62nd Street. Founded in 1903, it was the city's first social club organized by women for women. In 1933, Delano & Aldrich, the firm that had designed the Knickerbocker Club, constructed an elaborate Colonial building with extensive gymnasium and spa facilities as the **Cosmopolitan Club**, at 122 E 66th St. This was originally a place where rich women sent their governesses, but they eventually claimed the building for themselves. It's a strange apartment-like building, with white ironwork terraces reminiscent of New Orleans, and a private garden in the back.

On the corner of 65th Street and Fifth Avenue, America's largest reform synagogue, the **Temple Emanu-El**, strikes a more sober tone. The brooding Romanesque–Byzantine cavern manages to be bigger inside than it seems from outside. The interior melts away into darkness, making you feel very small indeed (Mon–Fri & Sun 9am–5pm).

The side streets off Fifth are a trim mix of apartment houses and elegant townhouses, typical Upper East Side stuff. One of the most beautiful private homes is the **Ernesto and Edith Fabbri House** at 11 E 62nd St, built for a Vanderbilt daughter around 1900 in a Parisian Beaux-Arts style with curving iron balconies. **The Sarah Delano Roosevelt Memorial House** at 47 E

65th St was commissioned by Mrs. Roosevelt as a handy townhouse for her son Franklin. After leaving the White House, Richard Nixon lived for a few years at no. 142 on the same street.

The Frick Collection

1 E 70th St. Subway #6 to 68th St–Lexington Ave. Tues–Sat 10am–6pm, Sun 1–6pm; $10, students $5, under 10 not admitted. Admission includes the use of ArtPhone, a dial-up audio guide to the rooms and exhibition pieces, which is available in six languages. A 22min audiovisual presentation in the Music Room tells Henry Clay Frick's story and details the mansion and its collection, every hour on the half hour. Concerts of classical music are held each month. ⓣ 212/288-0700 for details.

Housed in the former mansion of **Henry Clay Frick**, the immensely enjoyable Frick Collection comprises the art treasures hoarded by Frick during his years as one of the most ruthless of New York's robber barons. Vicious, uncompromising and anti-union, Frick broke strikes at his coal and steel plants with state troopers and was hated enough to attract a number of assassination attempts. However, the legacy of his ill-gotten gains – he spent millions on the best of Europe's art treasures – is a superb collection of works, and as good a glimpse of the sumptuous life enjoyed by New York's early industrialists as you'll find.

Opened in the mid-1930s, the museum has been largely kept as it looked when the Fricks lived there. Much of the furniture is heavy eighteenth-century French, but the nice thing about the place – and many people rank the Frick as their favorite New York gallery because of this – is that it strives hard to be as unlike a museum as possible. Ropes are kept to a minimum, fresh flowers are on every table, and even in the most sumptuously decorated rooms there are plenty of chairs you can freely sink into. When weary, take refuge in the central enclosed courtyard, whose cool marble floors, fountains and greenery are simply and classically arranged, and whose serenity you'd be hard pressed to beat.

A gallery on the ground level shows temporary exhibits from the permanent collection, as well as pieces on loan from other institutions (other temporary groupings may be shown in the Oval Room or the Garden Court). It is a more modern space, with pale, paneled walls and beige wall-to-wall carpeting, so it won't compete with whatever is on display. Accessible only by a narrow, steep spiral staircase just outside the entry hall, it's easy to miss unless you're looking for it.

The collection

The collection itself was acquired under the direction of Joseph Duveen, notorious – and not entirely trustworthy – adviser to the city's richest and most ignorant. For Frick, however, he seems to have picked out the cream of Europe's post-World War I private art collections, with a magnificent array of works by Rembrandt, Vermeer, Turner and Whistler, among other masters. In the rooms, each is set off dramatically by heavy marble tables with gilt accents.

Keep an open mind when you double back to start in the **Boucher Room** – which is not to twentieth-century tastes, with its heavily flowered, painted walls, overdone furniture and Boucher's succulent, rococo representations of the arts and sciences in gilded frames. Next along, the **Dining Room** is more reserved, its Reynoldses and Hogarths overshadowed by the one non-portrait in the room, **Gainsborough**'s *St James's Park* – a subtly moving promenade under an arch of luxuriant trees. Outside in the hall there's more lusty French painting (Boucher again – the *Four Seasons* canvases) and, in the next room, **Fragonard**'s *Progress of Love* series (1771), painted for Madame du Barry, mistress of Louis XV, and rejected by her soon after in favor of another artist's efforts.

Better paintings follow in the Living Hall, not least of them **Bellini**'s *St Francis*, which suggests his vision of Christ by means of pervading light, a bent tree and an enraptured stare. **Titian**'s *Portrait of a Man with a Red Cap* hangs pensively along one wall and **El Greco**'s *St Jerome*, above the fireplace, reproachfully surveys the riches all around. In the South Hall hangs an early **Vermeer**, *Officer and Laughing Girl*: suggestive and full of lewd allusions to anticipated sex. The Library holds a number of British works, most notably one of **Constable**'s *Salisbury Cathedral* series, **Turner's** idyllic *Fishing Boats Entering Calais Harbor* and a number of Gainsboroughs; and in the North Hall hangs Degas' *Rehearsal*, dancers rehearsing elegantly to a violinist's accompaniment, along with several soothingly pale, scenic works by **Corot**.

The **West Gallery**, beyond here, is the Frick's major draw, holding some of its finest paintings in a truly magnificent setting – a long elegant room with a concave glass ceiling and ornately carved wood trim. Two Turners, views of Cologne and Dieppe, hang opposite each other, each a blaze of orange and creamy tones; **Van Dyck** pitches in with a couple of uncharacteristically informal portraits of Frans Snyders and his wife – two paintings reunited only when Frick purchased them; there are several portraits by **Frans Hals**, and *Vincenzo Anastagi* by El Greco, a stunning portrait of a Spanish soldier resplendent in green velvet and armor. **Rembrandt**, too, is represented by a set of piercing self-portraits and the enigmatic *Polish Rider* – more fantasy piece than portrait.

At the far end of the West Gallery is a tiny room called the Enamel Room, so named because of the exquisite set of Limoges enamels on display, mainly sixteenth century. The trays, small boxes and tiny portraits are stunningly beautiful, and unlike anything you've seen. There is also a collection of small painted altarpieces by **Piero della Francesca**. At the other end of the West Gallery is the Oval Room with Houdon's sculpture of *Diana* and a quartet of spare, elegant portraits by Van Dyck and Gainsborough, all the same size and painted against similar backdrops – unintended matched sets. Past here, the **East Gallery** hosts a slew of famous paintings, anchored at the corners by **Whistler**'s full-length portraits with musically colorful titles. One is of fellow artist *Rose Corder (Arrangement in Brown and Gold)*; she often posed to the point where she would have to faint before Whistler would stop painting and let her leave. Other highlights of this final gallery include several massive Turner seascapes and a portrait of an expressive Spanish officer by **Goya.**

The Guggenheim Museum

1071 5th Ave (89th St). Subway #4, #5 or #6 to 86th St–Lexington Ave. Sun–Wed 9am–6pm, Fri & Sat 9am–8pm; $12, seniors & students $8, children under 12 free, Fri 6–8pm pay what you wish. ⓣ 212/423-3500 for exhibit information. The Guggenheim SoHo branch has changing exhibits culled from the Guggenheim permanent collection; *see* p.98.

Multistory parking garage or upturned beehive? Whatever you may think of the Guggenheim Museum collection, it's the building that steals the show. **Frank Lloyd Wright**'s structure, designed specifically for the museum and sixteen years in the making, caused a storm of controversy when it was unveiled in 1959, bearing little relation to the statuesque apartment buildings of this most genteel part of Fifth Avenue. Reactions ranged from disgusted disbelief to critical acclaim – "one of the greatest rooms erected in the twentieth century," wrote Philip Johnson. Wright didn't get to hear much criticism, however, as he died six months before construction was completed. The years have given the building a certain respectability and made it a widely recognized landmark much loved by New Yorkers and visitors alike. Any proposed changes can cause an uproar, as the debate over the museum's extension proved. From 1990 to 1992 the museum was closed, undergoing a $60 million facelift of the original Lloyd Wright building that opened the whole space to the public for the first time. Dull offices, storage rooms and bits of chicken wire were all removed to expose the uplifting interior spaces so that the public could experience the spiral of the central rotunda from top to bottom. At the same time a clever extension added the sort of tall, straight-walled, flat-floored galleries that the Guggenheim needed to offset its distinct shape. Though at the time the merits of the plans were hotly debated, the remodeled building is now a much better museum.

The museum's namesake, **Solomon R. Guggenheim**, was one of America's richest men, his mines extracting silver and copper – and a healthy profit – all over the US. As with other nineteenth-century American capitalists, the only problem for Guggenheim was how to spend his vast wealth, so he started collecting Old Masters – a hobby he continued half-heartedly until the 1920s, when various sorties to Europe brought him into contact with the most avant-garde and influential of European art circles. Abstraction in art was then considered little more than a fad, but Guggenheim, always a man with an eye for a sound investment, started to collect modern paintings with fervor, buying wholesale the paintings of **Kandinsky**, adding works by **Chagall**, **Klee**, **Léger** and others, and exhibiting them to a bemused American public in his suite of rooms in the *Plaza Hotel*. The Guggenheim Foundation was created in 1937; after exhibiting the collection in various rented spaces, it commissioned Wright to design a permanent home.

The collection

In addition to the works collected by Guggenheim himself, a number of acquisitions and donations have broadened the collection so that it spans the late 1800s through most of the twentieth century. In 1976, the collector Justin K. Thannhauser bequeathed masterworks by **Cézanne**, **Degas**, **Gauguin**, **Manet**, **Toulouse-Lautrec**, **Van Gogh** and **Picasso**, among others, greatly enhancing the museum's Impressionist and Post-Impressionist holdings. The Guggenheim's collection of American minimalist art from the 1960s is also especially rich. The **Robert Mapplethorpe** Foundation recently gave 196 photographs that span the artist's career, and they're now housed in a brand new gallery on the fourth floor. Other photographers are also well represented, though not in such quantity, including **Rineke Dijkstra** and **Bernd Becher**.

As a general rule of thumb, the permanent collection is housed on a rotating basis in the new tower and the small north rotunda, while **temporary exhibitions** based on aspects of the collection, picking up themes from the various styles and periods, are in the main rotunda – between the two, a significant part of the museum's collection is always on display. Even so, it's the original space itself that dominates; it's hard not to be impressed (or sidetracked) by the tiers of cream concrete that open up above like the ever-widening ribcage of some giant animal. Because the circular galleries rise upward at a not-so-gentle slope, you may prefer to start at the top of the museum and work your way down; most of the temporary exhibits are designed to be seen that way.

Though the entire museum can easily be seen in an afternoon, two galleries offer a representative sample of the Guggenheim's **permanent collection**: The first, on the second floor of the tower, gives a quick but enjoyable look at the **Cubists**. The other, in the restored small rotunda, offers a collection of **Impressionist**, **Post-Impressionist and early modern** masterpieces.

National Academy of Design

1083 5th Ave (89th St). Subway #4, #5 or #6 to 86th St–Lexington Ave. Wed–Thurs noon–5pm, Fri 10am–6pm & Sat–Sun 10am–5pm; $8, seniors & students $4.50, Fri 5–6pm free (pay as you wish). ⓣ *212/369-4880 for exhibition information.*

A group of artists, including Samuel Morse, founded the National Academy of Design in 1825 along the lines of London's Royal Academy, and a trip there is more like a visit to a favorite relative's house than to a museum. The building, donated to the academy by the husband of sculptor Anna Hyatt Huntington, is an imposing **Beaux-Arts townhouse**, complete with carpeted rooms and a twisting staircase. Anna Huntington's sculpture *Diana* gets pride of place below the cheerful rotunda.

The National Academy is a tripartite entity, consisting of the museum, the School of Fine Arts, and an exclusive membership of artists, who are required, when elected, to donate a work of art. More than 150 years' worth of these pictures are now held by the Academy and form the mainstay of the Selection from the Permanent Collection – varied throughout the year but always with a strong slant toward portraiture. Students from the school also exhibit their work.

Cooper-Hewitt National Design Museum (Smithsonian Institution)

2 E 91st St. Subway #4, #5 or #6 to 86th St–Lexington Ave. Tues 10am–9pm, Wed–Sat 10am–5pm, Sun noon–5pm; $8, students & seniors $5, free Tues 5–9pm. ⓣ *212/849-8400 for exhibition information. The permanent collection is on view by appointment only to design professionals and students (you must have a clear idea of what you want to see and meet with a curator beforehand).*

When he decided in 1898 to build at what was then the unfashionable end of Fifth Avenue, millionaire industrialist Andrew Carnegie asked for "the most modest, plainest and most roomy house in New York." What he got (after four years and $1.5 million) was a bit more than that: a beautiful, spacious mansion filled with dark wood-paneled walls, carved ceilings and parquet floors – too decorative to be plain, too large to be modest. These lovely rooms now constitute the gallery space for the Cooper-Hewitt National Design Museum run by the Smithsonian. Two floors of temporary exhibits focus on the history, nature and evolution of design and decorative arts – commercial, utilitarian and high art.

Very little of the large permanent collection is on view to the public, except when pieces are involved in a special exhibition. The adjacent **Design Resource Center** is open by appointment, and can provide access to the library, archives, and the Cooper-Hewitt's four curatorial departments, holding 40,000 objects in Applied Arts and Industrial Design, 160,000 works of art on paper in Drawings and Prints, and 40,000 examples of Wallcoverings and Textiles, some dating from the first century after Christ.

Skillful curating and insightful commentary make a trip to the Cooper-Hewitt highly entertaining, and the building itself is worth a look, too. Themes vary, so check what's on first. The gift shop sells some innovative and inexpensive items and books on every aspect of design.

Jewish Museum

1109 5th Ave (92nd St). Subway #4, #5 or #6 to 86th St–Lexington Ave. Sun 10am–5.45pm, Mon–Thurs 11am–5.45pm, Tues until 9pm, Fri 11am–3pm; $8, students $5.50, children under 12 free, free Tues 5–9pm. ☎ 212/423-3200 for exhibit information.

This is the largest museum of Judaica outside Israel. Its centerpiece is a permanent exhibition on the Jewish experience that seeks to answer the question, "What constitutes the essence of Jewish identity?" with a presentation of the basic ideas, values and culture developed over four thousand years. A collection of **Hanukkah lamps** is a highlight. More vibrant, however, are the changing displays of works by major international artists (including Chagall, shown in 2001), and theme exhibitions (for example, a recent major show on Freud containing nearly 200 artifacts from his Vienna offices). The Jewish Museum sponsors a varied media program, including a film festival.

Museum of the City of New York

1220 5th Ave (103rd St). Subway #6 to 103rd St–Lexington Ave. Wed–Sat 10am–5pm, Sun noon–5pm, Tues 10am–2pm for pre-registered tour groups only; suggested donation $7, students $4, families $12. ☎ 212/534-1672 for exhibit information.

Spaciously housed in a neo-Georgian mansion, the permanent collection of this museum provides a history of the city from Dutch times to the present. Prints, photographs, costumes and furniture are displayed on four floors, and a film about the city's history runs continuously. One of its permanent exhibits: **New York Toy Stories**, an engaging trip from the late 1800s to today that consists of all manner of motion toys, board games, sports equipment, and doll houses (one with original artwork by Duchamp and Lachaise). This is a comprehensive, worthwhile and fascinating look at the evolution of a city. (The museum is scheduled to relocate downtown to the Tweed Courthouse in the spring of 2003.)

Museo del Barrio

1230 5th Ave (104th St). Subway #6 to 103rd St–Lexington Ave. Wed–Sun 11am–5pm; suggested donation $5, students $3. ☎ 212/831-7272 for exhibition information.

Literally translated as "the neighborhood museum," the Museo was founded in 1969 by a group of Puerto Rican parents, educators and artists from Spanish Harlem who wanted to teach their children about their roots. In keeping with its "homegrown" vibe, the museum was born out of a school classroom and moved to several brownstones and El Barrio storefronts before graduating to its current location. Although the emphasis remains largely Puerto Rican, the museum embraces the whole of Latin America and nearby island cultures, with its one permanent exhibit examining **the Taino**, a highly developed and ritualized people from the Caribbean (1200-1500 AD). Relics from their civilization include intricately carved vomiting sticks (used to purify the body with the hallucinogen *cohaba* before sacred rites) and three-pointed fertility stones. Make sure to see the *santos de palo* – an exquisite collection of carved votive figures. Five major loan exhibits of painting, photographs and crafts each year are contributed by both traditional and emerging artists. In the summertime, the museum is open late one evening during the week, with a live band playing out front; call for the schedule.

Madison and Park avenues

Immediately east of Fifth is **Madison Avenue**, a strip that was entirely residential until the 1920s. Today it is mainly an elegant shopping street – though it too features a top modern museum in the **Whitney** (see below) – lined with top-notch designer clothes stores, some of whose doors are kept locked. At 699 Madison (63rd Street) is the tiny home of the **Margo Feiden Galleries**, which represent the work of the great New York caricaturist Al Hirschfeld, famous for his line drawings of Broadway stars. It's fun to admire the wedding dresses in **Vera Wang**'s bridal boutique at 991 Madison Ave (between 77th and 78th streets). One notable exception to the demure commercialism here is the stately **St James' Church** at 865 Madison Ave, with its graceful Byzantine altar, where the funeral service for Jacqueline Onassis was held.

A block away, **Park Avenue** is stolidly comfortable and often elegant. In the low 90s, the large black shapes of the **Louise Nevelson sculptures** stand out on the traffic islands. Just above 96th Street the neighborhood abruptly transforms into **Spanish Harlem** at the point where the subway line emerges from underground. One of the best features of this boulevard is the sweeping view south, as Park Avenue coasts down to the **New York Central** and **Met Life** (originally Pan Am) buildings.

Architectural gems and homes of the rich and (in)famous nestle in the side streets throughout the Upper East Side. The **Wildenstein family**, premier art dealers who came under attack for handling art stolen by the Nazis, have both their gallery and private mansion on East 64th Street between Park and Madison. **Andy Warhol** spent the last 13 years of his life, from 1974 to 1987, in a surprisingly conservative and extremely private narrow brick house at **57 E 66th St**: no friends were allowed inside, and when Warhol died he left behind oddities like a massive collection of cookie jars. While you're here, have a look at **no. 64** across the street, an elegant sandstone house with a green copper bay window and stained glass. At Park and East 66th Street are several **stables**, built a few blocks east of Fifth for use by the residents of its mansions, and now transformed into expensive art galleries (**no. 126**, with its Romanesque facade, is especially handsome).

Dominating a square block is the **Seventh Regiment Armory** (Park Ave between 66th and 67th streets), built in the 1870s with pseudo-medieval crenellations and, inside, a grand double stairway and spidery wrought-iron chandeliers – the only surviving building from the era before the New York Central's railroad tracks were roofed over and Park Avenue became an upscale residential neighborhood. There are two surviving interiors inside, executed by the firm that included Louis Comfort Tiffany and Stanford White – the Veterans' Room and the Library; call ahead for a tour (ⓣ212/744-8180; times vary). Frequent art and antique shows provide an opportunity to gawk at the enormous drill hall inside.

The Whitney Museum of American Art

945 Madison Ave (75th St). Subway #6 to 77th St–Lexington Ave. Tues-Thurs & Sat–Sun 11am–6pm, Fri 1–9pm ; $10, seniors and students with ID $8; Fri 6–9pm pay as you wish (free) with food, drink and special events; call for times for excellent free gallery talks. ⓣ212/570-3600 for exhibit information.

The Whitney, in a heavy, gray, arsenal-like building designed by Marcel Breuer in 1966, has, from the outside, an intimidating and suspiciously institutional air. Within, however, such impressions are quickly dispelled. This is some of the best gallery space in the city, and the perfect forum for one of the pre-eminent collections of twentieth-century American art.

Unlike most institutions in this neighborhood, the Whitney is best known for its superb temporary exhibitions, and devotes much of its time and rooms (and even the stairwells) to this end. Some of these are given over to retrospectives and debuts of lesser-known themes and artists. **Jasper Johns**, **Cy Twombly** and **Cindy Sherman** were all given their first retrospectives here. But the most thought-provoking exhibitions push the boundaries of art as a concept, with strong showings of late in the realms of video installations (incorporating names such as **Bill Viola** and **Nam June Paik**) and computer and digital technology. This type of exhibit makes the museum experience a more involving one: rather than just file past two-dimensional canvases, the visitor is forced to actively participate in, or even contribute to, the "art" created, and to more actively consider its implications. As such, the experience shouldn't be missed.

Every other year there is an exhibition – the **Whitney Biennial** – designed to give a provocative overview of what's happening in contemporary American art. Often panned by critics, sometimes for good reason, the Biennial is always packed with visitors. Catch it if you can between March and June in even-numbered years.

Some history

Gertrude Vanderbilt Whitney, a sculptor and champion of American art, established the Whitney Studio in 1914 to exhibit the work of living American artists who could not find support in established art circles. She was the first to exhibit Edward Hopper in 1920, and by 1929 she had collected more than 500 works of various artists that she offered, with a generous endowment, to the Met. When her offer was refused, she set up her own museum in Greenwich Village in 1930, with her collection as its core exhibit. The first Biennial was held two years later. The small museum soon outgrew its Village home, and, after several interim moves, relocated to its current spot in 1966.

The permanent collection

The museum owns more than 12,000 paintings, sculptures, photographs and films by almost two thousand artists as diverse as Calder, Nevelson, O'Keeffe, de Kooning, Rauschenberg and Le Witt. For an overview, see the **Highlights**

of the Permanent Collection, a somewhat arbitrary pick of the Whitney's best: the fifth floor takes you from Hopper to the mid-century, while the second floor brings you from Jackson Pollock up through today. The works form a superb introduction to twentieth-century American art, best evaluated with the help of the free gallery talks designed to explain the paintings and sculptures, and their place within various movements.

In deference to its origins, the collection is particularly strong on **Edward Hopper** (2000 of his works were bequeathed to the museum in 1970), and several of his best paintings are here. *Early Sunday Morning* is typical of many of his works focused on light and shadow, a bleak urban landscape, uneasily tense in its lighting and rejection of topical detail. The street could be anywhere (in fact it's Seventh Avenue); for Hopper, it becomes universal. Additional major bequests include a significant number of works by **Milton Avery**, **Charles Demuth** and **Reginald Marsh**. You may also find one of **Joseph Cornell**'s intricate shadowboxes, or one of surrealist **Yves Tanguy**'s alien landscapes populated with amoeba-like figures.

As if to balance the figurative works that formed the nucleus of the original collection, more recent purchases include an emphasis on abstract art. **Marsden Hartley**'s *Painting Number 5* is a strident work painted in memory of a German officer friend killed in the early days of World War I. **Georgia O'Keeffe** called it "a brass band in a closet," and certainly her own work is gentler, though with its own darkness: her *Abstraction* was suggested by the noises of cattle being driven to the local slaughterhouse. Have a look, too, at O'Keeffe's flower paintings; they verge on abstraction but hint at deeper organic, erotic forms.

The **Abstract Expressionists** are featured strongly, with great works by masters **Pollock** and **de Kooning**. **Mark Rothko** and the **Color Field** painters are also well-represented – though you need a sharp eye to discern any color in **Ad Reinhardt**'s *Black Painting*. In a different direction, **Warhol**, **Johns** and **Oldenburg** each subvert the meaning of their images in different ways. Warhol's silk-screened *Coke Bottles* fade into motif; Johns's celebrated *Three Flags* erases the emblem of patriotism and replaces it with ambiguity; and Oldenburg's lighthearted *Soft Sculptures*, with its squidgy toilets and melting motors, falls into line with his declaration, "I'm into art that doesn't sit on its ass in a museum."

The Whitney maintains a satellite museum in the Philip Morris building at 42nd Street and Park Avenue (see p.139).

Asia Society Museum

725 Park Ave (70th St). Subway #6 to 68th St–Lexington Ave. Tues–Sat 11am–6pm, Thurs until 8pm, Sun noon–5pm; $4, students/seniors $2; free Thurs 6–8pm. ⓣ 212/517-ASIA for exhibit information.

A prominent educational resource on Asia founded by John D. Rockefeller 3rd, the **Asia Society** offers an exhibition space dedicated to both traditional and contemporary art from all over Asia. In addition to the usually worthwhile temporary exhibits, intriguing performances, political roundtables, lectures, films and free events are frequently held.

Carnegie Hill

At the northernmost part of this stretch is **Carnegie Hill**, a Historic District bounded by 86th and 98th streets and Fifth and Lexington avenues. This well-tended and well-policed area retains the air of a gated community without the gates, and is largely inhabited by the more recently *riche*; you might catch a glimpse of celebrity tenants such as Bette Midler or Michael J. Fox, and their bodyguards, jogging down to Central Park. Aside from art and celebrity-sightings, the highlight here is the **Russian Orthodox Cathedral of St Nicholas** at 15 E 97th St, most notable for its polychromatic Victorian body and five onion domes on top. Get too much past here, and the upscale living quickly fades.

To get a good feeling (one that most tourists never experience) for the world of single-family luxury in Manhattan's most elegant townhouse district, pick a side street – almost any will do – and walk it from Fifth to Third or Second, then loop back on a parallel street. On a lambent spring or summer evening, stroll under arching London plane trees and in season delight in magnolia blossoms and beds of tulips, crocuses, forsythia, and many other flowering plants. After sunset, steal quick glances into an inaccessible (for most) environment of spiral staircases, glittery chandeliers, and floor-to-ceiling libraries. Sixty-fourth Street is especially recommended; 70th between Park and Lex is crème de la crème.

Lexington Avenue and east

Lexington Avenue is Madison without the class; as the western stretches of the Upper East Side became richer, property developers rushed to slick up real estate in the east. The signs of its 1960s economic heyday – hot bars like *Maxwell's Plum*, big stores like Alexander's – are gone, and this is now one of the cheaper areas on the east side for studio apartments. Much of the East 60s and 70s now houses young, unattached and upwardly mobile professionals – as the number of "happening" singles bars on Second and Third avenues will attest.

The southern stretches

On the southern perimeter of the Upper East Side, **Bloomingdale's** at 59th and Third is the celebrated American store for clothes and accessories, skillfully aiming its wares at the stylish and affluent (see p.404). Nearby, at 421 E 61st St between York and First Avenue, is the **Mount Vernon Hotel Museum and Garden** (Mon–Sat 11–4pm, Sun 1–5pm; closed in August; $4, students and senior citizens $3, children under 12 free; ⓣ212/838-6878), another eighteenth-century building that managed to survive by the skin of its teeth. Though formerly the Abigail Adams Smith Museum, this wasn't the actual home of Abigail Adams, daughter of President John Quincy Adams, just its stables, restored with Federal-period propriety by the Colonial Dames of America. The furnishings, knickknacks and the serene little park out back are more engaging than the house itself, but there's an odd sort of pull if you're lucky enough to be guided around by a chattily urbane Colonial Dame.

The house is hemmed in by decidedly unhistoric buildings and overlooked by the **Queensboro Bridge**, which may stir memories as the **59th Street Bridge** of Simon and Garfunkel's *Feelin' Groovy* or from the title credits of TV's *Taxi*. This intense profusion of clanging steelwork links Manhattan to Long Island City in Queens, but is utterly unlike the suspension bridges that elsewhere lace Manhattan to the boroughs. "My God, it's a blacksmith's shop!" was architect Henry Hornbostel's comment when he first saw the finished item in 1909.

Also in the neighborhood is the **Museum of American Illustration**, 128 E 63rd St (Tues 10am–8pm, Wed–Fri 10am–5pm, Sat noon–4pm; free; ⓣ212/838-2560 for exhibition information). Containing rotating selections from the museum's permanent collection of more than 2000 illustrations, it includes everything from wartime propaganda to political and other cartoons and drawing, to contemporary ads. Exhibitions center on a theme or illustrator – designed primarily for aficionados, but always accessible, well-presented and topical.

On East 67th Street, east of Lexington and beyond the rear of the Seventh Regiment Armory, look for a remarkable ensemble of fanciful **Victorian buildings** that narrowly escaped destruction and now resemble a movie set: the baby-blue-trimmed local **Police Precinct**, the **Fire Station** with its bright red garage doors, and the whimsical ochre **Park East Synagogue**, with its Moorish arches, floral stained glass and campanile.

Dozens of foreign consulates to the United Nations are scattered on Upper East Side blocks. Many countries – including poor ones spending more money than they can afford – have purchased handsome once-private homes, while the Russians occupy an entire apartment building on 67th between Lex and Third. Here and there you will notice a small kiosk occupied by a police officer - likely as not placed near a consulate of a country whose "politics" may tend to provoke street protests or unwelcome callers.

There's not much just north of here, until you hit the New York auction gallery of London-based **Sotheby's**, the oldest fine arts auctioneer in the world, at 1334 York Ave between East 71st and 72nd streets (ⓣ212/606-7000). Admission to a few of the largest auctions is by ticket only, but all viewings are open to the public. Sotheby's arch rival, **Christie's**, has two locations, at 502 Park Ave (ⓣ212/636-2000) and 219 E 67th St (ⓣ212/606-0400). With a little planning, attending an auction at either house can be quite amusing – like an upper-crust version of a garage sale.

Yorkville and around

It's left to **Yorkville**, originally a German-Hungarian neighborhood that spills out from East 77th to 96th streets between Lexington and the East River, to try to supply the Upper East Side with a tangible ethnicity. Much of New York's German community arrived after the failed revolution of 1848–49, to be quickly assimilated into the area around Tompkins Square in lower Manhattan. The influx of Italian and Slavic immigrants to the Lower East Side, the tragic sinking of an excursion steamer carrying Tompkins Square residents and the opening of the Elevated Railway, all around 1900, hastened their move uptown to Yorkville. Other groups followed not long after, and some splendid little townhouses were built for these newcomers, such as **The Cottages** on Third Avenue between East 77th and 78th streets, whose stylish English Regency facades and courtyard gardens remain intact.

Today, you have to search hard to detect a German flavor to the area, and the prospect of cheap rent with an Upper East Side address has lured many folks fresh-out-of-college who now blend amicably with the few elderly German-speaking residents who remain. There are some hints of the old neighborhood, such as the traditional German delicatessens **Schaller and Weber** at 1654 2nd Ave between 84th and 85th streets and **Bremen House** (218–220 E 86th St between Second and Third avenues). But otherwise, the area has succumbed to its newer residents: video stores and fast-food restaurants dominate.

Beginning on East 76th Street and East End Drive is **John Jay Park**, a lovely patch of green centering on a beautiful pool and gym – you need a Parks Department pass ($35 per year) to make use of either. Fronting the park on Cherokee Place between 77th and 78th streets are the **Cherokee Apartments**, originally the Shively Sanitarium Apartments, an understatedly elegant row with a splendid courtyard. Up the block at 81st Street is **John Finley Walk**, with its concrete promenade that runs north into the park named after **Carl Schurz**, a nineteenth-century German immigrant who rose to fame as Secretary of the Interior under President Rutherford B. Hayes and as editor of *Harper's Weekly* and the *New York Evening Post*. Winding pathways lead through this small, model park – a breathing space for elderly German speakers and East Siders escaping their postage-stamp apartments. The **FDR Drive** cuts beneath, and there are views across the river to Queens and the confluence of dangerous currents where the Harlem River, Long Island Sound and Harbor meet – not for nothing known as **Hell Gate**.

Gracie Mansion and Henderson Place

One of the reasons Schurz Park is so exceptionally well-manicured and maintained is the high-profile security that surrounds **Gracie Mansion** at 88th Street nearby. Built in 1799 on the site of a Revolutionary fort as a country manor house, it is one of the best-preserved colonial buildings in the city. Roughly contemporary with the Morris–Jumel Mansion (see p.231) and the Mount Vernon Hotel Museum, Gracie Mansion has been the official residence of the mayor of New York City since 1942, when Fiorello LaGuardia, "man of the people" that he was, reluctantly set up house, though "mansion" is a bit overblown for what's a rather cramped clapboard cottage.

After the very public breakup of their marriage in 2000, former mayor Giuliani and his wife continued to live in the mansion in a setting doubtless even more uncomfortable during the occasional visits of his female companion – and the ensuing lawsuit filed to bar her from the home. Visitors today will find the mansion more welcoming, for it is open for tours on Wednesdays, April through November, though you need to book in advance. (Suggested admission $4, $3 for seniors; you must make a reservation far enough in advance to receive a mailed confirmation, and there are no walk-ins. ⓣ212/570-4751.)

Across from the park and just below Gracie Mansion at East 86th Street and East End Avenue is **Henderson Place**, a set of old servants' quarters now transformed into an "historic district" of luxury cottages. Built in 1882 by John Henderson, a fur importer and real-estate developer, the small and sprightly Queen Anne-style wooden and brick dwellings were intended to provide close and convenient housing for servants working in the palatial old East End Avenue mansions, most of which have now been torn down. Ironically, these servants' quarters now represent some of the most sought-after real estate in the city, offering the space, quiet and privacy that most of the city's housing lacks.

Around Yorkville's outskirts

Just west of here is **Ruppert Park**, a shaded and civilized bit of village green between East 90th and 91st streets and Second and Third avenues. The **Church**

of the Holy Trinity (316 E 88th St between First and Second avenues) is a picturesque and discreet Victorian church with an enchanting little garden. On Third Avenue at East 96th Street is the **Islamic Cultural Center**, New York's first major mosque, whose orientation toward Mecca was precisely pinpointed with a computer. The funeral of **Betty Shabazz**, widow of **Malcolm X**, was held here in July 1997.

North of here, the mood begins to change rapidly, signaled by the bright turquoise facade of the diagonal housing projects on 97th Street and First Avenue and the busier streets and offshoots of El Barrio, the best-known part of New York's significant Latino community. The elevated tracks of the #4, #5 and #6 Bronx-bound trains surface at Park Avenue and 96th Street, denoting the end of Park Avenue's old-money dominance, while Madison and Fifth avenues retain their grandeur for only a few blocks more.

Roosevelt Island

An **aerial tramway** near **Queensboro Bridge** connects Manhattan with **Roosevelt Island** across the water. Though the island was connected by tunnel to the subway system in the 1990s, the tram is a much more fun way to arrive (trams run every 15min, Mon–Thurs & Sun 6am–2am, Fri–Sat 6am–3.30am; every 7½min during rush hours; $1.50 one way); from there, take the 25c bus to the northern part of the island.

Only two miles long and no more than 800 feet wide, Roosevelt Island was owned, inhabited and farmed by the **Blackwell** family from 1676 to 1826, and the brick paving and narrowness of **Main Street** preserve its small-town feel, virtually unavailable in any other part of the city. **Meditation Steps** and the

Welfare Island

On paper this should long have been an ideal residential spot, but Roosevelt Island's history as **"Welfare Island,"** a gloomy quarantine site of jail, poorhouse, lunatic asylum and smallpox hospital, for years put it out of bounds to Manhattanites. The stigma finally started to disappear in the 1970s when Johnson and Burgee's master plan spawned the Eastview, Westwood, Island House and Rivercross housing areas. Today these and other residential complexes house an ethnic stew of residents of diverse races and varying incomes. The narrow streets, bold signage and modular buildings are locally considered a triumph of urban planning; outsiders may find it reminiscent of the village in the TV series *The Prisoner*.

Grim reminders of Welfare Island remain. The **Octagon Tower**, now off-limits, at the island's north end was once an insane asylum (it briefly housed Mae West after an unpalatably lewd performance in 1927). At the northernmost point of the island the **Lighthouse** affords excellent views of the upper reaches of the East River and the surging waters of Hell Gate, and **Lighthouse Park** is a romantic retreat of grassy knolls and weeping willows.

To the south are the stabilized ruins of what was once the island's **Smallpox Hospital**, now a ghostly Gothic shell, and the **Strecker Laboratory**, the city's premier laboratory for bacteriological research when it opened in 1892. The ruins can be easily spotted from the Manhattan side of the East River but are all but impossible to see from the island itself, as the area surrounding the hospital is boarded up with rows of corrugated metal fencing.

River Walk, a walking and rollerblading path on the western side of the island, permit uncluttered views of Manhattan's East Side and the rattling grates of Queensboro Bridge's metalwork overhead.

The approach to Manhattan from Queens on the 59th Street Bridge provides a spine-tingling panorama of the city, the same one Nick Carraway described in F. Scott Fitzgerald's *The Great Gatsby*:

> ***Over the great bridge, with the sunlight through the girders making a constant flicker upon the moving cars, with the city rising up across the river in white heaps and sugar lumps all built with a wish out of non-olfactory money. The city seen from the Queensboro Bridge is always the city seen for the first time, in its wild promise of all the mystery and the beauty in the world . . . "Anything can happen now that we've slid over this bridge" I thought; "anything at all ..."***

21

The Upper West Side and Morningside Heights

Though dominated by some dazzling turn-of-the-nineteenth-century apartment buildings and the city's most prestigious performance space, the Upper West Side has always had a more unbuttoned vibe than its counterpart across Central Park. Rather than a stage for old wealth – mostly because the area was late to develop – it has seen its share of struggling actors, writers, opera singers and the like move into its spaces over the years, somewhat tempered by the gentrification of the Eighties and Nineties. This isn't to say it lacks glamour: there is plenty of money in evidence, especially along the lower stretches of **Central Park West** and **Riverside Drive**, and at **Lincoln Center**, New York's palace of culture, but this is less true as you move north. At its top end, marked at the edge by the monolithic **Cathedral of St John the Divine**, is **Morningside Heights**, home to Columbia University on the edge of Harlem.

The Upper West Side

North of 59th Street, paralleling the spread of Central Park, the somewhat tawdry Midtown West (see Chapter 17) becomes decidedly less commercial, less garish, and, above Lincoln Center, more of a residential and shopping neighborhood. The **Upper West Side** is one of the city's most desirable addresses, and tends to attract what might be called New York's cultural elite as well as new-money types, though there is also a small but jarringly visible homeless presence.

Bordered by Central Park to the east, the Hudson River to the west, Columbus Circle at 59th Street to the south, and 110th Street (the northernmost point of Central Park and beginning of Morningside Heights) to the north, the district's main artery is **Broadway**. Generally speaking, the further you stray east or west from there, the wealthier things become, until you reach the pinnacles of prosperity, the historic apartment houses of **Central Park**

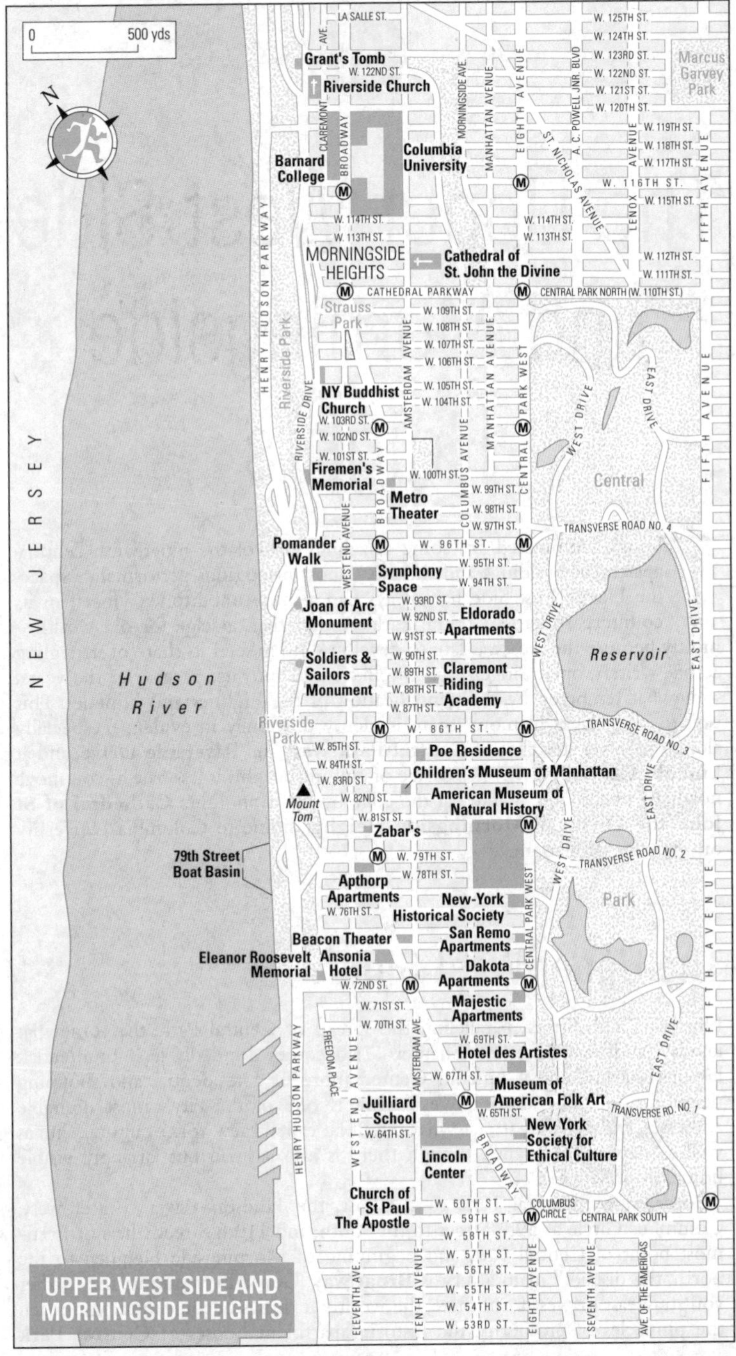
0 500 yds
N
LA SALLE ST.
W. 125TH ST.
W. 124TH ST.
W. 123RD ST.
W. 122ND ST.
W. 121ST ST.
W. 120TH ST.
Marcus Garvey Park
Grant's Tomb
W. 122ND ST.
Riverside Church
CLAREMONT
BROADWAY
MORNINGSIDE AVE.
MANHATTAN AVENUE
EIGHTH AVENUE
ST. NICHOLAS AVENUE
A. C. POWELL JNR. BLVD
LENOX AVENUE
FIFTH AVENUE
W. 119TH ST.
W. 118TH ST.
W. 117TH ST.
W. 116TH ST.
W. 115TH ST.
Barnard College
Columbia University
W. 114TH ST.
W. 113TH ST.
MORNINGSIDE HEIGHTS
Cathedral of St. John the Divine
W. 112TH ST.
W. 111TH ST.
CATHEDRAL PARKWAY
CENTRAL PARK NORTH (W. 110TH ST.)
HENRY HUDSON PARKWAY
Strauss Park
Riverside Park
W. 109TH ST.
W. 108TH ST.
W. 107TH ST.
W. 106TH ST.
W. 105TH ST.
W. 104TH ST.
AMSTERDAM AVENUE
MANHATTAN AVENUE
CENTRAL PARK WEST
COLUMBUS AVENUE
NY Buddhist Church
W. 103RD ST.
W. 102ND ST.
W. 101ST ST.
RIVERSIDE DRIVE
Firemen's Memorial
W. 100TH ST.
WEST DRIVE
EAST DRIVE
Central
W. 99TH ST.
Metro Theater
W. 98TH ST.
W. 97TH ST.
TRANSVERSE ROAD NO. 4
NEW JERSEY
Pomander Walk
WEST END AVENUE
W. 96TH ST.
W. 95TH ST.
Symphony Space
W. 94TH ST.
W. 93RD ST.
Joan of Arc Monument
W. 92ND ST.
Eldorado Apartments
W. 91ST ST.
W. 90TH ST.
Reservoir
Soldiers & Sailors Monument
W. 89TH ST.
W. 88TH ST.
W. 87TH ST.
Claremont Riding Academy
Hudson River
Riverside Park
W. 86TH ST.
TRANSVERSE ROAD NO. 3
W. 85TH ST.
Poe Residence
W. 84TH ST.
W. 83RD ST.
Children's Museum of Manhattan
Mount Tom
W. 82ND ST.
American Museum of Natural History
W. 81ST ST.
Zabar's
79th Street Boat Basin
W. 79TH ST.
TRANSVERSE ROAD NO. 2
W. 78TH ST.
Apthorp Apartments
W. 76TH ST.
New-York Historical Society
Park
Beacon Theater
San Remo Apartments
Eleanor Roosevelt Memorial
Ansonia Hotel
Dakota Apartments
W. 72ND ST.
W. 71ST ST.
W. 70TH ST.
Majestic Apartments
FREEDOM PLACE
AMSTERDAM AVE.
W. 69TH ST.
Hotel des Artistes
W. 67TH ST.
Museum of American Folk Art
Juilliard School
W. 65TH ST.
TRANSVERSE RD. NO. 1
W. 64TH ST.
New York Society for Ethical Culture
Lincoln Center
Church of St Paul The Apostle
W. 60TH ST.
COLUMBUS CIRCLE
CENTRAL PARK SOUTH
W. 59TH ST.
W. 58TH ST.
W. 57TH ST.
W. 56TH ST.
W. 55TH ST.
W. 54TH ST.
W. 53RD ST.
ELEVENTH AVE.
TENTH AVENUE
EIGHTH AVENUE
SEVENTH AVENUE
AVE. OF THE AMERICAS
UPPER WEST SIDE AND MORNINGSIDE HEIGHTS

West** and **Riverside Drive**. Sandwiched between these most prestigious of Manhattan addresses are modern high-rise apartment buildings and historic brownstones, dozens of restaurants, outdoor cafés and bars, clothing stores, gourmet food emporiums and a casual mix of people. Above 90th Street, particularly along Amsterdam and Columbus avenues (streets that further down in the 70s have become irreparably yuppified) you will still find enclaves of public housing, some shabby SRO ("single room occupancy") hotels, and down-beat street hustle that increase into the 100s where you'll find less-well-off Latino neighborhoods. However, even these areas have started to gentrify lately, with middle-class families moving into areas further north that they previously would have shunned.

Columbus Circle and around

Columbus Circle is located at the intersection of Broadway, Central Park West and 59th Street: a pedestrian's worst nightmare yet a good place to start investigating the Upper West Side. Christopher Columbus stands uncomfortably atop a lone column in the center of this odd cast of buildings grouped around a hazardous traffic circle. At the southern end stands an odd, white, vaguely Moorish, building that is one of the city's grand *folies*; when it went up in 1965, it was said to resemble a Persian brothel. It used to house the New York City Department of Cultural Affairs and a NY Conventions and Visitors Bureau, but, as of writing, stands empty awaiting a new tenant (besides the group of homeless camped outside).

Opposite the circle, on the park side, stands the **Maine Monument**, a large stone edifice with the prow of a ship jutting out from its base, crowned by a newly gilded and polished victory statue that shines above the entrance to the park. Erected in 1912, it is dedicated to the "valiant seamen who perished in the Maine" during the Spanish-American War. Across the street, at the junction of Broadway and Central Park West, is the glittering **Trump International Hotel** at 1 Central Park West, a new luxury hotel and residential condo, that during was touted as "The World's Most Prestigious Address" – just the latest example of Trump's extraordinary hubris. A large silver globe sits on the plaza in front of the hotel, a glitzy and completely unnecessary replica of the Unisphere that is on display at the 1964 World's Fair site in Queens.

For relief, go west a few blocks and contemplate the **Church of St Paul the Apostle** on Ninth Avenue between 59th and 60th streets, a beautiful Old Gothic structure housing Byzantine basilica features, such as Stanford White's high altar. A few steps further north the nearby **New York Society for Ethical Culture**, 2 W 64th St at Central Park West (☎212/874-5210), "a haven for those who want to share the high adventure of integrating ethical ideals into daily life." Founded in 1876 (though the building itself wasn't built until 1902), this distinguished organization also helped to found the National Association for the Advancement of Colored People and the American Civil Liberties Union. It holds regular Sunday meetings, and organizes occasional recitals and lectures on social responsibility, politics and other related topics. It also runs an elementary school here where J. Robert Oppenheimer, who directed the evolution of the first atomic bomb, was once a student.

Museum of American Folk Art

Moving away from the highbrow, the **Museum of American Folk Art**, 2 Lincoln Square, Columbus Ave, between 65th and 66th streets (Tues–Sun

11.30am–7.30pm; suggested admission $3; ⓣ212/595-9533, ⓦwww.folkart-museum.com), exhibits multicultural folk art from all over the US, with a permanent collection that includes over 3500 works from the seventeenth to twentieth centuries. The affiliated Folk Art Institute runs courses, lectures and workshops open to the public.

Lincoln Center

Broadway continues north from Columbus Circle to the **Lincoln Center for the Performing Arts**, an imposing group of white-marble and glass buildings arranged around a large plaza and fountain, on the west side between 63rd and 66th streets. Robert Moses came up with the idea of creating a cultural center on the west side in the 1950s as a way of "encouraging" gentrification of the area, an exercise in urban renewal that has been extremely successful. A number of architects worked on the plans, and the complex was finally built in the mid-1960s on a site that formerly held some of the city's poorest slums. After the slums were emptied (and the residents fled to ghettos further uptown), but before construction actually started, the run-down lots served as the open-air set for the 1960 filming of *West Side Story*, which was based on the musical that was set here.

Home to the Metropolitan Opera and the New York Philharmonic, as well as a host of other smaller companies, Lincoln Center is worth seeing even if you're not into catching a performance; the best way is to go on an **organized tour**, otherwise you'll only be allowed to peek into the ornate lobbies of the buildings. Tours leave daily at 10.30am, 12.30pm, 2.30pm and 4.30pm from the ticket booth at the Met, and take in the main part of the Center at a cost of $9.50 ($8 for students) for an hour-long tour. Be warned that they can get very booked up; best phone ahead (ⓣ212/875-5350) to be sure of a place. Backstage tours of the Met are also available; see p.208 for more information.

You could also stop by for **free entertainment**: there's the Autumn Crafts Fair in early September, folk and jazz bands at lunchtime throughout the summer, and dazzling fountain and light displays each evening. In addition, Lincoln Center hosts a variety of affordable summertime events, including Mostly Mozart, the country's first and most popular indoor summer chamber music series, and Midsummer Night Swing, a summertime dance series that allows you to swing, salsa, hustle and ballroom dance on an outdoor bandstand at the Lincoln Center Plaza Fountain. Contact **Lincoln Center Information** (ⓣ212/875-5000, ⓦwww.lincolncenter.org) for specifics.

The New York State Theater and Avery Fisher Hall

Philip Johnson's spare and elegant **New York State Theater**, on the south side of the plaza, is home to the New York City Ballet, the New York City Opera and the famed annual December performances of *The Nutcracker Suite*. Its foyer is ringed with balconies embellished with delicately worked bronze grilles and boasts an imposing, four-story-high ceiling finished in gold leaf. The ballet season runs from late November through February, and from early April through June; the opera season starts in July and runs through mid-November. Call ⓣ212/870-5570 for ticket information.

Johnson also had a hand in the **Avery Fisher Hall** opposite, on the north side of the plaza, where the New York Philharmonic plays. He was called in to refashion the interior after its acoustics were found to be below par. The seating space here, though, does not possess the magnificence of his glittery

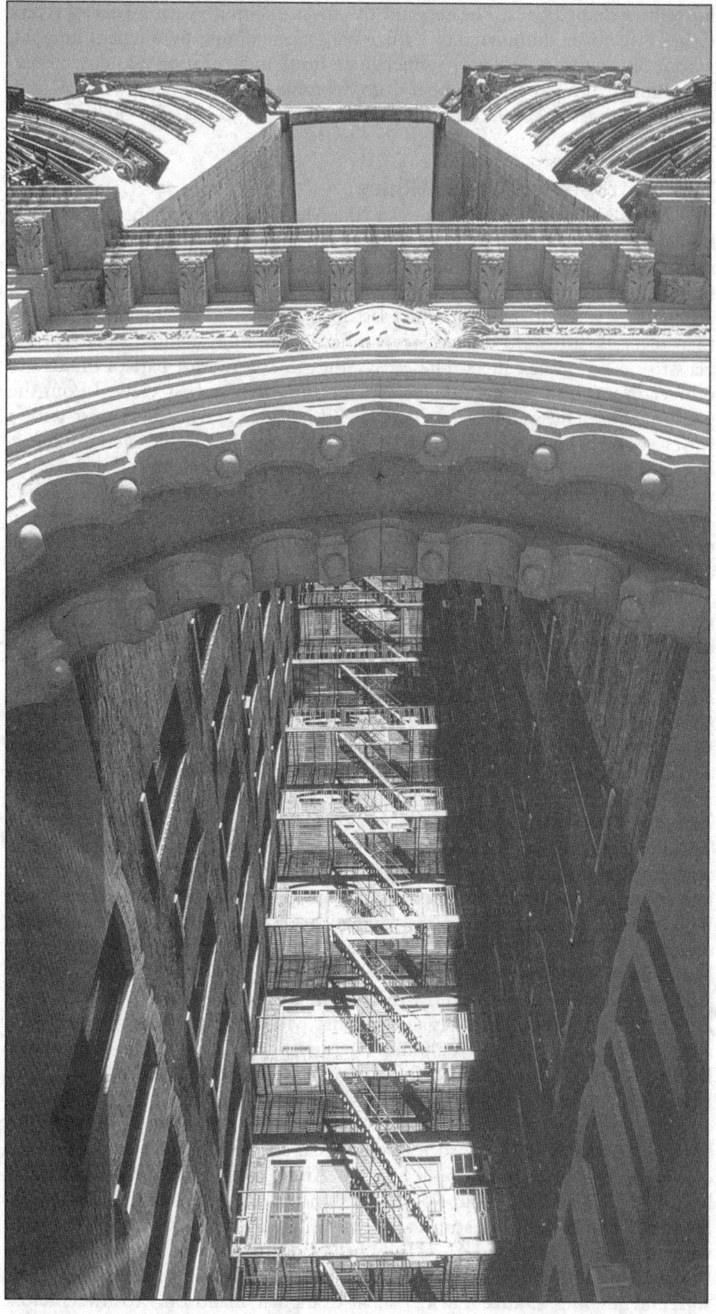

△ The Upper West Side is home to some of the city's most distinctive architecture

horseshoe-shaped State Theater, and the most exciting visual aspect of Avery Fisher is its foyer, dominated by a huge hanging sculpture by Richard Lippold, whose distinctive style you may recognize from an atrium or two downtown. The Philharmonic performs here from September though May, while Mostly Mozart concerts take place in July and August. Call ⓣ212/875-5030 for performance information.

The Metropolitan Opera House

The Metropolitan Opera House (aka "the Met"), the focal point of the plaza, is by contrast ornate, with enormous crystal chandeliers and red-carpeted staircases designed for grand entrances in gliding evening wear. Behind two of the high arched windows hang **murals** by Marc Chagall. The artist wanted stained glass, but it was felt these wouldn't last long in an area (at the time) still less than reverential toward the arts, so paintings were hung behind square-paned glass to give a similar effect. These days, they're covered for part of the day to protect them from the sun; the rest of the time they're best viewed from the plaza outside. The mural on the left, *Le Triomphe de la Musique*, is cast with a variety of well-known performers, landmarks snipped from the New York skyline and a portrait of Sir Rudolph Bing, the man who ran the Met for more than three decades – here garbed as a gypsy. The other mural, *Les Sources de la Musique*, is reminiscent of Chagall's renowned scenery for the Met production of *The Magic Flute*: the god of music strums a lyre while a Tree of Life, Verdi and Wagner all float down the Hudson River.

The opera house, with its elegant interior of African rosewood and red velvety chairs, says opulence, pure and simple. The acoustics and the singers make the music here; there is no electronic voice enhancement whatsoever (though the multilingual titling and translation system is definitely state-of-the-art). **Backstage Tours** of the Met cost $9 ($4 for students) and are given daily, October through June at 3.45pm and 10am on Saturday. As for performances, you'll find full details of what you can listen to and how to do it in Chapter 33, "The performing arts and film" or call ⓣ212/362-6000.

The rest of Lincoln Center

Two piazzas flank the Met; to the south there is Damrosch Park, a large space with rows of chairs facing the **Guggenheim Bandshell**, where you can catch free summer lunchtime concerts and various performances. To the north you will find a lovely, smaller plaza facing the **Vivian Beaumont Theater** designed by Eero Saarinen in 1965 and home to the smaller **Mitzi E. Newhouse Theater** in its basement. This square is mostly taken up by a rectangular reflecting pool, around which Manhattan office workers munch their lunch, while mid-pond reclines a lazy Henry Moore figure, given counterpoint at the edge by a spidery sculpture by Alexander Calder. **The New York Public Library for the Performing Arts** (ⓣ212/870-1630) is located behind the theater and holds over eight million items, and a museum that exhibits costumes, set designs and music scores. However, as of writing, the library is under renovation, so it's best to call ahead as exhibits and times are constantly changing. Across 66th Street is **Alice Tully Hall**, a recital hall that houses the Chamber Music Society of Lincoln Center, and the **Walter E. Reade Theater**, which features foreign films and retrospectives and, together with the Avery Fisher and Alice Tully halls, hosts the annual **New York Film Festival** in September. The celebrated **Juilliard School of Music** is in an adjacent building. **Dante Park**, a small triangular island on Broadway, across from the main Lincoln Center Plaza, is home to a statue designed in 1921 to commemorate the 600th anniversary of the poet's death. But that is no longer its greatest claim to fame: Movado (the Swiss watch designers) has erected *TimeSculpture* there, a stone sculpture with a series of large brass clocks designed by Philip Johnson, dedicated in May 1999 to the patrons of Lincoln Center.

Broadway

Broadway's **Verdi Square** is a good place to take a breather from Lincoln Center, offering contemplation of the ornate balconies, round corner towers and cupolas of the **Ansonia Hotel** at 2109 Broadway between W 73rd and W 74th streets. Completed in 1904, this dramatic Beaux-Arts building is still the artsy grande dame of the Upper West Side. Never a hotel but an upscale apartment house, it has welcomed such luminaries as Enrico Caruso, Arturo Toscanini, Lily Pons, Florenz Ziegfeld, Theodore Dreiser, Igor Stravinsky and even Babe Ruth. **The Beacon Theater**, on 2124 Broadway, between W 74th and 75th streets (ⓣ212/496-7070) is nothing particularly special from the outside. But step into the lobby, or better yet the 2700-seat auditorium (a designated landmark) to get the full effect of its extravagant Greco-Deco-Empire interior. It's a great venue for rock shows.

The enormous limestone **Apthorp Apartments**, at 2211 Broadway, occupies an entire block from Broadway to West End and West 78th to West 79th streets. Built in 1908 by William Waldorf Astor, the ornate iron gates of the former carriage entrance lead into a central courtyard with a large fountain, visible from Broadway (you won't be allowed in to stroll). Some of the best bagels in New York can be found nearby at **H&H Bagels**, at 2239 Broadway, at the corner of 80th Street, where they are said to bake over 50,000 bagels a day. Another culinary attraction is **Zabar's**, at 2254 Broadway, between 80th and 81st streets, the Upper West Side's principal gourmet shop and area landmark. Here you can find more or less anything connected with food; the ground floor is given over to things edible, the upper floor contains cooking implements and kitchenware, a collection which, in the obscurity of some of its items, must be unrivaled anywhere. What kitchen, for example, could do without a duck press?

Nearby the **Children's Museum of Manhattan**, 212 W 83rd St, between Broadway and Amsterdam Avenue (Tues–Sun 10am–5pm; $6; ⓣ212/721-1234, ⓦwww.cmom.org), fills a delightful five-story space that offers interactive exhibits that stimulate learning, in a really fun, relaxed environment for kids (and babies) of all ages. The Dr. Seuss exhibit and the storytelling room (filled with books kids can choose from) are particular winners. At 215 W 84th St, there's a plaque marking the one-time address of **Edgar Allan Poe** (he lived in a farmhouse on the site in 1844, while he finished *The Raven*), now sadly just a faceless condo. If you're a real Poe fan, head over to Riverside Park and sit on the rocky outcropping known as **Mount Tom** at 83rd Street, where Poe was said to have written a few works, such as the poem *To Helene*. Taking the theme even further is *Edgar's Café* (255 W 84th) and there's a green-topped street sign in his honor as well.

The northern part of the Upper West Side has seen a lot of changes in the last few years. Gentrification is slowly creeping northward, and the obligatory Starbucks have proliferated around here, as have chain clothing stores and (on the upside) nicer restaurants of all stripes. Check out one of the few real old-timer spots left in the neighborhood, **Barney Greengrass**, at 541 Amsterdam Ave, between 86th and 87th streets, which opened its doors in 1908 and still serves smoked fish and bagels with a *shmeer* (or a dollop) of cream cheese to loyalists.

Weaving your way north through Broadway's invariably crowded sidewalks, you will reach **Symphony Space**, 2537 Broadway between W 94th and 95th streets (Ⓣ212/864-5400, Ⓦwww.symphonyspace.org), one of New York's primary performing arts centers. Symphony Space regularly sponsors short story readings (called Selected Shorts), as well as classical and world music performances, but it is perhaps best known for its free, twelve-hour performance marathons, the uninterrupted reading of James Joyce's *Ulysses* every Bloomsday (June 16).

At 107th Street, Broadway and West End Avenue meet at **Strauss Park**, a small vest-pocket space centered on an **Augustus Lukeman statue** of a reclining woman gazing over a water basin. It was dedicated by Macy's founder Nathan Strauss to his brother/business partner, Isidor, and Isidor's wife, Ida, both of whom lived nearby and went down with the *Titanic* in 1912 – legend has it that Ida refused to leave Isidor for the lifeboats. Further down the block at no. 319, the **Roerich Museum** (Tues–Sun 2–5pm; free; Ⓣ212/864-7752) contains a small, weird and virtually unknown collection of strikingly original paintings by Nicholas Roerich, a Russian artist who lived in India and was influenced by Indian mysticism. The collection, centered on Himalayan scenes, rests in a comfortable brownstone.

Central Park West

North of Lincoln Center, as Broadway curves west, Ninth Avenue becomes chic Columbus Avenue, home to a multitude of outdoor cafés and eclectic boutiques, many of which are unfortunately being replaced by national chain stores, part of a citywide trend. The streets in the upper 60s and 70s between Columbus and **Central Park West** are quiet tree-lined blocks filled with beautifully renovated brownstones, many of which are one-family homes, making this neighborhood one of the most sought in the city.

On 67th Street, closer to Central Park West, is the **Hotel des Artistes**, specially built for artists in 1917, and the one-time Manhattan address of the likes of Noel Coward, Norman Rockwell, Isadora Duncan and Alexander Woollcott. It's now a swanky co-op apartment building. On the ground floor is the famous **Café des Artistes**, one of Manhattan's most romantic, and priciest, restaurants. If you can't afford to eat here, take a peek inside or have a drink at the renowned bar (but make sure you are dressed for it), just to absorb the ambience and see the nude-nymph murals by Howard Chandler Christy.

Taking up the entire block between 71st and 72nd streets on Central Park West, the **Majestic**, a mammoth pale yellow, Art Deco apartment house built in 1930, is best known for its twin towers and avant-garde brickwork. Across 72nd Street is the more famous **Dakota Building** (1 W 72nd St), so called because at the time of its construction in 1884 its Uptown location was considered to be as remote as the Dakota Territory. The grandiose German Renaissance-style mansion, with turrets, gables and other odd details, was built to persuade wealthy New Yorkers that life in an apartment could be just as luxurious as in a private house. Over the years there have been few residents here not publicly known in some way: big-time tenants included Lauren Bacall and Leonard Bernstein, and in the 1960s the building was used as the setting for Jack Finney's nostalgic novel *Time and Again*, and as Mia Farrow's home in Roman Polanski's film *Rosemary's Baby*. But the best-known resident of the Dakota was **John Lennon** (see box below). If you enter Central Park across the street you can see **Strawberry Fields**, and the mosaic dedicated to Lennon (for more on that, turn to p.170).

The death of John Lennon

Today most people know the Dakota Building as the former home of **John Lennon** – and present home of his widow, Yoko Ono, who owns a number of the building's apartments. It was outside the Dakota, on the night of December 8, 1980, that the ex-Beatle was murdered – shot by a man who professed to be one of his greatest admirers.

His murderer, Mark David Chapman, had been hanging around outside the building all day, clutching a copy of his hero's latest album, *Double Fantasy*, and accosting Lennon for his autograph – which he got. This was nothing unusual in itself – fans often used to loiter outside and hustle for a glimpse of the singer – but Chapman was still there when the couple returned from a late-night recording session, whereupon he pumped five .38 bullets into Lennon as he walked through the Dakota's 72nd Street entrance. Lennon was picked up by the doorman and rushed to the hospital in a taxi, but he died on the way from a massive loss of blood. A distraught Yoko issued a statement immediately: "John loved and prayed for the human race. Please do the same for him."

Why Chapman did this to John Lennon no one really knows; suffice it to say his obsession with the man had obviously unhinged him. Fans may want to light a stick of incense for Lennon across the road in Strawberry Fields (see p.170), a section of Central Park that has been restored and maintained in his memory through an endowment by Ono. Its trees and shrubs were donated by a number of countries as a gesture toward world peace. The gardens are pretty enough, if unspectacular, and it would take a hard-bitten cynic not to be a little bit moved by the *Imagine* mosaic on the pathway.

Built in 1930 and taking up the entire block, the **San Remo**, at 145–146 Central Park W between 74th and 75th streets, is one of the most integral components of the Central Park West skyline, with its ornate twin towers topped by columned, mock-Roman temples visible from most points in the park. It is also very exclusive: some years ago Madonna attempted to buy a multimillion dollar apartment here, but was roundly refused approval by the building's co-op board. Unaccountably, many other celebrities have been allowed to live here, including Warren Beatty and Diane Keaton (when they were an item), and Mary Tyler Moore. A block farther north is the **Central Park Historic District**, from 75th to 77th streets on Central Park West, and on 76th Street toward Columbus Avenue, where you will find a number of small turn-of-the-nineteenth-century rowhouses, and the **Kenilworth Apartments**, at 151 Central Park W, which was built in 1908 and boasts an unusual mansard roof and a wildly carved limestone exterior.

The New-York Historical Society

Further north is the oft-overlooked **New-York Historical Society**, 2 W 77th St at Central Park West (Tues–Sun 11am–5pm; suggested donation $5, students and seniors $3, children free; Ⓣ212/873-3400, Ⓦwww.nyhistory.org), which has a permanent collection of books, prints, portraits, and a research library. One room focuses on the work of **James Audubon**, the Harlem artist and naturalist who specialized in lovingly detailed watercolors of birds (the collection holds all 432 original watercolors of Audubon's *Birds of America*). Other galleries hold a broad sweep of **nineteenth-century American painting**, principally portraiture, and Hudson River School landscapes (among them Thomas Cole's famed and pompous *Course of Empire* series). A new permanent children's exhibit called **Kid City** offers interactive exhibitions, such as a child-size re-creation of a block on Broadway in 1901. More a museum of American than New York history, the society also features various temporary exhibitions that mix high and low culture with intelligence and flair; and the museum **library**, which holds 650,000 books, over two million manuscripts, letters and historical documents, and 30,000 maps and atlases, is worth further scrutiny. It boasts such diverse items as the original Louisiana Purchase document and the correspondence between Aaron Burr and Alexander Hamilton that led up to their duel (see p.230).

The American Museum of Natural History

Central Park W at 79th St. Subway B or C to 81st St–Central Park West. Sun–Thurs 10am–5.45pm, Fri & Sat 10am–8.45pm; suggested donation (which includes the Rose Center) $10, students $7.50, children $6; IMAX films, the Hayden Planetarium and certain special exhibits cost extra. Ⓣ *212/769-5100,* Ⓦ *www.amnh.org.*

An enormous complex of buildings full of fossils, gems, skeletons and other natural specimens, along with a wealth of man-made artifacts from indigenous cultures worldwide, the **American Museum of Natural History** is one of the best museums of its kind. This elegant giant fills four blocks with a strange architectural mélange of heavy Neoclassical and rustic Romanesque styles that was built in several stages, the first by Calvert Vaux and Jacob Wrey Mould in 1872. Founded in 1869, it is one of the oldest natural history museums as well as one of the largest, and once you've paced the length of its four floors of exhibition halls and witnessed a fair number of the 32 million items on display, you'll feel it in your feet. There's a fantastic amount to see, so be selective; depending on your interests, anything from a highly discriminating couple of hours to half a day should be ample. If you're not sure exactly where you are on a floor (and it can easily happen), check the pillars near each staircase and between exhibit halls – they contain good locator maps.

The collection

The Museum's vast marble front steps on Central Park West are a great reading-and-sunning place, with an appropriately haughty statue of Theodore Roosevelt looking out with a resolute gaze from his perch atop a horse, flanked by a pair of Native Americans marching gamely beside him. This entrance leaves you well placed for a loop of the more interesting halls on the **second** (entry-level) **floor**: principally the **Hall of Asian People** and **Hall of African People**, each filled with fascinating, often beautiful, art and artifacts, backed up with informal commentary and given atmosphere with piped-in drums and indigenous music. The Hall of African People displays ceremonial costumes, musical instruments and masks from all over the continent. The Hall of Asian People begins with Russian and Central Asian artifacts, moves on to Tibet – with a gorgeous re-creation of an ornate, gilded Tibetan Buddhist shrine – and then on to China and Japan, with displays of some fantastic textiles, rugs, brass and jade ornaments. Another highlight of this floor is the lower half of the **Hall of African Mammals**, a double-height room whose exhibits continue on to the third floor balcony. Don't miss (how can you?) the life-size family of elephants in the center of the room. Also worth seeing on the third floor are the **Reptiles and Amphibians Hall**, filled with samples of every such species one can think of, and the **Eastern Woodlands and Plains Indians** exhibit, a somewhat pedestrian display of artifacts, clothing and the like.

The **fourth floor** is almost entirely taken up with the wildly popular

Dinosaur Exhibit; renovated and expanded in 1996 into five spacious, well-lit and well-designed halls, it is the largest dinosaur collection in the world, with more than 120 specimens on display. Here, you can watch two **robotic dinosaur jaws** chew; walk on a transparent bridge erected over a fifty-foot-long Barosaurus spine; and **touch fossils**. The multilevel exhibits are also supplemented by interactive computer programs and claymation videos, which add a nice hands-on appeal to the exhibit.

Downstairs on the **first floor** (the floor below where you entered) is the **Hall of Gems and Minerals**, well laid-out and including some strikingly beautiful crystals – not least the Star of India, the largest blue sapphire ever found. The enormous double-height gallery dedicated to **Ocean Life** includes a 94-foot-long (life-size) **Blue Whale** disconcertingly hanging suspended from the high ceiling over a food court, and the exhibit of **North American Mammals** hasn't changed in ages – the dark halls, marble floors and illuminated diorama cases filled with stuffed specimens have seen fifty years' worth of children on school trips. The greatest draw on this floor, however, is the new **Hall of Biodiversity**. It focuses on both the ecological and evolutionary aspects of biodiversity, with multimedia displays on everything from the changes humans have wrought on the environment (with examples of solutions brought about by local activists and community groups in all parts of the world) to videos about endangered species. The centerpiece of the exhibit is a living re-creation of a **Central African Republic rainforest** that you can walk through, to the sounds of birdcalls and forest noises, accompanied by detailed texts about the ecology of the area and the need for conservation. The **NatureMax Theater**, located on this floor, presents some interesting nature-oriented IMAX films; check to see what's playing (there is an additional charge).

The Rose Center for Earth and Space

Across from the Hall of Biodiversity lies the first installation of the **Rose Center for Earth and Space** – the spanking new **Hall of Planet Earth**, a multilevel and multimedia exploration of how the earth works, with displays on a wide variety of subjects such as the **formation of planets**, underwater rock formation, plate tectonics and carbon dating. Items on display include a **2.7 billion-year-old specimen** of a banded iron formation and the **volcanic ash** from Mount Vesuvius. The centerpiece of the room is the **Dynamic Earth Globe**, where visitors seated below the globe are able to watch the earth via satellite go through its full rotation, getting as close as possible to the views astronauts see from outer space.

The Hall of Planet Earth links visitors to the rest of the Rose Center, which is made up of the new **Hall of the Universe** and the **Hayden Planetarium**. The center boasts an enormous **sphere**, 87 feet in diameter, which appears to be floating inside a huge metal and glass cube above the main arched entrance to the center. The sphere actually houses the planetarium itself, which includes two theaters, as well as research facilities and classrooms, and is illuminated rather eerily at night. Inside, the state-of-the-art **Space Theater** uses a Zeiss projector to create sky shows with sources like the Hubble telescope and NASA laboratories, and can take you to members of our solar system, the Milky Way or any other spacely destination, "to infinity and beyond."

On the second floor, the **Big Bang Theater** offers a multisensory re-creation of the "birth" of the universe. On the outer walkway stand the **Scales of the Universe**, an installation which gives a physical presentation of the relative sizes of things, from galaxies, stars and planets, down through cells and atoms, all in comparison to the central sphere. It is simple and effective, yet frustratingly complex to wrap your brain around.

Follow the **Cosmic Pathway**, a sloping spiral walkway that takes you through thirteen billion years of cosmic evolution via an interactive computerized timeline. It leads to the **Hall of the Universe**, which offers exhibits and interactive displays on the formation and evolution of the universe, the galaxy, stars and planets, including a mini-theater where visitors can journey inside a black hole through computerized effects. There is even a display here entitled **The Search For Life**, which examines on which of the planetary systems life could exist – in case you hadn't questioned the meaning of existence enough by this point.

Riverside Park and Riverside Drive

At the western edge of 72nd Street, **Riverside Park** begins to run north, bringing you as close to the **Hudson River** as you can get without bumping into the West Side Highway. Just south of here were the old **Penn Railroad Yards**, abandoned for nearly two decades and now being replaced by a towering luxury apartment development, spearheaded by none other than Donald Trump. **Riverside Drive** starts at 72nd Street and winds north, flanked by palatial townhouses and multistory apartment buildings put up in the early part of the twentieth century by those not quite rich enough to compete with the folks on Fifth Avenue. A number of historic, landmarked districts lie along it, particularly in the mid-70s, mid-80s, and low-100s.

The entrance to Riverside Park is marked by the **Eleanor Roosevelt Monument** on the corner of 72nd Street and Riverside Drive, dedicated in 1996 by then-First Lady Hillary Rodham Clinton. The monument consists of a large, planted base with a pensive statue of Eleanor Roosevelt standing in its center. The stone statue, by Penelope Jencks, surrounded by well-kept benches, makes it an inviting spot for contemplation.

One of only eight designated scenic landmarks in New York City, Riverside Park was conceived as a way of attracting the middle class to the (then) remote Upper West Side and covering the unappealing Hudson River Railway tracks that had been built along the Hudson in 1846. Not as imposing or spacious as Central Park, it was designed by the same team of architects; **Frederic Law Olmsted** started the plans in 1873, but it took 25 years to complete, and other architects, including his partner, **Calvert Vaux**, contributed designs. Rock outcroppings and informally arranged trees, shrubs and flowers surround its tree-lined main boulevards. The park was widened in the 1930s by **Robert Moses**, who typically added some of his own concrete touches, including the rotunda at the 79th Street Boat Basin. The **Warsaw Ghetto Memorial**, at 84th Street in the park will give you pause: a simple, open circular plaza with a small black iron-gated square is dedicated to the remembrance of the victims of World War II.

A delightful place for a break is the **79th Street Boat Basin**, with paths leading down to it located on either side of 79th Street at Riverside Drive (you'll hit a concrete rotunda first – keep going until you see water). Mostly overlooked by tourists, this is a small harbor where a couple of hundred Manhattanites live on the water in houseboats, while others just moor their motorboats and sailboats there. It's one of the city's most peaceful locations, and while the views across the water to New Jersey aren't exactly awesome, they're a tonic after the congestion of Manhattan proper.

Creative design is abundant along Riverside Drive: in the 70s, there are lovely turn-of-the-nineteenth-century townhouses, many with copper-trimmed mansard roofs and private terraces or roof gardens, and between 80th and 81st streets there are a row of historic **landmarked townhouses**, classics of the brownstone genre, with bowed exteriors, bay windows, and gabled roofs. You'll find other architectural surprises as well, as many of the residences in the 80s between Riverside and West End have stained glass transom windows, and the expressive faces in stone relief above the doorways seem to enjoy your passing through. The boulevard one block to the east, **West End Avenue**, is a unique New York avenue in that it is purely residential, lined with elegant prewar apartment buildings and townhouses, and few modern high-rises.

An exploration of Riverside Drive in the high 80s and low 100s reveals several notable monuments. **The Soldiers and Sailors Monument** (1902), a marble memorial to the Civil War dead, is located at Riverside Drive and 89th Street. The **Joan of Arc Monument** at West 93rd Street sits atop a 1.6-acre cobblestone and grass park in the middle of the Drive named Joan of Arc Island. Last, and most impressive, is the **Firemen's Memorial** at West 100th Street, a stately commemorative frieze designed in 1913 with the statues of *Courage* and *Duty* at its top. There are also two large, beautifully planted **community gardens** in Riverside Park, at 89th Street and just south of 96th Street, lovingly cared for by volunteers.

Further north on Riverside Drive, between 105th and 106th streets is a lovely block of historic apartments. It begins with **330 Riverside Drive**, now the Riverside Study Center, a glorious five-story Beaux-Arts house built in 1900 – note the copper mansard roof, stone balconies and delicate iron scrollwork. At **331 Riverside Drive** stands the current headquarters of the **New York Buddhist Church**, which was formerly the home of Marion Davies, a 1930s actress most famous for her role as William Randolph Hearst's mistress. Hearst actually had this small mansion built for her in 1902, and sometimes stayed here with her, while his family lived not too far away downtown. The odd little building next door is also part of the New York Buddhist Church and showcases a larger-than-life-size bronze statue of Shinran Shonin (1173–1262), the Japanese founder of the Jodo-Shinsu sect of Buddhism. It originally stood in Hiroshima and somehow survived the atomic explosion of August 1945. It was brought to New York in 1955 as a symbol of "lasting hope for world peace" and has been in this spot ever since. Local lore had it that the statue was still radioactive, so in the 1950s and 1960s children were told to hold their breath for protection as they went by. At **337 Riverside Drive**, the River Mansion, at the corner of 106th Street, was once home to Duke Ellington. In fact, this stretch of West 106th Street, between Riverside Drive and Central Park West, has been renamed Duke Ellington Boulevard to honor the great composer and musician.

Morningside Heights

One area just north of the Upper West Side has also undergone several waves of gentrification in the last decade. Happily, **Morningside Heights** has managed to retain its own slightly funky, college-town aura, resisting the urge (so far) to convert small stores to large impersonal chains or build luxury high-rise apartments. Filled with Columbia students and professors, middle-class families who can't quite afford the rents farther downtown, and a mix of whites, blacks, Latinos and Asians, it forms an eclectic, quintessentially New York neighborhood. There aren't a lot of sights in the area besides the Cathedral of St John the Divine and Columbia, but it is worth a trip just for those.

The Cathedral Church of St John the Divine

The Cathedral Church of St John the Divine at Amsterdam Ave at 112th St (☎212/316-7540), rises out of the urban landscape with a sure, solid kind of majesty. Far from finished, it is still one of New York's most impressive sights. Although frequently visited by dignitaries and world leaders, including the Dalai Lama, its uptown location ensures relative uncrowding, a rarity in this city.

Work on the Episcopal church began in 1892 to the specifications of a Romanesque design that, with a change of architect in 1911, became French Gothic. Work progressed quickly for a while but stopped with the outbreak of war in 1939 and only resumed again in the mid-1980s. The church declared bankruptcy in 1994, fraught with funding difficulties and hard questioning by people who think the money might be better spent on something of more obvious benefit to the local community, and has since launched a massive international fundraising drive in the hope of resuming building work soon.

That said, St John's is very much a community church, housing a soup kitchen and shelter for the homeless, AIDS awareness and health outreach initiatives, and other social programs, as well as a gymnasium and plans for an amphitheater. And some of the building work itself is being undertaken by local African-Americans who are trained by English stonemasons in the church's own sculpture/stone workshops. Though the cathedral appears finished at first glance (despite the ever-present scaffolding), when you gaze up into its huge, uncompleted towers, you realize how much is left to do. Only two-thirds of the cathedral is finished, and completion isn't due until around 2050 – assuming it goes on uninterrupted. If finished, St John the Divine would be the largest cathedral structure in the world, its floor space – at 600 feet long and at the transepts 320 feet wide – big enough to swallow both the cathedrals of Notre Dame and Chartres whole, or, as tour guides are at pains to point out, two full-size football fields.

The Portal of Paradise at the Cathedral's main entrance was completed in 1995, and is dazzlingly carved, with 32 biblical figures both male and female (despite the original design's focus on men only), and such startling images as a mushroom cloud rising apocalyptically over Manhattan, all chiseled in limestone and painted with metallic oxide. But progress is long and slow; the portal alone took ten years to complete.

Walking the length of the **nave**, these figures seem much more than just another piece of bigger-is-better Americana – the size is truly awe-inspiring and adds to the spiritual power of the space. Here, too, you can see the melding of the two styles, particularly in the choir, which rises from a heavy arcade of Romanesque columns to a high, light-Gothic vaulting, the temporary dome of the crossing to someday be replaced by a tall, delicate Gothic spire. For some idea of how the completed cathedral will look, glance in on the gift shop, where there's a scale model of the projected design, as well as an interesting array of books and souvenirs.

The open-minded, progressive nature of St John's is readily visible throughout the cathedral itself: note the intricately carved wood **Altar for Peace**, the **Poets Corner** (with the names of American poets carved into its stone block floor) and an altar honoring AIDS victims. The amazing stained-glass windows include scenes from American history among Biblical ones. All kinds of art, both religious and secular, grace the interior (teak prayer chests from Siam, tapestries from the 1600s, and Keith Haring's only religious work).

Next to the cathedral on the south side are the **Bestiary Gates**, their grillework adorned with animal imagery (celebrating the annual blessing of the animals ceremony held here on the Feast of St Francis), and a **Children's Sculpture Garden** showcasing small bronze animal sculptures that were created by local schoolchildren surrounding the **Peace Fountain**. It in turn circles Greg Wyatt's sizeable, scary black sculpture *Heaven and Hell*, which symbolically tells a tale of good triumphant over evil. Afterwards, take a stroll through the cathedral yard and workshop where, if work has begun again, you can watch Harlem's apprentice masons tapping away at the stone blocks of the future cathedral.

Public tours are given Tuesday through Saturday at 11am and Sunday at 1pm. Vertical tours (of the towers) are given the first and third Saturday of each month (call ⓣ212/932-7347 for reservations). If you happen to be here around Christmas, stop in for the Christmas Eve Candlelight Carol Service at 10pm, but, as with all things in New York, get here early – St John's is packed by the time the music begins, with even standing room hard to come by. Everyone is welcome, and if you want to leave after the caroling (and before the service), feel free; lots of people come from all over the city just for the music and the ambience.

Columbia University and the rest of Morningside Heights

The area to the east of the Cathedral is known as **Morningside Heights**, so called because of its large park of that name, acting as a buffer zone between East Harlem sprawling below and the academic, relatively affluent Columbia neighborhood up on the hill, bounded by Morningside Drive. **Morningside Park**, stretching from 110th to 123rd streets, was landscaped in 1887 by Frederick Law Olmsted; its foliage is lush and attractive, but after dark at least, it's to be treated with more than a bit of caution.

Two blocks west, Broadway is characterized by a livelier bustle, with numerous inexpensive restaurants, bars and cafés, and a few bookstores. The **West End**, 2911 Broadway, between 113th and 114th streets, was once the hangout of Jack Kerouac, Allen Ginsberg and the Beats in the 1950s, when it was "one of those nondescript places," as Joyce Johnson wrote, "before the era of white walls and potted ferns and imitation Tiffany lamps, that for some reason always made the best hangouts." While it still serves the student crowd from the nearby university, the *West End* has had several makeovers since the days of the Beats, and stand-up comedy and karaoke have replaced *Howl* as the performances of choice.

The **Columbia University** campus fills seven blocks between Broadway and Morningside Drive from 114th to 121st streets, with its main entrance at Broadway and 116th Street. It is one of the most prestigious academic institutions in the country (ranking with the other Ivy League colleges of the Northeast) and was established in 1754, making it the country's fifth oldest institution of higher learning. Columbia has a long and venerable history, from handing out the first MD degree in the country (through its medical college) to sponsoring groundbreaking atomic research in the 1940s. The Morningside

Heights campus, modeled after the Athenian *agora* (or town square), was laid out by McKim, Mead and White after it moved from midtown in 1897. Amid the rest of the structures in Italian Renaissance style, the domed and colonnaded **Low Memorial Library** stands center-stage at the top of a wide flight of stone steps. Built in 1902, and on the New York City Register of Historic Places, it is still a commanding sight, one that lent a dramatic focus to the somewhat violent demonstrations held here during the Vietnam War. Tours of the campus leave regularly Monday to Friday during the school year from the **information office** on the corner of 116th Street and Broadway. (Call ahead ⓣ212/854-4900 to schedule a tour or get additional information.) Across Broadway sits **Barnard College**. Part of Columbia University, it was the place where women had to study for their degrees until Columbia finally went coeducational in the mid-Eighties. Many women still choose to study here, and Barnard retains its status as one of America's elite "Seven Sisters" colleges.

Riverside Church, located north of here on Riverside Drive between 120th and 121st streets (daily 9am–4.30pm, Sun service 10.45am), has a graceful French Gothic Revival tower, loosely modeled on Chartres and, like St John the Divine, turned over to a mixture of community center and administrative activities for the surrounding parish. Take the elevator to the 20th floor and ascend the steps around the carillon (the largest in the world, with 74 bells) for some classic spreads of Manhattan's skyline, New Jersey and the hills beyond – and the rest of the city well into the Bronx and Queens. Take a look too at the church, whose open and restrained interior (apart from the apse, which is positively sticky with ornamentation) is in stark contrast to the darkened mystery of St John the Divine.

Up the block from the church is **Grant's Tomb**, at Riverside Drive and 122nd Street (daily 9am–5pm; free; ⓣ212/666-1640), a Greek-style memorial and the nation's largest mausoleum in which, Groucho Marx's old joke notwithstanding, conquering Civil War hero and blundering eighteenth US president Grant really is interred with his wife, in two black-marble Napoleonic sarcophagi. The National Parks Service refurbished the tomb in 1996, so current visitors will be spared the graffiti and trash that for some years decorated the resting place of a national hero.

22

Harlem

As goes Harlem, so goes Black America.

Langston Hughes

While **Harlem** earned a reputation for racial tension and urban decay from the outward neglect and internal strife throughout the 1940s, 1950s and 1960s, a visit here will reveal that's only part of a much bigger picture, one often simplified and jaundiced by some media hostility to black culture. The most famous African-American community in America – and, arguably, the bedrock of black culture in this century – does have its problems, yet it's a far less dangerous neighborhood than its reputation suggests, especially in light of solid city and neighborhood improvement efforts of the last decade. Visitors to Harlem's main thoroughfares, **125th Street**,

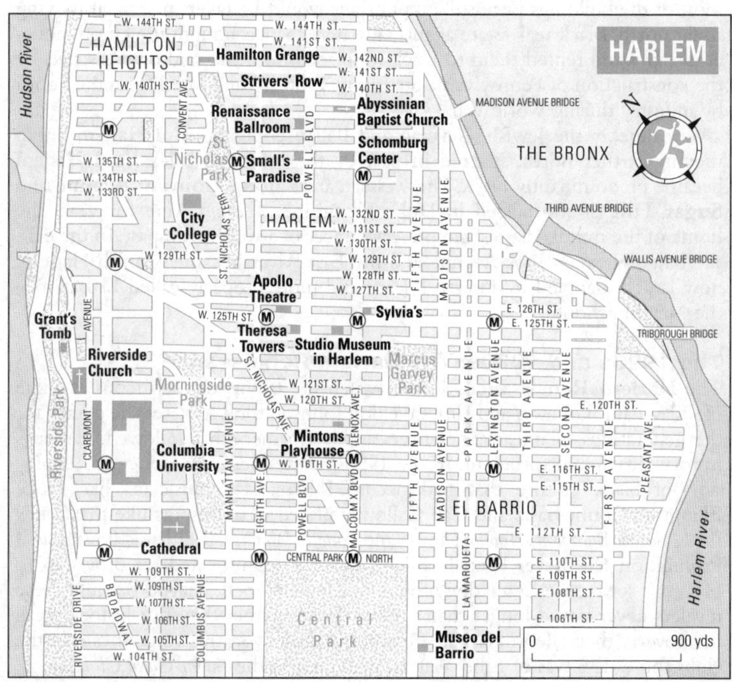

Adam Clayton Powell Jr Powell Boulevard, **Lenox Avenue** (officially renamed Malcolm X Boulevard but still known by its old name) or **116th Street**, should have no problem. Spanish Harlem – **El Barrio** – has an undeniably rougher edge to it, and reasons for visiting are far fewer than for Harlem proper.

Practically speaking, Harlem's sights are too spread out to amble between. You'll do best to make several trips, perhaps on a **guided tour** (see "Information, Maps and Tours" in Basics) to get acquainted with the area and to help you decide what to come back and see on your own. If you intend to tour Harlem on your own, it will serve you well to feel comfortable about where you're going beforehand, stick to the well-trodden streets and be relaxed once there. Thanks to their strong sense of community, Harlem residents are generally receptive to a friendly smile from passersby, and community businesses and organizations are actively seeking the tourist trade.

Harlem's beginnings

It was the Dutch who founded the settlement of **Nieuw Haarlem**, naming it after a town in Holland. Until the mid-nineteenth century the area was farmland, but when the New York and Harlem railroad linked the area with Lower Manhattan it attracted the better-off immigrant families (mainly German Jews from the Lower East Side) to newly built, elegant and fashionable brownstones in the steadily developing suburb. When work began on the IRT Lenox line later in the century, property speculators were quick to build good-quality homes in the expectation of seeing newly accessible Harlem repeat the success of the Upper West Side. They were too quick and too ambitious, for by the time the IRT line opened (it had reached what is now 129th Street by 1881) most of the buildings were still empty, their would-be takers uneasy at moving so far north. Black real-estate agents saw their chance, bought the empty houses cheaply and rented them to blacks displaced from the midtown districts by the construction of Pennsylvania Station in 1906–10 and lured from the South by industry during World War I.

Very quickly the Jewish, German and Italian populations of Harlem began moving farther north, spurred in part by the influx of blacks, and Harlem became predominantly black. The western areas **along Convent Avenue** and **Sugar Hill** (immortalized in Duke Ellington's *A Train*) were for years the home of the middle classes and preserve traces of a well-to-do past. In the east, the bulge between Park Avenue and the East River became Spanish Harlem, now largely peopled by Puerto Ricans and more properly called El Barrio – the Neighborhood.

The 1920s and 1930s: The Harlem Renaissance

The **Harlem Renaissance**, during which the talents of such icons as Billie Holiday, Paul Robeson and James Weldon Johnson took root, set the course for the generations of musicians, writers and performers that followed. Harlem's history is rich and turbulent. In the 1920s, whites began to notice the explosion of black culture that had occurred here: jazz musicians like Duke Ellington, Count Basie and Cab Calloway played in nightspots like the *Cotton Club*, *Savoy Ballroom*, *Apollo Theatre* and *Smalls Paradise*; the drink flowed as if Prohibition had never been heard of, and the sophisticated set drove up to Harlem's speakeasies after downtown had gone to bed. Maybe because these revelers never stayed longer than the last drink, neither they, nor history, recall the poverty then rife in Harlem. One of the most evocative voices heard in the clubs those days was of Ethel Waters, who sang in the *Sugar Cane Club*:

Rent man waitin for his forty dollars,
Aint got me but a dime and some bad news.
Bartender give me a bracer, double beer chaser,
Cause I got the low-down, mean, rent man blues.

Equally symbolic, if not more so, of the Harlem Renaissance was the literature of the time – the rich writings of Johnson, Langston Hughes, Jean Toomer and Zora Neale Hurston, among many others, which caught the fancy of blacks and whites alike – and the growing racial consciousness, evidenced by the popularity of Marcus Garvey, W.E.B. Du Bois, Charles S. Johnson, and their respective political causes. Still, all these cultural and political forces were not enough to sustain a neighborhood where most were on the economic brink; even before the Depression, it was hard to scrape out a living, and decline drove middle-class blacks out of Harlem.

Harlem today

The cramping together of people of diverse cultures (Caribbean and African) had long caused tensions and problems not easily understood by the city's bureaucracy. Dotted around Harlem were (and still are) buildings and projects that attested to an uneasy municipal conscience.

But by the early 1970s, the genesis of redevelopment had begun. Disgraceful living conditions brought residents to a boiling point and fingers were pointed at the slumlords and absentee landlords who were allowing Harlem to fall apart. The city, which had become accustomed to letting Harlem implode, was ultimately stirred into long-overdue action. A plethora of urban and community development grants were put into effect for commercial and retail development, housing and general urban renewal (unlike many so-called ghettos, the quality of the nineteenth-century housing here is excellent and ripe for modernization). Sometimes, amid the boarded-up storefronts and vacant lots, it's hard to believe you're but a mile or two away from the cozily patrician Upper East Side. Twenty-five years later, the initial investment is paying off: Harlem's historic areas are well maintained and everywhere you turn, construction seems to be in progress.

Currently, the federally established Upper Manhattan Empowerment Zone, encompassing Harlem and part of the South Bronx, is pumping $550 million into various area projects. Community-led development organizations involving ninety local churches, spearheaded by the Abyssinian Baptist Church, have become the developers and owners of a number of business sites. Further boosting the neighborhood's visibility was Bill Clinton's decision to move his first post-presidential office to 55 W 125th Street. Though his move in the summer of 2001 had its detractors – one activist labeled him the "the missionary of gentrification" – the community appears to have welcomed Clinton rather warmly.

But the opening of a Pathmark megastore supermarket on the corner of 125th Street and Lexington Avenue, its coffee-chain neighbor *Starbucks* on Lenox Avenue and an immense multiplex theater owned by Magic Johnson have been met with a mixed reception. Activists point out (with good reason) that community businesses have not been receiving the loans offered to the largely white-owned megastores and some have suggested that the revitalization effort is nothing more than a thinly veiled land-grab aimed at gentrifying the neighborhood for the benefit of affluent whites. Fortunately, many affluent blacks are making a point of moving back to Harlem already. In fact, Harlem residents have taken to saying that a Second Harlem Renaissance is under way.

Harlem's music venues

There were once plenty of black-owned nightspots in Harlem, which catered to a black audience only, many of them housed somewhat unglamorously in private brownstones. Most have been converted to other uses. However, several of Harlem's larger jazz venues have survived, and although their current boarded-up state is sobering, these beautiful buildings are slated for restoration and reuse. The Abyssinian Development Corporation has acquired the **Renaissance Ballroom**, on Adam Clayton Powell Blvd between 137th and 138th streets, a tile-trimmed, square- and diamond-shaped Twenties dance club that hosted Duke Ellington and Chick Webb, among others. The Rennie, as it was known, was a haven for middle-class blacks and today its original light-up Chop Suey sign (once considered an exotic and fashionable dish) can be seen rusting away on the exterior. The 1925 **Smalls Paradise**, a finial-topped brick building down the boulevard at 135th Street, hosted a mixed black and white crowd, and was once known as The Hottest Spot in Harlem. As such, when jazzmen met each other on the road in the 1930s, they would call to each other "See you at the Big Apple," after the name and appropriate illustration still decorating the outside of *Smalls*, and the term gained its greatest popularity as local newsmen started using it. *Smalls* was briefly revived by basketball great Wilt Chamberlain in the Sixties, and is also now owned by Abyssinian. Malcolm X worked as a waiter at *Smalls* while staying at the *YMCA* at no. 180 on 135th Street. The ground floor of the *Cecil Hotel* at 206–210 W 118th St still displays the light-up sign advertising **Mintons Playhouse**, birthplace of bebop (the precursor to improvisational jazz) in the 1940s, when Thelonious Monk, Dizzy Gillespie, Charlie Parker and John Coltrane would gather here for late-night jam sessions after playing at Harlem's jazz clubs. The hotel's current owner hopes to revive *Mintons*. For a look at a venue that has survived the decades check out the legendary **Apollo Theatre** at 253 W 125th St, which has been a supporter of black entertainment since the 1930s (see opposite). Another old-timer is **Lenox Lounge** at 288 Lenox Ave, where a $700,000 renovation has punched up the 1942 Art Deco palace; however, owing to changing tastes and economic times, its jazz shows are now primarily for tourists. Memorable in part for its unusual pairing of jazz, fried chicken and waffles was the now-defunct **Wells** at 2249 Powell Blvd. *Wells* had been in business since 1938 and played host to The Rat Pack (Sammy Davis Jr, Frank Sinatra, Dean Martin, Peter Lawford, Joey Bishop), Aretha Franklin and Nat King Cole, who tied the knot here.

Another famous name, the **Cotton Club** (originally at 142nd Street and Lenox Ave) was segregated. The major talent here, such as Cab Calloway, was black, as were some staff, but only whites were allowed to attend as patrons.

Combined with recent figures that show a dramatic drop in crime in the neighborhood and a renewed community spirit, this may not just be an overly optimistic view.

While brownstones triple in value and Harlem's physical proximity to the Upper West Side is touted, poverty and unemployment are still evident in large patches of Harlem. To fully understand New York and its ethnic and economic contradictions, however, it is necessary to explore this part of the city.

Along 125th Street

Along **125th Street** between Broadway and Fifth Avenue is the working center of Harlem and serves as its main commercial and retail drag. The subway lets you out here, and the **Adam Clayton Powell, Jr. State Office Building** on the corner of Seventh Avenue provides a looming concrete landmark. Commissioned in 1972, it replaced a constellation of businesses that included

Elder Louis Michaux's bookstore, one of Malcolm X's main rallying points. When construction began, the protests of squatters were so vehement that the city made several concessions: the bookstore was relocated one avenue eastward, and the building was named in the honor of Adam Clayton Powell Jr, Harlem's first black congressman. 125th Street was Malcolm X's beat in the 1950s and 1960s – this is where he strolled and preached, and photos of him and his followers have passed into legend.

The Apollo Theatre and around

Walk a little west from here and you reach the legendary **Apollo Theatre** at 253 W 125th St (Ⓣ212/531-5305). Not much to look at from the outside, this venue was, from the 1930s to the 1970s, the center of black entertainment in New York City and northeastern America. Today, it continues to launch and host great performers. Almost all the great figures of jazz and blues played here along with singers, comedians and dancers. Past winners of its famous Amateur Night have included Ella Fitzgerald, Billie Holiday, Luther Vandross, The Jackson Five, Sarah Vaughan, Marvin Gaye and James Brown. Since its heyday it's served as a warehouse, movie theater and radio station, and in its latest incarnation is the venue for a weekly TV show, *Showtime at the Apollo*. Today, the Apollo is enjoying somewhat of a renaissance of its own: a $6 million renovation project was announced in 2001, and a permanent show is being constructed. Chronicling 80 years of history through a variety of media, "Harlem Song" is expected to start in the summer of 2002, and other weekly productions, as well as a regular gig by the Dance Theater of Harlem, are being considered. An officially landmarked building, the Apollo offers daily 45-minute tours (call to arrange at Ⓣ212/531-5337).

Across the way at 125th Street and Seventh Avenue, the tall, narrow Theresa Towers office building was until the 1960s the **Theresa Hotel**: its gleaming white terra-cotta patterns with sunbursts at the top make it stand out from the shabbiness of the rest of the street. Desegregated only in 1940, it became known as the Waldorf of Harlem. Fidel Castro was a guest here in 1960 while on a visit to the United Nations, shunning midtown luxury in a popular political gesture. The hotel's first black manager was William Harmon Brown, whose son, Ron Brown, became President Clinton's Secretary of Commerce until his untimely death in a 1995 plane crash. At 230 W 125th St stands **Blumstein's**, fronted by its dilapidated neon sign. Founded by a German-Jewish immigrant in 1898 and once the largest department store in Harlem, Blumstein's refused to hire black workers except as menial laborers (like many white-owned local businesses) and was the focal point in 1934 of a community-wide boycott led by Adam Clayton Powell, Jr – pointedly called "Don't Buy Where You Can't Work." The campaign worked here: the department store not only began hiring blacks, but became the first in the area with a black Santa and black mannequins.

The Studio Museum in Harlem

Founded in 1968, the **Studio Museum in Harlem**, at 144 W 125th St, between Lenox and 7th ave (Wed–Thurs noon–6pm, Fri noon–8pm, Sat–Sun 10am–6pm; $5, students and seniors $3, under 12 $1, free admission on the first Sat of every month; Ⓣ212/864-4500, Ⓦwww.studiomuseuminharlem.org), has over 60,000 square feet of exhibition space dedicated to showcasing contemporary African-American painting, photography and sculpture. The permanent collection is displayed on a rotating basis and includes works by Harlem Renaissance-era photographer James Van Der Zee, and paintings and sculptures by post-war artists. A community-oriented perspective, skillful curating by Thelma Golden, and the supplementary lectures, author readings and music performances, combine to create thought-provoking work in an atmosphere like that of a community center.

Lenox Avenue and around: the Mount Morris Park Historical District

Centered on **Lenox Avenue** between West 118th and 124th streets, the area west of Mount Morris Park, now known as the **Mount Morris Park Historic District**, was one of the first to attract residential development after the elevated railroads were constructed. White Protestant downtown commuters gave way to the second largest neighborhood of Eastern European Jewish immigrants after the Lower East Side, and finally to black households starting in the late 1920s – complex demographics which explain the heavy concentration of religious structures here. The neighborhood is now on the National Register of Historic Places.

At 201 Lenox Ave (at 120th St) stands the **Mount Olivet Church**, a Greco-Roman-style temple that was once a synagogue, and one of literally hundreds of religious buildings dotted around Harlem. The somber, bulky, Gothic **St Martins**, at the southeast corner of Lenox Avenue and 122nd Street is among them, and both have been fortunate in avoiding decay as church and community declined. Elsewhere the Mount Morris district comprises some lovely rowhouses that went up in the speculative boom of the 1890s. Most outstanding of all are 133–143 W 122nd St, arguably the finest row of Queen Anne-style homes in the city, constructed by leading architect Francis H. Kimball in 1885–87 of gabled and dormered orange brick, with lovely stained glass. No. 131 is a Romanesque Revival house faced in Indiana limestone. Double back west and pause in front of **Hale House** at no. 154, established by Mother Clara Hale whose program for substance-addicted (and now HIV-infected) infants and mothers was one of the first in the country. A plaque in front is decorated with bronze faces of children and enfolds a statue of Mother Hale herself. Her daughter Lorraine, entrusted with the control of Hale House, was ousted in 2001 amid charges of mismanagement and embezzlement, tarnishing the facility's otherwise fine reputation.

When you reach **Mount Morris Park West**, the edge of the park itself, you may find it hard to appreciate some of the noteworthy houses, overshadowed as they are by one of Harlem's great architectural tragedies. Smack dab in the middle is a block of rowhouses so neglected that the facades of several have literally been torn away. Notoriously known as **The Ruins**, this ensemble was callously destroyed by New York State when, under the right of eminent domain, it began stripping several of the houses with plans to create a drug rehab center in 1968. Once again, late-Sixties community opposition was fierce: this proposal and later plans were shelved, and the future of the ghostly, crumbling block is unknown. Still, looking at Mount Morris Park West you can't help but feel that it too will go the way of the increasingly upmarket Lower East Side – the quality of building is so good, the pressures on Manhattan so great, it seems just a matter of time.

The former Mount Morris Park is now **Marcus Garvey Park**, taking its name from the black leader of the 1920s. It's an odd urban space, with jutting outcrops contradicting the precise lines of the houses around. At the summit, an elegant octagonal fire tower of 1856 is a unique example of the early-warning devices once found throughout the city – spiral your way to the top for a great view.

The Schomburg Center for Research in Black Culture

To look back at past times rather than the uncertain future, it's worth checking out the angular brick **Schomburg Center for Research in Black Culture** at 515 Lenox Ave (at 135th St) (Mon–Wed noon–8pm, Thurs–Sat 10am–6pm; ⓣ212/491-2200, ⓦwww.nypl.org/research/sc), a member of the New York Public Library system. Originally a lending branch, the (then) third floor Division of Negro Literature, History and Prints was created in 1925 after a community outcry for a library of its own, and grew dramatically the following year. Arthur Schomburg, a black Puerto Rican obsessed with documenting the black culture (and named by a peer as the "Sherlock Holmes of black history" for his efforts), had acquired over 10,000 manuscripts, photos and artifacts, and sold them to the NYPL for $10,000; he oversaw his own collection, sometimes using his own funds for upkeep, from 1932 until his death six years later. Since that time, the amassing of over five million items through donations, bequests and purchases have made the center the world's preeminent research facility for the study of black history and culture. Further enriching the site are the ashes of renowned poet Langston Hughes, perhaps most famously known for penning *The Negro Speaks of Rivers.* The poem inspired the "cosmogram" titled *Rivers* by Houston Conwill, a mosaic that graces one of the halls. Seven of Hughes' lines radiate out from a circle, and the last line, "My soul has grown deep like the rivers," located in a fish at the center, marks where he is interred.

Schomburg's five collection divisions consist of Art & Artifacts; General Research & Reference; Manuscripts, Archives & Rare Books (with 3.5 million works among these two, and where Alex Haley drew much of his research for *Roots*); Moving Image & Recorded Sound; and Photography & Prints (over 750,000 specimens). The Schomburg also features community heritage displays, book readings, art and music events in the two auditoriums, halls and gallery.

To recover from all the focus on the mind, stop at 328 Lenox Ave (between 126th and 127th streets), where the most famous soul food restaurant in New York, *Sylvia's*, will treat your stomach with equal reverence. Drop in afterwards at the recently renovated *Lenox Lounge* at 288 Lenox Ave (between 124th and 125th streets) for a drink or to hear some jazz. See p.369 & 345 for further restaurant and jazz listings.

Along 116th Street

Continue down Lenox Avenue to **116th Street** to find, at no. 102, the green onion-dome of the **Masjid Malcolm Shabazz** mosque, named after Malcolm X, who once preached here. Between Lenox and Fifth avenues on 116th Street, you'll pass the new home of the bazaar-like **Malcolm Shabazz Harlem Market**, its entrance marked by colorful fake minarets. The market's offerings include cloth, T-shirts, jewelry, clothing and more with a distinctly Afrocentric flavor. Ironically, the former street vendors, who used to run from police and clash with other local merchants, now pay taxes, accept credit cards, and take accounting courses at the mosque. Originally moved off the street by city authorities, the vendors were then moved down the block to make way for several massive construction projects being supervised by the mosque (which holds a huge role in the community, acquiring property and spurring development projects, much like the Abyssinian Development Corporation).

One of them is **Malcolm Shabazz Gardens**, a series of income-capped houses modeled on the derelict brownstones they replaced, lining 117th Street. At 116th and Fifth, the barn-like **Baptist Temple Church** was originally a synagogue; at 116th and Powell Boulevard, the fanciful blue-and-white 1912 Moorish-style Regent Theater, one of America's earliest movie palaces, has become the **Corinthian Baptist Church**. Many of black Harlem's churches are buildings built by other congregations or with other original intents; to see one of the few churches actually built by a black architect, head up to 134th Street between Frederick Douglass and Powell boulevards, and have a look at **St Philips Church**, an elegant brick and granite building constructed by Vertner Tandy in 1910–11.

Adam Clayton Powell Jr Boulevard

Above 110th Street, Seventh Avenue becomes **Adam Clayton Powell Jr Boulevard**, a broad sweep pushing north between low-built houses that for once in Manhattan allow the sky to break through. Since its conception Powell Boulevard has been Harlem's main concourse, and it's not difficult to imagine the propriety the shops and side streets had in their late nineteenth-century heyday. As with the rest of Harlem, Powell Boulevard shows years of decline in its graffiti-splattered walls and storefronts punctuated by demolished lots. The injection of funds into this area should impact it for the better; in fact if the current investments don't make some difference, its hard to say what will.

Abyssinian Baptist Church

At 132 W 138th St, just off Adam Clayton Powell Boulevard (Ⓣ212/862-7474), stands the **Abyssinian Baptist Church**, whose long-time minister was the **Reverend Adam Clayton Powell Jr**. In the 1930s, Powell was instrumental in forcing the mostly white-owned, white-workforce stores of Harlem such as Blumstein's to begin employing the blacks whose patronage ensured the stores' economic survival, Later he became the first black on the city council, then New York's first black representative in Congress, and he sponsored the first minimum-wage law in the country. His distinguished career came to an embittered end in 1967, when amid strong rumors of the misuse of public funds, he was excluded from Congress by majority vote. This failed to diminish his standing in Harlem, where voters twice re-elected him before his death in 1972. The scandal is almost forgotten now, and there's a fitting memorial on

Sunday gospel

The incredible **gospel music** has long attracted visitors up to Harlem. And for good reason: the music and the entire revival-style Baptist experience can be both amazing and invigorating. Gospel tours are becoming big business, and churches seem to be jockeying to get the most tourists. Many of the arranged tours (outlined in "Information, Maps and Tours" in Basics) are pricey, but they usually offer transportation Uptown and brunch afterwards. You can, however, easily go it on your own if you're looking for a more flavorful view. The choir at the Abyssinian Baptist Church is arguably the best in the city, but others of note include Metropolitan Baptist Church, 151 W 128th St at Adam Clayton Powell Jr Blvd (Ⓣ212/663-8990), Mount Moriah, 2050 5th Ave between W 126th & 127th St (Ⓣ212/289-9448) and Mount Nebo, 1883 7th Ave at W 114th St (Ⓣ212/866-7880). Keep in mind that this isn't a tourist attraction, but a real church where worship is taken especially seriously. Dress accordingly: jackets for men and skirts or dresses for women.

the boulevard that today bears his name. It's worth a trip if you can see the gut-busting **choir** – call ahead, or see "Information, Maps and Tours" in Basics for details.

Strivers Row

A block north of the Abyssinian Baptist Church lie some of the finest, most articulate blocks of rowhouses in Manhattan – **Strivers Row**. Commissioned during the 1890s housing boom, Strivers Row consists of 138th and 139th streets just west of Powell Boulevard. Three sets of architects were commissioned: James Brown Lord; Bruce Price and Clarence Luce; and the best, McKim, Mead and White's north side of 139th Street. The results are uniquely harmonious, a dignified Renaissance-derived strip that's an amalgam of simplicity and elegance. Note the unusual rear service alleys of the houses, reached via iron-gated cross streets. Within the burgeoning black community of the turn of the nineteenth century this came to be the desirable place for ambitious professionals (starting with organized rail porters) to reside – hence its nickname.

El Barrio

From Park Avenue to the East River is Spanish Harlem or **El Barrio**, dipping down as far as East 96th Street to collide head on with the affluence of the Upper East Side. The center of a large Puerto Rican community, it is quite different from Harlem. El Barrio was originally a working-class Italian neighborhood (a small pocket of Italian families survives around 116th Street and First Avenue) and the quality of building here was nowhere as good as that immediately to the west. The result is a more intimidating atmosphere. It has been predominantly Puerto Rican since the early 1950s, when the American government offered Puerto Ricans incentives to immigrate to the US under a policy known as "Operation Bootstrap" (so named in the theory that the scheme would help pull Puerto Rico up "by the straps of its boots" by reducing its overpopulation problem). But the occupants have had little opportunity to evolve Latino culture in any meaningful or noticeable way. The main space where cultural roots are in evidence is **La Marqueta** on Park Avenue between 111th and 116th streets, a five-block street market of Spanish products. Originally a line of pushcart street vendors hawking their wares, it's more regulated now, selling everything from tropical fruit and vegetables, jewelry, figurines and clothing to dried herbs and snake oils. To get some background on the whole scene, **Museo del Barrio** at Fifth Avenue and 104th Street (see p.194) is a showcase of Latin American art and culture and also includes **La Casa de la Herencia Cultural Puertorriqueña**, a Puerto Rican heritage library (☎212/722-2600). To the northeast, El Barrio's **International Art Gallery** at 309 108th St (between 3rd and Lexington avenues) is an alternative space for local artists of Latin, African-American and Asian origin.

23

Hamilton Heights, Washington Heights and the Cloisters Museum

The most northern stretch of Manhattan Island comprises a disparate group of localities. **Hamilton Heights** is largely residential, with an old Federal-style historic mansion and an excellent small museum as its main draws. Continuing uptown, **Washington Heights** is a patchy neighborhood with little in the way of attractions. You still may have reason to pass through because the **Cloisters Museum**, a mock medieval monastery that holds the Metropolitan Museum's superlative collection of medieval art and the most visited site north of Central Park, lies very near the top end of the island.

Hamilton Heights

The further uptown you venture, the less like New York your surroundings seem. Much of Harlem's western edge, between 135th and 145th streets, is taken up by the area known as **Hamilton Heights**, like Morningside Heights to the south, a mixed bag of campus, trash-strewn streets and slender parks on a bluff above Harlem. However, one stretch, the **Hamilton Heights Historic District** that runs down Convent Avenue to City College, pulls Hamilton Heights well up from the ranks of the untidily mediocre. During the Depression, the black professionals who made it up here and to Sugar Hill a little further north could glance down on poorer Harlemites with disdain: it's still a firmly bourgeois residential area – and one of the most attractive uptown. But even if this shabbiness around a well-heeled neighborhood is to your liking, there's little in the way of specific sights.

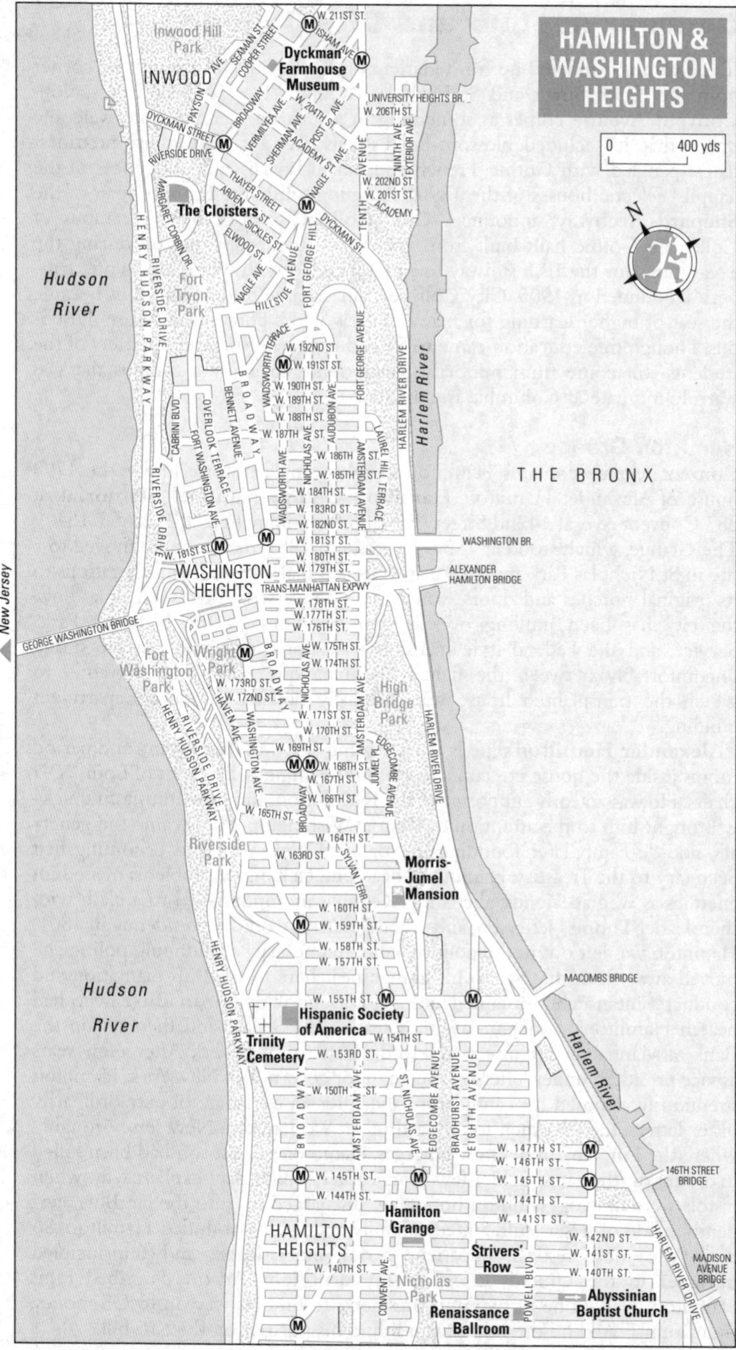
HAMILTON & WASHINGTON HEIGHTS
0 400 yds
N
Inwood Hill Park
INWOOD
Dyckman Farmhouse Museum
W. 211ST ST.
ISHAM AVE.
SEAMAN ST.
COOPER STREET
PAYSON AVE.
BROADWAY
VERMILYEA AVE.
W. 204TH ST.
SHERMAN AVE.
POST ST.
ACADEMY ST.
UNIVERSITY HEIGHTS BR.
W. 206TH ST.
TENTH AVENUE
NINTH AVE.
EXTERIOR AVE.
DYCKMAN STREET
RIVERSIDE DRIVE
THAYER STREET
ARDEN ST.
NAGLE AVE.
W. 202ND ST.
W. 201ST ST.
ACADEMY
The Cloisters
MARGARET CORBIN DR.
SICKLES ST.
ELWOOD ST.
DYCKMAN ST.
HENRY HUDSON PARKWAY
RIVERSIDE DRIVE
Fort Tryon Park
NAGLE AVE.
HILLSIDE AVENUE
FORT GEORGE HILL
Hudson River
WADSWORTH TERRACE
W. 192ND ST.
W. 191ST ST.
FORT GEORGE AVENUE
HARLEM RIVER DRIVE
Harlem River
BROADWAY
W. 190TH ST.
W. 189TH ST.
W. 188TH ST.
W. 187TH ST.
AUDUBON AVE.
CABRINI BLVD
OVERLOOK TERRACE
BENNETT AVENUE
LAUREL HILL TERRACE
W. 186TH ST.
W. 185TH ST.
NICHOLAS AVE.
AMSTERDAM AVENUE
FORT WASHINGTON AVE.
WADSWORTH AVE.
THE BRONX
W. 184TH ST.
W. 183RD ST.
W. 182ND ST.
W. 181ST ST.
W. 180TH ST.
W. 179TH ST.
WASHINGTON BR.
ALEXANDER HAMILTON BRIDGE
WASHINGTON HEIGHTS
TRANS-MANHATTAN EXPWY
W. 178TH ST.
W. 177TH ST.
W. 176TH ST.
New Jersey
GEORGE WASHINGTON BRIDGE
W. 175TH ST.
W. 174TH ST.
Fort Washington Park
Wright Park
W. 173RD ST.
W. 172ND ST.
HAVEN AVE.
High Bridge Park
W. 171ST ST.
W. 170TH ST.
W. 169TH ST.
W. 168TH ST.
W. 167TH ST.
W. 166TH ST.
JUMEL PL.
EDGECOMBE AVENUE
W. 165TH ST.
W. 164TH ST.
W. 163RD ST.
SYLVAN TERR.
Riverside Park
Morris-Jumel Mansion
W. 160TH ST.
W. 159TH ST.
W. 158TH ST.
W. 157TH ST.
MACOMBS BRIDGE
W. 155TH ST.
Hispanic Society of America
Trinity Cemetery
W. 154TH ST.
W. 153RD ST.
W. 150TH ST.
AMSTERDAM AVE.
ST. NICHOLAS AVE.
EDGECOMBE AVENUE
BRADHURST AVENUE
EIGHTH AVENUE
W. 147TH ST.
W. 146TH ST.
W. 145TH ST.
W. 144TH ST.
W. 141ST ST.
146TH STREET BRIDGE
Hamilton Grange
HAMILTON HEIGHTS
Strivers' Row
W. 142ND ST.
W. 141ST ST.
W. 140TH ST.
MADISON AVENUE BRIDGE
CONVENT AVE.
Nicholas Park
POWELL BLVD
Abyssinian Baptist Church
Renaissance Ballroom
HARLEM RIVER DRIVE

Convent Avenue and City College

If you've just wandered up from Harlem or up the hill and around the corner from the 135th Street and St Nicholas Avenue #B or #C subway station, **Convent Avenue** comes as something of a surprise – and a quite welcome one at that. Its secluded, blossom-lined streets have a garden suburb prettiness that's spangled with Gothic, French and Italian Renaissance influences in the happily eclectic houses of the 1890s. Running south, the feathery span of the **Shepard Archway** announces **City College**, a rustic-feeling campus of Collegiate Gothic halls built from gray Manhattan schist dug up during the excavations for the IRT subway line and mantled with white terra-cotta fripperies. Founded in 1905, City College didn't charge tuition, and thus became the seat of higher learning for many of New York's poor – and future illustrious. Though free education came to an end in the 1970s, three-quarters of the students still come from minority backgrounds to enjoy a campus that's as warmly intimate as Columbia is grandiose.

Hamilton Grange

Convent Avenue contains Hamilton Heights' single historic lure – the 1798 house of Alexander Hamilton, **Hamilton Grange National Memorial**, at 287 Convent Ave, at 142nd Street (Fri–Sun 9am–5pm; free; ⓣ212/666-1640). The Grange, which stood at 143rd Street until 1889, may soon be moved to a site in St Nicholas Park more similar to its original environment; alterations to its original porches and doors would also be reversed. For several years now, the city has been mulling over recommendations by the National Parks Service, and the Federal-style mansion waits for the decision, while sitting uncomfortably between the fiercely Romanesque St Luke's Church – to which the transplanted house was originally donated – and an apartment building.

Alexander Hamilton's life is as fascinating as it was flamboyant, and period rooms inside the house contain a few of his belongings, like a set of Louis XVI chairs. He was an early supporter of the Revolution, and his enthusiasm quickly brought him to the attention of George Washington. He became the general's aide-de-camp, later founding the Bank of New York and becoming first Secretary to the Treasury. Hamilton's headlong tackling of problems made him enemies as well as friends: alienating Republican populists led to a clash with their leader Thomas Jefferson, and when Jefferson won the presidency in 1801, Hamilton was left out in the political cold. Temporarily abandoning politics, he moved away from the city to his grange near here to tend his plantation and conduct a memorably sustained and vicious feud with **Aaron Burr**, who had beaten Hamilton's father-in-law to a seat in the Senate and then set up the Bank of Manhattan as a direct rival to the Bank of New York. After a few years as vice president under Jefferson, Burr ran for governor of New York; Hamilton strenuously opposed his candidature and, after an exchange of extraordinarily bitter letters, the two men fought a **duel** in Weehawken, New Jersey, roughly where the Lincoln Tunnel now emerges. Hamilton's eldest son had been killed in a duel on the same field a few years earlier, which may explain why, when pistols were drawn, Hamilton honorably discharged his into the air. Burr, evidently made of lesser stuff, aimed carefully and fatally wounded Hamilton. So died "the most restless, impatient, artful, indefatigable and unprincipled intriguer in the United States," as President John Adams described him. Hamilton is only one of two non-presidents to find his way on to US money (Benjamin Franklin's the other): you'll find his portrait on the $10 bill.

Washington Heights

Continue north above 145th Street for the largely uneventful walk and you'll note the change from Convent Avenue to Broadway is almost as abrupt as it was from Harlem to Convent Avenue. Broadway here is a once-elegant, now raggy sweep that slowly rises to the northernmost part of Manhattan Island, **Washington Heights**. Audubon Terrace at 155th and Broadway (easily reached by the #1 train to 157th and Broadway) is a weird, clumsy nineteenth-century attempt to glorify 155th Street with museums dolled up as Beaux-Arts temples. Officially the Washington Heights Museum Group, this Acropolis in a dead-end street was originally built in the vain anticipation of the movement north of New York's elite aristocratic society. Now the complex stands in mocking contrast to its still decrepit area. Included here are the American Academy of Arts and Letters, the American Numismatic Society and the Hispanic Society of America. As you might expect from something so far from the center of town, the complex is little known and little visited, though the Hispanic Society alone is worth the trip.

Containing one of the largest collections of Hispanic art outside Spain, the **Hispanic Society of America** (Tues–Sat 10am–4.30pm, Sun 1–4pm, Library closed Aug; free; ⓣ212/926-2234) owns over 3000 paintings, including works by Spanish masters such as Goya, El Greco and Velázquez, and more than 6000 decorative works of art. The collection ranges from a 965 AD intricately carved ivory box to fifteenth-century textiles to the joyful mural series *Provinces of Spain* by Joaquin Sorolla y Bastida (commissioned specifically for the society). Displays of the permanent collection rarely change, so you can be fairly certain you'll see the highlights. The library of 200,000 books, including over 16,000 printed before the eighteenth century, is a major reference site for Spanish and Portuguese art, history and literature topics.

If you've got time to kill, the **American Numismatic Society** (Tues–Fri 9am–4.30pm; free; ⓣ212/234-3130) just might surprise you with its changing exhibits on numismatic history, design and politics. Dedicated to the preservation and study of coins (the only such site in the country), the society's library contains an enormous number of numismatic periodicals, books and illustrations – all there for the researcher or intrigued collector.

Otherwise, one avenue east, at 155th Street and Amsterdam, is the **Trinity Church Cemetery**, its large, placid grounds dotted with some fanciful mausolea; the remains of robber baron John Jacob Astor are buried up here, as are naturalist James Audubon and Chelsea developer Clement Clark Moore. At 165th and Broadway, now controversially incorporated into the Columbia-Presbyterian Hospital complex, is the **Audubon Ballroom**, scene of Malcolm X's assassination in 1967.

The Morris–Jumel Mansion

Within easy walking distance of Audubon Terrace and the cemetery, the **Morris–Jumel Mansion**, at 65 Jumel Terrace at 160th Street and Edgecombe Avenue (Wed–Sun 10am–4pm; $3, $2 students/seniors; ⓣ212/923-8008), is another uptown surprise. Cornered by its garden, the mansion somehow survived the destruction all around, and today is one of the more successful house museums, its proud Georgian outlines faced with a later Federal portico. Inside, the mansion's rooms reveal some of its engaging history: built as a rural retreat in 1765 by Colonel Roger Morris, it was briefly Washington's headquarters before falling into the hands of the British. A leaflet describes the rooms and their historical connections, but curiously omits much of the later history. Wealthy wine merchant Stephen Jumel bought the derelict mansion in 1801 and refurbished it for his wife Eliza, formerly a prostitute and his mistress. New York society didn't take to such a past, but when Jumel died in 1832, Eliza married ex-vice president Aaron Burr (nemesis of Alexander Hamilton) – she for his connections, he for her money. Burr was 78 when they married, twenty years older than Eliza: the marriage lasted for six months before old Burr upped and left, only to die on the day of their divorce. Eliza battled on to the age of 91, and on the top floor of the house you'll find her obituary, a magnificently fictionalized account of a "scandalous" life.

Just opposite the entrance to the mansion's grounds is the quaint block of **Sylvan Terrace**, a tiny cobblestone mews lined with yellow and green wooden houses built in the 1880s – and seeming impossibly out of place just barely off the wide-open intersection of Amsterdam and St Nicholas avenues.

The George Washington Bridge

From most western stretches of Washington Heights you get a glimpse of the **George Washington Bridge**, linking Manhattan to New Jersey. It's arguable that the feeder road to the bridge splits two distinct areas: below is bleakly rundown, one of the biggest areas of illegal drug activity in the city; above, the streets relax in smaller, more diverse ethnic old-time neighborhoods of Jews, Greeks, Central Europeans and especially Irish, though a major Hispanic community has been building up since the Seventies. A skillful, dazzling sketch high above the Hudson, the bridge skims almost a mile across the channel in massive metalwork and graceful lines, a natural successor to the Brooklyn Bridge. "Here, finally, steel architecture seems to laugh," said Le Corbusier of the 1931 construction. And not only figuratively: the suspension cable looks like a gigantic smile, beaming upon midtown Manhattan's ambitious towers and workers in the distance.

The Cloisters Museum

What most visitors pass through Washington Heights to see is **The Cloisters Museum** (Subway #A to 190th St–Fort Washington Ave; Mar–Oct Tues–Sun 9.30am–5.15pm; Nov–Feb Tues–Sun 9.30am–4.45pm; suggested donation $10, students $5, including same-day admission to the Metropolitan Museum; ⓣ212/923-3700), which stands above the Hudson like some misplaced Renaissance palazzo-cum-monastery. Housed in Fort Tryon Park, the Metropolitan Museum's collection of medieval tapestries, metalwork, paintings and sculpture is a must, and you'll find an additional reward in the park itself, cleverly landscaped by Frederick Law Olmsted, Jr (son of the famed Central Park and Prospect Park architect). The stone-walled promenade overlooking the river and the English-style garden make for a sweepingly romantic spot. Inside the museum, the central cloister, its pink marble arcades and fountain purchased from the impoverished French monastery of Saint-Michel-de-Cuxa at the turn of the nineteenth century, might trick you into believing that you're really in southwestern France. Portions of five medieval cloisters (basically, covered walkways and their enclosed courtyards) are incorporated into the structure, the folly of collectors **George Grey Barnard** and **John D. Rockefeller, Jr**.

Some history

Barnard started a museum on this spot in 1914 to house his own medieval collection, mostly sculpture and architectural fragments acquired in France. Later, Rockefeller donated funds, enabling the Metropolitan Museum to purchase the site and its collection, along with 66 acres of land around it – now Fort Tryon Park – and, with commendable foresight, he also purchased 700 acres of land across the way in New Jersey to ensure perpetually good views. Barnard and Rockefeller each shipped over the best of medieval Europe to be part of the museum: **Romanesque chapels** and **Gothic halls**, dismantled and transplanted brick by brick, along with tapestries, medieval paintings and sculpture. Despite the hodgepodge of styles, it is all undeniably well carried off, superb in its detail and offering a great atmosphere. The completed museum opened in 1938, and is still the only museum in the US specializing in medieval art (it's actually a branch of the Metropolitan Museum of Art).

The collection

The best approach if you're coming from the 190th Street subway is directly across the park: the views are tremendous. Starting from the entrance hall and working counterclockwise, the collection is laid out in roughly chronological order. First off is the simplicity of the **Romanesque Hall**, featuring French remnants such as an arched, limestone doorway dating to 1150 and a thirteenth-century portal from a monastery in Burgundy. The frescoed Spanish **Fuentidueña Chapel** is dominated by a huge, domed twelfth-century apse from Segovia, that immediately induces a reverential hush. Hall and chapel form a corner on one of the prettiest of the five cloisters here, **St Guilhelm**, ringed by strong Corinthian-style columns topped by busily carved capitals with floral designs from thirteenth-century southern France. The nearby **Langon Chapel**, attractive enough in itself, is enhanced by a twelfth-century **ciborium** (a permanent altar canopy) that manages to be formal and graceful in just the right proportions, and an emotive wooden sculpture of the **Virgin and Child** beneath.

At the center of the museum is the **Cuxa Cloister**, from the twelfth-century Benedictine monastery of Saint-Michel-de-Cuxa near Prades in the French Pyrenees; its Romanesque capitals are brilliantly carved, with monkeys, eagles, crouching lions, and beasts whose open mouths reveal half-eaten human legs. Central to the scene is the garden, planted with fragrant, almost overpowering, herbs and flowers and offering (bizarrely) piped-in birdsong.

The museum's smaller **sculpture** collection is equally impressive. In the **Early Gothic Hall** are a number of carved figures, including one memorably tender and refined **Virgin and Child**, carved in France in the fourteenth century, probably for veneration at a private altar. The next room holds a collection of **tapestries**, including a rare surviving Gothic work showing the **Nine Heroes**. The heroes, popular figures of the ballads of the Middle Ages, comprise three pagans (Hector, Alexander and Julius Caesar), three Hebrews (David, Joshua and Judas Macabeas) and three Christians (Arthur, Charlemagne and Godfrey of Bouillon). Five of the nine are here, clothed in the garb of the day (around 1385) against a rich backdrop. The **Unicorn Tapestries** (*c.*1500, Netherlands) in the succeeding room are even more spectacular – brilliantly alive with color, observation and Christian symbolism, more so now than ever, as all seven were recently repaired, restored and rehung in a refurbished gallery with new lighting.

Most of the Met's medieval painting is to be found downtown, but one important exception is **Campin**'s *Altarpiece*, created for the private use of its owners. This fifteenth-century triptych depicts the Annunciation scene in a typical bourgeois Flemish home of the day, and is housed in its own antechamber, outfitted with a desk, chair, cupboard and other household articles from that period (though from different countries of origin). On the left of the altarpiece, the artist's patron and his wife gaze timidly on through an open door; to the right, St Joseph works in his carpenter's shop. St Joseph was mocked in the literature of the day, which might account for his rather ridiculous appearance – making a mousetrap, a symbol of the way the Devil traps souls. Through the windows behind, life goes on in a fifteenth-century market square, perhaps Campin's native Tournai. The **Late Gothic Hall** next door is filled with expressively detailed large sculptural **altarpieces** depicting biblical scenes. Especially noteworthy is the rarely depicted *Death (Dormition) of the Virgin* in dark wood, whose right side displays the girdle of the Virgin being dropped to St Thomas by an angel, conveying her assumption into heaven.

On the first floor, a large Gothic chapel boasts a high-vaulted ceiling and mid- to late-fourteenth-century Austrian stained-glass windows, along with the monumental **sarcophagus of Ermengol VII**, with its whole phalanx of (now sadly decapitated) family members and clerics carved in stone to send him off. Also here are two further cloisters to explore (one with a small café), along with an amazing **Treasury**, literally crammed with items, all worth your gaze. The *Belles Heures de Jean, Duc de Berry* is perhaps the greatest of all medieval Books of Hours; it was executed by the Limburg Brothers with dazzling miniatures of seasonal life and extensive border work in gold leaf. The *Reliquary Shrine of Elizabeth of Hungary* is a luminous enamel and gilded silver piece from the Rhine Valley, and the twelfth-century **altar cross** from Bury St Edmunds in England contains a mass of 92 tiny expressive characters from biblical stories. Finally, hunt out a golf-ball-sized **rosary bead** from sixteenth-century Flanders: with a representation of the Passion inside, it barely seems possible that it could have been carved by hand (it's made of separate tiny pieces of boxwood painstakingly fitted together with the aid of a magnifying glass).

Inwood

Fort Tryon Park joins **Inwood Park** by the Hudson River, and it is possible to walk across Dyckman Street and into Inwood Park. The path up the side of the river gives a beautiful view of New Jersey, surprisingly hilly and wooded this far upstream. Keep walking and you will reach the very tip of Manhattan, an area known as *Spuyten Duyvil* ("the spitting devil" in Dutch), nowadays Columbia University's Athletic Stadium. Inwood Park itself is wild and rambling, often confusing and a little threatening if you get lost. It was once the stomping ground for Indian cave dwellers, but unfortunately the site of their original settlement is now buried under the Henry Hudson Parkway. Inwood's main tourist attraction is the **Dyckman Farmhouse Museum** 4881 Broadway at 204th Street (Tues–Sun 10am–5pm; $1; ⓣ212/304-9422), an eighteenth-century Dutch farmhouse restored with period pieces – pleasant enough but hardly worth the journey.

24

Brooklyn

Maybe he's found out by now dat he'll neveh live long enough to know the whole of Brooklyn. It'd take a guy a lifetime to know Brooklyn t'roo an' t'roo. An' even den, you wouldn't know it at all.

Thomas Wolfe, *Only the Dead Know Brooklyn*

"The Great Mistake." So New York writer Pete Hamill later summed up the **Brooklyn** annexation in 1898. And, ever since, the borough of Brooklyn has endured secondary status to its proverbial big brother across the East River. Because Manhattan looms so large through the haze that often blankets the city, few tourists cross the river to experience all that Brooklyn has to offer. It's a city with an historic place in the creation of the nation; George Washington's Continental army fought the first major battle here after the signing of the Declaration of Independence.

If it were still a separate city, Brooklyn would be a popular tourist destination. It would be the fourth largest city in the United States, with a population of almost 2.5 million, nearly a million more than Manhattan. As well, Brooklyn has history, beautiful waterfront acreage and culture – 93 distinct ethnic groups. But until as recently as the early 1800s, it was no more than a group of loosely connected towns separated by heavy forests and farms, and relatively autonomous from already-thriving Manhattan across the East River. With the arrival of Robert Fulton's steamship service, linking the two, Brooklyn began to take on its present form, starting with the establishment of a leafy retreat in Brooklyn Heights and then spreading along the shorelines of Bay Ridge, Red Hook, Williamsburg and Greenpoint. But what really changed the borough was the opening of the **Brooklyn Bridge**, allowing immigrants to build communities of their own away from the already overcrowded and overcommercialized Manhattan. By 1900, Brooklyn was fully established as part of New York City, and its fate as Manhattan's perennial kid brother was sealed.

You can go to almost any neighborhood in Brooklyn and find something worthwhile, though you should schedule your day accordingly. Like Thomas Wolfe said above, Brooklyn is big – the second largest borough in New York City. The most visited district is **Brooklyn Heights**, on the East River opposite lower Manhattan. Though many never get past this point, the other areas around downtown – **Cobble Hill**, **Carroll Gardens** and **Park Slope** – offer a lively mix of culture, fine dining and some of the city's best-preserved brownstones. Young professional couples, writers and a thriving lesbian community call this area their home. There's also Frederick Law Olmsted and Calvert Vaux's **Prospect Park**, which for many is an improvement on their more famous bit of landscaping in Manhattan, Central Park. This oasis, surrounded by the Brooklyn Botanic Garden, Brooklyn Children's Museum and Prospect Park Zoo, make for a great afternoon for grownups and children. Then there's

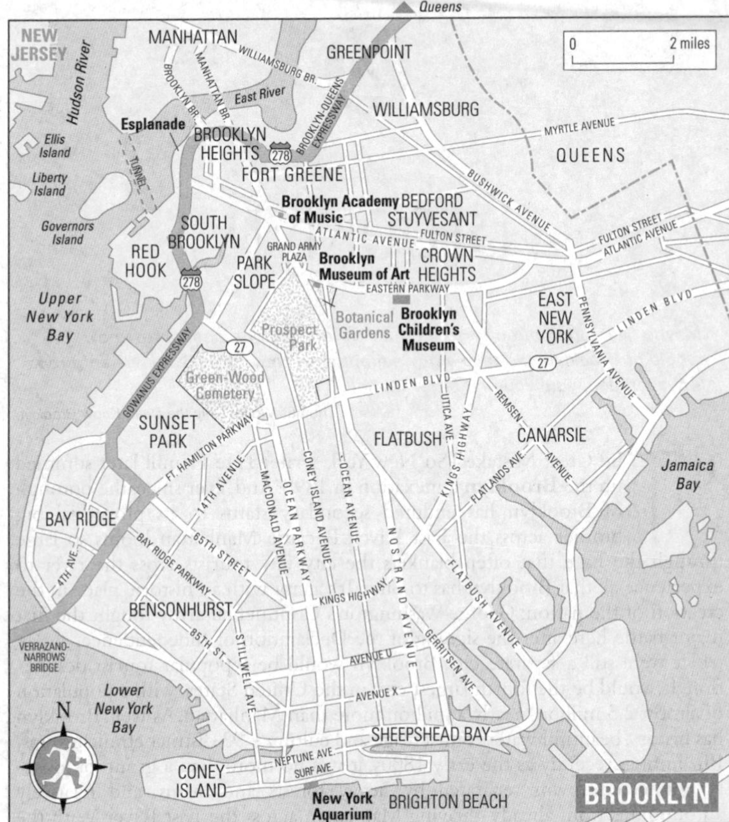

fringe Brooklyn, the up-and-coming neighborhoods like **Williamsburg**, which have already witnessed a flood of artists and hipsters seeking an East Village of the early twenty-first century, while neighborhoods like **Red Hook**, **Greenpoint** and **Gowanus** are just being discovered by Manhattan defectors. And if history has anything to say about it, these neighborhoods too will become *en vogue*. Rents will rise and the artists will pack up their easels looking for the next big thing, which might be other neighborhoods like **Bedford-Stuyvesant**, **Bensonhurst** and **Kensington** or coastal communities like **Bay Ridge**, **Sheepshead Bay** or **Coney Island**.

Downtown Brooklyn

This area encompasses the **Brooklyn Bridge**, the **Ferry District**, **Brooklyn Heights**, **Downtown**, **Fort Greene** and **Atlantic Avenue**, and stretches from the water to the Brooklyn Academy of Music, quickly moving from warehouses to brownstones to the staid buildings found in most any civic center. Getting there, if you choose to walk, could turn out to be the most exciting part of your trip.

Crossing the Brooklyn Bridge

If you are going to Brooklyn, consider walking across the **Brooklyn Bridge** – it's not too long (less than a mile) and it may hold the best views of Manhattan that you will get. The walkway begins at City Hall Park next to the Municipal Building and ends in Brooklyn either at the corner of Adams and Tillary streets or at the more convenient Cadman Plaza East staircase. If you're not up to walking (though it really is the best way), the #2, #3, #4, #5, #N, #R, #A, #C and #F subways all stop in downtown Brooklyn. A taxi from lower Manhattan will be about $10, and $15 from Midtown.

Arriving in Brooklyn from the bridge, walk down the stairs and bear right, following the path through the park at Cadman Plaza. If you cross onto Middagh Street, you'll soon be in the heart of Brooklyn Heights; follow Cadman Plaza West down the hill to Old Fulton Street, and you'll find yourself in the Fulton Ferry District.

Fulton Ferry District

Underneath the glowering shadow of the **Watchtower Building** (the world headquarters of the Jehovah's Witnesses) is the site where Robert Fulton's steam ferry put in to forge the East River (1814), helping the **Fulton Ferry District** grow into Brooklyn's first and most prosperous industrial neighborhood. With the coming of the Brooklyn Bridge the area fell into decline, but these days it's on the way up again: aging buildings are being snapped up and redesigned as loft spaces (check out the imposing **Eagle Warehouse**, 28 Old Fulton St; its penthouse, with the huge glass clock-window, is one of the city's most coveted apartments). Down on the ferry slip itself, a couple of barges-cum-restaurants – most notably the *River Café* – lure die-hard Manhattanites across the bridge by night, and Wall Street types come over for power lunches. Locals are more likely to follow their noses to the delicious and view-blessed Italian eatery, or the brick ovens of *Grimaldi's* (formerly *Patsy's Pizzeria*), which just might offer some of the best pizza in New York City.

If it's open, the **Brooklyn Bridge Anchorage** across Old Fulton Street is well worth a visit. A cavernous space, cool and quiet under (inside, actually) the bridge, it's home to sporadic art and performance art happenings. There's no central number to call for information, but call the events organization Creative Time (ⓣ212/206-6674) for the summer-only schedule or visit their website at ⓦwww.creativetime.org. Although no longer there, the Rome Brothers' Printshop, at Old Fulton and Cranberry streets, printed in 1855 the first copies of Walt Whitman's collection of poems *Leaves of Grass*.

Fulton Ferry State Park and DUMBO

Just north of here (walk through the garden of the *River Café*) is a waterfront warehouse district ripe for renewal. For now, the **Empire-Fulton Ferry State Park** offers a beautiful view of the river at river level – something increasingly rare – and occasional art and sculpture exhibits. Behind the park is an area that has become – in typical hip New York fashion (think SoHo and TriBeCa) – known as **DUMBO** (Down Under Manhattan Bridge Overpass), which is said to be the next artists' East Village, though some dot.coms have moved in too (and a few already moved out). There isn't a whole heck of a lot

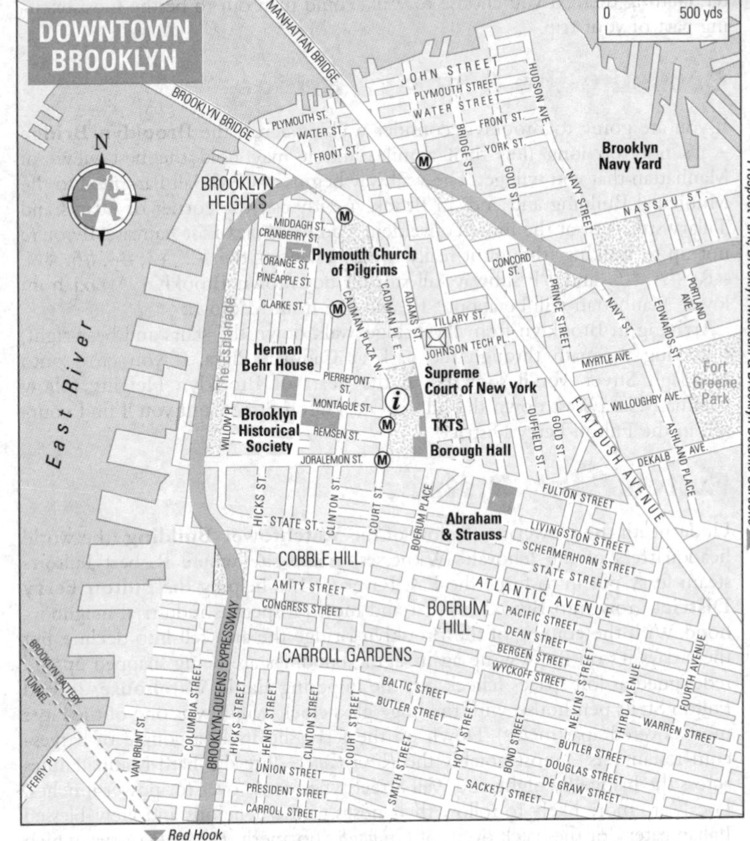

to see as of yet – though some waterfront redevelopment is planned – but the warehouse buildings and cobblestone streets are worth a gander if you're already over here during the day. If you visit during a weekend afternoon, expect to find a slew of open artists' studios.

Brooklyn Heights

Brooklyn Heights, Brooklyn's original city and its most coveted zip code, is one of New York City's most beautiful and historic neighborhoods. First occupied by the Canarsee Indians, the area was settled by the Dutch in the 1600s. From the early eighteenth century on, bankers and financiers from Wall Street lived exclusively along its tranquil shorefront, imagining themselves far from the tumult of Manhattan, yet close enough to keep an eye on the moneyed spires. Although many single-family brownstones were divided into apartments during the 1960s and 1970s, today the Heights, as it is often called, is not much different from what it was a hundred years ago.

Walk up the hill from Old Fulton Street and take Everett or Henry into the oldest part of the neighborhood, its streets lined with Federal-style brick buildings. You could take a self-guided walking tour just by following all the buildings with historical designation plaques; one house that has no plaque is **24 Middagh St** (at the corner of Willow), an unassuming but perfectly preserved wooden structure dating to 1824, it's the neighborhood's oldest house. Two streets down, on Orange between Hicks and Henry, the simple **Plymouth Church of the Pilgrims** went up in the mid-nineteenth century and became famous as the preaching base of **Henry Ward Beecher**, abolitionist and campaigner for women's rights. Horace Greeley, Mark Twain, even Abraham Lincoln all worshiped here on more than one occasion, drawn by Beecher's reputation as a great orator. The church was also a stop on the Underground Railroad, where slaves were hidden on their way to freedom. Henry Ward Beecher remains less known outside New York than his sister, Harriet Beecher Stowe, author of *Uncle Tom's Cabin*; his later years were marred by an adultery scandal; although he was acquitted he was never finally cleared in the public's eye. These days, you can see the barn-like interior only when a service is in progress.

South from here is **Pierrepont Street**, one of the Heights' main residential arteries, studded with delightful – and fantastic – brownstones. At its corner with Henry Street the **Herman Behr House**, a chunky Romanesque Revival mansion, has been, successively, a hotel, brothel, Franciscan monastery (the brothers added the horrific canopy) and, currently, private apartments. Further down Pierrepont, look in if you can on the **Brooklyn Unitarian Church** – originally known as the Church of the Savior – notable for its exquisite Neo-Gothic interior. Across the road at no. 128 is the **Brooklyn Historical Society** (Ⓦwww.brooklynhistory.org), which has temporarily shut its doors for a major renovation and expansion, though you can book an appointment (Ⓣ718/254-9830) to view a portion of their digitalized archives.

Walk west on any street between Clark and Remsen to reach the **Promenade** (aka "the Esplanade"), a boardwalk with one of the most renowned views in New York. It's hard to take your eyes off the Manhattan skyline, the water and the Statue of Liberty in the distance, but do turn around and notice between the trees the very large homes set back modestly from the walkway. The Heights has a history of housing writers, including W.H. Auden, Carson McCullers, Truman Capote, Tennessee Williams and Norman Mailer.

Leading off the southern end of the Promenade is **Montague Street**, Brooklyn Heights' hopping main thoroughfare, lined with shops, bars and restaurants. The street looks like it could be in Manhattan, but it feels more relaxed and subdued without the constant honk of cabs. After an afternoon of exploring, walk to **St. Ann's Church** (Ⓦwww.artsatstanns.org) at Montague and Clinton, which most nights offers a varied performing arts program, including experimental music, opera and theater.

Civic Center, Borough Hall and Fulton Street

Although the core of downtown Brooklyn has seen some hard times during the last several decades, it's on its way back, signaled by the first hotel built in these parts in 50 years, the *New York Marriott Brooklyn* at Renaissance Plaza, opened in November 1998 (still, a bed-and-breakfast in an adjoining neighborhood is a better option; see p.285 for more).

The eastern end of Montague Street is known as **"Bank Row"** – downtown Brooklyn's business center – and leads on to what is in effect the borough's

Civic Center, with the end of the residential Heights signaled by the tall Art Deco buildings of Court Street. Across the road the sober Greek-style **Borough Hall** is topped with a cupolated belfry; further east are the massive State Supreme Court and Romanesque **post office**, next to which stands a bronze statue of Henry Ward Beecher. There's little to linger for, but your tired feet should know that this is where to find the large Borough Hall subway station.

Beyond the civic grandeur, **Fulton Street**, the principal shopping street for the borough, leads east, becoming a pedestrianized mall in one strip, with more than 100 retail stores. The biggest draw is probably *Gage & Tollner*, one of Brooklyn's most famous restaurants, which serves seafood and steaks in a setting determinedly left unchanged since 1892. Another neighborhood landmark, and one more affordable, is *Junior's* on the corner of Flatbush and DeKalb avenues, famous for its cheesecakes (see p.347 for Brooklyn restaurant reviews).

New York Transit Museum

Just south of Fulton Mall, Adams Street turns into Boerum Place, and at the corner of Schermerhorn an old subway entrance leads to the **New York Transit Museum** (old subway entrance at Schermerhorn St and Boerum Place, Brooklyn. Subway #2, #3, #4, #5 or #F to Borough Hall. Tues–Fri 10am–4pm, Sat & Sun noon–5pm; $3, children $1.50; ⓣ718/243-3060, ⓦwww.mta.nyc.ny.us/museum). Housed in an abandoned 1930s subway station, this museum offers more than one hundred years' worth of transportation history and memorabilia, including antique turnstiles and more than twenty restored subway cars and buses dating back to around 1900 (including, amazingly, a wooden train car from 1914). A related gift shop, **New York Transit Museum Gallery and Store**, can be found on the main floor of Grand Central Station (see p.138).

Fort Greene

Going back a few steps to the corner of Fulton and Flatbush, you're at the border between downtown and **Fort Greene**, long a strong multiracial neighborhood, though now commonly associated with an upscale African-American community. Towering above the distinguished brownstones and grand churches, you should see the **Williamsburg Savings Bank** – Brooklyn's tallest building – the heart of the district. Just north of the Savings Bank, head into Fort Greene's Historic District down Fulton or Dekalb, and between Flatbush and Vanderbilt. While tours of homes can be arranged in May in even-numbered years and garden tours every year in June (ⓣ718/237-9031), you can also just stroll down streets like Oxford and South Portland to glimpse some of the better examples of the area's late-1800s housing stock.

If it's lunchtime, head to *Richlene*, 83 Lafayette Ave off Fulton (ⓣ718/243-2040), one of the area's many Caribbean-American cafés, and buy takeout for a picnic in **Fort Greene Park**, just north of DeKalb between Rockwell and Cumberland streets. An 1867 Olmsted and Vaux creation, the park holds at its summit a 148-foot **Prison Ship Martyrs Monument** (1906), commemorating the 11,500 American patriots who died in the British prison camps in old Wallabout Bay.

Fort Greene boasts America's oldest performing arts center, the **Brooklyn Academy of Music** (BAM to its fans, who come from all over the city) at 30 Lafayette Ave (ⓣ718/636-4100). The oldest performing arts center in America (1859), BAM, one of the borough's most hyped institutions, has played host over the years to a wide array of artists, from Charles Dickens and Booker T. Washington to Sergei Rachmaninoff and Philip Glass. BAM's four-screen, state-of-the-art cinema features art films and the occasional new release.

If you see what looks to be students with rucksacks on their backs and notebooks in their hands, they probably attend **Pratt Institute**, situated on a beautiful campus along Willoughby Avenue east of Fort Greene Park in the neighborhood **Clinton Hill**, which is also making a comeback. Founded in the 1880s by oil baron Charles Pratt, the pioneering institute admitted both males and females of all races to learn the new industrial trades. Today, Pratt offers degrees in architecture, art and design, information and library science, liberal arts and professional studies.

Atlantic Avenue

South of Brooklyn Heights is **Atlantic Avenue**, which runs from the East River all the way to Queens. The first stretch that divides Brooklyn Heights from Cobble Hill and Boerum Hill is the center of a vibrant Middle Eastern community. There are some fine and reasonably priced Yemeni and Lebanese restaurants and a good sprinkling of Middle Eastern grocers and bakeries. Wander through the **Sahadi Importing Co.** at no. 187, known throughout the city for nuts, dried fruit, halvah (crushed sesame seeds in a base of honey), and more than a dozen varieties of olives along with delicacies from other parts of the world. Walk east for a large concentration of antique stores, featuring Art Deco and Victorian furniture. Otherwise just head south down into gorgeous South Brooklyn.

South Brooklyn

Cobble Hill, **Carroll Gardens** and **Boerum Hill**, whose borders can be a blur – along with the old wharfing communities of **Red Hook** and the **Columbia Street Waterfront** – make up the area once known as **South Brooklyn**. (Geographically, much of the borough is actually south of this area.) Carroll Gardens and Boerum Hill once had the unfortunate distinction of being traversed by the Gowanus Canal, a once fetid and smelly stillwater canal. Although it's been slow going, residents have been fighting to reclaim the long-neglected artery, and recently won the battle to have city engineers open its drain so water could flow freely through the canal and into Gowanus Bay. In the future, this industrial neighborhood could be full of canal-side cafés and floating gondolas. But, at present, Court and Smith streets in Cobble Hill and Carroll Gardens hold the most interest, with their restaurants, cafés and shops. Take the F to Bergen or Carroll street stops to start your tour.

Cobble Hill

The main streets of **Cobble Hill** – Amity, Congress and Warren – are a mixture of solid brownstones and colorful red-brick rowhouses built between the 1840s and 1880s; most of them have long been a haven for the professional classes. The neighborhood got its name in the 1950s, when brownstone enthusiasts renovating the area discovered on a 1766 map that the neighborhood was once named "Cobles Hill," which referred to the since-removed conical hill near the corner of Court Street and Atlantic Avenue. The hill was an important Continental Army fortification during the Battle of Brooklyn.

Any who-was-who tour of Cobble Hill should take you to 197 Amity St, where **Jenny Jerome**, later Lady Randolph Churchill and mother of Winston Churchill, was born – the house is unfortunately disfigured by aluminum windows and a modern rustic facing. **Warren Place** is worth a look as well – easy to miss if you're not looking carefully. This tiny alley of late nineteenth-century workingman's cottages is a shelter of quiet on the westernmost block of Warren Street, just a stone's throw from the thunder of the Brooklyn-Queens Expressway.

On Congress Street, one block north of Warren Street, walk east away from the water. At Henry Street, look for the cobblestone alleyway – **Verandah Place** – lined by reclaimed and renovated mews built in the 1850s. The writer Thomas Wolfe lived at No. 40 and described the apartment in his novel *You Can't Go Home Again*. Verandah Place is also the southern edge of the lovely landscaped Cobble Hill Park, where during summer mornings couples read newspapers over coffee and croissants and then relax on the patches of green, sunlit grass.

For a real treat, look for Cobble Hill's hip and well-designed restaurants on Smith and Court streets, which are really just extensions of the bustling restaurant culture in neighboring Carroll Gardens.

Carroll Gardens

As you walk south along Court Street, Cobble Hill merges into **Carroll Gardens** around DeGraw Street. Originally a middle- and upper-class community of many nationalities, this part of South Brooklyn was invaded by a large number of Italian dockworking immigrants in the early 1900s. The area was named after Charles Carroll, the only Roman Catholic who signed the Declaration of Independence. Though plenty of youthful professionals have moved in from across the water, you'll still find plenty of pizza, pastries and cobblers hammering away on shoes in small storefronts. A strong sense of community prevails, as the lower-middle-class, family-oriented Italian population generally coexists quite peacefully with the newcomers.

Carroll Gardens residents are also known for their fantastic, often somewhat garish, **holiday decorations**. Although religious shrines and statues of the Virgin decorate many neighborhood gardens year-round, Christmas and Easter bring out the festivities in full force, as neighbors vie to outdo each other with flashing lights, incandescent monuments, and even appropriate music to produce the greatest display. A somber procession is held annually on Good Friday.

The progenitor of the South Brooklyn restaurant boom, Carroll Gardens' **Smith Street** is home to some of the best, not to mention quite a few designer shops and bric-a-brac furniture stores. Check out p.348 for restaurant reviews for the neighborhood.

Art lovers can check out **Jerard Studio**, 131 Union St at Columbia (tours by appointment only ⓣ718/852-4128), in an old bank building. It's the private studio for two local artists, John Gerard and Mary Crede, who have created puppets, mechanical costumes and stage sets for such Broadway shows as *The Beauty and the Beast* and *The Producers*, the Mel Brooks musical that won twelve Tony awards in 2001.

Boerum Hill

East of Cobble Hill, and south of Atlantic Avenue, Boerum Hill is scruffier and less architecturally impressive than its neighbors, though it has its share of sober Greek Revival and Italianate buildings – and gentrification has been under way for several years now. One of the more solidly integrated neighborhoods in Brooklyn, it's home to Italian- and Irish-descended families, Arabs and a long-established Puerto Rican population that has since become part of a more diverse Latino community. They bring salsa music and dancing to the stoops of the neighborhood brownstones and single-room storefront social clubs.

In the late 1960s, many local buildings were slated for demolition, but preservationists, community organizers and real-estate developers united to resurrect the neighborhood – after all, it was once home to **Washington Irving** and **James Fenimore Cooper**. During this time, the area was named after the Boerum family, which had farmed the land in colonial times. One interesting attraction, though under-recognized, is an abandoned **Long Island Rail Road tunnel**, the oldest in Brooklyn, built in 1844. Although the tunnel closed in 1859, rumors simmered about it being a secret passageway for bootleggers, smugglers and spies. In the 1980s, an eccentric Brooklynite, Robert Diamond, and a crew from the Brooklyn Union Gas Company lifted off a manhole that led to what was believed to be the tunnel. This is considered by some to be the world's first subway, predating the London Underground by sixteen years. The entrance, at the intersection of Atlantic and Court, is open on some summer Saturdays. Call for times or a guided tour (ⓣ718/941-3160).

Red Hook

After Carroll Gardens, the desolation of **Red Hook** is striking. Settled in 1636 and named because of the color of the soil and the shape of the land, Red Hook became one of the busiest and toughest shipping centers in the US. Elia Kazan's film *On the Waterfront* perfectly captured these times. But the growing automatization of the docking industry, vividly portrayed in the film and famous novel *Last Exit to Brooklyn*, left Red Hook behind. And the building of the Brooklyn-Queens Expressway in 1957 further isolated the area. To reach Red Hook, take the #F or #G train to Carroll Street and walk south on Court Street before crossing over the expressway.

Although Red Hook never recovered, community volunteers in 1995 presented their own ambitious urban renewal plan, though it has yet to be realized. Meanwhile, two arts organizations are helping to revitalize the waterfront area, where artists have taken over a number of Civil War-era warehouses that once stored supplies for the Union army. In fact, the **Brooklyn Waterfront Artists Coalition (BWAC)** holds its month-long Spring Show in May (ⓣ718/596-2507, ⓦwww.bwac.org) in the warehouses at the south end of Van Brunt Street. The view of the Statue of Liberty from this vantage point is stunning.

One street over is the **Hudson Waterfront Museum** at Pier 45, Conover Street at Beard Street (ⓣ718/624-4719, ⓦwww.waterfrontmuseum.org). Housed in a restored barge and run by a former professional clown, it sporadically sponsors both a circus and concerts – there's a shuttle bus available to fetch visitors from various Brooklyn neighborhoods. Red Hook is also home to **Picture Cars East** on Huntington Avenue, the largest provider of movie cars in the US. Still, change in this neighborhood is slow and it remains an area with little to experience, especially because it's not easily accessible.

Prospect Park and around

Where Brooklyn really asserts itself – architecturally, at any rate – as a city in its own right is not downtown, but on Flatbush Avenue in the vicinity of Grand Army Plaza (1870). At the plaza, traffic is funneled around a purely classical monument standing within the central open space. A cab ride from downtown Manhattan (about $10) is well worth the price. Otherwise, take the #2 or #3 train to the Grand Army Plaza stop.

Grand Army Plaza

Central Park architects Frederick Law Olmsted and Calvert Vaux designed Grand Army Plaza as a dramatic approach to their newly completed Prospect Park. The triumphal **Soldiers' and Sailors' Memorial Arch**, which you can climb during spring and autumn (weekends only), was designed in 1892 by John Duncan in tribute to the victory of the North in the Civil War. Inside the arch are bas reliefs, including one of Abraham Lincoln by Thomas Eakins and one of General Ulysses S. Grant by William O'Donovan, both installed in 1895. **The Victory Quadriga** (1898), a fiery sculpture atop the arch designed by Frederick William MacMonnies, depicts a rider, chariot, four horses and two heralds.

On the far side of the square, the creamy-smooth **Brooklyn Public Library** (Ⓦwww.brooklynpubliclibrary.org), finally finished in 1941 with the help of a $1.6 million donation from Andrew Carnegie in 1916, continues the heroic theme. Its facade is smothered with stirring declarations to its function as a fountain of knowledge, while above the entrance fifteen panels of decorative bronze screen sculptures by Thomas Hudson Jones reveal such favorite characters from American literature as Hawthorne's Hester Prynne, Twain's Tom Sawyer and Brooklyn's homegrown poet Walt Whitman.

Also in the neighborhood is the **Kurdish Library and Museum**, 144 Underhill Ave and Park Place (Subway #Q to 7th Ave, or #2 or #3 to Grand Army Plaza. Mon–Thurs 10am–3pm, Library open same hours; appointments are recommended; free; Ⓣ718/783-7930). A collection of 2000 volumes of Kurdish history, photographs, traditional costumes and crafts seeks to place in context the fourth largest group of people in the Middle East. Divided among several countries, the Kurds, despite vociferous protests, have no homeland of their own. The museum, American-founded and sponsored, is in a private brownstone and is the only institution of its kind in the Western hemisphere. It also publishes two journals about the Kurds; the library provides reference material of all kinds on their history, culture and politics.

The Brooklyn Museum of Art

To the east of Grand Army Plaza stands the **Brooklyn Museum of Art**, 200 Eastern Parkway (Subway #2 or #3 to Eastern Parkway-Brooklyn Museum. Wed–Fri 10am–5pm, Sat & Sun 11am–6pm, first Sat of every month 11am–11pm; $6, students $3; Ⓣ718/638-5000 for exhibition information or to schedule a tour, Ⓦwww.brooklynart.org). Built in 1915, the second largest museum in New York City announced a major renovation project in 2001. The Beaux-Arts entrance will be restored and the lobby space expanded. The expected completion date is early 2003. When Judy Chicago's *Dinner Party* was exhibited here in the early 1980s, people lined up all the way around the block.

Since then, however, the museum has reverted to its former status: good in its own right, but perpetually doomed to stand in the shadow of the Met.

A trip through the museum, one of the largest US art museums, with 1.5 million objects in its collection and **five floors of exhibits**, does require considerable selectivity. The permanent collection includes Egyptian, Classical and Ancient Middle Eastern Art; Arts of Africa, the Pacific and the Americas; Decorative Arts; Costumes and Textiles; Painting, Sculpture, Prints, Drawings and Photography; and 28 evocative **period rooms**, ranging from an early American farmhouse to a nineteenth-century Moorish castle.

Look in on the **American and European Painting and Sculpture galleries** on the top story, which progress from eighteenth-century portraits – including one of George Washington by **Gilbert Stuart** – and bucolic paintings by members of the **Hudson River School** to works by **Winslow Homer** and **John Singer Sargent** to pieces by **Charles Sheeler** and **Georgia O'Keeffe**. A handful of paintings by European artists – **Degas**, **Cézanne**, **Toulouse-Lautrec**, **Monet** and **Dufy**, among others – are also displayed, although nothing here approaches their best work. You will also find a large collection of **Rodin** sculptures. The museum's gift shop sells genuine ethnic items from around the world at reasonable prices.

Also nearby is the **Brooklyn Children's Museum**, 145 Brooklyn Ave at St. Mark's Avenue (Wed–Fri 2–5pm, Sat–Sun 10am–5pm; suggested donation $3. ⓣ718/735-4400). Founded in 1899, the first museum to explore culture, arts, science and the environment for children, it offers more than 10 galleries of hands-on exhibitions.

The Brooklyn Botanic Garden

The **Brooklyn Botanic Garden**, located at 1000 Washington Ave just south of the Brooklyn Museum of Art (Apr–Sept Tues–Fri 8am–6pm, Sat & Sun 10am–6pm; Oct–March Tues–Fri 8am–4.30pm, Sat & Sun 10am–4.30pm; $3, free Tues & Sat before noon; ⓣ718/623-7200, ⓦwww.bbg.org) is one of the most enticing park spaces in the city and a relaxing place to unwind after a couple of hours in the Brooklyn Museum of Art next door. Some 12,000 plants from around the world occupy 52 acres of manicured terrain. Sumptuous, but not overplanted, it offers a Rose Garden, Japanese Garden, a Shakespeare Garden (laid out with plants mentioned in the Bard's plays), the Celebrity Path (a winding walk studded with leaf-shaped plaques that honor Brooklyn's famous), and some delightful lawns draped with weeping willows and beds of flowering shrubs. A conservatory houses among other things the country's largest collection of bonsai, and a gift shop stocks a wide array of exotic plants, bulbs and seeds. The grounds may be rented for weddings and receptions.

Prospect Park

The Botanic Garden is about as far from Manhattan's bustle as you can get, but tear yourself away and explore Prospect Park (ⓣ718/965-895, ⓦwww.prospectpark.org) itself. Energized by their success with Central Park, Olmsted and Vaux landscaped this one in the early 1890s, completing it just as the finishing touches were being put to Grand Army Plaza outside. The park's 526 acres include a 60-acre lake on the east side, a 90-acre open meadow on the west side, and a 3.5-mile two-lane road primarily reserved for runners, cyclists, rollerbladers and the like.

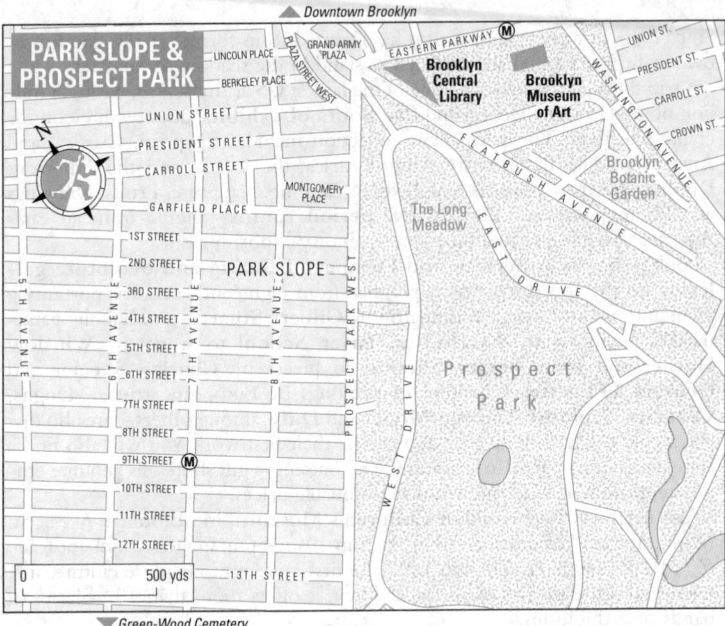

Unlike Central Park, Prospect Park has managed to retain its pastoral quality. Despite encroachments over the years – tennis courts, a skating rink and a zoo – it remains for the most part remarkably bucolic in feel. Architectural focal points include the **Lefferts Homestead**, an eighteenth-century colonial farmhouse moved here some time ago and now open, free of charge, on weekends, and the **Litchfield Villa** (95 Prospect Park W), built in 1857 by business tycoon Edwin Litchfield. **The Prospect Park Zoo** (Nov–Mar 10am–4.30pm; Apr–Oct Mon–Fri 10am–5pm, Sat & Sun 10am–5.30pm; $2.50, seniors $1.25, under 12 50¢) features a restored carousel and a lake. But probably the most redeeming element is the 90-acre **Long Meadow**, which cuts through the center of the park. On warm weekends you can find pickup soccer and volleyball matches, families hosting grand picnics and couples reading or romantically entwined.

Many attractions have been geared to children. Tired from walking? A free trolley bus (Ⓣ718/965-8967) makes the rounds of popular spots on weekends. The Boathouse has maps and information on events; dance, drama and music are performed in the bandshell on summer weekends (Ⓣ718/855-7882). The annual summer-long festival **Celebrate Brooklyn** (Ⓦwww.celebratebrooklyn.org) features music, art, film and dance.

Park Slope

The western exits of Prospect Park leave you on the fringes of Park Slope, an area settled in the seventeenth century by Dutch farmers and later fought over during the American Revolution. Learn some of the history at the **Old Stone House Museum** in J.J. Byrne Park, Fifth Avenue at Third Street (Sat–Sun 2–5pm; free; Ⓣ718/768-3195), where one of the bloodier skirmishes of the

Battle of Brooklyn took place. The house, rebuilt in the 1930s using original excavated stones, contains a small exhibit featuring a diorama of the house as it existed in the early days.

Today, Park Slope is an almost totally gentrified neighborhood sporting historic brownstones inhabited mostly by young professional couples with small children. If you come out of the park on its western perimeter, cross Prospect Park West while looking at the beautiful homes facing the park. Some of the finest Romanesque and Queen Anne residences in the US, they helped this area earn its nickname "The Gold Coast of Brooklyn." Walk down any quiet, tree-lined cross street to see why Park Slope, although a bit farther from Manhattan, has become a serious rival to Brooklyn Heights, with some of the city's highest property prices.

Walking west, you'll hit Seventh Avenue (you can also get there by the F train, 7th Avenue stop), lined with cafés, flower shops, wine stores, bakeries and book nooks. For home furnishings, don't miss Ecco, Artesana or The Clay Pot. The upscale **Flea Market on Seventh Avenue** (First to Third streets), is held every summer weekend (except when raining).

Although Seventh Avenue has plenty of restaurants, if it's fine dining you're after, beeline toward Fifth Avenue, Park Slope's burgeoning culinary capital. The king of the hill is no doubt *al di là*, a Northern Italian trattoria that gave life to this otherwise rundown strip. Early or late, expect at least a 45-minute wait (they don't take reservations), unless you are John Turturro, Steve Buscemi or Paul Auster, just a few of the many regulars. Other delicious places to dine include Park Slope veteran *Cucina*, at 256 Fifth Ave, and its new next door neighbor *Vaux Bistro*.

The Slope boasts one of the highest populations of gay, lesbian, bisexual and transgender people in the city, and hosted Brooklyn's first GLBT Pride Parade in June 1997. The **Brooklyn Pride Festival & Parade**, a colorful and fun-loving event, takes place every June. Since 1993, Park Slope has been the home of the Lesbian Herstory Archives (ⓣ718/768-DYKE for more information or to schedule a research appointment), one of the largest collections of lesbian research materials in the US. Key gay hangouts in Park Slope, all of them on edgier Fifth Avenue, include the crunchy *Rising Café*, at no. 186, the beer-soaked *Ginger's Bar*, at no. 363, and its loungy counterpart down the street, *Excelsior*, at no. 390.

South down Fifth Avenue, across Prospect Expressway, is the neighborhood of **Sunset Park** and the famed **Green-Wood Cemetery.** Almost as large as Prospect Park (478 acres to be exact) and very much the place to be buried in the nineteenth century if you could afford an appropriately flashy headstone or, better still, a mausoleum for the entire family. The main entrance at Fifth Avenue and 25th Street is distinguished by its cathedral-like Gothic revival gates, constructed in the 1860s by R.M. Upjohn, son of Trinity Church architect Richard Upjohn (both of whom are buried here). Other permanent residents include actress Mae West; politician and crusading newspaper editor Horace Greeley; William Marcy "Boss" Tweed, nineteenth-century Democratic chief and scoundrel; and the Steinway clan, of piano fame, at peace in their own 119-room mausoleum. Look out also for the tomb of one John Mathews, who made a fortune out of carbonated drinks and had himself a memorial carved with birds and animals, some fierce-looking gargoyles and (rather immodestly) scenes from his own life. You can stroll around and find all this for yourself, or catch one of the tours given by the **Brooklyn Center for the Urban Environment** (ⓦwww.bcue.org).

Flatbush

Southeast of Prospect Park is Flatbush, a busy though largely uninteresting residential and shopping area inhabited mostly by West Indians – though that makes it a good place to get food or other wares from that part of the world. There are other notable highlights. An exclusive (and exhaustively planned) community of large single-family houses developed in 1899, **Prospect Park South** is a surprising haven centered on several quiet, secluded streets around Albemarle Road – just walk south from Church Avenue (reachable from the park by the #Q train), on either Buckingham Road or Coney Island Avenue. Back on Church, at the corner of Flatbush Avenue, stands the **Reformed Protestant Dutch Church of Flatbush**, founded in 1654 by Peter Stuyvesant. This isn't the original building, but it's still attractive: the small **graveyard** in the back is a jewel. Many headstones have sunk into the ground or are hard to read; if you make out the names and inscriptions, you'll see that at least several are in Dutch. The large Gothic building across the street is **Erasmus Hall High School** (founded as a private academy by the church in 1786), Barbra Streisand's alma mater. To get a feel for this area during the 1940s, check out films like *Whistling in Brooklyn* (1944) and *It Happened in Flatbush* (1942). *The Lords of Flatbush* (1974) and *Sophie's Choice* (1982) recall more recent eras.

Central Brooklyn

The areas within **Central Brooklyn** are slightly rougher terrain, although they are no longer run by gangs and organized crime as they were up until the mid-1990s. Because of initiatives taken over the last decade, there's no place in New York City where you should feel unsafe during the daylight hours, and a trip here can be worth it for the under-appreciated historical appeal.

Bedford-Stuyvesant

Immediately east of Fort Greene, though quite different in feel, is **Bedford-Stuyvesant**, once one of the most elegant neighborhoods in the city and just maybe one of Brooklyn's best-kept secrets. Gothic, Victorian, French and other classic brownstones abound. Some of the more dignified streets include Chauncey, Macon, Decatur and Bainbridge; house tours are available in late October, but call ahead for scheduling (☎718/574-1979).

Bed-Sty is also the nation's second largest African-American community, second only to Chicago's South Side. Originally two separate areas, it was populated by both blacks and whites. The opening of the Brooklyn Bridge and later the construction of the A train brought a massive influx of African-Americans into the area. This led to increased hostility between the two groups, which in turn led to fighting, and in the 1940s the white population left, taking funding for many important community services with them. This was the start of the economic decline of Bed-Sty and, though the area has suffered the all-too-usual problems of inner-city neglect, today the African-American community here, which surpasses Harlem in size, is desperately trying to stop Bed-Sty's rot and take advantage of an architectural and cultural legacy.

The historical legacy here was largely forgotten until the 1960s and remains unknown to many outside the area. The nineteenth-century village of

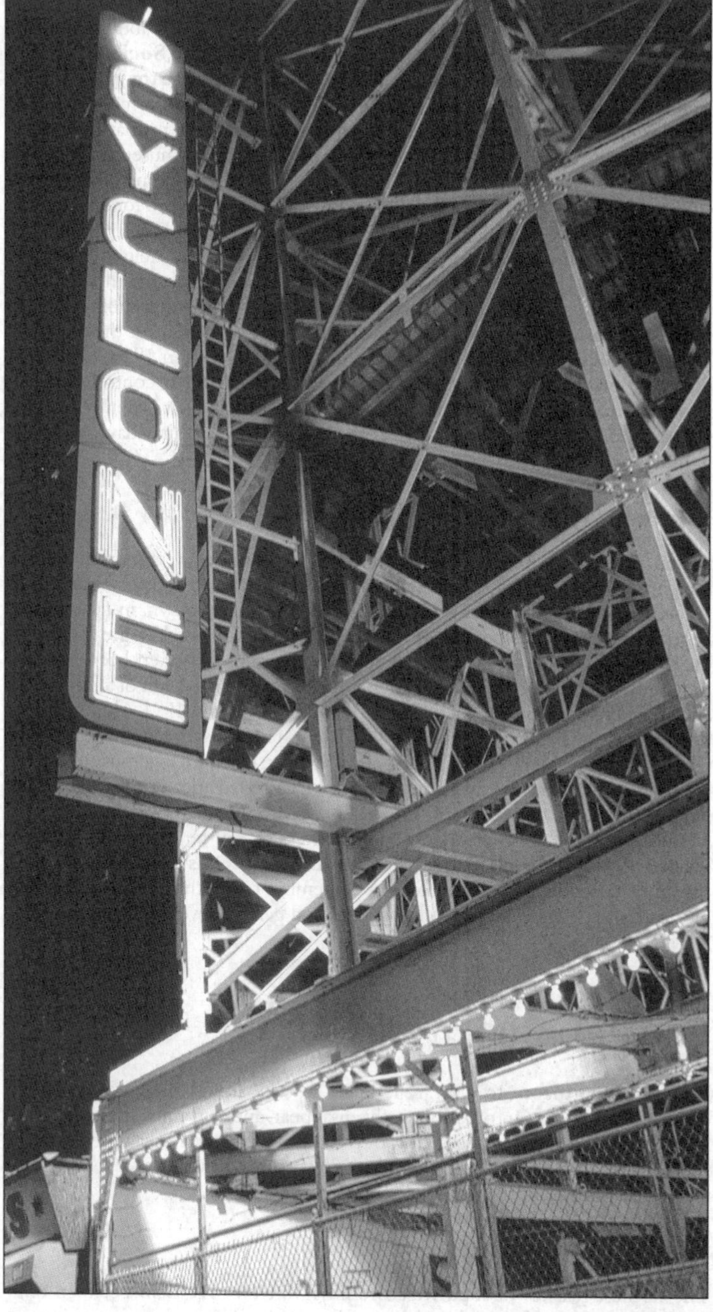

△ The creaky Cyclone rollercoaster is not for the timid

Weeksville – named after one of the first black landowners to move there – was a community of free blacks that evolved after slavery was abolished in the state in 1827. Little remains of Weeksville today, but the **Society for the Preservation of Weeksville and Bedford-Stuyvesant History**, 1698–1708 Bergen St, operates a museum of African-American history in these nineteenth-century houses and, while its efforts are directed primarily at local school groups, the society welcomes visitors. Although the museum is open to visitors (Tues–Sat 10am–4.30pm, Sun noon–6pm; $5, children under 18 $3; ⓣ718/756-5250, ⓦwww.weeksvillesociety.org), it's best to call for an appointment. To get to Weeksville take the #A train (of course) to Utica Avenue.

East of Bedford-Stuyvesant, there's not a lot to see. The neighborhood of **Brownsville** is notable for historic reasons: early in the twentieth century, it was a hotbed of prominent anarchists, Bolsheviks and other political freethinkers. **Emma Lazarus**, author of the spirited inscription on the Statue of Liberty ("Give me your tired, your poor . . . ."), lived here. In 1916, with more than 150 prospective clients waiting outside, the first birth control clinic in America opened here – only to be raided and closed nine days later by the vice squad; its founder, **Margaret Sanger**, was imprisoned for thirty days as a "public nuisance."

Crown Heights

Fulton Street and Atlantic Avenue separate Bedford-Stuyvesant from Crown Heights, home to the largest **West Indian neighborhood** in New York and to an active, established **community of Hasidic Jews**. Brooklyn, in fact, has the largest Afro-Caribbean population outside the Caribbean itself, a great many of them Haitian. Coexistence between these two groups has often been strained, though things have largely settled down since the accidental death of a black child and the subsequent murder of a Hasidic man set off riots in 1991. Although relations are getting better, the name Crown Heights remains synonymous with racial tension to many New Yorkers. Generally speaking, it's not dangerous to wander Crown Heights, and the lively atmosphere of Eastern Parkway, the world's first six-lane highway (reachable by the #2 or #3 to Eastern Parkway–Brooklyn Museum or the #2, #3 or #4 to Franklin Avenue), can be quite enjoyable. On Labor Day, this is the place to be; the annual **Mardi Gras Carnival** (aka West Indian Day Parade) bursts into life – in September rather than February because of the climate – with music, food, costumes and general revelry.

Coastal Brooklyn

It's possible, in theory, to walk, rollerblade or bike almost the entire southern **coast** of Brooklyn. On occasion, paths disappear, and you must share the service road off the highway with cars, but you'll never be on the highway itself. In short, it can be done. Even if you're of less sturdy stock, visit at least one of these areas to take in the often breathtaking views.

Bay Ridge

The farthest reaches of southwest Brooklyn, off the #R train between 65th and 101st streets, is the neighborhood of Bay Ridge. It is probably most known for Kleinfelds, the **world's largest bridal shop**, which welcomes 18,000 brides a year through its doors. A shuttle runs from Manhattan (Ⓣ718/765-8500, Ⓦwww.kleinfelds.com). In the shadows of the majestic Verrazano Narrows Bridge on a ridge overlooking the New York Bay, this hamlet's charm comes from the range of ethnicities represented – Irish, Italian, Russian, Muslims from Yemen and Lebanon, and Asians from China and Hong Kong – and the gorgeous old-world mansions (with yards and trees!) that line the shore. People from many cultures and income brackets coexist in a sort of Eden away from the hustle elsewhere. Newcomers and old-timers share space comfortably, as immortalized in the film *Saturday Night Fever*.

Get off the R train at Bay Ridge Avenue (locals call it 69th Street) and walk west to the **Shore Belt Cycle Club**, 29 Bay Ridge Ave (Ⓣ718/748-5077). For a great tour of the shoreline and the outer edges of Bay Ridge overlooking the water, rent a bike here for $6 an hour (25¢ extra for a bike with hand rather than foot brakes). Whether you ride or walk, continue west on 69th to the pier and the **Shore Road Bike Path**. Rollerbladers are welcome too, but stay on the #R train until 95th Street if you want skates. At Panda Sport, 9213 Fifth Ave and 92nd Street (Ⓣ718/238-4919), rentals are $15 for two hours or $20 for all day. Access the bike path at 95th Street.

The bike path offers great views of the Bay, the big homes, Staten Island and Lower Manhattan. The shimmering **Verrazano Narrows Bridge** (1964) flashes its minimalist message across the entry to Upper New York Bay. This slender, beautiful span was, until Britain's Humber Bridge opened, the world's longest at 4260 feet. In fact, the tops of the towers are visibly an inch or so out of parallel to allow for the curvature of the earth. The bridge, which connects Brooklyn to Staten Island and New Jersey, is named after the first explorer of New York Harbor, Giovanni da Verrazano.

John Paul Jones Park (Fourth Avenue at 101st Street) provides an excellent view of the bridge, though this park is not accessible from the bike path. Many parks lie along the bike path; packing a light lunch is a great idea for a lazy summer day. If you get on the path at 69th Street, you won't miss **Shore Road Park**, **Owl's Head Park** and the **Shore Parkway Promenade** (Ⓣ718/965-6524). If sitting amid roses and orchids is more your style, hit the **Narrows Botanical Gardens** (Shore Road between 69th and 72nd streets). A bit beyond the bridge is **Dyker Beach Park**, named after the beach that still exists underneath the lawn; at low tide, you can see sand at the water's edge. Old and young from the surrounding neighborhood come here for the sunshine and to fly kites.

The Dutch West India Company bought Bay Ridge from the Nyack Indians in 1652. This neighborhood was called Yellow Hook because of the yellow hues in the soil, but the name was changed in 1853 after New York City suffered a bout of yellow fever. A rural farming area until the late 1890s, Bay Ridge became a hotspot for rich Manhattanites who wanted to get away from the city. For a closer look at these **summer estates** of yesteryear, exit the Bike Path at 82nd Street, where a pedestrian bridge crosses the busy Belt Parkway. Shore, Narrows and River roads between 75th and 83rd are the best streets to glimpse some of the better Greek and Gothic Revival homes. The Howard E. and Jessie Jones House, sometimes referred to as the **Gingerbread House** (8220 Narrows Avenue and 83rd Street), looks like a witch's thatch-roofed backwoods lair. Known as Black Forest Art Nouveau, this architectural treasure was built in 1916.

Also worth a visit is the **US Army Garrison Fort Hamilton**, a historic military base at 101st Street and Fort Hamilton Parkway that houses 2000 military personnel and their families. Take the #R train to 95th Street and walk six blocks south, then four long blocks east, or take the B63 or B16 bus and ask the driver for the nearest stop to the fort. A self-guided walking tour will take you to the house occupied by **Robert E. Lee** (he served here as chief engineer from 1841 to 1846), the barracks, the commissary and the Officers Club. The **Harbor Defense Museum** (Mon–Fri 10am–4pm, second Saturday of each month 10am–4pm; ⓣ718/630-4349) is in a c1840 stone structure once used to protect the fort from a rear attack. Artifacts and weapons – guns, mines, missiles, cannons – tell the history of the defense of New York Harbor.

Coney Island

Accessible to anyone for the price of a subway ride, the beachfront amusement spot of **Coney Island** has long given working-class New Yorkers the kind of holiday they couldn't get otherwise. Buster Keaton movies and black-and-white photos from the early twentieth century give a sense of the fantasyland it was; take the subway to Stillwell Avenue (last stop on the #Q, #W, #F or #N) to see for yourself. These days, the music blares louder than it once did, the language of choice on the boardwalk is Spanish or Russian as often as English, and the rides look a bit worse for wear; but step out into the sunshine on a summer day and you'll feel the same excitement that filled generations of kids about to ride the Cyclone rollercoaster, the Parachute Jump or the Wonder Wheel for the first time.

You do have to be in the right frame of mind; this is not the sanitized, corporate-owned fun park you might be used to. On weekdays, rainy days and off-season, the festive atmosphere can totally disappear, making for an experience that's bittersweet, if not downright depressing and even a bit creepy. The beach can be overwhelmingly crowded on hot days, and it's never the cleanest place in or out of the water. But show up for the annual **Mermaid Parade** on the first Saturday of summer (late June, but check the newspapers), and you'll get caught up in the fun of what's got to be one of the oddest – certainly glitziest – small-town festivals in the country, where paraders dress as King Neptune and mermaids.

On arrival, head for **Nathan's**, the fast-food spot on the corner of Surf Avenue when you get off the subway. This is the home of the "famous Coney Island hot dog" advertised in *Nathan*'s branches elsewhere in the city, and while that delicacy is eminently skippable in Manhattan, only vegetarians have an excuse for missing it here. (*Nathan*'s holds an annual Hot Dog Eating Contest on July 4.) One block from *Nathan*'s is the boardwalk, where a leisurely stroll gives you ample opportunity to people-watch as you look for clues to Coney Island's past in the fading paint on the sides of buildings.

Go west to see the vine-covered, sunken remains of Coney Island's other wooden rollercoaster, the Thunderbolt, as well as the landmark parachute jump, now parachute-less and painted orange for no particular reason. These call up images of Coney Island's century-old heyday, when the entire area was abuzz and lit up with lights. In fact, it is said that Coney Island's lights were the first things immigrants could see as they entered the harbor making way for Ellis Island. Today, Coney Island's amusement area comprises several amusement parks, none of which offers a deal that makes a lot of sense unless you have kids (nearly all the children's rides are in Deno's Wonder Wheel Park) or plan on riding one ride more than four times. The **Wonder Wheel** ($3, plus a free children's ticket to the New York Aquarium, see below) is a must – after 75 years, it's still the tallest ferris wheel in the world, and the *only* one in the world on which two-thirds of the cars slide on serpentine tracks, shifting position as the wheel makes its slow circle twice around. The **Cyclone** roller coaster ($4, $3 for a repeat ride) is another landmark attraction, but if you're used to slick modern loop-coaster rides, be forewarned: this low-tech creaky wooden coaster is not for the faint of heart. Farther down the boardwalk, halfway to Brighton Beach, is the seashell-shaped **New York Aquarium**, Surf Avenue and West 8th Street (Mon–Fri 10am–5pm, Sat & Sun 10am–5.30pm; $9.75; ⓣ718/265-FISH). If you've never seen Sea World in Orlando, it's worth a visit if you have the time, especially the dolphin shows or during feeding hours.

The **Coney Island Museum** (ⓣ718/372-5159), maintained by a not-for-profit organization also known as Sideshows by the Seashore, is one indoor destination on the drab stretch of Surf Avenue that you won't want to miss. You may see such longstanding performers as Koko the Killer Clown, the Illustrated Man and Serpentina, or catch a nighttime burlesque or New Vaudeville performance. Shows start at 2pm and go until 10pm; price is $5. Unofficial, somehow more authentic, sideshows (such as the Two-Headed Baby, the Headless Woman and the Giant Killer Rat) abound on the side streets, but don't expect much for your money.

Brighton Beach

East along the boardwalk from Coney Island, at Brooklyn's southernmost end, is Brighton Beach, once an affluent seaside resort complete with a racetrack, casino and major hotel. Today, it's often called Little Odessa (the film of the same name was set here), and is home to the country's largest community of Russian emigrés, who arrived in the 1970s following a relaxation of restrictions on Soviet citizens entering the US. There's also a long-established and now largely elderly Jewish population. You know when you're out of Coney Island – not only have the amusements disappeared, but there's a residential aspect to the place that gives Brighton Beach appeal.

The neighborhood's main drag, **Brighton Beach Avenue**, parallels the boardwalk underneath the elevated subway until the train swings north (the #Q stops here). The street is a bustling mixture of **food outlets**, appetizing **restaurants** and shops selling every type of Russian souvenir imaginable. Eating is half the reason to go to Brighton Beach: for a taste of tradition, try the long-established *Mrs Stahl's Knishes* at Brighton Beach and Coney Island avenues, where the train turns. Even more fun is to order a picnic lunch at one of the many groceries or delis; *M & I International*, the largest Russian store, has all sorts of smoked fish, sausages, cheeses and breads. Sit-down food is also readily available, though you'd be better off waiting until evening, when the restaurants really heat up, becoming a near-parody of a rowdy Russian night out with lots of food, loud live music, lots of glass-clinking and free-flowing chilled vodka. Guests dress to the nines, and the dancing girls will have you feeling like you've landed in a foreign Vegas. The most popular and accessible spots are *National, Ocean* and *Odessa*, all on Brighton Beach Avenue at 273, 1029 and 1113, respectively. If you remember the movie *Moscow on the Hudson*, Robin Williams's character frequented the National. The action starts about 8.30pm and can last until 3am. Expect to spend $45 to $55 a head.

Sheepshead Bay

If you're returning to the heart of Brooklyn or Manhattan, the next stop on the #Q subway line is **Sheepshead Bay**, which claims distinction as "New

York's only working *fishing* village" (though City Island in the Bronx – p.270 – might beg to differ). It is much quieter than Coney Island or even Brighton Beach. **Emmons Avenue** maintains a definite salty charm, as locals stroll past the piers of fishing boats and relax at outdoor cafés whenever the weather is fine.

In the early evening, the adventurous shop the boats at the Emmons Avenue pier for what is undoubtedly **the freshest fish in the city**. At about 4pm on weekdays, boats unload heaps of bluefish, flounder and mackerel; arriving earlier, you can sample a previous catch anywhere along the strip. Truly dedicated fish fanatics can go out on one of the many boats that take out visitors for fishing and sightseeing trips. Half-day fishing trips (7am–1pm) go for about $25 – some boats vary in price. This isn't the best-run operation, which means you'll have to book your own trip. Ask the captain what is provided with the trip. Just show up at the piers before 7am and see who's around. Many boats also do sunset cruises (for $15) to various points of interest in New York Harbor. Show up at the pier at about 5pm on weekdays to see who's going out.

Just across the wooden Ocean Avenue Bridge from Sheepshead Bay is the affluent (if occasionally tacky) neighborhood of **Manhattan Beach**, where the beach of the same name is popular with locals and largely unknown to most New Yorkers. It's a very pleasant spot to swim, especially on less-crowded weekday afternoons. Northeast of Sheepshead Bay (although more easily accessible by bus from Flatbush) are the marshlands of **Marine Park** and **Floyd Bennett Field** – an old airfield that serves as headquarters for the Gateway National Recreation Area in **Jamaica Bay** (see p.264).

Northern Brooklyn

From the tip of Coastal Brooklyn, head northwest to the northern tip of Brooklyn to visit the neighborhoods of Polish **Greenpoint**, uber-hip North Williamsburg and Hasidic South Williamsburg, surely worth the better part of a day poking around.

Greenpoint

While there's not a whole lot to see and do in **Greenpoint**, it's worth a walk-through on your way to Williamsburg. After all, it is the birthplace of Mae West, and the epicenter of the oft-ridiculed Brooklynese accent. Reachable by the #G train to Greenpoint Avenue or the #L to Bedford Avenue, Greenpoint hasn't been green for a long time now. Purchased by the Dutch in 1638 from the Keshaechqueren Indians, this area in the mid-seventeenth century was known as *Boswijck* (or later Bushwick), meaning "the wooded district." But the Industrial Revolution changed all that. And while it was good to the economy, the environment certainly bears its legacy as a community of the "Black Arts" – printing, pottery, gas, glass and iron.

The abandoned **ironworks**, West Street between Oak and Calyer streets, was the site of the historic launching of the ironclad ship the *Monitor*, which went to sea on January 30, 1862, to fight just three months later the Confederate armored ram the *Merrimac*. Although the pollution was considerable, the industries that replaced them – primarily fuel and garbage – haven't really improved matters environmentally. That said, it's surprising to discover that

Greenpoint is a truly pleasant community. If you can, get a glimpse of the Manhattan skyline between the buildings.

The main strip is Manhattan Avenue, the heart of Greenpoint's Polish community (from Nassau to Java streets). Manhattan Avenue is mostly lined by mom-and-pop shops and bakeries, such as the Piekarnia Rzeszowska Bakery, 948 Manhattan Ave (Ⓣ718/349-7501), where you can buy a *babka*, the Polish cake made famous by *Seinfeld*, or a huge cheese Danish, which many say is the best New York City has to offer. Or if you want to pick up some fresh Polish meats or *pierogies*, markets like Steve's Meat Market, 104 Nassau St (Ⓣ718/383-1780) claim to make the best *kielbasa* in America. Detour down a side street for a different taste of Greenpoint; Slavic conversations float from the open windows of apartments, making you feel like you walked into a slice of Eastern Europe.

From Manhattan Avenue, turn right (west) on Nassau Street to **McCarren Park**, often considered the border between Greenpoint and Williamsburg. While the physical border might well be the park, the mental border is a little blurry, especially with North Williamsburg becoming such a hot spot among artists unable to afford Manhattan apartment and studio prices. At the south end of the park, a giant green dome hovers above the trees. This imposing structure is the **Russian Orthodox Church of the Transfiguration**, at N 12th St and Driggs Ave along Bedford Avenue and/or Berry Street. On Sunday this is the best place to witness what old Greenpoint is really about.

Williamsburg

South of Greenpoint, toward the Brooklyn-Queens Expressway, the neighborhood turns into **Williamsburg**, Hispanic at first, with a strong family atmosphere. Walk toward Bedford Avenue and you'll be in the hipster pocket of the neighborhood, where the streets are populated by scenesters wearing vintage clothes and jewlery, poking in and out of the coffee, record, book and clothes shops. This is also the heart of this area's blossoming art scene. Many dilapidated buildings have been put to creative use and the face of the neighborhood changes daily. Indeed, with easy access to Manhattan and excellent waterfront views, it's not hard to see why this area has exploded.

Out of the Bedford stop on the #L train, you'll emerge at the upper end of a string of cafés and bars. The **Brooklyn Brewery**, 79 N 11th St (Ⓣ718/486-7422, Ⓦwww.brooklynbrewery.com) hosts events all summer; hang out in their tasting room 6-10pm Fridays or take a free tour on Saturdays noon–5pm. Around 1900 there were nearly fifty breweries in Brooklyn, and this brewery is the first successful one in Brooklyn since Schaefer and Rheingold closed in 1976.

Williamsburg also boasts more than a dozen **contemporary art galleries** ranging in ambience from ultra-professional to makeshift, and run by an international coterie of artists; the most sophisticated is Pierogi 2000, 177 N 9th St (Ⓣ718/599-2144, Ⓦwww.pierogi2000.com). There's also Eyewash, in a tenement flat on the third floor of 143 N 7th St, and the tiny barn-like Holland Tunnel, at 61 S 3rd St. Farther south, in the shadow of the Williamsburg Bridge at 135 Broadway at Bedford Avenue (Ⓣ718/486-7372), is the imposing Victorian Kings County Savings Bank, now home to the somewhat misleadingly named **Williamsburg Art and Historical Center** (or "WAH," which means "harmony" in Japanese). One of several landmarked nineteenth-century banks in Williamsburg, founded to service local industrialists, the building was renovated and opened as a multimedia arts center in 1996 by Japanese artist

Yuko Nii, self-appointed grande dame of the Williamsburg art scene. Stop by or visit Ⓦwww.wahcenter.org for information on lectures and events.

For other things to do in Williamsburg, look west toward the water and let the old Pfizer smokestack lead you to **Grand Ferry Park**, one of the few waterfront parks left in Brooklyn. From here, ferries from 1800 to 1918 picked up and dropped off. This small oasis offers a great view of the Williamsburg Bridge.

South of the bridge, **Division Avenue** marks the traditional divide between the Hispanic community and the **Hasidic Jewish** part of Williamsburg, where men wear black suits, and long *payess* (curls) hang from under their hats. Women dress conservatively with scarves or wigs. The Jewish community has been prominent here since the **Williamsburg Bridge** linked the area to the Lower East Side, and many Jews from that neighborhood left for the better conditions across the East River (the bridge was unkindly nicknamed the "Jew Plank"). During World War II a further settlement of Hasidim, mainly from the ultraorthodox Satmar sect, established Williamsburg as a firmly Jewish area. Puerto Ricans began to arrive to the north and east, and the two communities coexist in a state of strained tolerance.

The best place to start exploring Jewish Williamsburg is **Lee Avenue**, or Bedford Avenue, which runs parallel (take the #J, #M or #Z to Marcy Avenue to get there). On both you'll see manifestations of the neighborhood's character: Glatt Kosher delicatessens line the streets; signs are written in both Yiddish and Hebrew. Don't take it personally if you're ignored – you may feel like you've dropped in from another planet, and the residents may feel like you have, too. Further south on Lee Avenue, you're far from any subway – the B44 bus will get you back to the Williamsburg Bridge; the B61 will take you to downtown Brooklyn.

At the southern tip of the neighborhood is the vast **Brooklyn Navy Yard**, a crucial World War II construction ground for famous battleships such as the *Iowa*, *New Jersey*, *Arizona* and *Missouri*. The famous *Monitor*, built in nearby Greenpoint, was clad in iron here, with an historic Civil War battle in its future. At its height in 1918, 18,000 workers were assembling and repairing ships. Closed in 1966, the Navy Yard is currently home to more than 200 companies, the most exciting of which is the as-yet-unfinished New York Studios (Ⓦwww.nystudios.com), a $160 million film and television production studio. Also on the scene are Robert De Niro and Miramax Studio's Weinstein brothers, building a Hollywood-style soundstage on a fifteen-acre portion of the Navy Yard.

25

Queens

Of New York City's four outer boroughs, its largest, **Queens**, named after Catherine of Braganza, queen of Charles II, is probably the least visited by outsiders – not counting when they arrive by Queens' airports: La Guardia or John F. Kennedy International. In fact, that's as far as most other New Yorkers get. Unlike Brooklyn or the Bronx – or even Staten Island, with its ferry – Queens has no hyped drawing card to pull visitors in. However, the individuality of its neighborhoods, a leftover from the fact it was never its own city before being incorporated into New York in 1898, just a county of separate towns and villages, should be reason enough to come explore.

While here, you can travel from Greek **Astoria** through Irish **Woodside** to Indian and South American **Jackson Heights** and finally Asian **Flushing**, which can feel as suburban as Long Island some days and as exotic as Hong Kong on others. You'll find a few underrated museums and no shortage of delicious ethnic foods – just follow the #7 train, which chugs through most of the borough; Turkish breads, Romanian sausage, Indonesian noodles, Tibetan pork, Argentinean steak, vegetarian Indian, Cantonese dim sum and some of the best Texas barbecue in the city await.

Long Island City and Astoria

Industrial **Long Island City** (which really was a city, and the largest community in Queens County from 1870 until incorporation) provides the first view of Queens for most people. Here, the #7 and #N subway trains cut above ground after crossing from Manhattan. The area has attracted artists to its affordable studio spaces for a number of years, although it hasn't been the mass migration some predicted. It's close to Manhattan, there's a thriving artist community and some new waterfront high-rise apartments with stellar views might finally make developers' dreams come true.

To explore Long Island City, take the #7 train to the Hunter's Point stop. Walk down Vernon Boulevard to 49th Street and take a left. The road ends at the newly refurbished and eccentrically designed **Gantry Plaza State Park**. There is a children's playground and three piers, one designated for fishing. If you're lucky you'll stumble upon a local fisherman pulling in a bluefish. The two huge cranes harken back to a day when boxcars were lifted from rail barges to eastbound trains. The **New York Waterway Ferry** connects Long Island City from this point to Manhattan's 33rd Street (☎1-800/533-3779 for information).

Long Island City Studios

Art Entrée and Sara Garden Armstrong Studio
48-18 Purves St (☎718/391-0011, Ⓦwww.artentree.com)
Crane Street Studio
46-23 Crane St (☎347/452-3757, Ⓦwww/ankiking.com)
Fardom Studio
25-17 41st Ave (☎718/752-0331, Ⓦwww.fardom.com)
Elinore Schnurr
10-09 50th Ave, 2nd floor (☎718/937-5229, Ⓦwww.elinoreschnurr.com)
Skewville
26-09 28th St (☎718/204-4795, Ⓦwww.skewville.com)

Sadly, there's not much else to see in this immediate vicinity, but this area is home to many **artists'** studios – viewable by appointment only (see sidebar; for a longer list, see the Queens' art map called **The Art Loop**). From the summer of 2002 through 2004, Queens is also the home of the Museum of Modern Art, while its new facility is being constructed on 53rd Street in Manhattan. **MoMA QNS**, 45-20 33rd St at Queens Blvd (#7 to 33rd Street stop; ☎212/708-9400, Ⓦwww.moma.org), in a reinvention of the Swingline Factory, will offer exhibitions and educational programs, along with a café and design shop. Highlights include a special installation of the museum's permanent collection and explorations of Pablo Picasso and Henri Matisse (see p.147 for more).

Another Long Island City draw is the **PS 1 Contemporary Art Center**, 20-25 Jackson Ave at 46th Ave (Wed–Sun noon–6pm; $5; ☎718/784-2084, Ⓦwww.ps1.org). Founded by Alanna Heiss in 1971, PS 1 has been devoted to showcasing cutting-edge artists, and even has club nights on Saturdays throughout the summer. In 2000, it became affiliated with the Museum of Modern Art.

Isamu Noguchi Garden Museum and Socrates Sculpture Park

While they are not in the most accessible part of Queens to get to, it's well worth going out of your way to visit the **Isamu Noguchi Garden Museum** and the Socrates Sculpture Park. To get to the Noguchi Museum's temporary location until Spring 2003 (Wed–Fri 10am–5pm, Sat & Sun 11am–6pm; suggested donation $4, free tours at 2pm; ☎718/204-7088, Ⓦwww.noguchi.org), take the #7 train to 33rd Street, walk three blocks east to 36th Street and turn on 43rd Avenue, where it can be found at no. 36-01. The museum is devoted to the works of the Japanese-American abstract sculptor Isamu Noguchi (1904–88), whose studio was in Queens. His pieces, in stone, bronze and wood, exhibit a Zen-like simplicity.

After Spring 2003, take the #N train to the Broadway (Queens) station and head west to Vernon Street – about 15 minutes. The permanent indoor-outdoor museum, 32–37 Vernon Blvd (April–Oct; same times and prices as above), is situated in a garden and former factory and showcases more than 250 works by Noguchi.

Although the **Socrates Sculpture Park**, Broadway at Vernon Blvd (daily 10am–sunset; Ⓦwww.socratessculpturepark.org), was in disrepair during a recent visit, it is the only space in New York City that gives artists room to create large-scale work. The park was an abandoned landfill until 1986, when artist Mark Di Suvero took the lead in transforming it into an outside studio.

Astoria

Head away from the river up Broadway and through the heart of **Astoria**; the #N or #R from Manhattan will also easily take you directly here. One of Queens' original communities, Astoria is known for two things: filmmaking and the fact that it has the largest concentration of Greeks outside Greece, or so it claims (whatever Melbourne, Australia, says to the contrary). Between 1920 and 1928, Astoria, where Paramount had its studios, was the capital of the silent film era and continued to blossom until the 1930s when the lure of

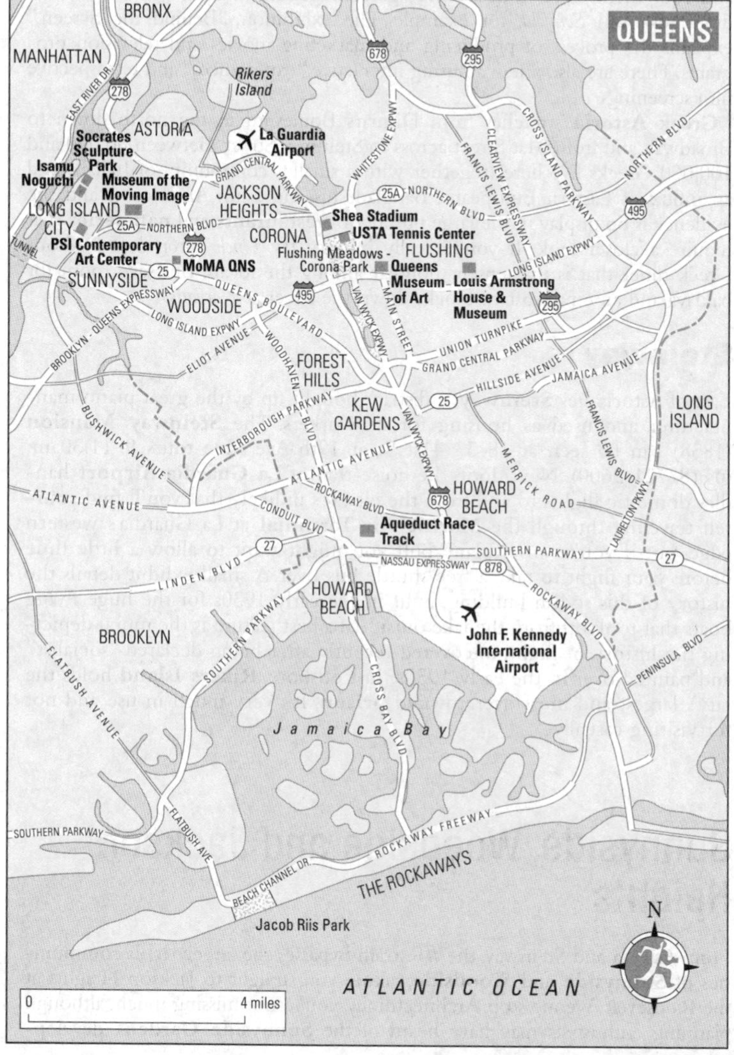

Hollywood's reliable weather left Astoria largely empty. So it remained until recently, when Hollywood's stranglehold on the industry weakened and interest – in New York in general and Astoria in particular – was renewed. After a major renovation, the **Kaufman Studios**, 34-12 36th St (Ⓣ718/392-5600, Ⓦwww.kaufmanstudios.com) are back open – bigger and better than ever. Early film stars such as Rudolph Valentino and W.C. Fields performed here, and films from *Beau Geste* to *The Wiz* were produced here.

The **American Museum of the Moving Image**, 35th Avenue at 36th Street (Tues–Fri noon–5pm, Sat & Sun 11am–6pm; $8.50; Ⓣ718/784-0077, Ⓦwww.ammi.org), is just around the corner in the old Paramount complex. It houses a stellar collection of more than 1000 objects, from posters to stills to sets and equipment, both from Astoria's golden age and more recent times – the diner set from *Seinfeld*, for example. The exhibition, "Behind the Screen," explains the process of producing and marketing movies and television programs. There are also a few amusing interactive "experiences" and retrospective film screenings.

Greek Astoria stretches from Ditmars Boulevard in the north down to Broadway, and from 31st Street across to Steinway Street. Between 80,000 and 100,000 Greeks live here (together with a smaller community of Italians and an influx of Eastern Europeans, Bangladeshis and Latin Americans) and the evidence is on display in the large number of **restaurants** and **patisseries** that require a closer look. If you're really hungry, try *Uncle George's*, a 24-hour Greek diner that is immensely popular among the locals. But save room for baklava and an espresso two blocks down the street at *Karyatis*.

Steinway

East of Astoria lies **Steinway**, a district bought up by the great piano manufacturer and used as housing for its workers. The **Steinway Mansion** (1858) can be seen at 18-33 41st St at 19th Ave (free tours 9–11.30am; Ⓣ718/721-2600). Next door, the noise-trap of **La Guardia Airport** handles domestic flights to and from the city. It's unlikely that you'll find yourself traveling through the **Marine Air Terminal** at La Guardia's western edge, but if you're an airplane buff you might want to allow a little time before your flight to take a free shuttle bus over. A small exhibit details the history of this stylish building, built in the early 1930s for the huge flying boats that took off from the lake outside. Its best feature is the mural depicting the history of flight, uncovered recently after being declared "socialist" and painted over in the early 1950s. Just offshore, **Rikers Island** holds the city's largest and most overcrowded **prison**. It's very much in use and not for visiting casually.

Sunnyside, Woodside and Jackson Heights

From Astoria and Steinway, the #R train bypasses the largely Irish communities of **Sunnyside** and **Woodside**, taking you straight to Jackson Heights at the Roosevelt Avenue stop. Architecturally, you're not missing much, although planning enthusiasts may have heard of the **Sunnyside Gardens** development, the first planned "garden city" in the United States. Started in 1924, it's not nearly as impressive to modern eyes, but if you'd like to see what it was all about, get off the #7 at the 46th Street stop and walk down 46th Street, on the opposite side of Queens Boulevard from the Art Deco "Sunnyside" sign.

Jackson Heights

East of Sunnyside the #7 train swings away from Queens Boulevard and up narrow Roosevelt Avenue, and the accent of the neighborhood changes. Get off at 74th Street and you'll find yourself in the heart of South American **Jackson Heights**, where at least 150,000 Colombians, half as many Ecuadorians and a good number of Argentinians and others from South America make their home in a self-contained area where English is rarely the language of choice. It's a raucous and lively area – as, for example, after a home-country team wins an important soccer match. The neighborhood didn't really get its start until 1917, when the elevated transit provided easy access. The area first became Hispanic in the 1960s, when huge influxes of people came over – many illegally – to find work and escape from the poverty and uncertain politics of their own countries, and it's now the largest South American contingent in the States. Tighter immigration controls, however, have radically cut the intake, and the community here is now more or less static.

Roosevelt Avenue and, running parallel, 37th Avenue between 82nd Street and Junction Boulevard are the focuses for the district, and eating-wise, there's no better part of Queens for exotic, unknown and varied **cuisines**. Along both streets you'll find Argentine steakhouses, Colombian restaurants, and pungent coffeehouses and bakeries stacked high with bread and pastries. But head back down 37th Avenue to 74th Street, and you'll see sudden contrast. With its proliferation of colorful sari, spice and video stores, **Little India** is the largest Indian community in New York, with numbers around 100,000; the restaurants here far surpass the fare on well-known 6th Street in Manhattan. A must stop is the *Jackson Diner*, 74th St at 37th Ave; see p.350 for a review.

Corona, Shea Stadium and Flushing Meadow Park

East of Jackson Heights you hit **Corona**, its subway yards ringed by menacing barbed wire and patrolled by dogs to deter graffiti artists. While there's not much to see here, Corona was home to Louis "Satchmo" Armstrong from 1943 until his death on July 6, 1971, at the now-designated **Louis Armstrong House Museum**, 107th Street, between 34th and 37th avenues (Mon-Fri 10am-5pm, Sat noon-5pm; free; ☎718/997-3670). A few steps away stands **Shea Stadium**, home of the New York Mets. The Beatles, too, played here in 1965 (originating the concept of the stadium rock concert) as did the Rolling Stones in 1989. Concerts out here are rare but appreciated; baseball games, on the other hand, are frequent and the Mets have a solid and loyal fan base. For details on the Mets and when they play, see Chapter 37, "Sports and outdoor activities."

Shea Stadium went up as part of the 1964 World's Fair (a repeat performance of the 1939-40 World's Fair), held in adjoining **Flushing Meadows-Corona Park**. The park is now the site of the US Tennis Association's **National Tennis Center**, the largest tennis facility in the world; it pays the city more than $400,000 a year in rent. The main event here is the US Open Tennis Championships at the end of each summer. Tickets to the early matches in the stadium are easy enough to come by; closer to the finals you may end up paying exorbitant rates from scalpers (see p.439 for info). Even if you can't get tickets to the Open, this is the best time of year to visit the park, because it's the only event for which air traffic is rerouted. At most other times, the roar of the jet engines can be deafening, marring what would otherwise be a truly lovely place to spend a day.

Flushing Meadows-Corona Park literally rose out of ashes – replacing a dumping ground known to locals as "Mount Corona" and described by F. Scott Fitzgerald in *The Great Gatsby* as "a fantastic farm where ashes grow like wheat into ridges and hills and grotesque gardens." Begun for the 1939–40 World's Fair, it took its present shape around the time of the later fair, and today it's a beautifully landscaped park with a couple of key attractions that may make the long haul out here well worthwhile.

From Shea, you'll easily find your way to the park. From the 111th Street stop on the #7 train (the stop before the stadium stop), it's not as obvious. However, if you walk south on 111th Street, you'll come to it, starting with the **New York Hall of Science**, 46th Ave and 111th St (special summer and fall hours, so call ahead; $7.50, $5 under 17; ⓣ718/699-0005, ⓦwww.nyhallsci.org), a concrete and stained-glass structure retained from the 1964 World's Fair (you'll see the best remaining structures deeper within the park). This is an interactive science museum kids will love; it's fun but can be exhausting for adults. The adjacent **Wildlife Center** (once the zoo) is interesting in that it features exclusively North American animals. But the main reason to come here is to see the **Unisphere** and the **Queens Museum of Art.**

Created for the 1964 World's Fair, the Unisphere is a 140-foot-high, stainless steel globe that weighs 380 tons – probably the main reason why it never left its place in the park. The great builder Robert Moses intended this park to be the "Versailles of America," and it's from this vantage point that you can see that plan in action: carefully designed pathways connect lawns, small pools and two lakes. On a summer day, the park is swarming with kids on bikes and roller blades; rent a bicycle yourself, or a boat.

The park puts out a good map, available free from inside the Queens Museum of Art, next to the Unisphere (Tues–Fri 10am–5pm, Sat & Sun noon–5pm; suggested donation $5; ⓣ718/592-9700, ⓦwww.queensmuse.org). Housed in a 1939 World's Fair building that served briefly as the first home of the United Nations, the Queens Museum holds a must-see in its **Panorama of the City of New York**, also built for the 1964 World's Fair. With one inch of the model equal to one hundred feet, the Panorama (and its 835,000 buildings, plus bridges, piers, rivers and airports) is the world's largest architectural model. It was recently updated, and new remodeling of the space allows you to walk all around (and occasionally over) the parameters of the five boroughs. Guided tours of the Panorama are also available. The rest of the museum is almost as fascinating: there are aerial photos, games, toys and other paraphernalia from the World's Fairs on view, plus a collection of glassworks by Louis Comfort Tiffany, who established his design studios in Corona in the 1890s.

Flushing

Beyond the eastern end of the park (Main Street, last stop on the #7 train) lies **Flushing**, most notable for its status as New York's second Chinatown. In actuality, Flushing is home to immigrants from many Asian countries – too many cuisines to choose from if you're only going to be there for an hour or so. Chinese, Japanese, Korean, Malaysian and Vietnamese restaurants, along with pastry shops and ubiquitous fruit stalls selling a variety of surprises, line Roosevelt Avenue and Main Street – although you may not always be able to read the signs to figure out what's what.

The **historic** side of Flushing is also interesting. The Quaker **Bowne House**, 37-01 Bowne St at Congressman Rosenthal Ave (☎718/359-0528), built in 1661, still stands, though it is currently undergoing a major reconstruction. Although it may be open on weekends starting in 2002, call and make an appointment in order to view seventeenth-, eighteenth- and nineteenth-century artwork and furniture belonging to nine generations of the Bowne family. John Bowne helped Flushing acquire the tag "birthplace of religious freedom in America" by resisting official discrimination at a time when anyone who wasn't a Calvinist was persecuted by the Dutch. You'll run into Bowne Street walking east on Roosevelt; just make a left, and the house will be a few blocks up, between 37th and 38th avenues. More information about Queens history (and a map for a do-it-yourself walking tour of the historic sites) can be had at the **Queens Historical Society** (Mon–Fri 9.30am–5pm; free; ☎718/939-0647) at the Kingsland Homestead across the way – a historic house in its own right, shifted here from its original site about a mile away and reputedly the first house in Flushing to release its slaves. The houses are worth visiting if you're out here for ethnic eats – *Kum Gang San*, a Korean restaurant on 138-28 Northern Blvd at Union Street is recommended – but it might not be worth a special trip. And while you're in an Asian mood, East Flushing has some great Buddhist temples, such as the modern **Nichiren Shoshu Temple**, 42-32 Parsons Blvd at Ash, and the ornate **Won Buddhist Temple**, 43-02 Burling St and Cherry.

Forest Hills, Rego Park and Kew Gardens

South of Flushing Meadows, the stretch of Queens Boulevard through **Rego Park**, **Forest Hills** and **Kew Gardens** is a comfortable, residential area that's more than sixty percent Jewish – manifest in the abundance of synagogues and Jewish centers. The Rego Park stretch isn't much of a draw, and you may as well take the #E or #F straight to 71st Street – Continental Avenue in the heart of Forest Hills. Incidentally, the name "Rego" comes from the "Real Good Construction Company" – the outfit responsible for much of the original development here.

Forest Hills was for a long time one of the choicest Queens neighborhoods. The West Side Tennis Club once hosted the US Open and still holds important matches. The priciest part of Forest Hills is still largely unchanged: **Forest Hills Gardens**, a mock Tudor village interesting not for what it is but for what it might have been, since it was built originally as housing for the urban poor until the rich grabbed it for themselves. Walk through to see for yourself and, if you do, wind your way to *Eddie's Sweet Shop,* a longstanding soda shop and confectionery on the corner of Metropolitan and 72nd avenues, for one of the best ice cream sundaes you'll find anywhere.

Further east on Queens Boulevard (at the Union Turnpike stop on the #E or #F) is another planned neighborhood, **Kew Gardens**, which extends south from Queens Boulevard and skirts the edge of Forest Park. It has a pleasant English feel (it was named after the London suburb), but is altogether an unspectacular wilderness. Around 1900, Kew Gardens was a watering hole popular with aging New Yorkers, complete with hotels, lakes and a whole tourist infrastructure. That's all gone now, but Kew Gardens remains, in a leafy and dignified kind of way, one of Queens' most visually enticing districts. The Q10 bus to JFK Airport gives you a nice view if you don't actually wish to visit.

Jamaica Bay and the Rockaways

JFK Airport is on the edge of the wild, island-dotted marshlands of 9,155-acre **Jamaica Bay Wildlife Refuge**, named for the Jameco Indians whose territory this was. Near Broad Channel on the largest of these islands (take the A train to Broad Channel and walk a half-mile; the Q53 bus from Rockaway or Jackson Heights also stops there), you can hike the trails and observe the diverse habitats of more than 325 varieties of migrating **birds**, including several endangered species – a serious birder's dream. A unit of the Gateway National Recreation Area, this is one of the most important urban wildlife areas in the United States. However, the birds pose a danger for the people on the planes. A crew patrols the tarmacs with falcons to help keep away the birds so they do not get in the way of planes. This is the only US commercial airport using live falcons as a deterrent. For information on the refuge, call ⓣ718/318-4340 or, to find out about the federally administered **Gateway National Recreation Area**, call ⓣ718/388-3799.

Partly enclosing the bay, the narrowing spit of the Rockaways stretches for ten miles back toward Brooklyn – most of it strollable along the boardwalk. The action really centers around Beach 116th Street (a subway stop serviced by the A or the Rockaway Shuttle, depending on the time of day), where the boardwalk bustles and the surfers gather. The only place to surf in New York City proper is popular with expat Californians.

At the western end of the spit, **Jacob Riis Park**, also part of the Gateway NRA, has a quieter beach, much less built up, mostly because the subway doesn't go there (take the Q22 bus from Beach 116th or the Q35 from Flatbush in Brooklyn). Named for the crusading journalist who battled for better housing and recreation facilities, it features architecture reminiscent of less accessible beaches created by Robert Moses, including a stately brick bathhouse and an outdoor clock that have been New York City landmarks since the 1930s. Each summer, the country's only all-women lifeguard tournament is held here, a popular athletic event (call Gateway for dates, or ⓣ718/318-4300 for specific info). In the eastern corner of the beach, nude bathing is tolerated (if not officially allowed); the area is frequented by predominantly gay male devotees of nudism.

26 The Bronx

The city's northernmost borough, **The Bronx**, has long fought a (one-time admittedly deserved) reputation as a tough crime-ridden district; indeed, there was no other part of the city about which people were so ready to roll out their most gruesome horror stories. Nowadays its poorer reaches still suffer from urban deprivation, but much of the borough has undergone a successful civic and economic transformation (parts were in any case always prime residential territory), even in the notorious **South Bronx** –

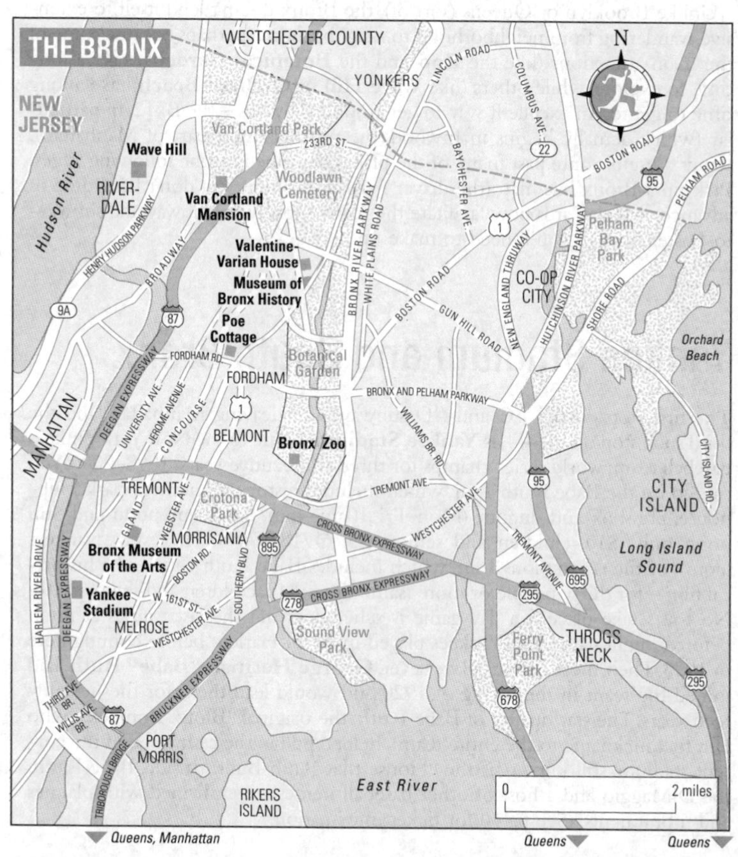

where landlords once burned their own buildings to collect insurance money. There were always plenty of attractions, beautiful parks and vistas in the Bronx, including a world-class botanical garden and zoo, but thanks to community efforts, the outlook these days is better than ever. Find out more from the **Bronx Tourism Council**, 198 E 161st St (Ⓣ718/590-3518), also good for a visitor's pass, which will get you some discounts on your wanderings.

The Bronx is New York's only mainland borough; as might be expected it has more in common geographically with Westchester County to the north than it does with the islands of New York City: steep hills, deep valleys and rocky outcroppings to the west, and marshy flatlands along Long Island Sound to the east. Economically, the Bronx developed – and declined – more quickly than any other part of the city. First settled in the seventeenth century by a Swedish landowner named Jonas Bronck, like Brooklyn and Queens it only became part of the city proper at the turn of the nineteenth century – in two stages, with the area west of the Bronx River being annexed in 1874, and the area to its east in 1895. From 1900 onward things moved fast, and the Bronx became one of the most sought-after parts of the city in which to live, its main thoroughfare, the **Grand Concourse**, becoming edged with increasingly luxurious Art Deco apartment buildings. This avenue runs the length of the borough; many places of interest lie on it or reasonably close by.

Unlike Brooklyn or Queens (sort of), the Bronx doesn't lend itself to extensive wandering from neighborhood to neighborhood, perhaps because some of the main attractions (like the **Zoo** and the **Botanical Gardens**) take a long time to explore, while others (like **Wave Hill** or **Orchard Beach**) take a long time to get to. An excellent way to get around is by bus – the Bx12, in particular (which actually begins in Inwood, the northernmost part of Manhattan), winds a useful route past many of the places described on the following pages. Pick up a Bronx bus map (the driver may have one if you don't have time in advance). MetroCards now facilitate the many subway-to-subway and subway-to-bus exchanges you'll need to make up here.

Yankee Stadium and South Bronx

The first stop on the #C and #D subways after leaving Manhattan, and the third such stop on the #4, is **Yankee Stadium**, home to the New York Yankees baseball team, world series champs for three consecutive years, 1998–2000. You can go on the Babe Ruth Tour, which includes history, monument park, clubhouse, pressbox and dugout (Mon–Fri 10am–4pm, Sat 10am–noon and Sun noon only; $10, children and seniors $5; Ⓣ718/579-4531, Ⓦwww.yankees.com), or the Champions Tour, which includes Babe Ruth Tour and a historical film – for thirty people or more (same times; $15, children and seniors $10). No tours take place if a day game is scheduled, and the last tour is at noon before a night game. The Yankees played in north Harlem before coming here in 1923. Their most famous player ever, **George Herman "Babe" Ruth**, had joined the team in the spring of 1920 and would lead them for the next fifteen years. The star quality of Babe Ruth, the original "Bronx Bomber" (who lent that nickname to the entire team), helped pull in the cash to build the current stadium, still known as the "House that Ruth Built." Inside, Babe Ruth, Joe DiMaggio and a host of other baseball heroes are enshrined with plaques and monuments. (See p.440 for ticket information.)

A trip on the elevated #4 train up to Yankee Stadium affords a good view of the South Bronx if you have no time to explore on foot. The **Grand Concourse**, in its lower reaches, is appealing, and quite safe during the day. On the Concourse is the ever-busy **Bronx County Court House**, at 161st Street and, farther along at 1040 Grand Concourse and E 165th Street, the greenhouse-like **Bronx Museum of the Arts** (Wed noon–9pm, Thurs–Sun noon–6pm; suggested donation $3, students and seniors $2, children under 12 free, Wed free; ⓣ718/681-6000). Housed in a converted synagogue, this small collection of twentieth-century American art holds a few Romare Beardens, works by local artists, and graffiti art, which was more or less born here.

If you get off at the first stop on the #4 train out of Manhattan at 138th Street–Grand Concourse, you're near **Port Morris**, an industrial part of town whose small outpost of antique shops is a good example of the South Bronx's resurgence. Local antique dealers, like Tigris & Euphrates, 79 Alexander St, no doubt hope that restaurants are soon to follow; for now, the *Schlitz Inn* at 767 E 137th St and Willow Ave is a 1950s-era best bet for German pub food and Schlitz beer (open weekdays only). Poke around this industrial zone a bit if you have the chance: colorful sunken row houses (built before the street grade level was raised) are on 137th and 136th streets, and the dark, satanic-looking hulk of the **Philips Knitting Mills** is on 136th Street and Bruckner Blvd (closer to the #6 train stop at 3rd Ave–138th St).

In the Sixties, the **South Bronx** earned its negative connotations from the rapidly declining areas south of Fordham Road. This was the first part of the borough to become urbanized, then scarred in the 1960s until fairly recently by huge squares of rubble, leveled apartments sprawling between gaunt-eyed tenements and groups of aimless teenagers. Steps for renewal were begun later through various city and federal government programs, though local heroes like Catholic Father Louis Gigante of Longwood and his South East Bronx Community Organization (SEBCO) had been trying to improve housing since the late 1960s. Indigenous art forms, meanwhile, developed with the times: early explosions of graffiti, rap and break dancing occurred in the South Bronx during the 1970s.

Once the most famous slum in the country, the infamous **Charlotte Street** (east of Crotona Park and north of Morrisania, now called Charlotte Gardens) is the symbolic ground zero of a revitalization effort now over twenty years in the works. Presidents Carter and Reagan visited the desolate site of wholesale demolition in 1977 and 1980, respectively, and in 1978 Deputy Mayor Herman Badillo, a former Bronx Borough president, began actively seeking to redevelop the South Bronx. By the late 1990s the entire area had become known as the "Bronx Miracle," and by the time President Clinton visited Charlotte Street in 1997, it had been transformed into the pleasantly, if eerily, suburban Charlotte Gardens. Elsewhere in the South Bronx, abandoned buildings have been renovated into co-operative apartments; backed by federal funds, private investments and a myriad of involved community groups, retailers long missing in this area – basic ones such as food and drug chains – have moved in. That said, it's still best to exercise caution in the somewhat downtrodden areas.

Central Bronx

Fordham Road, which runs west-east at the level of 183rd to 190th streets, can be said to divide the South and North Bronx. Get off the #B, #D or #4 train at the junction of Fordham Road and the Grand Concourse, and you will find yourself between two main **shopping districts**. East Fordham and West Fordham roads are the focus of Saturday afternoon shopping, with Fordham Road boasting every fast-food franchise imaginable, and hundreds of families and street vendors vying for space on the crowded sidewalk. If you take East Fordham Road downhill (or get on the Bx12 bus, which will do it for you) you'll arrive at the Fordham University Campus: continue east, and Arthur Avenue will branch off to your right. Arthur Avenue is the main thoroughfare of **Belmont**, a mixture of tenements and clapboard houses that is home to one of the largest segments of New York's Italian community – and the most authentically provisioned. It's a small area, bordered to the east by the zoo and the west by Third Avenue, with the intersection of Arthur Avenue and 187th Street forming its axis. Although there has been a small influx of other ethnic groups – most notably Haitians, Mexicans and Albanian Yugoslavs (who love Italian food) – the staunch Italian community is still the dominant force.

Few tourists come here: a shame, because where real Italian flavor is concerned, Belmont makes Little Italy look like Disneyland. There's no better part of the Bronx if you want to eat, particularly if you're on your way to the zoo. Choose restaurants on Arthur Avenue with care: swanky *Mario's* at no. 2342 (supposedly where the scene in *The Godfather* in which Al Pacino shot the double-crossing policeman was filmed) is popular but pricey. Other local-recommended, moderately priced spots include *Pasquale Rigoletto* and *Emilia's* restaurants at nos. 2311 and 2331, respectively.

The Bronx Zoo

Follow 187th east to the edge of the **Bronx Zoo/Wildlife Conservation Park** (Mon–Fri 10am–5pm, Sat & Sun 10am–5.30pm; $9, seniors and kids $5, free Wed, parking $7, rides and some exhibits are an additional charge; ⓣ718/367-1010, ⓦwww.wcs.org), accessible either by its main gate on Fordham Road or by a second entrance on Bronx Park South. (The latter is the entrance to use if you come directly here by subway – the East Tremont Ave stop on the #2 or #5.)

The zoo is probably the only reason many New Yorkers from outside the borough ever visit the Bronx. Opened in 1899 and surrounding a cluster of original buildings, this is arguably America's greatest zoo, its largest urban one, and one of the first to realize that animals both looked and felt better out in the open – something that's been artfully achieved through a variety of simulated natural habitats. Visit in summer to appreciate it at its best; in winter, a surprising number of animals are kept in indoor enclosures without viewing areas.

One of the most interesting parts is the **Wild Asia** exhibit, an almost forty-acre wilderness through which tigers, elephants and deer roam relatively freely, viewable either by walking or (May–Oct only; $2) from an elevated monorail train. Look in also on the **World of Darkness** (a re-creation of night, holding nocturnal species) and a simulation of a Himalayan mountain area, with endangered species like the red panda and snow leopard. In the children's section, kids climb spider webs and wriggle through prairie dog tunnels. As a park, the zoo functions particularly well, too, making for nice strolling.

New York Botanical Garden

Across the road from the zoo's main entrance is the back turnstile of the **New York Botanical Garden** (Tues–Sun 10am–6pm; $3, seniors and students $2, kids under 12 $1, free to all on Wed, parking $5; ⓣ718/817-8700, ⓦwww.nybg.org). Incorporated in 1891, the garden, in its southernmost reaches, is as wild as anything you're likely to see upstate. Its scientific facilities include a museum, library, herbarium and a research laboratory. Further north, near the main entrance, are more cultivated stretches. The Enid A. Haupt Conservatory, a landmark, turn-of-the-nineteenth-century crystal palace, showcases jungle and desert ecosystems, a palm court and a fern forest, among other seasonal displays ($5, students and seniors $4, kids $2). The Everett Children's Adventure Garden contains eight acres of plant and science exhibits for children ($3, $2, $1). In addition, there are tram tours and plant sales, and other gardens enormous enough to wander around happily for hours.

The Poe Cottage and the Museum of Bronx History

Leave the garden by the main entrance and walk west on Fordham Road to East Kingsbridge Road, where you will take a right (or simply take the #D or #4 train to Kingsbridge Road) – and you'll come eventually to the **Edgar Allan Poe Cottage**, Grand Concourse and E Kingsbridge Rd (Sat 10am–4pm, Sun 1–5pm, otherwise by appointment only; $2; ⓣ718/881-8900) built in 1812 and now in Poe Park. This tiny, white-clapboard anachronism in the midst of a now-working-class Hispanic neighborhood was Edgar Allan Poe's rural home for the last three years of his life, from 1846 to 1849, though it was moved here only recently when threatened with demolition. Never a particularly stable character and dogged by financial problems, Poe was rarely happy in the cottage, but he did manage to write the short, touching poem *Annabel Lee* and other famous works, including *The Bells*. The cottage was finally purchased by the City of New York in 1913 and made into a museum in 1917. A film about Poe and a small gallery of 1840s artwork and photographs are on view.

A bit north of here is the Valentine-Varian House, an eighteenth-century Georgian stone farmhouse that now houses the **Museum of Bronx History**, 3266 Bainbridge Ave (#D train to 205th St–Bainbridge Ave, or #4 to Kingsbridge Rd; Sat 10am–4pm, Sun 1–5pm; $2; ⓣ718/881-8900). The museum is more notable for its historic building than for its exhibitions of Bronx-related artifacts from the pre-Colonial era to the Depression. Yet, considering how much the Bronx has changed – there was still plenty of farm country left in the 1940s – the old photographs and lithographs can be fascinating.

North Bronx

The **North Bronx** is the topmost fringe of the city; anyone who makes it up here wants to see the luminary-filled **Woodlawn Cemetery**. Accessible from Jerome Avenue at Bainbridge (last stop, Woodlawn, on the #4), this is a prime example of how New Yorkers in the 1850s took in the air: before the age of public parks, they went to visit the dead (and the idea of city parks grew out of the popularity of such excursions). For many years, Woodlawn has been a celebrity cemetery and, like Green-Wood in Brooklyn (see p.247), boasts a number of tombs and mausoleums that are memorable mainly for their garishness. It's a huge place, but some monuments do stand out: one Oliver Hazard Belmont, financier and horse dealer, lies in a dripping Gothic fantasy near the entrance, modeled on the resting place of Leonardo da Vinci in Amboise, France. F.W. Woolworth has himself an Egyptian palace guarded by sphinxes. Jay Gould, not a popular businessman when alive, takes it easy in a Greek-style temple. Pick up a guide from the office at the entrance to locate the many larger-than-life individuals buried here: they include Herman Melville, Irving Berlin, George M. Cohan, Fiorello LaGuardia, Robert Moses, Miles Davis and Duke Ellington.

Van Cortlandt Park

West of the cemetery lies **Van Cortlandt Park**, a forested and hilly all-purpose recreation space, used in fall and spring by high school cross-country track teams. Apart from the pleasure of hiking through its woods, the best thing here is the **Van Cortlandt House Museum**, nestled in its southwest corner not far from the subway station. This is the Bronx's oldest building, an authentically restored Georgian structure built in 1748. During the Revolution it changed hands a number of times, and was used as an operations headquarters by both the British and the Patriots. On the hills above, New York City's archives were buried for safekeeping during the Revolution, and it was in this house that George Washington slept before heading his victory march into Manhattan in 1783 (Tues–Fri 10am–3pm, Sat & Sun 11am–4pm; $2, seniors and students $1.50, kids free; ⓣ718/543-3344).

Riverdale and Wave Hill

Immediately west rise the moneyed heights of **Riverdale** – one of the most desirable neighborhoods in the city, and so far from the South Bronx in feel and income it might as well be on the moon. This part of the Bronx (and it is part of the Bronx, though some residents and real-estate agents would prefer to forget that) is difficult to get to without a car; Metro-North to Riverdale or the #1 or #9 to West 242nd Street are the closest rail options, and even the buses cover little of the residential streets. If you do make the trip, you'll be rewarded with suburban escape and – when you can get through the trees – spectacular views.

Well worth a visit is **Wave Hill**, 249th St at Independence Ave (Apr 15–Oct 14 Tues–Sun 9am–5.30pm; Oct 15–Apr 14 Tues–Sun 9am–4.30pm; $4, $2 seniors and students, Nov 15–Mar 14 free; ⓣ718/549-3200, ⓦwww.wavehill.org), a small country estate overlooking the Hudson River and the towering Palisades on its western bank. In 1960, Wave Hill was donated to the city; in previous years, it was briefly home to Mark Twain and, later, Teddy Roosevelt. This is the only house open for view that millionaires built in this area during the late nineteenth century. The delightful grounds boast gorgeous botanical gardens, and the mansion is now a forum for temporary art installations, concerts and workshops.

City Island

On the east side of the Bronx, **City Island**, a 230-acre island that is, historically, a fishing community, juts out into Long Island Sound. While much of the fishing has gone, the atmosphere remains, despite the proximity of the urban

Bronx. A short causeway takes the Bx29 bus – pick it up at the Pelham Bay Park subway stop on the #6 – to and from the mainland. With all the historic house moving that goes on these days, it's easy to believe that City Island was imported from Maine or Massachusetts by some nautically minded philanthropist. Yet the truth is, that in 1761 a group planned a port to rival New York's, but when that plan went nowhere, locals started fishing and building boats.

Most people come here for the **restaurants** – in fact, on a weekend night, it's nearly impossible for the bus to get down the traffic-clogged City Island Avenue, and the restaurants overflow with "off islanders." You're better off making the trip on a weekday; not only will the "clamdiggers" (as those born on the island call themselves) be friendlier, but you'll stand a better chance of getting something fresh when you order your dinner. Try the *Lobster House*, 691 Bridge St, or *JP Waterside Restaurant*, 703 Minneford Ave, for seafood and outdoor seating.

Aside from the restaurants, City Island is interesting primarily for its New England-style houses and its small-town feel. You can easily walk the length of it, and though walking back and forth can be tiring, both the main drag and the back roads deserve a look. On **City Island Avenue**, small **shops** are the rule of the day – stop in at Mooncurser Antiques to see one of the largest collections of **vinyl records** assembled anywhere. In recent years, an **arts community** has begun to thrive here too, led by CIAO Gallery and Arts Center, 278 City Island Ave (☎718/885-9316), where you can pick up a brochure listing other spaces to view and buy arts and handicrafts; as well, there's an annual arts and crafts fair here during the last weekend of May. Heading back toward the causeway, turn right on Fordham Street and then left on King Street. The bigger houses on City Island have remained on King and Minneford streets; to make yourself really envious, look back behind the houses at the private piers and beaches.

Also consider a stop at the **North Wind Undersea Institute**, 610 City Island Ave (Mon–Fri 1–5pm, Sat & Sun noon–5pm; $3, students and seniors $2; ☎718/885-0701), a quaint museum co-founded by Woodstock concert legend Richie Havens. Housed in a renovated Victorian mansion and an attached 100-year-old tugboat, its exhibits pay particular attention to the institute's role in the rehabilitation and rescue of threatened and stranded marine life. Prowl around to see the collection of old diving gear, whaling artifacts and bones dating back to 1502 and a superb collection of scrimshaw (whalebone etched with intricate designs), which many consider to be the first true American folk art form.

Pelham Bay Park and Orchard Beach

From City Island, it's an easy walk to **Orchard Beach**, the easternmost part of the expansive **Pelham Bay Park** – just make a right after the causeway, and take the scenic park path. These days, Orchard is known locally as the "Spanish Riviera," and beach and boardwalk pulse constantly with a salsa beat. **Free concerts** in summer are common, and even if nothing is going on, wander long enough and you're bound to hear impromptu jam sessions (complete with dancing).

At the northern end of the boardwalk, a sign for the **Kazimiroff Nature Trail** takes you into a wildlife preserve that's also part of Pelham Bay Park. It's named after Theodore Kazimiroff, the noted naturalist who helped stop these wetlands from being turned into a landfill. The trail winds through meadow, shrubland, forest and marsh, and is serene and peaceful – a stark contrast with much of the rest of the park, now crisscrossed by highways that take away from its original charm. Without a car, unfortunately, exploring the further reaches of Pelham Bay Park is difficult.

The **Bartow-Pell Mansion Museum and Gardens** (Wed, Sat & Sun noon–4pm; $2, students and seniors $1, kids free; ☎718/885-1461) is a national landmark worth seeing for its beautifully furnished interior and magnificent formal gardens that overlook Long Island Sound, but to get there you must go back to the Pelham Bay Park subway #6 station and take bus Bx45 (no service Sunday).

Staten Island

Like all of New York City, **Staten Island**, the common name for what's officially Richmond County, was settled by the Dutch in the seventeenth century. The name derives from States General, Holland's governing body. Until about 40 years ago, Staten Island was still predominantly isolated. Getting to it meant a ferry trip or long ride through New Jersey (to which it's physically closer). Staten Islanders enjoyed an insular, self-contained rural life in the state's least populous borough – and still do for the most part. The stretch of water to Manhattan marks a cultural as much as physical divide.

In 1964 the **Verrazano Narrows Bridge**, connecting Staten Island with Brooklyn, changed things; land-hungry Brooklynites found cheap property on the island and swarmed over the bridge to buy their parcel of suburbia. Today Staten Island has swollen into tightly packed residential neighborhoods, forming endless backwaters of tidy, look-but-don't-touch homes. The roughly triangular island is 13.9 miles long and 7.5 miles wide – 2.5 times the size of Manhattan. The major topography of the island includes marshlands, hardwood forests and beaches on the South Shore, and the island is still the most verdant borough. It's no wonder that in 1843 Henry David Thoreau, who lived on Staten Island for six months as a private tutor, wrote, "The whole island is like a garden."

If New Yorkers from other boroughs know anything about Staten Island – and it's not guaranteed that they would – it's probably limited to garbage and secession movements. Though recycling efforts have significantly reduced the amount of garbage the city produces, more than 75,000 tons a week were dumped in Staten Island's Fresh Kills Landfill, incorporated in 1947 on 2100 acres of the western shore of the island. The **world's largest landfill** – though at the time of publication scheduled to be closed, and replaced gradually by parkland – holds 2400 million cubic feet of refuse (that's 25 times the size of the Great Pyramid at Giza), and it's a claim to fame that residents strongly resent, especially in light of citywide political reforms that have left Staten Island vulnerable to decisions made by the votes in the more populous boroughs. Partially due to this size discrepancy, over the years there's been much talk of Staten Island seceding from the city. A 1996 referendum had 65 percent of Staten Islanders voting to secede, but that vote has since stalled in the state assembly.

It's no wonder that nine out of ten tourists take the **Staten Island ferry** for the views it provides of Manhattan, then promptly return to the big city. Hard to berate anyone for that, but should you decide to stay, your efforts in seeing the somewhat far-flung attractions will be rewarded.

The Staten Island Ferry and around

The **Staten Island ferry** sails from the southern tip of Manhattan Island (at the Battery) around the clock, with departures every 15-20 minutes during rush hours (between 7–9am and 5–7pm), every 30 minutes midday and evenings, and every 60 minutes late at night – weekends less frequently. It is truly New York's best bargain: since 1997, an absolutely free ride with wide-angled views of the city and the Statue of Liberty becoming more spectacular as you retreat. (For more information about the Staten Island ferry: ⓣ718/727-2508, ⓦwww.siferry.com). By the time you arrive on Staten Island, the Manhattan skyline stands mirage-like, often filtered through haze: the romantic, heroic city of a thousand and one posters.

Although the Staten Island terminal lacks the grandeur of the Battery terminal, it is conveniently attached to the Staten Island Railway and the bus station, which offer the transportation you need to get anywhere on the island. (MetroCards will provide a free transfer if you took the subway to the ferry.) Because Staten Island can be tricky to get around, arm yourself with a map, and – if you can find one – a *Staten Island Sites and Scenes* brochure (available free in the ferry terminals), and you're on your way.

Around the terminal: Lighthouse Museum and St George

Several long blocks east of the ferry along the North Shore Esplanade (enter at the junction of Richmond Terrace and Bay Street), some old buildings are being reconstructed as a **National Lighthouse Center and Museum**, including the original US Lighthouse Service Depot. The first exhibits open in July 2002; until then, tours of the existing site are available (Wed & Sat 11am–3pm & Sun 1–3pm, reservations required; suggested donation $2; ⓣ718/556-1681, ⓦwww.lighthousemuseum.org).

The surrounding town of **St George**, on the hill above the ferry terminal, is a strange, underutilized place despite its obvious potential. The landmarked historic district includes portions of St Marks Place, Carroll Place, Westervelt Avenue, Hamilton Avenue, the Phelps Place dead end and short stretches of Richmond Terrace. The wonderful residential buildings include examples of shingle, Queen Anne, Greek Revival and Italianate styles – a large number designed by Staten Island architect Edward Alfred Sargent (1842–1914).

Snug Harbor Cultural Center

In contrast, the **Snug Harbor Cultural Center**, 1000 Richmond Terrace (ⓣ718/448-2500, ⓦwww.snug-harbor.org), in nearby New Brighton (take the S40 bus from the ferry terminal or walk from St George), thrives with signs of cultural growth. This arts center's 28 buildings are spread out over a campus that once served as a retirement home for sailors. The galleries and studios for up-and-coming artists, the annual outdoor Summer Sculpture Festival and events and concerts year-round (including summer performances by the Metropolitan Opera and New York Philharmonic – good music in outdoor surroundings more intimate than anywhere in Manhattan) draw visitors from all over the borough and beyond. The lively Harmony Street Fair is held annually on the second Sunday in June. In the same park area, the **Staten Island Children's Museum** (Sept–June noon–5pm; July–Aug 11am–5pm; $4, free under 2; ⓣ718/273-2060) offers permanent exhibits like "Adventures in Three Dimensions" and "Bugs and Other Insects." Snug Harbor also has the borough's only public garden, the **Staten Island Botanical Garden** (Tues–Sun 10am–5pm; $5, children $4; ⓣ718/723-8200, ⓦwww.sibg.org). This 86-acre sanctuary, built in 1977, includes a White Garden, Butterfly Garden and Herb Garden. The center's grounds are open all the time, free to the public; free tours are given on weekend afternoons.

The Alice Austen House

If you pack a picnic lunch for Staten Island, or pick up a sandwich along the way, plan to enjoy it on the grounds of the **Alice Austen House**, 2 Hylan Blvd (Thurs–Sun noon–5pm; suggested donation $3; ⓣ718/816-4506). Easily reachable by the S51 bus from the ferry dock to Hylan Boulevard (walk down the hill), or on the Staten Island Railroad (SIR) to Clifton Station (walk south on Edgewater Street), this Victorian cottage faces the waters of the Narrows, and from the front lawn one can understand why Alice Austen's grandparents called their house Clear Comfort – today the spectacular view takes in the Verrazano Bridge as well as the Brooklyn shore.

But the attraction of this place is actually the story of Alice Austen herself, a pioneering photographer whose work comprises one of the finest records of c1900 American life. At a time when photography was both difficult and expensive, she developed her talent and passion for the art expertly. Her tragedy is that she never considered the possibility of going professional, even when the stock market crash of 1929 lost her the family home and left her in the poorhouse, and her work was rediscovered only shortly before her death in 1952. The house exhibits a relatively small selection of her photographs (the whole collection is owned by the Staten Island Historical Society), but they're fascinating to look at, and as more of the rooms are restored and refurnished, the museum can only improve.

Along the coast and inland

Stretching below the Verrazano Narrows, along the eastern part of the island, are several public beaches, starting with **South Beach**, a once-thriving resort for New York's wealthy, and continuing down to **Great Kills Park** (take the Great Kills stop on the SIR), a place surfed by locals. Few visitors come to New York for its beaches, and those who do most likely head to the Rockaways in Queens – for good reason – but these aren't bad if you're looking for less crowded and more casual alternatives. At South Beach, reachable by the S51 bus from the ferry dock, a two-and-a-half-mile boardwalk – the fourth longest in the world – provides a great place to jog or rollerblade; otherwise, just hit its fairly quiet sands for sunning. Great pizza can be had at *Good Fellas Brick Oven Pizza*, on 1718 Hylan Blvd – a good mile and a half walk inland from the beach, or just nearby the SIR Dongan Hills stop.

The Jacques Marchais Museum of Tibetan Art

In the middle of Staten Island's residential heartland, the **Jacques Marchais Museum of Tibetan Art**, 338 Lighthouse Ave (Apr–Nov Wed–Sun 1–5pm; Dec–Mar Wed–Fri 1–5pm; $5, seniors and students $3, kids $2; ⓣ718/987-3500, ⓦwww.tibetanmuseum.com), is an unlikely find. The bus drivers might not know it's there, so ask to be let off at Lighthouse Avenue. Hike about a mile up the steep hill until you hit it on your right, or take the SIR to the Grant City stop and walk right one block along South Railroad Avenue to Grant City Cars for car service to the museum (for around $4.50 one way). Jacques Marchais was the alias of Jacqueline Klauber, a New York art dealer who reckoned she'd get on better with a French name in the 1920s and 1930s. She did, and used her own comfortable income and that of her husband to indulge her passion for Tibetan art. Eventually she assembled the largest collection in the Western world, and reproduced a *gompah*, or Buddhist temple, on the hillside in which to house it in 1947. Even if you know nothing about such things the exhibition is small enough to be accessible, with magnificent bronze *Bodhisattvas*, fearsome deities in union with each other, musical instruments, costumes, and decorations from the mysterious world of Tibet. Best time to visit is on a Sunday, when lectures focus on different aspects of Asian culture around the world, and in early October when the Tibetan festival takes place: Tibetan monks in maroon robes perform traditional ceremonies, and Tibetan food and crafts are sold. Phone ahead for the exact date.

While you're on this hill, stroll past two other places of interest, neither of which is open to the public. The **Staten Island Lighthouse** on Ediboro Road can be seen from Lighthouse Avenue, though it's a strange thing to see so far inland. The lighthouse has been in pretty much constant use since it first guided ships into New York Harbor in 1912. Around the corner, at **48 Manor Court**, the private home known as Crimson Beech was designed by Frank Lloyd Wright – the only Wright residence within the city limits.

Historic Richmond Town

Back on the main Richmond Road, a short walk or the S54 bus from the Great Kills stop brings you to **Historic Richmond Town** (July–Aug Wed–Fri 10am–5pm, Sat & Sun 1–5pm; Sept–June Wed–Sun 1–5pm; $4, students, seniors and under-18s $2.50; ⓣ718/351-1611), home to the Staten Island Historical Society and a charming "reinvention" of the seventeenth-to-nineteenth-century village of Richmond. The restoration includes about thirty historic houses original to the town, some transplanted from their original sites. Richmond was the nexus of old Staten Island and the frontier outpost-like crossroads of the route from Manhattan to New Jersey. Starting from the Historical Museum, half-hourly tours negotiate such gems as the 1695 Dutch-style Voorlezer's House, the nation's oldest existing school building; a picture-book general store whose contents span the nineteenth and twentieth centuries; and the atmospheric Guyon-Lake-Tysen House of 1740. Costumed volunteer craftspeople use traditional techniques to make wooden water buckets, bake bread and weld tin; all are enthusiastic experts on their activities and the houses and shops in which they "work." It's all carried off to picturesque and ungimmicky effect, and by the end of your visit you're likely to want to work there yourself – or at least come back for one of their special events. The rustic setting makes it difficult to believe you're just twelve miles from downtown Manhattan.

Conference House

At the far southern tip of the island is the **Conference House**, 7455 Hylan Blvd (SIR to Tottenville exit; Mar–Dec Wed–Sun 1–4pm; $2, $1 seniors and under-12s; ⓣ718/984-6046), a stately seventeenth-century stone structure whose claim to fame is acting as host to failed peace talks, led by Ben Franklin and John Adams, during the American Revolution. It certainly feels like it hasn't seen much action since, other than perhaps the manicuring of its rolling lawns, which offer a lovely beachfront view of Perth Amboy, New Jersey. Today, the house is open for tours; step inside for a peek at the period furnishings and its original kitchen, now restored to working order.

listings

listings

28

Accommodation

Accommodation in New York definitely eats up the lion's share of a traveler's budget. Many **hotels** in the city charge somewhere in the neighborhood of $150–200 a night, not to mention the **taxes** tacked on to that, and some go well beyond that price. With some planning, it is possible to get a decent-sized clean room for $150 or less, but in truth it's far easier to hunt splurges than bargains. Bearing that in mind, make your **reservations** as far ahead as possible; most hotels cite "supply and demand" as the main influence on their room rate. On the other hand, you may luck out by calling the day before, but don't even think of doing this during high season: at certain times of the year – Christmas and summer particularly – you're likely to find everything (and we mean this) chock full. If you're looking for lodging in a particular area, refer to the Accommodation map, pp.282–283, for help.

You can book a room in a hotel yourself, by phoning direct to the hotel or by going through a **travel agent** – which can sometimes work out cheaper (see "Getting there" in Basics for addresses). Using the corporate "800" numbers will usually, but not always, net you a higher rate. Bear in mind, too, the possibilities of all-included flight and hotel package vacations, again detailed under "Getting there." Booking services – see box, p.287 – reserve rooms at discount prices and usually for no extra charge. Also, you might try booking through hotel websites, or travel websites listed on p.11, for the occasional special deal.

For the young and sociable there are plenty of **hostels** with dormitory accommodation. Other budget options include private rooms in a **YMCA/YWCA**, which run to around $50 for a double, or a **bed and breakfast**, which basically means staying in somebody's spare room, but with all the amenities of a private apartment. These rooms go for $75 and up for a double and can be booked through any agency listed in the appropriate section below.

Hostels and YMCAs

Hostels and **YMCAs** are just about the only option for cash-strapped backpackers in New York, with dorm beds going for as little as $25 a night. Most hostels are fine as long as you don't mind sleeping in a bunk bed and sharing a room with strangers (if you're traveling in a group of four or six you could often get a room to yourselves), though they do vary in quality. YMCAs are better if you want privacy because they have private single and double rooms, though they tend to have a more institutional feel than the more relaxed hostels. Note that hostels are especially busy – and fairly rowdy – in August and September when the legions of camp counselors descend on the city. For a

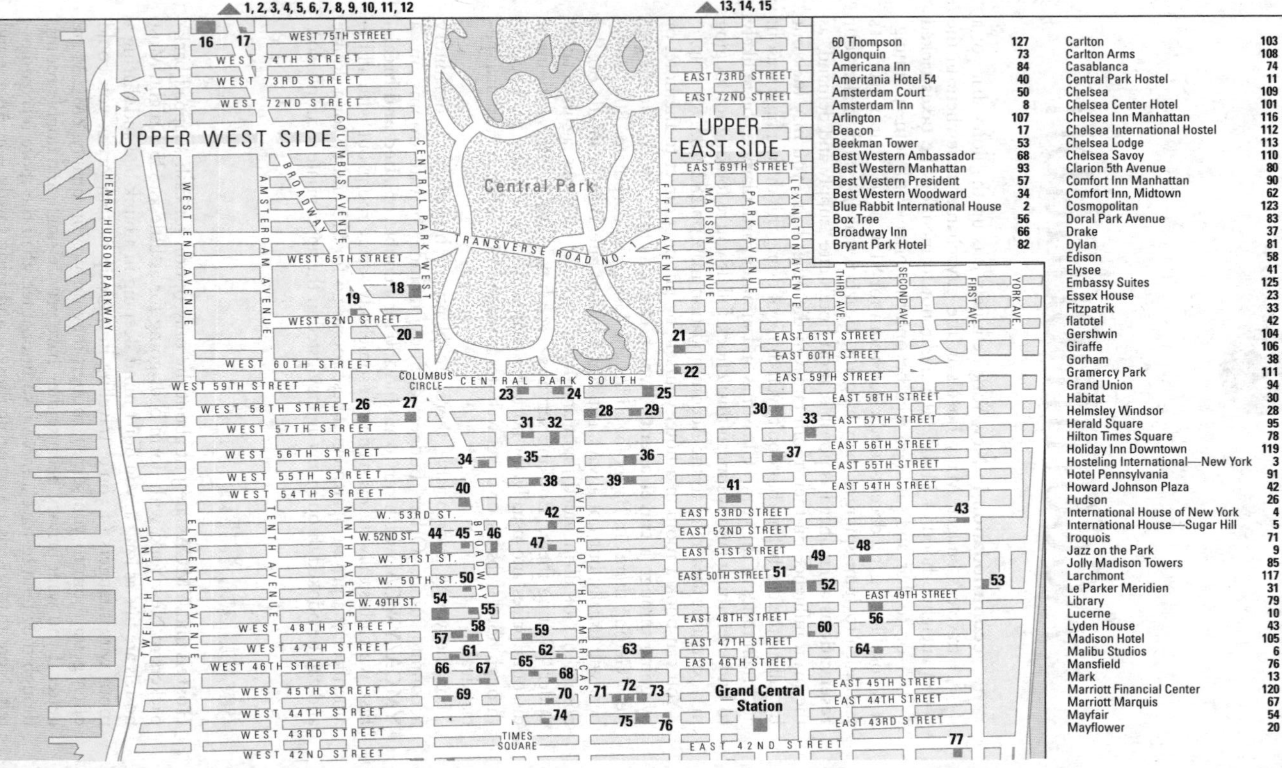

Hotel	No.
60 Thompson	127
Algonquin	73
Americana Inn	84
Ameritania Hotel 54	40
Amsterdam Court	50
Amsterdam Inn	8
Arlington	107
Beacon	17
Beekman Tower	53
Best Western Ambassador	68
Best Western Manhattan	93
Best Western President	57
Best Western Woodward	34
Blue Rabbit International House	2
Box Tree	56
Broadway Inn	66
Bryant Park Hotel	82
Carlton	103
Carlton Arms	108
Casablanca	74
Central Park Hostel	11
Chelsea	109
Chelsea Center Hotel	101
Chelsea Inn Manhattan	116
Chelsea International Hostel	112
Chelsea Lodge	113
Chelsea Savoy	110
Clarion 5th Avenue	80
Comfort Inn Manhattan	90
Comfort Inn, Midtown	62
Cosmopolitan	123
Doral Park Avenue	83
Drake	37
Dylan	81
Edison	58
Elysee	41
Embassy Suites	125
Essex House	23
Fitzpatrik	33
flatotel	42
Gershwin	104
Giraffe	106
Gorham	38
Gramercy Park	111
Grand Union	94
Habitat	30
Helmsley Windsor	28
Herald Square	95
Hilton Times Square	78
Holiday Inn Downtown	119
Hosteling International—New York	3
Hotel Pennsylvania	91
Howard Johnson Plaza	42
Hudson	26
International House of New York	4
International House—Sugar Hill	5
Iroquois	71
Jazz on the Park	9
Jolly Madison Towers	85
Larchmont	117
Le Parker Meridien	31
Library	79
Lucerne	10
Lyden House	43
Madison Hotel	105
Malibu Studios	6
Mansfield	76
Mark	13
Marriott Financial Center	120
Marriott Marquis	67
Mayfair	54
Mayflower	20

MANHATTAN HOTELS & HOSTELS
Hudson River
0 500 yds
N
THEATER DISTRICT
MURRAY HILL
CHELSEA
GREENWICH VILLAGE
Port Authority Bus Terminal
Penn Station
GREELEY SQUARE
Madison Square Park
Union Square Park
TWELFTH AVENUE
ELEVENTH AVENUE
TENTH AVENUE
NINTH AVENUE
EIGHTH AVENUE
SEVENTH AVENUE
AVENUE OF THE AMERICAS
FIFTH AVENUE
PARK AVENUE
LEXINGTON AVENUE
THIRD AVENUE
SECOND AVENUE
FIRST AVENUE
BROADWAY
IRVING PLACE
FOURTH AVENUE
WEST STREET
WEST 41ST STREET
WEST 40TH STREET
WEST 39TH STREET
WEST 38TH STREET
WEST 37TH STREET
WEST 36TH STREET
WEST 35TH STREET
WEST 34TH STREET
WEST 33RD STREET
W. 30TH ST.
W. 29TH ST.
W. 28TH ST.
W. 27TH ST.
WEST 26TH STREET
WEST 25TH STREET
WEST 24TH STREET
WEST 23RD STREET
WEST 22ND STREET
WEST 21ST STREET
WEST 20TH STREET
WEST 19TH STREET
WEST 18TH STREET
WEST 17TH STREET
WEST 16TH STREET
WEST 15TH STREET
WEST 14TH STREET
WEST 13TH STREET
WEST 12TH STREET
WEST 11TH STREET
WEST 10TH STREET
WEST 9TH STREET
WEST 8TH STREET
EAST 41ST STREET
EAST 40TH STREET
EAST 39TH STREET
EAST 38TH STREET
EAST 37TH STREET
EAST 36TH STREET
EAST 35TH STREET
EAST 34TH STREET
EAST 33RD STREET
EAST 32ND STREET
EAST 26TH STREET
EAST 25TH STREET
EAST 24TH STREET
EAST 23RD STREET
EAST 22ND STREET
EAST 21ST STREET
EAST 20TH STREET
EAST 19TH STREET
EAST 18TH STREET
E. 17TH ST.
EAST 15TH STREET
EAST 14TH STREET
EAST 13TH STREET
EAST 12TH STREET
E. 11TH STREET
E. 10TH STREET
EAST 9TH STREET
ST. MARK'S PLACE
EAST 7TH STREET
GREENWICH AVENUE
GANSEVOORT ST.
HORATIO ST.
JANE ST.
W. 12TH ST.
WASHINGTON ST.
GREENWICH STREET
HUDSON STREET
BETHUNE ST.
78
79
80
81
82
83
84
85
86
87
88
89
90
91
92
93
94
95
96
97
98
99
100
101
102
103
104
105
106
107
108
109
110
111
112
113
114
115
116
117
118
120, 121, 122, 123, 124, 125, 126, 127
119
Mercer 124
Metro 88
Michelangelo 47
Milburn 16
Milford Plaza 69
Millennium Broadway 70
Morgans 86
Murray Hill Inn 100
Muse 65
Novotel 45
Off SoHo Suites 121
On the Ave 1
Paramount 61
Park Savoy 24
Pickwick Arms 48
Pierre 21
Plaza 25
Portland Square 59
Quality Hotel on Broadway 12
Quality Midtown 63
Radisson Empire 19
Riverside Tower 7
Roger Smith 60
Roger Williams 96
Roosevelt 72
Royalton 75
Salisbury 32
San Carlos 52
Seventeen 115
Shelburne Murray Hill 87
Sheraton Manhattan 46
Sherry Netherland 22
Shoreham 36
Soho Grand 122
Southgate Tower 97
Stanford 92
Thirty One 99
Thirty Thirty 102
The Time 55
Tribeca Grand 126
UN Crowne Plaza 77
Uptown Hostel 14
Vanderbilt YMCA 64
W 49
W Union Square 114
Waldorf Astoria 51
Wales 15
Warwick 39
Washington Square 118
Webster Apartments 89
Wellington 35
Westpark 27
Westside YMCA 18
Wolcott 98
Wyndham 29

comprehensive listing of hostels in New York and across North America, obtain *The Hostel Handbook* for $4 plus shipping by phoning ⓣ212/926-7030 or emailing ⓔinfohostel@aol.com. Or, you can visit the Internet Guide to Hosteling at ⓦwww.hostelhandbook.com. The following is a small selection of the best hostels and Ys.

Blue Rabbit International House 730 St Nicholas Ave (at 146th Street), NY 10031 ⓣ1-800/6-HOSTEL or 212/491-3892, ⓔbluerabbit@hostelhandbook.com. Opened by the owners of *International House – Sugar Hill*, four doors away (see below), this Harlem hostel chargesthe same price ($25) for dorms. With a limited number of double rooms, available only on a first-come, first-served basis, for $30 per person per night (plus $10 deposit), maybe the cheapest doubles in the city. Check-in between 9am and 10pm. Has kitchens, and bed linen is included in the price.

Central Park Hostel 19 W 103rd St (near Central Park West), NY 10025 ⓣ212/678-0491, ⓕ678-0453, ⓔinfo@CentralParkHostel.com. New Upper West Side hostel has dorm beds for 4, 6 or 8 people ($26–36), and some private two-bed rooms in a five-story renovated walk-up. All rooms share clean bathrooms, and lockers are available (bring a padlock). Sheets and blankets included, payment in cash or travelers' checks only; you must have a foreign passport or international student ID.

Chelsea Center Hostel 313 W 29th St (near 8th Ave), NY 10001 ⓣ212/643-0214, ⓕ473-3945, ⓦwww.chelseacenterhostel.com. Reputable, clean, safe and friendly, the *Chelsea Center Hostel* has beds for $30 with breakfast and clean sheets and blankets included. The privately run hostel has no sign outside, which adds to its security, and it's well situated for Midtown West, Chelsea and the West Village (the hostel also has a second location in the East Village if that's where you want to be). Book well in advance in high season (as it sleeps a total of only twenty) and facilities include a safe for valuables and summer barbecues in the garden courtyard. Office hours are 8.30am to 11pm, there's no curfew, and most importantly, cash only.

Chelsea International Hostel 251 W 20th St, NY 10011 ⓣ212/647-0010, ⓕ727-7289, ⓦwww.chelseahostel.com. Situated in the heart of Chelsea, between 7th and 8th aves, this is the closest hostel to downtown and, with a police precinct across the street, one would assume it's also pretty safe. Beds (130 in all) are $27 a night, including tax, and the rooms, which sleep four or six, are small with bathrooms in the hall (though larger rooms for six at the back of the hostel have bathrooms). Private rooms for two are $65 a night. There are communal areas, free lockers, a laundry room, a backyard, and free pizza parties once a week. Accommodation is rudimentary, as befits the price, but the location is the hostel's main attraction. Desk open 8am–9pm, and there are security guards and sign-in at night. Passport required.

Gershwin Hotel 7 E 27th St, NY 10016 ⓣ212/545-8000, ⓕ684-5546. A fun hostel/hotel in the Flatiron district, just off Fifth Avenue, and handy for just about any part of town. Beds in dorms (which sleep four to twelve) are $35 a night including tax, and private full beds are $59. The catch is they accept only a limited number of reservations – mostly it's a first-come, first-served basis. Imaginatively decorated with a Pop Art theme that spills out onto the sidewalk, and geared toward young travelers. There's an astroturfed rooftop terrace (for their summer weekend parties), a small bar, a well-priced restaurant and friendly staff. Expect only the barest necessities in sleeping arrangements, but there's so much going on here you'll probably want to be awake.

Hosteling International – New York 891 Amsterdam Ave (at 103rd St), NY 10025 ⓣ212/932-2300, ⓕ932-1600. This historic Upper West Side building has 480 dormitory-style beds for $29–35 for IYHA members (on-the-spot membership is $25 for US citizens or $18 for those with a foreign address); $3 extra for nonmembers per night. Facilities include a library, kitchen, lounge, coffee bar and a large patio. Though the place is large, it may be heavily booked; reserve at least 24 hours in advance (at least a week in the summer). Open 24 hours.

International House of New York **500 Riverside Drive (at 122nd St), NY 10027 ⓣ212/316-8400.** This graduate student residence hall near Columbia University also functions as a hostel for travelers, though the cheapest rooms, with shared bathrooms, are available only to nonstudents during Christmas and summer, and cost $45 a night, or $35 if you stay fifteen days or more. Singles with private bathroom are available year-round for $100-115, doubles and triples slightly more.

International House – Sugar Hill **722 St Nicholas Ave (at 145th St), NY 10031 ⓣ212/926-7030, ⓔsugarhill@hostelhandbook.com.** Friendly, well-run dorm hostel in a safe, middle-class neighborhood on the border of Harlem and Washington Heights. $25 per night, tax included, no curfew, no chores and no lockout during the day. Hostel sleeps about 25 with six people per dorm. Check-in between 9am and 10pm. Book in advance for Aug and Sept. Also a limited number of double rooms, available only on a first-come, first-served basis, for $30 per person per night. Take the A or D train to 145th St – the hostel is just above the subway station.

Jazz on the Park **36 W 106th St (at Central Park W), NY 10025 ⓣ212/932-1600, ⓕ932-1700, ⓦwww.jazzhostel.com.** This groovy bunkhouse, just a stone's throw from the park, boasts a TV-gameroom, rooftop barbecues, the *Java Joint Café*, plus activities galore. The rooms, sleeping between two and fourteen, are clean, bright and air-conditioned. Beds cost between $30 and $35 a night (including tax, linen and a light breakfast); a two-bed room is $88. Reservations essential June–Oct and over Christmas and New Year's (when rates are a little higher).

Uptown Hostel **239 Lenox Ave (at 122nd St), NY 10027 ⓣ212/666-0559, ⓕ663-5000.** Small hostel just north of Central Park, well situated for the clubs, restaurants and shopping in Harlem. Clean bunk beds for four to six people a night at $22 per person. Decent-size hall bathrooms, communal kitchen and pleasant common area. Summer lockout from 11am–4pm. Very helpful staff.

Vanderbilt YMCA **224 E 47th St (between 2nd and 3rd aves), NY 10017 ⓣ212/756-9600.** Smaller and quieter than most of the hostels above, and neatly placed in midtown Manhattan, just five minutes' walk from Grand Central Station. Inexpensive restaurant, swimming pool, gym and laundromat. Singles start at $70, doubles at $85. All rooms are air-conditioned; handicapped access and nonsmoking rooms available.

Westside YMCA **5 W 63rd St, NY 10023 ⓣ212/875-4173 or 875-4273, ⓕ875-1334.** A wonderfully situated Y next to Central Park and Lincoln Center with single rooms for $70/$110 per night (with or without bath), doubles for $80/$120, and free use of two pools, saunas, gym and sports facilities. All rooms air-conditioned. Early booking advisable.

Bed and breakfast

Choosing a **bed and breakfast** can be a good way of staying right in the center of Manhattan at a reasonably affordable price. But don't expect to socialize with your temporary landlord/lady – chances are you'll have a self-contained room and hardly see them – and don't go looking for B&Bs on the streets. All rooms – except for a few which we've found off the beaten track (listed below) – are let out via the following official agencies and they all recommend making your reservations as far in advance as possible, especially for the cheapest rooms. In cases where landlords/ladies prefer that visitors reserve in advance rather than show up on their doorsteps, we have omitted addresses.

B&B agencies

Affordable New York City **21 E 10th St, NY 10003 ⓣ212/533-4001, ⓕ387-8732, ⓦwww.affordablenewyorkcity.com.** Established network of 120 properties (B&Bs and apartments) around the city, with detailed descriptions. B&B accommodations from $85 (shared bath) and $100 (private), unhosted studios $140–175 and one-bedrooms $175–225. Cash or travelers' checks only; three-night minimum. Very customer-oriented and personable.

Bed and Breakfast Network of New York 130 Barrow St, NY 10014 ⓣ1-800/900-8134 or 212/645-8134, Mon–Fri 8am–6pm. Growing network with hosted singles for $80–100, doubles $110–150; prices for unhosted accommodation run from $130 to luxury multibedded apartments for $400. Weekly and monthly rates also available. For an assured booking write at least a month in advance; make short-notice reservations by phone.

City Lights Bed & Breakfast PO Box 20355, Cherokee Station NY 10021 ⓣ212/737-7049, ⓕ535-2755, ⓔreservations@citylightsbandb.com. More than 400 carefully screened B&Bs (and short-term apartment rentals) on its books, with many of the hosts involved in theater and the arts. Hosted singles run $90–125, doubles $95–135. Unhosted accommodation costs $135 to $300 per night depending on whether it's a studio or four-bedroom apartment. Minimum stay two nights, with some exceptions. Reserve well in advance. In business 16 years, City Lights is consistently reliable and helpful.

CitySonnet.com Village Station, PO Box 347, NY 10014 ⓣ212/614-3034, ⓕ425/920-2384, ⓦwww.CitySonnet.com. Small, personalized B&B/short-term apartment agency with accommodations all over the city, but specializing in downtown and the West Village. Singles start at $80; doubles $100–155; unhosted flats start at $140.

Colby International 139 Round Hey, Liverpool L28 1RG, England ⓣ0151/220 5848, ⓦwww.colbyintl.com. If you want guaranteed B&B accommodation, Colby International is without doubt your best bet – and they can fix up accommodation from the UK. Excellent-value double rooms start at $95 a night, singles are $80 (not in private room), and apartments range from $125–300, depending on size and location: book as far ahead as possible in high season, though it's worth trying for last-minute reservations.

Gamut Realty Group 301 E 78th St, ground floor, NY 10021 ⓣ212/879-4229 or 1-800/437-8353, ⓕ517-5356, ⓔGamut@GamutNYC.com, ⓦwww.GamutNYC.com. Fully automated agency that can fax or email sample listings of available rooms and apartments for nightly or longer-term stays. Unhosted studio apartments for $120–150, and one-bedroom apartments for $165 and up. Some apartments possible for $95. Has accommodation all over Manhattan, some in luxury buildings or artists' lofts.

New World Bed & Breakfast Suite 837, 150 5th Ave, NY 10011 ⓣ212/675-5600, outside city 1-800/443-3800, ⓕ675-6366. Hosted singles ($90) and doubles ($100). Larger apartments are available from $130 up; call for a brochure.

B&B properties

Angelique Bed & Breakfast 405 Union St, Brooklyn NY 11231 ⓣ718/852-8406, ⓔsspoerri@ezaccess.net. A four-room Victorian brownstone in historic Carroll Gardens. Singles $75, doubles $125 (two-night minimum).

Baisley House ⓣ718/935-1959. Another charming Victorian brownstone, this one dating from 1865. Singles $95, doubles $125–150, all with shared bath. There is a two-night minimum.

Bed & Breakfast on the Park ⓣ718/499-6115, ⓕ718/499-1385, ⓦwww.bbnyc.com. A handsome 1892 Park Slope limestone townhouse with views over Prospect Park, with eight double rooms ranging $125–300 a night (two-night minimum).

Chelsea Brownstone ⓣ212/206-9237, ⓕ388-9954. Conveniently situated on a safe, quiet street in Chelsea, this well-maintained, family-run brownstone contains a number of private, self-contained apartments (recently upgraded) starting at $130 for studios and $150 for one-bedrooms, per night (with good discounts for stays of more than a week), each with its own TV, phone, bathroom and fully equipped kitchen. One has its own patio, and one has access to a back garden. Best to book well in advance by phone, though last-minute bookings are possible.

Foy House ⓣ718/636-1492. Small, beautiful 1894 brownstone (with only three guest rooms) in the heart of Park Slope's Historic District. Rooms range from $120 to $150. In business since 1984. Smoking not permitted. Close to subways.

Inn at Irving Place 56 Irving Place, NY 10003 ⓣ1-800/685-1447 or 533-4600, ⓕ533-4611, ⓦwww.innatirving.com. It costs $295–500 a night for one of the twenty rooms – each named after a famous architect, designer or actor – in this handsome pair of 1834 brownstones, which must rank as one of the most exclusive guesthouses in the city. Frequented by celebrities, the Inn offers five-course high teas, along with free access to a local gym. A very special place for a very special occasion.

New York Bed and Breakfast 134 W 119th St (at Lenox Ave), NY 10026 ⓣ212/666-0559, ⓕ663-5000. This lovely old brownstone just north of Central Park in the heart of Harlem features nice double rooms for $65 a night for two people. The owner also runs the *Uptown Hostel* a few blocks up the road (see p.285).

Hotels

Most of New York's hotels are in midtown Manhattan, which is fine if you want to be close to theaters and the main tourist sights (and large clusters of tourists), but it's hardly the makings of a stressless, restful vacation. There are a growing number of downtown options, mainly of the fancy kind, with a few affordable ones mixed in. The Upper West or Upper East sides should do if your taste runs more to Central Park and the high culture of museums and Lincoln Center's offerings. The selections below cover the gamut from the cheapest to New York's most luxurious and/or hippest, the latter a small and select group of "special" places for which you may want to empty your wallet. Finally, it's worth mentioning the latest fad in hotel design and marketing – the so-called "boutique" hotel. These are typically smaller establishments (100 or fewer rooms), where your dollars buy less square footage in floor space but gain the added benefits of heightened style, comfort and ambience that more than compensate.

Hotels are listed alphabetically within each neighborhood group below. For a visual overview of where to find a listed hotel, see the Accommodation map on pp.282–3.

Taxes and other hidden costs

Taxes are added to your hotel bill, and hotels will nearly always quote you the price of a room before tax. The good news is that New York City and State hotel taxes have dropped considerably in the past few years. Taxes will add 13.25 percent to your bill (state tax 8.25 percent, city tax 5 percent), andthere is also a $2 per night "occupancy tax." This will add about $15 to a $100 room. The price codes at the end of each of the following listings represent the price of the hotel's cheapest double room inclusive of all taxes.

Hotel booking services

Accommodations Express ⓣ609/391-2100 or 1-800/444-7666, ⓕ609/525-0111, ⓦwww.accommodationsexpress.com
CRS ⓣ407/740-6442 or 1-800/950-0232, ⓕ407/740-8222, ⓦwww.reservation-services.com
Express Reservations (weekdays only) ⓣ1-800/356-1123 or 303/440-8481, ⓕ303/440-0166, ⓦwww.expressreservations.com
Hotel Reservations Network ⓣ1-800/964-6835, ⓦwww.hoteldiscount.com
Meegan's Services ⓣ1-800/441-1115 or 718/995-9292, ⓕ718/995-4439
The Room Exchange 450 7th Ave, NY 10123 ⓣ1-800/846-7000 or 212/760-1000, ⓕ760-1013

Hotel price codes

The code in the following listings refers to the price of a hotel's cheapest double room and includes all taxes (state tax at 8.25 percent, city tax at 5 percent and occupancy tax of $2). Where there's a significant seasonal variation, the high season rate is usually given. Prices based on a per-person rate are given in dollars. Hotels in each geographical section are listed alphabetically.

❶ under $100	❺ $200–250
❷ $100–130	❻ $250–300
❸ $130–160	❼ $300–350
❹ $160–200	❽ over $350

Most hotels do not offer free breakfast, though continental breakfasts are becoming increasingly popular. If you have to pay for breakfast, you'll get better value at a nearby diner. At the more upmarket hotels, tipping is expected: unless you firmly refuse, a bellhop will grab your bags when you check in and expect $5 to carry them to your room. The cleaning staff will really appreciate your tip when you leave (figure $2 minimum per day for cheaper hotels, $5 a day for the nicer establishments). The luxuriously stocked minibars, with booze and chocolate goodies at astronomical prices, are formulated to appeal to your sense of laziness and/or unshakeable case of the munchies; these and the hotel shops that sell basic necessities at three times the street price should generally be avoided. Also, it's worth checking on the hotel's phone charge policy: some will charge excessively for any call, even if you use toll-free numbers or your own calling card, so beware.

Discounts and special deals

The best advice is simply to ask – discounts may also be available in the form of promotional specials or corporate rates. Off-season summer rates are always competitive; in 2001, summer yielded some of the best rates in years, as the city-wide occupancy rate declined 7.6 percent in the first quarter from the previous year, a result of a slower economy and a boom in hotel rooms. If you stay long enough, you may also be able to pay a special weekly rate, maybe getting one night in seven for free. Some hotels also lay on special weekend discounts (especially downtown choices, as they tend to be devoid of their usual business travelers then), or discounts for staying additional nights, though these are often not available during the busiest season from September through December. In truth, there is usually one form of discount or another to help offset the cost.

The internet is also worth a try: Ⓦwww.nycvisit.com has listed specials, especially in brutally hot July and August (which come with a list of restrictions, and require that you pay with an American Express card). Furthermore, several consolidator-type sites are available (try Ⓦwww.hotres.com, Ⓦwww.travelscape.com, or Ⓦwww.hoteldiscounts.com) where you plug in your requirements, and seal the deal by entering your credit card number (you pay these venues directly, instead of the hotels).

With almost any hotel room it's possible to cut costs slightly if you can fill a double with three or even four people. Contrary to some other parts of the world, you're generally charged by the room, not for each person, and management rarely minds, providing an extra bed or two for an extra $20 or so. In some pricier hotels, especially those recently renovated, you may find in-room CD players, VCRs (along with a CD/video library at the front desk), modem connections, a health club and business center, so even if you are paying top dollar, you may be saving money or time otherwise. For full hotel listings and prices, consult the New York Convention and Visitors Bureau leaflet, *Hotels in New York City*, available from one of their offices.

Downtown: Below 14th Street

60 Thompson **60 Thompson St (between Spring and Broome sts), NY 10012 ⓣ212/431-0400, ⓕ431-0200, ⓦwww.60thompson.com.** With excellent proximity to SoHo's chic restaurants and vibrant galleries, the handsome *60 Thompson* offers 100 modern guestrooms and suites with full-leather or suede wall panels. It further indulges visitors with a rooftop garden, in-house DVD library, linens by Frette and even personal stationery. Upstairs rooms look out over SoHo's rooftops. ❽.

Cosmopolitan **95 W Broadway, NY 10007 ⓣ1-888/895-9400 or 212/566-1900, ⓕ566-6909, ⓦwww.cosmohotel.com.** Great TriBeCa location, with smart, well-maintained rooms at a steal of a price. Excellent value. ❸.

Embassy Suites **102 North End Ave, NY 10281 ⓣ1-800/EMBASSY or 212/945-0100, ⓕ945-3012, ⓦwww.embassynewyork.com.** Quiet location near Battery Park City esplanade means you're a little out of the loop, despite the 16-screen theater next door. But it also means a great value if your stay includes a weekend – the roomy bedroom and living area have tons of amenities, passes get you in to the New York Sports Club, and a cook-to-order breakfast is included (unheard of in these parts). Brand new, with a super staff. ❼, with weekend rates at ❺.

Holiday Inn Downtown **138 Lafayette St (at corner of Howard St), NY 10013 ⓣ212/966-8898 or 1-800/HOLIDAY, ⓕ966-3933.** Just north of busy Canal St where Chinatown spills over into Little Italy, this idiosyncratic member of the well-known chain is also a stone's throw from SoHo and TriBeCa, where hotels are few and far between. Though the rooms are small for the highish price, the rates fluctuate according to availability so booking early should get you a better deal. ❹.

Larchmont **27 W 11th St (between 5th and 6th aves), NY 10011 ⓣ212/989-9333, ⓕ989-9496.** Budget hotel in the heart of the West Village, on a beautiful tree-lined street, just off Fifth Avenue. Hotels are a rarity in this residential area, so this is a real find. Rooms are small but nicely decorated and clean, and all have TV, air conditioners, phones and washbasins. Small kitchens and bathrooms with showers are on each corridor. Prices include continental breakfast. Very small singles as low as ❶; doubles at ❷.

Marriott Financial Center **85 West St (between Carlisle and Albany sts), NY 10006 ⓣ212/385-4900.** On summer weekends, doubles at ❺ make this civilized business hotel with superb views of the Hudson and New York Harbor fairly affordable. Weekdays are a different story, but the high rates (❽) are well worth it. Service is excellent.

The Mercer **147 Mercer (at Prince St), NY 10012 ⓣ1-888/918-6060 or 212/966-6060, ⓕ965-3838.** The last word in discreet "boutique" chic. Rooms are stylish with simple furnishings, high ceilings, walk-in closets and over-sized bathrooms. The occasional celebrity will share your sofa in the smart lobby, and trendy *Mercer Kitchen* provides your room service 24 hours. All this in the heart of SoHo. ❽.

Off SoHo Suites **11 Rivington St (between Christie St and Bowery), NY 10002 ⓣ1-800/OFF-SOHO or 212/979-9808, ⓕ979-9801, ⓦwww.offsoho.com.** These small, apartment-style suites are well situated for Little Italy, East Village, SoHo and Chinatown, but are in a somewhat depressed Lower East Side neighborhood. Very good value for two or four, the suites include fully equipped kitchen, TV, and use of laundry and fitness room. Suite for two with a shared bathroom ❷; suites for four with private bath ❺.

Soho Grand Hotel **310 W Broadway (at Grand St), NY 10013 ⓣ1-800/965-3000 or 212/965-3000, ⓕ965-3200, ⓦwww.sohogrand.com.** Great location at the edge of SoHo, and many guests exude the attitude that comes with the territory: rock stars, models, actors and the like. Still, the staff is surprisingly helpful, the rooms are stylishly appointed, if a bit small, with classic New York photographs from a local gallery and an optional goldfish (ask and you shall receive). The hotel also boasts an elegant bar, restaurant and fitness center. ❽.

Tribeca Grand Hotel **2 Ave of the Americas (between White and Walker sts), NY 10013 ⓣ1-877/519-6600 or 212/519-6600, ⓕ965-3244, ⓦwww.tribecagrand.com.** Unlabeled, and hidden by a brick facade like a brand new

Rooms with a view

Amazing vistas can be had (for a price) at these hotels:
Essex House, 160 Central Park S (between 6th and 7th aves); see p.295.
Hilton Times Square, 234 W 42 St (between 7th and 8th aves); see p.295.
Marriott Marquis, 1535 Broadway at 45th St; see p.296.

train station, the *Tribeca Grand* is close to *Soho Grand* in location and spirit. Once inside, the *Church Lounge*, one of the more striking hotel public spaces, beckons with a warm orange glow. The rooms are stylish yet on the understated side, though each bathroom boasts a phone and built-in TV. The black-clad staff are extra attentive, and decidedly gorgeous. Off-season weekends can be as low as ❺ ; for most weekdays, count on rates in the ❽ bracket.

Washington Square **103 Waverly Place, NY 10011 ⓣ212/777-9515 or 1-800/222-0418, ⓕ979-8373.** An ideal location: bang in the heart of the West Village, just off Washington Square Park, and a stone's throw from the NYU campus. The rooms are more than adequate and some have views over the park. Continental breakfast and use of the exercise room are included in the price. Book two months in advance for the summer. ❹ .

Chelsea and the West Side: W 14th to 36th streets

Arlington Hotel **18 W 25th St (between 6th Ave and Broadway), NY 10010 ⓣ212/645-3990, ⓕ633-8952.** Chinese-run hotel with very good prices and clean rooms near Madison Square Park and equidistant from downtown and midtown. ❸ , with two-room suites for four at ❹ .

Best Western Manhattan **17 W 32nd St (between 5th Ave and Broadway), NY 10001 ⓣ1-800/567-7720 or ⓣ212/736-1600, ⓕ563-4007.** Recently refurbished hotel, whose tranquil black, white and lilac Art Deco lobby offers a welcome respite from this rather hectic part of town. Doubles at ❸ , with suites starting at ❹ .

Chelsea Hotel **222 W 23rd St (between 7th and 8th aves), NY 10011 ⓣ212/243-3700, ⓕ675-5531, ⓦwww.hotelchelsea.com.** One of New York's most noted landmarks, both for its aging neo-Gothic building and, more importantly, its long list of alumni, from Dylan Thomas to Bob Dylan (see p.119 for a fuller cast). It's still something of a haunt of musicians and art-school types, though these days it's as much an apartment building as a hotel with a majority of guests being semi-permanent. If you check into the *Chelsea* you may find yourself staying in somebody's apartment, surrounded by their belongings. Ask instead for a renovated room with polished wood floors, log-burning fireplaces, and plenty of space to cram a few extra friends into. ❹ for a double room, ❼ for a suite.

Chelsea Inn **46 W 17th St, NY 10011 ⓣ212/645-8989, ⓕ645-1903.** A long-term hostel as well as hotel in the heart of Chelsea, not too far from the West Village. It's low on services and a bit rough around the edges, but with a choice of guestrooms (with or without bathroom), studios and suites, most equipped with kitchenettes, it can be a good deal. Studio with bathroom ❹ .

Chelsea Lodge **318 W 20th St, NY 10011 ⓣ212/243-4499, ⓕ243-7852.** When you step through the (unmarked) door, this new gem in a converted boarding house greets you with cheery Early American/Sportsman decor (globes, wooden ducks and a stuffed swordfish hover near the ceiling), and simple comfortable Americana is the theme throughout. The plaid-papered "lodge" rooms (with sink and shower – the shared toilet is down the hall) are a little small for two, but the few deluxe rooms (❹) are a great value and have new full bathrooms. There's also a choice of four one-room suites (❺) that can sleep four (there's a pull-out bed) and have a kitchenette (and two have access to a small patio/garden). You must give a credit card number to guarantee your reservation, and a three-day cancellation policy applies. Note: lodge quarters don't have in-room phones.

Chelsea Savoy Hotel **204 W 23rd St, NY 10011 ⓣ212/929-9353, ⓕ741-6309.** A few doors away from the *Chelsea Hotel*, the *Savoy* has none of its neighbor's funky charm but its rooms, though small, are clean and nicely decorated and the staff is helpful. Try to avoid rooms facing the main drags outside. ❸.

Comfort Inn Manhattan 42 W 35th St, NY 10001 ⓣ212/947-0200. The best thing about the *Comfort Inn* is the free deluxe continental breakfast and free newspapers in the elegant lobby each morning. It's a solid, good-value place to stay but the management can be unhelpful – you may not be able to see a room before you hand over your cash, for example. ❺.

Herald Square 19 W 31st St (between 5th Ave and Broadway), NY 10001 ⓣ1-800/727-1888 or 212/279-4017, ⓕ643-9208, ⓦwww.heraldsquarehotel.com. The original home of *Life* magazine, *Herald Square* still features Philip Martiny's golden sculptured cherub *Winged Life* over the doorway of this Beaux-Arts building. Inside it's meticulously clean, but without much in the way of extras, and somewhat soulless. ❸; triples and quads ❹. Very small single rooms go for as low as $76 a night with shared bathroom.

Hotel Pennsylvania 401 7th Ave, NY 10001 ⓣ1-800/223-8585 or 736-5000, ⓕ502-8712. Boasting the same telephone number since 1917 (the "Pennsylvania six five thousand" of the Glenn Miller song), this is across from Madison Square Garden, and offers every possible convenience in its 1705 rooms, though you can't help thinking it looked better "back in the day." ❹, dropping to ❸ in summer.

Southgate Tower 371 7th Ave (at 31st St), NY 10001 ⓣ1-800/ME SUITE or 212/563-1800, ⓕ465-3697. A member of the excellent Manhattan East Suites chain, *Southgate Tower* is opposite Penn Station and Madison Square Garden. All double rooms are suites with kitchens. ❻.

Stanford,43 W 32nd St (between Broadway and 5th Ave), NY 10001 ⓣ1-800/365-1114 or 212/563-1500, ⓕ629-0043. Clean, inexpensive hotel on the block known as "Little Korea." Rooms are a tad small, but attractive and very quiet, and the hallways are well-lit, if a little narrow. The *Stanford* offers free continental breakfast and valet laundry, a cocktail lounge and good Korean cuisine (in the very relaxing surroundings of the *Gam Mee Ok* restaurant), and the efficient and friendly staff would be welcome in hotels twice this price. ❹.

Wolcott 4 W 31st St (between 5th Ave and Broadway), NY 10001 ⓣ212/268-2900. A surprisingly relaxing budget hotel, with a gilded, ornate Louis XVI-style lobby full of mirrors and lion reliefs (even the ceiling is lavish). The rooms, while much more staid, are more than adequate, all with (somewhat old-fashioned) bathrooms. ❸.

Union Square to Murray Hill: E 14th to 42nd streets

Carlton 22 E 29th St (at Madison Ave), NY 10016 ⓣ1-800/542-1502 or 212/532-4100, ⓕ889-8683, ⓦwww.carltonhotelny.com. A fairly well-priced, nicely modernized hotel in a Beaux-Arts building. Two pluses: you're in the safe residential area of Murray Hill, and you get room and valet service, not often associated with hotels in this price bracket. ❻; with summer rates ❹.

Carlton Arms 160 E 25th St (between 3rd and Lexington aves), NY 10010 ⓣ212/679-0680. One of the city's latest Bohemian hangouts, with eclectic interior decor by would-be artists, very few comforts, and a clientele made up of Europeans, down-at-the-heel artists and long-staying guests. People either love it or hate it – so check it out before you commit yourself to staying. Discount rates available for students and foreign travelers, with an extra 10 percent discount if you pay for seven nights in advance. Singles with bath can be as low as $75 plus tax. Reserve well in advance for summer. ❷.

Clarion 5th Avenue 3 E 40th St (between 5th and Madison aves), NY 10016 ⓣ1-800/228-5151 or 212/447-1500. This motel-style hotel, owned by a Canadian chain, has helpful,friendly staff. Rooms are bright and well-furnished; there's a comfortable lounge and restaurant on the premises. ❻; with summer rates from ❹.

Doral Park 70 Park Ave (at 38th St), NY 10016 ⓣ1-800/223-6725 or 212/687-7050, ⓕ808-9029, ⓦwww.doralparkavenue.com. A multimillion-dollar restoration has turned the *Doral Park* into one of the snazziest deluxe hotels, with re-creations of classical friezes and frescoes and original designs for lighting and furnishings. Rooms are in shades of turquoise/green and orange (it's not as bad as it sounds). Service is excellent. ❻; promotional rates ❹.

Dylan **52 E 41st St, NY 10017 ⓣ1-866/55-DYLAN or ⓣ212/338-0500, ⓕ338-0569.** The hardwood floors, warm citrus light and vaguely lemony-tasting air floating through the lobby are indicative of the whole experience – classy and clever. Even the hallways are cool, with room numbers sticking out of the upper walls (unintentionally?) looking like back-lit yellow-and-black pills. The rooms show attention to detail and design, and 11-foot ceilings make the rooms look much larger than usual (those chemists must have been tall). If you have the green, book the Alchemy Suite, a one-of-a-kind Gothic bedchamber with a vaulted ceiling and unusual stained-glass windows. The notable *Virot* restaurant is just downstairs. ❽.

Gershwin Hotel **7 E 27th St, NY 10016 ⓣ212/545-8000, ⓕ684-5546.** A young person's hotel just off Fifth Avenue in the Flatiron district that also functions as a hostel (see p.284). The 110 private double rooms with bathrooms cost about $169 a night (plus tax); weekends are $15 extra. Imaginatively decorated with a Pop Art theme, the *Gershwin* has an astroturfed rooftop (where parties are held on the weekend), a small bar, a well-priced restaurant and a friendly staff. Try to book well in advance. ❹.

Giraffe **365 Park Ave South (at 26th St), NY 10016 ⓣ1-877/296-0009 or 212/685-7700, ⓕ685-7771, ⓦwww.hotelgiraffe.com.** Similar in tone and with similar amenities to sister hotels the *Library* and *Casablanca*, the *Giraffe* borrows its decor from the Moderne period of the 1920s and 1930s. ❻.

Gramercy Park **2 Lexington Ave (at 21st St), NY 10010 ⓣ1-800/221-4083 or 212/475-4320, ⓕ505-0535.** Pleasant enough hotel perfectly situated in a delightful area next to the only private park in the city (residents get a key) and popular with Europeans. It boasts one of the most unsuspecting bar scenes in New York, where a mix of hotel guests, locals and publishing types buzz over stiff drinks. Nonsmoking rooms can be requested, though not guaranteed; there's a mixture of fairly recently redone and tatty rooms. ❹.

Grand Union **34 E 32nd St (between Madison and Park aves), NY 10016 ⓣ212/683-5890, ⓕ689-7397.** Comfortable budget hotel. Well situated and well priced, perfect for those who won't mind its lackluster appearance. With one bed ❷, with two ❸.

Jolly Madison Towers **22 E 38th St (at Madison Ave), NY 10016 ⓣ212/802-0600, ⓕ447-0747.** Italian chain hotel with restful, clean, fairly spacious rooms and the nautical themed *Whaler Bar*. ❺; occasional promotional rates at ❹.

Library **299 Madison Ave (at 41st St), NY 10022 ⓣ1-877/793-READ or 212/983-4500, ⓕ204-5401, ⓦwww.libraryhotel.com.** The *Library* must have the most intriguing concept in New York hoteldom: each floor is devoted to one of the ten major categories of the Dewey Decimal System, and each room's artwork and books reflect a different pursuit within that group. Only those with a serious sense of purpose could design 60 unique rooms and handpick more than 6,000 books for the place, and the dedication shows in other ways, notably in the monstrous black card catalog at the front desk, and the lovely Poet's Garden on the roof (within sight of the "motherland," the New York Public Library). Rooms in shades of brown and cream are average in size but nicely appointed (the stone bathrooms are big, though). Continental breakfast is included, tasty snacks and coffee drinks are given away all the time, and the hotel throws a wine and cheese get-together every weekday. ❼.

Madison Hotel **21 E 27th St (between Madison and 5th aves), NY 10017 ⓣ1-800/9-MADISON or 212/532-7373, ⓕ686-0092, ⓦwww.madison-hotel.com.** Clean, if basic, rooms, all with air conditioning and private bathroom and a free continental breakfast. ❸; winter at ❶.

The Metro **45 W 35th St, NY 10001 ⓣ1-800/356-3870 or 212/947-2500, ⓕ279-1310, ⓦwww.hotelmetronyc.com.** A very stylish hotel – it's Art Deco sensible, with old Hollywood posters on the walls, a delightful rooftop terrace, spacious communal areas, clean rooms and free continental breakfast. A few more extras (like a fitness room, and the highly recommended *Metro Grill* restaurant on the ground floor) than normally expected in this category. ❺; summer specials ❹.

Morgans **237 Madison Ave (between 36th and 37th sts), NY 10016 ⓣ1-800/334-3408 or 212/686-0300, ⓕ779-8352.** Created by the instigators of *Studio 54* (the now-vanished notoriously druggy disco), this is one of the most chic flophouses in town. Discreet furnishings are by André Putnam, and good-looking young staffers clothed in Klein and Armani are welcoming. Although the black-white-gray decor is starting to look too self-consciously 1980s, stars still frequent the place, able as they are to slip in and out unnoticed. And you do get a Jacuzzi, a great stereo system and cable TV in your room. Great bar downstairs. ❼; summer promotional specials at ❺.

Murray Hill Inn 143 E 30th St (between Lexington and 3rd aves), NY 10016 ⓣ1-888/996-6376 or 212/683-6900, ⓕ545-0103, ⓦwww.murrayhillinn.com. It's easy to see why young travelers and backpackers line the Inn's narrow halls. Although the rooms are smallish, they are air-conditioned and all have telephone, cable TV, and sink; some also have private bathrooms. With a friendly staff and a residential locale that offers a breather from the bustle. Rates per room: singles $75, doubles $95 (shared bath), $125 (private), additional costs if more than two in a room. They also have weekly rates for single rooms. ❶.

Roger Williams 131 Madison Ave (at 31st St), NY 10016 ⓣ1-888/448-7788 or 212/448-7000, ⓕ448-7007, ⓦwww.rogerwilliamshotel.com. At some point during its $2 million "boutique" renovation, this hotel made a turn onto Madison and its prices shot up exponentially. Still, Rafael Vinoly's mellow, Scandinavian/Japanese fusion rooms with Aveda bath gels and fluted zinc pillars in the lobby make it well worth the extra bucks. European breakfast, and 24-hour espresso/cappuccino bar. ❻; September through December ❼.

Seventeen 225 E 17th St (between 2nd and 3rd aves), NY 10003 ⓣ212/475-2845, ⓕ677-8178. Budget accommodation as you'd expect it to look: rudimentary bedrooms, and bathrooms on the corridors that have seen better days. But *Seventeen* is clean and friendly, and it can't be beaten either for location – it's on a pleasant, tree-lined street and very handy if you want to spend your time in the East Village, only a few blocks away. Singles ❶, doubles ❷.

Shelburne Murray Hill 303 Lexington Ave (between 37th and 38th), NY 10016 ⓣ1-800/ME-SUITE or 212/689-5200, ⓦwww.mesuite.com. Luxurious Manhattan East Suite hotel, in the most elegant part of Murray Hill. All the rooms have kitchenettes; the *Secret Harbour Bistro* presents, each Wednesday and Thursday, a Maryland crab bash. ❻; promotional rates drop to ❺.

Thirty-One 120 E 31st St (between Lexington and Park aves), NY 10016 ⓣ212/685-3060, ⓕ532-1232. A new hotel in Murray Hill brought to you by the folks who own *Seventeen* (see above). The rooms are clean and the street is quiet and pleasant. ❶ (shared bathroom) or ❸ (private bathroom).

Thirty Thirty 30 E 30th St, NY 10016 ⓣ1-800/804-4480 or 212/689-1900. Small welcoming budget hotel, with a few small but welcome design touches, like the framed black and white scenes of old New York in the rooms. ❸.

W Union Square 201 Park Ave (at Union Square), NY 10003 ⓣ1-877/W-HOTELS or 212/253-9119, ⓕ253-9229. The newest (for now) outpost of David Rockwell's growing hotel empire, with rooms slightly bigger than the *W* in midtown. Located in the former Guardian Life Building, this is really the only upscale hotel in the area, and boasts Todd English's *Olives* restaurant as well as a bar scene that lasts from after work to after hours. The artificial green grass and corkscrewing bamboo in the lobby is just a prelude to the rooms with deep purple accents, which are called "Wonderful," "Spectacular" or "Mega"; all will set you back. ❽.

Expense account hotels

Make sure the bill goes to someone else to enjoy these locations with no worries:

Bryant Park Hotel, 40 W 40th St (between 5th and 6th aves); p.294.

The Mercer, 147 Mercer (at Prince St); p.289.

The Plaza, 768 5th Ave (at Central Park S); p.297

Sherry Netherland, 781 5th Ave(between 59th and 60th sts); p.301.

Soho Grand Hotel, 310 W Broadway (at Grand St); p.289.

Midtown West: W 36th to 60th streets

Algonquin **59 W 44th St (between 5th and 6th aves), NY 10036 ⓣ1-800/555-8000 or 212/840-6800.** New York's classic literary hangout for the past century, as created by Dorothy Parker and her associates (see p.142) and perpetuated by the likes of Noel Coward, George Bernard Shaw and Irving Berlin. The cabaret in the *Oak Room* perpetuates the air of hushed sophistication. Some decor remains little changed, but the rooms, bathrooms and lobby were handsomely refurbished in 1998. From ❺.

Americana Inn **69 W 38th St (between 5th and 6th aves), NY 10018 ⓣ1-888/HOTEL58 or 212/840-6700, ⓕ840-1830.** Fifty fairly basic, renovated, clean rooms (with semi-private baths) a few blocks from both Macy's and the Empire State Building. Associated with a mid-scale hotel group (not an independent), it's a slightly better bet than other budgeters. ❶.

Ameritania Hotel 54 **230 W 54th St (at Broadway), NY 10019 ⓣ1-800/922-0330 or 212/247-5000.** One of the coolest-looking hotels in the city. The well-furnished rooms come with marble bathroom, cable TV and CD player; and there's a bar/restaurant off the high-tech, neo-classical lobby. $5 off their basic rates if you mention *Rough Guides*. ❻, with July and August specials at ❸.

Amsterdam Court Hotel **226 W 50th St (between Broadway and 8th), NY 10019 ⓣ1-800/341-9889 or 212/459-1000, ⓕ265-5070.** Well-positioned and affordable, the *Amsterdam Court* had an overhaul a few years ago, and with it a significant price increase. Still worth a look. ❺.

Best Western Ambassador **132 W 45th St (between 6th Ave and Broadway), NY 10036 ⓣ1-800/242-8935 or 212/921-7600, ⓕ719-0171.** On the edge of the theater district, this newly redecorated hotel is an oasis of calm in a bustling part of town. The spacious suites can easily accommodate four people; decor is in the English Georgian tradition. Continental breakfast is included in the price. ❺, with rates dropping as low as ❷ in January and February.

Best Western President **234 W 48th St (between 8th Ave and Broadway), NY 10036 ⓣ1-800/826-4667 or 212/246-8800, ⓕ974-3922.** A solid, easygoing chain hotel with an Italian restaurant, it offers small tasteful rooms. ❺.

Best Western Woodward **219 W 55th St (at Broadway), NY 10019 ⓣ1-800/336-4110 or 212/247-2000.** This renovated Beaux-Arts building is very handy for visiting the Museum of Modern Art. ❺; in summer and January/February ❷.

Broadway Inn **264 W 46th St, NY 10036 ⓣ1-800/826-6300 or 212/997-9200, ⓕ768-2807, ⓦwww.broadwayinn.com.** Cozy, reasonably priced bed-and-breakfast hotel in the heart of the theater district on the corner of charmless 8th Ave, but a skip away from Times Square and Restaurant Row. All rooms are pleasantly decorated and have private bathrooms. Continental breakfast is included in the price and all guests get a 20 percent discount at the restaurant downstairs. A reportedly excellent staff makes up for the lack of an elevator. ❹.

Bryant Park Hotel **40 W 40th St (between 5th and 6th aves), NY 10018 ⓣ1-877/640-9300 or 212/869-0100.** The hotel, in the American Radiator building (see p.137), is new and ready for the party. Designer David Chipperfield put the whole thing together, and it shows off his edgy attitude – note the burning-heart red elevator alcove, and the funky *Cellar Bar* downstairs, filled with "media people." If you get a craving for Cherry Garcia frozen yogurt or a hummus dip at 3am, there's a butler on each floor, at your beck and call 24 hours a day, which is as it should be at this price. ❽.

Casablanca **147 W 43rd St (between 6th and 7th aves), NY 10036 ⓣ1-888/9-CASABLANCA or 212/869-1212, ⓕ391-7585, ⓦwww.casablancahotel.com.** Moorish tile, ceiling fans and, of course, *Rick's Cafe* are all here in this unusual, thoughtful and understated theme hotel. While the feeling is Morocco in the 1940s, the features (dataports for laptops, VCRs) are all up-to-date, and bottled water and Belgian chocolates appear at turndown. Continental breakfast is laid out daily in the café, and drinks and snacks are available in front of the wide-screen TV all afternoon. ❻.

Comfort Inn Midtown **129 W 46th St (between 6th and 7th aves), NY 10036 ⓣ1-800/567-7720 or 212/221-2600, ⓕ764-7481.** A clean chain hotel that doesn't look like one. Rooms, which were redone in 1998, are on the small side, but cozy and light. Excellent location in Times Square. ❹.

Edison 228 W 47th St (just west of Broadway), NY 10036 ⓣ1-800/637-7070 or 212/840-5000, ⓕ596-6850, ⓦwww.edisonhotelnyc.com. The most striking thing about the distinctly funky 1000-room *Edison* is its beautifully restored brown and gold Art Deco lobby, a re-creation of the original from 1931. All rooms were redone in the 1990s. ❹.

Essex House 160 Central Park S (between 6th and 7th aves), NY 10019 ⓣ1-800/WESTIN-1 or 212/247-0300, ⓕ315-1839. A beautiful hotel for a special occasion, *Essex House* was restored by its previous Japanese owners to its original Art Deco splendor. The best rooms have spectacular Central Park views. Despite the excellent service and marble lobby, the atmosphere is not at all formal or hushed. ❽, dropping to ❻ on weekends.

flatotel 135 W 52nd St (between 6th and 7th aves), NY 10019 ⓣ1-800/352-8683 or 212/887-9400, ⓦwww.flatotel.com. Maybe the 'flat' refers to apartments (these rooms used to be condos, and they're all gigantic). Maybe it has to do with the linear room treatments (all the bed and furniture box shapes, the vertical lines of the floor-to-ceiling curtains). In any case, a very comfortable (if colorless) entry in the heart of midtown. Excellent service. ❼; weekend, summer and other specials ❺.

Gorham 136 W 55th St (between 6th and 7th aves), NY 10019 ⓣ1-800/735-0710 or 212/245-1800, ⓕ582-8832. Cosmopolitan midtown hotel transformed to reflect its original opening in 1929. Handy for Central Park and the Museum of Modern Art. All the rather generous rooms have convenient self-service kitchens; suites have whirlpool baths. Doubles ❻, with occasional promotional specials at ❺.

Helmsley Windsor 100 W 58th St (between 6th and 7th aves), NY 10019 ⓣ1-800/221-4982 or 212/265-2100, ⓕ315-0371. Enjoy coffee on the house each morning in the richly decorated, wood-paneled lobby. Like other Helmsley hotels, the *Windsor* has a pleasantly old-fashioned air, with plenty of useful extras in the rooms. Central Park is a block north. ❺; summer weekends at ❹.

Hilton Times Square 234 W 42 (between 7th and 8th aves), NY 10036 ⓣ1-800/HILTONS or 212/840-8222, ⓕ840-5516, ⓦwww.timessquare.hilton.com. Gorgeous property starts on the 20th floor of the building, with modern boxy furniture in the lobby and stripes of bright yellow light to draw you in to the chic *Pinnacle* bar/*Above* restaurant. The rooms done in chocolate, tan and cream are good-sized, with an attractive desk and dresser in light wood. Very new, and on a famous block, with awesome views up- and downtown. Rates start at ❺; ask reservations about packages or specials.

Howard Johnson Plaza 8th Ave (at 52nd St), NY 10019 ⓣ212/581-4100. Don't worry - it bears no resemblance to the company's orange-roofed motels spread over the Atlantic coast. Rooms are decorated primarily in maroon and dark wood, there's space to spread out and a *Beefsteak Charlie's* restaurant next door. ❹.

Hudson 356 W 58th St, NY 10022 ⓣ1-800/444-4786 or 212/554-6000, ⓕ554-6001. An elevator whisks you to one of 1000 cramped rooms with tiny TVs in this latest model from hotelier Ian Schrager (co-founder of the notorious *Studio 54* disco in the late 1970s). However, rooms are only a small part of the experience here. The brick-walled atrium lobby is neat, but the main attraction happens after hours. The scene, incorporating two bars (a glowing yellow *Hudson Bar* with a ceiling fresco and the intimate *Library Bar*) and the *Hudson Cafeteria*, has been christened the New (Ultra West) Hamptons, with all the required attitude, but without the sand. The publicized $95 room can be available, but only weeks in advance, and only for solo travelers. Starts at ❺.

Iroquois 49 W 44th St (between 5th and 6th aves), NY 10036 ⓣ1-800/332-7220 or 212/840-3080, ⓕ398-1754, ⓦwww.iroquoisny.com. What was once a haven for down-at-the-heel rock bands has reinvented itself as a somewhat stuffy "boutique" hotel with comfortable, tasteful rooms with Italian marble baths and the usual amenities (health center, library and five-star restaurant). One of the hotel's noted visitors is immortalized in the lounge named for him: James Dean lived here from 1950 to 1953, and some say his room (#803) still retains an element of magic. ❼.

Le Parker Meridien 118 W 57th St (between 6th and 7th aves), NY 10019 ⓣ212/245-5000, ⓕ247-4698, ⓦwww.parkermeridien.com. Five years and $60 million transformed the famous *Parker Meridien*. Gone are the fussy French colonial rooms, in favor of comfortably modern ones, filled with thoughtful touches like an Aeron chair, ergonomic features and a rotating 32-inch flat screen TV. The mood has been lightened as well: the breakfast-only *Norma's* restaurant has fun with its many inventive options, room numbers (and doorbells) emit a cobalt glow, and classic cartoons and film shorts play in the elevators. With a huge fitness center, a rare rooftop swimming pool, and 24-hour room service, this is hard to pass up, with weekends at ❺. Weekday pricing is at ❼.

Mansfield 12 W 44th St, NY 10036 t1-877/847-4444 or 212/944-6050, Ⓕ764-4477, Ⓦwww.mansfieldhotel.com. A makeover by the Boutique Hotel Group has transformed a rather mangy midtown flophouse into one of the loveliest hotels in the city. The *Mansfield* manages, somehow, to be both grand and intimate. With its recessed floor spotlighting, copper-domed salon, clubby library, nightly jazz and Tamara de Lempicka's *Polo Player* welcoming guests from behind the front desk, there's a charming, slightly quirky feel about the place – an echo, perhaps, of its turn-of-the-nineteenth-century role as a pad for New York's most eligible bachelors. With the European breakfast, all-day cappuccino and jazz in the lounge, a great deal at ❺.

Marriott Marquis 1535 Broadway (at 45th St), NY 10036 Ⓣ212/398-1900. The enormous *Marquis* is perfect for conference and convention guests; it's worth dropping by to gawk at the split-level atrium and to ride the glass elevators to NY's only revolving bar and restaurant, but the rooms themselves are modest for the high price. ❻.

Mayfair 242 W 49th St (between Broadway and 8th Ave), NY 10019 Ⓣ1-800/556-2932 or 212/586-0300, Ⓕ307-5226, Ⓦwww.mayfairnewyork.com. This new, non-smoking, "boutique"-style hotel, across the street from the St Malachay Actor's Chapel, has beautifully decorated rooms, its own restaurant and a charming "old-world" feel, emphasized by the historic photographs on loan from the Museum of the City of New York that are everywhere on display. ❺, with summer rates at ❸.

Michelangelo 152 W 51st St (between 6th and 7th aves), NY 10019 Ⓣ1-800/237-0990 or 212/765-0505, Ⓕ541-6604. An Italian chain took over and created a palazzo on Broadway, with acres of marble, and no expenses spared in the luxurious and super-large rooms. In terms of decor, the suites offer a choice of Art Deco, Empire or Country French styles. On weekends and some holidays prices drop from ❽ to ❻.

Milford Plaza 270 W 45th St (at 8th Ave), NY 10036 Ⓣ1-800/221-2690 or 212/869-3600, Ⓕ944-8357. Rooms are tiny in this Ramada hotel and the atmosphere is impersonal, but hordes of theater-goers still flock here for the "Lullabuy [sic] of Broadway" deals. ❹.

Millennium Broadway 145 W 44th St (between Broadway and 6th), NY 10036 Ⓣ1-800/622-5569 or 212/768-4400, Ⓕ768-0847. Black marble and modern Italian wall-to-ceiling artworks dominate the *Millennium Broadway* lobby; the sleek lines continue in the beautiful off-white bedrooms. A good place for an intimate after-theater supper, even if you decide against the (justifiably) high room rates. ❼; weekends sometimes ❻.

Muse 130 W 46th St (between 6th Ave and Broadway), NY 10036 Ⓣ1-877/NYC-MUSE or 212/485-2400, Ⓕ485-2900. This small hotel in the center of Times Square caters to Europeans. The slightly chilly staff and off-putting lobby (which looks more like reception at a brokerage house, with its absence of a front desk) contrasts with the more traditional, very airy, rooms, plainly decorated in muted colors, with feather beds to lull you to sleep. Weekdays at ❽, weekends at ❺.

Novotel 226 W 52nd St (on Broadway), NY 10019 Ⓣ212/315-0100, Ⓕ765-5369. This chain hotel is large enough to offer a decent range of facilities, while small enough to avoid anonymity. The decor is clean, featuring uncluttered wood with blue accents, the food good (as you would expect from a French-owned establishment) and the hotel offers special rooms for the disabled. ❻, with summer rates dropping to ❺.

Paramount 235 W 46th St (between Broadway and 8th Ave), NY 10036 Ⓣ212/764-5500. For the past few years, this has been one of the hippest places to stay, popular with a pop and media crowd that comes to enjoy the theatrical public space (blue-lit staircase strewn with tea candles, gift shop as concession stand) designed by Philippe Starck. The very white rooms are tiny (though rooms on lower floors are slightly bigger), but you won't hang out in them anyway. You'll be waited on everywhere by sleek young things, and a branch of *Dean and DeLuca* off the lobby, the *Whiskey Bar* and the *Coco Pazzo Teatro* restaurant are all busy and fun. ❺, with some rates as low as ❹.

Park Savoy 158 W 58th St (between 6th and 7th aves), NY 10019 ⓣ212/245-5755. With colorful, cozy rooms, all with private baths, and just a block from Central Park, this hotel offers good value for the area. ❹.

The Plaza 768 5th Ave (at Central Park S), NY 10019 ⓣ1-800/527-472 or 212/759-3000, ⓕ546-5234. The last word in New York luxury, at least by reputation, and worth the money for the fine old pseudo-French chateau building if nothing else. Doubles start at $365 and run to $15,000 (no kidding!) for a specialty suite, and that's before taxes. A place to stay if someone else is paying. ❽.

Portland Square 132 W 47th St (between 6th and 7th aves), NY 10036 ⓣ1-800/388-8988 or 212/382-0600, ⓕ382-0684, ⓦwww.portlandsquarehotel.com. A theater hotel since 1904, and former home to Jimmy Cagney and other members of Broadway casts, the *Portland* has a few more comforts than its sister hotel *Herald Square*, but is still a budget operation, good for a few nights' sleep but not for hanging out. The cheapest rooms go as low as $65 plus tax for a small single with a shared bathroom. Doubles ❸; triples and quads ❹.

Quality Midtown 59 W 46th St (between 5th and 6th aves), NY 10036 ⓣ1-800/567-7720 or 212/719-2300, ⓕ790-2760. Near Diamond Row and a stone's throw from Rockefeller Center. All rooms in this comparatively inexpensive chain hotel come with private bath, cable TV and telephone. Free continental breakfast. ❹.

Royalton 44 W 44th St (between 5th and 6th aves), NY 10036 ⓣ1-800/635-9013 or 212/869-4400, ⓕ869-8965. Owned by the same management as the *Paramount*, the *Royalton* attempts to capture the market for the discerning style-conscious, with white-draped chairs and candle-filled interiors designed by Philippe Starck (see p.142). It has tried to become the new *Algonquin*, and is as much a power-lunch venue for NY's media and publishing set as a place to stay. ❼, with discounts sometimes available at ❻.

Salisbury 123 W 57th St, NY 10019 ⓣ1-888/NYC-5757 or 212/246-1300, ⓕ977-7752, ⓦwww.nycsalisbury.com. Good service, large bright rooms and proximity to Central Park and 57th Street's shops are the main attractions of this quality hotel. Offers reduced rate access to the Health and Racquet Club and Spa. ❻.

Sheraton Manhattan 790 7th Ave (between 51st and 52nd sts), NY 10019 ⓣ1-800/223-6550. There's a bigger (translate more expensive) *Sheraton* across the street, but this one is quiet, classy and nicer than you'd expect. Rooms are decorated in understated dark golds and browns. You can look out on the bustling tourists on the avenue from *Russo's Steak & Pasta*, or, if that's too much effort, unwind in the health club with an indoor pool and a sundeck. ❺; specials at ❹.

Shoreham 33 W 55th St, NY 10019 ⓣ1-877/847-4444 or 212/247-6700, ⓕ765-9741. Winner of the Best Hotel Design Award for 2001 from *Interiors* magazine (and home to the best-smelling rooms in town), the *Shoreham* is everything it proclaims itself to be: "Urbane. Mindful. Discreet. Comfortable." You get the idea from the lobby, done in cool white marble, pool blue wall accents and polished steel columns and fixtures, and from the spiky-haired staff all in black. The neutral-colored rooms are average size, but, as with other boutique hotels, you get amenities galore, and the dark-lit, media-populated *Shoreham Bar* is only an elevator flight away. Start at ❽; ❼ for summer.

The Time 224 W 49th St, NY 10019 ⓣ1-877/TIME NYC or 212/246-5252, ⓕ245-2305, ⓦwww.thetimeny.com. *Tempus fugit* – and everything here reminds you to spend it wisely, from the waist-level clock in the lobby, to the hallways bedecked with Roman numerals (you can even catch some TV while waiting for the elevator). Designer Adam Tihany created a hip hotel that may see a Clinton one day, a rap impresario or a heavy metalhead the next. Modern styling in a minimalist environment equals lots of black and white rectangles in the lobby and active bar, and one primary color allotted to each room for the bedspread. Small-to-medium size rooms are tricked out with the latest accoutrements (dual-line phones, ergonomic work station, in-room fax) and a minibar. Not terribly expensive for what you get. ❺.

Warwick **65 W 54th St (at 6th Ave), NY 10019 ⓣ1-800/223-4099 or 212/247-2700.** Stars of the 1950s and 1960s – including Cary Grant, Rock Hudson, the Beatles, Elvis Presley and JFK – stayed here as a matter of course. Although the hotel has lost its showbiz cachet, it's a pleasant place, from the elegant lobby to the *Ciao Europa* restaurant and *Randolph's* cocktail lounge. The staff is helpful and friendly. ❽; summer specials at ❺.

Wellington **7th Ave (at 55th St), NY 10019 ⓣ1-800/652-1212 or 212/247-3900, ⓕ581-1719, ⓦwww.wellingtonhotel.com.** The gleaming, mirror-clad lobby is the result of fresh renovations, and similar attention has been paid to the rooms. Some have kitchenettes, and family rooms offer two bathrooms. Close to Carnegie Hall and handy for Lincoln Center, the hotel's a good value for this stretch of town. ❹.

Westpark **6 Columbus Circle (off 8th Ave), NY 10019 ⓣ1-866/WESTPARK or 212/445-0200, ⓕ246-3131, ⓦwww.westparkhotel.com.** The best rooms look out over Columbus Circle and the southwestern corner of Central Park. The staff is somewhat reserved but helpful, and it's a great deal for the area, with Lincoln Center and the park nearly right outside the door, and a daily continental breakfast buffet. Reserving on the internet will save a few bucks from the call-in rates. ❹.

Wyndham **42 W 58th St (between 5th and 6th aves), NY 10019 ⓣ1-800/257-1111 or 212/753-3500, ⓕ754-5638.** The large rooms and suites vary enormously in terms of decor and it's the kind of place where the hotel's devotees – many of whom are actors and actresses – request their favorite on each visit. All the rooms are homely, though, and the place feels more like an apartment building than a hotel. ❹; summer specials ❸.

Midtown East: E 42nd to 59th streets

Beekman Tower **3 Mitchell Place (at 49th St and 1st Ave), NY 10017 ⓣ1-800/ME-SUITE or 212/320-8018, ⓕ465-3697.** One of the more expensive hotels in the Manhattan East Suite chain and also one of the most stylish. All the rooms are suites and come with fully equipped kitchens. The Art Deco *Top of the Towers* restaurant offers superb East Side views. ❻; in summer prices can drop to ❹. Weekend and extended stay rates also available.

Box Tree **250 E 49th St (between 2nd and 3rd aves), NY 10017 ⓣ212/758-8320, ⓕ308-3899, ⓦwww.theboxtree.com.** Thirteen elegant rooms and suites fill two adjoining eighteenth-century townhouses and make one of New York's more eccentric lodgings. The Egyptian-, Chinese- and Japanese-style rooms have fur throws on the beds, great lighting, and ornaments and decoration everywhere. A credit of up to $100 toward the hotel bill is offered to weekend diners in the excellent *Box Tree Restaurant*. Worth it for a splurge. ❻; weekend rates are $100 more expensive.

Drake **440 Park Ave (at 56th St), NY 10022 ⓣ212/421-0900.** A first-class hotel, and member of the Swissotel chain, with bustling cocktail bar and superb seafood restaurant (*Quantum 56*), a spa and gym. This was once an apartment building, so the rooms are large (and the suites are super-large and expensive), and a bit more stylish than most others of the same level. ❼, with weekends closer to ❺.

Elysee **60 E 54th St, NY 10022 ⓣ212/753-1066.** The *Elysee* was until recently celebrated for its eccentric, theatrical style, but, sadly, the enthusiastic new management has refurbished the whole place in the best possible taste. A fine place to stay, if you can afford it, with a great bar and close to Fifth Avenue. ❻ for summer, ❽ otherwise.

Fitzpatrick Manhattan **687 Lexington Ave (between 56th and 57th sts), NY 10022 ⓣ212/355-0100 or 1-800/367-7701, ⓕ355-1371.** Opened in 1991, this handsome Irish-owned and Irish-themed hotel is perfectly situated for midtown shopping, Upper East Side museums and Central Park. A hearty Irish breakfast is served all day. Doubles and suites for ❻, with weekend deals and summer rates available.

Habitat **130 E 57th St (between Lexington and Park), NY 10022 ⓣ1-800/255-0482 or 753-8841, ⓕ829-9605, ⓦwww.stayinny.com.**

Centrally situated in a very classy part of town, this hotel was once the women-only *Allerton House*. Remodeled in 2000, its rooms are small, yet perfectly adequate. ③ (with private bathroom); ② (without).

Lyden House 320 E 53rd St (between 1st and 2nd aves), NY 10022 ⓣ212/888-6070. One of the friendliest of the Manhattan East Suite chain, the *Lyden* is situated in exclusive Sutton Place. Even the smallest suites are apartment-sized by New York standards and most could sleep four (second two adults at $20 plus tax per person per night). All suites have eat-in kitchens and a maid to do the dishes. ⑥; off-season rates can drop to ⑤ if available.

Pickwick Arms 230 E 51st St, NY 10022 ⓣ212/355-0300. A thoroughly pleasant budget hotel and, for the price, one of the best deals you'll get on the East Side. All 400 rooms are air-conditioned, with cable TV, direct-dial phones and room service. The open-air roof deck with stunning views and café are added attractions. A single room with a shared bathroom is $75. ③.

Roger Smith 501 Lexington Ave (at 47th St), NY 10017 ⓣ1-800/445-0277 or 212/755-1400, ⓕ319-9130. One of the best midtown hotels with very helpful service, individually decorated rooms, a great restaurant, and artworks and sculpture on display in the public areas (and in the Roger Smith Gallery next door). Breakfast is included in the price, along with a refrigerator and coffee-maker in all rooms and VCRs in most with 2000 videos available from the hotel's library. Popular with bands and guests who like the artsy ambience. ⑥; summer rates drop to ④.

Roosevelt 45 E 45th St (at Madison Ave), NY 10017 ⓣ1-888/TEDDY NY or 212/661-9600, ⓕ885-6161. The hotel's heyday was in the Railway Age, when its proximity to Grand Central Station meant that thousands of travelers came to stay. It has lately undergone extensive renovations, with new suites and the prices to match. Has a nice, if traditional, bar and restaurant. ⑦; summer rates at ⑥.

San Carlos 150 E 50th St (between Lexington and 3rd aves), NY 10022 ⓣ1-800/722-2012 or 212/755-1800, ⓕ688-9778, ⓦwww.sancarloshotel.com. It is well-situated near plenty of bars and restaurants; most of the large rooms have fully equipped kitchenettes. This is a useful standby when everything else is booked solid. ⑤; summer rates can drop to ④.

UN Crowne Plaza 304 E 42nd St (between 1st and 2nd aves), NY 10017 ⓣ212/986-8800, ⓕ986-1758. One of the more stylish hotels close to Grand Central Station. Rooms are deluxe, with minibars, cable and in-room movies, hair dryers and opulent marble bathrooms. There's a fitness room and sauna too. Service is excellent. ⑧; promotional specials at ⑤.

W 541 Lexington Ave (between 49th and 50th sts), NY 10022 ⓣ212/755-1200, ⓕ319-8344. If the crowd hanging out in the *Whiskey Blue* bar, dining at *Heartbeat* or just posing in the Living Room (that's the feel of the lobby, and its name, too) are anything to go by, the *W* might well be the hippest dosshouse in town. Clean, stylish rooms and other perks: Egyptian cotton on the feather beds, business services, gym and spa. ⑧, though weekend specials are available.

Waldorf-Astoria 301 Park Ave (at E 50th St), NY 10022 ⓣ1-800/WALDORF or 212/355-3000, ⓕ872-7272. One of the great names among New York hotels, and restored to its 1930s glory, making it a wonderful place to stay if you can afford it or someone else is paying. ⑧; promotional rates can drop to ⑤.

Pet-friendly hotels

These hotels, among others, allow some of your (small) best friends to stay. Call ahead for details.

Best Western President 234 W 48th St (between 8th Ave and Broadway); p.294.
Le Parker Meridien 118 W 57th St (between 6th and 7th aves); p.295.
Marriott Marquis 1535 Broadway (at 45th St); p.296.
Mayflower 15 Central Park W (at 61st St); p.300
Novotel 226 W 52nd St (on Broadway); p.296.

The Upper West Side: Above W 59th Street

Amsterdam Inn 340 Amsterdam Ave (at 76th St), NY 10023 ⓣ212/579-7500, ⓕ579-6127, ⓦwww.amsterdaminn.com. From the owners of the lauded *Murray Hill Inn*, this new addition is within walking distance of Central Park, Lincoln Center and the American Museum of Natural History. Rooms are basic (no closets) but clean, and the front desk is two long flights up. There's a friendly, helpful staff, plus rooms have TVs, phones and maid service. Singles with shared bath ❶; doubles ❷; rooms with private bath ❸.

Beacon 2130 Broadway (at 75th St), NY 10023 ⓣ1-800/572-4969 or 212/787-1100, ⓕ724-0839, ⓦwww.beaconhotel.com. A pleasantly buzzing hotel with good-sized rooms, deep closets, cable TV and fully equipped kitchenettes. *Zabar's*, NY's famous gourmet deli, is a few blocks up Broadway, and Fairway market, with all the fresh strawberries and peaches you can carry, is across the street. ❹.

Lucerne 201 W 79th St (at Amsterdam Ave), NY 10024 ⓣ1-800/492-8122 or 212/875-1000, ⓕ721-1179. This beautifully restored 1904 brownstone, with its extravagantly baroque red terra-cotta entrance, charming rooms and friendly, helpful staff is a block from the American Museum of Natural History and close to the liveliest restaurant stretch of Columbus Ave. ❺, with summer rates ❹.

Malibu Studios 2688 Broadway (at 103rd St), NY 10025 ⓣ212/222-2954, outside the city 1-800/647-2227, ⓕ678-6842. Excellent value budget accommodation, within walking distance of plenty of restaurants and nightlife because of the nearby presence of Columbia University. Prices, all before taxes, range from $79 for a single room with shared facilities to $149 for a double/double with private bathroom. Also triples and quads. Renovated in 2001. Mention the *Rough Guides* and pay for three nights or more upfront and get a ten percent discount on any room. Friendly, helpful management, too. Credit cards not accepted. ❶.

Mayflower 15 Central Park W (at 61st St), NY 10023-7709 ⓣ1-800/223-4164 or 212/265-0060, ⓕ265-0227, ⓦwww.mayflowerhotel.com. A slightly down-at-the-heel but very comfortable hotel a few steps from Central Park and Lincoln Center. It's so close to the latter, in fact, that performers and musicians are often seen in the hotel's very good *Conservatory Café*. ❻, with occasional promotional rates.

Milburn 242 W 76th St ⓣ212/362-1006 or 1-800/833-9622, ⓕ721-5476. Welcoming and well-situated suite hotel, great for families, redone in a gracious style. There are studios and one-room suites with fully equipped kitchenettes, bathrooms and TV. Practical extras are in-room safes, laundry and maid service. ❹; summer ❸.

On the Ave 2178 Broadway (at 77th St), NY 10024 ⓣ1-800/509-7598 or 212/362-1100, ⓕ787-9521, ⓦwww.ontheave-nyc.com. Relatively new, it has a modern but slightly weary feeling, with stainless steel sinks in the minimalist baths and dark wood platforms for the beds. Not packed with amenities, it is still clean, comfortable and relatively inexpensive. ❹.

Quality Hotel on Broadway 215 W 94th St, NY 10025 ⓣ1-800/228-5151 or 212/866-6400, ⓕ866-1357. Reliable chain hotel popular with the younger crowd, with decent rooms but not many extras. Convenient to #1 and #9 subway. ❸, or in summer ❷. Weekends are about $40 more than weekdays.

Radisson Empire 44 W 63rd St (at Broadway), NY 10023 ⓣ1-888/822-3555 or 212/265-7400, ⓕ315-0349. A lavishly refurbished member of the Radisson chain, the *Empire* will suit music lovers: it is opposite the Metropolitan Opera House and Lincoln Center, and each (box-sized) room comes with a CD player and VCR. ❻, but summer rates can drop to ❹.

Riverside Tower 80 Riverside Drive (at W 80th St), NY 10024 ⓣ1-800/724-3136 or 212/877-5200, ⓕ873-1400. Although the hallways are plain as can be and rooms – all with small refrigerators – are ultra basic, it's the location in this exclusive and safe neighborhood, flanked by one of the city's most beautiful parks and with (on upper floors) stunning views of the Hudson River, that sets this budget hotel apart from the others. And it's worth noting that quads work out at around $35 per person, per night. Reservations a few weeks in advance are recommended. For a few dollars more than the double, get the two-room suite for two people. ❷.

Upper East Side: Above E 59th Street

Mark 25 E 77th St (at Madison Ave), NY 10021 ⓣ212/744-4300, ⓕ744-2749. A hotel that really lives up to its claims of sophistication and elegance. A redesign has kitted the lobby out with Biedermeier furniture and sleek Italian lighting. In the guest rooms, restaurant and invitingly dark *Mark's Bar*, there's a similar emphasis on the best of everything. ❼.

Pierre 795 5th Ave (at 61st St), NY 10021 ⓣ1-800/332-3442 (US), 1-800/268-6282 or 212/940-8101, ⓕ758-1615. The *Pierre* has consistently retained its reputation as one of New York's top hotels and is certainly luxurious. It was Salvador Dalí's favorite in the city, but the only surreal aspects today are the prices. If these prohibit a stay, have afternoon tea in the gloriously frescoed *Rotunda*, or experience a power breakfast in the *Café Pierre*. ❼.

Sherry Netherland 781 5th Ave (between 59th and 60th sts), NY 10022 ⓣ212/355-2800. With its stunning views of Central Park, this is the place to rent a whole floor and live in permanently, if a large sum of money ever comes your way. Many of the guests do this, and the service is geared to satisfying their every whim. Room service is by renowned restaurateur Harry Cipriani. ❽.

Wales 1295 Madison Ave (at 92nd St), NY 10128 ⓣ1-877/847-4444 or 212/876-6000. Almost in Spanish Harlem, though very definitely Upper East Side in feel. Excellent prices for the high standard of accommodation: the original oak moldings and mantles have been lovingly restored, and tea, cookies and classical music are served up every afternoon in the parlor. ❼; summer rates ❺.

Airport hotels

If your flight gets in at an ungodly hour, or if your eyes don't open before noon and the plane's taking off at 5.30am, it may benefit your sanity to stay at one of the area's airport hotels. Usually comfortable and conveniently near the tarmac (though not to say always quiet), these offerings exist simply to ease the getting-to-the-airport stress associated with inconvenient traffic delays and hearing-impaired taxi drivers ("You wanted Newark? I thought you said JFK…").

JFK

Holiday Inn JFK 144-02 135th Ave, Queens, NY ⓣ718/659-0200

Radisson 13530 140th St, Queens, NY ⓣ718/322-2300

Ramada Plaza JFK Van Wyck Expressway, Queens, NY ⓣ718/995-9000

La Guardia

Crowne Plaza La Guardia 104-04 Ditmars Blvd, Queens, NY ⓣ718/457-6300

Sheraton La Guardia East 135-20 39th Ave, Queens, NY ⓣ718/460-6666

Wyndham Garden 100-15 Ditmars Blvd, Queens, NY ⓣ718/426-1500

Newark

Courtyard Rt 1-9 South at Rt 78, Newark, NJ ⓣ973/643-8500

Holiday Inn 160 Frontage Rd, Newark, NJ ⓣ973/589-1000

Marriott Airport Newark, NJ ⓣ973/623-0006

29

Cafés, snacks and light meals

Like the restaurants in New York, the city's **cafés and bakeries** run the gamut of its population's ethnic and cultural influences. They can be found in every neighborhood, with the usual French, Italian and American favorites very visible, but Chinese and Greek outposts are there as well, for the traveler in the know. Middle Eastern snacks, vegetarian wraps, beignets, pizza, homemade candy, bagels and ice cream are all available and ready to be gulped up.

New York has a number of **coffee houses and tearooms**, which don't always serve alcohol but concentrate instead on providing fresh coffee and tea, fruit juices, pastries and light snacks, and sometimes full meals. Many of the more long-established cafés are downtown, congenial places with a European emphasis; indeed they're often determinedly Left Bank in feel (like the grouping at the junction of Bleecker and MacDougal streets) and perfect for lingering or just resting up between sights. The more upscale midtown hotels are good places to stop for formal tea too, if you can afford the prices they charge for the English country-house atmosphere they often try to contrive.

Financial District

Sandwiches and snacks

Ruben's Empanadas **64 Fulton St ☎212/962-5330, 15 Bridge St ☎212/509-3825.** The Spanish pastries come in savory (meat or vegetable) or sweet (cherry, apple, guava and cheese), with two egg options for breakfast.

Specialty eating

We've highlighted particular types of snacks and lighter meal options and listed them in boxes on the following pages.

Bagels p.307
Breakfast: coffee shops and diners p.304
Some atmospheric cafés p.307
Ice cream p.311
Juice bars p.312
Pizza by the slice p.309
Tea in Chinatown opposite

Chinatown, Little Italy and the Lower East Side

Bakeries and cafés

Café Gitane 242 Mott St (between Prince and Houston sts) ⓣ212/334-9552. Sunny little café serving coffee and creative light lunch fare.

Caffè Biondo 141 Mulberry St (between Grand and Hester sts) ⓣ212/226-9285. A little brick-walled cappuccino shop with excellent Italian desserts.

Caffè Roma 385 Broome St (between Mulberry and Mott sts) ⓣ212/226-8413. Old Little Italy *pasticceria*, ideal for a drawn-out coffee and pastry. Try the homemade Italian cookies, exceptionally good cannoli (plain or dipped), or gelato at the counter in back.

Ceci-Cela 55 Spring St (at Mulberry St) ⓣ212/274-9179. Tiny French *patisserie* with a stand-up counter and bench out front for immediate consumption of coffee and delectable baked goods. The croissants and palmiers are divine.

Dragon Land Bakery 125 Walker St ⓣ212/219-2012. Satisfy your cravings here, whether for mango buns, red bean cookies, or (what can only be described as) shredded pork donuts.

Fay Da Bakery Corp 83 Mott St (south of Canal St) ⓣ212/791-3884. More Eastern bakery items and specialty drinks in a rather plainly decorated shop.

Ferrara's 195 Grand St (between Mott and Mulberry sts) ⓣ212/226-6150. The best-known and most traditional of the Little Italy coffee houses, this neighborhood landmark has been around since 1892. Try the cheesecake, cannoli or *granite* (Italian ices) in summer. Outside seating. See also the newer midtown locations at 1700 Broadway (at 53rd St) and 201 W 42nd St (at 7th Ave).

Kossar's 367 Grand St (at Essex St) ⓣ212/473-4810. Jewish baker whose bialys may be the best in New York.

Kwong Wah Cake Company 234 Canal St (at Lafayette St) ⓣ212/925-3614. You can't get more authentically Chinese than this cake establishment on teeming Canal Street.

Saint's Alp Teahouse 51 Mott St ⓣ 212/766-9889. Great stopoff in Chinatown's heart if you don't want the full restaurant experience, with hot green tea, Chinese fruit drinks and shakes, and a good choice of snacks – try the vegetable dumplings or preserved eggs.

Yonah Schimmel's 137 E Houston St (between Forsyth and Eldridge sts) ⓣ212/477-2858. Knishes, baked fresh on the premises, and wonderful bagels. Unpretentious and patronized by a mixture of wrinkled old men wisecracking in Yiddish and – on Sundays especially – young uptowners slumming it while they wade through the Sunday papers.

Sandwiches and snacks

Chinatown Ice Cream Factory 65 Bayard St (between Mott and Elizabeth sts) ⓣ212/608-4170. An essential stop after sampling one of the restaurants nearby, but the wondrously unusual flavors make it good any time. Specialties include green tea, ginger, almond cookie and lychee ice cream.

Doughnut Plant 379 Grand St (between Essex and Norfolk sts) ⓣ212/505-3700. A world of

Tea in Chinatown

The Chinese, who have always revered **tea**, have positioned it for a new set of consumers. The following modern versions of the teahouse (aside from the traditional ones) feature milk-added or fruit-flavored teas enhanced with pearl tapioca (termed bubble tea or pearl tea). The tapioca beads, which can come in white or purple-black, impart a minor flavor, but a significant textural double take – sucked up through double-wide straws, the chewy bubbles either pop in the mouth or slide whole down the esophagus. Though a bit unsettling at first, it makes tea a fun proposition.

Fay Da Bakery Corp 83 Mott St ⓣ212/791-3884
Green Tea Café 45 Mott St ⓣ212/693-2888
Sago Tea Cafe South St Seaport, Pier 17, 89 South St ⓣ212/ 212/267-8316
Saint's Alp Teahouse 51 Mott St ⓣ212/766-9889

fried dough, with all the fillings and toppings ever invented.

Grilled Cheese 168 Ludlow St (between Houston and Stanton sts) ⓣ212/982-6600. Great salads and (go figure!) grilled cheese sandwiches any way you want them; very tiny dining space.

Ray's 27 Prince St ⓣ212/966-1960. While countless pizzerias in the city claim to be the "original Ray's," this Little Italy mainstay is the best. Their Sicilian slices are particularly good.

SoHo and TriBeCa

Bakeries and cafés

Balthazar Bakery 80 Spring St (between Crosby St and Broadway) ⓣ212/965-1414. Next door to the celebrated *Balthazar* brasserie, this bakery has wonderful breads and pastries both simple and ornate, without the attitude, name-droppers or the smoke.

Bouley Bakery Cafe 120 W Broadway (between Duane and Reade sts) ⓣ212/964-2525. *Wunderkind* David Bouley's latest, a tiny bakery-restaurant with truly great breads and baked goods, as well as reasonably priced light food. Make sure to turn right once through the door, or you'll end up in the *très* expensive restaurant.

Breakfast: coffee shops and diners

You rarely have to walk more than a block or two in Manhattan to find somewhere that serves breakfast. Coffee shops and diners all over town serve up much the same array of discounted specials before 11am. But when you're desperate for a shot of early morning coffee, the following checklist should help you avoid traipsing too far from wherever you happen to be staying. You'll find full reviews elsewhere in this chapter; otherwise just expect standard American burgers, sandwiches and breakfasts.

Downtown Manhattan

Around the Clock 8 Stuyvesant St (between 2nd and 3rd aves) ⓣ212/598-0402
Bendix Diner 219 8th Ave (at 21st St) ⓣ212/366-0560
Jones Diner 371 Lafayette (at Great Jones St) ⓣ212/673-3577
KK Restaurant 192–194 1st Ave (between 11th and 12th sts) ⓣ212/777-4430
Odessa 117–119 Ave A (between 7th St and St Mark's Place) ⓣ212/473-8916
Triumph Restaurant 148 Bleecker St (between LaGuardia and Thompson sts) ⓣ212/228-3070
Veselka 144 2nd Ave (between 9th St and St Mark's Place) ⓣ212/228-9682
Waverly Restaurant 385 6th Ave (between 8th St and Waverly Place) ⓣ212/675-3181

Midtown Manhattan

Broadway Diner 590 Lexington Ave (at 52nd St) ⓣ212/486-8838; 1726 Broadway (at W 55th St) ⓣ212/765-0909
Chez Laurence 245 Madison Ave (between 37th and 38th sts) ⓣ212/683-0284
Ellen's Stardust Diner 1377 6th Ave (at 56th St) ⓣ212/307-7575; 1650 Broadway (at W 51st St) ⓣ212/956-5151
Jerry's Metro Delicatessen 790 8th Ave (at 48th St) ⓣ212/581-9100
Market Diner 572 11th Ave (at 43rd St) ⓣ212/695-0415
Olympic Restaurant 809 8th Ave (between 48th and 49th sts) ⓣ212/956-3230
Westway Diner 614 9th Ave (between 43rd and 44th sts) ⓣ212/582-7661

Uptown Manhattan

EJ's Luncheonette 433 Amsterdam Ave (between 81st and 82nd sts) ⓣ212/873-3444
Googie's Diner 1491 2nd Ave (at 78th St) ⓣ212/717-1122
Gracie Mews Diner 1550 1st Ave (at 81st St) ⓣ212/861-2290
Tom's Restaurant 2880 Broadway (at 112th St) ⓣ212/864-6137
Tramway Coffee Shop 1143 2nd Ave (at 60th St) ⓣ212/758-7017
Viand 673 Madison Ave (between 61st and 62nd sts) ⓣ212/751-6622

Le Pain Quotidien 100 Grand (at Mercer St) ⓣ212/625-9009; 833 Lexington Ave (between 63rd and 64th sts) ⓣ212/755-5810, 50 W 72nd St ⓣ212/712-9700, 1131 Madison Ave (between 84th and 85th sts) ⓣ212/327-4900. Wonderful French bakery.

Once Upon a Tart 135 Sullivan St (between Houston and Prince sts) ⓣ212/387-8869. Tiny café serving good coffee and homemade muffins and scones.

Yaffa Tea Room 19 Harrison St (at Greenwich St) ⓣ212/966-0577. Hidden in an unassuming corner of TriBeCa next to the *Yaffa Bar*, this restaurant serves Mediterranean-style dinners, good brunch and a cozy high tea (reservations required). Eclectic decor composed of flea market bric-a-brac finds.

Sandwiches and snacks

Bassett Café 123 West Broadway (at Duane St) ⓣ212/349-1662. Salads, light bites and an assortment of sides in spare but pleasant surroundings.

Café Bari 529 Broadway (at Spring St) ⓣ212/431-4350. A cornucopia of wholesome choices, on a SoHo corner good for people-watching. Juices, too.

Hampton Chutney 68 Prince (at Crosby) ⓣ212/226-9996. The American sandwich takes a detour through Indian breads and ingredients. Out of the ordinary, and quite good.

Rocky Mountain Chocolate Factory 125 Chambers St (near West Broadway), ⓣ212/349-7553. Chocolate (and other sweets) in every configuration you can think of – even sugar-free.

Snack 105 Thompson (between Prince and Spring sts) ⓣ212/925-1040. Some fresh Greek food and mezzes will only set you back $10 or so at lunch. Be prepared to wait for a table at this thimble-sized space.

West Village

Bakeries and cafés

A Salt and Battery 112 Greenwich Ave ⓣ212/691-2713. Manhattan's only true chippie, run by the Brits from *Tea and Sympathy* next door, and an authentic enough affair, with decent battered cod and plaice, great chips and mushy peas, all washed down with a mug of tea. However, it may be the most expensive chippie in the world, with a fish supper costing you a good twenty bucks.

Café Le Figaro 184 Bleecker St (at MacDougal St) ⓣ212/677-1100. Former Beat hangout during the 1950s, now ersatz Left Bank, serving cappuccino and pastries. If you want to watch weekend tourists flooding West Village streets, this is a good place to do it.

Caffè Dante 79 MacDougal St (between Bleecker and Houston sts) ⓣ212/982-5275. A morning stopoff for many locals since 1915. Good cappuccino, double espresso and caffè alfredo with ice cream. Often jammed with NYU students and teachers.

Caffè Reggio 119 MacDougal St (between Bleecker and 3rd sts) ⓣ212/475-9557. One of the first Village coffee houses, dating back to the 1920s, always crowded and with tables outside for people- or tourist-watching in warm weather.

Caffè Vivaldi 32 Jones St (between Bleecker and 4th sts) ⓣ212/929-9384. An old-fashioned Viennese-style coffee house with fireside coziness.

Magnolia Bakery 401 Bleecker Street (at 11th St) ⓣ212/462-2572. Like you've died and gone to cake heaven: huge beautiful slabs of moist crumbly cake, that homemade smell in the air and staff frosting cakes while you watch. In addition to chocolate, vanilla, hummingbird (an awesome mix of carrots, pineapple, coconut and nuts) and red velvet, there's banana pudding with wafer cookies and cupcakes. There are only three tables, so count on finishing as you walk around the block.

Tea and Sympathy 108 Greenwich Ave (between 12th and 13th sts) ⓣ212/807-8329. Self-consciously British tearoom, serving an afternoon high tea full of traditional British staples like jam roly-poly and treacle pud, along with shepherd's pie and scones. Perfect for British tourists feeling homesick.

Thé Adoré 17 E 13th St (between 5th Ave and University Place) ⓣ212/243-8742. Charming little tearoom with excellent pastries, scones, croissants and coffee. Sit upstairs and have a sandwich and a tasty bowl of soup. Daytime hours only; closed Sundays;

generally closed Saturdays in August, but it varies so call ahead.

Zito's **259 Bleecker St (between 6th and 7th aves) ☎212/929-6139.** Long-established Italian baker, renowned for its fine round *pane di casa*.

Sandwiches and snacks

Bagel Buffet **406 6th Ave (between 8th and 9th sts) ☎212/477-0448.** Wide selection of fillings and good-value bagel and salad platters for around $5. Open 24 hours.

Elixir **523 Hudson St (between 10th and Charles sts) ☎212/352-9952; also in TriBeCa, 95 West Broadway (between Reade and Chambers sts) ☎212/233-6171.** Casual, friendly joint where you can order juices, smoothies, seasonal elixirs – Femme: peppermint, rosemary, nettle and dandelion, or Belly: spearmint, fennel and catnip (!) – or just park yourself and think healthy.

Peanut Butter and Company **240 Sullivan St (at W 3rd) ☎212/677-3995.** Peanut butter, on sandwiches and otherwise, in ways you never imagined.

Two Boots-to-go West **75 Greenwich Ave (between 7th Ave and 11th St) ☎212/633-9096; also in the East Village 42 Ave A (at 3rd St) ☎212/505-5450; in Grand Central Terminal Food Concourse; and Park Slope Brooklyn ☎718/499-3253.** Great thin-crust pizzas with a cornmeal dusting and Cajun flavor. Take a slice of a Newman (sopressata, sweet sausage and ricotta) or Mrs. (Emma) Peel (round vegetable Sicilian).

Village Delight **323 Bleecker St (between Christopher and Grove sts) ☎212/633-9275.** Healthy-sized sandwiches of whole turkey or roast beef (made daily), with an assortment of Middle Eastern side dishes.

East Village

Bakeries and cafés

Caffè Della Pace **48 E 7th St (at 2nd Ave) ☎212/529-8024.** Dark and cozy East Village café with decent food and a great selection of coffees and desserts, especially the tiramisu.

Cloister Café **238 E 9th St (between 2nd and 3rd aves) ☎212/777-9128.** Don't come here for the food, which hovers somewhere between mediocre and really bad. Come for the spacious garden dining area and a big mug of coffee. Popular late-night spot.

Moishe's **115 2nd Ave (between 7th St and St Mark's Place) ☎212/505-8555.** Good prune danishes, excellent *humentashen*, seeded rye and other kosher treats.

Sticky Fingers **121 1st Ave (between 7th St and St Mark's Place) ☎212/529-2554.** Friendly East Village refuge with kids' artwork on the wall. Good coffee, pastries and breads.

Taylor's **175 2nd Ave (between 11th and 12th sts) ☎212/378-2892; 523 Hudson St (between 10th and Charles sts) ☎212/378-2890; 228 W 18th St (between 7th and 8th aves) ☎212/378-2895.** *Taylor's* offers soups and salads, but you should come for the oversized muffins and astonishing pastries. Try the monkey bread (a kind of sugary baked doughnut), zebra brownies, flourless chocolate soufflé cake or blueberry muffins.

Veniero's **342 E 11th St (between 1st and 2nd aves) ☎212/674-4415.** An East Village bakery and neighborhood institution since 1894,

Some atmospheric cafés

Coffee is big business in New York, and as such the city has been invaded by cookie-cutter coffee chains, large and small, each professing to offer the final word in the java experience. While the profusion of chains like *Starbuck's*, *Xando* and *New World Coffee* has encroached upon the smaller establishments there are still some more atmospheric options.

Café Mozart 154 W 70th St, p.309
Caffè Vivaldi 32 Jones St, p.305
Tea and Sympathy 108 Greenwich Ave, p.305
Thé Adoré 17 E 13th St, p.305
Veniero's 342 E 11th St, see above

Bagels

Theories abound as to the origin of the modern bagel. Most likely, it is a derivative of the pretzel, with the word bagel coming from the German *beigen*, "to bend." Modern-day bagels are probably softer and have a smaller hole than their ancestors – the famous hole made them easy to carry on a long stick to hawk on street corners. Whatever their birthplace, it is certain that bagels have become a New York institution. Since they are boiled before being baked, bagels have a characteristically chewy texture. They are most traditionally (and famously) served with cream cheese and lox (smoked salmon), though of course they can be topped with anything you like. In the past five years, there has been an expansion in the roster of bagel varieties; while many can't do without a blueberry or cheese bagel, others are outraged, decrying the invention of the new flavors which, they say, turn the revered bagel into a lower-class muffin alternative.

Until the 1950s bagels were still handcrafted by eastern European Jewish immigrants in two- or three-man cellars scattered around New York's Lower East Side. Today they can be found almost everywhere, but many New Yorkers would say only a few places serve the real thing. Here is a list of some of the better bagelsmiths. (And if you prefer bialys, a drier flatter bagel without a hole, head straight to *Kossar's*, p.303.)

Bagel Buffet 406 6th Ave (between 8th and 9th sts) ⓣ212/477-0448
Bagelry 1324 Lexington Ave (between 88th and 89th sts) ⓣ212/996-0567
Bagels on the Square 7 Carmine St (between Bleecker St and 6th Ave) ⓣ212/691-3041
Columbia Hot Bagels 2836 Broadway (between 110th and 111th sts) ⓣ212/222-3200
Ess-A-Bagel 359 1st Ave (at E 21st St) ⓣ212/260-2252
H & H Bagels 2239 Broadway (at W 80th St) ⓣ212/595-8000
Yonah Schimmel's 137 E Houston St (between Forsyth and Eldridge sts) ⓣ212/477-2858

Veniero's sells wonderful pastries and has an expanded seating area in the back. Desserts and decor are fabulously over-the-top. The ricotta cheesecake and homemade gelati are great in the summer.

Sandwiches and snacks

B & H Dairy 127 2nd Ave (between 7th St and St Mark's Place) ⓣ212/505-8065. This tiny luncheonette serves homemade soup, challah and latkes. You can also create your own juice combination to stay or go. Good veggie choice.

Damask Falafel 89 Ave A (between 5th and 6th sts) ⓣ212/673-5016. One of the better Middle Eastern snack providers in the area.

Bulgin' Waffles 49 1/2 1st Ave (at 3rd St) ⓣ212/477-6555. Homemade waffles with a variety of sweet fruity toppings. Despite its fast-food look, it takes a while if crowded.

Des Moines 41 Ave A (at 3rd St) ⓣ212/614-8015. Airy casual room with mismatched chairs where you can seemingly stay all day with a book and a snack.

Hero's Sweet Potatoes 30 E 13th St (between 5th Ave and University) ⓣ646/336-1685. Baked, chipped or fried, a welcome change from the same old.

Juicy Lucy's 85 Ave A (between 5th and 6th sts) ⓣ212/777-LUCY. This very small but congenial juice bar is extremely comprehensive in its offerings.

Live Juice 1st Ave at 1st St, no phone. Sidewalk shack relative of *Lucy's* with a couple of tables at the head of First Avenue.

Lucky's Juice Joint 11th St at 2nd Ave ⓣ212/358-0300. Over 30 kinds of juice and smoothie combos, with options like Reggae Rumba and Bulldozer.

Panya 10 Stuyvesant St (between 3rd Ave and 9th St) ⓣ212/777-1930. A Japanese take on the sandwich shop. It's tiny – look for the logo, a cute, Hello Kitty-style animal.

Pomme Frites 123 2nd Ave (between 7th and 8th sts) ⓣ212/674-1234. Arguably the best fries in the city, with Belgian-style gooey toppings available.

Sanctuary 25 1st Ave (between 1st and 2nd sts) ⓣ212/780-9786. Spiritual pamphlets abound, yoga classes are given upstairs, and the breezy lunch café's got appropriate, cool wall decorations you can buy and take home. But *Sanctuary* is a haven for foodies, too, as the natural ingredients are extra flavorful.

Uncle Louis G's 49 1/2 1st Ave (at 3rd St) ⓣ212/477-6555. Consistently good ice cream in the same room as *Bulgin' Waffles*.

Chelsea

Bakeries and cafés

Big Cup **228 8th Ave (between 21st and 22nd sts) ⊕212/206-0059.** Popular coffee shop with fresh muffins and (big) hot cups of joe. Comfortable couches and chairs make it the perfect place to read the papers and relax into your day.
News Bar **2 W 19th St (between 5th and 6th aves) ⊕212/255-3996.** Tiny minimalist café with equally great selections of pastries and periodicals. Draws photographer and model types as well as regular people, making it good for people-watching.
Wild Lily Tea Room **511 W 22nd St (between 5th and 6th aves) ⊕212/691-2258.** Convenient for a gallery tour of west Chelsea, the shop has over forty different brews, and strange-sounding but delicious tea sandwiches.

Sandwiches and snacks

Amy's Bread **75 9th Ave (between 15th and 16th sts) ⊕212/462-4338.** You can find Amy's Bread in fine stores citywide – but it's freshest here.
F&B **269 W 23rd St (between 7th and 8th aves) ⊕646/486-4441.** Unusual premise and a chic (for a slender storefront) execution: all manner of franks (vegetarian too) and beignets (awesome with apricot dip), with fries of course. Humorous menu, and classy cheap joint. Eat in or takeout.
Petite Abeille **107 W 18th St (at 6th Ave) ⊕212/604-9350.** French for "little bee," this charming Belgian place is perfect for a light snack or a bigger lunch after shopping at any of the department stores in the neighborhood.
Ronnybrook Farms Dairy **75 9th Ave (between 15th and 16th sts) ⊕212/741-6455.** Natural ice cream and dairy products, mostly for take-out, made in Long Island.

Union Square, Gramercy Park, Murray Hill

Bakeries and cafés

Chez Laurence **245 Madison Ave (corner of 38th St) ⊕212/683-0284.** Well-placed, friendly little *patisserie* that makes cheap breakfasts and decent, inexpensive lunches – and good coffee at any time of the day. Closed Sun.
City Bakery **22 E 17th St (between Broadway and 5th Ave) ⊕212/366-1414.** Minimalist bakery that uses fresh Greenmarket ingredients from around the corner. Serves reasonable soups and light lunch fare, but above all masterfully delicate tartlets, creamy hot chocolate, and *crème brûlée*. Closed Sun.
La Boulangère **49 E 21st St (between Broadway and Park Ave S) ⊕212/475-8772; 66 Mercer (between Broome and Spring sts) ⊕212/475-8582.** French bakery-café featuring breads, pastries, soups and salads; good for a midday pick-me-up.

Sandwiches and snacks

Eisenberg's Sandwich Shop **174 5th Ave (between 22nd and 23rd sts) ⊕212/675-5096.** This narrow little restaurant is a Flatiron institution. A tuna sandwich and some matzoh ball soup will cure what ails you.
Cosi **21st St and Park Ave South ⊕212/598-9300, with many locations in the city.** Though the fillings are good, they're not exceptional – what people come for is *Cosi*'s bread, which falls somewhere on the spectrum between focaccia and pita, and is made on the premises every day. Expensive as sandwiches go. In many sites, it is paired with *Xando* coffee bar.

Midtown West

Bakeries and cafés

Algonquin Hotel **59 W 44th St, lobby (between 5th and 6th aves) ⊕212/840-6800.** The archetypal American interpretation of the English drawing room, located in the airy, attractive lobby of the hotel (home of the notorious Round Table). Good for afternoon teas (not high tea, though), or a drink.
Brasserie Centrale **1700 Broadway (at W 53rd**

St) ☎212/757-2233. A rare midtown place where you can linger over coffee, freshly baked treats or a full meal. The menu offers a range of burgers, soups, salads, pastas and average French-tinged brasserie standards (stick with the simpler items on the menu). Large outdoor seating area. Open 24 hours.

Cupcake Café **522 9th Ave (at W 39th St) ☎212/465-1530.** A delightful little joint, offering decent soup and sandwiches at bargain prices, and great cakes, cupcakes and pies. Anything with fruit is a must.

Poseidon Bakery **629 9th Ave (between 44th and 45th sts) ☎212/757-6173.** Decadent baklava and other sweet Greek pastries, strudels and cookies, as well as spinach and meat pies. Known most of all for the hand-rolled phyllo dough that it makes on the premises and supplies to many restaurants in the city. Closed Sun and Mon.

Sandwiches and snacks

Schlotzky's **1380 6th Ave (at 56th St) ☎212/247-2867.** Reliably tasty sandwiches on specialty bread, or mini-pizzas with sourdough crust.

Soup Kitchen International **259A W 55th St (off 8th Ave), ☎212/757-7730.** The real-life counterpart of Jerry Seinfeld's friend the Soup Nazi, with rich soups highly priced but worth it. Closed in summer.

Souperdog **692 8th Ave (between 43rd and 44th sts) ☎212/221-9280.** Hopping soup and sausage establishment, with a focus on non-beef wursts.

Pizza by the slice

Mariella p.311
Ray's p.304
Schlotzky's (personal pizza) see above
Two Boots p.306
Vinnie's p.311

Midtown East

Sandwiches and snacks

Little Pie Company **Grand Central Station (Lower Food Concourse), no phone; but also at 424 W 43rd St (between 9th and 10th aves) ☎212/736-4780 and 407 W 14th St (between 9th and 10th aves) ☎212/414-2324.** True to its name, the *Little Pie Company* serves three-berry pies that are to die for, while the peach-raspberry, available in summer, has been known to provoke rioting. If it's just you, pick up a five-inch personal pie.

La Maison du Chocolat **30 Rockefeller Concourse (between 49th and 50th sts) ☎212/265-9404; also 1018 Madison Ave (between 78th and 79th sts) ☎212/744-7117.** Go soak up the French vibe: the original *Maison* is in Paris.

Shoebox Cafe **Grand Central Station (Lower Food Concourse) ☎212/986-5959.** Instead of taking the train to the deep South, just stop here, with authentic fried chicken and bourbon and pecan country ham available. The muffins (sweet and savory options) are also worthy, if heavy. No cook on Sundays.

Upper West Side and Morningside Heights

Bakeries and cafés

The Bread Shop **3139 Broadway (at W 123rd St) ☎212/666-4343.** Rich homemade breads and buttermilk biscuits in the bakery section, and soup and pizza in the cozy little restaurant section. A good place to rest up if you're in the neighborhood.

Café Lalo **201 W 83rd St (between Amsterdam and Broadway) ☎212/496-6031.** The spirit of Paris, complete with cramped tables and inconsistent service. Try the "shirred" eggs (made fluffy with a cappuccino machine) with all sorts of herbs and add-ins, or the wonderful Belgian waffles. Great desserts.

Café Mozart **154 W 70th St (between Central Park W and Columbus Ave) ☎212/595-9797.** This faded old Viennese coffee house serves rich tortes and apple strudel.

Caffè la Fortuna **69 W 71st St (between Central Park W and Columbus Ave) ☎212/724-5846.** The walls are covered with records and black-and-white photos of opera personalities.

The best things in life are free

Down to your last $20 bill? Not to worry, it is possible to eat for free in the city. Not an entire meal, perhaps, but maybe just enough of a snack to hold you through until supper. The following options are usually offered in a limited timeframe…so plan your day's itinerary accordingly.

Gourmet stores

Generally a weekend afternoon pursuit, and hit or miss. You may feast on fish at Zabar's or chew on cheese at Citarella. Sometimes the giveaways are listed on a flier outside, sometimes not. And you'll have to fight off a particularly energetic crowd.

Happy hours

Many bars, especially in midtown, give away bar grub as an incentive to stop in, usually 5–7pm weeknights. But as you'll have to shell out for the sometimes pricey drinks, it's not much in the way of a bargain.

Wine tastings

With some winemakers trying to appeal to regular people as more of an everyday drink than one for special occasions, a little education (and a big sip) can go a long way. Many wine merchants have tastings on Friday evenings or Saturday afternoons, where you can pick up grape history and learn the proper way to taste. Best Cellars, 1291 Lexington Ave (between 86th and 87th sts) has tastings every night during the week; from 1pm to 4pm on Saturday, the featured drink is usually paired with a nibble of sorts. Best of all, the wines for sale are all about $10, and all good.

The atmosphere is dark, comfy and inviting. You can sip a coffee all day long in the shade of their peaceful garden, and their Italian pastries are heavenly.

Drip 489 Amsterdam Ave (between 83rd and 84th sts) ☎212/875-1032. Not only can you find rich coffee and homemade desserts here, but also (maybe) a date for the evening – a set of three-ring binders in the back has completed questionnaires from hopefuls hoping to meet you on *Drip*'s comfortably worn couches.

Edgar's Café 255 W 84th St (between West End Ave and Broadway) ☎212/496-6126. A pleasant coffee house with good (though expensive) desserts and light snacks, great hot cider in the winter, and well-brewed coffees and teas all the time. Named for Edgar Allan Poe, who at one time lived a block or so farther east on 84th St.

Ecce Panis 282 Columbus Ave ☎212/362-7189; 1260 Madison Ave ☎212/348-0040; and three other locations. The knowing New Yorker's favorite bakers of fine bread.

Hadleigh's 1900 Broadway (between 63rd and 64th sts) ☎212/580-0669. Upscale and imported edible luxuries, and sandwiches you can eat at the shaded tables outside.

Hungarian Pastry Shop 1030 Amsterdam Ave (between 110th and 111th sts) ☎212/866-4230. This simple, no-frills coffee house is a favorite with Columbia University students and faculty alike. You sip your espresso and read all day if you like; the only problem is choosing amongst the pastries, cookies and cakes, all made on the premises.

Sandwiches and snacks

Euforia Cafe 167 W 83rd St (between Amsterdam and Columbus aves) ☎212/712-1500. Juices and smoothies, one flight down, in addition to a full-service flower shop.

Gray's Papaya 2090 Broadway (at W 72nd St) ☎212/799-0243. Order two all-beef franks and a papaya juice for a true New York experience. No ambience, no seats, just good cheap grub.

Hot & Crusty 2062 Broadway ☎212/799-6269; 2387 Broadway ☎212/496-0632; and other locations. Despite a name that sounds lifted out of *The Simpsons*, this chain bakery maintains excellent quality baked goods (the carrot and chocolate layer cake slices for $2.95 are better than in many elite cafés) and offers sandwiches, wraps and soups.

It's a Wrap 2102 Broadway (between 69th and 70th sts) ☎212/362-7922. The wrap sandwiches with funny names are more filling than you'd expect. The smoothies have funny names, too.

Nussbaum & Wu 2897 Broadway (at W 113th St) ☎212/280-5340. Baked goods and lunch items. For *Seinfeld's* idea of true New York, get one of their black-and-whites (though you can also get an all-black, all-white, or a mocha-and-white).

P&W Sandwich Shop 1030 Amsterdam Ave (between 110th and 111th sts) ⓣ212/222-2245. A recently opened luncher from the *Hungarian Pastry Shop* people next door.

V&T Pizzeria 1024 Amsterdam Ave (between 110th and 111th sts) ⓣ212/663-1708. Checked tablecloths and a low-key, down-home feel describes this pizzeria near Columbia that draws a predictably college-aged crowd. Good though, and very inexpensive.

Vinnie's Pizza 285 Amsterdam Ave (between 73rd and 74th sts) ⓣ212/874-4332. Some say the best, cheesiest pizzas on the Upper West Side. Cheap too.

Zabar's 2245 Broadway (at W 80th St) ⓣ212/787-2000. Pre-made but still tasty sandwiches and some limited hot lunch items, in addition to the usual suspects, compete for attention here at the café annex of the Upper West Side institution.

Upper East Side

Bakeries and cafés

Food Attitude 127 E 60th St (between Lexington and Park aves) ⓣ212/980-1818. Sweet fruit tarts and chocolate truffle cakes make this tiny café a good place to rest up between sights. A display of crusty bread creatures graces the front window. Closed Sun.

Les Friandises 922 Lexington Ave (between 70th and 71st sts) ⓣ212/988-1616. A paradise of French pastries on the Upper East Side. Wonderful croissants and brioches and a sublime tarte tatin.

Payard Patisserie & Bistro 1032 Lexington Ave (between 72nd and 73rd sts) ⓣ212/717-5252. This is real Parisian pastry – buttery, creamy and over the top. Cookies, cakes and *crème brûlée* made to the exacting standards of the kitchen staffs of local millionaires.

Serendipity 3 225 E 60th St (between 2nd and 3rd aves) ⓣ212/838-3531. Long-established eatery and ice-cream parlor adorned with Tiffany lamps. Has been a favorite spot for sweet sixteen parties and after-the-movie first dates for years. The frozen hot chocolate, a trademarked and copyrighted recipe, is out of this world, and the wealth of ice cream offerings are a real treat too.

Sandwiches and snacks

Mariella Pizza 151 E 60th St (between Lexington and 3rd aves) ⓣ212/319-5999; 180 3rd Ave ⓣ212/777-1220; 960 8th Ave ⓣ212/757-3016. Substantial slices make this a fine noontime option.

Wildgreen Café 1555 3rd Ave (at E 88th St) ⓣ212/828-7656. A small-town feel adds to the draw of this shop "where natural foods become gourmet." Muffins, salads, wraps and juices.

Ice cream

As a departure from the chain store **ice creams** (Ben & Jerry's, Haagen Dazs) found in your freezer and everywhere else, check out the following:

Avalanche 311 E 92nd St ⓣ212/987-9771
Chinatown Ice Cream Factory 65 Bayard St, see p.303.
Ciao Bella 227 Sullivan St ⓣ212/505-7100; 200 W 57th St ⓣ212/956-5555; 27 E 92nd St ⓣ212/831-5555
Cones 272 Bleecker St ⓣ212/414-1795
Custard Beach Grand Central Terminal Dining Concourse ⓣ212/983-9155
Howard Johnson's 1551 Broadway (at W 46th St) ⓣ212/354-1445
Moondog 612 Metropolitan Ave, Brooklyn ⓣ718/384-0333
Petrossian Cafe 911 7th Ave ⓣ212/245-2217
Uncle Louis G's 49 1/2 1st Ave, see p.307.
Uncle Luigi's 362 Coney Island Ave, Brooklyn ⓣ718/436-6914

Harlem, Washington Heights, Inwood

Bakeries and cafés

Wilson's Bakery and Restaurant 1980 Amsterdam Ave (at W 158th St) ☎212/923-9821. Luscious Southern specialties, like sweet potato pie and peach cobbler, but much more than desserts – try the chicken and waffle combination.

Brooklyn

Bedouin Tent 405 Atlantic Ave (at Bond St), Brooklyn Heights ☎718/852-5555. Original and best branch of small Middle-Eastern chain that has since migrated to Manhattan (originally known as *Moustache*.

Bergen Street Beat 440A Bergen St (between Flatbush & 5th Ave), Park Slope ☎718/623-1934. Try the delicious panini sandwiches, Brazilian coffee and plate combinations at this laid-back café/music shop. There's even a computer terminal for those out for some surfing.

Bliss 191 Bedford St, Williamsburg ☎718/599-2547. This earthy-crunchy stop tries to make you forget you're eating healthy.

Brooklyn Egg Cream Corp 424 Greenwood Ave, Park Slope ☎718/435-5914. One of the last habitats of a dying tradition, authentic egg creams have been made here since 1991.

Bruno Bakery 602 Lorimer St (between Skillman Ave and Conselyea St), Williamsburg ☎718/349-6524. Relaxing Italian bakery, open daily 9am–7pm.

Chip Shop 383 5th Ave, Park Slope ☎718/832-7701. English pub fare that the UK expats seem to love. Kid-friendly atmosphere.

City Sub 450 Bergen St, Park Slope ☎718/398-2592. Fresh local bread is a key ingredient of these sandwiches.

Connecticut Muffin 206 Prospect Park W, Park Slope ☎718/965-2067. Coffee and muffins, good to take to the park nearby.

Damascus Bakery 56 Gold St, Brooklyn Heights ☎718/855-1456. Syrian bakery, long established, with the city's best supply of different pita breads, as well as a dazzling array of pastries and desserts.

Fortunato Brothers 289 Manhattan Ave (at Devoe St), Williamsburg ☎718/387-2281. Old World Italian coffee shop with character to spare.

Leaf 'n' Bean 83 7th Ave (between Union and Berkeley sts), Park Slope ☎718/638-5791. Exotic coffees and teas plus excellent homemade soups and gourmet truffle candies. Brunch for about $10 on weekends. Outdoor seating when the weather cooperates.

Living Room Cafe 188 Prospect Park W, Park Slope ☎718/369-0824. Fun, cozy place where the locals go.

Mrs Stahl's 1001 Brighton Beach Ave (at Coney Island Ave), Brighton Beach ☎718/648-0210. Longstanding knish purveyor with over 20 different varieties.

Nathan's Famous Surf and Stillwell aves, Coney Island ☎718/266-3161. New York's most famous hot dogs and crinkle-cut French fries. Not the ultimate in gastronomy but a legend nonetheless.

Once Upon a Sundae 7702 3rd Ave (at 77th St), Bay Ridge ☎718/748-3412. Turn-of-the-nineteenth-century ice-cream parlor.

Juice Bars

Des Moines p.307
Elixir p.306
Euforia p.310
It's a Wrap p.310
Juicy Lucy's p.307
Live Juice p.307
Lucky's Juice Joint p.307
Wildgreen Café p.311

Queens

Athens 32-01 30th Ave, Astoria ☎718/626-2164. The Greekest of cafés, with spinach pies and specialty desserts.

Ommonia Café 32-20 Broadway, Astoria ☎718/274-6650. Despite the horrible name and the eatery's gaudy blue neon, *Ommonia* serves decent sandwiches and café items.

30

Restaurants

A large part of visiting New York City is experiencing not just the food but the **culture of dining**. New York is a rich port city that can get the best foodstuffs from anywhere in the world and, as a major immigration gateway, it attracts chefs who know how to cook the world's cuisines properly, even exceptionally. So not only can you get Senegalese, Brazilian, French regional, or any other kind of food you can think of, you can also get outstanding versions of it. As you stroll through the streets of New York, heavenly odors seem to emanate from every corner: pizza fresh from the oven, honey roasted nuts from streetside vendors, the sweet smell of Indian curry, or tantalizing halal meats being grilled on skewers. It's not hard to work up an appetite.

Although many hotels serve a breakfast of some kind, it is usually much cheaper (not to mention more interesting) to go out to a coffee shop for the first meal of the day. Most diners offer **breakfast specials** until 11am, allowing you to eat and drink until you're full for under $7. See "Cafés, snacks and light meals," Chapter 29, for more breakfast options.

Most restaurants open at lunchtime. In addition to diners, one of the best **lunchtime deals** can be had in **Chinatown**, where you can get a massive plate of pork, chicken or beef with noodles or rice for around $5 or, if you're feeling a little more adventurous, feast at a dim sum restaurant for around $8.

Another option for lunch – and one that's not just limited to Manhattan – is to get a **sandwich "to go"** from a **deli**. New York is known for its over-sized sandwiches; you can expect to pay around $4–7 per, and it is often a meal in itself.

Lunch is also the perfect time to sample some of New York's more expensive dining options, as many have prix-fixe deals making them actually quite affordable. Some restaurants have cottoned on to targeting this price with the current year, thus a two- or three-course lunch coming out at $20.02 in 2002.

Brunch is something of a New York institution, usually served on weekends between 11am and 3pm. Lox and cream cheese on a bagel, omelettes, French toast, eggs Benedict and pancakes are favorite brunch items. Many restaurants compete for customers by offering a special well-priced brunch menu – sometimes including a free Bloody Mary or Mimosa – basically, because the place specializes in dinner fare and wants to fill some seats in the afternoon. There's a list of recommended brunch venues on p.332. But be careful, brunch is also

Be sure to **tip** fifteen to twenty percent pretty much wherever you go, unless the service is terrible. As far as actual **payment** is concerned, most – although by no means all – restaurants take credit cards; travelers' checks are also widely accepted (see Basics, "Money and Banks").

a time for socialites to get in their daily gab, so at most places you should expect a wait.

Restaurant prices

New York's ethnic make-up is at its most obvious and accessible in the city's restaurants. Don't, however, make the mistake of assuming all ethnic food is necessarily inexpensive. Often it's not. You pay Manhattan's highest **prices** for the better Italian, French and Japanese eateries; Greek and Spanish food, too, often work out to be expensive, and really only Chinese, Jewish, Mexican and Eastern European are dependably low-budget. One other thing to bear in mind is that these days many of New York's most interesting and affordable ethnic restaurants are in Brooklyn, the Bronx and Queens. The listings that follow are by neighborhood and then country of origin or ethnic group, with a closing section on vegetarian options.

Eating on a budget

Street food – falafel, cheesesteaks, hot dogs and so on – can make for a cheap, greasy and sometimes sublimely satisfying meal; also, for around $1.75 you can always get a slice of pizza. In any case, you should never have to resort to fast-food chains to get good inexpensive eats.

Diners are another option, for filling breakfasts, burgers and French fries, hot and cold sandwiches, soups, salads and other basic fare from a usually enormous menu, which often includes lunchtime specials. We've listed the best of these below, along with **cafés** that serve up full meals; if you don't find it here, check for spots listed in Chapter XX, "Cafés, snacks and light meals," which may also offer sandwiches and cheap takeout.

Cuisines

American cooking, as served by New York restaurants, tends to be served in huge portions. Main dishes include steaks and burgers, fried chicken, fish and different types of seafood. Side dishes will almost certainly include a choice of French fries, rice or baked potato, and an assortment of vegetables. You'll also find many American restaurants offering a rich array of regional specialties such as **Southern**, **Cajun**, **Southwestern** and **Tex-Mex**, everything from jambalaya to crab cakes to grits to barbecue spare ribs. **Continental** cuisine is generally a hybrid of American, Italian and French influences, featuring pastas, meat and poultry in light sauces, fish, seafood and an array of nightly specials.

Be prepared to confront a startling variety of **ethnic cuisines**. In New York, none has had so dominant an effect as **Jewish food**, to the extent that many Jewish specialties – bagels, pastrami, lox and cream cheese – are now considered archetypal New York. Others retain more specific identities. **Chinese** food, available not just in Chinatown but all over Manhattan and the outer boroughs, includes the familiar Cantonese, as well as spicier Szechuan and Hunan dishes – most restaurants specialize in one or the other. Chinese prices are usually among the city's lowest, especially in the numerous takeout places (which are usually not very good). **Japanese** food is generally expensive, but very good; sushi, sashimi, even places specializing in fresh soba noodles, have all become quite popular the past decade or so. Other Asian cuisines include **Indian** – best in Jackson Heights, Queens – and a broad and increasing sprinkling of **Thai**, **Korean**, **Vietnamese** and **Indonesian** restaurants, all of which tend to be pricier than Chinese but not prohibitively so.

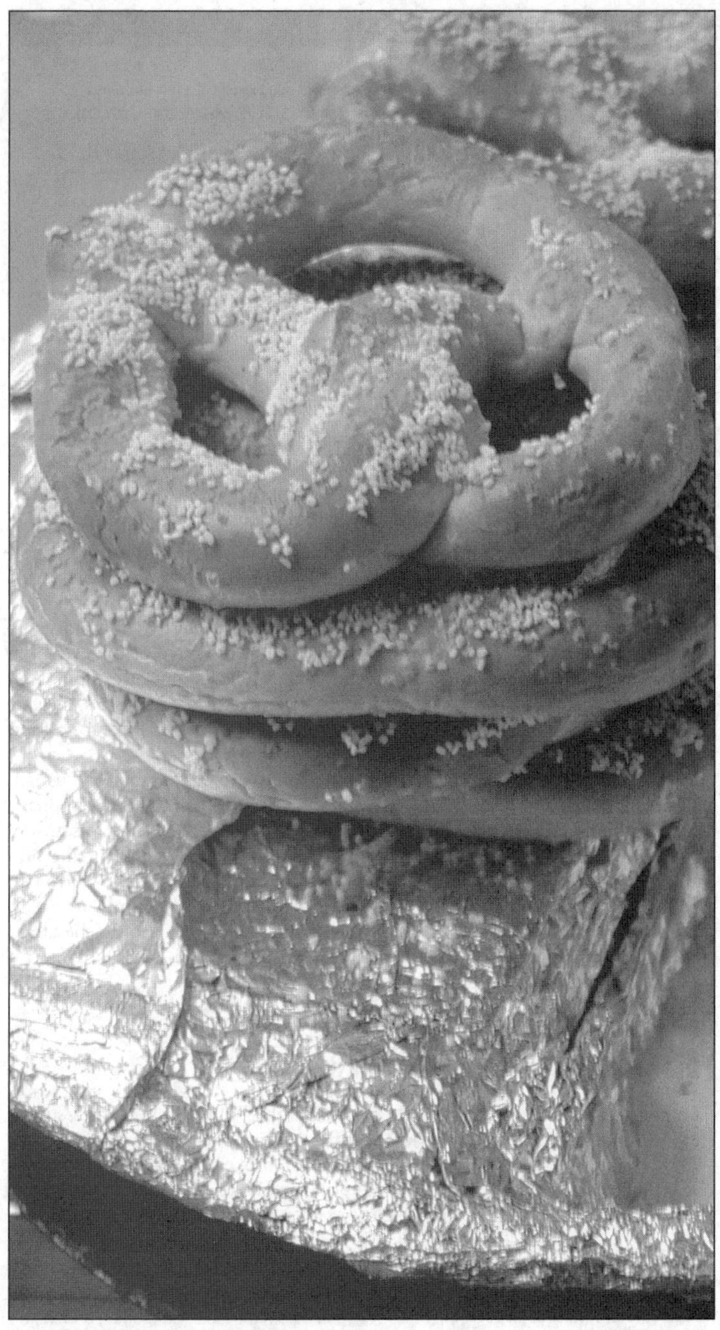

△ Typical New York street food

Specialty eating

We've highlighted particular types and styles of restaurant, and places to eat that can't easily be listed elsewhere, and listed them in boxes in the text. We've also picked out a few favorites in the city, which is very hard to do; most of the places recommended in the chapter are exactly that – recommended – but this might give you an easy guide:

Favorites

Types

Irish food is found mostly in city bars, with the occasional exception. **Italian** cooking is also widespread and not terribly expensive, especially if you stick to pizza or pasta; **Spanish** food, though not as common, can be a good deal if you order the huge seafood paella dishes – an economical night out for those in a group (and don't forget the large pitchers of sangria). **French** restaurants tend to be pricier, although there are an increasing number of bistros and brasseries turning out authentic and reliable French nosh for attractive prices. A fading trend is **Belgian** food: a surprising number of Belgian brasseries and steak frites joints opened in the last several years, offering steamed mussels, *pommes frites* and Trappist ales. Yet, many have since shut their doors. In New York, food trends come and go.

There is also a whole range of **Eastern European** restaurants – Russian, Ukrainian, Polish and Hungarian – that serve well-priced, filling fare (emphasis on the filling). **Caribbean**, **Central** and **South American** restaurants are on the rise in New York, and often offer a good deal and a large, satisfying and often spicy meal. Other places include weird hybrids like Chinese-Peruvian, Japanese-Brazilian, and any number of **vegetarian** and **wholefood** eateries to cater to any taste or fad. The key is to keep your eyes peeled and not be afraid to be adventurous. Eating is one of the great joys of being in New York, and it would be a shame to waste it on the familiar.

Financial District and City Hall area

The culinary focal point of lower Manhattan is the Fulton Fish Market, so not surprisingly many of the restaurants in this area serve seafood. Unfortunately, with few exceptions, most overcharge the power-broker lunch regulars for relatively unimpressive fare. Remember, the place revolves around trading hours, so many restaurants close early, and are closed or have reduced hours on weekends.

American and Continental

Bridge Café **279 Water St (at Dover St) ☎212/227-3344.** They say there's been a bar here since 1794, but this place looks very up-to-the-minute. The good crabcakes come from the local fish market, and there are plenty of upscale beers with which to wash them down. The rare eighteenth-century frame house, painted red with black trim, is well worth a look. Entrees are priced between $15–25.

Harry's at Hanover Square **1 Hanover Square (between Pearl and Stone sts) ☎212/425-3412.** Clubby bar that gets into its stride when the floor traders come in after work. Great burgers, but only open on weekdays.

Hudson River Club **4 World Financial Center, 250 Vesey St, Upper Level (at West St) ☎212/786-1500.** Worth the $70 or so per head for the view over the harbor to the Statue of Liberty. The food is American, with special emphasis on cooking from New York State's Hudson River Valley. Start with the seafood martini (shrimp, lobster and lump crabmeat with a citron aioli) or just go straight for the apricot-glazed halibut entree.

Jeremy's Alehouse **254 Front St (at Dover St) ☎212/964-3537.** Once a sleaze bar in the shadow of the Brooklyn Bridge, *Jeremy's* fortunes changed with the aggrandizement of the nearby South Street Seaport. However, it still serves well-priced pint mugs of beer and excellent fish fresh from the adjacent Fulton Fish Market, as well as burgers. Expect to spend $10–15 per person.

Paris Café **119 South St ☎212/240-9797.** Established in 1873, this old-fashioned bar and restaurant serves plentiful servings of traditional American fare – including very fresh fish and seafood; entrees are about $18–25.

Rough Guide favorites

Burgers

Big Nick's Upper West Side, p.340
Corner Bistro West Village, p.323
Diner Williamsburg, p.349
Hamburger Harry's Midtown West, p.335
Viand Upper East Side, p.343

Vine Restaurant and Bar **25 Broad St (enter on Exchange Place) ☎212/344-8463.** Relatively new, located just steps away from the Stock Exchange (expensive and stuffy), the food is American eclectic.

Caribbean, Central and South American

Radio Mexico **259 Front St (at Dover St) ☎212/791-5416.** Good Tex-Mex food in enjoyable, if often crowded Seaport surroundings. About the only such choice in the neighborhood, it's fun, reliable and has good margaritas. Entrees between $6 and $12.

Italian

Carmine's Bar and Grill **140 Beekman St (at Front St) ☎212/962-8606.** In business since 1903, this place specializes in Northern Italian-style seafood and exudes a comfortable if run-down ambience. Try a glass of the house wine and a bowl of linguini in clam sauce for lunch.

Chinatown and Little Italy

Three of New York's most prominent cuisines huddle together in these crowded adjoining neighborhoods. If authentic Chinese, Thai and Vietnamese food is what you're after, best head for the busy streets of **Chinatown**. Dim sum (literally meaning "your heart's delight") is highly recommended and consists of small dishes that you choose from a moving trolley and pay for at the end, according to the empty dishes in front of you.

Mulberry Street is **Little Italy**'s main drag, and though often crowded with Bridge and Tunnel weekend tourists, the Southern Italian food and carnival atmosphere can make dinner and coffee a worthwhile excursion.

Asian

Bo Ky **80 Bayard St (between Mott and Mulberry sts) ☎212/406-2292.** Cramped Chinese-Vietnamese serving very inexpensive noodle soups and seafood dishes. The house specialty is a big bowl of rice noodles with shrimp, fish or duck.

Canton **45 Division St at the Manhattan Bridge (between Bowery and Market sts)**

☎212/226-4441. Fairly upscale compared to other Chinatown restaurants in terms of decor, style and service, but only marginally more expensive. Seafood is the specialty here; bring your own booze. Closed Mon and Tues.

Excellent Dumpling House 111 Lafayette St (between Canal and Walker sts) ☎212/219-0212. The thing to order is obviously the most excellent dumplings, any way you like them. Their scallion pancakes are also delicious.

Goody's 1 East Broadway ☎212/577- 2922. If the lines at *Joe's* are too long, this Shanghai specialist – the sister restaurant of a longer-established Queens eatery – is a great alternative, with soup dumplings that are at least as good, and wonderful duck and pork shoulder specials.

Joe's Shanghai 9 Pell St (between Bowery and Mott sts) ☎212/233-8888. Probably Chinatown's most famous restaurant, this place is always packed, with good reason. Start with the soup dumplings and work through some seafood dishes for the main course; communal tables.

New York Noodletown 28 Bowery (at Bayard St) ☎212/349-0923. Despite the name, noodles aren't the real draw at this down-to-earth eatery – the soft-shell crabs are crisp, salty and delicious. Good roast meats (try the baby pig) and soups too.

Nice Restaurant 35 E Broadway (between Catherine and Market sts) ☎212/406-9510. This vast Cantonese restaurant is especially good for dim sum (and barbecued duck). Usually crowded and noisy, particularly on Sundays.

Silver Palace 50 Bowery (between Bayard and Canal sts) ☎212/964-1204. A predominantly dim sum restaurant. Take the escalator up to the enormous dining room with dragon pillars and peacock murals. Not recommended for vegetarians.

Sweet 'n' Tart Restaurant 20 Mott St (at Canal St) ☎212/964-0380. The place for shark's-fin soup and other Hong Kong-style seafood delicacies, as well as superb dim sum. Very popular, so expect to wait. The older establishment, with a more limited menu, is located just up the street at 76 Mott St.

Thailand Restaurant 106 Bayard St (at Baxter St) ☎212/349-3132. The well-priced Thai food is eaten at long communal tables here. The whole fish dishes, crispy and spicy, are standouts.

Vietnam 11–13 Doyers St (between Bowery and Pell sts) ☎212/693-0725. This hard-to-find underground eatery doesn't offer much in the way of decor, but the inexpensive Vietnamese fare is among the city's best: you can't go wrong here with the ginger whole fish, caramel pork or sautéed watercress.

Italian

Il Fornaio 132a Mulberry St (between Hester and Grand sts) ☎212/226-8306. Stylish, bright, tiled Italian restaurant with good lunch deals – fine calzone and pizza for $4. Affordable and tasty Southern Italian cooking: pastas, Italian stews and the like.

La Luna 112 Mulberry St (between Canal and Hester sts) ☎212/226-8657. One of Little Italy's longest established and best value choices. The attitude of the waiters is gruff, and the food only middling – but the atmosphere is fun and it's a popular joint, packing in a crowd.

Lombardi's 32 Spring St (between Mott and Mulberry sts) ☎212/941-7994. Arguably some of the best pizza in town, including an amazing clam pie; no slices though. Ask for roasted garlic on the side.

Peasant 194 Elizabeth St (between Prince and Spring sts) ☎212/965-9511. A bit of a hangout after-hours for city chefs, here you'll pay around $22–30 for hearty grilled entrees, such as lamb or fish, served from an open kitchen.

Pellegrino 138 Mulberry St (between Hester and Grand sts) ☎212/226-3177. Laid-back Little Italy restaurant serving good homemade pastas and other dishes at good prices.

Puglia 189 Hester St (between Mulberry and Mott sts) ☎212/226-8912. One of Little Italy's more affordable (and tacky) restaurants, where they cut costs and sharpen the atmosphere by sitting everyone at communal trestle tables. Consistently good Southern Italian food, consumed loudly and raucously. Closed Mon.

Vincent's Clam Bar 119 Mott St (at Hester St) ☎212/226-8133. A Little Italy mainstay that serves fresh, cheap and spicy seafood dishes – clams, mussels and squid.

Lower East Side

In spots, the **Lower East Side** seems like a throwback to early immigrant sweatshop days; at others it's a place where the city's hipsters hang out. Either way, it's still the best place to get a pickle.

American and Continental

71 Clinton Fresh Food 71 Clinton St (at Rivington St) ⓣ212/614-6960. Popular with foodies and hipsters alike, this cozy spot serves some of the best food in the city. Either the beer-braised short ribs or sea bass crusted with edamame will send you for a loop; start with the potato torte or salmon-avocado tartare.

Lansky Lounge & Grill 104 Norfolk St (between Delancey and Rivington sts) ⓣ212/677-9489. With a hidden, back-alleyway entrance, this former speakeasy was once a haunt of gangster Meyer Lansky. With a bone-in ribeye that's fit for a king and a lounge that hops late at night, this hotspot has all the makings of a sinful evening.

Caribbean, Central and South American

El Cibao corner of Clinton and Rivington sts, no phone. The best of a slew of Dominican and Puerto Rican restaurants in the Lower East Side. Hearty and inexpensive fare, with great sandwiches, particularly the *pernil* (pork), toasted crisp in a sandwich press.

El Sombrero 108 Stanton St (at Ludlow St) ⓣ212/254-4188. Known to the local demimonde as "The Hat," this unprepossessing Mexican restaurant serves generous portions of food and wonderful frozen margaritas.

Jewish and Eastern European

Katz's Deli 205 E Houston St (between Essex and Ludlow sts) ⓣ212/254-2246. Cafeteria-style or sit down and be served. The overstuffed pastrami or corned beef sandwiches, doused with mustard and with a side pile of pickles, should keep you going for about a week. Also famous for their egg creams; open seven days a week. Don't lose your meal ticket or they'll charge you an arm and a leg.

Sammy's Roumanian Restaurant 157 Chrystie St (between Delancey and Rivington sts) ⓣ212/673-0330. The food, at around $25 or so for a full meal, is undeniably good, but most people come for the raucous live music.

TriBeCa

Still one of New York's trendiest neighborhoods, here you often pay for the vista rather than the victuals. Yet who can argue with sitting outside at a sidewalk café and feeling like you've traveled (rather cheaply) to Europe? Even so, there are appropriately divine meals, and occasional deals, to be had in **TriBeCa** – and the people-watching is not bad either.

American and Continental

Bubby's 120 Hudson St (between Franklin and N Moore sts) ⓣ212/219-0666. A relaxed TriBeCa restaurant serving homely health-conscious American food. Great scones, mashed potatoes, rosemary chicken and soups. A good, moderately priced brunch spot, too – the trout and eggs is a killer!

City Hall 131 Duane St (between Church and West Broadway) ⓣ212/227-7777. With a nod toward old-time New York City, *City Hall* is all class, with amazing steaks and always-fresh oysters. Though a little pricey, the open-room ambience, great service and opportunity to rub shoulders with celebs make the splurge worth it.

Odeon 145 W Broadway (at Thomas St) ⓣ212/233-0507. *Odeon* has shown surprising staying power, perhaps because the eclectic food choices are actually pretty good and the people-watching still can't be beat. Entrees go for around $15–20 and, on the whole, are worth it.

Screening Room 54 Varick St (at Laight St)

☎212/334-2100. This restaurant-bar with a small movie theater makes for those perfect evenings you don't want to schlep all over town to this restaurant, that movie theater and then this bar. At $35, the dinner and a movie deal can't be beat.

TriBeCa Grill **375 Greenwich St (at Franklin St) ☎212/941-3900.** As it is owned by Robert De Niro, some people come for a glimpse of the actor when they should really be concentrating on the food – fine American cooking with Asian and Italian accents at around $30 a main course. The setting is nice too; an airy, brick-walled eating area around a central Tiffany bar. Worth the money as a treat, despite the trendy scene and gawking tourists.

Asian

Nobu **105 Hudson St (at Franklin St) ☎212/219-0500.** Robert De Niro's best-known New York restaurant, whose lavish woodland decor complements really superlative Japanese cuisine, especially sushi, at the ultra-high prices you would expect. If you can't get a reservation, try *Next Door Nobu*, located just next door.

Thai House Café **151 Hudson St (at Hubert St) ☎212/334-1085.** Small, friendly TriBeCa Thai restaurant, popular for its inexpensive authentic food. The *pad thai* and red curries are excellent. Closed Sun.

Mexican

El Teddy's **219 W Broadway (between Franklin and White sts) ☎212/941-7070.** Eccentrically decorated restaurant that serves creative Mexican food, like goat cheese quesadillas, and the best margaritas in town. Try the fried tortillas wrapped around spicy chicken for starters. Entrees, around $15–19, feel a bit pricey for what you get.

French and Belgian

Bouley **165 Duane St (between Greenwich and Hudson sts) ☎212/608-3852.** One of New York's best French restaurants, serving modern French food made from the freshest ingredients. Popular with city celebrities, but costs for the magnificent meals can be softened by opting for the prix-fixe lunch and dinner options. (For details on next-door *Bouley Bakery* see p.304)

Capsouto Frères **451 Washington St (at Watts St) ☎212/966-4900.** Tucked away in a discreet corner of TriBeCa is this wonderful, if pricey, French bistro with a lofty feel. Dinner entrees are about $14–24. Try the duck with ginger and cassis, and don't miss the dessert soufflés.

Chanterelle **2 Harrison St (at Hudson St), ☎212/966-6960.** Some say while in New York you should live on stale bread all week and spend all your money on the haute French cuisine here, which is of the finest order. The wines are so rare, you are advised to reserve your bottle ahead of time so they can properly decant it. Very pricey.

Montrachet **239 West Broadway (between Walker and White sts) ☎212/219-2777.** A greybeard of the Drew Nieporent restaurants, *Montrachet* is pricey but oh so delicious. The milk-poached veal loin and the mustard-crusted sweetbreads are fantastic. Amazing wine list. Closed Sun.

Greek and Middle Eastern

Delphi **109 W Broadway (at Reade St) ☎212/227-6322.** Accommodating Greek restaurant with good menu, great portions and unbeatable prices. The antipasti and fish are excellent value at $9–12 or there's kebabs and the like from $7–10 and sandwiches as low as $5. Best Manhattan choice for bargain Greek eating.

Layla **211 W Broadway (at Franklin St) ☎212/431-0700.** Middle Eastern-themed restaurant, where you can get a very nice $26 kebab, as well as calamari stuffed with merguez sausage. Wild, rich Persian-style decor and belly dancers add a great deal to the experience. Expensive.

Indian

Pakistan Tea House **176 Church St (between Reade and Duane sts) ☎212/240-9800.** Great cheap Pakistani, $5–7 entrees, with made-to-order flatbreads.

Rough Guide favorites

Sushi

Blue Ribbon Sushi SoHo, see opposite
Bond Street East Village, p.326
Nobu TriBeCa, see above
Tomoe Sushi West Village, p.323
Yama West Village, p.323

SoHo

Some of the city's trendiest – and most celebrated – restaurants can be found in **SoHo**, covering a wide array of cuisines. And while they tend toward the expensive, the people-watching can be amazing.

African

Ghenet **284 Mulberry St (between Houston and Prince sts) ☎212/343-1888.** Atmospheric and relatively inexpensive Ethiopian restaurant serving a changing menu of unusual spicy dishes that you can eat with your hands and sop up with homemade bread. Try the lamb stew.

American and Continental

Jerry's Restaurant **101 Prince St (between Greene and Mercer sts) ☎212/966-9464.** Casual American-continental restaurant with a funky, upscale diner atmosphere. Good lox for brunch, though often crowded. Moderate prices. Closed Sun night.

Moondance Diner **80 6th Ave (between Grand and Canal sts) ☎212/226-1191.** This authentic old diner car turns out cheap and filling meals of great burgers, onion rings, omelets and apple pancakes. Open 24 hours on weekends; to midnight all other nights.

Rialto **265 Elizabeth St (between Houston and Prince sts) ☎212/334-7900.** Serious homestyle American cooking in unlikely surroundings – an elegant room with curved red leather banquettes, filled with beautiful, chic people, and a refreshing garden in back. Not as expensive as the clientele looks either.

Spring Street Natural Restaurant **62 Spring St (at Lafayette St) ☎212/966-0290.** Not wholly vegetarian, but very good, freshly prepared health food served in a large airy space. Moderately priced, with entrees from $9 on up. Very popular with locals, but crowds add to sometimes already slow service.

Asian

Blue Ribbon Sushi **119 Sullivan St (between Prince and Spring sts) ☎212/343-0404.** Widely considered one of the best sushi restaurants in New York, the lines for a table can be long and it doesn't allow reservations. Our advice: have some cold sake and relax – the kitchen is open until 2am.

Kelley and Ping **127 Greene St (between Prince and W Houston sts) ☎212/228-1212.** Sleek pan-Asian tea room and restaurant that serves a tasty bowl of noodle soup. Dark wooden cases filled with Thai herbs and cooking ingredients add to the casually elegant (and unusual) setting.

Rice **227 Mott St (between Prince and Spring sts) ☎212/226-5775.** Small, inexpensive pan-Asian spot, where you mix-and-match various rices (black, sticky, etc) with interesting meat choices (lemongrass chicken, beef salad and the like).

Caribbean, Central and South American

Brisa del Caribe **489 Broadway (at Broome St) ☎212/226-9768.** Very good and very cheap rice and beans in an unlikely SoHo no-frills eatery.

Café Habana **17 Prince St (at Elizabeth St) ☎212/625-2001.** Small and always crowded, this Cuban-South American eatery features some of the best skirt steak and fried plantains this side of Havana.

Mexican Radio **19 Cleveland Place (between Kenmare and Spring sts) ☎212/343-0140.** Although the move to this new, larger location meant losing some of *MR*'s original charm, you can still get the same creative Mexican fare… and now even possibly a seat.

French and Belgian

Alison on Dominick **38 Dominick St (between Hudson and Varick sts) ☎212/727-1188.** About as tucked away and romantic as you can get in the middle of a huge city, with great Southwestern French food that is served with a creative, light touch. Very expensive, but worth it for a special occasion with the one you love.

Balthazar **80 Spring St (between Crosby St and Broadway) ☎212/965-1414.** After around five years this is still one of the hottest reservations in town. The tastefully ornate Parisian decor and nonstop beautiful people keep your eyes busy until the food arrives; then all you can do is savor the fresh oysters and mussels, the exquisite pastries and everything in between. It's worth the money and the attitude.

L'Ecole 462 Broadway (at Grand St) ☎212/219-3300. Students of the French Culinary Institute serve up affordable French delights – and they rarely fail. The three-course prix-fixe dinner costs $29.95 per person; book in advance. Closed Sun.

Le Jardin Bistro 25 Cleveland Place (between Kenmare and Spring sts) ☎212/343-9599. Unpretentious French bistro with a garden in the back and reliably good food, including cassoulet and very fresh seafood. Romantic and moderately priced for what you get, with entrees around $16–20.

Le Pescadou 18 King St (off 6th Ave, south of W Houston St) ☎212/924-3434. A chic seafood bistro in a charming French setting. Moderate prices.

Manhattan Bistro 129 Spring St (between Greene and Wooster sts) ☎212/966-3459. Your basic bistro – familiar French dishes, plus pastas and focaccia sandwiches – that has lasted in a fad-obsessed neighborhood because the food is well prepared and not overpriced, and the room is classy and quiet.

Provence 38 MacDougal St (between Prince and Houston sts) ☎212/475-7500. Very popular SoHo bistro that serves such excellent dishes as rabbit at around $18–25 for a main course. A nice place for a special occasion, *Provence* features a lovely, airy eating area and a garden for the summer.

Raoul's 180 Prince St (between Sullivan and Thompson sts) ☎212/966-3518. French bistro seemingly lifted from Paris. The food, especially the steak *au poivre* and crayfish risotto, plus service are wonderful – as you'd expect at the high prices you'll find here. Reservations recommended. Closed Aug.

Vandam 150 Varick St (at Vandam St) ☎212/352-9090. A brand new restaurant from the people who brought you *Balthazar*, with sumptuous decor and pricey French food with a Latin American twist. Want some yucca with your *foie gras*? Now you can have it. Closed Sun.

Italian

Mezzogiorno 195 Spring St (at Sullivan) ☎212/334-2112. Bright SoHo restaurant that's as much a place to people-watch as eat. A little overpriced, but a good and inventive menu, including excellent wood-burning-oven pizzas, great salads and *carpaccio* – thinly sliced raw beef served in various ways.

Oro Blu 333 Hudson St ☎212/645-8004. Great Italian food in a modern airy setting – a mixture of savory classics and more innovative fare. It is a good option in a fairly sparse part of town – well off the main SoHo track.

West Village

The bohemian edge that once characterized the **West Village** became the most seductive of marketing ploys, attracting visitors from near and far. Now many restaurants are overcrowded and overpriced, particularly in and around New York University, along Seventh Avenue and, increasingly, in the red-rope meatpacking district, an area of the Village that sprawls into Chelsea. In spite of tourist traffic, the hub of Italian cafés around Bleecker and MacDougal remains a good place to recuperate with a healthy infusion of sugar and caffeine, and tucked away gems continue to impress.

American and Continental

Anglers & Writers 420 Hudson St (at St Luke's Place) ☎212/675-0810. Village café serving high tea from 4pm to 7pm, as well as decent continental fare – soups and desserts are a specialty. A good place to just have a coffee, a snack or a full meal.

Brother's Bar-B-Q 255 Varick St (corner of Clarkson) ☎212/727-2775. A huge airy room with firehouse decor, kitschy Dixie-ana displays, big booths and piped-in country/blues music, serving some pretty good BBQ – for NYC. The ribs, mashed potatoes and collard greens are not to be missed. Cheap too – two people can eat handsomely for around $25.

Corner Bistro 331 W 4th St (at Jane St) ☎212/242-9502. Down-home pub with cavernous cubicles, paper plates and maybe the best burger and fries ($6.50) in town. Longstanding haunt of West Village literary and artsy types, a mix of locals and die-hard fans line up nightly; but don't be discouraged, the line moves faster than it looks.

Cowgirl Hall of Fame 519 Hudson St (at 10th St) ☎212/633-1133. Down-home Texan-style barbecue amidst cowboy kitsch and memorabilia. Huge selection of tequilas served in a glass cowboy boot. Try the meaty ribs or fried chicken.

Fressen 421 W 13th St (between 9th Ave and Washington St) ☎212/645-7775. Unique New American fusion menu and warm yet industrial design (cement walls) makes this a happening spot for dinner and late night drinks.

Grange Hall 50 Commerce St (at Barrow St) ☎212/924-5246. Tucked away in one of the most beautiful West Village neighborhoods, this depression-era designed eatery is a hit for dinner, brunch and drinks. Cranberry pork chops and potato pancakes are recommended. Entrees $11–17.

Home 20 Cornelia St (between Bleecker and 4th sts) ☎212/243-9579. *Home* is one of those rare restaurants that manages to pull off quaint and cozy with flair. The creative and reasonably priced American food is always fresh and wonderful, perhaps a better deal at lunch than dinner. Try the cumin-crusted pork chops.

One if by Land 17 Barrow St (between 7th Ave and 4th St) ☎212/228-0822. One of the most romantic restaurants in the city, it's also one of the priciest ($59 prix fixe). Once occupied by Aaron Burr, this cozy, classy space is rounded out by delicate piano music.

The Pink Teacup 42 Grove St (between Bleecker and Bedford sts) ☎212/807-6755. Longstanding Southern soulfood institution in the heart of the Village, with good smothered pork chops, cornbread and the like. Brunch too, but no credit cards.

Shopsin's General Store 63 Bedford St (at Morton St) ☎212/924-5160. Leave your attitude at the door when you come to *Shopsin's*. This tiny, family-run restaurant serves a Bible-length menu of homemade soups and sandwiches. Closed weekends just because they feel like it. No credit cards.

White Horse Tavern 567 Hudson St (at 11th St) ☎212/989-3956. There's no better spot for beer and burgers, especially during summer at the outdoor picnic tables. See p.357 for details on the bar.

Asian

Chow Bar 230 W 4th St (at 10th st) ☎212/633-2212. Pan-Asian soups and noodles are available at this centrally located West Village institution at very fair prices.

Little Basil 39 Greenwich Ave ☎212/645-8965. Such Thai staples as green and red curries, *pad thai* and the like are served here, along with more pan-Asian dishes like crispy duck, with upscale panache in a comfortably casual environment.

Sushi Samba 7 87 7th Ave (at Barrow St) ☎212/691-7885. Hard to miss, as the garish colors and buzzy feel spill onto the street, this Japanese-South American sushi-ceviche restaurant manages to serve up unique, tasty and eminently fresh seafood concoctions, along with exotic and potent drinks.

Tomoe Sushi 172 Thompson St (between Bleecker and Houston sts) ☎212/777-9346. While the nightly lines might look daunting, the wait is worth it for some of the best sushi in Manhattan. If they have soft shell crab, get it rolled.

Toons 417 Bleecker St (at Bank St) ☎212/924-6420. Despite relatively high prices, this low-lit, homey Thai-community favorite has an intimate atmosphere and offers tasty authentic *pad thais* and red or green curries.

Yama 40 Carmine St ☎212/989-9330. This initimate yet bustling Japanese restaurant features great sushi, great everything. Try the wasabi shumai dumplings.

Caribbean, Central and South American

Benny's Burritos 113 Greenwich Ave (at Jane St) ☎212/727-0595; 93 Ave A (at 6th St)

☎212/254-2054. Huge, tasty burritos with all kinds of fillings; speedy service, great margaritas and low prices.

Caribe **117 Perry St (between Hudson and Greenwich sts) ☎212/255-9191.** A funky Caribbean restaurant filled with leafy jungle decor and blasted with reggae music. Jerk chicken, washed down with wild tropical cocktails, makes it the place for a fun night out. Entrees around $9–16.

Day-O **103 Greenwich Ave (at 12th St) ☎212/924-3161.** A young crowd enjoys the food and lively atmosphere at this downtown Caribbean/Southern joint. Highlights include fried catfish, jerk chicken, coconut shrimp and a choice of two veggie dishes – not to mention the deadly tropical drinks.

Mi Cocina **57 Jane St (at Hudson St) ☎212/627-8273.** Authentic Mexican food in a simple setting. Good prices – entrees in the range of $11–15. Often crowded, so be prepared to wait.

Tortilla Flats **767 Washington St (at 12th St) ☎212/243-1053.** Cheap West Village Mexican dive with great margaritas, a loud jukebox and plenty of kitsch. Be careful, gets really crowded.

French and Belgian

Bar Six **502 6th Ave (between 12th and 13th sts) ☎212/691-1363.** Varied French-Moroccan fare in this small bistro with outdoor seating on the street and a hopping happy hour.

Café de Bruxelles **118 Greenwich Ave (at 13th St) ☎212/206-1830.** Very authentic and popular Belgian restaurant in the West Village. Try the *waterzooi*, a rich and creamy chicken stew, or mussels served every way you like.

Chez Brigitte **77 Greenwich Ave (between Bank St and 7th Ave) ☎212/929-6736.** Only a dozen people fit in this tiny restaurant, which serves stews, all-day roast meat dinners for under $10, and other bargains from a simple menu.

Cornelia Street Café **29 Cornelia St (between Bleecker and W 4th) ☎212/989-9319.** As much American as French, there is no more comfortable café on a more beautiful street in NY. Pastas, salads and great brunch. Also jazz, poetry and performance art in downstairs cabaret.

Florent **69 Gansevoort St (between Washington and Greenwich sts) ☎212/989-5779.** Ultra-fashionable bistro on the edge of the meat-packing district that serves good French food, either à la carte or from a prix-fixe menu ($20.95, or $18.95 before 7.30pm). Coffee shop decor, always busy. The mussels are so good it almost doesn't matter how obnoxious the waiters are. Open 24 hours, it's a favorite late-night hangout for clubbers and low-level celebrities.

Markt **401 W 14th St ☎212/727-3314.** Very large and very noisy brasserie, serving decent Belgian standards – mussels, *waterzooi*, and of course frites – along with one of the city's best choice of Belgian ales. A less formal alternative to *Café de Bruxelles* (see above), but not the place for a quiet tête-à-tête.

Paris Commune **411 Bleecker St (between 11th and Bank sts) ☎212/929-0509.** Romantic West Village bistro with reliable French home cooking and a fireplace. Memorable French toast and wild mushroom ravioli at moderate prices. Long lines for brunch.

Pastis **9-11 Little W 12th St (at 9th Ave) ☎212/929-4844.** Brightly colored almost pedantically authentic Parisian brasserie. The food is great; the service can be hit-and-miss, unless you are one of the many local celebs who frequent during busy weekend brunch. For dinner try the crispy monkfish.

Petite Abeille **466 Hudson St ☎212/791- 6479.** Another popular remnant of the Belgian food craze that swept the city a few years back. Though it's very small and not really the place for an intimate dinner, the omelettes, mussels and such are well worth sampling.

Tartine **253 W 11th St (at 4th St) ☎212/229-2611.** With no more than ten tables packed in this popular bistro, crowds line the street almost any night of the week. But bring your own bottle of wine, have the waitress cork it, and converse amongst yourselves or others while you wait. The warm asparagus salad is to die for.

Titou **259 W 4th St (between Charles and Perry sts) ☎212/691-9359.** Kid sister of *Tartine* just up the block, *Titou* offers affordable fare in an unpretentious setting. The roasted chicken with truffle mashed potatoes is so smooth and flavorful you'll never want to eat anything else.

Italian

Arturo's Pizza 106 W Houston St (at Thompson St) ⓣ212/475-9828. Coal-oven pizzas, no slices, that rival some of the best pies in town. While-you-eat entertainment often includes live jazz, and there are a couple of outdoor tables on busy Houston St.

Babbo 110 Waverly Place (between 6th Ave and MacDougal St) ⓣ212/777-0303. This eatery offers delicious, creative Italian dishes – beef cheek ravioli and various takes on scrapple garner much of the praise – attentive service and an interesting selection of wine; it's quite popular, so reserve in advance. Expect to pay at least $50 or so a head.

Cent' Anni 50 Carmine St (between Bleecker and Bedford sts) ⓣ212/989-9494. Small, low-key, old-time Village restaurant serving consistently delicious, and sometimes pricey, Florentine dishes.

Cucina Della Fontana 368 Bleecker St (at Charles St) ⓣ212/242-0636. From the outside this place looks like a normal bar, but out in the back there's a plant-filled atrium where you can eat fine Italian food, such as mussels, fish and pasta.

'ino 21 Bedford St (between Downing St and 6th Ave) ⓣ212/989-5769. This closet-sized restaurant serves bruscetta and panini sandwiches, sumptuous cheeses and wine by the glass; the truffled egg toast is an excellent brunch option.

John's Pizzeria 278 Bleecker St (between 6th and 7th aves) ⓣ212/243-1680. No slices, no takeaways. A full-service restaurant that serves some of the city's best and most popular pizza, with a crust that is thin and coal-charred. Be prepared to wait in line. Uptown branches at 408 E 64th St (between 1st and York aves) ⓣ212/935-2895 and 48 W 65th St (between Columbus Ave and Central Park W) ⓣ212/721-7001.

Lupa 170 Thompson St (between Bleecker and Houston sts) ⓣ212/982-5089. *Lupa* serves hearty, rustic Italian specialties such as *osso buco*, *saltimbocca* and gnocchi with fennel sausage. Hint: go before 6.30pm and you'll have no problem getting a table.

Piccolo Angolo 621 Hudson St (at Jane St) ⓣ212/229-9177. While owner Renato Migliorini and his sons constantly bicker, this no-frills pasta joint offers some of the best walnut cream sauce and chicken *rollatini* in town. Always ask for daily specials, but listen up because Migliorini talks fast and with a heavy accent.

Po 31 Cornelia St (between Bleecker and 4th sts) ⓣ212/645-2189. Serving delicious and creative Italian food, made with fresh, interesting ingredients, *Po*'s pastas are amazing. Reserve well in advance, as it's still one of the hotspots in the Village. Entrees run about $25.

Spanish

Sevilla 62 Charles St (at 4th St) ⓣ212/929-3189. Wonderful Village old-timer that is still a favorite neighborhood haunt. Dark, fragrant (from garlic) restaurant with good, moderately priced food. Terrific paella and large pitchers of strong sangria.

Spain 113 W 13th St (between 7th and 8th aves) ⓣ212/929-9580. Modest prices (entrees are $9–18) and large portions are the prime attractions of this cozy Spanish restaurant. Casual atmosphere and tacky decor in the larger back dining room – this neighborhood place has been here forever. Order the paella and split it with a friend.

Vegetarian

Eva's 11 W 8th St (between 5th and 6th aves) ⓣ212/677-3496. Healthy food in a coffee-shop setting. Nice grub, speedily served, and very cheap. Try the vegetarian falafel combo.

Souen 210 6th Ave (at Prince St) ⓣ212/807-7421; 28 E 13th St (between 5th Ave and University Place) ⓣ212/627-7150. This vegetarian and macrobiotic restaurant serves organic vegetables, fish, shrimp and grains.

East Village

The gritty **East Village** is a mixed bag of radicals, artists, students, immigrants (mostly Puerto Ricans and older Eastern Europeans), and an increasingly large number of young professionals and trendy transplants. It seems a new upscale Italian restaurant, sushi bar or chic café opens every day. By contrast the homely and cheap restaurants of Little India, E 6th St between First and Second avenues, and Little Ukraine, around E 7th to E 9th St between First and Third avenues, remain consistently good and satisfying.

American and Continental

Around the Clock 8 Stuyvesant St (between 2nd and 3rd aves) ⓣ212/598-0402. Centrally situated East Village restaurant serving crepes, omelets and pasta at reasonable prices. Open 24 hours.

First 87 1st Ave (between 5th and 6th sts) ⓣ212/674-3823. Sophisticated East Village spot serving innovative combinations of New American fare, like tuna steak *au poivre* and double-thick pork chops. Moderately priced – entrees average about $16–24, but there is a cheaper "anytime" menu for those watching their wallets.

Gotham Bar & Grill 12 E 12th St (between 5th Ave and University Place) ⓣ212/620-4020. This restaurant serves marvelous American fare by one of the early vertical food proponents in an airy, trendy setting. Generally reckoned to be one of the city's best restaurants, and it's at least worth a drink at the bar to see the city's beautiful people drift in.

Miracle Grill 112 1st Ave (between 6th and 7th sts) ⓣ212/254-2353. Moderately priced Southwestern specialties (catfish tacos are excellent) with interesting taste combinations and an attractive garden out back. Save room for the vanilla bean flan.

Prune 54 E 1st St (between 1st and 2nd aves) ⓣ212/677-6221. The star addition to what has become the East Village's most popular restaurant row, *Prune*'s rustic country fare (rabbit, capon, bacon-wrapped pork chop) comes with some surprises (a rye omelette here, a deviled egg there). Slightly confusing menu, as appetizers, entrees and side dishes aren't designated as such, but the pricing (not cheap) will clue you in. Closed Mon.

Stingy Lulu's 129 St Mark's Place (between 1st Ave and Ave A) ⓣ212/674-3545. This retro diner offers decent, simple American fare served by trashy drag queens. Open late, it caters to clubbers who stumble in and float out.

Time Café 380 Lafayette St (between Great Jones and 4th sts) ⓣ212/533-7000. Happening restaurant with a reasonably priced eclectic California-Southwestern menu and a large outdoor seating area perfectly positioned for people-watching. Downstairs the *Fez* lounge (see p.367) offers poetry readings, regular live jazz (usually on Wednesdays) and periodic campy 1970s music revues – along with strong drinks and tasty appetizers. There's an Upper West Side branch at 2330 Broadway (at 85th St) ⓣ212/579-5100.

Asian

Bond Street 6 Bond St (between Broadway and Lafayette) ⓣ212/777-2500. Very hip multileveled, super-suave Japanese restaurant (with happening bar on ground floor). The sushi is amazing, the miso-glazed sea bass exquisite, and steak a treat. Fairly pricey.

Daily Chow 2 E 2nd Street (at Bowery St) ⓣ212/254-7887. Eat pan-Asian family style upstairs or create your own dish at the downstairs Mongolian barbecue wok. The bar serves a rich mix of potent cocktails and martinis.

Dok Suni's 119 1st Ave (between 7th St and St Mark's Place) ⓣ212/477-9506. This dimly lit, somewhat cramped East Village restaurant has fast become a favorite for Korean home cooking like *bibimbop*, seafood pancake or *kim chee* rice; moderately priced.

Elephant 58 E 1st St (between 1st and 2nd sts) ⓣ212/505-7739. The menu is a delicious fusion of fairly priced Thai and French delicacies, featuring innovative fish specials and superb noodle dishes. The bright blue-and-yellow awning makes sure you can spot this tiny, crowded, eclectic East Village favorite.

Indochine 430 Lafayette St (between 4th St and Astor Place) ⓣ212/505-5111. Not the kind of place you go to save money; more to lap up the elegant surroundings and excellent French-Vietnamese food. Good for people-watching, too.

Mee Noodle Shop 219 1st Ave (between 13th and 14th sts) ⓣ212/995-0333; 922 2nd Ave (at 49th St) ⓣ212/888-0027; 795 9th Ave (at 53rd St) ⓣ212/765-2929. You can create endless combinations of noodles, broths and toppings at *Mee*. The food is so inexpensive that you won't notice the lack of decor. Try the Mee Fun Soup with chicken or the Dan Dan noodles, served with black mushrooms in a spicy meat sauce.

Mingala Burmese **21 E 7th St (between 2nd and 3rd aves) ☎212/529-3656.** Indian, Thai and Chinese cuisines combine in Burmese food – made well and relatively inexpensively. Try the delicious Thousand Layer Pancakes and the crispy lentil fritters.

Shabu Tatsu **216 E 10th St (between 1st and 2nd aves) ☎212/477-2972.** This place offers great and moderately priced Korean barbecue. Choose a combination of meat or seafood platters, and have them cooked right at your table.

Takahachi **85 Ave A (between 5th and 6th sts) ☎212/505-6524.** Superior sushi, the best in the neighborhood, at affordable prices. For dinner you'll probably have to wait – they don't take reservations.

Caribbean, Central and South American

Boca Chica **13 1st Ave (at 1st St) ☎212/473-0108.** This is real South American stuff, piled high and washed down with black beer and fancy, fruity drinks. It gets crowded, especially late and on weekends, and the music is loud, so come in a party mood and bring your dancing shoes. Inexpensive.

Casa Adela **66 Ave C (between 4th and 5th sts) ☎212/473-1882.** Slightly off the beaten path, this neighborhood is a great spot to taste true Puerto Rican food. Try the *mofungo* (fried plantains mixed with pork and garlic) or the roast pork. All entrees between $6.50–8. Cash only.

French and Belgian

Casimir **103 Ave B (between 6th and 7th sts) ☎212/358-9683.** Dark, spacious French bistro, specializing in straightforward pleasures. Try the filet mignon or the thick-cut pork chop, both excellent – and, surprisingly, well-priced – cuts of meat.

Chez Es Saada **42 E 1st St (between 1st and 2nd sts) ☎212/777-5617.** The decor evokes visions of underground Tangiers in the early 1950s while rose petals line the stairs. The menu is a mix of French and Moroccan fare, and is very expensive.

Rough Guide favorites

Quintessential New York

Katz's Delicatessen Lower East Side, p.319
Peter Luger's Steakhouse Brooklyn, p.349
Sammy's Romanian, Lower East Side, p.319
Second Avenue Deli East Village, p.328
Sylvia's, Harlem, p.346

Meanwhile, the bar scene is hopping and nightly DJs pull in the black-clad crew – it's worth it to get a drink and an appetizer and take it all in.

Danal **90 E 10th St (between 3rd and 4th aves) ☎212/982-6930.** Charming and cozy French café in what used to be an antiques store. French toast made with croissants and topped with cinnamon apples. Great for dinner, brunch and high tea on weekends from 4–6pm.

Jules **65 St Mark's Place (between 1st and 2nd aves) ☎212/477-5560.** Comfortable and authentic French restaurant, a rarity in the East Village, serving up moderately priced bistro fare and a good-value brunch on weekends.

Greek and Middle Eastern

Khyber Pass **34 St Mark's Place (between 2nd and 3rd aves) ☎212/473-0989.** Afghan food, which, if you're unfamiliar, is filling and has plenty to offer vegetarians (pulses, rice and eggplant are frequent ingredients). The lamb dishes are tasty. Excellent value for around $10.

Indian

Gandhi **345 E 6th St (between 1st and 2nd aves) ☎212/614-9718.** One of the best and least expensive of the E 6th St Indian restaurants – also one of the more spacious, with two open dining areas. Try the lamb *muglai* and the light, fluffy *poori* bread.

Mitali East **334 E 6th St (between 1st and 2nd aves) ☎212/533-2508.** Though more expensive than the other 6th St Indians, this one is well worth it, and still at half the price of spots further uptown. There's another branch across town, *Mitali West*, at 296 Bleecker St (at 7th Ave) ☎212/989-1367.

Rose of India **308 E 6th St (between 1st and 2nd aves) ⓣ212/533-5011.** Good workmanlike curries, and if you tell them it's your birthday they'll turn on the "disco lights" and bring you a free dessert.

Italian

Cucina di Pesce **87 E 4th St (between 2nd and 3rd aves) ⓣ212/260-6800.** There are better Italian restaurants around, but not at these prices. The room is attractive and underlit, and the help is friendly. Squid-ink linguini and various seafood specials are the standouts. There's a big local crowd at dinnertime; get a drink at the bar and nibble on the free stewed mussels while you wait.

Frank **88 2nd Ave (between 5th and 6th sts) ⓣ212/420-0202.** This tiny neighborhood favorite serves basic, traditional Italian dishes at communal tables. It's packed every night with hungry locals looking for the closest thing to a home-cooked meal at a very reasonable price.

Il Buco **47 Bond St (between Lafayette and the Bowery) ⓣ212/533-1932.** While leaning more toward Italian, this cash-only eatery boasts French and Spanish flares as well. Once an antique store and sometime eatery, *Il Buco* now serves food full-time. In fact, the food is amazing. The wine cellar is alleged to be the inspiration for Poe's story "The Cask of Amontillado."

La Foccaceria **128 1st Ave (between 7th and 8th sts) ⓣ212/254-4946.** Cheap, filling Sicilian meals in a tiny, down-home setting, with wine served in water glasses.

Lanza Restaurant **168 1st Ave (between10th and 11th sts) ⓣ212/674-7014.** A prix-fixe lunch and a late-night prix-fixe at 9–11pm makes this basic Italian fare, like linguini with white clam sauce, seem extra-special.

Jewish and Eastern European

B & H Dairy **127 2nd Ave (between 7th St and St Mark's Place) ⓣ212/505-8065.** Good veggie choice, this tiny luncheonette serves homemade soup, challah and latkes. You can also create your own juice combination to stay or go.

Christine's **208 1st Ave (between 12th and 13th sts) ⓣ212/254-2474.** Longstanding Polish coffee shop, one of several such places in the area – great soups, blintzes and pierogies.

Second Avenue Deli **156 2nd Ave (between 9th and 10th sts) ⓣ212/677-0606.** An East Village institution, serving up marvelous burgers, hearty pastrami sandwiches, matzoh ball soup and other deli goodies in ebullient, snap-happy style – and not nearly as cheap as you'd think. The star plaques in the sidewalk out front commemorate this area's Yiddish theater days.

Veselka **144 2nd Ave (corner of 9th St) ⓣ212/228-9682.** East Village institution that offers fine homemade hot borscht (and cold in summer), latkes, pierogies and great burgers and fries. Open 24 hours.

Spanish

Xunta **174 1st Ave (between 10th and 11th St) ⓣ212/614-0620.** This electric East Village gem buzzes with hordes of young faces perched on rum barrels downing pitchers of sangria and choosing from the dizzying tapas menu – try the mussels in fresh tomato sauce, shrimp with garlic and the mushrooms in brandy. You can eat (and drink) very well for around $20.

Vegetarian

Anjelica Kitchen **300 E 12th St (between 1st and 2nd aves) ⓣ212/228-2909.** Vegetarian macrobiotic restaurant with various daily specials for a decent price. Patronized by a colorful downtown crowd and considered by many to be the best veggie food in NYC.

Kate's Joint **58 Ave B (at 4th St) ⓣ212/777-7059.** While hit and miss overall, her hummus, soups, tofu and mock meat dishes are fantastic. You can eat well here for no more than $10.

Chelsea

Retro diners, Cuban-Chinese greasy spoons along Eighth Avenue, increasingly trendy restaurants and cute brunch spots characterize **Chelsea**. Perhaps the best and most reasonably priced offerings are to be had in the area's Central American establishments, though there is also a mosaic of international cuisines

– Thai, Austrian, Mexican, Italian and traditional American. Chelsea is the heart of gay-friendly dining in the city as well.

American and Continental

Cafeteria 119 7th Ave (at 17th St) ☎212/414-1717. Don't let the name fool you! While *Cafeteria* is open 24 hours and has great chicken fried steak, meat loaf and macaroni and cheese, this place is anything but a trucker's dream. Modern, plastic-designed and always packed with beautiful diners and a sexy waitstaff.

Eighteenth and Eighth 159 8th Ave (between 17th and 18th sts) ☎212/242-5000. Ever so tiny, upscale Chelsea coffee shop popular with a hip, gay crowd. Great for homely brunch fare, especially the brioche French toast.

Empire Diner 210 10th Ave (between 22nd and 23rd sts) ☎212/243-2736. With its gleaming chrome-ribbed Art Deco interior, this is one of Manhattan's original diners, still open 24 hours and still serving up plates of simple (if not much better than average) American food such as burgers and grilled cheese sandwiches.

Food Bar 149 8th Ave (between 17th and 18th sts) ☎212/243-2020. The food at this Chelsea restaurant, part of the Chelsea gay scene, is not quite as good as the view. Even so, well-priced salads and sandwiches.

Mare 198 8th Ave (at 20th St) ☎212/675 7522. This fish and seafood restaurant is a welcome addition to Chelsea's burgeoning restaurant ghetto, with good fish dishes and a raw bar.

Moran's 146 10th Ave (at 19th St) ☎212/627-3030. Listed in the phone book as "Moran's Chelsea Sea Food," but while you can get good swordfish, lobster and sole here, it's the steaks and chops that impress – as well as the plush stained-wood decor. Try and get the cozy back room, especially in winter, when the fireplace is roaring.

The Old Homestead 56 9th Ave (between 14th and 15th sts) ☎212/242-9040. Steak. Period. But really gorgeous steak, served in an almost comically old-fashioned walnut dining room by waiters in black vests. Huge portions, but expensive.

O'Reilly's 56 W 31st St (between Broadway and 6th Ave) ☎212/684-4244. Posh Irish pub/restaurant with standard American dishes at $7–13. Good value.

Asian

Bright Food Shop 216 8th Ave (between 21st and 22nd sts) ☎212/243-4433. Fusion of Asian and Mexican food make this Chelsea eatery an eye-opener. Always crowded, and while prices are cheap, they're certainly not a steal.

Meri Ken 189 7th Ave (at 21st St) ☎212/620-9684. Stylish Art Deco sushi place, with reliably fresh fish and a faithful crowd. Bento boxes are the deal.

Monster Sushi 158 W 23rd St (between 6th and 7th aves) ☎212/620-9131. As the name implies, "monster" portions of sushi are served. But what they are known for is their creative and brightly colored rolls. Not the cheapest sushi in town, but good.

Pad Thai 114 8th Ave (at 16th St) ☎212/691-6226. Good noodle dishes, stews and other classics, all at very low prices. Also a wide array of vegetarian choices.

Royal Siam 240 8th Ave (between 22nd and 23rd sts) ☎212/741-1732. Reasonably priced Thai restaurant, with surprisingly flavorful renditions of the old standards.

Caribbean, Central and South American

Blue Moon Café 150 8th Ave (between 17th and 18th sts) ☎212/463-0560; 1444 1st Ave (at 75th St) ☎212/288-9811. Standard Mexican food at moderate prices. Hockey fans may be interested to know the restaurant was once owned by the NY Rangers. Try their large Blue Moon margaritas – yes, they're blue; they're also quite potent.

Cuba Libre 200 8th Ave (between 20th and 21st sts) ☎212/206-0038. Tapas, mojitos and hip-swinging music make this airy, reasonably priced eatery a Chelsea favorite with the gay crowd.

Kitchen 218 8th Ave (between 21st and 22nd sts) ☎212/243-4433. Tasty Mexican cuisine, with a slew of daily burrito specials.

La Taza de Oro 96 8th Ave (between 14th and 15th sts) ☎212/243-9946. Changing daily specials, each served with a heaping of rice and beans makes this a cheap place to get a tasty, filling meal with a Puerto Rican twist.

Mary Ann's 116 8th Ave (at 16th St) ☎212/633-0877. Considered by many to be, if not the best Mexican food in Manhattan, the most consistent. Great prices and great margaritas round out this mainstay, with three other locations around the city.

Negril 362 W 23rd St (off 9th Ave) ☎212/807-6411. An enormous aquarium and colorful decor add to the pleasure of eating at this Jamaican restaurant. Spicy jerk chicken or goat, stews and other dishes keep 'em coming, as do the reasonable prices (around $10–12 for an entrée).

Greek

Periyali 35 W 20th St (between 5th and 6th aves) ☎212/463-7890. Gourmet Greek food that's a cut above the rest, both in quality and price, in a cheerful Mediterranean setting. Closed Sun.

Italian

Bottino 246 10th Ave (between 25th and 26th sts) ☎212/206-6766. One of Chelsea's most popular restaurants, *Bottino* attracts the in-crowd looking for some honest Italian food served in a very downtown atmosphere. The homemade leek tortellini (winter months only) is truly tantalizing.

Chelsea Trattoria 108 8th Ave (between 15th and 16th sts) ☎212/924-7786. A brick-walled Northern Italian restaurant that's cozy and enjoyable as much for the ambience as the moderately priced food.

Daniella Ristorante 320 8th Ave (at 26th Street) ☎212/807-0977. Convenient to Penn Station and Madison Square Garden, this is a great find in a pretty food-poor neighborhood.

Frank's 85 10th Ave (at 15th St) ☎212/243-1349. Long-established Italian-American steakhouse, with pasta and other Italian dishes from $10 up. The casual atmosphere provides a real taste of old New York.

Le Madri 168 W 18th St (at 7th Ave) ☎212/727-8022. Named after the Italian "mothers" who work in the kitchen, this elegant Tuscan eatery's marvellous food and wine are only slightly marred by the snooty service and clientele. On the pricey side, but worth it. Try and get a table in the patio outside.

Spanish

El Quijote 226 W 23rd St (between 7th and 8th aves) ☎212/929-1855. Has changed very little over the years; it was not too long ago used as the setting for a dinner scene in *I Shot Andy Warhol* (which takes place in 1968) with minimal makeover. Still serves lovely *mariscos* and fried meats amidst the deep burgundy lighting and dark-stained wood setting.

Union Square

The area around **Union Square**, known variously as the Flatiron district and Park Avenue South, has experienced an increase in fancyish spots – though whether that will remain in the wake of the dot-com fall is hard to say (NY's Silicon Alley is/was right along here).

American and Continental

Alva 36 E 22nd St (between Broadway and Park Ave S) ☎212/228-4399. Mirrors and photos of Thomas Alva Edison cover the walls in this eclectic continental restaurant. Specialties include grilled duck, double garlic roast chicken and soft-shell crabs. It's expensive, but the weekday pre-theater prix-fixe dinner (served 5.30–7pm; 3 courses and a glass of wine for about $30) is good value. Beware heavy smoking (cigars as well as cigarettes) at the bar.

Angelo & Maxie's 233 Park Ave S (at 19th St) ☎212/220-9200. Often considered one of the best steaks in the city, *A&M's* is a little more stylish than its meaty counterparts. But beware, this huge, high-ceilinged establishment is loud and cigar smoke will upset some.

Blue Water Grill 31 Union Square W (at 16th St) ☎212/675-9500. This is the place to go for seafood – if you can get a reservation.

Outdoor seating during the summer or after your meal listen to some jazz in the downstairs bar. Never a complaint, but be careful of the prices.

Chat 'n' Chew 10 E 16th St (between 5th Ave and Union Square W) ☎212/243-1616. Riding the "trailerpark chic" wave, this trendy spot offers up some of the best macaroni and cheese, meatloaf, grilled cheese and turkey dinners in the city. The kitsch decor adds to the Americana theme and brings a pleasant, relaxed feeling to this part of town.

City Crab 235 Park Ave S (at 19th St) ☎212/529-3800. A large and very popular joint that prides itself on a large selection of fresh East Coast oysters and clams, which can be had in mixed sampler plates. Overall, a hearty place to consume lots of bivalves and wash 'em down with pints of ale. Sometimes with jazz at weekend brunch. Roughly $20–30 per person for a full dinner.

Coffee Shop 29 Union Square W (at 16th St) ☎212/243-7969. A unique American coffee shop that serves salads, burgers and grilled meats with a Brazilian twist. Open 24 hours, this corner eatery sees a varied yet usually hip and modish crowd. Come more for the bar scene or the live music; while the food has its highlights the *caipirinhas* will get you higher.

Mesa Grill 102 5th Ave (between 15th and 16th sts) ☎212/807-7400. One of lower Manhattan's more fashionable eateries, serving eclectic Southwestern grill fare at relatively high prices. During the week it's full of publishing and advertising types doing lunch – at dinner things liven up a bit.

Union Square Café 21 E 16th St (between 5th Ave and Union Square W) ☎212/243-4020. Choice California-style dining with a classy but comfortable downtown atmosphere. No one does salmon like they do. Not at all cheap – prices average $100 for two – but the creative menu (and great people-watching) is a real treat. Don't miss it if you have the bucks.

Asian

Republic 37 Union Square W (between 16th and 17th sts) ☎212/627-7172. Pleasant decor, fast service, low prices and serviceable noodle dishes make this a popular pan-Asian spot. The tasty appetizers are the best part.

Zen Palate 34 Union Square E (at 16th St) ☎212/614-9291; 663 9th Ave (at 46th St) ☎212/582-1669; 2170 Broadway (between 76th and 77th sts) ☎212/501-7768. Stylish and modern, with what it calls a "Zen atmosphere," these reliable restaurants serve up health-conscious vegetarian Asian food prepared to look, and sometimes even taste, like meat. Sit at the counter and pick an appetizer from the extensive list of "Tasty Morsels" for quick snacks alone.

French and Belgian

L'Acajou 53 W 19th St (between 5th and 6th aves) ☎212/645-1706. This small, homely (the staff eats together every night) bistro for years has attracted an eclectic clientele. The bar gets smoky and crowded at happy hour and the tables are often full for lunch and dinner. Specials include omelets and French fries and daily dinner tarts.

L'Express 249 Park Ave S (at 20th St) ☎212/254-5858. A good, airy bistro with the usual food at somewhat reasonable prices, but with two important points of distinction: the waiters are actually friendly, and it's open 24 hours – by far the classiest all-night place in the neighborhood.

Pitchoune 226 3rd Ave (at 19th St) ☎212/614-8641. Provençal French bistro fare served by a friendly waitstaff in a comfortable, relaxed setting. The sidewalk tables, when whether permits, add to the pleasant ambience. Entrees are $15–20 and well worth it.

Steak Frites 9 E 16th St (between Union Square W and 5th Ave) ☎212/463-7101. Classic European feel, with an upscale ambience and good service. As the name suggests, great steak and frites, for around $25.

German

Rolf's 281 3rd Ave (at 22nd St) ☎212/473-8718. A nice, dark, chintz-decorated Old World feeling dominates this East Side institution. Schnitzel and sauerbraten are always good but somehow taste better at the generous bar buffet, commencing around 5pm all through the week.

Brunch

Weekend brunch is a competitive business in New York, and the number of restaurants offering it is constantly expanding. Selections below (most of which are covered in more detail elsewhere in the listings) all offer a good weekend menu, sometimes for an all-inclusive price that includes a free cocktail or two – though offers of freebies are to be treated with suspicion by those more interested in the food than getting blitzed. Above all, don't regard this as a definitive list – call to determine price and menu. You'll find other possibilities all over Manhattan.

Downtown Manhattan

Aggie's 146 W Houston St (at MacDougal St) ⓣ212/673-8994
Balthazar 80 Spring St (between Broadway and Crosby sts) ⓣ212/965-1414
Bubby's 120 Hudson St (at N Moore St) ⓣ212/219-0666
Cupping Room Café 359 W Broadway (between Broome and Grand sts) ⓣ212/925-2898
Danal 90 E 10th St (between 3rd and 4th aves) ⓣ212/982-6930
Elephant and Castle 68 Greenwich Ave (between 6th and 7th aves) ⓣ212/243-1400
Home 20 Cornelia St (between Bleecker and 4th sts) ⓣ212/243-9579
Jerry's Restaurant 101 Prince St (between Greene and Mercer sts) ⓣ212/966-9464
Jules 65 St Mark's Place (between 1st and 2nd aves) ⓣ212/477-5560
Nadine's 99 Bank St (at Greenwich St) ⓣ212/924-3165
Old Devil Moon 511 E 12th St (between aves A and B) ⓣ212/475-4375
Paris Commune 411 Bleecker St (between 11th and Bank sts) ⓣ212/929-0509

Midtown Manhattan

Cafeteria 119 7th Ave (at 17th St) ⓣ212/414-1717
Cibo 767 2nd Ave (between 41st and 42nd sts) ⓣ212/681-1616
Eighteenth and Eighth 159 8th Ave (between 17th and 18th sts) ⓣ212/242-5000
Food Bar 149 8th Ave (between 17th and 18th sts) ⓣ212/243-2020
Friend of a Farmer 77 Irving Place (between 18th and 19th sts) ⓣ212/477-2188
The Globe 373 Park Ave South (between 26th and 27th sts) ⓣ212/545-8800
Jubilee 347 E 54th St (between 1st and 2nd aves) ⓣ212/888-3569
Les Halles 411 Park Ave South (between 28th and 29th sts) ⓣ212/679-4111
Rive Guache 560 3rd Ave (at 37th St) ⓣ212/949-5400

Italian

Campagna 24 E 21st St (between Broadway and Park Ave South) ⓣ212/460-0900. Rather small, pricey, but delicious Northern Italian dishes are served at this Flatiron district eatery.

Spanish

Bolo 23 E 22nd St (between Broadway and Park Ave South) ⓣ212/228-2200. Another Bobby Flay favorite (see *Mesa Grill* above) that has been pumping out tasty victuals, such as fennel-dusted rabbit and asparagus risotto, for many years now. The prices are quite heady.

Gramercy Park, Murray Hill and the Garment District

While not the best neighborhoods for dining in NYC, **Gramercy Park**, **Murray Hill** and the **Garment District** are picking up the pace. The area around Lexington Avenue in the upper 20s is a good place to sample cheap and filling Indian fare. It's also a fantastic place to find cheap Vietnamese, not to mention a number of crowded sushi bars and small French bistros.

American and Continental

El Rio Grande 160 E 38th St (between Lexington and 3rd aves) ⓣ212/867-0922. Long-established Murray Hill Tex-Mex place with a gimmick: you can eat Mexican, or if you prefer, Texan, by simply crossing the "border" and walking through the kitchen.

Uptown Manhattan

1295 Madison Ave (between 92nd and 93rd sts) ☎212/410-7335
Annie's 1381 3rd Ave (between 78th and 79th sts) ☎212/327-4853
Barking Dog Luncheonette 1678 3rd Ave (at 94th St) ☎212/831-1800
Barney Greengrass (The Sturgeon King) 541 Amsterdam Ave (between 86th and 87th sts) ☎212/724-4707
Copeland's 547 W 145th St (between Broadway and Amsterdam Ave) ☎212/234-2357
E.A.T. 1064 Madison Ave (between 80th and 81st sts) ☎212/772-0022
EJ's Luncheonette 433 Amsterdam Ave (between 81st and 82nd sts) ☎212/873-3444
Emily's 1325 5th Ave (between 111th and 112th sts) ☎212/996-1212
Good Enough to Eat 483 Amsterdam Ave (between 83rd and 84th sts) ☎212/496-0163
Popover Café 551 Amsterdam Ave (between 86th and 87th sts) ☎212/595-8555
Sarabeth's Kitchen 423 Amsterdam Ave (between 80th and 81st sts) ☎212/496-6280
Shark Bar 307 Amsterdam Ave (between 74th and 75th sts) ☎212/874-8500
Sylvia's Restaurant 328 Lenox Ave (between 126th and 127th sts) ☎212/996-0660

Outer boroughs

Banania 241 Smith St (at Douglass St), Carroll Gardens ☎718/237-9100
Christina's 853 Manhattan Ave (at Milton St), Greenpoint ☎718/383-4382
Harvest 218 Court St (at Warren Street), Cobble Hill ☎718/624-9267
Max & Moritz 426A 7th Ave (at 14th St), Park Slope ☎718/499-5557
Montague Street Saloon 122 Montague St (between Henry and Hicks sts), Brooklyn Heights ☎718/522-6770
New City Bar & Grill 25 Lafayette Ave (between Ashland Place and St. Felix St), Fort Greene ☎718/875-7197
New Prospect Café 393 Flatbush Ave (between Plaza and Sterling Place), Prospect Heights ☎718/638-2148
Oznot's Dish 79 Berry (at N 9th St), Williamsburg ☎718/599-6596
Rose Water 787 Union St (at 6th Ave), Park Slope ☎718/783-3800

Personable and fun – and the margaritas are earth-shattering.

Friend of a Farmer 77 Irving Place (between 18th and 19th sts) ☎212/477-2188. Rustic Gramercy café known for its old-fashioned chicken pot pie and homely "comfort meals." Also a popular brunch spot.

Reuben's 244 Madison Ave (at 38th St) ☎212/867-7800. A busy midtown diner that makes a fine and filling haven in between the sights and shops of lower Fifth Avenue. Get the reuben sandwich: you'll be impressed.

Scotty's Diner 336 Lexington Ave (at 39th St) ☎212/986-1520. Conveniently placed midtown diner, close to Grand Central and the Empire State Building. Solid diner food, good breakfasts until 11am and a friendly Spanish owner. Open 24 hours.

Soul Fixin's 37 W 34th St (between 8th and 9th aves) ☎212/736-1345. Though the soulfood is good, it's by no means down home. Stick with the fried chicken and sweet potatoes, but stay away from the collards unless you're in the mood for a salt fix.

Verbena 54 Irving Place (between 17th and 18th sts) ☎212/260-5454. This simple and elegant restaurant serves a seasonal menu of creative (and pricey) New American food. Don't miss the *crème brulée* with lemon verbena, the herb for which the restaurant was named. Try to get seated in the garden, and reserve in advance.

Asian

Asia de Cuba 237 Madison Ave (between 37th and 38th sts) ☎212/726-7755. If you feel like treating yourself, this Asian-Latin American hotspot is where to go. Designed by "it man" Philippe Starck, *Asia de Cuba* attracts celebrities by the dozen. An enormous communal dining table, flavorful menu and upstairs bar full of beautiful people have kept the buzz alive.

Choshi 77 Irving Place (at 19th St) ⓣ212/420-1419. Reasonably priced Gramercy Japanese serving first-rate fresh sushi. The $22 dinner prix-fixe menu is a good deal, including drinks, soup, appetizer, main dish (even sushi) and dessert.

Hangawi 12 E 32nd St (between 5th and Madison aves) ⓣ212/213-0077. A strictly vegetarian and vegan-safe Korean restaurant. The autumn rolls are a great starter. A little pricey, but quite good.

Jaiya Thai 396 3rd Ave (between 28th and 29th sts) ⓣ212/889-1330. This spicy, delicious and affordable restaurant features *pad thai* for $8.95.

L'Annam 393 3rd Ave (at 28th St) ⓣ212/686-5168. Fast Vietnamese in hip dining room. $5.25 lunch specials can't be beat.

French and Belgian

Les Halles 411 Park Ave S (between 28th and 29th sts) ⓣ212/679-4111. Noisy, bustling bistro with carcasses dangling in a butcher's shop in the front. Very pseudo Rive Gauche, serving rabbit, steak frites and other staples. Entrees range from $15–25. Not recommended for veggies.

Park Bistro 414 Park Ave S (between 28th and 29th sts) ⓣ212/689-1360. This friendly bistro is sister to *Les Halles* and similar in prices and style, though a little less hectic.

Indian

Curry in a Hurry 119 Lexington Ave (between 27th and 28th sts) ⓣ212/683-0900. A local favorite, offering quick, inexpensive and delicious buffet-style Indian cuisine where you can eat for around $8.

Madras Mahal 104 Lexington Ave (between 27th and 28th sts) ⓣ212/684-4010. A kosher vegetarian's dream . . . and really good for everyone else, too. Entrees are around $10.

Italian

Cinque Terre 22 E 38th St (between Madison and Park aves) ⓣ212/213-0910. A good, reliable Italian in a neighborhood not blessed with a huge number of restaurants of any kind. Specializes in the food of Liguria: expect seafood, chickpeas and pesto sauces.

Midtown West

While the majority of Manhattan's best dining occurs downtown, some manifold good meals await you in **Midtown West**, a neighborhood whose restaurants encompass Greek, South American, Japanese, African, French and everything in between. Restaurant Row (West 46th Street between Eighth and Ninth avenues) is a frequent stopover for theatergoers seeking a late-night meal, though Ninth Avenue offers cheaper and generally better alternatives. Be advised that most restaurants in the Times Square area are overpriced and not great quality, with exceptions to that rule noted below.

American and Continental

'21' Club 21 W 52nd St (between 5th and 6th aves) ⓣ212/582-7200. Manhattan's longest surviving speakeasy, *'21'* is haute at its height: cigars, incredible wine cellar, rare art and fine American food. Step into the past.

Aquavit 13 W 54th St (between 5th and 6th aves) ⓣ212/307-7311. Superb Scandinavian food – pickled herrings, salmon, even reindeer – in a lovely atrium restaurant with a mock waterfall cascading down one of the walls. A real treat, and priced accordingly; reserve well ahead.

Arriba Arriba 762 9th Ave (at 51st St) ⓣ212/489-0810. Boozy Tex-Mex place, popular with the after-work crowd for the great margaritas as much as the inexpensive meals.

Atlas 40 Central Park South (between 5th and 6th aves) ⓣ212/759-9191. Stylishly designed by Larry Bogdanow, *Atlas* is worth the hefty prices for great fusion foods and an exceptional wine list. Play it safe with succulent lamb chops or be daring and go for the *foie gras* in sea urchin broth.

Bryant Park Grill **25 W 40th St (between 5th and 6th aves) ☎212/840-6500.** The food is standard-upscale (Caesar salad, grilled chicken, rack of lamb, hake), but the real reason to come is atmosphere, provided by the park, whether viewed from within the spacious dining room or enjoyed al fresco on the terrace. *The Café at Bryant Park*, next door on the terrace (May–Sept), serves less expensive, lighter options, but beware: it's a huge singles scene.

Hamburger Harry's **145 W 45th St (between Broadway and 6th Ave) ☎212/840-0566.** Handy diner just off Times Square; some claim its burgers are the best in town.

Joe Allen's **326 W 46th St (between 8th and 9th aves) ☎212/581-6464.** Tried and true formula of checkered tablecloths, old-fashioned barroom feel, and reliable American food at moderate prices. The calf's liver with spinach and potatoes has been on the menu for years. Popular pre-theater spot, so reserve well in advance unless you can arrive after 8pm.

Landmark Tavern **626 11th Ave (at 46th St) ☎212/757-8595.** A long-established Irish tavern popular with a yuppie crowd. Tasty menu with large portions, and the Irish soda bread is baked fresh every day.

Market Diner **572 11th Ave (at 43rd St) ☎212/695-0415.** The ultimate 24-hour diner, chrome-furnished and usually full of weary clubbers filling up on breakfast. A good place to refuel early evening, too.

Rock Center Cafe **20 W 50th St (at Rockefeller Plaza) ☎212/332-7620.** Gazing at the Rockefeller Center ice skating rink and plaza is what this place has going for it.

Stage Deli **834 7th Ave (between 53rd and 54th sts) ☎212/245-7850.** Another reliable all-night standby and longtime rival to the *Carnegie Deli*, p.337. More genuine New York attitude and big overstuffed sandwiches, but it's not at all cheap.

The Supper Club **240 47th St (between Broadway and 8th Ave) ☎212/921-1940.** Enormous restaurant/swing club, with an eclectic menu derived from the menus of famous old nightclubs of the 1940s and 1950s, great period decor and a talented big band orchestra. If you enjoy the style, you'll love this grand palace (formerly a Broadway theater). Call ahead for the schedule and to book a table – it's still a hotspot and, as you might expect, not at all cheap.

Virgil's Real BBQ **152 W 44th St (between Broadway and 6th Ave) ☎212/921-9494.** Hardcore ribs and biscuits for barbecue enthusiasts, though the ambience leaves something to be desired. A bit pricey, so order light – chances are you'll still end up with too much. Very popular with tourists, especially pre-theater, so despite its huge size waits can be long. Also very noisy.

West Bank Café **407 W 42nd St (at 9th Ave) ☎212/695-6909.** Some French, some American, all delicious and not as expensive as you'd think – pastas and entrees range from $11–20. Very popular with theater people before and especially after a performance.

Asian

China Grill **52 W 53rd St (between 5th and 6th aves) ☎212/333-7788.** An eclectic, pretentious see-and-be-seen pan-Asian eatery that always seems to be busy. Fun destination whether you're seeking lunch, dinner or drinks.

Dish of Salt **133 W 47th St (between 6th and 7th aves) ☎212/921-4242.** Tired of the linoleum-table Cantonese fare in Chinatown? For approximately five times as much money, you can dig into roast plum duckling and spinach with crabmeat, served impeccably at huge polished-wood tables at this midtown institution.

Ollie's Noodle Shop **190 W 44th St (between Broadway and 8th Ave) ☎212/921-5988; also 2315 Broadway (at 84th St) ☎212/362-3111; 2957 Broadway (at 116th St) ☎212/932-3300.** Good Chinese restaurant that serves marvellous noodles, barbecued meats and spare ribs. Not, however, a place to linger. Very cheap, very crowded and very noisy. Also very popular pre-theater place, so don't be alarmed if there are long lines – due to the rushed service, they move fast.

Pongsri Thai Restaurant **244 W 48th St (between Broadway and 8th Ave) ☎212/582-3392; 106 Bayard St (at Baxter St) ☎212/349-3132; 311 2nd Ave (at 18th St) ☎212/477-4100.** Restaurant popular at lunchtime with local businesspeople for its extensive and good-value lunch menu – the rice and noodle combos a specialty. The menu in the evenings is massive.

Caribbean, Central and South American

Cabana Carioca 123 W 45th St (between 6th Ave and Broadway) ☎212/581-8088. Animated restaurant decorated with colorful murals. A great place to try out Brazilian-Portuguese specialties, like *feijoada* (black bean and pork stew), washed down with fiery *caipirinhas*. Portions large enough for two make it reasonably inexpensive.

Churrascaria Plataforma 316 W 49th St (between 8th and 9th aves) ☎212/245-0505. Crowded bar serving strong *caipirinhas* and huge open dining room where meat is the fare of choice, served by waiters walking around tables with swords stabbed with succulent slabs of grilled pork, chicken and lots of beef. But be careful, while the all-you-can-eat price is a hefty $38.95, the drinks are even more expensive.

El Papasito 370 W 52nd St (at 9th Ave) ☎212/265-2225. Inexpensive and tasty Dominican fare, this small eatery offers excellent pork *chicharrones* (fried on the bone), *asopado* (thick garlic rice soup) and for dessert flan that will melt in your mouth.

Via Brasil 34 W 46th St (between 5th and 6th aves) ☎212/997-1158. Another excellent place to taste *feijoada*, Brazil's national dish. A bit pricey, though; entrees are in the range of $15–23. Live music Wed-Sat nights.

Victor's Café 52 236 W 52nd St (between Broadway and 8th Ave) ☎212/586-7714. A well-established hangout, serving real Cuban food at moderate prices. Great black bean soup and sangria.

Zuni 598 9th Ave (at 43rd St) ☎212/765-7626. Pricey haute Mexican cuisine in an informal setting. They make the guacamole fresh at your table.

French and Belgian

Brasserie Centrale 1700 Broadway (at 53rd St) ☎212/757-2233. A rare midtown place where you can linger over coffee, freshly baked treats or a full meal. The menu offers a range of burgers, soups, salads, pastas and average French-tinged brasserie standards (stick with the simpler items on the menu). Large outdoor seating area. Open 24 hours.

Rough Guide favorites

Haute Cuisine

71 Clinton Fresh Food Lower East Side, p.319
Aquavit Midtown West, p.334
Bouley TriBeCa, p.320
Gotham Bar & Grill East Village, p.326
Le Bernardin Midtown West, see below

Chez Napoleon 365 W 50th St (between 8th and 9th aves) ☎212/265-6980. Due to this neighborhood's proximity to the docks, it became a hangout for French soldiers during World War II, leading to the creation of several highly authentic Gallic eateries here in the 1940s and 1950s. This is one of them, and it lives up to its reputation. A friendly, family-run bistro; bring a wad to enjoy the tradition, though.

Hourglass Tavern 373 W 46th St (between 8th and 9th aves) ☎212/265-2060. Tiny midtown French restaurant, which serves an excellent-value, two-course prix-fixe menu for between $12.75 and $15.75. The gimmick is the hourglass above each table, the emptying of which means you're supposed to leave and make way for someone else. In reality they seem to last more than an hour, and they only enforce it if there's a line. Cash only.

La Bonne Soupe 48 W 55th St (between 5th and 6th aves) ☎212/586-7650. Traditional French food at reasonable prices. Steaks, omelets, snails and fondues from $15.

Le Bernardin 155 W 51st St (between 6th and 7th aves) ☎212/489-1515. One of the finest French restaurants in the city; the chef, Eric Ripert, offers an excellent smoked salmon gravalax topped with scallop *ceviche*. Prix fixe: $45 lunch and $77 dinner.

Le Madeleine 403 W 43rd St (between 9th and 10th aves) ☎212/246-2993. Pretty midtown French bistro with good service, above-average food (including some knockout desserts) and moderate to expensive prices. Get a seat in the outdoor garden if you can. Usually crowded pre-theater.

German

Hallo Berlin 402 W 51st St (between 9th and 10th aves) ☎212/541-6248. The owner used to sell his wursts stuff from a pushcart, and made enough to open a restaurant; it's a pleasant bench-and-table beer-garden setting in which to enjoy all manner of German sausages, washed down with unusual ales.

Greek and Middle Eastern

Afghanistan Kebab House 155 W 46th St (between 6th and 7th aves) ⊕212/768-3875; 1345 2nd Ave (between 70th and 71st sts) ⊕212/517-2776. Inexpensive lamb, chicken and seafood kebabs, served with a variety of side dishes. Complete dinners for under $15.

Ariana Afghan Kebab 787 9th Ave (between 52nd and 53rd sts) ⊕212/262-2323. A casual neighborhood restaurant serving inexpensive kebab (chicken, lamb and beef) and vegetarian meals.

Lotfi's Couscous 358 W 46th St (between 8th and 9th aves) ⊕212/582-5850. Moderately priced Moroccan hidden away on the second floor. Lots of spicy dishes, vegetarian options and inexpensive salads. Closed in Aug.

Uncle Nick's 747 9th Ave (between 50th and 51st sts) ⊕212/315-1726. A clean, sunny little restaurant with unimpassioned but filling Greek standards.

Italian

Becco 355 W 46th St (between 8th and 9th aves) ⊕212/397-7597. At *Becco*, a welcome addition to Restaurant Row (and as such is busy with the pre-theater crowd), you get generous amounts of antipasto and pasta for around $20.

Carmine's 200 W 44th St (between Broadway and 8th Ave) ⊕212/221-3800; also 2450 Broadway (between 90th and 91st sts) ⊕212/362-2200. This restaurant made a name for itself with its combination of decent (and decently priced) Southern Italian food in mountainous portions meant to be shared and for the noisy, convivial atmosphere in which it's served. Try the fried calamari ($18) or the *osso buco* (for around $30), either of which could easily feed 3 to 4 people. Reservations for groups of 6 or more; otherwise be prepared to wait in line.

Julian's 802 9th Ave (between 53rd and 54th sts) ⊕212/262-4800. Light and inventive Mediterranean fare in a bright, pleasing room and clever dining garden tucked in an alley. Whether you want sandwiches or scaloppine, this is a safe bet in Hell's Kitchen.

Supreme Macaroni Co. 511 9th Ave (between 38th and 39th sts) ⊕212/564-8074. A macaroni shop with a small, divey but lovable restaurant attached.

Trattoria dell'Arte 900 7th Ave (between 56th and 57th sts) ⊕212/245-9800. Unusually nice restaurant for this rather tame stretch of midtown, with a lovely airy interior, excellent service and good food. Great, wafer-thin crispy pizzas, decent and imaginative pasta dishes for around $20 and a mouth-watering antipasto bar – all eagerly patronized by an elegant out-to-be-seen crowd. Best to reserve.

Jewish and Eastern European

Carnegie Deli 854 7th Ave (between 54th and 55th sts) ⊕212/757-2245. This place is known for the size of its sandwiches – by popular consent the most generously stuffed in the city, and a full meal in themselves. The chicken noodle soup is good, too. Not cheap, however, and the waiters are among New York's rudest.

Firebird 365 W 46th St (between 8th and 9th aves) ⊕212/586-0244. A marble foyer leads to a lush dining room covered in rich reds and golds in this standout Russian eatery. It is an expensive but worthwhile dining experience – pre-theater prix-fixe menu is between $30–36, depending on what day of the week it is.

Russian Tea Room 150 W 57th St (between 6th and 7th aves) ⊕212/265-0947. One of New York's favorite places to hobnob with the literati. Rates are perhaps not as high as in the city's top French dining spots, and it's easier to get a table (though unless you're a celeb you may get relegated to the second floor dining room). The wonderfully garish interior makes eating here a real occasion, too, though choose carefully on the rather overrated menu, and stick to the old favorites – blinis, borscht and chicken Kiev.

Uncle Vanya Café 315 W 54th St (between 8th and 9th aves) ⊕212/262-0542. Moderately priced delicacies, including more than just the obligatory borscht and caviar.

Vegetarian

Great American Health Bar 35 W 57th St (between 5th and 6th aves) ⊕212/355-5177.

This Manhattan chain comes highly praised, but in reality the food can be rather bland and uninviting. For committed veggies only.

Zenith Vegetarian **888 8th Ave (at 52nd St) ☎212/489-8263.** The best and most creative vegetarian fare in midtown, if you go in for the mock meats and such.

Midtown East

Catering mostly to lunchtime office-going crowds that swarm the sidewalks on weekdays, **Midtown East** overflows with restaurants, most of them on the pricey side. You probably won't want to make it the focal point of too many culinary excursions but, that said, there are a few timeworn favorites in the neighborhood.

American and Continental

Broadway Diner **590 Lexington Ave (at 52nd St) ☎212/486-8838; 1726 Broadway (at 55th St) ☎212/765-0909.** An upscale coffee shop with 1950s-style ambience.

Comfort Diner **214 E 45th St (between 2nd and 3rd aves) ☎212/867-4555; 142 E 86th St at Lexington Ave ☎212/369-8628.** One of the friendliest spots in town, this retro diner serves up hearty staples like meatloaf, fried chicken, and macaroni and cheese. It's a great place to fill up and rest the weary toes.

Four Seasons **99 E 52nd St (between Park and Lexington aves) ☎212/754-9494.** Housed in Mies van der Rohe's Seagram Building, this is one of the city's most noted restaurants, not least for the decor, which includes murals by Picasso, sculptures by Richard Lippold and interior design by Philip Johnson. The food isn't at all bad either, and there's a relatively inexpensive pre-theater menu – $55 – if you want to try it. Somewhat stuffier than the other top restaurants.

Goldwater's **988 2nd Ave (between 52nd and 53rd sts) ☎212/888-2122.** Fish dishes in huge portions for $15–22 a head. Primarily a seafood restaurant, though some steaks and pastas are served. Recently renovated, the new slick look serves it well – occasional live music as well.

Lipstick Café **885 3rd Ave (at 54th St) ☎212/486-8664.** Unlike most restaurants in the neighborhood, this one serves up delectable lunchtime food at affordable prices. Tasty homemade soups, salads and delicious baked goods. Closed weekends.

Oyster Bar **Lower Level, Grand Central Terminal (at 42nd St and Park Ave) ☎212/490-6650.** Atmospheric turn-of-the-nineteenth-century place located down in the vaulted dungeons of Grand Central Station, where midtown execs and others break for lunch. The oyster appetizers are particularly good, while seafood entrees go for a minimum of $25 per dish. If you're hard up, just saddle up to the bar for a bowl of excellent clam chowder, or great creamy bowls of pan-roasted oysters or clams.

Rosen's Delicatessen **23 E 51st St (between 5th and Madison aves) ☎212/541-8320.** Enormous Art Deco restaurant, renowned for its pastrami and corned beef, and handily situated for those suffering from midtown shopping fatigue. Good breakfasts too.

Smith and Wollensky **797 3rd Ave (at 49th St) ☎212/753-1530.** Clubby atmosphere in a grand setting, where waiters – many of whom have worked here for twenty years or more – serve you the primest cuts of beef imaginable. Quite pricey – you'll pay at least $33 a steak – but worth the splurge. Go basic with the sides and wines.

Asian

Hatsuhana **17 E 48th St (between 5th and Madison aves) ☎212/355-3345; 237 Park Ave (at 46th St) ☎212/661-3400.** Every sushi lover's favorite sushi restaurant now has two branches. Not at all cheap, so try to get there for the prix-fixe lunch.

Mee Noodle Shop and Grill **547 2nd Ave ☎212/779-1596.** The antidote to the pricier Asian places in this area, *Mee* is a standard in-and-out joint that does great soup noodles and other Chinese classics very fast and very well.

Vong **200 E 54th St (between 2nd and 3rd aves) ☎212/486-9592.** This is an eccentrically,

Restaurants with views

This is a brief checklist of – mainly Manhattan – restaurants that draw many people just for their views or location. Some of the restaurants are covered in more detail in other sections: where they're not, it's worth bearing in mind that the quality of the views will almost invariably be reflected in the size of your bill.

Boat Basin Café W 79th St (at the Hudson River) ⓣ212/496-5542
Boathouse Café Central Park Lake (east side, near 72nd St entrance) ⓣ212/517-2233
River Café 1 Water St (at the East River), Brooklyn 718/522-5200
Tavern on the Green W 67th St (at Central Park W) ⓣ212/873-3200
Terrace in the Sky 400 W 119th St (between Amsterdam Ave and Morningside Drive) ⓣ212/666-9490
The Water Club 500 E 30th St (at the East River; access from 34th St) ⓣ212/683-3333

exotically decorated restaurant everyone continues to talk about, which means it's hot enough to make your wallet smoke. The chefs take a French colonial approach to Thai cooking, doing things like putting mango in *foie gras*, and sesame and tamarind on Moscovy duck. Somehow it works. You can get a "tasting menu" of samples for the bargain price of $72 per person.

Caribbean, Central and South American

Zarela 953 2nd Ave (between 50th and 51st sts) ⓣ212/644-6740. If you've ever wondered what regional home-cooked Mexican food really tastes like, this festive restaurant is the place to go. It's noticeably more expensive than most Mexican places, but worth every bit.

French

Le Cirque 2000 New York Palace Hotel, 455 Madison Ave (between 50th and 51st sts) ⓣ212/794-9292. Recently relocated, it is still widely considered to be one of the city's best restaurants, though not quite as good as it used to be. Very orchestrated, very expensive, and frequented over the years by the likes of Liza Minnelli, Richard Nixon and Ronald Reagan.

Lutèce 249 E 50th St (between 2nd and 3rd aves) ⓣ212/752-2225. Still rated one of the best restaurants in the country, and a favorite of many well-to-do New Yorkers. The classic French food is top-notch, the service elegant and understated. What's surprising is how low-key and completely unpretentious it is, though you do need big bucks and reservations in advance. Worth every penny.

Rive Gauche 560 3rd Ave (at 37th St) ⓣ212/949-5400. Pleasant, if unremarkable neighborhood French bistro, serving soups, salads and classic entrees at a reasonable price (for French food), $13.95–20.95 an entrée or between 5–7pm the prix fixe is $19.95.

Italian

Luna Piena 243 E 53rd St (between 2nd and 3rd aves) ⓣ212/308-8882. One of the better local Italians in a neighborhood of many mediocre restaurants. The food is good, the service is friendly, and there's a nice enclosed garden for warm summer evenings.

Spanish

Solera 216 E 53rd St (between 2nd and 3rd aves) ⓣ212/644-1166. Tapas and other Spanish specialties in a stylish townhouse setting. As you'd expect from the surroundings and the ambience, it can be expensive.

Upper West Side

Restaurants on the **Upper West Side** offer a wide array of ethnic and price choices (particularly if you avoid the overpriced Lincoln Center area). There are lots of generous burger joints, Chinese restaurants, friendly coffee shops and delectable, if a bit pricey, brunch spots, so you'll never be at a loss for good meals.

American and Continental

Big Nick's 2175 Broadway (between 76th and 77th sts) ☎212/362-9238. If you want a hamburger or pizza on the Upper West Side, this is a fun, New York kind of place. In his crowded, chaotic little wooden-table restaurant, Big Nick has been serving them up all night long to locals for 20-plus years.

Boat Basin Café 79th St at the Hudson River (access through Riverside Park) ☎212/496-5542. An outdoor restaurant, open May through September, with informal tables covered in red-and-white checked cloths, some under a sheltering overhang. The food is standard, but inexpensive considering the prime location – burgers with fries ($7.75), hot dogs, sandwiches and some more serious entrees like grilled salmon ($14.50). On weekend afternoons a violin trio adds to the ambience.

Boathouse Café Central Park Lake (72nd St entrance) ☎212/517-2233. Peaceful retreat from a hard day's trudging around the Fifth Avenue museums. You get great views of the famous Central Park skyline and decent American/continental cuisine, but at very steep prices. Closed from Oct to March.

Dock's Oyster Bar 2427 Broadway (between 89th and 90th sts) ☎212/724-5588; also 633 3rd Ave (at 40th St) ☎212/986-8080. Some of the best seafood in town at this popular uptown restaurant, with a raw bar, great mussels and a wide variety of high-quality fresh fish. The Upper West Side is the original and tends to have the homier atmosphere – though both can be noisy and service can be slow. Reservations recommended on weekends.

EJ's Luncheonette 447 Amsterdam Ave (between 81st and 82nd sts) ☎212/873-3444. Diner that does its best to look retro, with mirrors, booths upholstered in turquoise vinyl, and walls adorned with 1950s photographs. Unpretentious, affordable American food that includes pancakes in many guises and banana splits to die for. Also great French-fried sweet potatoes. Expect long lines for brunch on Sun.

Fish 2799 Broadway (at 108th St) ☎212/864-5000. A nice compromise between nouvelle and old-fashioned; the dishes here aren't fussy, just incredibly tasty. Fried calamari with anchovy butter is a good example; prawns roasted with bacon, cognac and scallions is another. Or just content yourself with impeccably fresh raw oysters.

Good Enough to Eat 483 Amsterdam Ave (between 83rd and 84th sts) ☎212/496-0163. Cutesy Upper West Side restaurant known for its cinnamon-swirl French toast, award-winning meatloaf and excellent brunch value.

Hi-Life Bar & Grill 477 Amsterdam Ave ☎212/787-7199. A cozy bar/restaurant that serves an odd combination of classic American food and cocktails and sushi. Good prices and excellent service.

Josephina 1900 Broadway (between 63rd and 64th sts, across from Lincoln Center) ☎212/799-1000. Large airy restaurant painted with colonial murals (albeit cut in half by the banquette seating). Good salads, soups and the like; moderate prices.

Positively 104th St 2725 Broadway (between 104th and 105th sts) ☎212/316-0372. It's questionable whether Bob Dylan would be impressed with decent steaks and a friendly atmosphere; a good choice for this part of town. Reasonably priced, too.

Santa Fe 72 W 69th St (between Columbus Ave and Central Park W) ☎212/724-0822. Upscale Southwestern cuisine in lovely surroundings – muted earth tones, large arrangements of fresh flowers and a cozy fireplace. The food is first-rate and the prices steep; be prepared to spend about $30 per person.

Sarabeth's Kitchen 423 Amsterdam Ave (between 80th and 81st sts) ☎212/496-6280; 1295 Madison Ave (between 92nd and 93rd sts) ☎212/410-7335. Best for brunch, this country-style restaurant serves delectable baked goods and impressive omelets. Dinner is very pricey, so you're better off at brunch. But expect to wait in line.

Tom's Restaurant 2880 Broadway (at 112th St) ☎212/864-6137. Cheap, greasy-spoon fare. This is the *Tom's* of *Seinfeld* and Suzanne Vega fame, usually filled with students from Columbia. Great breakfast deals – a large meal for under $6.

Asian

Fujiyama Mama 467 Columbus Ave (between 82nd and 83rd sts) ☎212/769-1144. One of the Upper West Side's best – and most boisterous – sushi bars, with high-tech decor and loud music.

Hunan Park 235 Columbus Ave (between 70th and 71st sts) ☎212/724-4411. Some of the best Chinese food on the Upper West Side is served here, in a large, crowded room, with typically quick service and moderate prices. Try the spicy noodles in sesame sauce and the dumplings. A good, less expensive option within a few blocks of Lincoln Center.

Jaya 494 Amsterdam Ave (at 84th St) ☎212/769-9585. A good standby in this part of town if you're craving Malaysian or Indonesian food – not a cuisine you find that often in Manhattan. Well priced, too.

Lenge 200 Columbus Ave (at 69th St) ☎212/799-9188. This decent Japanese restaurant offers plenty of sushi choices at average prices.

Neo 2298 Broadway (at 83rd St) ☎212/769-1003. Great and highly unusual sushi, beautifully prepared and served – but extremely pricey.

Ollie's Noodle Shop 2315 Broadway (at 84th St) ☎212/362-3111; 2957 Broadway (at 116th St) ☎212/932-3300; 190 W 44th St (between Broadway and 8th Ave) ☎212/921-5988. Good Chinese restaurant that serves marvellous noodles, barbecued meats and spare ribs. Not, however, a place to linger. Very cheap, very crowded and very noisy.

Rikyu 210 Columbus Ave (between 69th and 70th sts) ☎212/799-7847. A wide selection of Japanese food, including sushi made to order. Inexpensive lunches and early-bird specials make this place a relative bargain.

Caribbean, Central and South American

Café con Leche 424 Amsterdam Ave (at 80th St) ☎212/595 7000. Great neighborhood Dominican that serves fantastic roast pork, rice and beans, and some of the hottest chili sauce you've ever tasted. Cheap and very cheerful.

Calle Ocho 446 Columbus Ave (between 81st and 82nd sts) ☎212/873-5025. Very tasty Latino fare, such as *ceviches* and *chimchuri* steak with yucca fries, is served in an immaculately designed restaurant with a hopping bar, whose mojitos are as potent as any in the city.

Flor de Mayo 2651 Broadway (at 101st St) ☎212/663-5520. Very cheap, very popular Cuban-Chinese restaurant with coffee-shop decor and lots of food, though not much for vegetarians – spicy chicken, Cuban-style steaks, etc. You can eat well for around $12.

La Caridad 2199 Broadway (at 78th St) ☎212/874-2780. This is something of an Upper West Side institution, a tacky, no-frills eatery that doles out plentiful and cheap Cuban-Chinese food to hungry diners (the Cuban is better than the Chinese). Bring your own beer, and expect to wait in line.

Rosa Mexicano 51 Columbus Ave (at 62nd St) ☎212/977-7700. High-end Mexican fare, served in a smartly designed space – complete with water cascading down the 30-foot stairway wall. The guacamole is not to be missed (made tableside), and the mole sauce is definitely something to be sampled.

French and Belgian

Café Luxembourg 200 W 70th St (between Amsterdam and West End aves) ☎212/873-7411. Trendy Lincoln Center area bistro that packs in (literally) a self-consciously hip crowd to enjoy its first-rate contemporary French food. Not too pricey – two people can eat for $60 or so.

Jean Georges Trump International Hotel, 1 Central Park W (between 60th and 61st sts) ☎212/299-3900. This is French at its finest, crafted by star chef Jean-Georges Vongerichten. Definitely the place for a special occasion when you don't mind dropping a pretty penny. For the more money conscious, the frontroom, *Nougatine* has a prix-fixe summer brunch for $20. But whatever you do, don't miss the rhubarb tart for dessert.

La Boite en Bois 75 W 68th St (between Central Park W and Columbus Ave) ☎212/874-2705. Rustic, moderately priced Lincoln Center bistro that has good country French food.

Indian

Indian Café 2791 Broadway (between 107th and 108th sts) ☎212/749-9200. This light, airy restaurant serves good Indian food at moderate prices. A pleasant spot for lunch or dinner (weekday lunch specials run from $6.95 to $8.95).

Mughlai **320 Columbus Ave (at 75th St) ☎212/724-6363.** Uptown, upscale Indian with prices about the going rate for this strip: $11–16 an entree. The food, though, is surprisingly good.

Italian

Caffè la Fortuna **69 W 71st St (between Central Park W and Columbus Ave) ☎212/724-5846.** The walls are covered with records and black-and-white photos of opera personalities. The atmosphere is dark, comfy and inviting. You can sip a coffee all day long in the shade of their peaceful garden, and their Italian pastries are heavenly.

Ernie's **2150 Broadway (at 75th St) ☎212/496-1588.** Casual, extra-large Upper West Side Italian, serving staple, decent food at slightly inflated prices.

Gennaro **665 Amsterdam Ave (between 92nd and 93rd sts) ☎212/665-5348.** A tiny outpost of truly great Italian food, with room only for about fifty people (and thus perpetual lines to get in). Standouts include a warm potato, mushroom and goat cheese tart (incredible) and braised lamb shank in red wine. The desserts are also worth the wait. Moderate prices – open for dinner only.

Jewish and Eastern European

Barney Greengrass (The Sturgeon King) **541 Amsterdam Ave (between 86th and 87th sts) ☎212/724-4707.** A West Side deli and restaurant that's been around since time began. The smoked salmon section is a particular treat. Cheese blintzes are tasty too.

Restaurants with outdoor seating

The following is just a brief checklist of restaurants that regularly have outdoor seating in summer. Many Manhattan restaurants put at least a few tables out on the sidewalk when the weather gets warm.

Downtown Manhattan

Cloister Café 238 E 9th St (between 2nd and 3rd aves) ☎212/777-9128
The Coffee Shop 29 Union Square W (between 16th and 17th sts) ☎212/243-7969
KK Restaurant 192-194 1st Ave (between 11th and 12th sts) ☎212/777-4430
Miracle Grill 112 1st Ave (between 6th and 7th sts) ☎212/254-2353
Pisces 95 Ave A (between 6th and 7th sts) ☎212/260-6660
Provence 38 MacDougal St (between Prince and Houston sts) ☎212/475-7500
Radio Perfecto 190 Ave B (between 11th and 12th sts) ☎212/477-3366
Spring Street Natural Restaurant 62 Spring St (at Lafayette St) ☎212/966-0290
Time Café 380 Lafayette St (at Great Jones St) ☎212/533-7000

Midtown Manhattan

Brasserie Centrale 1700 Broadway (at 53rd St) ☎212/757-2233
Bryant Park Grill 25 W 40th St (between 5th and 6th aves) ☎212/840-6500
Caffè Bondo 7 W 20th St (between 5th and 6th aves) ☎212/691-8136
Empire Diner 210 10th Ave (between 22nd and 23rd sts) ☎212/243-2736
Le Madeleine 403 W 43rd St (between 9th and 10th aves) ☎212/246-2993
Pete's Tavern 129 E 18th St (at Irving Place) ☎212/473-7676

Uptown Manhattan

Boat Basin Café W 79th St (at the Hudson River) ☎212/496-5542
Boathouse Café Central Park Boating Lake (72nd St entrance) ☎212/517-2233
Caffè la Fortuna 69 W 71st St (between Central Park W and Columbus Ave) ☎212/724-5846
The Saloon 1920 Broadway (at 64th St) ☎212/874-1500

Fine & Schapiro **138 W 72nd St (between Broadway and Columbus Ave) ⓣ212/877-2721.** Longstanding Jewish deli that's open for lunch and dinner and serves delicious old-fashioned kosher fare – an experience that's getting harder to find in New York. Great chicken soup.

Upper East Side

Upper East Side restaurants cater mostly to a discriminating mixture of well-heeled clientele and young professionals from Wall Street; many of the best French and Italian restaurants call this neighborhood home. Otherwise, the cuisine here is much like that of the Upper West Side: a mixture of Asian, standard American and more reasonable Italian cafés. For a change of pace, try a wurst and some strudel at one of Yorkville's old-world German luncheonettes.

American and Continental

Barking Dog Luncheonette **1678 3rd Ave (at 94th St) ⓣ212/831-1800.** Puppy motif at this uptown diner with extra-special mashed potatoes and grilled-cheese sandwiches. Expect lines for brunch.

Brother Jimmy's **1485 2nd Ave (between 77th and 78th sts) ⓣ212/288-0999.** A raucous beer and sports bar that serves some mighty good barbecue. Be ready to belch with the rest of the crowd.

Canyon Road **1470 1st Ave (between 76th and 77th sts) ⓣ212/734-1600.** Yuppie Upper East Side place effecting a Santa Fe atmosphere. Moderate prices.

E.A.T. **1064 Madison Ave (between 80th and 81st sts) ⓣ212/772-0022.** Expensive and crowded but excellent food (celebrated restaurateur and gourmet grocer Eli Zabar is the owner, so that's no surprise) – especially the soups and breads, and the ficelles and Parmesan toast. Unlike most in the city, the mozzarella, basil and tomato sandwiches are fresh and heavenly.

Elaine's **1703 2nd Ave (between 88th and 89th sts) ⓣ212/534-8103.** Remember the opening shots of Woody Allen's *Manhattan*? That was *Elaine's*, and today her restaurant is still something of a favorite with New York celebrities – though it's hard to see why. Nevertheless, if you want to star-gaze there's no better place to come.

Googie's Diner **1491 2nd Ave (at 78th St) ⓣ212/717-1122.** Artsy diner with funky decor and Italian-influenced American food.

Madhatter **1485 2nd Ave (between 77th and 78th sts) ⓣ212/628-4917.** This casual pub serves decent burgers and other simple food in a lively, sometimes loud setting.

Post House **26 E 63rd St ⓣ212/935-2888.** Classic American food in an elegant and comfortable, typically Upper East Side setting. It's reasonably unpretentious for the area, and does very good steaks and chops, though not all that cheaply.

Rathbones **1702 2nd Ave (between 88th and 89th sts) ⓣ212/369-7361.** Opposite Elaine's and an excellent alternative for ordinary humans. Take a window seat, watch the stars arrive, and eat for a fraction of the price. Steaks and fish for around $15 – and a wide choice of beers.

Viand **673 Madison Ave (between 61st and 62nd sts) ⓣ212/751-6622.** A bit pricier than most diner fare but worth it for the enormous turkey sandwiches, remarkable burgers and tasty vanilla Cokes.

Asian

Pig Heaven **1540 2nd Ave (between 80th and 81st sts) ⓣ212/744-4333.** Good-value Chinese restaurant decorated with images of pigs, serving lean and meaty spare ribs, among other things. In case you hadn't guessed, the accent is on pork.

Sala Thai **1718 2nd Ave (between 89th and 90th sts) ⓣ212/410-5557.** Restaurant serving creative combinations of hot and spicy Thai food for about $15 a head. Pleasant decor, good service and the best Thai food in the neighborhood.

Wu Liang Ye **215 E 86th St (between 2nd and 3rd aves) ⓣ212/534-8899.** Excellent, authentic Szechuan food. The menu here features dishes you've never seen before and, if you like spicy food, you will not be disappointed. Perhaps one of the best Chinese restaurants in the whole city.

Caribbean, Central and South American

Bolivar **206 E 60th St (between 2nd and 3rd aves) ⓣ212/838-0440.** New South American venue serving mostly Peruvian dishes and large Argentine steaks and grilled meats. Entrees run about $16–20. The next-door café section is cheaper and more casual, serving essentially the same food in smaller portions.

El Pollo **1746 1st Ave (between 90th and 91st sts) ⓣ212/996-7810.** Delicious – and very cheap – Peruvian-style restaurant, serving rotisserie chicken, flavored with a variety of spices to eat in or take out.

French and Belgian

Aureole **34 E 61st St (between Madison and Park aves) ⓣ212/319-1660.** Magical French-accented American food in a gorgeous old brownstone setting. The prix-fixe options should bring the cost down to $70 per head. Actually though, the late lunch special (after 2pm) is truly affordable (and a steal) at $20.

Bistro du Nord **1312 Madison Ave (at 93rd St) ⓣ212/289-0997.** A cozy bistro with excellent Parisian fare. Very stylish atmosphere with moderate to expensive prices – entrees run from $19–26. Try the duck confit.

Daniel **60 E 65th St (between Madison and Park aves) ⓣ212/288-0033.** Upscale and expensive fare from celebrated chef Daniel Boulud. The fava-encrusted halibut is amazing. One of the best French restaurants in New York City.

Le Refuge **166 E 82nd St (between Lexington and 3rd aves) ⓣ212/861-4505.** Quiet, intimate and deliberately romantic old-style French restaurant situated in an old city brownstone. The bouillabaisse and other seafood dishes are delectable. Expensive but worth it; save for special occasions. Closed Sun during the summer.

Les Friandises **922 Lexington Ave (between 70th and 71st sts) ⓣ212/988-1616.** A paradise of French pastries on the Upper East side. Wonderful croissants and brioches and a sublime tarte tatin.

Mme Romaine de Lyon **29 E 61st St (between Madison and Park aves) ⓣ212/758-2422.** The best place for omelets: they've got 350 on the lunch menu, and dinner features an expanded non-omelet menu (though honestly, why bother? Eggs are the thing here).

Patisserie & Bistro **1032 Lexington Ave (between 72nd and 73rd sts) ⓣ212/717-5252.** This is real Parisian pastry – buttery, creamy and over the top. Cookies, cakes and *crème brulée* made to the exacting standards of the kitchen staffs of local millionaires.

Greek and Middle Eastern

Uskudar **1405 2nd Ave (between 73rd and 74th sts) ⓣ212/988-2641.** Authentic Turkish cuisine at a rather spartan Upper East Side venue. Great prices – plan on $30 or so for two.

Indian

Dawat **210 E 58th St (between 2nd and 3rd aves) ⓣ212/355-7555.** One of the most elegant gourmet Indian restaurants in the city. Try the Cornish game hen with green chili or the leg of lamb. A bit pricey – entrees average about $17. For an extra charge, Beverly will give you a tarot card reading.

Italian

Caffè Buon Gusto **243 E 77th St (between 2nd and 3rd aves) ⓣ212/35-6884.** This stretch of the Upper East Side has plenty of cool, Italian joints: what *Buon Gusto* lacks in style it makes up for in taste and low prices. The vodka sauce is excellent.

Carino **1710 2nd Ave (between 88th and 89th sts) ⓣ212/860-0566.** Family-run Upper East Side Italian, with low prices, friendly service and good food. Two can eat here for under $30.

Contrapunto **200-206 E 60th St (at 3rd Ave) ⓣ212/751-8616.** More than twenty fresh pastas daily at this friendly neighborhood Italian restaurant. Reasonably priced as well.

Ecco-La **1660 3rd Ave (between 92nd and 93rd sts) ⓣ212/860-5609.** Unique pasta combinations at very moderate prices make this place one of the Upper East Side's most popular Italians. A real find if you don't mind waiting.

Il Vagabondo **351 E 62nd St (between 1st and 2nd aves) ⓣ212/832-9221.** Hearty family-style Southern Italian food in a casual setting that includes the restaurant's own bocci court.

Rough Guide favorites

Pizza by the pie

Arturo's West Village, p.325
Grimaldi's Brooklyn, p.347
John's West Village, p.325
Lombardi's SoHo, p.318
Trattoria dell'Arte Midtown West, p.337

Jewish and Eastern European

Heidelburg 1648 2nd Ave (between 85th and 86th sts) ⓣ212/628-2332. The atmosphere here is mittel-European kitsch, with gingerbread trim and waitresses in Alpine goatherd costumes. But the food is the real deal, featuring excellent liver dumpling soup, Bauernfrühstück omelets, and pancakes (both sweet and potato). And they serve weissbier the right way, too – in giant, boot-shaped glasses.

Ideal Restaurant 238 E 86th St (between 2nd and 3rd aves) ⓣ212/535-0950. Before renovations a few years back, this was *the* place. Now, we're not so sure, but you can still get wursts and sauerkraut in huge portions for paltry prices.

Mocca Hungarian 1588 2nd Ave (between 82nd and 83rd sts) ⓣ212/734-6470. Yorkville restaurant serving hearty portions of Hungarian comfort food – schnitzel, cherry soup, goulash and chicken paprikash, among others. Moderately priced, but be sure to come hungry.

Upper Manhattan: Morningside Heights, Harlem, Washington Heights, Inwood

Cheap Cuban, African, Caribbean and the best soulfood restaurants in the city abound in and around **Harlem**; even institutions like *Sylvia's*, touristy and crowded as it may be, remain reasonably priced. It's well worth the trip up, though some of the other spots, like Inwood, you'll likely only want if you happen to be visiting the odd sight up this way.

African

Koryoe Restaurant and Café 3143 Broadway (between Tiemann Place and LaSalle St) ⓣ212/316-2950. Huge portions of West African specialties served with your choice of meat and sauce. Try the *wacheay*, rice with black-eyed peas, plantains and your choice of meat. Most everything is under $10. Also vegetarian selections.

Zula 1260 Amsterdam Ave (at 122nd St) ⓣ212/663-1670. High-quality and inexpensive ($8–up) Ethiopian food that's popular with the folk from Columbia University. Spicy chicken, beef and lamb dishes mainly, though a few veggie plates too.

American and Continental

Amy Ruth's 113 W 116th St (between Lenox and 7th aves) ⓣ212/280-8779. Surprisingly cheap, considering its enormous portions, this new soulfood spot draws Harlemites and visitors with its outstanding fried chicken and ribs. The desserts are excellent, too.

The Bread Shop 3139 Broadway (at 123rd St) ⓣ212/666-4343. Rich homemade breads and buttermilk biscuits in the bakery section, and soup and pizza in the cozy little restaurant section. A good place to rest up if you're in the neighborhood.

Copeland's 547 W 145th St (between Broadway and Amsterdam Ave) ⓣ212/234-2357. Soulfood at good prices for dinner or Sunday Gospel brunch, with a more reasonably priced cafeteria next door. Try the Louisiana gumbo. Live jazz on Fri and Sat nights.

Emily's 1325 5th Ave (at 111th St) ⓣ212/996-1212. Barbecued chicken and some of the best chopped bbq pork sandwiches in New York in a convivial atmosphere.

Londel's 2620 8th Ave (between 139th and 140th sts) ⓣ212/234-6114. A little soulfood, a little Cajun, a little Southern-fried food.

Twenty-four-hour food

This is simply a checklist for late-night – and mainly budget-constrained – hunger. For details, either check the individual listings, or assume they serve a straight coffee-shop menu. If you're nowhere near any of the addresses below, don't despair. There are numerous additional all-night delis (for takeout food), and in most neighborhoods of the city you'll also find at least one 24-hour Korean greengrocer – good for most food supplies.

Downtown Manhattan

Around the Clock 8 Stuyvesant St (between 2nd and 3rd aves) ☎212/598-0402
Bagel Buffet 406 6th Ave (between 8th and 9th sts) ☎212/477-0448
Dave's Pot Belly 94 Christopher St (at Bleecker St) ☎212/242-8036
Florent 69 Gansevoort St (between Washington and Greenwich sts) ☎212/989-5779
French Roast Café 456 6th Ave (at 11th St) ☎212/533-2233
Greenwich Café 75 Greenwich Ave (between 7th Ave S and Bank St) ☎212/255-5450
L'Express 249 Park Ave S (at 20th St) ☎212/254-5858
Triumph Restaurant 148 Bleecker St (between LaGuardia and Thompson sts) ☎212/228-3070
Veselka 144 2nd Ave (between 9th St and St Mark's Place) ☎212/228-9682
Waverly Restaurant 385 6th Ave (between 8th St and Waverly Place) ☎212/675-3181
Wo Hop 17 Mott St (between Canal St and Park Row) ☎212/267-2536.
Yaffa Café 97 St Mark's Place (between Ave A and 1st Ave) ☎212/677-9001

Midtown Manhattan

Brasserie Centrale 1700 Broadway (at 53rd St) ☎212/757-2233
Empire Diner 210 10th Ave (between 22nd and 23rd sts) ☎212/243-2736
Gemini Diner 641 2nd Ave (at 35th St) ☎212/532-2143
Lox Around the Clock 676 6th Ave (at 21st St) ☎212/691-3535
Market Diner 572 11th Ave (at 43rd St) ☎212/695-0415
Sarge's 548 3rd Ave (between 36th and 37th sts) ☎212/679-0442
Stage Deli 834 7th Ave (between 53rd and 54th sts) ☎212/245-7850
West Side Diner 360 9th Ave (at 31st St) ☎212/560-8407

Uptown Manhattan

Big Nick's 2175 Broadway (between 76th and 77th sts) ☎212/362-9238
Gray's Papaya 2090 Broadway (at 72nd St) ☎212/799-0243
Green Kitchen 1477 1st Ave (at 77th St) ☎212/988-4163
H & H Bagels 2239 Broadway (at 80th St) ☎212/595-8000
Tramway Coffee Shop 1143 2nd Ave (at 60th St) ☎212/758-7017

This is an attractive down-home place where you can eat upscale items like steak Diane or more common treats such as fried chicken; either way, follow it up with some sweet potato pie.

Sylvia's Restaurant **328 Lenox Ave (between 126th and 127th sts) ☎212/996-0660.** The most well-known Southern soulfood restaurant in Harlem – so famous that Sylvia herself even has her own package food line. While some find the barbecue sauce too tangy, the fried chicken is exceptional at $16.95 and the garlic mashed potatoes and candied yams are justly celebrated. Also famous for the Sunday Gospel brunch but be prepared for a 30-minute wait.

Caribbean, Central and South American

Caridad Restaurant **4311 Broadway (at 184th St) ☎212/781-0431.** Not to be confused with the Upper West Side restaurant of (almost) the same name, this place serves mountains of Dominican food at cheap prices. Try the *mariscos* or seafood, the specialty of the house to be eaten with lots of *pan y ajo*, thick slices of French bread, grilled with olive oil and plenty of garlic. Be sure to go feeling hungry.

French

Terrace in the Sky **400 W 119th St (between Amsterdam Ave and Morningside Drive)**

☎212/666-9490. This rooftop eclectic yet classy eatery is best known for its incredible views of the city (and possibly as the place Columbia University students most often take their parents to dinner). Fairly expensive, but if Dad's paying, who cares?

Brooklyn

In **Brooklyn**, lower Atlantic Avenue offers some of the city's best Middle Eastern food; Brighton Beach features the most authentic Russian food in NYC; and Park Slope, Carroll Gardens, Cobble Hill and Fort Greene all have burgeoning restaurant rows.

Atlantic Avenue

Fatoosh Babecue 311 Henry St (at Atlantic Ave) ☎718/596-0030. Call it "hippie Middle Eastern" – fresh, hearty falafel and babaganoush.

La Bouillabaisse 145 Atlantic Ave (between Clinton and Henry sts) ☎718/522-8275. French bistro popular with the locals; said to be the place to try sweetbreads if you never have before. Affordable and crowded most nights.

Moroccan Star 205 Atlantic Ave (between Court and Clinton sts) ☎718/643-0800. Perhaps New York's best Moroccan restaurant, offering wonderful tajines and couscous with lamb. The chef once worked at the *Four Seasons*, and the quality of his cooking remains undiminished. Entrees are generally around $9.

Petite Crevette 127 Atlantic Ave (between Henry and Clinton sts) ☎718/858-6660. Reasonably priced, comfortable French bistro with many simple fish dishes.

Tripoli 156 Atlantic Ave (at Clinton St) ☎718/596-5800. Lebanese restaurant serving fish, lamb and vegetarian dishes for a low $8 or so. Miniature lamb pies in yogurt sauce are a standout.

Waterfront Ale House 155 Atlantic Ave ☎718/522-3794. This inexpensive and good fun old-style pub serves good spicy chicken wings, ribs and killer Key Lime pie (made locally and only available in Brooklyn).

Brooklyn Heights

Grimaldi's Pizza19 Old Fulton St (between Water and Front sts) ☎718/858-4300. Delicious, thin and crispy pies that bring even Manhattanites across the water – cheap and crowded.

Heights Café 84 Montague St (at Hicks St) ☎718/625-5555. Near the Esplanade overlooking the East River and the Manhattan skyline, this mainstay offers a great environment for a drink and appetizers at the bar or a decent-priced American eclectic meal at one of the sidewalk tables.

Henry's End 44 Henry St (at Cranberry St) ☎718/834-1776. Neighborhood bistro with a wide selection of reasonably priced seasonal dishes, appetizers and desserts. Normally crowded, and don't expect it to be all that cheap. Known for its wild-game festival in fall and winter.

Montague Street Saloon 122 Montague St (between Henry and Hicks sts ☎718/522-6770. Burgers and salads for under $10; good fried calamari and Cajun catfish.

Teresa's 80 Montague St (between Hicks St and Montague Terrace) ☎718/797-3996. Large portions of Polish home cooking – blintzes, pierogies and the like – make this a good lunchtime stop-off for those on tours of Brooklyn Heights.

Bay Ridge

101 Café 10018 4th Ave (at 101st St) ☎718/833-1313. Italian eatery and bar that attracts hip, younger Bay Ridge crowd.

Elia 8611 3rd Ave (between 86th and 87th sts) ☎718/748-9891. Simple, piquant Greek food that some say is not only better than anything in Astoria, but maybe even in Greece itself. Can't lose with any of the grilled fish on the menu.

Tuscany Grill 8620 3rd Ave (between 86th and 87th sts) ☎718/921-5633. Always full of locals dining on simple Italian and fantastic thin crust pizzas.

Brighton Beach

Mrs Stahl's 1001 Brighton Beach Ave (at Coney Island Ave) ☎718/648-0210. This longstanding knish purveyor features over twenty different varieties.

Odessa **1113 Brighton Beach Ave (between 13th and 14th sts) ⓣ718/332-3223.** Excellent and varied Russian menu at unbeatable prices. Dancing and music nightly.

Primorski **282 Brighton Beach Ave (between 2nd and 3rd sts) ⓣ718/891-3111.** Perhaps the best of Brighton Beach's Russian hangouts, serving up a huge menu of authentic Russian dishes, including blintzes and stuffed cabbage, at absurdly cheap prices. Live music in the evening.

Boerum Hill, Cobble Hill, Carroll Gardens

Banania **241 Smith St (at Douglass St) ⓣ718/237-9100.** French bistro serving brunch and dinner for quite reasonable prices; steaks and fish dishes, like pan-roasted cod, stand out. Average price for entrees is $14; cash only.

Ferdinando's **151 Union St (between Hicks and Columbia sts) ⓣ718/855-1545.** Authentic Italian, cooked and served by the family that owns this tiny dining room. Nothing fancy, just your basic sauces, meats and pastas made the same way they've been making them out here for decades.

Grocery **288 Smith St (between Sackett and Union sts) ⓣ718/596-3335.** Small and tasty New American restaurant, with entrees, including a number of game dishes, ranging from $17 to 23. Highlights include duck breast with toasted bulghur and nightly homemade sausage specials.

Sam's **238 Court St (between Baltic and Kenneth sts) ⓣ718/596-3458.** Long-established restaurant serving standard Italian fare at reasonable prices.

Saul **140 Smith St (at Bergen St) ⓣ718/935-9844.** Former *Bouley* star Saul Bolton's New American food is one of the reasons to come out to happening Smith Street; the cucumber and avocado soup is great for a hot summer day.

Smith Street Kitchen **174 Smith St (between Warren and Wyckoff sts) ⓣ718/858-5359.** Very good seafood, like the Individual Clam Bake (clams, mussels, lobster, sausage, corn and potatoes in a sweet broth), that runs about $16–20 an entree. Outside garden a plus.

Coney Island

Carolina **1409 Mermaid Ave (at 15th St) ⓣ718/714-1294.** Inexpensive, family-run Italian restaurant that's been around forever. Great food, great prices.

Gargiulo's **2911 W 15th St (between Surf and Mermaid aves) ⓣ718/266-4891.** A gigantic, noisy family-run Coney Island restaurant famed for its large portions of cheap and hearty Neapolitan food.

Downtown Brooklyn

Gage & Tollner **372 Fulton St (between Jay and Boerum sts) ⓣ718/875-5181.** Old-fashioned seafood restaurant with an extensive menu that's long been part of the downtown Brooklyn eating scene. One of the oldest restaurants in New York (c 1879), it's not as expensive as it looks. Serves great crab cakes, Charleston she-crab soup and clam bellies.

Junior's **386 Flatbush Ave (at DeKalb Ave) ⓣ718/852-5257.** Open 24 hours in a sea of lights that makes it worthy of Vegas, *Junior's* offers everything you can imagine, from chopped liver sandwiches to ribs and meatloaf. Whatever you do, save room for the cheesecake, which many consider to be NYC's finest.

River Café **1 Water St (at the East River) ⓣ718/522-5200.** This elite eating establishment, situated at the base of the Brooklyn Bridge, provides spectacular views of Manhattan. While dishes like the potato-crusted oysters are excellent, the $70 prix fixe (dinner only) is a little steep.

Fort Greene

A' Tabla **171 Lafayette Ave (at Adelphi St) ⓣ718/935-9121.** Gallic comfort food, with outdoor seating in summer.

Richlene **83 Lafayette Ave (between Elliot and Portland sts) ⓣ718/243-2040.** Real Caribbean dishes, including oxtail, jerk chicken and *rotis*. If you're in the neighborhood during lunch make a pit stop whether you're hungry or not

Sol **229 DeKalb Ave (between Adelphi and Clermont sts) ⓣ718/222-1510.** Serving unique Caribbean-Asian fusion food, *Sol* offers a killer mushroom risotto and tasty duck springrolls. There is also a menu full of exotic mixed drinks.

Greenpoint

Old Poland Bakery and Restaurant 190 Nassau Ave ☎718/349-7775. Cheap and delicious Polish food as served in the old country. Pork shank with mashed potatoes and vegetables is the way to go.

Park Slope

Al Di Là 248 5th Ave (at Carroll St) ☎718/783-4565. Venetian country cooking at its finest at this husband-and-wife-run eatery. Standouts include beet ravioli, grilled sardines, *saltimbocca* and salt-baked striped bass. Invariably crowded.

Aunt Suzie's 247 5th Ave (between Garfield Place and Carroll St) ☎718/788-3377. Neighborhood Italian serving decent food for as little as $10 a person. Not a restaurant to drive from Manhattan for, but if you happen to be in the area, it's one of the best-value places around.

Coco Roco 392 5th Ave (between 6th and 7th sts) ☎718/965-3373. Peruvian rotisserie chicken, roasted pork, *ceviches* and *jalea* (seafood lightly fried in purple corn meal). Manhattan taste at Brooklyn prices: $9–17 for entrees.

Cucina 256 5th Ave (between Garfield Place and Carroll St) ☎718/230-0711. Warm and inviting Italian restaurant serving exemplary food for affordable prices.

Geido 331 Flatbush Ave (at 7th Ave) ☎718/638-8866. This reasonably priced sushi might be some of Brooklyn's best; the Sharon roll is a must. Get in good with chef Osamu and he may pour you a glass of his special sake.

Rose Water 787 Union St (at 6th Ave) ☎718/783-3800. Intimate Mediterranean-American bistro, serving excellent food at moderate cost: under $15 for dishes that would be twice as much across the water. Good for a special meal, and you won't soon forget the flavors either.

Williamsburg

Brick Oven Pizza Gallery 33 Havemeyer St (between N 7th & N 8th sts) ☎718/963-0200. The perfect pitstop before heading to nearby *Pete's Candy Store* (see p.364), this unassuming eatery serves authentic and superb wood-fired pizzas, best washed down with not quite superb $2 glasses of table wine.

Charleston Bar and Grill 174 Bedford Ave ☎718/782-8717. A local dive that's more bar than grill – come here primarily for the good cheap pizza and to listen to the assortment of bands that play nightly.

Diner 85 Broadway (at Berry St) ☎718/486-3077. Located in a refurbished dining car under the Williamsburg Bridge, this local favorite dishes out a superb array of food that includes fantastic burgers, French standards and a wealth of daily specials. Kitchen open nightly to 2am.

Oznot's Dish 79 Berry St (at N 9th St) ☎718/599-6596. Technically Moroccan and Middle Eastern, this colorful spot is more Middle-East-Village in spirit. Plop down on one of the antique chairs and try grilled shrimp with jalapeño vinaigrette served on a grilled mango, or lamb chunks over basmati rice with melted leeks and *tomatillos*.

Peter Luger's Steak House 178 Broadway (at Driggs Ave) ☎718/387-7400. Catering to carnivores since1873, *Peter Luger's* may just be the city's finest steakhouse. The service is surly and the decor plain, but the porterhouse steak – the only cut served – is divine. Cash only; expect to pay at least $60 a head.

Planet Thailand 141 N. 7th (between Bedford Ave and Berry St) ☎718/599-5758. Excellent, affordable Thai and Japanese food served up in an artsy warehouse-sized space that buzzes with conversation and dj-spun tunes. Bars at both entrances make the usual half-hour wait somewhat palatable.

Vera Cruz 195 Bedford Ave (between N 6th and N 7th sts) ☎718/599-7914. Reasonably priced, imaginatively prepared Mexican food – the grilled corn-on-the cob starter coated in mayonnaise and cheese is superb – best enjoyed in the back garden. Skip the overly sweet margaritas in favor of one of their many Mexican brews.

Queens

The most ethnically diverse of all the boroughs, **Queens** holds the city's largest Greek, South American, Slavic and Asian communities, thus some of the best examples of those types of food – not to mention the Indian available in Jackson Heights.

Long Island City and Astoria

Elias Corner **24-02 31st St (at 24th Ave), Astoria ☎718/932-1510.** Pay close attention to the seafood on display as you enter, for *Elias Corner* does not have menus and the staff is not always forthcoming. This informal Astoria institution, with open-air seating when weather permits, serves some of the best and freshest fish as well as a myriad of salads. Try the swordfish kebabs.

Karyatis **35-03 Broadway, Astoria ☎718/204-0666.** Upscale Greek that doesn't miss a beat in service, food or price. Save room for the baklava. Often has live music.

Uncle George's **33-19 Broadway (at 34th St), Astoria ☎718/626-0593.** This 24-hour joint serves excellent and ultra-cheap authentic Greek food, including some of the top Greek BBQ and *spanakopita* in the city.

Jackson Heights and Corona

Green Field Churrascaria **108-01 Northern Blvd, Corona ☎718/672-5202.** A huge Brazilian meatery, where waiters by the dozen swarm your table offering every sort of grilled meat under the sun.

Inti-Raymi **86-14 37th Ave (between 86th and 87th sts), Jackson Heights ☎718/424-1938.** Unpretentious restaurant serving substantial low-priced Peruvian food in a jovial atmosphere. Try the *ceviche de mariscos* (raw fish in lime juice) or the Peruvian version of lo mein. Limited hours, however: it is open for dinner only on Thurs & Fri, lunch and dinner on Sat & Sun, and closed the rest of the week.

Jackson Diner **37-47 74th St (between 37th and Roosevelt Ave), Jackson Heights ☎718/672-1232.** Come here hungry and stuff yourself silly with amazingly light and reasonably priced Indian fare. Samosas and mango lassis are not to be missed.

La Pequeia Colombia **83-27 Roosevelt Ave (at 84th St), Jackson Heights ☎718/478-6528.** Literally "Little Colombia," this place doles out heaped portions of seafood casserole, pork and tortillas. Try the fruit drinks too, *maracuay* (passion fruit) or *guanabana* (sour soup).

Tabaq 74 **73-21 37th Ave (between 74th and 75th sts) ☎718/898-2837.** Pakistani barbecue of the highest order. If you don't like beef brains (the house specialty), you can have chicken, lamb or quail, generously spiced and prepared with skill and care.

Flushing, Forest Hills, Kew Gardens

Jade Palace **136-14 38th Ave, Flushing ☎718/353-3366.** Fantastic and very inexpensive dim sum. The *har gow* (shrimp dumplings) and taro cakes are a great place to start.

Mardi Gras **70-20 Austin St (between 70th Rd and 69th Ave), Forest Hills ☎718/261-8555.** Tiny Cajun eatery, serving crawfish, *muffalleta* sandwiches and other tasty treats at moderate prices.

Pastrami King **124-24 Queens Blvd (at 82nd Ave), Kew Gardens ☎718/263-1717.** The home-smoked pastrami and corned beef are better than any you'll find in Manhattan. Closed Sat.

The Bronx

In the **Bronx**, Belmont is one of the best places in the city to eat authentic Italian cuisine.

The Crab Shanty **361 City Island Ave (at Tier St) ☎718/885-1810.** While the decor is cheesy to say the least, the fried clams and Cajun fried fish specials at this City Island favorite are worth the trip.

Dominick's **2335 Arthur Ave (at 187th St) ☎718/733-2807.** All you could hope for in a Belmont neighborhood Italian: great, rowdy atmosphere, communal family-style seating, wonderful food and low(ish) prices. As there are no menus, pay close attention to your waiter. Stuffed baby squid, veal parmigiana and chicken *scarpariello* are standouts.

Mario's **2342 Arthur Ave (between 184th and 186th sts) ☎718/584-1188.** Pricey but impressive Italian cooking, from pizzas to pastas and beyond, enticing even die-hard

Manhattanites to the Belmont section of the Bronx.

Mister Taco **2255 White Plain Rd ☎718/882-3821.** Makes for a great snack or meal after walking around the nearby Bronx Botanical Garden. The tamales are the call here. No English spoken.

Sam's **596-598 Grand Concourse, ☎718/665-5341.** Located just a hop away from Yankee Stadium, *Sam's* makes for a tasty, cheap pre-game meal. Stay with the chicken, jerked or fried.

Schlitz Inn **767 E 137 St ☎718/993-3979.** Hankering for some boiled beef, goulash and a can of Schlitz? Probably not, but this would be the place to go for it.

Staten Island

Aesop's Tables **1233 Bay St (at Hylan Blvd) ☎718/720-2005.** Cozy and rustic restaurant serving interesting American regional variations. Try the catfish over greens or jerk chicken.

Killmeyer's Old Bavaria Inn **4254 Arthur Kill Rd (at Sharrott's Rd) ☎718/984-1202.** This Bavarian establishment has everything you might expect: men in lederhosen, a beer garden, bratwurst, potato pancakes and large hunks of meat served on the bone. Entrees are large enough to feed two.

31

Drinking

You can't walk a block along most Manhattan avenues (and many of the side streets) without passing one or two bars. The **bar scene** in New York City is a varied one, with a broader range of places to drink than in most American cities, and prices to suit most pockets. Bars generally open from mid-morning (around 10am) to the early hours – 4am at the latest, when they have to close by law. Bar kitchens usually stop operating around midnight or a little before.

As for prices, in a basic bar you'll be paying around $4–5 for a pint of beer "on tap," although in a swankier and/or more fashionable environment, this may go up considerably. You can swig drafts at your local dive or sip martinis in the city's plushest hotel bars. Look out for "happy hour" bargains (see box below) and two-for-the-price-of-one deals, but avoid bars or clubs that offer "free drinks for ladies" unless you are looking for cattle markets – or worse. Wherever you go, even if you just have a drink you'll be expected to tip about a buck a drink.

Happy hours and free stuff

At the turn of the nineteenth century, Bowery barkeeps offered a "free lunch" of pickles and boiled eggs to attract workingmen during their midday break. This practice has evolved into **happy hour**, now designed to pull in the after-work crowds. It's generally a two-hour period, often 5–7pm, sometimes with an extra hour tacked on either end, Monday to Friday only. Discounts are offered, either in two-for-one deals, or sometimes with special prices on specific drinks – "well" drinks, for example, which are the cheapest "house" liquors. A diminishing number of tatty bars put out thirst-inducing snacks like popcorn or pretzels during happy hour, and a few glitzy midtown joints offer free hors d'oeuvres, though this practice is on the decline. For happy-hour devotees, there are possibilities in addition to those listed: just check out the more upscale midtown bars and hotels. Alternatively, head to Chelsea or SoHo on a Wednesday or Friday night, and do a "gallery hop," taking advantage of the free wine as you go. (Openings are listed in *The Gallery Guide*, available from most of the establishments it mentions, and also on-line at ⓦwww.galleryguide.org.)

What to drink

When you've made your choice of bar, the problem is deciding **what to drink**.

Beer

Beer is enjoying something of a renaissance these days – it's not unusual to see ten taps of draft and a half-dozen bottled beer options behind the bar – with a choosy clientele knowing just what they want.

△ New York's bar scene has something for every tippler

Microbrews are particularly popular: Sam Adams, Pete's Wicked and Anchor Steam are drunk almost as frequently as the insipid American stalwarts Budweiser, Miller or Coors – something you wouldn't have seen fifteen years ago. Belgian beers have stormed the market, edging out their European brethren vying for space. You'll find many bars have Stella Artois or Hoegaarden on tap alongside German brands like Spaten and Paulaner – not to mention the usual assortment of Heineken, Guinness, Newcastle and Bass. There's also an increasing selection of Asian beers, such as Sapporo and Tiger, available. Beer usually costs around $5 a pint, bottles are usually cheaper at $4 a pop. If price is a problem, then bear in mind you can walk into any supermarket or corner store and buy bottles of beer at around $1.25 apiece.

Wine

Not only is **American wine** generally very good, but the price is pretty reasonable too, at around $13–18 a bottle in a liquor store. If you wish to sample something decent, try the varieties from the Napa or Sonoma valleys, just north of San Francisco, which between them produce some of the best-quality wines in the country. New York State also produces wine, though of a lesser quality than California. French, Italian and Australian wines are often less costly. In all cases, however, wine demands a better-filled wallet when in a restaurant or bar: expect 100 percent mark-up (at least!) on the bottle.

Spirits and liquor

As for the **hard stuff**, there are a number of points of potential confusion for overseas visitors. First bear in mind that whether you ask for a drink "on the rocks" or not, you'll most likely get it poured into a glass full to the brim with ice; if you don't want it like this ask for it "straight up." Don't forget either that if you ask for whiskey you will get one of the American kinds, most likely rye, of which the most common brand is Seagram's 7. If you want bourbon, Scotch or Irish whiskey you should ask for them by name. Pick a brand if you want something better than "speed rack" liquor (the cheap stuff a bartender serves if a brand choice is not indicated); it will cost more, but it will also be infinitely more drinkable.

Non-alcoholic drinks

By law, all NYC bars must serve selections of non-alcoholic drinks. Even if you plump for (say) the dubious delights of the alcohol-free beers so popular in the early 1990s, quaffing a Kaliber in an Irish bar is a bit like having a bath with your raincoat on. See "Some atmospheric cafés" box on p.307 for details of places specializing in genteel refreshment – and those that will provide you with a serious caffeine hit.

The age rage

The **drinking age** in New York is 21. Order any kind of alcohol and you're likely to be "carded" or "proofed" – carry ID just in case. If you're underage, you won't get in trouble for trying to buy alcohol; just prepare yourself for embarrassment if you're turned down. It's also not uncommon for staff to ask for proof of your age even when you're obviously well over 21. Since the Giuliani era, neighborhoods with a high youth population (ie, near colleges) have been subject to "sweeps" by local police, so if you aren't carded at a place one day, don't count on being so fortunate the next.

Buying your own booze

When buying your own alcohol or wine, you'll need to find a liquor store – supermarkets only have beer, just one of New York State's complex licensing laws. Other regulations worth keeping in mind are that you have to be over 21 to buy or consume alcohol in a bar or restaurant (and you'll be asked to provide evidence if there's any dispute); that it's against the law to drink alcohol on the street (which is why you see so many people furtively swigging from brown paper bags, though this still doesn't make it legal); and that on a Sunday you can't buy your own booze anywhere, other than beer, which is only available after noon.

The bar scene

The selections that follow are personal favorites. The potential choice is a lot wider below 14th Street, and the **West Village** takes in a wide range of taste, budget and purpose. (Bear in mind that many places double as bar and restaurant, and you may therefore find them listed not here but in the previous chapter, "Restaurants.") Some of the best hunting grounds are in the **East Village**, **NoLita**, **SoHo** and the more western reaches of the **Lower East Side**; there's a good choice of midtown bars – though here bars tend to be geared to an after-hours office crowd and (with a few notable exceptions) can consequently be pricey and rather dull; the **Upper West Side** has a good array of bars, some interesting, although most tend to cater to more of a clean-cut and dully yuppie crowd; and the bars of **Harlem**, while not numerous, offer some of the city's most affordable jazz in a relaxed environment.

While most visitors to New York may not have time or occasion to check out the bar scenes in the outer boroughs, those that venture to **Williamsburg**,

Cocktails

Bacardi	White rum, lime and grenadine
Black Russian	Vodka with coffee liqueur, brown cacao and Coke
Bloody Mary	Vodka, tomato juice, Tabasco, worcestershire sauce, salt and pepper. A brunch staple.
Cosmopolitan	Pink martini made with vodka, cranberry juice and lime juice
Daiquiri	Dark rum, light rum and lime, often frozen and with fruit such as banana or strawberry
Harvey Wallbanger	Vodka, galliano, orange juice
Highball	Any spirit plus a soda, water or ginger ale
Kir Royale	Champagne, cassis
Long Island Iced Tea	Gin, vodka, white rum, tequila, lemon juice and Coke
Manhattan	Vermouth, whiskey, lemon juice and soda
Margarita	Tequila, triple sec and lime (or strawberry) juice
Mimosa	Champagne and orange juice, often offered with prix fixe brunch
Mint Julep	Bourbon, mint and sugar
Mojito	Light rum, sugar, fresh mint and fresh lime juice
Piña Colada	Dark rum, light rum, coconut, cream and pineapple juice
Screwdriver	Vodka and orange juice
Tequila Sunrise	Tequila, orange juice and grenadine
Tom Collins	Gin, lemon juice, soda and sugar
Vodka Collins	Vodka, lemon juice, soda and sugar
Whisky Sour	Bourbon, lemon juice and sugar
White Russian	Vodka, white cacao and cream

Park Slope, **Brooklyn Heights** and **Fort Greene** in Brooklyn or to **Astoria** in Queens will find bars that range in feel from the neighborly to the hip.

Groupings follow, approximately, the chapter divisions outlined in the Guide. For ease of reference, however, all specifically gay and lesbian bars are gathered together in "Gay and Lesbian New York," Chapter 34.

Financial District and South Street Seaport

Jeremy's Alehouse **254 Front St (at Dover St) ☎212/964-3537.** An earthy bar near the South Street Seaport, housed in an old garage, *Jeremy's* also happens to serve some of the city's best calamari and clams.

North Star Pub **93 South St (at Fulton St) ☎212/509-6757.** "British" alehouse where you can wash down your bangers & mash with a pint of Newcastle Brown Ale – or choose from some 80 single malt Scotch whiskies. Fairly small, the *North Star* is very popular with Wall Street types and visiting Limeys.

TriBeCa

Grace **114 Franklin St (between Church St and W Broadway) ☎212/343-4200.** An excellent cocktail and olives spot teeming with old-school class – there's a 40ft mahogany bar. Top-notch drink selection for a twenty-something clientele.

Knitting Factory Tap Bar **74 Leonard St (between Church St and Broadway) ☎212/219-3006.** Street-level bar and cozy downstairs taproom with 18 draft microbrews and free live music – usually some revolutionary form of jazz – from 11pm. (For details on the jazz venue upstairs, see "Nightlife," p.367.)

Liquor Store Bar **225 W Broadway (at White St) ☎212/226-7121.** Homely little wood-paneled pub with sidewalk seating that feels like it's been around since colonial times. A welcome respite from the trendy local scene.

No Moore **234 W Broadway (at White St) ☎212/925-2901.** Sprawling, friendly lounge with live music at weekends (some weeknights too). No food but, oddly, you can order in or bring your own dinner.

Puffy's Tavern **81 Hudson St (at Harrison St) ☎212/766-9159.** Small but friendly TriBeCa bar with lunchtime food and bar pizza, cheap booze and a great jukebox, specializing in old 45s of the likes of James Brown and Patsy Cline.

SoHo and NoLita

Bar 89 **89 Mercer St (between Spring and Broome sts) ☎212/274-0989.** Slick, modern lounge with soft blue light spilling down over the bar, giving the place a trippy, pre-dawn feel. Check out the clear liquid crystal bathroom doors that go opaque when shut ($10,000 each, reportedly) and the strong, pricey drinks that pay for them.

Ear Inn **326 Spring St (between Washington and Greenwich sts) ☎212/226-9060.** "Ear" as in "Bar" with half the neon "B" chipped off. Be that as it may, this cozy pub, a stone's throw from the Hudson River, has a good mix of beers on tap, serves basic, reasonably priced, American food and claims to be the second oldest bar in the city.

Fanelli **94 Prince St (at Mercer St) ☎212/226-9412.** Established in 1872, *Fanelli* is one of the city's oldest bars, relaxed and informal and a favorite of the not-too-hip after-work crowd. The food is simple American fare: burgers, salads and such.

Pravda **281 Lafayette St (between Houston and Prince sts) ☎212/334-5015.** Very tasteful, pseudo-exclusive bar, maybe a little too grandiose for most tastes. There's nothing Communist about the place – think caviar and cocktails, all washed down with champagne.

The Room **144 Sullivan St ☎212/477-2102.** Dark but homely two-room bar with exposed brick walls and plush comfortable couches that eschews spirits for an impressive array of domestic and international beers.

Sweet and Vicious **5 Spring St (between Bowery and Elizabeth sts) ☎212/334-7915.** A neighborhood favorite, it's the epitome of rustic chic with its exposed brick and wood, replete with antique chandeliers. The atmosphere makes it seem all cozy, as does the back garden.

Toad Hall **57 Grand St (between W Broadway and Wooster St) ☎212/431-8145.** With a pool table, good service and excellent bar snacks, this stylish alehouse is a little less hip, more of a local hangout than *Lucky Strike* next door.

West Village

55 **55 Christopher St (between 6th and 7th aves) ☎212/929-9883.** A gem of an underground dive bar, this is a local favorite, with a great jazz jukebox, congenial clientele and live music seven nights a week.

Blind Tiger Ale House **518 Hudson St (at 10th St) ☎212/675-3848.** You could easily leave here with things looking a bit foggy after you choose from the 24 beers on tap and eclectic bottled selection. Come on Sunday between 1pm and 6pm for the free brunch of bagels and cream cheese with complimentary newspapers.

Cedar Tavern **82 University Place (between 11th and 12th sts) ☎212/741-9754.** The original *Cedar Tavern*, situated just a block away, was a legendary Beat and artists' meeting point in the1950s. The new version, a homely bar with food, reasonably priced drinks and occasional poetry readings, retains the bohemian feel, though. All year round you can eat under the stars in their covered roof garden.

Chumley's **86 Bedford St (between Grove and Barrow sts) ☎212/675-4449.** It's not easy to find this former speakeasy, owing to its unmarked entrance, but it's worth the effort – offering up a good choice of beers and food, both reasonably priced. Best arrive before 8pm if you want to eat at one of the battered tables.

Hogs & Heifers **859 Washington St (at 13th St) ☎212/929-0655.** Hogs as in the burly motorcycles parked outside; heifers as in, well, ladies. Though officially there's no more bar dancing (Julia Roberts was famously photographed doing so here), those bold enough to venture into this rough-and-tumble meat-packing district joint can still drink to excess.

Kava Lounge **605 Hudson St (at 12th St) ☎212/989-7504.** Maori-style murals grace the walls of this charming, intimate and truly original Village bar, which serves mainly Australian and New Zealand wines – as well as smoothies – to a fairly moneyed crowd.

Kettle of Fish **59 Christopher St (at 6th Ave) ☎212/414-2278.** It may have moved from its longtime Third Street location, but the *Kettle of Fish* is still a refreshing dive, which houses the locals and old-timers in the area looking for a cheap drink in a laid-back atmosphere.

Peculier Pub **145 Bleecker St (between La Guardia and Thompson sts) ☎212/353-1327.** Popular local bar whose main claim to fame is the number of beers it sells – more than 300 in all and examples from just about any country you care to mention.

Reservoir **70 University Place (between 10th and 11th sts) ☎212/598-0055.** The regular size TVs (6 of them) disqualify this affable NYU hangout from being listed as a fully-fledged sports-bar (which may be to its credit!). Still, it's a good place to enjoy a beer and watch a game – and that's not too easy to find in this part of town. $2 pints Sat, Sun and Wed nights and live music on Sundays from 9pm.

White Horse Tavern **567 Hudson St (at 11th St) ☎212/243-9260.** Greenwich Village institution where Dylan Thomas supped his last before being carted off to hospital with alcoholic poisoning. The beer and food are cheap and palatable here, and outside seating is available in the summer.

Hotel bars

There's no better place to go for a martini, Cosmo or Mojito in New York when you're feeling fabulous. Hotel bars are posh watering holes for the well-bred and well-maintained and, lest you forget, their sole purpose is comfort. Sure the drinks are expensive, but you're paying for atmosphere, too. Sink back into a comfy banquette, sip your precious booze slowly and with dignity, and watch the parade of foreign dignitaries, royalty, well-groomed businesspeople, media celebs, chic socialites and mysterious strangers conducting important affairs.

Bemelman's The Carlyle, 35 E 76th St (at Madison Ave) ☎212/744-1600
The Blue Bar The Algonquin Hotel, 59 W 44th St (between 5th and 6th aves) ☎212/840-6800
Cellar Bar Bryant Park Hotel, 40 W 40th St (between 5th and 6th aves) ☎212/642-2260
Cherry W Tuscany, 120 E 39th St ☎212/519-8508
Church Lounge TriBeCa Grand, 2 6th Ave ☎212/519-6600
Cibar The Inn at Irving Place, 54 Irving Place (between 17th and 18th sts) ☎212/460-5656
Etoile 109 E 56th St (between Park and Lexington aves) ☎212/750-5656
Grand Bar SoHo Grand Hotel, 310 W Broadway (between Grand and Canal sts) ☎212/965-3000
Hudson Bar & Hudson Library Bar Hudson Hotel, 356 W 58th St (between 8th and 9th aves) ☎212/554-6343 and 554-6317
King Cole Bar St Regis Hotel, 2 E 55th St (between 5th and Madison aves) ☎212/753-4000
Oak Room at the Algonquin 59 W 44th St (between 5th and Broadway) ☎212/840-6800
The Oak Bar The Plaza Hotel, 768 5th Ave (at 59th St) ☎212/546-5330
The Pierre Hotel Bar 2 E 61st St (at 5th Ave) ☎212/838-8000
Serena Chelsea Hotel, 222 W 23rd St ☎212/255-4646
Spread Marcel Hotel, 323 3rd Ave (at 24th St) ☎212/683-6880
Thom's Bar 60 Thompson St at 60 Thompson Hotel ☎212/219-2000
Twist Lounge Ameritania Hotel, 230 W 54th St (at Broadway) ☎212/247-5000
Underbar W Hotel Union Square, 201 Park Ave South ☎212/358-1560
The View The Marriott Marquis, 1535 Broadway (at 45th St) ☎212/398-1900
Wet Bar W Hotel, 130 E 39th St (at Lexington Ave) ☎212/592-8844
Whiskey Bar Paramount Hotel, 235 W 46th St (between 8th Ave and Broadway) ☎212/819-0404
Whiskey Blue The W, 541 Lexington Ave (between 49th and 50th sts) ☎212/755-1200

Lower East Side and Chinatown

Angel **174 Orchard St (between Houston and Stanton sts) ☎212/780-0313.** A heavenly designed lounge, it boasts a rare high ceiling and some super-comfy chairs, manages to keep it a little more real – in both prices and attitude – than some of its chi chi neighbors in the Lower East Side.

Barramundi **147 Ludlow St (between Stanton and Rivington sts) ☎212/529-6900.** Laid-back bar with a magical, fairy-lit garden that provides sanctuary from the increasingly hip Lower East side. Come 10pm though, the garden closes and you've got to move inside.

bOb **235 Eldridge St (between Stanton and Houston sts) ☎212/777-0588.** Lounge and dance club that is beautifully languid during the week and stark crazy at the weekends.

Double Happiness **174 Mott St (at Broome) ☎212/941-1282.** Low ceilings, dark lighting and lots of nooks and crannies make this Asian-theme bar an intimate place to be. If the decor doesn't seduce you, one of the house specialties – a green tea martini – should soon loosen you up.

Idlewild **145 Houston St (between 1st and 2nd aves) ☎212/477-5005.** Hugely popular super-sleek bar themed on all things airplane – a 1967 747 to be exact – and the owners have done everything to make the experience as authentic as possible. Beware the cocktails – you know what they say about alcohol at a high altitude.

Kush **183 Orchard St (between Stanton and Houston sts) ☎212/677-7328.** Beguiling Moroccan bar with live music, belly dancing and excellent salty bar snacks. If you're looking for something different, this is the place to be.

Luna Lounge **171 Ludlow St (between Houston and Stanton sts) ☎212/260-2323.** Friendly spot without any attitude. Long, comfy bar serves up pints in the front, noisy rock bands or stand-up comedians perform in the back.

Max Fish **178 Ludlow St (between Houston and Stanton sts) ☎212/529-3959.** Visiting indie rock bands come here in droves, lured by the unpretentious but arty vibe and the jukebox which, quite simply, rocks any other party out of town.

Orchard Bar **200 Orchard St (between Houston and Stanton sts) ☎212/673-5350.** A Lower East Side stalwart that features walls lined with glass display cases, filled with nature and neon lights; cozy recesses to whisper in and some of the nicest bar staff in town.

Sapphire Lounge **249 Eldridge St (between Houston and Stanton sts) ☎212/777-5153.** Very small, very dark and very popular with the cocktail-dress and martini-glass tribe.

Swim **146 Orchard St (between Rivington and Stanton sts) ☎212/673-0799.** Sleek two-floor bar that packs in a hip and rich crowd with its strong DJ listings, its strong drinks and maybe a bite of sushi or two.

Karaoke

Yep, it's still going strong. If you have the guts (and the stamina) to join in, these places are all guaranteed to give you a memorable, crazy night.

Arlene Grocery 95 Stanton St (between Ludlow and Orchard sts) ☎212/358-1633. Not your run-of-the-mill *Islands In the Stream*-style karaoke here, oh no, but rather punk and rock karaoke, accompanied by a live band. Be it Teenage Lobotomies or Teenage Kicks, you'll be able to sing it here. Monday nights at 10pm.

Asia Roma 40 Mulberry St (between Worth and Bayard sts) ☎212/385-1133. Despite the fact that this is one of the few places in the city where you can sing for free, it's often devoid of crowds (and atmosphere). Good to practice that rendition of *Cry Me a River*, though.

Nibankan 919 2nd Ave (between 48th and 49th sts), third floor ☎212/935-2329. You have to climb two flights of stairs and ring a buzzer before you even get in the door of this midtown gem, but once you're there it's worth it. Portable microphones, $1 per song and a lengthy playlist all add to the joy, as do the sweet velvet couches.

Village Karaoke 27 Cooper Square (between 5th and 6th sts) ☎212/254-0066. Bright lights, private rooms ($30 per hour for four people) and no booze for sale make this spot a place for those who want to sing and sing well, rather than get drunk and make a fool of themselves. However, it is open until 6am at the weekends.

Winnie's 104 Bayard St (between Mulberry and Baxter sts) ☎212/732-2384. Tiny Chinatown bar where the most dedicated New Yorkers go to belt out a few. It's seedy and sleazy, but nowhere else in the city will you find such a social hodgepodge united in a common cause: singing.

East Village

7B **108 Ave B (at 7th St) ☎212/473-8840.** Quintessential East Village hangout with an extremely mixed crowd that has often been used as a sleazy set in films and commercials – recall the bar brawls in *Crocodile Dundee*. It features deliberately mental bartenders, strong, cheap booze and one of the best punk jukeboxes in the Village.

Ace **531 E 5th St (between aves A and B) ☎212/979-8476.** Behind the architectural glass brick is a noisy and strangely cavernous neighborhood bar, with pool table, darts, pinball machines and an amazing collection of childhood lunch boxes. An alternative rock jukebox augments the old school East Village feel.

Angel's Share **8 Stuyvesant St (between 9th St and 3rd Ave), second floor ☎212/777-5415.** This tiny haven, where serene bartenders serve the most exquisite martinis in Manhattan, was once the city's best-kept secret. Then it was discovered by the masses, but it is well worth the wait.

Baraza 133 Ave C (between 8th and 9th sts) ☎212/539-0811. Quirky yet welcoming, this gem of a bar plays great music, serves great drinks and is the jewel in the crown of the Loisaida.

Bowery Bar 40 E 4th St (at Bowery) ☎212/475-2220. Once the place to see and be seen, the *Bowery Bar* still pulls in a high volume of celebrities and beautiful people – as well as commoners – who come to sip cocktails or share a bottle of wine in the serene, fairy-lit garden.

Burp Castle 41 E 7th St (at 2nd Ave) ☎212/982-4756. The bartenders wear monks' habits, choral music is piped and you are encouraged to speak in tones below a whisper. Oh, and there's over 550 different types of beer.

d.b.a. 41 1st Ave (between 2nd and 3rd sts) ☎212/475-5097. A beer lover's paradise, *d.b.a.* has at least 60 bottled beers, 14 beers on tap and an authentic hand pump. Garden seating is available in the summer.

Decibel 240 E 9th St (between 2nd and 3rd aves) ☎212/979-2733. Great, beautifully decorated underground sake bar with a rocking atmosphere (and good tunes). The inevitable wait for a wooden table will be worth it, guaranteed.

Detour 349 E 13th St (between 1st and 2nd aves) ☎212/533-6212. Comfortable jazz bar with live music seven nights a week and no cover.

Drinkland 339 E 10th St (between aves A and B) ☎212/228-2435. Dizzying psychedelic decor fused with top quality DJs spinning big-beat and trip-hop make this place a favorite among downtown hipsters. Strong mixed drinks, too.

Holiday Cocktail Lounge 75 St Mark's Place (between 2nd and 3rd aves) ☎212/777-9637. Unabashed dive with a mixed bag of customers, from old-world grandfathers to the younger set, and a bona-fide character tending bar (more or less). Good place for an afternoon beer. Closes early.

KGB 85 E 4th St (between 2nd Ave and Bowery) ☎212/505-3360. A lovely dark bar on the second floor, which claims to have been the HQ of the Ukrainian Communist party. The Eastern European edge remains, making it popular with off-off-Broadway theater crowds and wannabe Beats.

Lakeside Lounge 162 Ave B (between 10th and 11th sts) ☎212/529-8463. Opened by a local DJ and a record producer who have stocked the jukebox with old rock, country and R&B. A down-home hangout, with live music four nights a week.

McSorley's 15 E 7th St (between 2nd and 3rd aves) ☎212/473-9148. New York City's longest-established watering hole, so it claims, and a male-only bar until a 1969 lawsuit. These days it retains a saloon look, with mostly an out-of-towner crowd. There's no trouble deciding what to drink – you can have McSorley's ale, and you can have it dark or light.

Open Air 121 St Mark's Place (between 1st Ave and Ave A) ☎212/979-1459. A little newcomer that is the antithesis of St Mark's: beautifully designed, it somehow divides itself into a chill-out lounge, an eerie middle space lit by flickering flat screens and a front bar, all imbued with the same well-spun tunes from the DJ.

St Dymphna's 118 St Mark's Place (between 1st Ave and Ave A) ☎212/254-6636. With a tempting menu and perhaps the city's best Guinness, this snug and tasteful (no fake shamrocks here) Irish watering hole is, understandably, a favorite among young East Villagers.

Standard 158 1st Ave (between 9th and 10th sts) ☎212/387-0239. Tiny, narrow lounge that glows green onto the street at night – obey your impulse and venture inside, where you'll find a few stylish loungers, somewhat pricey drinks and a DJ spinning laid-back tunes.

Union Square, Gramercy Park, Murray Hill and Midtown East

Belmont Lounge 117 E 15th St (between Park Ave S and Irving Place) ☎212/533-0009. Oversized couches, dark cavernous rooms and an outdoor garden reel in a continuous stream of twenty-something singletons. The strong drinks help things, too.

British Open 320 E 59th St (between 1st and 2nd aves) ☎212/355-8467. Shamelessly

Anglophile pub/sports bar that has five TVs and a fetish for the royal and ancient game.

Cibar **56 Irving Place (between 17th and 18th sts) ☎212/460-5656.** Innovative cocktails, elegant decor and a sweet garden make this cozy hotel bar a local hotspot.

Divine Bar **244 E 51st St (between 2nd and 3rd aves) ☎212/319-9463.** Although it's often packed with corporate types communing with their cellphones, this swanky tapas lounge has a great selection of wines and imported beers, not to mention tasty appetizers and outdoor seating – a treat round here.

Flute **205 W 54th St (between Broadway and 7th Ave) ☎212/265-5169.** Housed in a former speakeasy, this champagne bar has kept the decor but not the ethos. These days, you can find over 100 types of bubbly, fancy chocolates and cigars here, making it about as cutting-edge as a blunt knife.

Heartland Brewery **35 Union Square W (between 16th and 17th sts) ☎212/645-3400.** Even with seating sprawled out onto the sidewalk, this vast space still gets packed some nights. Good selection of beers brewed on the premises.

No Idea **30 E 20th St (between Broadway and Park Ave S) ☎212/777-0100.** Bizarre palace of inebriation has something for most barflies – from $4.50 pints of mixed drinks, to a pool room, TV sports and even a drink-for-free-if-your-name's-on-the-wall night.

Old Town Bar and Restaurant **45 E 18th St (between Broadway and Park Ave S) ☎212/529-6732.** One of the oldest and still one of the very best bars in the city, although it can get packed, especially when the suits from the Flatiron district get off work to enjoy its excellent, if standard, menu of chili, burgers and the like. It was regularly featured on the old *David Letterman Show*.

Paddy Reilly's **519 2nd Ave (between 29th and 30th sts) ☎212/686-1210.** A good place to enjoy a few Guinness drafts, listen to live music and pretend you're Irish. $5 cover some nights.

Pete's Tavern **129 E 18th St (at Irving Place) ☎212/473-7676.** Former speakeasy that claims to be the oldest bar in New York – opened in 1864 – though these days it inevitably trades on its history, which included such illustrious patrons as John F Kennedy Jr and O. Henry, who allegedly wrote *The Gift of the Magi* in his regular booth here.

P.J. Clarke's **915 3rd Ave (between 55th and 56th sts) ☎212/759-1650.** One of the city's most famous watering holes, this is a spit-and-sawdust alehouse with a not-so-cheap restaurant out the back. You may recognize it as the setting of the film *The Lost Weekend*.

Revival **129 E 15th St (between Irving Place and 3rd Ave) ☎212/253-8061.** Walk down the stairs and into this friendly narrow bar with great outdoor seating in its backyard. Popular with fans waiting for a rock show at Irving Plaza (see p.367) around the block.

Chelsea, Garment District and Midtown West

Chelsea Commons **242 10th Ave (at 24th St) ☎212/929-9424.** Not only a personable bar but a great place to eat, with reasonably priced and excellent burgers and other such pub grub. Popular local hangout with a summer garden, winter fireplace and the occasional impromptu puppet show.

Citron 47 **401 W 47th St (between 9th and 10th aves) ☎212/397-4747.** Charming hybrid of a French bistro, hip bar and New England farmhouse situated in gentrified Hell's Kitchen. Great place to knock a few back.

The Collins Bar **735 8th Ave (between 46th and 47th sts) ☎212/541-4206.** Sleek, stylish bar has choice sports photos along one side, original art works along the other – not to mention perhaps the most eclectic juke in the city.

Half King **505 W 23rd St (between 10th and 11th aves) ☎212/462-4300.** Media bar on the far west side that is run by *Perfect Storm* author Sebastian Junger and some other literary types, and is a pleasant, warm place, kind of like an antique living room.

Jimmy's Corner **140 W 44th St (between Broadway and 6th Ave) ☎212/221-9510.** The walls of this long, narrow corridor of a bar, owned by ex-fighter/trainer Jimmy Glenn, are a virtual Boxing Hall of Fame. You'd be hard pressed to find a more characterful dive anywhere in the city – or a better jazz/R&B jukebox.

Park **118 10th Ave (between 17th and 18th sts) ☎212/352-3313.** It's easy to get lost in this vast warren of rooms filled with fireplaces, geodes and even a Canadian redwood in the middle of the floor. The garden is a treat though, and the servers are the best dressed in New York.

Passerby **436 W 15th St (between 9th and 10th aves) ☎212/206-7321.** Funky space that is connected to Gavin Brown's art gallery next door. As you might suspect, it's full of black-clad lovelies, weird mirrors and art-world gossip.

Rudy's Bar and Grill **627 9th Ave (between 44th and 45th sts) ☎212/974-9169.** One of New York's cheapest, friendliest and liveliest dive bars, a favorite with local actors and musicians. *Rudy's* offers free hot dogs and a backyard that's great in the summer.

Russian Vodka Room **265 W 52nd St (between Broadway and 7th Ave) ☎212/307-5835.** They have several different kinds of vodka, as you might expect, and a lot of Russian and Eastern European expatriates.

Serena **222 W 23rd St (between 7th and 8th aves) ☎212/255-4646.** Retro basement bar is a fairly new addition to the tired old *Chelsea Hotel*, bringing in a new, younger and infinitely more self-assured brand of local. Be prepared to pay for the legend, though, and beware the bouncers and the somewhat pricey drinks.

St.Andrews **120 W 44th St (between 6th Ave and Broadway) ☎212/840-8413.** A friendly Scottish bar that is a welcome addition to Midtown, with a huge collection of draught beers and the city's largest selection of single malts.

Ye Olde Tripple Inn **263 W 54th St (between Broadway and 8th Ave) ☎212/245-9849.** No frills Irish bar that serves inexpensive food at lunchtime and early evening. A useful place to know in this part of town.

Upper West Side

Abbey Pub **237 W 105th St (between Broadway and Amsterdam Ave) ☎212/222-8713.** Half-a-century old and the *Abbey* is still charming locals and students alike with its stained-glass windows and overheard learned conversations whispered in wooden booths. Not to mention the cheap beer.

Dead Poet **450 Amsterdam Ave (between 81st and 82nd sts) ☎212/595-5670.** You'll be waxing poetical and then dropping down dead if you stay for the duration of this sweet little bar's happy hour: it lasts from 8am to 8pm and offers draft beer at $3 a pint. There's a back room with armchairs, books and even a pool table, too, so you can both exercise and educate yourself while you drink.

Dublin House **225 W 79th St (between Broadway and Amsterdam Ave) ☎212/874-9528.** Noisy, atmospheric Irish bar with a young crowd, good jukebox and inexpensive drinks.

Potion Lounge **370 Columbus Ave (between 78th and 79th sts) ☎212/721-4386.** A little more expensive than most of the bars around here, *Potion* is also a little better thought out. A bubble motif reigns throughout, from the windows to the futuristic bar to the house "potions" that will intoxicate you for a mere $10 a pop.

Prohibition **530 Columbus Ave (between 84th and 85th sts) ☎212/579-3100.** A pool table, live jazz and pavement tables all combine to make this one of the liveliest singles scenes on the Upper West Side.

Shark Bar **307 Amsterdam Ave (between 74th and 75th sts) ☎212/874-8500.** Ultra-elegant African-American lounge with great soulfood and a beat to go with it.

Smoke **2751 Broadway (at 105th St) ☎212/864-6662.** Seductively mellow jazz lounge – a real find in this neighborhood. Live music most nights. $8 cover at the weekend.

Time Out **349 Amsterdam Ave (between 76th and 77th sts) ☎212/362-5400.** What an anomaly… a sports bar with a pleasant atmosphere! Good selection of cheap beers and pub grub, friendly bonhomie and 24 screens of sporting entertainment. $10 cover for special events.

Upper East Side

American Trash **1471 1st Ave (between 76th and 77th sts) ☎212/988-9008.** Self-styled "professional drinking establishment" has a friendly barstaff, a pool table, a sing-a-long jukebox and a happy hour dedicated to getting you there.

Bear Bar East **1770 2nd Ave (between 92nd and 93rd sts) ☎212/987-7580.** Raucous, spit 'n' sawdust sports bar with hip hop on a Friday, free drinks on Mondays for the "ladies" and too many cheap beer 'n' wings deals to list here.

The Cocktail Room **334 E 73rd St (between 1st and 2nd aves) ☎212/988-6100.** Fancy-schmanzy bar, with couches, dim lighting and a modish 1960s' theme. Popular with singles, and groups who go to lounge on the couches in the back, this neighborhood anomaly throbs on weekends.

Metropolitan Museum of Art **1000 5th Ave (at 82nd St) ☎212/535-7710.** It's hard to imagine a more romantic spot to sip a glass of wine, whether it's up on the Cantor Roof Garden (open only in warm weather, see p.181), enjoying one of the very best views in the city or on the Great Hall Balcony listening to live chamber music (Fri and Sat from 5–8pm).

Phoenix Park **206 E 67th St (between 2nd and 3rd aves) ☎212/717-8181.** Nothing special about this Irish pub, except it's sociable, has a jukebox, TVs and a pool table – and there's very little else happening in this part of town.

Subway Inn **143 E 60th St (at Lexington Ave) ☎212/223-8929.** Downscale neighborhood dive bar across the street from Bloomingdale's. A great spot for a late-afternoon beer.

Harlem

Lenox Lounge **288 Lenox Ave (between 124th and 125th sts) ☎212/427-0253.** Elegant Art Deco Harlem landmark, formerly graced by Billie Holiday, is celebrated for its swanky Zebra Room, whose ceiling is adorned with zebra skins. Jazz is played on weekends.

Showmans **375 W 125th St (between Morningside and St Nicholas aves) ☎212-864-8941.** This small yet long-established blues, jazz and gospel music haunt is often packed with Harlemites and occasional tourists. Jazz shows on Thurs, Fri and Sat nights; no cover charge.

Sugar Shack **2611 Frederick Douglass Blvd (at 139th St) ☎212/491-4422.** Just west of Strivers Row, this bar-café comes alive at night with reggae, blues, comedy and hip-hop acts. The soulfood's also worth the trip.

Brooklyn

Brooklyn Inn **148 Hoyt St (at Bergen St), Boerum Hill ☎718/625-9741.** Locals – and their dogs – gather at this friendly Boerum Hill favorite with high ceilings and a friendly bar staff. Great place for a daytime buzz or shooting pool in the smoky back room.

Frank's Bar and Grill **660 Fulton St, Fort Greene ☎718/625-9339.** A stone's throw from the Brooklyn Academy of Music, this mellow bar with a classic-to-modern R&B jukebox comes alive at night when DJs spin hip hop and the party spreads upstairs.

Galapagos **70 N 6th St (between Wythe and Kent aves), Williamsburg ☎718/782-5188.** Gorgeous design – this converted factory features watery pools and candelabras – and avant-garde movies on Sunday and Monday nights.

The Gate **321 5th Ave, Park Slope ☎718/768-4329.** An extensive array of beers and patio seating lure Park Slopers to this roomy, congenial staple of the Fifth Avenue bar scene.

Iona **180 Grand St (between Bedford Ave and Driggs St), Williamsburg ☎718/384-5008.** An Irish bar for the young and the hip, *Iona* provides a calm, tasteful respite from the moody lighting and incestuous hip of the other bars all around. A sweet outdoor garden and a great selection of beer only add to this gem's appeal.

Enid's **560 Manhattan Ave (at Driggs St), Greenpoint ☎718/349-3859.** It may be out-of-the-way, but as the hordes from the village and the 'Burg that come here will attest,

Enid's cheap beer, ample seating and relaxed ambience is well worth the trek.

Moe's 80 Lafayette Ave (at South Portland St) Fort Greene ☎718-797-9536. Bright, airy and extremely friendly bar welcomes everyone to share in its so-understated-it's-excusable *Simpsons* theme. Don't bother with the Duff beer, however, even for the novelty.

Pete's Candy Store 709 Lorimer St (between the BQE and McCarren Park), Williamsburg ☎718/302-3770. Once a Mafia joint fronting as a soda parlor, and now a haven of punk rock and seedy, cheap cocktails, *Pete's* retains an underground vibe.

Stinger Club 241 Grand St (between Driggs and Roebling sts), Williamsburg ☎718/218-6662. Super-cool joint for super-cool artists, with a pool table, dim red lighting and a jukebox that loves your ears.

Yabby 265 Bedford Ave (between N 1st and Grand sts) Williamsburg ☎718/384-1664. Cheap pints and loads of comfy outdoor couches make this totally attitude-free place the perfect location for a lazy afternoon of inebriation.

Queens

Bohemian Hall and Park 29-19 24th Ave, Astoria ☎718/728-9776. Old-world Czech Bohemians and twenty-something bohemians mingle at New York's largest beer garden, which features a variety of pilsners. Summer bands range in style from polka to rock to hip hop.

Café-Bar 32-90 34th Ave, Astoria ☎718/204-5273. With its plush couches and outdoor seating, the ultra-relaxed *Café-Bar* is the perfect place to kill time before a matinee at the nearby American Museum of the Moving Image.

32

Nightlife

New York's **music scene** reflects the city's diversity. Traditional and contemporary **jazz** are still in abundance, with the annual JVC and *Knitting Factory*'s "What Is Jazz?" festivals bringing top international talent to the city every year. The downtown **avant-garde** scene – best personified by John Zorn, Arto Lindsay and Laurie Anderson – still exists; its attendant art noise bands – the most famous being Sonic Youth – continue to influence the area's musicians both directly (the band runs the Sonic Youth Recordings label, and Thurston Moore does informal talent scouting) and indirectly (Kim Gordon's X-Girl fashion line). Spoken word performers, along with the current crop of singer/songwriters, are reviving the Beats' poetry scene. And, if you travel uptown or to the outer boroughs, you'll find pockets of Brazilian music, West Indian music, reggae and hip hop. But if you stay downtown, **indie rock** will fill your ears. The city's guitar bands have become more inventive in the last decade, with the punk revival giving way to acts that incorporate every type of gadget, pedal and sample into their tunes. Techno, hip hop and electronica – and every hybrid form thereof, from classical violin played over skrawking German beats on the subway to experiments in mixology at your local bar – are everywhere; dance music has finally taken New York and New York is playing it in every place it can.

Despite what the designers on any avenue would like you to believe, New York is not uptight about appearance. In the most expensive, glitzy **clubs**, however, appearances do matter: acolytes must adhere to the current look, with bouncers guarding the doors against the gauche. But if you just want to dance, there are plenty of more casual places, especially the city's **gay clubs**, which often offer more creative music and less hassle.

The sections that follow provide accounts of the cream of current venues. Remember, though, that the music – and especially the club scenes – change continually. To ensure that the Great British house night isn't now a drag-queen party (or vice versa), consult weekly **listings** publications. Excellent freebies include the *Village Voice* (Ⓦwww.villagevoice.com), *New York Press* (Ⓦwww.nypress.com), *Homo Xtra* (Ⓦwww.hx.com) and the monthly club sheet *Flyer* (which all contain detailed club, theater and venue listings for the straight and gay scenes; you can find them in corner self-serve newspaper boxes and music stores). Also on the web and on the ball are *Time Out New York* (Ⓦwww.timeoutny.com) and *Citysearch* (Ⓦwww.newyork.citysearch.com). It may seem a ridiculous and puritanical requirement, but you will undoubtedly be "carded" at the door in New York, so it's imperative to bring your **ID** (driver's license or passport) with you when you go out. Venues and bars do enforce the legal drinking age of 21 and you must be 18 to enter some music venues.

Rock music

New York's rock music scene is still built on white-boy guitar bands, with three-chord rock the default setting. That said, many foreign acts – especially British bands – travel to New York's shores first when trying to break into America. Frequently you'll have the opportunity to see these groups play in small venues at low admission prices.

Rising rents have forced many musicians out of Manhattan and into the outer boroughs and New Jersey; although the scene is still in Manhattan, the center has become more diffuse. There is a thriving off-Manhattan hub in Hoboken, New Jersey, centering on *Maxwell's* (see opposite); and in Brooklyn and Queens, large Latin, South American, Indian and reggae contingents exist – although the venues themselves are way off the average tourist circuit.

In Manhattan, most of the energy is provided by bars and venues located in the East and West villages. The listings below will point you to the primary spots where you should find something for your ears, no matter what you're looking for.

Big performance venues

Madison Square Garden 7th Ave at W 32nd St ⓣ212/465-6741. New York's principal large stage, the Garden hosts not only hockey and basketball but also a good proportion of the stadium rock acts that visit the city. Seating 20,000-plus, the arena is not the most soulful place to see a band, but it may be the only chance that you get.

Meadowlands Stadium Route 120, East Rutherford, New Jersey ⓣ201/935-3900. The city's other really large venue, again with room for 20,000 of your closest friends.

Radio City Music Hall 1260 6th Ave (at 50th St) ⓣ212/247-4777. Not the prime venue it once was; most of the acts that play here now are firmly in the mainstream. The building itself has as great a sense of occasion, though, despite a recent renovation, and Rockette dolls are still sold in the gift shop.

Smaller venues

Apollo Theatre 253 W 125th St (between 7th and 8th aves) ⓣ212/749-5838 (show info) ⓣ212/531-5305 (tkts) ⓣ212/531-5337 (tours), ⓦwww.apolloshowtime.com. Stars are born and legends are still made at the Apollo, where everyone from Billie Holiday to Aretha Franklin and Duke Ellington had their day. Now the just-renovated theater features a cast of black music acts, comedy and weekly amateur nights (Wed). $13–35.

Arlene Grocery 95 Stanton St (between Ludlow and Orchard sts) ⓣ212/473-9831. An intimate, erstwhile bodega that hosts nightly free gigs by local, reliably good indie bands – and there's no cover charge during the week. Frequented by musicians, some talent scouts and open-minded rock fans. Go on Monday nights for the metal and punk karaoke, where you can sing along with a live band. $3 Fri & Sat, $5 Sun.

Baby Jupiter 170 Orchard St (at Stanton St) ⓣ212/982-2229. Restaurant in front, performance space in back. Hosts a spectrum of rock (indie to avant-garde) bands and experimental performances. $2–5.

Beacon Theater 2124 Broadway (between 74th St and 75th Sts) ⓣ212/496-7070. Once the quirky Upper West Side host of off-the-mainstream names, now featuring the more mature artist – from Spinal Tap to Cher. $25–100.

The Bitter End 147 Bleecker St ⓣ212/673-7030. Young MOR bands in an intimate club setting. The famous people who've played the club are listed by the door: don't expect to see them there nowadays. Cover $5, with a two-drink minimum.

The Bottom Line 15 W 4th St (corner of Mercer St) ⓣ212/228-7880. Not New York's most adventurous venue but one of the better known – where you're most likely to see singer-songwriters. Cabaret setup, with tables crowding out any suggestion of a dance floor. Cover varies, with shows at 7.30pm & 10.30pm. Cash only.

Bowery Ballroom 6 Delancey St (corner of Bowery) ⓣ212/533-2111. A minimum of attitude among staff and clientele, great sound, and even better views has earned this site praise from fans and bands alike. Great bar and solid line-up. Shows $10–20.

Brownies **169 Ave A (between 10th and 11th sts) ⓣ212/420-8392, ⓦwww.browniesnyc.com.** The place to see major-label one-offs, bands on the cusp of making it big and impressive local talent. Around $7-10.

CBGB (and OMFUG) **315 Bowery (at Bleecker St) ⓣ212/982-4052.** After 20+ years the black, sticker-covered interior may be the last of its kind in New York, but this legendary punk bastion (see box, p.103) is not as cutting-edge as it was. Noisy rock bands are the order now, often five or six a night. Shows begin at 7 or 8pm; occasional Sun matinees at 5pm. Prices about $5–10.

CB's 313 Gallery **313 Bowery (at Bleecker St) ⓣ212/677-0445.** Seven nights a week, CBGB's clean, spacious counterpart features folk, acoustic and experimental music. $5.

Continental **25 3rd Ave (between St Mark's Place and E 9th St) ⓣ212/529-6924.** Loud alternative rock, with the odd guest appearance by the likes of Iggy Pop. Shows start on the hour; buy a beer and get $2 shots at all times. Free entrance Sun–Tues, $5 Wed–Sat.

The Cooler **416 W 14th St (between 9th and 10th aves) ⓣ212/229-0785.** Maybe it's the indigo lighting that lends a *Blue Velvet* feel to this underground bunker – or perhaps it's because the club is a former meat refrigerator. Adventurous indie rock and avant-garde attract a youthful, hip crowd. Mon–Thurs shows begin at 9pm; Fri & Sat shows start at 10pm. Free–$12; advance tix from X-Large (see p.365).

Don Hill's **511 Greenwich St (at Spring St) ⓣ212/334-1390.** Some of the most sexually diverse parties in the city happen here, where Brit-poptastic bands warm up the crowd before the real stars – the DJs – take the stage. $10–15.

Fez **380 Lafayette St (at Great Jones St) ⓣ212/533-2680.** The mirrored bar and sparkling gold stage curtain suggest a disco fantasy; poetry readings and acoustic performances are high caliber. Around $10.

Hammerstein Ballroom **311 W 34th St (between 8th and 9th aves) ⓣ212/564-4882.** Refurbished ballroom that hosts a few shows a month, mostly indie rock and electronic music, in a 3600-seat venue. Uptight bouncers limit movement between seating levels and prohibit smoking on the balconies. Cover varies, but upwards of $18.

Irving Plaza **17 Irving Place (between 15th and 16th sts) ⓣ212/777-6800.** Once home to an off-Broadway musical (hence the dangling chandeliers and blood-red interior), now host to an impressive array of rock, electronic and techno acts. The uproom has wildly divergent acoustics; stand toward the back on the ground floor for truest mix of sound. $10–25.

Knitting Factory **74 Leonard St (between Church St and Broadway) ⓣ212/219-3055, ⓦwww.knittingfactory.com.** While this intimate downtown space is known for its avant-garde jazz, you can hear all other kinds of aural experimentation – from art rock to electronica – here, too. Recommended.

The Living Room **84 Stanton St ⓣ212/533-7235.** Comfortable couches and a friendly bar make for a relaxed setting in which to hear up-and-coming folk and rock. No cover, one drink minimum.

Maxwell's **1039 Washington (at 11th St), Hoboken, New Jersey ⓣ201/798-0406.** Neighborhood rock club hosting up to a dozen bands a week: some big names and one of the best places to check out the tri-state scene. Admission $6–12.

Mercury Lounge **217 E Houston St (Essex St) ⓣ212/260-7400.** Dark, medium-sized, Lower East Side mainstay which hosts a mix of local, national and international rock acts. It's owned by the same crew as Bowery Ballroom, but generally houses less established bands. Around $7–12.

Roseland Ballroom **239 W 52nd St (between Broadway and 8th Ave) ⓣ212/249-0200.** A historic ballroom that opened in 1919 and was once frequented by Adele and Fred Astaire, among others. Now a ballroom dancing school that, six times a month, turns into a concert venue, hosting big names and various pop and electronic acts. Take a gander at the shoes and photographs displayed in the entry hall. $10–50.

SOB's **(Sounds of Brazil) 204 Varick St (at Houston St) ⓣ212/243-4940.** Premier place to hear hip hop, Brazilian, West Indian, Caribbean and world music acts within the confines of Manhattan. Vibrant, with a high quality of music. Two shows nightly, times

vary. Admission $10–20 with $10-15 minimum cover at tables.

The Supper Club 240 W 47th St (between Broadway and 8th Ave) ⓣ212/921-1940. White linen tablecloths, a large dance floor and upscale lounge jazz/hip-hop groups. Fri and Sat at 8pm, Eric Comstock and the Supper Club's house big band swing with a vengeance. $25 before 11pm; $15 after.

Surf Reality 172 Allen St ⓣ212/673-4182, ⓦwww.surfreality.com. Welded metal parts make up the doorway to this velvet-draped offbeat venue, featuring contemporary vaudeville and open-mike performances, some of them truly bizarre. $3 open mike Sun 8pm. Other times $6–8.

Terra Blues 149 Bleecker St (between Thompson and LaGuardia sts) ⓣ212/777-7776. Great venue hosting jazz, blues and funk. Mon–Fri $5–15 cover, Sat & Sun $5 cover + two-drink minumum.

Village Underground 130 W 3rd St (between Macdougal and 6th Ave) ⓣ212/777-7745, ⓦwww.thevillageunderground.com. This no-smoking-yet-smoky wee place is one of the most intimate and innovative spaces around, where you might catch anyone from Guided By Voices to RL Burnside.

Jazz

The late 1980s and early 1990s were tough times for New York jazz. The city's clubs went through a rough patch, from which many a joint – including the landmark *Village Tavern* – did not recover. A clutch of new clubs has revived the scene, however, and there still are more than forty locations in Manhattan that present jazz regularly. Look mostly to **Greenwich Village** or **Harlem** for a good place; midtown jazz clubs tend to be slick dinner-dance joints – expensive and overrun by businesspeople looking for culture.

To find out who's playing, check the usual sources, notably the *Voice*, *New York Magazine* and *Hothouse*, a free monthly magazine sometimes available at the venues; or the jazz monthly *Downbeat*. The city's jazz-oriented **radio stations** are also sources of information: two of the best are WBGO (88.5 FM), a 24-hour jazz station, and WKCR (98.7 FM), Columbia University's radio station. As a final resort, **Jazzline** (ⓣ212/479-7888) provides recorded information about the week's events.

Price policies vary from club to club, but at most there's a hefty cover ($10–30) and always a minimum charge for food and drinks. An evening out at a major club will cost at least $15 per person, and more along the lines of $25–30 per person if you'd like to eat. Piano bars – smaller and often more atmospheric – come cheaper; some have neither an admission fee nor a minimum, but expect to pay inflated drink prices.

Jazz venues

55 55 Christopher St (between 6th and 7th aves) ⓣ212/929-9883. Really, really special underground jazz bar; the best of the old guard. See p.357.

Arthur's Tavern 57 Grove St ⓣ212/675-6879, ⓦwww.arthurstavernnyc.com. Small, amiable piano bar with some inspired performers and no cover or minimum. Drinks are pricey.

Birdland 315 W 44th St (between 8th and 9th aves) ⓣ212/581-3080, ⓦwww.birdlandjazz.com. Not the original place where Charlie Parker played, but an established supper club nonetheless. Hosts some big names. Sets nightly at 9pm and 11pm. Music charge of $20–35, with a $10 food/drink minimum and a complimentary drink if you sit at the bar.

The Blue Note 131 W 3rd St (at 6th Ave) ⓣ212/475-8592, ⓦwww.bluenote.net. Famous names here aren't really worth the attendant high prices, cattle-herd atmosphere and minimal legroom. Cover charges vary wildly, from $7 to $65, plus a $5 minimum per person at the tables or a one-drink minimum at the bar; all of which leads to a very regulated, controlled ambience – the antithesis of the free flow of jazz. Sets are at 9pm & 11.30pm. On Fri & Sat, the jam sessions after 1am are free if you've seen the previous set, $5 if you haven't. Also offers a decent Sunday brunch for $18.50 that includes live music.

Café Carlyle **The Carlyle Hotel, 35 E 76th St (at Madison Ave) ⓣ212/744-1600.** This intimate, special place is home to both Bobby Short and Woody Allen, who does the jazz thang here on Monday nights. $30–60 cover, no minimum.

Detour **349 E 13th St (at 1st Ave) ⓣ212/533-6212.** Coffee and cocktail bar that fancies itself a bit of Paris in the East Village and is probably the best place to catch free jazz in the city. Modern jazz and avant-garde experimentation nightly, no cover.

Iridium Jazz Club **44 W 63rd St (at Columbus Ave) ⓣ212/582-2121.** Contemporary jazz performed 7 nights a week in a surrealist decor described as "Dolly meets Disney." The godfather of electric guitar Les Paul plays every Monday. Shows at 8.45pm and 10.45pm, extra Fri & Sat show at 12.15am. Cover $20–35, $10 food and drink minimum; Sunday jazz brunch.

Izzy Bar **166 1st Ave (at 10th St) ⓣ212/228-0444.** Popular with a European crowd, this cavernous hangout is more lounge than bar – but hosts jazz sessions and a variety of other music acts nightly. Admission is $5–10.

Jazz At Noon **Café St Barts, 109 E 50th St (at Park Ave) ⓣ212/888-2664, ⓦwww.jazzatnoon.com.** Every Friday at noon the Friday Faithful perform upstairs at this restaurant, accompanied by a special guest performer from the upper echelons of the jazz world.

Jazz Standard **116 E 27th St ⓣ212/576-2232, ⓦwww.jazzstandard.com.** A spacious underground room with great sound and even better performers has earned this club high praise and a loyal clientele. Sets Mon–Thurs at 8pm and 10pm, Fri and Sat 8pm, 10.30pm and midnight, Sun at 7pm and 9pm. Mon $15; Tues–Thurs & Sun $18; Fri & Sat $25; all with $10 minimum.

Joe's Pub **425 Lafayette St ⓣ212/539-8777, ⓦwww.joespub.org.** Stylishly classic bar in Joe Papp's Public Theater attracts the entertainment crowd. Performances six days a week, ranging from Broadway songbooks to readings from the *New Yorker*'s fiction issues, with the likes of salsa, Indian music and jazz thrown in. Open daily 5pm–4am. $10–25.

Kavehaz Jazz Club **123 Mercer St ⓣ212/343-0612, ⓦwww.kavehaz.com.** Sweet little SoHo gallery/club that plays host to decent jazz and decent drinks for no cover charge.

Knitting Factory **74 Leonard St (between Broadway and Church St) ⓣ212/219-3005.** The refurbished club – two performance spaces, two bars and a microbrewery with eighteen beers on draft – has won the cool kids back, and it's now the place to see avant-garde jazz, experimental acts and big-name rock bands in an intimate setting. $15–20, with shows beginning from 8–10pm.

Lenox Lounge **288 Malcolm X Blvd (between 74th and 75th sts) ⓣ212/427-0253.** This recently renovated Harlem staple is elegantly laid-back, and retains the area's legendary jazz aura as it plays host to jazz on the weekends and jam sessions on Monday nights.

Rose Center for Earth and Space, American Museum of Natural History **81st St and Central Park West ⓣ212/769-5920.** The planetarium, well worth a visit in its own right (see p.213), hosts a three-hour Friday night live jazzfest called Starry Nights. Performances begin at 5.45pm.

Roulette **228 W Broadway (between Franklin St and Broadway) ⓣ212/219-8242, ⓦwww.roulette.org.** Focusing on fringe music this TriBeCa living room hosts (very) experimental musicians performing jazz, rock and "new music." All shows begin at 8.30pm. $10.

Savoy Lounge **355 W 41st St ⓣ212/947-5255, ⓦwww.savoylounge.com.** Just behind the Port Authority Bus Terminal, this midtown joint has live jazz and blues nightly, live jams frequented by Broadway pit musicians, super-cheap drinks and an increasingly rare Hammond organ. Sets Sun–Wed at 9pm, 10.30pm and midnight, no cover; jam session Thurs 11.30pm–4am, $5; sets Fri–Sat at 10pm, 11.30pm, 1am, $7.

Sista's Place **456 Nostrand Ave (at Jefferson Ave), Brooklyn ⓣ718/398-1766.** Excellent and intimate place to hear innovative jazz, albeit a long way from Manhattan in Bedford-Stuyvesant.

Smalls **183 W 10th St (at 7th Ave) ⓣ212/929-7565, ⓦwww.smallsjazz.com.** Tiny West Village club has the best jazz bargain in NY: four to 13 hours of music for $10, from 10pm to dawn. The weekday program comprises two sets and a late-night jam, by well-knowns and unknowns; the weekends also have an early bird set at 7.30pm. Free juice and non-alcoholic beverages, or BYOB. Highly recommended.

Smoke 2751 Broadway (between 105th and 106th sts) ⓣ212/864-6662, ⓦwww.smokejazz.com. Voted the best club in the city by *New York* magazine, this Upper West Side joint is a real neighborhood treat. Sets start at 9pm, 11pm and 12.30am, the first two weekend sets are smoke free, and there's a retro happy hour with $3 cocktails Mon–Sun 5–8pm.

Tonic 107 Norfolk St (between Rivington and Delancey sts) ⓣ212/358-7503, ⓦwww.tonicnyc.com. Hip Lower East Side avant-jazzerie on two levels, with no cover charge to the lower, *Subtonic* lounge. Occasional movies and Klezmer brunch on a Sunday. Cover varies.

Village Vanguard 178 7th Ave (at 11th St) ⓣ212/255-4037. A NYC jazz landmark that celebrated its sixtieth anniversary a few years back, the *Vanguard* supplies a regular diet of big names. Mon–Thurs admission is $15, with a $10 minimum; Sat–Sun entry is $20, with a $10 minimum. Sets are at 9.30pm and 11.30pm, with a 1am set Sat and Sun.

Zinc Bar 90 W Houston (at LaGuardia Place) ⓣ212/477-8337, ⓦwww.zincbar.com. Great jazz venue with strong drinks and a loyal bunch of regulars. The blackboard above the entrance announces the evening's featured band. Cover is $5 with a one-drink minimum. Hosts new talent and established greats such as Max Roach, Grant Green and Astrud Gilberto; also poetry readings on Sun at 6.30pm and comedy on Tues at 8pm.

Folk, country and spoken word venues

13 35 E 13th St ⓣ212/979-6677. Monday night and this cozy bar is home to A Little Bit Louder, a superior evening of open mike and poetry slams. You can dance here, too – outside in summer – a rare treat.

Gathering of the Tribes 285 E 3rd St (between aves C & D) ⓣ212/674-3778. This super-cool venue hidden away in the lowest of the Lower East Side hosts one of the city's finest open mikes from 5–7pm on Sunday nights. $3.

NuYorican Poet's Café This is the godfather of all slam venues, often featuring stars of the poetry world who pop in unannounced. SlamOpen on Wednesdays and the Friday Night Slam both cost $5 and come highly recommended.

People's Voice Café 45 E 33rd St (between Park and Madison aves) ⓣ212/787-3903. Tucked into the Workmen's Circle Building, this space draws those in search of original music and cultural acts. $10 cover; seats about eighty.

Poetry Project at St Mark's Church 131 E 10th St (at 2nd Ave) ⓣ212/674-0910, ⓦwww.poetryproject.com. The late Allen Ginsberg, a Poetry Project protégé, said "the poetry project burns like red hot coal in New York's snow." Make of that what you will, the thrice-weekly reading series held here features some truly, ahem, hot stuff. Closed July and August.

Rodeo Bar 375 3rd Ave (at 27th St) ⓣ212/683-6500, ⓦwww.rodeobar.com. Dust off your spurs, grab your partner and head down to the *Rodeo* for live country tunes seven days a week. No cover.

Nightclubs

New York's – especially Manhattan's – **club life** is a rapidly evolving creature. While many of the name DJs remain the same, venues shift around, opening and closing according to finances and fashion. Musically, techno, electronica and house hold sway at the moment, with the emphasis on the deep, vocal style that's always been popular in the city; but reggae, hip hop, funk, ambient and drum'n'bass all retain interest.

In the past decade, former Mayor Giuliani introduced a conservative strain into the city's nightlife. Under the guise of "quality of life" improvements,

Giuliani enacted laws requiring each nightspot to have a cabaret license in addition to an alcohol license if it intends to allow dancing. So while many bars might have a DJ playing in the corner, only the ones with the costly extra paperwork will permit their patrons to shake their hips. Perhaps the city's new mayor will enjoy a jig more than Rudy, yet that remains to be seen.

Another problem that has dampened the scene came from within. Peter Gatien, the owner of New York's three largest nightclubs – *Limelight*, *Tunnel* and the *Palladium* – was indicted in 1996 on drug distribution and conspiracy charges. *Limelight* was closed after the debacle but has now reopened, while the *Palladium* was not so lucky, and has closed its doors permanently. Though drugs are regarded by many as a natural accompaniment to clubbing, a word of warning: if you feel you must indulge, be very discreet. Door searches are thorough, and guaranteed.

Despite all this, clubs in New York can offer a good night out. The scene constantly changes, so to ensure that the party is still there, check such listings mags as *Time Out New York*, *Paper Magazine* or *Homo Xtra* – or freebies like the *Village Voice* and the *New York Press*.

Clubbing can be costly. In order to get the most for the least amount of money, here are some guidelines:

- The best time to go is during the week. Crowds are smaller, prices are cheaper, service is better and clubbers are more savvy than during the weekend, which is when out-of-towners ("Bridge and Tunnel" or "BT") flood the floor.
- The fliers placed in record and clothing stores in the East Village and SoHo are the best way to find out about the latest clubs and one-off nights. Many fliers also offer substantial discounts.
- Style can be important, so make an effort and you'll probably get beyond the velvet rope (if there even is one).
- Nothing much gets going before midnight, so many places offer reduced admission before then.
- Expect to be thoroughly frisked by security before entering the larger dance clubs. Drugs, weapons and hip flasks will be confiscated; any sharp objects that could be used as weapons (Swiss Army knives, metal combs) will be held at the door, as will pepper sprays and bottles of water. Basically, if you'd like to keep it, don't take it to the club.
- When you eventually stagger out into the morning light, keep your wits about you. If you're taking a cab, specify the most direct route home, or you might find yourself taking a tour of the city.

13 **35 E 13th St, second floor ☎212/979-6677.** Cute and cozy dance club with an outdoor roof deck and a laid-back, unpretentious clientele. The free Thursday night Eighties' night is infinitely more fun than the mediocre $5 weekends.

Baktun **418 W 14th St ☎212/206-1590.** If you're in the mood to make the trek this far west the rewards are vast in this multimedia lounge, one of the city's most innovative and unpretentious nightclubs. They finally got their cabaret license, making "Direct Drive" Saturdays one of the best nights out a Manhattanite can have. Great time guaranteed. $7.

bOb **235 Eldridge St (at E Houston St) ☎212/777-0558.** A friendly, 20-something art-school crowd lounges on the sofas while DJs spin hip hop, house and soul grooves. Nightly; free.

Centro-Fly **45 W 21st St ☎212/627-7770.** If you can stand the attitude, the wait, the rough bouncers and the rope, *Centro-Fly* hosts some of the biggest names in commercial house at the weekends, especially at their Friday night GBH (Great British House) parties ($20, $10 on guestlist ☎212/539-3916). Downstairs in the *Pinky* things are a little more low-key and sedate. Open till 6am.

Cheetah 12 W 21st St (between 5th and 6th aves) ☎212/206-7770. A club for lounging around on faux leopard skin in-between the occasional dance… much less effort than the sanctimonious *Centro-Fly* down the road.

China Club 268 W 47th St (between Broadway and 8th Ave) ☎212/398-3800. Huge fancy schmanzy temple of MOR spinnery, with occasional live tunes thrown in. The occasional live tunes are occasionally performed by the likes of Bowie and the Boss.

Don Hill's 511 Greenwich St (at Spring St) ☎212/219-2850. Drag queens, creative types and slumming stars congregate at this dive on the outskirts of SoHo. Less trendy than it used to be, but still the place where your rubber gear won't get a second glance. Saturday night is the ever-popular Tiswas, featuring live bands and the best of all things Britpop. $10–15.

Filter 14 432 W 14th St ☎212/366-5680. This not-quite-finished (ever) space was once home to *Mother*, and almost to *Armani* (hence the perpetual unfinished appearance). The Friday night deep house parties here are superb, with the talent of such guests as David Morales adding to the top-quality tunes.

Frying Pan Pier 63, Chelsea Piers at 23rd St ☎212/439-1147. This old lightship is one of the coolest club venues in the city – great views, consistently good parties and a relaxed door policy all lend themselves to a damn fine time. $10.

Fun 130 Madison St ☎212/964-0303. This eclectic space under the Manhattan Bridge is fun, funky and as unpretentious as they come. Urban bible *Flyer* hosts parties here on the last Thursday of the month, to which a hugely varied selection of hipsters and international DJs come and play. $5–15.

Giant Step venues vary, call ☎212/414-8001 for time and place. After singlehandedly flooding NY with acid jazz, *Giant Step* has mercifully reinvented itself as a proponent of drum'n'bass, trip-hop and underground house. Hosts low-key shows that aren't well publicized, offering the chance to see name acts for cheap prices in small venues. $10–15.

Limelight 37 W 20th St (at 6th Ave) ☎212/807-7059. This is one of the most splendid party spaces in New York: a church designed by Trinity Church-builder Richard Upjohn. A scandalous past involving jail bird Michael Alig has lead the club to clean up its ways and it now plays host to more measured monthly events such as Gatecrasher. $30.

Nell's 246 W 14th St (between 7th and 8th aves) ☎212/675-1567. First of the so-called "supper clubs," opened by *Rocky Horror*'s Nell Campbell, and still a plush venue with late supper and live music upstairs, and DJ dancing down. Open-mike night on Tues with the occasional celebrity walk-on; soul Wed, reggae Thurs. Some nights the bridge-and-tunnel crowd is in full force; but in general, it's a multiracial, well-dressed crowd. $10–15.

Ohm 16 W 22nd St (between 5th and 6th aves) ☎212/229-2000. A glam supper club with three-level lounge area and upstairs dance space as well as a mellower black-lacquered dance floor downstairs. Big names in Latin music and sensuously performed salsa – the only place in central Manhattan where the twain do meet. Regrettably, it's frequented by a serious bridge-and-tunnel contingent at the weekends, with serious drink prices to match. Open for dinner and dancing Thurs–Sat; admission $5–20.

Sapphire Lounge 249 Eldridge St (at Houston St) ☎212/777-5153. Pleasantly sleazy lounge, with a black-lit interior and "arty" films in the back room. Frequented by hip Lower East Siders. Music of all kinds, from soulful Social Sundays to hip-hop Touch Tuesdays (with half-price drinks 'till 10pm) and Latin- and reggae-tinged 'Infinity' on Saturday. Open every night; free–$5.

Shine 285 W Broadway (at Canal St) ☎212/941-0900. Looking every bit what a nightclub should: velvet ropes and angry bouncers outside, high ceilings, plush red curtains and dim lights inside. Once important for up-and-coming rock bands, it's still the place for music industry parties; Thursday nights host Giant Step ($10; see above) while Fridays are slamming with the popular Touch parties (guest list ☎212/502-3532). $10–20.

Spa 76 E 13th St ☎212/388-1062. This funky new space, complete with stage, chill-out room and loads of pretty boys and girls, plays host to hip DJs like Paul Sevigny (brother of Chloe) at their popular Wednesday night party ($20, free on guest list ☎212/714-5075) and the talented Jackie Christie and Lady Bunny on Thursday nights ($20).

True **28 E 23rd St (between 5th and Madison aves) ☎212/252-4127.** Kitschy, Eighties, Glam and Goth are all favorite themes of this cute, two-level club. $5–15.

Tunnel **220 12th Ave (at W 27th St) ☎212/695-4682.** A superclub-style techno and house hall occupying a never-completed subway station, a tad the worse for wear. Check out the Kenny Scharf room with cartoonish decor by the artist and the unisex bathroom with full bar and lounge. The lounge downstairs offers a little sanctuary but watch out for giant crowds of out-of-towners – and the gay college crowd – on the weekends. Open Fri–Sun; $15–30.

Vinyl **6 Hubert St (between Hudson and Greenwich sts) ☎212/343-1379.** Considered one of New York's hottest venues, this big, dark, low-ceilinged warehouse is a techno sweatshop: packed full of beat junkies who don't even get started until 1am. Li'l Louis Vega spins here each Sat; expect to wait in line for a long time. On Sundays from 3–10pm, DJ François K dishes up heavy house at this afternoon party. Popular with a mid-20s crowd that prefers dancing to body piercings. Fri–Sun; $12–20.

The Warehouse **141 E 140th St, Bronx ☎718/992-5974.** Even the most dedicated Manhattanites seem to make an effort to come way up here, where the attitude is non-existent, the decor is school disco and the music all hip hop and Chicago house. They even sell deep-fried snacks to compensate for all that break dancin'… $15.

Webster Hall **125 E 11th St (between 3rd and 4th aves) ☎212/353-1600.** A microcosmic venue with myriad private rooms, four floors of techno, acid jazz, jungle and the like, nooks and crannies – even a coffee shop. Expect to meet frat boys, bridge-and-tunnel types, homeboys, queens, Goths and the Wall Street crowd. $10–20.

33 The performing arts and film

From Broadway glitter to Lower East Side grunge, from the high-culture polish of Lincoln Center to the rawest experimentalism of the Kraine, the range and variety of the **performing arts** in New York is exactly what you might expect. And prices, of course, vary accordingly, from $100 nights at the opera to free bring-your-own-chair performances of Shakespeare in downtown parking lots. Broadway, and even Off-Broadway theater, is notoriously expensive, but if you know where to look, there are a variety of ways to get tickets cheaper, and on the Off-Off-Broadway fringe you can see a play for little more than the price of a movie ticket. As for dance, music and opera: again, the big mainstream events are extremely expensive, but smaller ones are often equally as interesting and far cheaper. For movies, New York gets the first run of most American films and many foreign ones long before they reach Europe, and has a very healthy arthouse and revival scene.

"What's on" listings for the arts can be found in a number of places. The most useful sources are the clear and comprehensive listings in *Time Out New York*, the free *Village Voice* (especially the pull-out "Voice Choices" section), or the also-free *New York Press*, all especially useful for things downtown and vaguely "alternative." For tonier events try the "Cue" section in the weekly *New York Magazine*, the "Goings On About Town" section of the *New Yorker*, or Friday's "Weekend" or Sunday's "Arts and Leisure" sections of the *New York Times*. Specific Broadway listings can be found in the free *Official Broadway Theater Guide*, available at theater and hotel lobbies or at the New York Convention and Visitors' Bureau (see "Information, Maps and Tours" in Basics). Even more useful, if you want to plan your itinerary before you leave home, websites such as Ⓦnewyork.citysearch.com and Ⓦwww.timeoutny.com have up-to-the-minute information on arts and events in New York, as well as the sites ⓌNYTheatre.com and Ⓦwww.offbroadwayonline.com, both useful sources of information about local theater.

Theater

Theater venues in the city are referred to as **Broadway**, **Off-Broadway**, or **Off-Off-Broadway**, groupings that represent a descending order of ticket price, production polish, elegance and comfort (but don't necessarily have much to do with the address) and an ascending order of innovation, experimentation and theater for the sake of art rather than cash. Broadway, for years dominated by grandiose tourist-magnet musicals, has, over the past few years, been getting its act together and getting serious. In recent years, Neil Simon's *The Dinner Party*, Peter Brook's *Hamlet*, and especially an adaptation of Mel Brooks's movie *The Producers*, starring Matthew Broderick and Nathan Lane, have taken the city by storm. On top of that, lively, imaginative musicals like *The Lion King*, *Kiss Me Kate*, *Rent*, *Chicago* and *Annie Get Your Gun* continue to draw crowds and acclaim.

Off-Broadway, while less glitzy, is the best place to discover new talent and adventurous new American drama and musicals like the Blue Man Group's recent sensation *Tubes* or the outrageous *Naked Boys Singing*. It's Off-Broadway where you'll find social and political drama, satire, ethnic plays and repertory: in short, anything that Broadway wouldn't consider a surefire money-spinner. Lower operating costs also mean that Off-Broadway often serves as a forum to try out what sometimes ends up as a big Broadway production.

Off-Off-Broadway is New York's fringe. Unlike Off-Broadway, Off-Off doesn't have to use professional actors, and shows range from shoestring productions of the classics to outrageous and experimental performance art. Prices for Off-Off range from cheap to free, and quality can vary from execrable to electrifying. Use weekly reviews as your guide; the listings here should give you an idea of which venues and companies are worth a look.

For the record, the size of the theater technically determines the category it falls into: under 100 seats and a theater is Off-Off; 100 to 500 and it's Off. Most Broadway theaters are in the blocks just east or west of Broadway between 41st and 53rd streets; Off- and Off-Off-Broadway theaters are sprinkled throughout Manhattan, with a concentration in the East and West villages and Chelsea; several are in the 40s and 50s west of the Broadway theater district.

Tickets

Tickets for Broadway shows can cost as much as $75 for orchestra seats (sometimes even $100 for the hottest show in town) and as little as $15 for day-of-performance rush tickets for some of the longer-running shows. Off-Broadway's best seats are cheaper than those on Broadway, averaging $25–55. Off-Off Broadway tickets, however, should rarely set you back more than $15 at most. Here's how to get cheap seats on and Off-Broadway:

- Line up at the **TKTS booth** run by the Theater Development Fund (Ⓣ212/768-1818, Ⓦwww.tdf.org), where you can obtain cut-rate tickets on the day of performance (up to half off plus a $2.50 service charge) for many Broadway and Off-Broadway shows (though not always for the more recently opened popular shows). The booth at Duffy Square, where Broadway and Seventh Avenue meet between 45th and 47th streets, has long lines and is open Mon–Sat 3–8pm, 10am–2pm for Wed and Sat matinees, and 11am–7pm for all Sun performances. Both booths take cash or travelers' checks only; best days for availability and short lines are Tues, Wed and Thurs. Bear in mind that changes in availability can occur on an hourly basis, as people cancel, but that you can *never* get tickets for one of the top shows in town, and you generally cannot get prime seats for any show whatsoever.
- Look for **twofer discount coupons** in the New York Convention and Visitors' Bureau and many shops, banks, restaurants and hotel lobbies. These entitle two people to a hefty discount (though the

days when they really offered two-for-the-price-of-one are long gone) and, unlike TKTS, it's possible to book ahead, though don't expect to find coupons for the latest shows. The Hit Show Club, 630 9th Ave at 44th St (Ⓣ212/581-4211) also provides discount vouchers up to 50 percent off that you present at the box office.

• Same-day standing-room tickets are also available for some sold-out shows for $10–20. Check listings magazines for availability.

• If you're prepared to pay full price you can, of course, go directly to the theater, or call one of the following ticket sales agencies. **Tele-Charge** (Ⓣ212/239-6200 or 1-800/432-7250 outside NY) and **Ticketmaster** (Ⓣ212/307-4100 or 1-800/755-4000 outside NY) sell tickets over the phone to Broadway shows, but note that no show is represented by both these agencies. You will need a credit card and should expect to pay a $5–7 surcharge per ticket. Make sure to ask the operator to explain where your seats will be – if you are unhappy with the seating arrangements, you must say so now. **Tickets Central** (Ⓣ212/279-4200) sells tickets to many Off-Broadway theaters 1–8pm daily. All these services charge a service fee of a couple of dollars or more. You can also buy theater tickets over the Internet at individual theater websites or at Ⓦwww.ticketmaster.com and Ⓦwww.telecharge.com.

Though you will want to check out the aforementioned journals to see what's playing, the following theaters are worth attention for their specialized repertoire or for their long-running shows.

On and Off-Broadway

Actor's Playhouse 100 7th Ave S Ⓣ212/463-0060. West Village venue specializing in gay-themed theater, and home of the recent Off-Broadway hit, *Naked Boys Singing*.

Astor Place Theater 434 Lafayette St Ⓣ212/254-4370. Showcase for much exciting work since the 1960s, when Sam Shepard's *The Unseen Hand* and *Forensic and the Navigators* had the playwright on drums in the lobby. Since 1992, however, the theater has been the home of the comically absurd but very popular performance artists The Blue Man Group (Ⓦwww.blueman.com).

Brooklyn Academy of Music 30 Lafayette Ave, Brooklyn Ⓣ718/636-4100, Ⓦwww.bam.org. Despite its name, BAM regularly presents theater on its three stages. The academy has imported a number of stunning productions directed by Ingmar Bergman in recent years and played host to Peter Brook's wonderful *Hamlet*. Every autumn the annual Next Wave Festival is the city's most exciting showcase for large-scale performance art by the likes of Robert Wilson, Robert LePage, Laurie Anderson and Pina Bausch. Not so much Off-Broadway as Off-Manhattan, but well worth the trip.

Century Center Theatre 111 E 15th St (at Union Square) Ⓣ212/982-6782. This new theater has a June festival entitled "Oh Shaw, Don't Be A Coward, Go Wilde! Ibsen's Watching" that consists of a series of readings of plays by . . . those dramatic giants.

Daryl Roth Theatre 20 Union Square E (at 15th St) Ⓣ212/239-6200. Site of the rambunctious, airborne frat-party of a show that is *De La Guarda*. Wear old clothes and be prepared to be hoisted in the air by swooping performance artistes.

Irish Repertory Theater 132 W 22nd St Ⓣ212/727-2737, Ⓦwww.irishrepertorytheatre.com. Specializes in quality Irish or Irish-themed drama. Wheelchair accessible.

Jane Street Theatre at the Hotel Riverview Ballroom, 113 Jane St at West Side Hwy Ⓣ212/239-6200. Way out west in the meat-packing district, this little upstairs venue spawned the hugely popular transsexual German rock opera *Hedwig and the Angry Inch* in 1999 and then the equally successful *Tick, Tick... Boom!* in 2001. Incidentally, the survivors of the *Titanic* were housed in this hotel in 1912. Wheelchair accessible.

The Joseph Papp Public Theater 425 Lafayette St Ⓣ212/239-6200, Ⓦwww.publictheater.org. This major Off-Broadway venue produces serious and challenging theater from new, mostly American, playwrights year-round, and is the major presenter of Shakespeare productions in the city. In the summer the Public runs the free Shakespeare Festival at the open-air Delacorte Theater in Central Park (ⓣ212/861-8277). Tickets are available on the day both at the Public downtown and the Delacorte uptown, but expect long lines. For information about Shakespeare in the Park, call ⓣ212/539-8750 or see p.172.

Manhattan Theater Club **131 W 55th St ⓣ212/581-1212, ⓦwww.mtc-nyc.org.** Major midtown venue for serious new theater, many of whose productions eventually transfer to Broadway. See them here first. Wheelchair accessible.

New Amsterdam Theater **214 W 42nd St ⓣ212/307-4100.** Disney's recently renovated Times Square palace is home to Julie Taymor's Tony award-winning extravaganza *The Lion King*. Wheelchair accessible.

Orpheum Theater **126 2nd Ave (at St Mark's Place) ⓣ212/477-2477.** One of the biggest theaters in the East Village, known for showing David Mamet and other new American theater, and home for the last few years to the incredibly annoying British percussion performance troupe Stomp (ⓦwww.stomponline.com). Wheelchair accessible.

St James Theatre **246 W 44th St ⓣ212/239-6200.** *The Producers*, NYC's most popular musical, has its run at this large Broadway theater.

Shubert Theater **225 W 44th St ⓣ212/239-6200.** Fred Astaire and Katharine Hepburn are just two of the stars to have graced the Shubert's stage. These days, it's home to the well-known musical called *Chicago*.

Studio 54 **524 W 54th St ⓣ212/239-6200, ⓦwww.cabaret-54.com.** The disco legend has been recently transformed into the perfect setting for the Tony award-winning revival of *Cabaret*.

Vivian Beaumont Theater and the **Mitzi E. Newhouse Theater** **Broadway at W 65th St at Lincoln Center ⓣ212/239-6200.** Technically Broadway theaters, though far enough away from Times Square in distance and, usually, quality, to qualify as Off. The place to see new work by Stoppard, Guare and the like.

Westside Theater **407 W 43rd St ⓣ212/315-2244.** Two small theaters, on two levels, known for productions of Shaw, Wilde, Pirandello and the like. The downstairs one has wheelchair access.

Off-Off-Broadway and performance art spaces

Bouwerie Lane Theater **330 Bowery (at Bond St) ⓣ212/677-0060.** Home of the Jean Cocteau Repertory, which produces plays by Genet, Sophocles, Shaw, Strindberg, Sartre, Wilde, Williams, etc.

Collective Unconscious **145 Ludlow St, ⓣ212/254-5277, ⓦwww.weird.org.** Very experimental theater and performance art, often political and usually of a high caliber.

Dixon Place **309 E 26th St (between 1st and 2nd aves) ⓣ212/532-1546, ⓦwww.dixonplace.org.** Very popular small venue dedicated to experimental theater, dance, readings and the like. On the first Wednesday of the month, Dixon Place has an "Open Performance Night," where the first ten people to sign up can present ten minutes of anything goes.

Expanded Arts **113 Ludlow St (below Delancey) ⓣ212/358-5096.** Lower East Side performance venue that also produces the summer-long "Shakespeare in the Park(ing Lot)" series of free performances at the Municipal Parking Lot at Broome and Ludlow.

Franklin Furnace Archive **45 John St #611, ⓣ212/766-2606, ⓦwww.franklinfurnace.org.** An archive dedicated to installation work and performance art, the Franklin Furnace has launched the careers of performers as celebrated and notorious as Karen Finley and Eric Begosian. Performances do not take place at the TriBeCa Furnace but at related downtown venues.

Here **145 6th Ave (at Spring St) ⓣ212/647-0202, ⓦwww.here.org.** A very open-minded, intriguing space supporting artists in their early careers. Puppetry and performance art are special strengths, as is the café.

Hudson Guild Theater **441 W 26th St (between 9th and 10th aves) ⓣ212/760-9800.** Inside a Chelsea community center, this theater introduces new American and European playwrights.

Knitting Factory **74 Leonard St (between Broadway and Church St) ⓣ212/219-3006, ⓦwww.knittingfactory.com.** This much-loved alternative music venue hosts theater and performance art too, here at the Tribeca Alterknit Theater.

Kraine 85 E 4th St (between 2nd and 3rd aves) ⓣ212/539-7686. This much-loved East Village Theater plays host to many fine – mainly comedic – plays.

La Mama E.T.C. (Experimental Theater Club) 74A E 4th St (between the Bowery and 2nd Ave) ⓣ212/475-7710, ⓦwww.lamama.org. The mother of all Off-Off-theaters and venue for some of the most exciting theater, performance and dance seen in the city for more than 30 years.

New York Theater Workshop 79 E 4th St (between Bowery and 2nd Ave) ⓣ212/460-5475, ⓦwww.nytw.org. Innovative and respected space that seems to choose cult hit shows – it was the original host of the hugely successful *Rent*.

Nuyorican Poets Café 236 E 3rd St (between aves B and C) ⓣ505-8183, ⓦwww.nuyorican.org. For a number of years now the *Nuyorican* in Alphabet City has been one of the most talked-about performance spaces in town. Its "poetry slams" made it famous, but they also host theater and film script readings, occasionally with well-known downtown stars.

Ontological-Hysteric Theater at St. Mark's Church 131 E 10th St (at 2nd Ave) ⓣ212/533-4650, ⓦwww.ontological.com. Produces some of the best radical theater in the city; especially famous for the work of independent theater legend Richard Foreman.

Performing Garage 33 Wooster St ⓣ212/966-3651, ⓦwww.woostergroup.org. The well-respected experimental Wooster Group (whose most famous member is Willem Dafoe) perform regularly in this SoHo space. Tickets are gold dust but worth every effort.

P.S. 122 150 1st Ave (at 9th St) ⓣ212/477-5288, ⓦwww.ps122.org. A converted school in the East Village that is a perennially popular venue for a jam-packed schedule of radical performance art, dance and one-person shows.

St Mark's Theater 94 St Mark's Place (between 1st Ave and Ave A) ⓣ212/473-8312. An exciting venue for new work by both established and rising stars.

Surf Reality 172 Allen St (between Stanton and Rivington sts) ⓣ212/673-4182, ⓦwww.surfreality.org. Eclectic performance art and comedy space on the Lower East Side.

Theater for the New City 155 1st Ave (at 10th St) ⓣ212/254-1109. Known for following the development of new playwrights and integrating dance, music and poetry with drama. TNC also performs outdoors for free at a variety of venues throughout the summer and hosts the Lower East Side Festival of the Arts at the end of May.

Thread Waxing Space 476 Broadway, 2nd floor (between Broome and Grand sts) ⓣ212/966-9520, ⓦwww.threadwaxing.org. Beautifully named performance space in SoHo, inside an old factory, mostly used for music, but often hosts performance-based art too.

Literary Events and Readings

New York's long-held status as a literary mecca, in combination with the city's proliferation of competitive literary bookstores (see "Books," p.420), means that you can see someone perform wordy wonders any night of the week. Every author has Manhattan on his or her book tour, and someone, somewhere, is always reading to a crowd.

Barnes & Noble The city's numerous B&Ns host a surprisingly diverse range of readings almost every night of the week. See "Books," (p.421) for store locations and contact details.

KGB 85 E 4th St ⓣ212/505-3360. This wonderful wee bar, once owned by Mafia capo Lucky Luciano, hosts a wonderful, cozy and very cool reading series at 7.30 on Sunday nights and on the third Thursday night of the month. Top publishing houses beg for their authors to perform here.

Makor 35 W 67th St ⓣ212/601-1000, ⓦwww.makor.org. This Jewish spirituality/arts center, open since 1999, has fast become one of the hottest spots in New York's art world. Their programming is superb, and the poetry reading series perhaps the best in the city.

92nd St Y Unterberg Poetry Center 1395 Lexington Ave ⓣ212/415-5500, ⓦwww.92ndsty.org. Quite simply, the definitive place to hear all your Booker, Pulitzer and Nobel Prize-winning favorites, as well as many other exciting new talents.

Symphony Space **2537 Broadway (at 95th St) ⓣ212/864-5400, ⓦwww.symphonyspace.org.** The highly acclaimed Selected Shorts series, in which actors read the short fiction of a variety of authors, packs the Symphony Space theater and can be heard across the country on the radio.

Dance

With the astounding success of Broadway dance shows like *Fosse*, *Tap Dogs*, *Riverdance* and anything starring Savion Glover, **dance** is surging in popularity in New York. And, as with theater, the range of dance offered in the city is vast. New York has five major ballet companies, dozens of modern troupes and untold thousands of soloists, and you would have to be very particular indeed in your tastes not to find something of interest. Events are listed in broadly the same periodicals and websites as music and theater – though you might also want to pick up *Dance Magazine* or check out ⓦwww.danceline.com. The official dance season runs from September to January and April to June. The following is a list of some of the major dance venues in the city, though a lot of the smaller, more esoteric companies and solo performers also perform at many of the spaces like the Kitchen and P.S.122, which are listed above under "Off-Off Broadway and performance art spaces." Dance fans should also note that the annual **Dance on Camera Festival** (ⓣ212/727-0764, ⓦwww.dancefilmsassn.org) of dance films takes place at the Walter Reade Theater at Lincoln Center in January.

Brooklyn Academy of Music **30 Lafayette St (between Flatbush Ave and Fulton St), Brooklyn ⓣ718/636-4100, ⓦwww.bam.org.** Universally known as BAM, America's oldest performing arts academy is one of the busiest and most daring producers in New York. In the autumn, BAM's Next Wave Festival showcases the hottest international attractions in avant-garde dance and music; in winter visiting artists appear, and each spring BAM hosts the annual DanceAfrica Festival, America's largest showcase for African and African-American dance and culture, now in its twentieth year. A great venue and one definitely worth crossing the river for.

City Center **131 W 55th St (between 6th and 7th aves) ⓣ212/581-1212 or 581-7907, ⓦwww.citycenter.org.** This large, midtown venue hosts some of the most important troupes in modern dance, such as the Merce Cunningham Dance Company, the Paul Taylor Dance Company, the Alvin Ailey American Dance Theater, the Joffrey Ballet and the Dance Theater of Harlem.

Cunningham Studio **55 Bethune St (at Washington St) ⓣ212/691-9751 x30.** The home of the Merce Cunningham Dance Company stages performances once a week by emerging modern choreographers.

Dance Theater Workshop's Bessie Schönberg Theater **219 W 19th St (between 7th and 8th aves) ⓣ212/924-0077, ⓦwww.dtw.org.** Founded in 1965 as a choreographers' collective to support emerging artists in alternative dance, DTW boasts more than 175 performances from nearly 70 artists and companies each season. On the second floor of a former warehouse, the theater has an unintimidating, relaxed atmosphere and ticket prices are very reasonable.

Danspace Project **St Mark's-Church-in-the-Bowery, 131 E 10th St (at 2nd Ave) ⓣ212/674-8194, ⓦwww.danspaceproject.org.** Experimental contemporary dance, with a season running from September to June in one of the more beautiful performance spaces.

The Joyce Theater **175 8th Ave (at 19th St) ⓣ212/242-0800, ⓦwww.joyce.org.** Situated in Chelsea, the Joyce is perhaps the best-known downtown dance venue. It hosts short seasons by a wide variety of acclaimed dance troupes such as Pilobolus, the Parsons Dance Company and Donald Byrd/The Group. In a space in SoHo at 155 Mercer St (between Prince and Houston sts) ⓣ212/431-9233, the Joyce hosts a three-week concert series of collaborating choreographers each spring.

The Judson Church 55 Washington Square S (at Thompson St) ⓣ212/477-0351. Greenwich Village's historic venue for experimental dance, but no performances in summer.

Juilliard Dance Workshop Juilliard Theater, 155 W 65th St (at Broadway) ⓣ799-5000. The dance division of the Juilliard School often gives free workshop performances, and each spring six students work with six composers to present a "Composers and Choreographers" concert.

Lincoln Center's Fountain Plaza 65th St (at Columbus Ave) ⓣ212/875-5766, ⓦwww.lincolncenter.org. Open-air summer venue for the enormously popular offering, "Midsummer Night Swing," where you can learn a different dance en masse each night (everything from polka to rockabilly) and watch a performance all for $12. Tickets go on sale at 5.45pm on the night.

Metropolitan Opera House 65th St (at Columbus Ave), Lincoln Center ⓣ212/362-6000, ⓦwww.metopera.org. Home of the renowned American Ballet Theater, which performs at the Opera House from early May into July. Prices for ballet at the Met range from $275 for the best seats at special performances to $12–16 for standing-room tickets, which go on sale the morning of the performance.

New York State Theater 65th St (at Columbus Ave), Lincoln Center ⓣ212/870-5570, ⓦwww.lincolncenter.org. Lincoln Center's other major ballet venue is home to the revered New York City Ballet, which performs for a nine-week season each spring.

Pace Downtown Theater Schimmel Center for the Arts, Spruce St (between Park Row and Gold St) ⓣ212/346-1715, ⓦwww.pace.edu/schimmel/main.html. Venue for the Yangtze Repertory Theatre Company, which stages work by Asian choreographers.

92nd Street Y 1395 Lexington Ave (at 92nd St) ⓣ212/415-5500, ⓦwww.92ndsty.org. Hosts performances and discussions, often for free, at the Y's Harkness Dance Center.

Classical music and opera

New Yorkers take **serious music** seriously. Long lines form for anything popular, many concerts sell out, and summer evenings can see a quarter of a million people turning up in Central Park for free performances by the New York Philharmonic. The range of what's available is wide – but it's big names at big venues that pull in the crowds.

Opera venues

Amato Opera Theater 319 Bowery (at 2nd St) ⓣ212/228-8200, ⓦwww.amato.org. This Bowery venue presents an ambitious and varied repertory of classics performed by up-and-coming young singers and conductors. Performances at weekends only; closed in the summer.

Juilliard School 60 Lincoln Center Plaza (at Broadway and 65th St) ⓣ212/799-5000, ⓦwww.juilliard.edu. Right next door to the Met, Juilliard students often perform under the control of a famous conductor, usually for low ticket prices.

Metropolitan Opera House Columbus Ave (at 64th St), Lincoln Center ⓣ212/362-6000, ⓦwww.metopera.org. Known as the Met, New York's premiere opera venue is home to the Metropolitan Opera Company from Sept to late April. Tickets are expensive and can be quite difficult to obtain, though 175 standing-room tickets for $12–16 go on sale every Sat morning at 10am (the line has been known to form at dawn).

The New York State Theater in Lincoln Center ⓣ212/870-5570 is where the New York City Opera plays David to the Met's Goliath. Its wide and adventurous program varies wildly in quality – sometimes startlingly innovative, occasionally mediocre, but seats go for less than half the Met's prices.

Concert halls

The Avery Fisher Hall in Lincoln Center ⓣ212/875-5030, ⓦwww.Lincolncenter.org. Permanent home of the New York Philharmonic, and temporary one to visiting orchestras and soloists. Ticket prices for the Philharmonic are in the range of $12–50. An often fascinating bargain are the NYP open rehearsals at 9.45am on concert days. Tickets for these,

Free summer concerts

In the light of high concert ticket prices, it's welcoming that so many events in the city, especially in summer, are free. **The SummerStage Festival** (ⓣ212/360-2777, ⓦwww.SummerStage.org) in **Central Park** puts on an impressive range of free concerts of all kinds of music throughout the summer. Performances take place at the Rumsey Playfield (near the 72nd St and 5th Ave entrance). Pick up a calendar of events around town or look in *Time Out New York* or the *Village Voice* for details. On occasional Wednesday nights the **New York Grand Opera** performs Verdi operas at SummerStage. Central Park is also one of the many open-air venues for the **New York Philharmonic's Concerts in the Park** series (ⓣ212/875-5709, ⓦwww.nyphilharmonic.org) of concerts and fireworks displays that turns up all over the city and the Outer Boroughs in July, and the similar **Met in the Parks** series (ⓣ212/362-6000, ⓦwww.metopera.org) in June and July. All summer, **Lincoln Center Out-of-Doors** (ⓣ212/875-5108, ⓦwww.lincolncenter.org) hosts a varied selection of free performances of music and dance on the plaza, while the beautifully redesigned **Bryant Park** has free concerts on the grass. And at MoMA the **Summergarden** series (ⓣ212/708-9491, ⓦwww.moma.org) presents free music concerts in the sculpture garden on Friday and Saturday evenings in July and August.

The **Festival of Creative Communities** brings emerging and established music and dance companies together to perform on a couple of weekend afternoons in the summer, as well as for a fortnight in September. And there is free classical music and jazz in the Village at the **Washington Square Music Festival** on Tuesdays at 8pm throughout July. On July and August weekends the **Prospect Park Bandshell** serves as venue for the **Celebrate Brooklyn Festival** (ⓣ718/855-7882, ⓦwww.brooklynx.org/celebrate).

nonreservable, cost just $14. Avery Fisher also hosts the very popular annual Mostly Mozart Festival (ⓣ875-5103) in Aug.

The Alice Tully Hall **ⓣ212/721-6500, also in Lincoln Center,** is a smaller venue for chamber orchestras, string quartets and instrumentalists. Prices similar to those in Avery Fisher.

Bargemusic **Fulton Ferry Landing, Brooklyn ⓣ718/624-4061 or ⓣ718/624-2803, ⓦwww.bargemusic.org.** Chamber music in a wonderful river setting below the Brooklyn Bridge on Thurs and Fri at 7.30pm, and Sun at 4pm. Tickets are $30, $25 for senior citizens, $15 for students.

Brooklyn Academy of Music **30 Lafayette Ave (near Flatbush Ave), Brooklyn ⓣ718/636-4100, ⓦwww.bam.org.** See "Dance," p.379.

Cathedral of St. John the Divine **1047 Amsterdam Ave (at 112th St) ⓣ212/662-2133, ⓦwww.stjohndivine.org.** Magnificent Morningside Heights setting that hosts both classical and New Age performances. Prices range from free to $60; call ⓣ212/316-7540 for details.

Carnegie Hall **154 W 57th St (at 7th Ave) ⓣ212/247-7800, ⓦwww.carnegiehall.org.** The greatest names from all schools of music performed here in the past, from Tchaikovsky and Toscanini to Gershwin and Billie Holiday. Labeled "one of the finest orchestral showplaces on the planet" by Alex Ross in the *New Yorker*.

Kaufman Concert Hall **in the 92nd St Y (see p.378) at 1395 Lexington Ave ⓣ212/996-1100, ⓦwww.92ndsty.org.**

Lehman Center for the Performing Arts **250 Bedford Park Blvd, Bronx ⓣ718/960-8232, ⓦwww.lehman.cuny.edu.** First-class concert hall drawing the world's top performers.

Merkin Concert Hall **129 W 67th St (between Broadway and Amsterdam Ave) ⓣ212/501-3330, ⓦwww.merkinconcerthall.org.** In the Elaine Kaufman Cultural Center, this intimate and adventurous venue is a great place to hear music of any kind. Plays host to the New York Guitar Festival in September.

Symphony Space **2537 Broadway (at 95th St) ⓣ212/864-5400, ⓦwww.symphonyspace.org.** Jazz, classical, a world music center and a free annual 12-hour music marathon, a gift to the people of New York.

Town Hall **123 W 43rd St (between 6th and 7th aves) ⓣ212/840-2824.** An eclectic bill of fare hallmarks this midtown venue.

Cabaret and comedy

Comedy clubs and **cabaret spots** are rife in New York, with shows varying from stand-up and improvised comedy to singing waiters and waitresses, many of whom are professional performers waiting for their big break. Most clubs have shows every night, with two at weekends, and charge a cover and usually a two-drink minimum. The list below represents the best-known venues in town, but performances may be found at a multitude of bars, clubs and art spaces all over the city. Check *Time Out New York* and *Village Voice* for the fullest and most up-to-date listings.

Boston Comedy Club **82 W 3rd St (between Thompson and Sullivan sts) ⓣ212/477-1000.** This long-running club in the heart of the Village has what *New York Magazine* calls "an *Animal House* ambience," so be warned. You might even be accosted on the street by house MC Lewis Schaffer hustling up an audience. $8 cover Sun–Thurs, $12 Fri–Sat. Two-drink minimum.

Brandy's Piano Bar **235 E 84th St (between 2nd and 3rd aves) ⓣ212/650-1944.** Small, Upper East Side piano bar featuring bar staff and waitresses who sing popular Broadway show hits and old TV theme tunes. Performances begin at 9.30pm when there's a two-drink minimum charge at the tables but no cover.

Caroline's on Broadway **1626 Broadway (at 49th St) ⓣ212/757-4100.** Having moved to Times Square from the Seaport, *Caroline's* still books some of the best stand-up acts in town. $12–15 cover Sun–Thurs, $17–21.50 Fri and Sat. Two-drink minimum. Also has a restaurant, *Comedy Nation*, upstairs.

Chicago City Limits Theater **1105 1st Ave (at 61st St) ⓣ212/888-5233.** Improvization theater playing one show nightly, two on weekends. Closed Tues. Admission is $20, $10 on Mon. New York's oldest improv club.

Comedy Cellar **117 MacDougal St (between W 3rd and Bleecker sts) ⓣ212/254-3480.** Popular Greenwich Village comedy club now in its third decade. A good late-night hangout. $5 cover Sun–Thurs, $12 Fri–Sat. Two-drink minimum.

Comic Strip Live **1568 2nd Ave (between 81st and 82nd sts) ⓣ212/861-9386.** Famed showcase for stand-up comics and young singers going for the big time. Cover $8 Sun–Thurs, $12 Fri and Sat. Two-drink minimum.

Dangerfield's **1118 1st Ave (between 61st and 62nd sts) ⓣ212/593-1650.** Vegas-style new talent showcase founded by Rodney Dangerfield. Cover $12.50–15, with, unusually, no minimum drink charge.

Don't Tell Mama **343 W 46th St (between 8th and 9th aves) ⓣ212/757-0788.** Lively and convivial west midtown piano bar and cabaret featuring rising stars and singing waitresses. Shows at 8pm and 10pm. Cover varies, two-drink minimum.

Duplex **61 Christopher St (at 7th Ave) ⓣ212/841-5410.** West Village cabaret popular with a boisterous gay and tourist crowd; Joan Rivers was discovered here. Has a rowdy piano bar downstairs and a cabaret room upstairs. Hosts a "Star Search" show on Fri nights. Open 4pm–4am. Cover $3–12, two-drink minimum.

Gotham Comedy Club **34 W 22nd St (between 5th and 6th aves) ⓣ212/367-9000, ⓦwww.gothamcomedyclub.com.** A swanky and spacious comedy venue in the Flatiron district, highly respected by NY media types. Cover $10 Sun–Thurs, $15 Fri and Sat. Two-drink minimum.

Judy's Chelsea **169 8th Ave (near 18th St) ⓣ212/929-5410, ⓦwww.judyschelsea.com.** A cosy supper club, piano bar and cabaret with performances seven nights a week. $10 minimum in cabaret room, cover varies.

Stand Up New York **236 W 78th St (at Broadway) ⓣ212/595-0850, ⓦwww.standupny.com.** Upper West Side all-ages forum for established comics, many of whom have appeared on Leno, Letterman and the like. Hosts the Toyota Comedy Festival in June. Nightly shows, three on weekends. Weekdays $7 cover, Fri & Sat $12. Two-drink minimum.

Surf Reality **172 Allen St (between Stanton and Rivington sts) ⓣ212/673-4182, ⓦwww.surfreality.org.** The Sunday night open mikes here are some of the most raucous – and amusing – in town. $3–10 cover.

Upright Citizens Brigade Theater 161 W 22nd St (at 7th Ave) ⓣ212/366-9716, ⓦwww.ucbtheater.com. Consistently hilarious sketch-based comedy, seven nights a week. Thurs night is improv night, with a mere $5 cover.

Film

New York is a **movie-lover's dream**. New state-of-the-art movie theaters are popping up all over the city, with more than a hundred new screens being added. Most will be in multiscreen complexes with all the charm of large airports but with the advantages of superb sound, luxurious seating and perfect stadium-seating sightlines, as in the megaplexes at Union Square and Kips Bay. Times Square, whose cinemas, except for the enormous **Astor Plaza** (44th St and Broadway ⓣ212/869-8340) and the four-screen **State Theater** in the Virgin Megastore (1540 Broadway ⓣ212/391-2900), have tended to be small and noisy, has had an overhaul in keeping with its ongoing gentrification.

For a movie-going experience with more character, the venerable **Ziegfeld** (54th St at 6th Ave ⓣ212/765-7600) is an old-style midtown movie palace that makes almost any film look good. Also worth a trip, if only to sit in an old-time balcony, is the **Paris Fine Arts** (58th St and 5th Ave ⓣ212/980-5656). For new foreign and independent films visit the six-screen **Lincoln Plaza** (Broadway at 62nd St ⓣ212/757-2280), on the Upper West Side; the ever popular, but increasingly less adventurous six-screen **Angelika Film Center** (corner of Houston and Mercer sts ⓣ212/995-2570), whose spacious café lobby is a great place to meet; the smaller four-screen **Quad** (13th St at 6th Ave ⓣ212/255-8800); the three-screen **Cinema Village** (22 E 12th St ⓣ212/924-3363); the TriBeCa **Screening Room** (54 Varick St at Canal St ⓣ212/334-2100), which has its own cocktail bar and restaurant and does a *Breakfast at Tiffany's* Sunday Brunch; or the Brooklyn Academy of Music, which has the excellent four-screen **Rose** arthouse cinema (ⓣ718/623-2770, ⓦwww.bam.org). The **Film Forum** (see p.384) also screens a popular selection of new low-budget films and documentaries. For Imax films (both 3-D and 2-D) visit the **Sony Lincoln Square** (1998 Broadway at 68th St ⓣ212/336-5000), near Lincoln Center.

Festivals

There always seems to be some **film festival** or other running in New York. The granddaddy of them all, the **New York Film Festival**, starts at the end of September and runs for two weeks at the Alice Tully Hall at Lincoln Center, and is well worth catching if you're in town. Unfortunately, tickets sell out quickly in mid-September for the most popular films, but it's often possible to purchase tickets on the night from people selling unwanted tickets at face value outside the theater (especially if the film has been panned that morning in the *New York Times*). Other New York film festivals include the **New York Jewish Film Festival** in January; **New Directors/New Films Festival** – which speaks for itself – at the Museum of Modern Art, and the rival downtown **Underground Film Festival**, both in March; the **GenArt Film Festival** of American independents, the **Women's Film Festival**, and the **Avignon/New York Festival** of French and American films in April; **Docfest** (the International Documentary Festival), the **Human Rights Watch Film Festival**, the **Lesbian and Gay Film Festival** in June; the **Asian American International Film Festival** and the **New York Video Festival** in July; the **Harlem Week Black Film Festival** in August; the **Hong Kong Film Series** at the Cinema Village in August and September; and the **Margaret Mead Festival** of anthropological films at the Museum of Natural History in October.

For **listings** your best bets are the weekly *Village Voice* or the *New York Press* (both free), *Time Out New York*, or the daily papers on Fridays, when reviews come out. The weekly magazines (*New York*, the *New Yorker*) publish listings but without showtimes. Beware that listings in papers are not *always* entirely accurate, but you can phone ⓣ212/777-FILM or visit the website ⓦwww.moviefone.com for accurate showtimes and computerized film selections. Ticket prices have risen to as high as $10.50, and there are no reduced matinee prices in Manhattan, nor cheap evenings. Senior discounts are often available. Note that theaters are very busy on Friday and Saturday nights, and tickets for hot new releases can sell out early in the day on opening weekends.

Revivals

Outside of Paris, New York may well be the best city in the world to see a wide selection of old movies, but the cinema landscape has changed considerably in the past decade. The old repertory houses showing a regular turnover of scratchy prints of old chestnuts and recent favorites have all gone. But what remains, or has sprung up in its place, is an impressive selection of museums and revival houses showing an imaginatively programmed series of films – whether retrospectives of particular directors or actors, series from particular countries, or programs of particular genres. The theaters showing these films range from the dryly academic to the purely pleasurable, but what most of them have in common is an emphasis on good-quality prints (there are exceptions of course) and comprehensiveness. Of course, as a visitor, what you get to see is a matter of chance. If you're lucky your trip may coincide with retrospectives of your favorite director or your movie heartthrob, or that series of Lithuanian silents you'd been waiting all your life to see.

Schedules can be found in the publications listed above, and all the following revival houses and museums publish calendars available at the box office.

The American Museum of the Moving Image 35th Ave (at 36th St), Astoria, Queens ⓣ718/784-0077, ⓦwww.ammi.org. Showing films only on weekends during the day, AMMI is well worth a trip out to Queens (it's not as far as it sounds – call ⓣ718/784-4777 for directions) either for the films – serious director retrospectives, silent films and a good emphasis on cinematographers – or for the cinema museum itself.

Anthology Film Archives 32 2nd Ave (at 2nd St) ⓣ212/505-5181, ⓦwww.anthologyfilmarchives.org. The bastion of experimental filmmaking where programs of mind-bending abstraction, East Village grunge flicks, auteur retrospectives and the year-round Essential Cinema series rub shoulders.

Cinema Classics 332 E11th St ⓣ212/677-6309, ⓦwww.cinemaclassics.com. It's a grungy, sit-on-folding-chairs affair, but the film selections are excellent, the café's sofas and cakes divine and all tickets are $5.50. They also have an esoteric collection of cult videos for sale.

Film Forum 209 W Houston St (between 6th and 7th aves) ⓣ212/727-8110, ⓦwww.filmforum.com. The cozy three-screen Film Forum has an eccentric but famously popular program of new independent movies, documentaries and foreign films on two screens, and a repertory program in Film Forum 2 specializing in silent comedy, camp classics and cult directors. With its cappuccinos and popcorn and lively crowds, Film Forum is always worth a visit.

Millennium 66 E 4th St (between 2nd Ave and the Bowery) ⓣ212/673-0090. Just around the corner from Anthology, the Millennium keeps the experimental candle burning with occasional screenings of new abstract and avant-garde work in film and classes in low-budget filmmaking.

The Museum of Modern Art 11 W 53rd St ⓣ212/708-9480, ⓦwww.moma.org. Famous among local cinephiles for its vast collection of films, its exquisite programming and its regular audience of cantankerous senior citizens. Films range from Hollywood screwball comedies to hand-painted Super 8, and entry to either of MoMA's large movie theaters is free with museum admission. (Call first! MoMA is being renovated. See p.147.)

Ocularis 70 N 6th St (between Whythe and Kent sts), Williamsburg, Brooklyn ⓣ718/388-8713, www.billburg.com/ocularis. This small space housed inside the *Galapagos* bar is transformed into an independent cinema on Sunday nights, screening rarely seen cult classics, foreign gems and pioneering work by new directors.

Two Boots Pioneer Theater 155 E 3rd St (at Ave A) ⓣ212/254-3300, ⓦwww.twoboots.com. Sunday nights are for short films, Tuesdays for rarely-seen and underrated gems and the rest of the week for themed programming throughout the year.

Walter Reade Theater 165 W 65th St (between Broadway and Amsterdam Ave) ⓣ212/496-3809, ⓦwww.filmlinc.com. Programmed by the Film Society of Lincoln Center, the Walter Reade is simply the best place in town to see great films. Opened in 1991, this beautiful modern theater with perfect sightlines, a huge screen and impeccable sound elevates the art of cinema to the position it deserves within Lincoln Center. The emphasis is on foreign cinema and the great auteurs.

Other venues

Come summer, New Yorkers have been known to sit through terrible movies just to reap the benefits of the modern theaters' intensive air-conditioning systems in the heat of the afternoon. However, if you don't mind the heat and would rather watch your movies outside, **Bryant Park** (6th Ave and 42nd St ⓣ212/512-5700, ⓦwww.bryant-park.org) hosts free, outdoor screenings of old Hollywood favorites on Monday nights at sunset throughout the summer, while **River Flicks** at Chelsea Piers (ⓣ212/533-PARK) has free summer screenings of cult crowd-pleasers Wednesday nights at Pier 54 and Friday nights at Pier 25. Though primarily music venues, **Symphony Space** (2537 Broadway at 95th St ⓣ212/864-5400) hosts a repertory program of old favorites on Tuesday nights, and the **Knitting Factory** (74 Leonard St ⓣ212/219-3006) occasionally shows silent films with live modern accompaniment. There are also regular screenings, often of experimental cinema, at the **Whitney Museum** (945 Madison Ave at 75th St ⓣ212/570-3676, ⓦwww.whitney.org) in conjunction with its exhibitions.

German, Asian, Japanese and French cinema can often be found at, respectively, the **Goethe Institute** (1014 5th Ave ⓣ212/439-8700), the **Asia Society** (725 Park Ave at 70th St ⓣ212/288-6400, ⓦwww.asiasociety.org), the **Japan Society** (333 E 47th St ⓣ212/832-1155, ⓦwww.jpnsoc.com) and the **French Institute's Florence Gould Hall** (55 E 59th St ⓣ212/355-6160, ⓦwww.fiaf.org). And for night owls, there are special midnight screenings on Friday and Saturday nights at the **Angelika Film Center** and the **Screening Room** (see p.383).

34

Gay and lesbian New York

There are few places in America – indeed in the world – where **gay culture** thrives as it does in New York. A glance at the pages of the *Village Voice*, where gay theater, gossip and politics share space with more mainstream goings-on, gives you an idea of how proudly the gay and lesbian community shows its many faces. By some estimates, about twenty percent of New Yorkers are lesbians or gay males; when you extend that category to include bisexuals and transgender individuals, the numbers climb even further – as they do when you take into account the numbers of gay newcomers who come to New York each day for the welcome refuge the city can offer them.

The largely liberal orientation of New York politics has been generally beneficial to the gay community since the 1969 riots at the *Stonewall Inn* protesting police harassment marked the onset of the gay-rights movement. The passage of the Gay Rights Bill contributed significantly to the high visibility of lesbians and gay men in local government. Until around a decade ago, the New York State governor, the mayor, the City Council president and controller and the Manhattan borough president all employed full-time liaison officers to work with gay and lesbian groups. However, the election of a Republican governor and a Republican mayor in the mid-1990s resulted in some movement away from what had been nearly automatic support for gay-oriented initiatives. Although the gay community has a widespread political base and can resist any onslaught on the battles already won, negative effects have been felt in the most time-sensitive areas of gay activism: HIV/AIDS legislation and research. The urgent need to confront this devastating epidemic – which still affects the gay community more than any other – is one reason the outspoken New York gay community will not lapse into complacency.

Socially, lesbians and gay men are fairly visible, and while it's not recommended that you and your partner hold hands in public before checking out the territory, there are neighborhoods in the city where you'll find yourself in a comfortable majority. Chelsea (centered on Eighth Avenue between 14th and 23rd streets) and the East Village are the largest of these, and have largely replaced the West Village as the hub of gay New York. A strong presence lingers in the vicinity of Christopher Street in the West Village, but it's in Chelsea that gay socializing is most out and open. The other haven is Brooklyn's Park Slope, though perhaps more for women than for men; it's primarily a residential area and so a little harder to get to know, but talk to enough Chelsea regulars and you're bound to find a bunch who call Park Slope home.

Several free **newspapers** serve New York's gay community: *Blade*, *Next* and *HX* are all published weekly, while *LGNY News* is biweekly. You'll find these at the Center (see below) and at bars, cafés, lesbian and gay bookshops and occasionally at newsstands, along with glossy national mags such as *Out*, *The Advocate*, *Girlfriends*, *Diva*, etc and the useful *MetroSource*. If you're looking for some serious, full-blown action, *Next* lists private parties, dungeon events and orgies in the subculture section of its events listings – or check out Ⓦwww.nextmagazine.net/events/subculture. Other useful resources are listed in this chapter. In addition, we've listed gay-run (and gay-friendly) hotels, gay bars and nightclubs.

Lesbian and gay resources

The Lesbian, Gay, Bisexual & Transgender Community Services Center 208 W 13th St, NY 10014 (west of 7th Ave) Ⓣ212/620-7310, Ⓦwww.gaycenter.org. The Center's free paper, *Center Voice*, is mailed to more than 55,000 households, which should give you an idea of how it's grown since it opened here in 1983 in an abandoned school. The just-renovated, glistening new Center, which houses countless diverse organizations (from ACT UP to the Metro Gay Wrestling Alliance), also sponsors workshops, dances, movie nights, guest speakers, youth services, programs for parents and kids, an archive and library, the annual Center Garden Party and lots more. Even the bulletin boards are fascinating. All in all, you really can't beat it as a place to start.

General Help and Advice

Association of the Bar of the City of New York - Committee on Lesbian & Gay Rights, 42 W 44th St, NY 10036 Ⓣ212/382-6600. The committee recommends legal policies for employers and law schools, and addresses general policy issues regarding lesbian and gay rights.

The Audre Lorde Project 85 S Oxford St, Brooklyn, NY 11217 Ⓣ718/596-0016 (community information), Ⓦwww.alp.org. Center for LGBT and people of color.

Bisexual Information and Counseling Services, Inc. 599 West End Ave, Suite 1A, NY 10024 Ⓣ212/595-8002, Ⓦwww.bisexualcounseling.org. Help on health and relationship issues; general and professional discussion groups.

Black Pride NYC PO Box 20399, London Terrace Sta., NY 10011-0004 Ⓣ212/613-0097. This empowerment and awareness group organizes a four-day festival in early August, including cultural celebration, community forum, literary reading, workshops, interfaith service and a beach party.

Brooklyn Pride PO Box 150508, Brooklyn, NY 11215 Ⓣ718/670-3337, Ⓦwww.worldconx.com/brooklynpride. Organizes Brooklyn Pride Festival and Parade.

Empire State Pride Agenda Matt Foreman, Executive Director, 647 Hudson St, NY 10014 Ⓣ212/627-0305, Ⓦwww.espany.org. Political organization lobbies legislature and governor, helps elect gay-supportive candidates through financial/campaign assistance, organizes constituent pressure, educates public about lesbian/gay life.

Gay and Lesbian National Hotline Ⓣ1-888/THE GLNH or 212/989-0999, Ⓦwww.glnh.org (Mon–Fri 6–10pm, Sat noon–5pm). Information, help and referrals.

Gay Yellow Pages PO Box 533, Village Station, NY 10014-0533 Ⓣ 212/674-0120, Ⓦwww.gayellowpages.com. Annual directory of gay/lesbian businesses and resources.

GLAAD-NY (Gay and Lesbian Alliance Against Defamation) 150 W 26th St at 7th Ave, Suite 503 Ⓣ212/807-1700, Ⓦwww.glaad.org. Monitors the portrayal of gays, lesbians and bisexuals in the media, and organizes caucuses and discussion groups on media topics. Volunteers and visitors welcome.

International Gay and Lesbian Human Rights Commission (New York) c/o Human Rights Watch, 350 5th Ave, 34th floor Ⓣ212/216-1814 or 212/216-1876, Ⓦwww.iglhrc.org.

Lambda Legal Defense and Education Fund **120 Wall St, 15th floor, NY 10005 ⓣ212/809-8585, ⓦwww.lambdalegal.org.** Active against discrimination affecting people with AIDS and the lesbian, gay, bisexual and transgender community; publications, speakers and newsletter.

The Names Project/New York City Chapter **75 Varick St, Suite 1404 ⓣ212/226-2292, ⓦwww.aidsquilt-nyc.org.** New York makers of the huge AIDS memorial quilt.

New York Area Bisexual Network ⓣ212/459-4784. Call for information on bisexual support groups, discussions, social events and other activities.

Exclusively lesbian organizations

See also "Women's New York," p.45.

Astraea **116 E 16th St, 7th floor, #520, NY 10003 (between Park Ave S and Irving Place) ⓣ212/529-8021, ⓦwww.astraea.org.** National lesbian foundation offering financial support, education and networking to lesbian organizations and projects.

Center for Anti-Violence Education/Brooklyn Women's Martial Arts **421 5th Ave, 2nd floor, Brooklyn, NY 11215 ⓣ718/788-1775, ⓦwww.cae-bkln.org.** Self-defense and martial arts classes integrate a political understanding of violence; not-for-profit, feminist and anti-racist.

Lesbian Herstory Archives **PO Box 1258, NY 10116 ⓣ718/768-DYKE, ⓦwww.datalounge.com/lha.** Celebrated and unmissable. Call or write for an appointment or for schedule of events in Park Slope.

Radical Women **32 Union Square E, #907 ⓣ212/677-7002.** Multi-racial socialist feminist organization.

Social Activities for Lesbians (SAL) **PO Box 2270, Church Street Station ⓣ212/330-6582.** A social group that organizes dinners, parties, cultural excursions, video nights and the like. Call for details and calendar.

Health and well-being

Callen-Lorde Community Health Center **356 W 18th St (between 8th and 9th aves) ⓣ212/271-7200, ⓦwww.callen-lorde.org.** Clinic with sliding pay-scale based on income that can either treat or refer patient. Mon–Thurs 9am–8pm (closed Wed 1–5pm).

Center for Mental Health and Social Services **at the Center, 208 W 13th St ⓣ212/620-7310.** Free confidential counseling and referrals.

Identity House **39 W 14th St, Suite 205 (between 5th and 6th aves) ⓣ212/243-8181, ⓦwww.erols.com/identityhouse.** Psychological counseling, referrals, groups and workshops for the lesbian, gay, bisexual and transgender community.

SAGE: Senior Action in a Gay Environment **305 7th Ave (at 27th St) ⓣ212/741-2247.** Also at the Center, 208 W 13th St; advice and numerous activities for gay seniors.

AIDS/HIV-related organizations

ACT UP (AIDS Coalition to Unleash Power) **332 Bleecker St, Suite G5, NY 10014 ⓣ212/966-4873, ⓦwww.actupny.org.** The first and most prolific of the direct action groups, ACT UP advocates group empowerment and action, advocating that silence will only equal death. Meets Mondays, 7.30 pm, at the Center, 208 W 13th St.

A & U **25 Monroe St, Suite 205, Albany, NY 12210-2743 ⓣ518/426-9010 or 1-888/245-4333, ⓦwww.aumag.org.** America's AIDS Magazine.

AIDS Hotline **ⓣ212/447-8200. Information, counseling and referrals available 7 days a week, 9 am–9 pm.** AIDS Service Center of Lower Manhattan, 80 5th Ave, 3rd floor, NY 10011 ⓣ 212/645-0875, ⓦwww.asclm.org. AIDS/HIV services.

AIDS Theatre Project **c/o Educational Alliance, 197 E Broadway ⓣ212/780-2300, ext 305.** Educational outreach theater. Actors with HIV/ AIDS perform plays about their experiences in community areas.

AIDS Treatment Data Network (The Network) **611 Broadway, Room 613, NY 10012 ⓣ212/260-8868 or free call 1-800/734-7104, ⓦwww.aidsinfonyc.org/network.** Not-for-profit community-based organization provides information on treatment, counseling and referral services to people with HIV/AIDS.

American Foundation for AIDS Research (AmFAR) **120 Wall St, 13th floor, NY 10005 ⓣ212/806-1600, ⓦwww.amfar.org.** Nation's leading not-for-profit organization supporting AIDS research and advocating sound AIDS-related public policy.

Brooklyn AIDS Task Force **502 Bergen St (Carlton St at 6th Ave), Brooklyn, NY 11217 ⓣ718/622-2910,**

Gay bath houses

Let's be honest, you're not going to get clean here. But you are going to be careful. Among the **bath houses** are such standouts as the **East Side Club** 227 E 56th St (☎212/753-2222), whose three floors of 24-hour steam, sauna and porno flick action are well worth $21 temporary membership. The **West Side Club** 27 W 20th St (☎212/691-2700) has no sauna, showers or steam but charges the same entrance price as the East Side Club nonetheless – if you want a locker, that is. Open 24 hours. The **Wall Street Sauna** 1 Maiden Lane (☎212/233-8900) is more refined, with a lounge area and even the occasional straight stockbrocker. Open Mon–Fri 11am–8pm, Sat noon–6pm. $11.

@www.pages.prodigy.net/batf. Counseling on gay and lesbian issues.

Bronx AIDS Services (BAS) One Fordham Plaza, Suite 903, Bronx, NY 10458 ☎718/295-5605, @www.basnyc.org.

Gay Men's Health Crisis (GMHC) 119 W 24th St (between 6th and 7th aves) ☎212/807-6664, @www.gmhc.org. Despite the name, this organization – the oldest and largest not-for-profit AIDS organization in the world – provides information and referrals to everyone.

HIV/AIDS Legal Service Project Legal Action Center, 153 Waverly Place, NY 10014 ☎212/243-1313. Free childcare, discrimination, housing and health planning services for people with AIDS/HIV.

New York State Department of Health AIDS Institute Gay/Lesbian Unit, Special Populations Bureau, 5 Penn Plaza, 1st floor north, NY 10001 ☎212/268-6234. Responsible for public education and health care.

Shades of Lavender 502 Bergen St, Park Slope ☎718/622-2910 ext 103. Division of the Brooklyn AIDS Task Force. Regular events, social and support groups. A small but friendly operation popular with the Park Slope crowd.

Accommodation

A few suggestions if you're looking for a place to rest your head: these places are friendly to gays and lesbians and convenient for the scene. See Hotel price codes, p.288.

Chelsea Mews Guest House 344 W 15th St, NY 10011 (between 8th and 9th aves) ☎212/255-9174. All-male gay guesthouse. Local calls are included. ❷–❸.

Chelsea Pines Inn 317 W 14th St (between 8th and 9th aves) ☎212/929-1023, @www.chelseapinesinn.com. Well-priced hotel, whose guests are mostly gay, housed in an old brownstone on the Greenwich Village/Chelsea border that offers clean, comfortable, attractively furnished rooms. Best to book in advance. ❶–❹; 3-night minimum stay at weekends.

Chelsea Savoy Hotel 204 W 24th St (at 7th Ave) ☎212/929-9353, @www.chelseasavoynyc.com. This relative newcomer, housed in a new building, makes up for a lack of charm with clean and modern amenities in every room. ❷.

Colonial House Inn 318 W 22nd St, NY 10011 (between 8th and 9th aves) ☎212/243-9669, @www.colonialhouseinn.com. Economical, 20-room bed-and-breakfast in the heart of Chelsea. Also welcomes straight guests. Boasts a clothing-optional roofdeck. ❶, with 15% off in Jan & Feb.

Hotel 17 255 E 17th St, NY 10003 ☎212/475-2845, @www.hotel17.citysearch.com. Woody Allen's *Manhattan Murder Mystery* was filmed here, and the 120 rooms have just been tastefully redone. Good neighborhood, too. ❶, with single room rates available.

Incentra Village House 32 8th Ave (between 12th and Jane sts), NY 10014 ☎212/206-0007. Twelve-room townhouse, some rooms with kitchenette. Three-night minimum stay at weekends. Also welcomes straight guests. ❷.

Arts and media

There's always a fair amount of gay theater going on in New York: check the listings in the *Village Voice* and the free papers noted above.

All Out Arts 107 Suffolk St, Suite 310, NY 10002 ⓣ212/477-9945, ⓦwww.alloutarts.org. A nonprofit group that produces a two-week-long festival of lesbian and gay arts.
The Advocate 80 8th Ave, #305, NY 10011 ⓣ212/242-8100, ⓦwww.advocate.com. National gay and lesbian newsmagazine.
Broadway Night Out PO Box 387, NY 10028-0007 ⓣ212/289-1741. This society offers low-priced group-rate tickets for Broadway and off-Broadway shows and hosts socializing dinners before shows. Call for membership information.
Dyke TV PO Box 101, Old Chelsea Station, NY 10011 ⓣ718/230-4770, ⓦwww.dyketv.org. Media and arts center with half-hour show Tuesday nights at 8pm on Manhattan Cable Channel 34 covering news, arts, politics, sports and other features – including current issues in lesbian activism. Also offers training for lesbians in video and computer technologies.
Gay Cable Network 133 W 25th St, Suite 6E, NY 10001 ⓣ212/727-8825, ⓦwww.gcntv.com. A variety of programs featuring news, interviews, entertainment reviews and more, mainly for men. Broadcast on Manhattan Cable Channel 35 on Thursday at 11pm and on other cable networks in the city.
Gay Parent Magazine PO Box 750852, Forest Hills, NY 11375-0852 ⓣ718/997-0392, ⓦwww.gayparentmag.com.
Heritage of Pride 154 Christopher St, Suite 1D, NY 10014 ⓣ212/80-PRIDE (807-7433), ⓦwww.nycpride.org. The group that organizes the bulk of citywide events for June, Gay Pride Month.
HX Magazine c/o Two Queens, 230 W 17th St, 8th floor, NY 10011 ⓣ212/352-3535, ⓦwww.hx.com. Vital homosexual listings mag.
Lesbian Central QCom, 25 Leroy St, NY 10014 ⓣ212/242-0536. World's first lesbian TV talk show.
Lesbian & Gay New York (LGNY) newspaper, 150 5th Ave, Suite 600, NY 10011 ⓣ212/691-1100 ext 11, ⓦwww.lgny.com.
Leslie-Lohman Gay Art Foundation 127b Prince St (between Wooster St and W Broadway) ⓣ212/673-7007, ⓦwww.leslie-lohman.org. The foundation maintains an archive and permanent collection of lesbian and gay art, with galleries open to the public from September to June.
Metrosource Magazine 180 Varick St, 5th floor, NY 10014 ⓣ212/691-5127, ⓦwwwmetrosource.com. National gay and lesbian lifestyle magazine with a local directory of gay-friendly professionals and businesses.
New Festival (aka **New York Lesbian and Gay Film Festival**) 47 Great Jones St, 6th floor, NY 10012 ⓣ212/254-7228, ⓦwww.newfestival.org. The festival takes place each June.
New York City Gay Men's Chorus 262 W 38th St, Suite 604, NY 10018 ⓣ212/398-5888, ⓦwww.nycgmc.org. Gay men's choral group. Call for concert schedule and membership information.
Out Magazine 110 Greene St, Suite 600, NY 10012 ⓣ212/334-9119, ⓦwww.out.com. A lifestyle magazine covering everything from politics to health.

Bars

Gay men's **bars** cover the spectrum: from relaxed, mainstream cafés to some hard-hitting clubs full of glamour and attitude. Most of the more established places are in Greenwich Village and Chelsea, and along Avenue A in the East Village. The areas around Murray Hill and Gramercy Park (the east 20s and 30s) are up-and-coming. For women, Park Slope in Brooklyn is the center of the Sapphic universe, while, in the East Village and along Hudson Street in the West, dyke bars are cropping up at a crazy rate. Things tend to get raunchier further west as you reach the bars and cruisers of the wild West Side Highway and meat-packing districts, both of which are pretty hard-line. Check local weeklies, like the *Village Voice* and *MetroSource*, which is published every two months and gay-specific 'zines like *HX* for up-to-the minute listings.

Mainly for men

The Bar 68 2nd Ave (at E 4th St) ⓣ212/674-9714. A longstanding neighborhood hideaway with a pool table in the East Village. Fairly relaxed on weeknights, cruisier at the weekend.
Barracuda 275 W 22nd St (between 7th and

8th aves) ☎212/645-8613. A favorite spot in New York's gay scene, and as laid-back as you'll find in Chelsea. Two-for-one happy hour from 4–9pm during the week, crazy drag shows and pick-up lines and a hideaway lounge out back.

The Boiler Room 86 E 4th St (between 1st and 2nd aves) ☎212/254-7536. NYU/ local bar with a pool table.

Brandy's Piano Bar 235 E 84th St (between 2nd and 3rd aves) ☎212/744-4949. Handsome uptown cabaret/piano bar with a crazy mixed and generally mature clientele. Definitely worth a visit.

The Break 232 8th Ave (between 21st and 22nd sts) ☎212/627-0072. Hard-core Chelsea pick-up dive with cheap drinks, a pool table and free summer barbeques each Saturday in the back yard.

Chase 255 W 55th St (between 8th Ave and Broadway) ☎212/333-3400. This sweet and almost too-designed bar is all about Feng Shui and feeling good, rather than grabbing your neighbor's buns.

The Cock 188 Ave A (at 12th St) ☎212/777-6724. Unashamed of its theme, but without the overblown muscles and the tiny white tee. With amateur "talent" contests and strip karaoke to kill for, it's dirty, sleazy and a social hodgepodge – and a whole lot of fun.

Dick's 192 2nd Ave (at 12th St) ☎212/475-2071. Local bar with a pool table, an interesting jukebox and a good age mix.

The Dugout 185 Christopher St (at Weehawken St) ☎212/242-9113. Right by the river, this friendly West Village hangout with TV, pool table and video games might be the closest you'll find to a gay sports bar.

Dusk Lounge 147 W 24th St (between 6th and 7th aves) ☎212/ 924-4490. A place to chill out and unwind, this Chelsea stalwart is perfect on a weekday afternoon.

Excelsior 390 5th Ave (between 6th and 7th streets), Park Slope ☎718/832-1599. Amusing versatile jukebox, a friendly rather than overtly cruisy clientele and a little outside area make this one of Brooklyn's best bars for guys.

FC29 29 2nd Ave (between 1st and 2nd sts) ☎212/777-9660. A rare thing in the ever-slicker East Village: a gay dive bar. The locals are somewhat territorial though, so be nice.

g 223 W 19th St (between 7th and 8th aves) ☎212/929-1085. Nearly as stylish as its "guppie" clientele, this large and deservedly very popular lounge also features a regular DJ and juice bar.

Hannah's Lava Lounge 923 8th Ave (between 54th and 55th sts) ☎212/974-9087. Friendly neighborhood bar with charity bingo on the weekends 4–8pm – free shot if you get no. 69!

Hell 59 Gansevoort St (between Greenwich and Washington sts) ☎212/727-1666. A friendly, upscale lounge in the hip meat-packing district with a mixed and fairly restrained clientele.

Julius 159 W 10th St (at Waverly Place) ☎212/929-9672. As the oldest gay bar in the city, this quaint, wooden affair deserves at least one drink.

The Lure 409 W 13th St (between 9th Ave and Washington St) ☎212/741-3919. It's S&M and it's serious. But if that's your bag . . .

Marie's Crisis 59 Grove St ☎212/243-9323. Well-known cabaret/piano bar popular with tourists and locals alike. Features old-time singing sessions on Fri and Sat nights. Often packed, always fun.

The Monster 80 Grove St (at Waverly Place) ☎212/924-3558. Large, campy bar with drag cabaret, piano and downstairs dance floor. Very popular, especially with tourists, yet has a strong "neighborhood" feel.

Phoenix 447 E 13th St (between 1st Ave and Ave A) ☎212/477-9979. This relaxed East Village favorite is much loved by the so-not-scene-they're-scene boys and guys who really just want a drink.

Rawhide 212 8th Ave (at 21st St) ☎212/242-9332. Hell-bent for leather, Chelsea's Rough Rider Room opens at 8am for those who have beer for breakfast (and closes fairly late too).

The Spike NYC 120 11th Ave (at 20th St) ☎212/243-9688. Chelsea institution with a mostly middle-aged jeans-and-leather crowd, conveniently situated on the West Side Highway. $3 beers.

Stonewall 53 Christopher St (between Waverly Place and 7th Ave S) ☎212/463-0950. Yes, that *Stonewall*, site of the seminal 1969 riot, mostly refurbished and flying the pride flag like they own it – which, one supposes, they do.

Wonder Bar 505 E 6th St (between aves A and B) ☎212/777-9105. Cramped, festive and lesbian-friendly, this is a truly wonderful and unpretentious find for the thinking boy. Still mainly for the men, though.

The Works **428 Columbus Ave (at 81st St) ☎212/799-7365.** Kitschy tropical theme bar with a fairly mixed crowd and friendly, laid-back atmosphere. One of the few options for this part of town.

Mainly for women

Ginger's **363 5th Ave, Park Slope, Brooklyn ☎718/788-0924.** This new addition to Park Slope's sapphic scene is dark and moody yet has a great happy hour.

Henrietta Hudson **438 Hudson St (between Morton and Barrow sts) ☎212/924-3347.** Laid-back in the afternoon but brimming by night, especially on weekends. Lounging, pool and dancing areas are all separated and guys are welcome too.

Julie's **204 E 58th St (between 2nd and 3rd aves) ☎212/688-1294.** Fairly sedate and couply throughout the week, except for Thursday nights when the single girls come out to play. One of your few choices around midtown or uptown.

Meow Mix **269 E Houston St (at Suffolk St) ☎212/254-0688.** Still one of the city's hottest girl venues, way east downtown. Bands or performances most nights, for which men are welcome if they behave themselves.

The Rising **186 5th Ave (at Sackett St), Park Slope, Brooklyn ☎718/789-6340.** A relaxed neighborhood favorite with a touch of Lilith Fair, this laid-back brunch spot has live music on Wed, Fri and Sun and a DJ on Sat nights.

Rubyfruit Bar & Grill **531 Hudson St (at 10th St) ☎212/929-3343.** A cozy, friendly place for grown-up dykes, *Rubyfruit* is all about couches, cheap drinks and good company.

Clubs

Gay and lesbian **clubs** in New York can be some of the most outrageous in the world, while many of the city's nondenominational nightspots have a very open-door policy (as regards sexuality) and often host weekly gay parties. Again, check out the *Village Voice* (Ⓦwww.villagevoice.com) and *HX* (Ⓦwww.hx.com) for the latest in homosexual hip. The places below have their much-coveted cabaret license; therefore, go forth and dance.

The Cock **188 Ave A (at 12th St) ☎212/777-6254.** See above.

Don Hill's **511 Greenwich St (at Spring St) ☎212/334-1390.** An open-to-all-up-for-anything place, where you will find Britpop drag queens, mod rock dominatrixes and the occasional submissive metal fan. Pole dancers and porn complete the vibe.

Henrietta Hudson **438 Hudson St (at Morton St) ☎212/924-3347.** West Side spot of choice for the girls. See above.

J's Hangout **675 Hudson St (at 14th St) ☎212/242-9292.** Very cruisey late-night spot with very dark rooms and a "buff" Saturday night. Open nightly from midnight.

La Nueva Escuelita **301 W 39th St (at 8th Ave) ☎212/631-0588.** Exclusive and elusive, this is also one of the city's very best gay clubs. It's all about kitsch, dress-up, salsa and drag and (wo)men. Expect to wait in line for a while.

Meow Mix **269 E Houston St (at Suffolk St) ☎212/254-0688.** See above for details.

The Monster **80 Grove St (at Sheridan Square) ☎212/924-3558.** Every night here brings something different, from Latin grooves to retro hits and a Sunday afternoon tea dance (free before 8pm, $3 after). Free during the week, $5 at the weekend.

The Web **40 E 58th St ☎212/978-9988.** A predominantly Asian crowd congregates here for theme-party nights and drag competitions ($5–10), as well as Wednesday night bingo and karaoke Sundays (free).

Religion

There are numerous **gay religious organizations** in New York.

Congregation Beth Simchat Torah **57 Bethune St, NY 10014 ☎212/929-9498.** Lesbian and gay synagogue with Friday night services at 8.30pm.

Dignity/New York **☎212/818-1309.** Catholic liturgy and social each Saturday at 8pm at

the Center, 208 W 13th St.
Metropolitan Community Church **446 W 36th St, NY 10018 (between 9th and 10th aves) ☎212/242-1212.** Services each Sunday at 10.30am, 12.30pm (in Spanish) and 7pm.

Shopping

Be it a waterproof pocket rocket, that Quentin Crisp biography or some third-wave feminist tract, New York's stores are guaranteed to satisfy the most fantastical of consumerist dreams.

Bluestockings **172 Allen St (between Stanton & Rivington sts) ☎212/777-6028, ⓦwww.bluestockings.com.** Collectively-run feminist bookstore on the Lower East Side.
Columbia Fun Maps **118 E 28th St, NY 10016 ☎212/447-7877, ⓦwww.funmaps.net.** Publishes maps and guides serving gay and lesbian travelers throughout the Western world.
Creative Visions **548 Hudson St (between Perry and Charles sts) ☎212/645-7573 or 1-800/997-9899, ⓦwww.creativevisions.citysearch.com.** A well-stocked gay bookstore that also has a huge range of S&M videos and some vintage magazines.
Housing Works Used Book Café **126 Crosby St (between Prince and Spring sts) ☎212/334-3324.** An old library, this store holds more than 45,000 used books and records and a café. All the profits go to Housing Works, which provides housing, health care, etc for homeless New Yorkers with HIV and AIDS.
The Oscar Wilde Memorial Bookshop **15 Christopher St (between 6th & 7th aves) ☎212/255-8097, ⓦwww.oscarwildebooks.com.** The world's first gay and lesbian store. Unbeatable.
Out of the Closet Thrift Shop **220 E 81st St, NY ☎212/472-3573.** This excellent fundraising thrift store for AIDS groups sells everything from books to designer apparel. Tues–Sat 10am–5pm.

35

Commercial galleries

Art, and especially contemporary art, is big in New York: there are roughly 500 **art galleries** in the city, the majority in SoHo and Chelsea, and as many as 90,000 artists living in those neighborhoods. Even if you have no intention of buying, many of these galleries are well worth seeing, as are some of the alternative spaces, run on a nonprofit basis and less commercial than mainstream galleries.

Broadly, galleries fall into five main areas: in the 60s and 70s on the Upper East Side for antiques and the occasional (minor) Old Master; 57th Street between Sixth and Park avenues for big, established modern and contemporary names; SoHo for established but hip artists; Chelsea for trendy and up-and-comers; and TriBeCa for more experimental displays. The large old warehouse spaces in Chelsea offer better space for the money and are perfectly suited for galleries. Williamsburg in Brooklyn also hosts an exciting scene, although recently the area has "done a SoHo" and become almost as expensive as downtown Manhattan in terms of accommodation, pushing the less-established artists further out of the city again. There are still lots of spaces, though, and a few worthwhile galleries are listed if you want to check out what's going on in the independent world of art in New York City.

A few of the more exclusive galleries are invitation only, but most accept walk-ins (sometimes with a bit of attitude). One of the best ways to see the top galleries is with Art Tours of Manhattan (see p.29), which runs informed (if pricey) guided tours. Also, pick up a copy of the *Gallery Guide* – available upon request in the larger galleries – for listings of current shows and each gallery's specialty. The weekly *Time Out New York* offers broad listings of the major commercial galleries.

Listed below are some of the more interesting options in Manhattan. Opening times are roughly Tues–Sat 10am–6pm, but note that many galleries have truncated summer hours and are closed during August. The best time to gallery-hop is on weekday afternoons; the absolute worst time is on Saturday, when out-of-towners flood into the city's trendy areas. Openings – usually free and identifiable by crowds of people drinking wine from plastic cups – are excellent times to view work and eavesdrop on art gossip. A list of openings appears in the *Gallery Guide* and at ⓦwww.galleryguide.org.

SoHo and TriBeCa galleries

14 Sculptors Gallery 332 Bleecker St, Suite K35 ⓣ212/966-5790, ⓦwww.14sculptors.com. Just as the name implies, a gallery formed by fourteen sculptors to exhibit non-commercial figurative and abstract contemporary art. Open by appointment only.

123 Watts 123 Watts St (between Greenwich and Hudson Sts) ⓣ212/219-1482, ⓦwww.123watts.com. Trendy gallery known for its photography, along with other forms of contemporary art; has shown work by Robert Mapplethorpe, Arturo Cuenca and Bruno Ulmer.

The Drawing Center 35 Wooster St ⓣ212/219-2166, ⓦwww.drawingcenter.org. Offers shows of contemporary and historical works on paper, with an emphasis on emerging artists.

John Gibson 568 Broadway at Prince St, Suite 101 ⓣ212/925-1192, ⓦwww.johngibson.com. Avant-garde and old school American painting, sculpture and prints, with an emphasis on conceptual art and abstract works.

Lehmann Maupin 39 Greene St ⓣ212/965-0753. Shows a range of established international and American contemporary artists working in a wide range of media, amongst them Tracy Emin, Juergen Teller and Gilbert & George. Also showcases diverse new talent.

Louis Meisel 141 Prince St (at W Broadway) ⓣ212/677-1340, ⓦwww.meiselgallery.com. Specializes in Photorealism – past shows have included Richard Estes and Chuck Close – as well as Abstract Illusionism (Meisel claims to have invented both terms).

O K Harris 383 W Broadway ⓣ212/431-3600, ⓦwww.okharris.com. Named after a mythical traveling gambler, O K is the gallery of Ivan Karp, a cigar-munching champion of Super-Realism. One of the first SoHo galleries and, although not as influential as it once was, worth a look. Also displays an interesting array of collectibles and Americana.

Sperone Westwater 142 & 121 Greene St ⓣ212/431-3685, ⓦwww.speronewestwater.com. High-quality European and American painting and works on paper. Artists have included Francesco Clemente, Frank Moore and Susan Rothenberg.

Chelsea galleries

Several large **warehouse spaces** in this neighborhood hold multiple galleries and are worth exploring as a group – in particular check out the four floors of galleries at 529 W 20th St, especially the likes of I-20, Derek Eller and Andrew Kreps – in addition to some of the ones listed below, which are also part of larger groups of galleries.

303 Gallery 525 W 22nd St ⓣ212/255-1121, ⓦwww.303gallery.com. A comprehensive range of media employed by fairly established contemporary artists is on show here.

Andrea Rosen 525 W 24th St ⓣ212/627-6000, ⓦwwwRosenGallery.com. A long-established and well-respected gallery with a permanent video and film library screening room, featuring hundreds of tapes.

Annina Nosei 530 W 22nd St, 2nd floor ⓣ212/741-8695. Global works, especially contemporary pieces by emerging Latin American and Middle Eastern artists. Mon–Fri 11am-6pm.

Barbara Gladstone Gallery 515 W 24th St ⓣ212/206-9300, ⓦwww.gladstonegallery.com. Paintings, sculpture and photography by hot contemporary artists such as Matthew Barney and Rosemarie Trockel.

Brent Sikkema 530 W 22nd St ⓣ212/929-2262, ⓦwwwkyung.com/sikkema. A controversial space that takes risks with its exhibitions, such as the work of Kara Walker which was received by a great press hullabaloo.

Edward Thorp 210 11th Ave, 6th floor ⓣ212/691-6565. Mainstream, contemporary American and European painting and sculpture.

Feature 530 W 25th St ⓣ212–675–7772. This Chelsea space tends towards briefly exhibiting fairly cerebral modern artists and the controversial likes of Richard Kern (of New York Girls fame) rather than extensively highlighting a select few.

Gavin Brown's Enterprise 436 W 15th St ⓣ212/627-5258. An ultra-hip space featuring the young, cool and fearless of the mixed media art world (who, incidentally, hang out at Gavin's *Enterprise* bar next door).

Gagosian Gallery 555 W 24th St ⓣ212/228-2828, ⓦwww.gagosian.com. This stalwart of the New York scene, owned by an ex-LA poster salesman, features modern and contemporary art in all its manifestations, including work by the likes of Damien Hirst, David Salle, Eric Fischl, Richard Serra and Andy Warhol. There's also a branch uptown, at 980 Madison Ave, Sixth Floor, where you can see work by Jackson Pollock, Jasper Johns and others.

Greene Naftali 526 W 26th St, 8th floor ⓣ212/463-7770. A wide-open, airy space noted for its top-notch large group shows and conceptual installations.

Holly Solomon *The Chelsea Hotel*, **222 W 23rd St, Rm #425 ⓣ212/924-1191**
A dramatic display space with an emphasis on installations and multimedia; artists have included Laurie Anderson, William Wegman and Nam June Paik.

Mary Boone Gallery 541 W 24th St ⓣ212/752-2929. An extension of her uptown gallery, this Chelsea space has facilities for large-scale works and installations by the up-and-coming darlings of the art world.

Matthew Marks Gallery 522 W 22nd St (between 10th and 11th aves) ⓣ212/243-0200. The centerpiece of Chelsea's art scene, it shows the work of such well-known minimalist and abstract artists as Cy Twombly, Ellsworth Kelly and Lucien Freud. See also the branch at 523 W 24th St.

Pat Hearn 530 W 22nd St ⓣ212/727-7366. This long-time venue was an influential presence in its former SoHo location, and continues to specialize in abstract and conceptual artists, and risky exhibits.

Paula Cooper 534 W 21st St ⓣ212/255-1105. An influential gallery that shows a wide range of contemporary painting, sculpture, drawings, prints and photographs, particularly minimalist and abstract works. Recently relocated from SoHo

Robert Miller 524 W 26th St, 1st floor ⓣ212/366-4774, ⓦwww.robertmillergallery.com. Exceptional shows of twentieth-century art, including paintings by David Hockney and Lee Krasner, and photographs by artists such as Diane Arbus and Robert Mapplethorpe.

Rupert Goldsworthy Gallery 435 W 17th St ⓣ212/414-4560. Very cool venue featuring the likes of Richard Hell, John Rand and other such mavens.

Sonnabend 536 W 22nd St ⓣ212/627-1018. A top gallery featuring cross-the-board painting, photography and video from contemporary American and European artists, including Robert Morris and Gilbert & George.

Team Gallery 527 W 26th St ⓣ212/279-9219. Beautiful, voyeuristic and sexually evocative work is shown here; past exhibitions have included the work of Tracy Emin and Genesis P-Orridge.

Upper East Side and midtown galleries

Gemini G.E.L. at Joni Moisant Weyl 58 W 58th St (between 5th & 6th aves) ⓣ212/308-0924, ⓦwww.joniweyl.com. Contemporary graphics, with some vintage prints; has shown works by Roy Lichtenstein and Robert Rauschenberg. By appointment only.

Knoedler & Co. 19 E 70th St ⓣ212/794-0550. Highly renowned gallery specializing in abstract and Pop artists, and Post-War and Contemporary Art with a focus on the New York School. Shows some of the best-known names in twentieth-century art, including Stella, Rauschenberg and Fonseca.

Leo Castelli 59 E 79th St ⓣ212/249-4470, ⓦwww.castelligallery.com. One of the original dealer-collectors, Castelli was instrumental in aiding the careers of Rauschenberg and Warhol, and offers big contemporary names at big prices.

Marlborough/Marlborough Graphics 40 W 57th St ⓣ212/541-4900, ⓦwww.marlboroughgallery.com.
Internationally renowned galleries show the cream of modern and contemporary artists and graphic designers. The broad sweep includes works by Red Grooms, Francis Bacon, R.B. Kitaj and others.

Mary Boone 745 5th Ave, 4th floor ⓣ212/752-2929. Leo Castelli's protégé who specializes in installations, paintings and works by up-and-coming European and American artists. A top gallery, now with an interesting Chelsea addition. (See opposite.)

PaceWildenstein 32 E 57th St ⓣ212/421-3292, ⓦwww.pacewildenstein.com. This celebrated gallery has carried works by most of the great modern American and European artists, from Picasso to Calder to Rothko. Also has a good collection of prints and African art. A SoHo satellite located at 142 Greene St (ⓣ212/431-9224) specializes in edgier works and large installations.

Williamsburg galleries

Eyewash 143 N 7th St, 3rd floor ⓣ718/387-2714. Housed in a tenement flat, this gallery showcases the works of local rising stars.

Holland Tunnel 61 S 3rd St (between Berry St and Wythe Ave) ⓣ718/384-5738. Situated in the garden of Dutch artist Paulien Lethen, this tiny barn-like gallery is a gem. Open Sat & Sun 1–5pm and by appointment – best to call ahead before visiting.

Pierogi 2000 177 N 9th St ⓣ718/599-2144, ⓦwww.pierogi2000.com. This stark-white former workshop mounts installations of various kinds. It is noted in the art world for its "flatfiles," a collection of gray folders containing the work of 600 or so artists and stored clinically and provocatively in metal, sliding cabinets. Peirogi also provides the names and addresses of other Williamsburg galleries. Open Fri–Mon noon–6pm & by appointment.

Brooklyn Heights

The Rotunda Gallery 33 Clinton St, Brooklyn ⓣ718/875-4047, ⓦwww.brooklynx.org/rotunda. This not-for-profit exhibition space features the work of Brooklyn-affiliated contemporary artists in all media.

Alternative spaces

The galleries listed above are part of a system designed to channel artists' work through the gallery spaces and, eventually, into the hands of the collector. While initial acceptance by a major gallery is an important rite of passage for an up-and-coming artist, it shouldn't be forgotten that the gallery system's philosophy is centered on making money for the owners, who normally receive fifty percent of the sale price. In these galleries, for an artist's work to be non-commercial is perhaps even more damning than to be socially or politically unacceptable. The galleries below, often referred to as alternative spaces, provide a forum for the kind of risky and non-commercially viable art that many other galleries may not be able to afford to show. Those mentioned here are at the cutting edge of new art in the city.

55 Mercer 55 Mercer St, 2nd floor ⓣ212/226-8513. An artist-run co-operative that shows mostly abstract works by New York-area artists. High-quality group and solo shows.

Apex Art 291 Church St (between Walker & White Sts) ⓣ212/431-5270, ⓦwww.apexart.org. A nonprofit exhibition space which invites dealers, artists, writers, critics and international art world bods to act as curators and mount idea-based shows, along with lectures and associated events.

Art in General 79 Walker St (between Broadway & Lafayette St) ⓣ212/219-0473, ⓦwww.artingeneral.org. An experimental gallery with multimedia exhibits and performances, and an emphasis on multicultural themes.

Artists Space 38 Greene St, 3rd floor ⓣ212/226-3970, ⓦwww.artistsspace.org. One of the most respected alternative spaces, with frequently changing theme-based exhibits, film screenings, videos and installations, as well as events. In over thirty years of existence, it has presented the work of more than 5000 emerging artists.

Clocktower 108 Leonard St ⓣ212/233-1096. Temporary exhibitions, and an annual studio program run by PS1, in which artists work in the studio space within the clock tower. When this is happening, you're allowed to wander around and talk to the artists about their work. Go just to see the incredible views of downtown.

DIA Center for the Arts 548 W 22nd St ⓣ212/989-5566, ⓦwww.diacenter.org. The pre-eminent Alternative Art Foundation's largest gallery space shows year-long exhibitions of work by artists such as Joseph Beuys, Dan Graham, Robert Ryman and Kids of Survival. The exhibition space on the roof has a café and chairs designed by artists. Other exhibit spaces include the New York Earth Room (see below), and "the Broken Kilometer" exhibit at 383 W Broadway (ⓣ212/925-9397).

Dumbo Arts Center 30 Washington St, DUMBO ⓣ718/624-3772 ⓦwww.dumboartscenter.org. A huge warehouse space, this is dedicated to showing innovative new group work.

Exit Art/The First World 548 Broadway, 2nd floor ⓣ212/966-7745, ⓦwww.exitart.org. A young, hip crowd frequents this huge alternative gallery that favors big installations, multimedia, and edgy cultural and political subjects. Make sure to have some espresso and ginger cookies from the café.

Flipside 84 Withers St, 3rd floor, Brooklyn ⓣ718/389-7108, ⓦwww.flipsideart.com. This gallery, opened in 1997 to provide a space for the exchange of diverse ideas and methods, features experimental work and installations by emerging and established artists.

New York Earth Room 141 Wooster St (between Prince and Houston sts) ⓣ212/473-8072, ⓦwww.diacenter.org. An incredible permanent exhibit by Walter de Maria, featuring a room filled, as the name suggests, with masses of dirt. Also changing exhibitions, installations and performances by contemporary artists.

P.S.1 Contemporary Arts Center 22-25 Jackson Ave at 46th St, Long Island City, Queens ⓣ718/784-2084, ⓦwww.ps1.org. $2 suggested donation. Part of the same organization (the Institute for Art and Urban Resources) as Clocktower, and based in an old schoolhouse, this is the place for avant-garde and experimental new art – so new that some downtown galleries cull new talent from the exhibits here. Now affiliated with MoMA.

P.S.22 150 1st Ave ⓣ212/228-4249. Nonprofit gallery space open from September to June, which highlights emerging artists.

White Columns 320 W 13th St (enter on Horatio St) ⓣ212/924-4212, ⓦwww.whitecolumns.org. Focuses on emerging artists, and is considered very influential. Check out the changing group shows.

36

Shops and markets

The consumer capital of the world, New York's **shops** cater to every possible taste, preference, creed and perversity, in any combination and in many cases at any time of the day or night. As such, they're a great reason for visiting the city, even if the invasion of America-wide superstores and chains, like Barnes & Noble, Filene's Basement, T.J. Maxx, Bradley's and even the world's largest K-Mart have caused some worry. And there seems to be a Gap on every corner. Nevertheless, many of the oddest and oldest stores remain, and nothing beats discovering a quirky, independent shop that may specialize only in vintage cufflinks or rubber stamps.

When to shop, how to pay

Most parts of the city are at their least oppressive for shopping early weekday mornings, and at their worst around lunchtimes and on Saturday. There are few days of the year when most everything closes (really only Thanksgiving, Christmas and New Year's Day) and many shops, including the big midtown department stores, are open on Sunday. Chinatown is open all day every day, while the stores of the Financial District follow the area's nine-to-five routine and for the most part are shut all weekend.

Opening hours in midtown Manhattan are roughly Monday–Saturday 9am–6pm, with late closing on – usually – Thursday; downtown shops tend to stay open later, at least until 8pm and sometimes until about midnight; bookstores especially are often open late.

As far as **payment** goes, credit cards are as widely accepted as you'd expect: even the smallest of shops will take Visa, American Express, MasterCard (Access) and Diners Club; many department stores also run their own credit schemes. Remember that an 8.25 percent sales tax will be added to your bill; this is bypassed sometimes when paying cash in a market or discount store. Finally, wherever you're shopping, be careful. Manhattan's crowded, frenzied stores are ripe territory for pickpockets and bag-snatchers.

Shopping neighborhoods of Manhattan

As in most large cities, New York stores are concentrated in specific neighborhoods, so if you want something particular you invariably know exactly where to head.

Shopping Categories

South Street Seaport and the Financial District

South Street Seaport contains stores that you can easily find elsewhere and is very touristy. Nevertheless it is very historic and very pleasant, with a great view of the Brooklyn Bridge. There aren't too many other places to shop around the **Financial District**, with the notable exception of Syms (42 Trinity Place).

Lower East Side

Bordered by Canal Street on the south and Houston Street on the north, Orchard Street is the main artery of the Jewish **Lower East Side**. It's worth a trip for its cheap clothing stores, especially on Sunday when its shops are open only to pedestrians. With merchandise out on the street, it becomes an open-air bazaar. Some shops, like Ben Freedman, at 137 Orchard St, have been there since its pushcart heyday around 1900.

Chinatown

Always bustling with energy and activity, **Chinatown** holds great interest for food shopping, especially along Mott Street, where produce is beautiful, fresh and remarkably cheap. You can also get prepared food (noodles, fried rice, etc) for a few dollars from carts on the south side of Canal Street. Pearl River (277 Canal St) is a popular Chinese department store, while Pearl Paint across the street is one of the world's best art supply stores (see p.426).

SoHo

The area **So**uth of **Ho**uston, north of Broome and between Lafayette and Sixth Avenue is one of the most lively and fashionable in the city. Along Broadway, from Canal Street up to Astor Place, shoes, jeans and sneaker stores fill the blocks – most notably Canal Jeans Co, 504 Broadway, where the assortment of clothes, old and new, is almost overwhelming. West of here, along Prince and Spring streets, you encounter high fashion, trendy shoes, beautiful antiques and home furnishings along with all of the accompanying attitude.

Just east of SoHo and north of Little Italy is NoLita (from Lafayette to the Bowery, and between Prince and Houston). Many local artists, jewelry-makers and designers, such as at Push Jewelry (240 Mulberry St) and Kelly Christy (235 Elizabeth St), have set up shop here.

West Village

The **West Village** plays host to a wide variety of more offbeat stores: small boutiques, secondhand bookshops and almost pedantically specialized stores, selling nothing but candles or a hundred different types of caviar. On Christopher Street, west of Seventh Avenue, several stores cater to gays, with all sorts of merchandise options; 8th Street is shoe central (erring on the hip side). Most shops are small and charming and can be found on streets that fit the same description; the atmosphere makes this a fun shopping neighborhood.

East Village

To shop on the funkier side of life, hit the **East Village** – at its best along 9th Street and down Avenue A. This neighborhood is crammed with one-of-a-kind shops and boutiques like Kimono House (93 E 7th St at 1st Ave) and Body Worship (nearby at 102 E 7th), with its stylish fetish wear. For vintage clothes, head southwest of Tompkins Square Park, mostly along 7th Street.

Chelsea

Sixth Avenue in **Chelsea** is lined with places to shop, mostly giant superstores. However, as you move west toward Seventh and Eighth avenues you encounter some smaller, more unusual shops like Eclectic Home (224 8th Ave at 21st St) and Roger & Dave (123 7th Ave between 17th and 18th sts), the latter good for kitschy T-shirts. Chelsea is also the home of the city's most gay-friendly stores. The Chelsea Antiques Fair and Flea Market, at 26th Street and 6th Avenue on weekends, enjoys wide renown.

The Flower District, nearby on Sixth Avenue between 26th and 30th streets, has the city's largest concentration of plants and flowers. If you can't find what you want here, be it houseplant, tree or dried, cut or artificial flower, then it's likely not available anywhere in New York.

Finally, Chelsea is a best bet for warehouse sales of clothes and shoes (you're likely to get handed fliers on the street), and lingerie wholesalers are concentrated around and east of Broadway and West 28th Street. The blocks between Sixth and Seventh avenues in the 30s can be a good place to pick up designer clothes, fabric and trimmings (beads, buttons and ribbon) at a discount. There's an office here for just about every women's garment retailer and manufacturer in the country, and though some are wary of selling to non-wholesale customers, you can pick up some enviable bargains at sample sales. Dave's A & N Jeans (779 6th Ave) is Manhattan's best spot for discount jeans; for a wonderful array of tassels and buttons, start at M & J Trimming (1008 6th Ave at 38th St).

Lower 5th Avenue/Flatiron District

Between the Flatiron Building at 23rd Street and Union Square at 14th Street, **Fifth Avenue and Broadway**, and their side streets, have become a great shopping neighborhood. You'll find standards like Banana Republic (17th St and 5th Ave), as well as designers such as Eileen Fisher (5th Ave between 17th and 18th sts) and Matsuda (5th and 20th St). ABC Carpet and Home (19th Street and Broadway) and Domain (Broadway at 22nd St) rule over home furnishings, and vintage gravy boats can be procured at Fish's Eddy (19th St and Broadway).

Herald Square

The small triangular park where Sixth Avenue and Broadway intersect, at 34th Street, is named **Herald Square**, an unlikely center of New York's busiest shopping district. Locals and tourists alike come here for clothes, shoes and accessories; during holidays, the crowds are almost fathomless. The main reason, of course, is Macy's department store, where 35,000 shoppers visit daily. Some bargain stores surround the madness.

Fifth Avenue

Just south of Central Park, **Fifth Avenue** in the 50s is a neighborhood filled with the best-known international designer stores: department stores like Henri Bendel (at 56th St), Saks (at 50th St, across the street from Rockefeller Center) and Takashimaya (between 54th and 55th sts); jewelry stores such as Bulgari (at 57th St) and Cartier (at 52nd St); and designer boutiques including Christian Dior (at 55th St) and Gucci (at 54th St). Unfortunately, there's a lot of tourist tat among the riches here. As you travel downtown on Fifth Avenue, the prices and merchandise get more downscale. On Diamond Row, at W 47th Street between Fifth and Sixth avenues, you can browse the jewelry marts and select your own gems and settings. South of 42nd Street you'll find Lord & Taylor (at 39th St), many electronics and camera stores and inexpensive "going-out-of-business" stores selling fakes.

57th Street

One of the most exclusive shopping streets in the world is bracketed by Lexington Avenue on the east and Seventh Avenue and Carnegie Hall on the west. Almost all top designers, often found elsewhere only in Paris, Milan and LA, have boutiques on **57th Street**. Among them are Bergdorf Goodman, Tiffany, Chanel, Escada and Tourneau. The junction of 57th Street and Fifth Avenue isn't steeped only in luxury, as evidenced by chains like Pottery Barn, Victoria's Secret, Limited Express, Bolton's and a Borders superstore. On Lexington, the glitter returns at fast and fun Bloomingdale's department store (two blocks north at 59th St), which is surrounded by Banana Republic, Urban Outfitters and the Levi's 501 store.

Upper West Side

The **Upper West Side** has perhaps the city's greatest concentration of intellectuals, especially if judged by the number of bookstores and cafés. There are enough off-the-wall stores, antique shops, secondhand clothing shops and craft and design shops to challenge any funky area in the city. They include Allan & Suzi (416 Amsterdam at 80th St), which claims to have restarted the platform shoe craze and features chain-mail bikinis in its ever-changing window. On upper Broadway and Columbus Avenue you'll find such staples as Laura Ashley, Ann Taylor, Gap, Body Shop, Limited Express, Pottery Barn and Talbots, as well as unusual clothes and home shops and upper-crust thrift shops like Housing Works (306 Columbus Ave). The Green Flea Market, in the I.S. 44 schoolyard at 77th and Columbus, has become a neighborhood institution, with clothing, jewelry, collectibles, vintage clothes, lingerie and a farmer's market, and is nicely complemented in the spring and summer by the white canvas booths of art and fine jewelry vendors ranged alongside the American Museum of Natural History across the street.

Upper East Side

Madison Avenue in the 60s, 70s and 80s – the major artery of the **Upper East Side** shopping neighborhood – is filled with exclusive clothiers and antique and art dealers. Between 62nd and 72nd streets there are no fewer than twenty designer shoe stores, as well as dozens of European fashion boutiques including Armani, Gianni Versace, Krizia, Valentino and Prada. Ralph Lauren (at 71st St) is one of the few American designers here; also unusual is the designer discount store Bis (24 E 81st). Because this is also a residential neighborhood, there's a smattering of children's stores, coffee shops, restaurants and bars. The waning German community influence is most visible at the intersection of 82nd Street and Second Avenue, with Kramer's Pastries and Schaller & Weber butchers. Most of the museums on

△ Cartier is one of Fifth Avenue's most elegant jewellery stores

Museum Mile have elegant shops (museums unto themselves) – most notably the Metropolitan Museum, with its exquisite jewelry reproductions from all eras of history.

Harlem

The main shopping district of **Harlem** runs along 125th Street between Park Avenue, where the MetroNorth commuter trains stop, and Frederick Douglass Boulevard (or Eighth Avenue), where the new Harlem USA theme mall houses a Disney Store, an HMV, a Gap and a Cineplex Odeon. The stores are mostly mundane and the goods mainly cheap. Mart 123 (125th St between Frederick Douglass and Adam Clayton Powell blvds) holds nearly forty vendors, selling everything from fresh produce and T-shirts to incense and kitchen appliances. Don't miss the Malcolm Shabazz Harlem Market, in its new minaret-framed home between Lenox and Fifth, for beautiful African imports, and the museum store at The Studio Museum in Harlem (144 W 125th St). The best shop in the city for African crafts is African Paradise (27 W 125th St), with its herbal medicines, black soaps, baskets, musical instruments and much more; Our Black Heritage at 2295 Adam Clayton Powell Blvd sells tapes of great speeches by black leaders and greetings cards and books with a black theme.

Department stores and malls

Saks 5th Avenue, Lord & Taylor, Bloomingdale's and Macy's are among the world's greatest (and most beautiful) **department stores**. However, the last decades of the twentieth century saw a number of the long-established ones close down. Others have gone upmarket, making them less places to stock up on essentials and more outlets for designer clothes and chichi accessories. Most department stores offer restaurants and complimentary personal shopping, alterations and concierge service: they'll make your dinner reservations, secure tickets to the theater, call a taxi and more. Ask for details at each store's information desk.

Manhattan also has a number of **shopping malls**. Housed in purpose-built locations or in conversions of older premises, several of them are a lot of fun to shop in – and a far cry from the megamalls of the American suburbs. The larger and more important ones are listed below.

Department stores

Barney's 600 Madison Ave at 61st St ⓣ212/826-8900. Mon–Fri 10am–8pm, Sat 10am–7pm. Though a proper department store, Barney's actually concentrates on clothes, particularly men's, with the emphasis on high-flying, up-to-the-minute designer garments and women's wear. If you've got the money, you're sure to find something original and very you (darling) here.

Bergdorf Goodman 754 5th Ave (at 57th St) ⓣ212/753-7300. Mon–Fri 10am–8pm, Sat 10am–7pm, Sun 11am–6pm. Come if only to ogle the windows, which approach high art with their rhinestone-encrusted diaphanous dress displays. Everything about Bergdorf's speaks of its attempt to be New York City's most elegant and wealth-oriented department store. Lucky that most of the folk who shop here have purses stacked with charge cards – the rustle of money would utterly ruin the feel. The men's store is across 5th Ave.

Bloomingdale's 1000 3rd Ave (at 59th St) ⓣ212/705-2000, ⓦwww.bloomingdales.com. Mon–Fri 10am–8.30pm, Sat 10am–7pm, Sun 11am–7pm. When an Upper East Side matron dies, "Bloomies," not "Rosebud," is more likely to be the last word on her lips. New Yorkers adore this store's class, sense of style and, perhaps most importantly, its ability to inject a little whimsy into a major department store. It has the atmosphere of a large, bustling bazaar, packed with concessionaires offering perfumes and designer clothes. Stand in front of one of their exquisitely designed model apartments and hold hands with someone you love.

Henri Bendel **712 5th Ave (between 55th and 56th sts) ⓣ212/247-1100. Mon–Wed, Fri & Sat 10am–7pm, Thurs 10am–8pm, Sun noon–6pm.** This store, more gentle in its approach than the biggies – its refinement thanks in part to its classy reuse of the Coty perfume building, with windows by René Lalique – has a name for exclusivity and top modern designers. There's an excellent array of top-shelf make-up at street level and gorgeous designer clothing – with price tags to send heart-rates soaring – in the glamorous upper echelons. The powder rooms seem designed for a princess.

Lord & Taylor **424 5th Ave (at 39th St) ⓣ212/391-3344, ⓦwww.lordandtaylor.com. Mon, Tues & Sat 10am–7pm, Wed & Fri 10am–8.30pm, Thurs 9am–8.30pm, Sun 11am–7pm.** The most venerable of the New York specialty stores, in business since 1826 and to some extent the most pleasant, has a more traditional feel than Macy's or Bloomingdale's. Though no longer at the forefront of New York fashion, it's still good for classic designer fashions, petites, winter coats, household goods and accessories and the more basic items.

Macy's **151 W 34th St (on Broadway at Herald Square) ⓣ212/695-4400 or 1-800-289-6229, ⓦwww.macys.com. Mon–Sat 9am–9pm, Sun 11am–7pm.** Quite simply, the largest department store in the world, with two buildings, two million square feet of floor space and ten floors (four for women's garments alone). Unfortunately it's not the hotbed of top fashion it ought to be: most merchandise is of mediocre quality (particularly the jewelry), although real fashion – in the guise of popular high-street names – is steadily returning. But the downstairs housewares department, The Cellar, is arguably the best in the city.

Saks 5th Avenue **611 5th Ave (at 50th St) ⓣ212/753-4000, ⓦwww.saks5thavenue.com. Sun–Wed, Fri & Sat 10am–6.30pm, Thurs 10am–8pm.** The name is virtually synonymous with style and, although Saks has retained its name for quality, it has also updated itself to carry the merchandise of all the big designers. Shopping here is more like a stroll, along Saks' unique winding pathways. In any case, with the glittering array of celebrities that use the place regularly, Saks can't fail. The ground floor is lovely when decorated with sparkling white branches at Christmas time.

Sterns **899 6th Ave (at 33rd St) ⓣ212/244-6060. Daily 10am–8pm.** The focus of the Manhattan Mall, this store is similar in look and merchandise to ones found in suburbs across the nation. Go to shop, not to soak in atmosphere.

Takashimaya **693 5th Ave (between 54th and 55th sts) ⓣ212/350-0100. Mon–Sat 10am–8pm, Sun noon–5pm.** This beautiful Japanese department store offers a scaled-down assortment of expensive merchandise, simply displayed, and exquisitely wrapped purchases. The café, *The Tea Box*, on the lower level, has an assortment of teapots and loose tea.

Shopping malls

Manhattan Mall **100 W 33rd St (at 6th Ave) ⓣ212/465-0500. Mon–Sat 10am–8pm, Sun 11am–6pm.** Perhaps because it is just a block from Macy's, this large, mirror-fronted and rather glitzy multilevel shopping center has never really been a success. The humdrum string of mainstream stores resembles nothing so much as a suburban shopping mall.

South Street Seaport **12 Fulton St ⓣ212/732-7678. Mon–Sat 10am–9pm, Sun 11am–8pm.** Again, not quite the shopping experience it's cracked up to be, what with the preponderance of mall-style vendors, but the barn-like building and its historic surroundings of ships, docks and old warehouses are fascinating and fun, the river views from the deck are lovely, and The Sharper Image stocks some terrifying and ingenious toys for adults.

Trump Tower **725 5th Ave (between 56th and 57th sts) ⓣ212/832-2000. Mon–Sat 10am–6pm, Sun noon–5pm.** Donald Trump's retail triumph was constructed in his own image. This gaudy caterer to the wealthy offers a range of exclusive boutiques set around a deep, marbled atrium with a several-story goldtone waterfall – a tourist attraction in itself.

Clothes and fashion

Dressing right is important to many in Manhattan, and fashion is a key reference point, though you may find that **clothes** are more about status here than setting trailblazing trends. Although New York may be far in front of the rest of the country fashion-wise, compared with the cutting-edge in Europe it can sometimes seem slightly behind, unless you are in an international designer's boutique. If you are prepared to search the city with sufficient dedication you can find just about anything, but it's the **designer clothes** and the snob values that go with them that predominate. **Secondhand clothes**, of the "vintage" or "antique" variety, have caught on of late, and upscale designer vintage stores abound. Unfortunately this popularity has driven the prices up, but it is still possible to find bargains here and there.

Chain stores

Ann Taylor 575 5th Ave (at 47th St; flagship store) ⓣ212/922-3621, ⓦwww.anntaylor.com. Medium-priced business and elegant casual clothing for women. More than ten branches throughout the city.

Banana Republic 655 5th Ave (at 52nd St; flagship store) ⓣ212/644-6678. Owned by the same company that owns the Gap. More than ten branches throughout the city; check the phone book for locations.

Benetton 597 5th Ave at 48th St ⓣ212/317-2501. Italian chain offering youthful, contemporary, casual, bright-colored clothing for women, men and children. The flagship store is in the landmark Scribners building, an insult to many serious book buyers.

Brooks Brothers 346 Madison Ave ⓣ212/682-8800. Something of an institution in New York. This flagship store, founded in 1915, sells classic conservative style, selling tweeds, gabardines and quietly striped shirts and ties.

Burberry's 9 E 57th St (between 5th and Madison aves) ⓣ212/371-5010. Classic plaids and tweeds, with a distinctly British feel to the conservative designs.

Club Monaco 160 5th Ave; 121 Prince St; 520 Broadway; 1111 3rd Ave and 2376 Broadway ⓣ212/352-0936. Understated simplicity is the theme at this newish chain of stylish and well-priced clothing for men and women.

Diesel 770 Lexington (at 60th St) ⓣ212/308-0055. One of five US stores that sell this Italian-designed label. Funky, some vintage-inspired clubwear, lots of denim. The two floors include a café.

Eileen Fisher 103 5th Ave between 17th and 18th sts ⓣ212/924-4777, ⓦwww.eileenfisher.com. This is the largest of their five NY shops full of loose and elegantly casual clothes for women. Their outlet is on 9th St between 1st and 2nd aves ⓣ212/529-5715.

Gap 60 W 34th St and Herald Square (flagship store) ⓣ212/643-8960. Branches are on every other corner of the city; check the phone book for locations. Circular sale racks in the back of many stores offer terrific reductions.

H&M 34th St and Herald Square (flagship store) ⓣ646/473-1164. Wildly cheap and equally popular Swedish clothing store with an ever-changing array of affordable, up-to-the-minute designer rip-offs. To be avoided on the weekend. Branches also at 51st St and 5th Ave and Broadway between Prince and Spring.

J. Crew 99 Prince St (at Mercer; flagship store) ⓣ212/966-2739. Better known as a mail-order company, but plenty of retail stores are popping up across the country. Casual clothing for men and women.

Laura Ashley 398 Columbus Ave (at 79th St) ⓣ212/496-5110. Expanding beyond its familiar floral prints, this store offers contemporary cotton, linen and silk clothing for women and children as well as country-style home furnishings.

The Limited **691 Madison Ave (at 62nd St) ⓣ212/838-8787.** Moderately priced casual clothing for women.

Urban Outfitters **628 Broadway (between Houston and Bleecker sts); 360 6th Ave at Waverly Place; 162 2nd Ave at 10th St and 127 E 59th St at Lexington Ave ⓣ212/475-0009, ⓦwww.urbn.com.** Stylish and trendy chain with prices that have risen dramatically but with designs that are still irresistible.

Zara **750 Lexington Ave (at 59th St); 580 Broadway (at Prince St); 39 W 34th St and 101 5th Ave (at 18th St) ⓣ212/754-1120, ⓦwww.zara.com.** Quality, elegant European fashion at affordable prices from this influential Spanish chain. Check out the Zara Basic and Trafaluc ranges for cheaper, trendy buys.

Designer stores

As you might expect, New York has an unrivaled selection of designer clothing stores, and if you have any interest in clothes at all these should not be missed, even if only for an afternoon of people-watching. Internationally known design houses are concentrated uptown on Fifth Avenue in the 50s and on Madison Avenue in the 60s and 70s. Downtown the newer, younger designers are found in SoHo, NoLita, the East and West villages and TriBeCa. In these neighborhoods you can easily walk from one to another. Dress well, and you'll be welcomed whether browsing or buying. Most are open Mon to Sat 10am–6pm, but call to check.

agnès b **women's 116–118 Prince St (between Greene and Wooster sts) ⓣ212/925-4649; men's 79 Greene St ⓣ212/431-4339; 13 E 16th St ⓣ212/741-2585 and 1063 Madison Ave (between 80th and 81st sts) ⓣ212/570-9333, ⓦwww.agnesb.fr.**

Anna Sui **113 Greene St (between Prince and Spring sts) ⓣ212/941-8406.**

April Cornell, **487 Columbus Ave (at 83rd St) ⓣ212/779-4342, ⓦwww.aprilcornell.com.** Pastoral designs reminiscent of *Little House on the Prairie*, delicate dresses, lingerie, jewelry and colorful housewares as well.

Bagutta **402 W Broadway ⓣ212/925-5216.** A confluence of top designers including Helmut Lang, Prada, Gaultier, Plein Sud, Dolce & Gabbana.

Beau Brummel **421 W Broadway (between Prince and Spring sts) ⓣ212/219-2666.**

Betsey Johnson **138 Wooster St (near Houston St) ⓣ212/995-5048; 248 Columbus (at 71st St) ⓣ212/362-3364; 251 E 60th St (at Lexington Ave) ⓣ212/319-7699 and 1060 Madison Ave (at 81st St) ⓣ212/734-1257, ⓦwww.betseyjohnson.com.**

Calvin Klein **654 Madison Ave (at 60th St) ⓣ212/292-9000.**

Chanel **15 E 57th St and 139 Wooster St ⓣ212/355-5050, ⓦwww.chanel.com.**

Chloe Boutique **850 Madison (at 70th St) ⓣ212/717-8220.**

Christian Dior **21 E 57th St ⓣ212/931-2950.**

Comme des Garçons **520 W 22nd St (at 10th Ave) ⓣ212/604-0013 and 116 Wooster St (between Prince and Spring sts) ⓣ212/219-0660.**

Cynthia Rowley **112 Wooster St (between Prince and Spring sts) ⓣ212/334-1144.**

Daryl K **208 E 6th St (between 2nd and 3rd sts) ⓣ212/475-1255; 21 Bond St at Broadway ⓣ212/777-0713.** This Irish designer is quite the darling of the New York fashion cognoscenti.

D & G **434 W Broadway (at Spring St) ⓣ212/965-8000, ⓦwww.dolcegabbana.it.**

Diesel Style Lab **416 W Broadway (near Spring St) ⓣ212/343-3863, ⓦwww.diesel.com.**

DKNY **655 Madison Ave (at 60th St) ⓣ212/223-3569.**

Dolce & Gabbana **825 Madison Ave (between 68th and 69th sts).**

Donna Karan **817 Madison Ave (between 68th and 69th sts).**

Emanuel Ungaro **792 Madison Ave (between 66th and 67th sts) ⓣ212/249-4090.**

Emporio Armani **110 5th Ave (at 16th St) and 601 Madison Ave (between 57th and 58th sts).** Here you'll find the lower-priced, more mass-produced Armani line; for his most relaxed, inexpensive look, head for Armani Exchange, 568 Broadway (at Prince St) ⓣ212/431-6000 and 645 5th Ave (at 51st St) ⓣ212/980-3037, ⓦwww.armaniexchange.com.

Clothing and shoe sizes

Women's dresses and skirts									
American	4	6	8	10	12	14	16	18	
British	8	10	12	14	16	18	20	22	
Continental	38	40	42	44	46	48	50	52	
Women's blouses and sweaters									
American	6	8	10	12	14	16	18		
British	30	32	34	36	38	40	42		
Continental	40	42	44	46	48	50	52		
Women's shoes									
American	5	6	7	8	9	10	11		
British	3	4	5	6	7	8	9		
Continental	36	37	38	39	40	41	42		
Men's suits									
American	34	36	38	40	42	44	46	48	
British	34	36	38	40	42	44	46	48	
Continental	44	46	48	50	52	54	56	58	
Men's shirts									
American	14	15	15½	16	16½	17	17½	18	
British	14	15	15½	16	16½	17	17½	18	
Continental	36	38	39	41	42	43	44	45	
Men's shoes									
American	7	7½	8	8½	9½	10	10½	11	11½
British	6	7	7½	8	9	9½	10	11	12
Continental	39	40	41	42	43	44	44	45	46

Gianni Versace 647 5th Ave (between 51st and 52nd sts) ⓣ212/317-0224, 815 Madison Ave (at 68th St) ⓣ212/744-6868.
Giorgio Armani 760 Madison Ave (at 65th St) ⓣ212/988-9191, ⓦwww.giorgioarmani.com.
Gucci 685 5th Ave (at 54th St) ⓣ212/826-2600.
Helmut Lang 80 Greene St (at Spring) ⓣ212/925-7214, ⓦwww.helmutlang.com.
Hermes 11 E 57th St ⓣ212/751-3181.
Issy Miyake 992 Madison Ave (between 77th and 78th sts).
Krizia 769 Madison Ave (between 65th and 66th sts) ⓣ212/879-1211, ⓦwww.krizia.net.
Meaghan Kinney Studio 312 E 9th St (between 1st and 2nd aves) ⓣ212/260-6329. By designing clothes with classic lines complimenting the female form, Ms Kinney has made herself a standout on 9th St.
Miu Miu 100 Prince St ⓣ212/334-5156. Gorgeous fashion for women.
Nicole Farhi 10 E 60th St (between 5th and Madison aves) ⓣ212/223-8811.
Paul Smith 108 5th Ave (at 16th St) ⓣ212/229-2471. Excellent sophisticated menswear.
Paul Stuart Madison Ave at 45th St ⓣ212/682-0320. Classic men's garb, not unlike Brooks Brothers but more stylish.
Philosophy di Alberta Ferretti 452 W Broadway (at Prince St) ⓣ212/460-5500.
Pleats Please 128 Wooster St (at Prince) ⓣ212/226-3600, ⓦwww.pleatsplease.com.
Polo Ralph Lauren 867 Madison Ave ⓣ212/606-2100 and Polo Sport Ralph Lauren, 888 Madison Ave ⓣ212/434-8000.
Prada 724 5th Ave (between 56th and 57th sts) ⓣ212/664-0010 and 841 Madison Ave (at E 70th St) ⓣ212/327-4200; 45 E 57th St (near Park Ave) ⓣ212/308-2332.
Valentino Boutique 747 Madison Ave (at 65th St) ⓣ212/772-6969.
Vivienne Tam 99 Greene St (between Prince and Spring sts) ⓣ212/966-2398.
Yohji Yamamoto 103 Grand St (at Mercer St) ⓣ212/966-9066.
Yves Saint Laurent Boutique 855 Madison Ave (between 70th and 71st sts) ⓣ212/988-3821.

Funky, Trendy, Hip

Whatever you want to call it, you know what you're looking for. Check out 7th Street and 9th Street between Third Avenue and Avenue A for a prodigious number of stores carrying the above-mentioned desirables. And definitely search through Ludlow, Mott and Elizabeth streets south of Houston.

555-Soul 290 Lafayette St ⓣ212/431-2404. A must-visit for hip-hop kids and skateboarders, this store is chockablock full of baggy pants, hats, T-shirts and bags for every B-boy and girl.

Antique Boutique 712 Broadway (at Washington Place) ⓣ212/460-8830. Ultra-hip, funkily cut, avant-garde labels for a young and moneyed crowd. Good vintage section at the back.

Big Drop 174 Spring St (between Thompson St and W Broadway) ⓣ212/966-4299. Clothes for forward-thinking women.

Calypso St Barth's 280 Mott St ⓣ212/965-0990. Forget black, color is the game here. Vibrant fashions imbued with a rich hippie aesthetic – think string bikinis at $75 a pop.

Canal Jean Co 504 Broadway (between Spring and Broome sts) ⓣ212/226-1130. Enormous warehousey store sporting a prodigious array of jeans, jackets, T-shirts, dresses, hats and more, new and secondhand. Young, fun and reasonably cheap.

Diesel Style Lab 416 W Broadway (at Spring St) ⓣ212/343-3863, ⓦwww.diesel.com. The ultra-hip top-shelf branch of this Italian chain has taken New York by storm.

Final Home 241 Lafayette St (at Spring St) ⓣ212/966-0202. Intimidatingly futuristic designs and accessories for techno beans. Mainly for the boys.

New York Firefighter's Friend 263 Lafayette (between Spring and Broome sts) ⓣ212/226-3142. Get those NY Fire Dept tees and trucks here; an NYPD section is next door.

Old Japan 382 Bleecker St (at Perry St) ⓣ212/633-0922. Gorgeous, authentic Japanese clothes and trinkets, with a fantastic selection of antique kimonos.

Patricia Field 10 E 8th St (between 5th Ave and University Place) ⓣ212/254-1699 and 382 W Broadway (between Broome and Spring sts) ⓣ212/966-4066. Touted as founder of Manhattan's most inventive clothing store, Pat Field was one of the first NYC vendors of "punk chic" and has since blossomed into one of the few downtown emporia that yuppies will actually visit.

Pierre Garroudi 139 Thompson St (between Houston and Prince sts) ⓣ212/475-2333. A limited design line with unusual fabrics, colors and styles. Bias-cut dresses, wedding gowns and tailored suits. All of the clothes are made on the premises and they can make any item for you overnight. Reasonable prices.

TG-170 170 Ludlow St (between Houston and Stanton sts) ⓣ212/995-8660, ⓦwww.tg170.com. Small, unique store featuring emerging local designers. A favorite with the East Village girls.

Trash 'n' Vaudeville 4 St Mark's Place (between 2nd and 3rd aves) ⓣ212/982-3590. Great clothes, new and "antique," in the true East Village spirit, including classic lace-up muscle shirts.

X-Large 267 Lafayette St ⓣ212/334-4480. Check out the Mini line for women, X-Large for men. Cutting-edge streetwear for B-boys and gals. Sonic Youth's Kim Gordon and the Beastie Boys' Mike D are part owners.

Vintage/secondhand

The East Village is the neighborhood for this kind of shopping. Wander back and forth along the side streets between Third Avenue and Avenue B, where the stores are too numerous to mention. But there are many good options throughout the city.

a tempo couture 290 Columbus Ave (between 73rd and 74th sts) ⓣ212/769-0368. Exquisite vintage dresses and evening gowns.

Alice Underground 481 Broadway (between Broome and Grand sts) ⓣ212/431-9067, ⓦwww.aliceundergroundnyc.com. A large assortment contained in bins you have to dig through. A good selection of vintage linens, dresses, lingerie and shoes.

Allan & Suzi 416 Amsterdam Ave (at 80th St) ⓣ212/724-7445. Beautiful far-out fashion from the last several decades. Claims to have single-handedly restarted the platform shoe craze.

Andy's Chee-pees 691 Broadway (at 3rd St) ⓣ212/420-5980. *The* place to go for those all-American bowling shirts, pump-attendant tees and beat-up denimwear.

Antique Boutique 712–714 Broadway (at Washington Place), 227 E 59th St (between 2nd and 3rd aves) ☎212/460-8830. Wedding dresses from the 40s, used Levis, suede jackets and Diesel, Betsey Johnson and Pat Field meet up at this vintage institution.

Cheap Jack's 841 Broadway (at 13th St) ☎212/777-9564. Not as cheap as it once was, but still a good and comprehensive source of used clothing and accessories.

Darrow Vintage 7 W 19th St (between 5th and 6th aves) ☎212-255-1550. Designer and never-worn vintage, with a friendly and helpful staff. Popular with top models.

The Fan Club 22 W 19th St (between 5th and 6th aves) ☎212/929-3349. An amazing selection of vintage clothes, many from movies, TV and theater, with a good supply of Marilyn Monroe frocks usually on display in the front window. The store benefits three AIDS charities.

Honeymoon Antiques 105 Ave B ☎212/477-8768. A mix of old T-shirts and vintage fashion in the heart of Alphabet City. You won't leave empty-handed.

Love Saves the Day 119 2nd Ave (at 7th St) ☎212/228-3802. Fairly cheap vintage as well as classic lunchboxes and other kitschy nostalgia items, including valuable Kiss and Star Wars dolls.

Michael's: The Consignment Shop 1041 Madison Ave (between 79th and 80th sts) ☎212/737-7273. For bridal wear as well as slightly used designer women's clothing from names like Ungaro, Armani and Chanel.

Out of the Closet 220 E 81st St ☎212/472-3573. One of the Upper East Side's most charming thrift shops, with an antique feel and a greenhouse. Established to help AIDS sufferers.

Out of Our Closet Consignment 136 W 18th St (between 5th and 6th aves) ☎212/633-6965. Specializing in top-end designers like Gucci, Prada and Helmut Lang. You can also find new clothes direct from the showroom.

Reminiscence 50 W 23rd St ☎212/243-2292. Remember the everything-with-palm-trees craze of the 1980s? Relive it here (the store's logo is a palm tree). They also carry funky secondhand and new clothes for men and women. Staples include Hawaiian shirts, tie-string overalls and tube tops.

Resurrection East 123 E 7th St (between 1st Ave and Ave A) ☎212/228-0063 and 217 Mott St ☎212/625-1374. Specializing in designer vintage (Pucci, Christian Dior) in excellent condition at reasonable prices. Attracts designers and models.

The Ritz Thrift Shop 107 W 57th St (between 6th and 7th aves) ☎212/265-4559. New York's venerable and best source for used furs, known as "The Miracle on 57th Street." Imagine, get a $15,000 mink for only $2000!

Screaming Mimi's 382 Lafayette St (between 4th St and Great Jones) ☎212/677-6464. One of the most established vintage stores in Manhattan. Vintage clothes (including lingerie), bags, shoes and housewares at reasonable prices.

Stella Dallas Look 218 Thompson St (between Bleecker and 3rd sts) ☎212/674-0447. A relatively small selection, but very nice quality vintage clothing with a beautiful selection of scarves (most $1–3). Also hand-embroidered vintage linens.

Tokio 7 64 E 7th St (between 1st and 2nd aves) ☎212/353-8443, Ⓦwww.tokio7.com. Attractive secondhand and vintage designer consignment items – a little pricier than most, but a good selection.

The Village Scandal 19 E 7th St (between 2nd and 3rd aves) ☎212/253-2002. Small and friendly shop, with fashionable clothing at decent prices.

What Comes Around Goes Around 351 W Broadway (between Broome and Grand sts) ☎212/343-9303, Ⓦwww.nyvintage.com. Established and well-loved downtown vintage store.

Thrift Stores

Decidedly cheaper and less self-consciously "cool" than vintage stores, these are the places where you have to work to find your coveted, one-off wares. Even if the clothes seem a little too Golden Girls for your taste, there's usually an excellent selection of books at around 25¢ a pop. There are tiny stores all over the city – these are some of the bigger (and more time-consuming) finds:

Domsey's 431 Kent Ave, Williamsburg, Brooklyn ☎718-384-6000, Ⓦwww.domsey.com. Discreetly embedded along the East River's decrepit warehouse district, this five-story thrift store sells everything from boutique to boot-camp salvage . . . by the pound!

Housing Works Thrift Shop 143 W 17th St (between 6th and 7th aves) ⓣ212/366-0820; 306 Columbus Ave ⓣ212/579-7566; 202 E 77th St ⓣ212/772-8461. Upscale thrift shops where you can find secondhand designer wear in very good condition. All proceeds benefit Housing Works, an AIDS social service organization.

Salvation Army Thrift Store 536 W 46th St (between 10th and 11th aves) ⓣ212/757-2311; 220 E 23rd St (between 2nd and 3rd) ⓣ212/289-9617; 208 8th Ave (at 21st St) ⓣ212/929-5214 and seven other city locations.

St George's Thrift Shop 209 E 16th St (at 3rd Ave) ⓣ212/475-5510. Smaller than most of the others, but with a high volume of cheap, good-quality tat.

St Luke's Thrift Shop 487 Hudson St (between Christopher and Grove sts) ⓣ212/924-9364. A crazy wee treasure trove of stuff.

Discount clothing

Aaron's 627 5th Ave (between 17th and 18th sts), Brooklyn ⓣ718-768-5400. This 10,000-square-foot store carries discounted designer fashions ranging from Jones New York to Adrienne Vittadini at the beginning of each season, not the end. Prices are marked down about 25 percent. It's 30 minutes from Manhattan – take the R train to Brooklyn, get off at the Prospect Ave Station/4th Ave and 17th St in Brooklyn. Walk one block east to 5th Ave.

Century 21 472 86th St (between 4th and 5th aves), Bay Ridge, Brooklyn ⓣ718/748-3266 (take the R train to 86th St and 4th Ave). A department store with designer brands for half the cost, a favorite among budget-yet-label-conscious New Yorkers. Only snag – no dressing rooms.

Daffy's Five locations in Manhattan; the biggest one is at Herald Square, 6th Ave and 34th St ⓣ212/736-4477. Name-brand clothes at discount prices for men, women and children. Specializes in Italian designers such as Les Copian.

Dave's Army & Navy Store 581 6th Ave (between 16th and 17th sts) ⓣ212/989-6444. Comes recommended as the best place to buy jeans in Manhattan. Helpful assistants, no blaring music, and brands other than just Levi's.

Filene's Basement A relative newcomer to NY's discount shopping, a favorite in the suburbs. 620 6th Ave (at 18th St) is the

Sample sales

At the beginning of each season, designers' and manufacturers' showrooms are full of **leftover merchandise** that is removed via these informal sales. You'll always save at least fifty percent off the retail price, though you may not be able to try on the clothes and you can never return them. As well, while some take credit cards, be prepared with cash. The best times for sample sales are spring and fall. Short of waiting for advertisement fliers to be stuffed into your hands while walking through the garment district, the following sources (particularly the up-to-the-minute websites) are helpful.

Daily Candy An ultra-hip, up-itself website dedicated to the spendthrift in all of us. The place to find out about coveted designs at bargain rates before the city's fashionistas commence their stampede. ⓦwww.dailycandy.com.

Nice Price 493 Columbus Ave (at 84th St) ⓣ212/362-1020. The owners of this terrific designer outlet store run regular sample sales. Pick up a printed card at the store or call their sample sale hotline ⓣ212/947-8748.

S&B Report Find out about designer showroom sales, as well as the best retail sales, and consignment and thrift shops in *Sales and Bargains* magazine. It is published monthly by NYC's other bargain expert, Elysa Lazar, whom *Redbook* magazine called "the world's smartest shopper." Send $9.95 for the month's issue that coincides with your trip to NY, or you can subscribe for $59 a year. The *Black Belt Bulletin*, which lists latebreaking sales, is $3 an issue; $124 is the yearly rate for both. Address: Lazar Media Group, Inc. 56 1/2 Queen St, Charleston, SC 29401 ⓣtoll free 1-877/579-0222, ⓦwww.lazarshopping.com.

ⓦwww.styleshop.com. This website is a goldmine of detailed information about current designer sample sales, including collections, locations and dates.

bigger one ⊕212/620-3100; another is at Broadway and 79th St ⊕212/873-8000.

Labels for Less biggest branch is at 1345 6th Ave (at 54th St) ⊕212/956-2450. The name says it all – a national chain with 13 stores in Manhattan selling discount designer labels for women.

Loehmann's biggest branch is at 101 7th Ave (between 16th and 17th sts) ⊕212/352-0856, ⊛www.loehmanns.com. New York's best-known department store for designer clothes at knockdown prices. No refunds and no exchanges, but there are individual dressing rooms. Other locations are Seaport Plaza, 2807 E 21st St, Sheepshead Bay, Brooklyn ⊕718/368-1256 and the original store at 5740 Broadway, Riverdale, the Bronx ⊕718/543-6420.

Nice Price 493 Columbus Ave (at 84th St) ⊕212/362-1020 and 134 W 37th St, 2nd floor ⊕212/947-8748. An unprepossessing boutique chock-full of overruns and factory seconds from major designers like Max Studio, whose prices drop to unbelievable lows during clearance blitzes. Nice Price also runs sample sales.

Syms 42 Trinity Place ⊕212/797-1199 and 54th St and Park Ave ⊕212/317-8200. "Where the educated consumer is our best customer."

T.J. Maxx 620 6th Ave (between 18th and 19th sts) ⊕212/229-0875. Another suburban discount chain, a lot like Filene's, and in the same shopping center.

Shoes

Most department stores carry two or more **shoe** salons – one for less expensive brands and one for finer shoes. Both Bloomingdale's and Lord & Taylor are known for their shoe departments, and Loehmann's has a vast selection of designer shoes at discount prices. You'll find shoe stores in all clothes-shopping areas, such as 34th Street, Columbus Avenue, Broadway from Astor Place to Spring Street, and Bleecker going south to Sixth Avenue. The greatest concentration of bargain shoe shops in hip fashions is on West 8th Street between University Place and Sixth Avenue in the Village and on Broadway below West 8th Street. Shoes on Sale is the largest shoe sale open to the public, with more than 50,000 pairs of shoes. It is held each year around the second week in October, in a tent in Central Park at Fifth Avenue and 60th Street. Check the newspaper for details.

Bruno Magli 777 5th Ave (at 66th St) ⊕212/752-7900, ⊛www.brunomagli.com. Elegant, comfortable and skillfully designed shoes.

Camper 125 Prince St (at Wooster) ⊕212/358-1842. Cult and no longer underground Spanish footwear, based on eccentric twists on the bowling shoe.

Charles Jourdan 612 Madison Ave ⊕212/585-2238, ⊛www.charlesjourdan.com. Outstanding French designer of fine shoes, who strikes a delicate balance between traditional and contemporary looks.

DDC Lab 180 Orchard St (at Houston St) ⊕212/375-1647. The place to go for those elusive Green Flash, Converse or other hard-to-find hip designs.

Jimmy Choo 645 5th Ave (at 51st St) ⊕212/593-0800. Popular British designer has a huge Manhattan following.

John Fluevog 104 Prince St ⊕212/431-4484, ⊛www.fluevog.com. Innovative designs for a walk about town. Mostly casual, ever-big and always hip shoes.

Juno 550 Broadway (between Prince and Spring sts) ⊕212/924-6415. High-quality imitations of designer shoes for kids.

Kenneth Cole 353 Columbus Ave (at 77th St) ⊕873-2061, ⊛www.kencole.com. Call for more locations. Classic and contemporary shoes, beautiful bags, excellent full-grain leather.

Manolo Blahnik 31 W 54th St (between 5th and 6th aves) ⊕212/582-3007. World-famous strappy stilettos – good for height (of fashion), hell for feet.

Manuela di Firenze (Maraolo) 131 W 72nd St ⊕787-6550; 782 Lexington Ave ⊕212/832-8182 and 835 Madison Ave (at 69th St) ⊕212/628-5080. Attractive, inexpensive Italian shoes in various styles. Seems to be holding a permanent clearance sale.

New Balance, New York 51 W 42nd St (at 6th Ave) ⊕212/997-9112,

The Diamond District

The strip of 47th Street between Fifth and Sixth avenues is known as the **Diamond District**. Crammed into this one block are more than 100 shops: combined they sell more jewelry than any other block in the world. The industry has traditionally been run by Hasidic Jews, and you'll run into plenty of black-garbed men with *payess* (sidelocks) in this area.

At the street level are dozens of retail shops and more than twenty "exchanges" – marts containing booths where many different dealers sell very specific merchandise. For example, 55 W 47th St is home to 115 independent jewelers and repair specialists. Lesser known is the Swiss Center at 608 5th Ave at 49th St, specializing in antique and estate jewelry and housed in an historic Art Deco building.

There are different dealers for different gems, for gold and silver – even dealers who will string your beads for you, and "findings" stores where you can pick up the basic silver makings of do-it-yourself jewelry, like chains and earring posts. Some jewelers trade only among themselves; some sell retail; and others do business by appointment only. Most shops are open Monday through Saturday 10am–5.30pm, though a few close on Friday afternoon and Saturday for religious reasons, and the standard vacation time is from the end of June to the second week in July.

It is very important that you go to the exchanges educated. Research what you are looking for and be as specific as possible. It's always better to go to someone who has been recommended to you if possible. Some good starting points are Andrew Cohen, Inc (579 5th Ave, 15th floor), for diamonds; Myron Toback (25 W 47th St), a trusted dealer of silver findings; and Bracie Company Inc (608 5th Ave, suite 806), a friendly business specializing in antique and estate jewelry. Once you buy, there's AA Pearls & Gems (10 W 47th St), the industry's choice for pearl and gem stringing; and, if you want to get your gems graded, the Gemological Institute of America (580 5th Ave, 2nd floor).

ⓦwww.newbalance.com. Super-fine sneakers guaranteed to be made in Europe or the USA, by workers paid at least that country's minimum wage.

Nine West **675 5th Ave (at 53rd St) ⓣ212/319-6893, ⓦwww.ninewest.com.** Immensely popular designer look-a-likes, often with good seasonal reductions. Call for other locations.

Otto Tootsi Plohound **137 5th Ave (at 20th St) ⓣ212/460-8650 and 38 E 57th St (near Park Ave) ⓣ212/231-3199.** If you want to run with a trendy crowd, these shoes will help. Very current designs.

Prada **45 E 57th St (between Madison and Park) ⓣ212/308-2332.** This branch of the Italian fashion police is strictly for the feet.

Salvatore Ferragamo **661 5th Ave (at 52nd St) ⓣ212/759-3822 (women's) and 725 5th Ave (at 56th St), in Trump Tower ⓣ212/759-7990 (men's).** Wonderful Italian shoes, as well as accessories and clothing.

Shoe **197 Mulberry St (at Kenmare St) ⓣ212/941-0205.** A wee gem of a store with a stock of unusual shoes from all around the world.

Sigerson Morrison **242 Mott St (at Prince St) ⓣ212/219-3893.** Kari Sigerson and Miranda Morrison make rather timeless, simple and elegant shoes for women.

Steve Madden **150 E 86th St (between Lexington and 3rd aves) ⓣ212/426-0538; 540 Broadway (near Prince St) ⓣ212/343-1800; 2315 Broadway (near 86th St) ⓣ212/799-4221 and 41 W 34th St (at 6th Ave) ⓣ212/736-3283.** Very popular copies of up-to-the-minute styles, well-loved for their ability to take on New York's "shoe-killing" streets.

Tod's **650 Madison Ave (at 59th St) ⓣ212/644-5945, ⓦwww.tods.com.** Seriously comfortable and very well-made loafers, shoes and boots; made for walking.

Unisa **701 Madison Ave (at 63rd St) ⓣ212/753-7474, ⓦwww.unisa.com.** The only retail shop for these comfortable affordable shoes imported from Spain and Brazil.

Accessories and finishing touches

As a rule of thumb you will find these accessories in major department stores and in areas where there is a high concentration of shopping such as SoHo and the Upper East Side. You can spend very little or a fortune – whatever suits you. What follows is a sampling of the best.

Bags

Fendi **720 5th Ave (at 56th St) ☎212/767-0100.** This beautifully decorated store is a treat in itself; the accessories are luxurious, unnecessary treats.

Kate Spade **454 Broome St (at Prince St) ☎212/274-1991.** All the rage for several years running, these boxy fabric bags with the little logo-label are a generic assertion of "Manhattan chic."

Manhattan Portage **242 W 30th St ☎212/594-7068; 333 E 9th St ☎212/995-5490.** The now-classic canvas messenger bag with the red skyline-printed label appeared in 1980, then these practical, rugged New York carryalls skyrocketed to chic-dom. These days, they're a bit too common to be cool.

Glasses

Alain Mikli Optique **880 Madison Ave (between 71st and 72nd sts) ☎212/472-6085.** A wide selection of European and vintage frames for men and women.

Cohen's Fashion Optical **117 Orchard St ☎212/674-1986, with branches all over town – call for locations.**

Morgenthal-Frederics **944 Madison Ave (near 75th St) ☎212/744-9444; 685 Madison Ave ☎212/838-3090 and 399 W Broadway (at Spring St).** Nice custom-made spectacles and excellent service, including emergency fittings.

Oliver Peoples **366 W Broadway (at Broome St) ☎212/925-5400 and 755 Madison Ave (at 65th St) ☎212/585-3433.** This LA cult eyewear designer's New York outpost offers understated frames for $200–400.

Robert Marc **575 Madison Ave ☎212/319-2000 and four other locations.** Exclusive New York distributor of designer frames like Lunor and Kirei Titan; also sells Retrospecs, restored antique eyewear from the 1890s to the 1940s. Very expensive and very hot.

Hair

Astor Place Hair Designers **2 Astor Place ☎212/475-9854.** People line up six deep here. They'll do any kind of unusual style, and, most important, don't cost the earth – $15 and up for a straight cut.

Chelsea Barber **465 W 23rd St ☎212/741-2254.** Bertilda "Betty" Garcia is drawing some of the glitterati away from their $300 haircuts; hers are closer to $15.

Jean Louis David **367 Madison Ave ☎212/808-9117; call for more locations.** They're everywhere if you need an inexpensive, respectable cut. You don't need an appointment but it helps.

Dramatics NYC **77 5th Ave (at 15th St) ☎212/243-0068 and seven other locations.** Their motto is "cut, shampoo and entertainment." You have been warned.

Snip 'n' Sip **204 Waverly Place ☎212/242-3880.** This cute two-chair salon filled with 1930s nostalgia is possibly the only place in the city where you can get a cut, a coke and a trip down memory lane.

Warren Tricomi **16 W 57th St ☎212/262-8899, ⓦwww.warrentricomi.com.** Super-quick and very stylish cuts from this on-the-ball salon. Cuts from $90–200.

Make-up

If you're looking for make-up lines such as Clinique, Elizabeth Arden, Bobbi Brown and the like, go to any department store, because they all have large cosmetics departments. If you are looking for something a little different check out the following:

Aveda **233 Spring St (between 6th Ave and Varick St – 7th Ave) ☎212/807-1492, ⓦwww.aveda.com.** Call for more locations.

Body Shop **747 Broadway (at 8th St) ☎212/979-2944.** Environmentally and animal-friendly products that will make you smell like fruit salad, marshmallows or cherry pie.

MAC **14 Christopher St (between 6th and 7th aves) ☎212/243-4150 and 113 Spring St ☎212/334-4641, ⓦwww.maccosmetics.com.** These cruelty-free cosmetics are hugely popular among America's models and actresses.

Make-up Forever **409 W Broadway (between Prince and Spring sts) ☎212/941-9337, ⓦwww.makeupforever.fr.** High-quality French make-up.

Mary Quant Colour Concept Shop **520 Madison Ave (at 53rd St) ☎212/980-7577, ⓦwww.maryquant.com.** Mod make-up in every conceivable shade, all with the so-cool 60s' flower motif.

L'Occitane **343 Spring St (between Wooster St and W Broadway)☎212/343-0109.** French-African soaps and bath scrubs for the spoiled little mademoiselle in your life.

Origins **402 W Broadway (at Spring St)**

☎212/219-9764, ⓦwww.origins.com. Plant-based creams, lotions and natural-look make-up. Call for other locations.

Ricky's 590 Broadway (between Houston and Prince sts) ☎212/226-5552 and four other Manhattan locations. New York's haven of the overdone, the brash and the OTT. Also stocks cool brands such as Urban Decay and Tony & Tina. Think drag, darling.

Sephora 555 Broadway ☎212/625-1309 and 636 5th Ave (at 51st St) ☎212/245-1633. Breathtaking "warehouse" of perfumes, make-up and body-care products. You have to see (or smell) it to believe it.

Shu Uemura 121 Greene St (at Prince St) ☎212/979-5500. Elegant make–up with an Oriental influence.

Sporting goods

The **sporting goods** scene is dominated by chains such as Foot Locker, The Athlete's Foot, Sports Authority and Modell's, though there are a few other options – "theme park" sports clothes stores, as well as stores tightly focused on one sport. Use them for merchandise as well as a wealth of information about that sport in NY.

Superstores

Niketown 6 E 57th St (between 5th and Madison aves) ☎212/891-6453, ⓦwww.nike.com. You can enter this sneaker temple through Trump Tower, literally hearing crowds cheer as you pass through the door. Every 30 minutes, a screen descends the full five stories of the store and shows Nike commercials. The tons of memorabilia relate most notably to Michael Jordan. Oh, and you can also purchase Nike clothing and accessories at full price.

Reebok Store 160 Columbus Ave ☎212/595-1480. This is the flagship Reebok store, although there is an outlet at Chelsea Piers. Not as dazzling as Niketown, but it does show ads on two big screens, houses the Reebok Sports Club and features European Reebok lines not found anywhere else in the States.

Specialty stores

Bicycle Habitat 244 Lafayette St ☎212/431-3315. This unassuming store is frequented by bike messengers. Buy a bike here, and they'll service your brakes forever.

Bicycle Renaissance 430 Columbus Ave (at 81st St) ☎212/724-2350. A classy place with competitive prices, custom-bike building and usually same-day service. Trek and Cannondale bikes and Campagnolo and Shimano frames in stock.

Blades, Board & Skate 120 W 72nd St (between Broadway and Columbus Ave) ☎212/787-3911 and five other locations, including one in the Manhattan Mall. Rent or buy rollerblades, snowboards and the like.

Eastern Mountain Sports (EMS) 20 W 61st St (between Broadway and Columbus Ave) ☎212/397-4860 and 611 Broadway (at Houston St) ☎212/505-9860, ⓦwww.emsonline.com. Top-quality merchandise covering almost all outdoor sports, including skiing and kayaking.

Mason's Tennis Mart 56 E 53rd St ☎212/755 5805. New York's last remaining tennis specialty store – they let you try out all racquets.

Paragon Sporting Goods 867 Broadway (at 18th St) ☎212/255-8036, ⓦwww.paragonsports.com. Family-owned, with three levels of general merchandise.

Soccer Sport Supply Company 1745 1st Ave (between 90th and 91st sts) ☎212/427-6050. Half-century-old international soccer and rugby supply company with a professional staff.

Super Runners Shop 1337 Lexington Ave (at 89th St) ☎212/369-6010; 360 Amsterdam Ave (at 77th St) ☎212/787-7665 and 416 3rd Ave (at 29th St) ☎212/213-4560. Experienced runners work at all four locations; co-owner Gary Muhrcke won the first NYC Marathon in 1970.

The World of Golf 147 E 47th St (between Lexington and 3rd aves) ☎212/755-9398. Known for their large selection and discounts.

Food and drink

Food – the buying as much as the consuming of it – is a New York obsession. Nowhere do people take eating more seriously than in Manhattan, and there's no better place in the world to shop for food. Where to buy the best bagels, who stocks the widest – and weirdest – range of cheeses, are questions that occupy New Yorkers a disproportionate amount of time. The proliferation of delis boasting diverse fresh salad bars packed to overflowing (and selling beautiful flowers on the side) will confirm for you that America is indeed the Land of Plenty. More sophisticated places, gourmet or specialty shops for example, will be enough to make you swoon – and new ones are opening every day in affluent neighborhoods.

The listings below, while comprehensive, are by no means exhaustive. Wander the streets and you'll no doubt uncover plenty more besides. If you're after drink, remember that you can only buy liquor – ie, wines, spirits or anything else stronger than beer – at a liquor store, and that you need to be 21 or over to do so.

Supermarkets, delis and greengrocers

For the most general food requirements, there are a number of supermarket chains that pop up all over the city. Big Apple, Sloan's, Gristedes and Food Emporium you'll find pretty much everywhere; D'Agostino and Whole Foods tend to appear in the fancier neighborhoods. In addition, many of the department stores listed on pp.405–406 – principally Macy's and Bloomingdale's – have food halls.

On a smaller scale, delis and greengrocers sell basic food and drink items, as well as sandwiches and coffee to take away, and sometimes hot ready meals and the chance to dip into a salad bar. You should never have to walk more than a couple of blocks to find one, and most are open late or all night.

Gourmet markets

In the late seventies there were three: Balducci's in the Village, Dean and Deluca in SoHo, and Zabar's on the Upper West Side. But in recent years new gourmet markets have glutted the scene. A step up from delis, they are gloriously stocked places, selling all manner of choice edible items in a super-abundant environment that will make your taste buds jump.

Agata & Valentina 1505 1st Ave (at 79th St) ⓣ212/452-0690. A spinoff of Balducci's (see below); very classy, with an authentic Sicilian atmosphere.

Around the Clock Center, Chelsea Market 75 9th Ave (between 15th and 16th sts) ⓣ243-6005. A complex of eighteen former industrial buildings, among them the late-19th-century Nabisco Cookie Factory. A true smorgasbord of stores, including Amy's Bread, Bowery Kitchen Supplies, the Chelsea Wholesale Flower Market, the Chelsea Wine Vault, Hale & Hearty Soups, the Lobster Place and the Manhattan Fruit Exchange.

Balducci's 424 6th Ave (between 9th and 10th sts) ⓣ212/673-2600, ⓦwww.balducci.com. The long-time rival of the Upper West Side's Zabar's, this is a family-run store that's no less appetizing – though some say it's slightly pricier.

Citarella 2135 Broadway (at 75th St) and 1313 3rd Ave (at 75th St); both ⓣ212/874-0383. Famous fish store gone full-service gourmet market (see also p.418).

Dean and Deluca 560 Broadway (between Prince and Spring sts) ⓣ212/226-6800. One of the original big neighborhood food emporia. Very chic, very SoHo and not at all cheap. There's also a café on Prince St.

EAT Gourmet Foods 1064 Madison Ave (at 80th St) ⓣ212/772-0022. A brother to Zabar's (and run by Eli Zabar, brother of Zabar's owner; see below), and packed with gourmet delights. Try the wonderful Eli's bread. Like Dean and Deluca, it has its own "Gourmet Café" next door. .

Eli's Manhattan 1411 3rd Ave (at 80th St) ☎212/717-8100. A slick, expensive counterpoint to Zabar's, run by Eli Zabar, owner of EAT.

Faicco's 260 Bleecker St (between 6th and 7th aves) ☎212/243-1974. Very authentic Italian deli. Specializing in sausages and other pork products.

Fairway 2127 Broadway (between 74th and 75th sts) ☎212/595-1888. Long-established Upper West Side grocery store that for many locals is the better-value alternative to Zabar's. They have their own farm on Long Island, so the produce is always fresh, and their range in some items is enormous. Fantastic organic selection upstairs.

Fine & Schapiro 138 W 72nd St (between Broadway and Columbus Ave) ☎212/877-2874. Excellent, principally kosher, meals to go and renowned sandwiches and cold meats. Also a restaurant – see p.343.

Garden of Eden 162 W 23rd St (between 6th and 7th aves) ☎212/675-6300 and 310 3rd Ave ☎212/228-4627. Foodie treats and gourmet picnic fare; the olive and pickle bar is a treat.

Gourmet Garage 453 Broome St (at Mercer) ☎212/941-5850; 301 E 64th St ☎212/535-5880; 2567 Broadway ☎212/663-0656 and 117 7th Ave ☎212/699-5980. Excellent value on cheeses, olives, produce and ready-made sandwiches. Purveyors to *Le Cirque 2000* and *The Four Seasons*.

Grace's Marketplace 1237 3rd Ave (at 71st St) ☎212/737-0600. Gourmet deli offspring of Balducci's that is a welcome addition to the Upper East Side food scene. An excellent selection of just about everything.

Grand Central Market Main Concourse, Grand Central Station (Lexington Ave and 43rd St). A traveler's dream: fresh fruit, fish, salads and meats for that long journey ahead.

Russ & Daughters 179 E Houston St (between Allen and Orchard sts) ☎212/475-4880. Technically, this store is known as an "appetizing" – the original Manhattan gourmet shop, set up about 1900 to sate the appetites of homesick immigrant Jews, selling smoked fish, caviar, pickled vegetables, cheese and bagels. This is one of the oldest.

Schaller & Weber 1654 2nd Ave (between 85th and 86th sts) ☎212/879-3047. Culinary heart of the Upper East Side's now sadly diminished German-Hungarian district of Yorkville, this shop is a riot of cold cuts, salami and smoked meats. Not for vegetarians.

Todaro Brothers 555 2nd Ave (between 30th and 31st sts) ☎212/532-0633. An excellent selection of imported and domestic gourmet foods, plus a bakery.

Zabar's 2245 Broadway (between 80th and 81st sts) ☎212/787-2000. The apotheosis of New York food-fever, Zabar's run by Saul Zabar, is still the city's most eminent foodstore. Choose from an astonishing variety of cheeses, cooked meats and salads, fresh baked bread and croissants, excellent bagels, and cooked dishes to go. Upstairs, shop for shiny kitchen and household implements to help you put it all together at home; there are often good bargains on electric items like fans and European coffee-makers. Not to be missed.

Bakeries and patisseries

From Italian cakes to Hungarian pastries, New York's **bakeries and patisseries** offer an alluring range of baked goods.

Balthazar p.304.
Ceci-Cela p.303.
Cupcake Café p.309.
Damascus Bakery p.312.
Ecce Panis p.310.
Ferrara's p.303.
H&H Bagels p.307.
Hungarian Pastry Shop p.310.
Kossar's p.303.
Little Pie Company p.309.
Magnolia Bakery p.305.
Moishe's Homemade Kosher Bakery p.306.
Once Upon a Tart p.305.
Payard Patisserie p.311.
Sticky Fingers p.306.
Taylor's p.306.
Veniero's p.306.
Yonah Schimmel's p.303.
Zito's p.306.

Cheese and dairy

Alleva Latticini **188 Grand St (at Mulberry St) ☎212/226-7990.** Oldest Italian cheesery in America; also a grocer. Makes own smoked mozzarella and ricotta.

Di Paolo's Dairy Store **206 Grand St (at Mott St) ☎212/0226-1033.** A wide array of different cheeses, including fresh Italian dairy varieties made on the premises. Very high quality.

East Village Cheese **40 3rd Ave ☎212/477-2601.** A huge, but not particularly exotic selection at bargain-basement prices.

Ideal Cheese Shop **1205 2nd Ave (between 63rd and 64th sts) ☎212/688-7579.** A fine cheese emporium.

Joe's Dairy **156 Sullivan St (between Houston and Prince sts) ☎212/677-8780.** Family store considered New York's best bet for fresh mozzarella in several varieties.

Murray's Cheese Shop **257 Bleecker St (between 6th and 7th aves) ☎212/243-3289.** A variety of more than 300 fresh cheeses and excellent fresh panini sandwiches, all served by knowledgeable staff. Free tastings on Saturday afternoons.

Fish and seafood

Barney Greengrass **541 Amsterdam Ave (between 86th and 87th sts) ☎212/724-4707.** "The Sturgeon King" – an Upper West Side smoked-fish brunch institution since 1908 that also sells brunch-makings to go.

Caviarteria **502 Park Ave (enter on 59th St between Park and Madison aves) ☎212/759-7410 and 310 W Broadway ☎212/925-5515.** Mainly caviar – more than a dozen varieties – and a stock of smoked fish and patés. Tasting bars, too.

Central Fish Company **527 9th Ave (between 39th and 40th sts) ☎212/279-2317.** Friendly, knowledgeable staff, stocks 35 species, including fresh Portuguese sardines and live carp, at any given time – and at very reasonable prices.

Citarella **2135 Broadway (at 75th St) ☎212/874-0383).** The largest and most varied fish and seafood source in the city, now with gourmet baked goods, cheese, coffee, meat and prepared food. Still, the specialty is seafood; there's a wonderful bar serving prepared oysters, clams and the like to take away. Famous for its artistic window displays, which make graceful use of squid.

Fulton Fish Market For New York's freshest fish if you're up at 5am (see p.72). The market itself is a lively affair to visit.

Murray's Sturgeon Shop **2429 Broadway (between 89th and 90th sts) ☎212/724-2650 and 38 E 9th St (between 5th and Madison aves) ☎212/473-3000.** Another popular Upper West Side haunt, this place specializes in smoked fish and caviar. The downtown branch is equally fine.

Petrossian **182 W 58th St (at 7th Ave) ☎212/245-2214.** This well-known shop imports only the finest Russian caviar, alongside a range of other gourmet products – smoked salmon and other fish mainly – as well as pricey implements to eat it all with. Quite the most exclusive place to shop for food in town, and with a restaurant attached to complete the experience.

Health food, vegetarian and spice shops

Angelica's Herbs & Spices **147 1st Ave (at 9th St) ☎212/529-4335.** An excellent selection of herbs, tinctures, spices and books.

Aphrodisia **264 Bleecker St (between 6th and 7th aves) ☎212/989-6440.** For herbs, spices and seasoning oils only, this place is hard to beat.

Bell Bates Natural Food Market **97 Reade St (at Hudson St) ☎212/267-4300.** Manhattan's largest health food store.

Commodities Natural Foods **117 Hudson St (between N Moore and Franklin sts) ☎212/334-8330 and 165 1st Ave (at 9th St) ☎212/260-2600.** The Hudson Street branch is huge, and has a health food café.

Good Food Co-op **58 E 4th St.** Cooperatively run but open to the public. Full market with a good amount of organic food.

Healthy Pleasures **93 University Place (between 11th and 12th sts) ☎212/353-3663; 489 Broome St (between W Broadway and Wooster St) ☎212/431-7434 and 2493 Broadway (between 92nd and 93rd sts).** These giant stores have juice bars, incredible salad-bar selections and all manner of healthy delights. The bottom floor of the Broadway branch is entirely kosher.

Kalustyan's **123 Lexington Ave (between 28th and 29th sts) ☎212/685-3451.** The best of the groceries in the tiny Little India district of Manhattan. Good spice selection.

Integral Yoga Natural Foods 229 W 13th St ☎212/243-2642. This popular store has a wide range of fresh, organic vegetables and buy-in-bulk grains, nuts and seeds.
Prana 125 1st Ave (between St Mark's and 7th St) ☎212/982-7306. Good value, friendly wholefood shop where you can make your own peanut butter.

Ice cream and frozen yogurt

Two national chains have largely divided the city's appetite for ice cream and frozen yogurt between them: Baskin-Robbins and the considerably better Häagen-Dazs; frozen yogurt mega-chain TCBY ("The Country's Best Yogurt") has only a few Manhattan locations (check Yellow Pages for addresses).

Die-hard New York ice-cream freaks swear by a few smaller operators, though in the ultra-competitive marketplace that is Manhattan a number have melted away. Ben & Jerry's (222 E 86th St; 680 8th Ave at 43rd St; 41 3rd Ave between 9th and 10th sts; Bryant Park kiosk at 42nd St and 6th Ave; and Rockefeller Center) still gives the impression of being the jolly place it set out to be, even if it's resolutely more commercial – and their esoteric ice cream and frozen yogurt flavors are hard to beat. Chelsea Baking and Ice Company at 259-263 W 19th St (between 7th and 8th aves) offers 100 flavors of ice cream, 20 of gelati and 80 sorbets. Emack & Bolio's, inside Macy's and at 389 Amsterdam Ave (between 78th and 79th sts) serves up delicious Bostonian ice cream and frozen yogurt. The Chinatown Ice Cream Factory (65 Bayard St, south of Canal between Mott and Elizabeth sts) serves up tasty and exotic flavors like mango, green tea and lychee. Vegetarians are urged to try Michael and Zoe's (2nd Ave between 5th and 6th sts), where you can get a totally vegan and very delicious tofu ice-cream fix in chocolate or vanilla, and then choose your own "mix-ins" from a selection of fresh fruit, candy and nuts.

Sweets, nuts and chocolate

Bazzini 339 Greenwich St (at Jay St) ☎212/334-1280. Nice selection of expensive gourmet nuts and sweets in all shapes and sizes, but a far cry from the unpretentious wholesaler it used to be.
Bespeckled Trout 422 Hudson St (at St Luke's Place) ☎212/255-1421. Wonderful old-fashioned candy shop with jars of colorful sweets and rows of homemade lollypops.
Economy Candy 108 Rivington St (between Essex and Ludlow sts) ☎212/254-1832. A candy junk shop on the Lower East Side, selling tubs of sweets, nuts and dried fruit at low prices.
Elk Candy Co 1628 2nd Ave (between 84th and 85th sts) ☎212/650-1177. A Yorkville candy store selling Yorkville-style candies – rich and marzipaned.
Godiva 701 5th Ave (between 54th and 55th sts) ☎212/593-2845. This renowned Belgian chocolatier has branches all over Manhattan – unbeatable for satisfying anyone's chocolate craving.
Leonidas 485 Madison Ave (between 51st and 52nd sts) ☎212/980-2608. The only US franchise of the famous Belgian confectioner.
Lexington Candy Shop 1226 Lexington Ave (between 83rd and 84th sts) ☎212/288-0057. The best place in the city for that New York sickly stalwart, egg cream made from scratch.
Li-Lac 120 Christopher St (between Hudson and Bleecker sts) ☎212/242-7374. Delicious chocolates that have been handmade on the premises since 1923, including fresh fudge and hand-molded Liberties and Empire States. One of the city's best treats for those with a sweet tooth.
Neuchatel 2 W 59th St (inside Plaza Hotel) ☎212/751-7742 and 60 Wall St ☎212/480-3776. Hand-made Swiss chocolates, made on the premises and at a price. Try the truffles for a true taste of Alpine heaven.
Teuscher 620 5th Ave (between 49th and 50th sts) ☎212/246-4416 and 25 E 61st St (at Madison Ave) ☎212/751-8482. Upper East Side Swiss chocolate importer renowned for its beautifully presented truffles.
Treat Boutique 200 E 86th St (at 3rd Ave) ☎212/737-6619. Six different kinds of homemade fudge and a broad selection of dried fruit and nuts.

Tea and coffee

Empire Coffee and Tea Co 568 9th Ave (between 41st and 42nd sts) ⓣ212/268-1220. This store for the serious addict has been fueling New York's caffeine habits since 1908.

McNulty's 109 Christopher St (between Bleecker and Hudson sts) ⓣ212/242-5351. Expensive personalized coffee blends and a wide selection of teas, since 1895.

Oren's Daily Roast 31 Waverly Place (between University and Greene sts) ⓣ212/420-5958; call for other locations along the East Side. Among the best – and the freshest – beans in the city.

Porto Rico Importing Company 201 Bleecker St (between 6th Ave and McDougal St) ⓣ212/477-5421; 40 1/2 St Mark's Place (off 2nd Ave) and 107 Thompson St (between Prince and Spring sts). Best for coffee, and local rumor has it that the house blends are as good as many of the more expensive coffees. The Thompson St branch has a smaller selection and is primarily a café.

Sensuous Bean of Columbus Avenue 66 W 70th St (just off Columbus Ave) ⓣ212/724-7725. Mostly coffee, with some tea.

Liquor stores

Prices for all kinds of liquor are controlled in New York State and vary little from one shop to another. However, a number of places either have a particularly good selection or tend to be a touch less expensive. They are listed here. A state law forbids the sale of hard liquor and wine on Sundays; supermarkets may sell beer, but not wine or spirits.

Acker, Merrall & Condit 160 W 72nd St (between Broadway and Columbus Ave) ⓣ212/787-1700. The oldest wine store in America, founded in 1820, has a very wide selection from the US, especially California.

Astor Wines and Spirits 12 Astor Place (at Lafayette St) ⓣ212/674-7500. Manhattan's best selection and some of the city's most competitive prices. Good kosher and organic wine section.

Best Cellars 1291 Lexington Ave (between 86th and 87th sts) ⓣ212/426-4200. Wine store with 100 carefully chosen selections, each for under $10, and a very knowledgeable staff.

Chelsea Wine Vault 75 9th Ave (in Chelsea Market) ⓣ212/462-4244. These incredibly knowledgeable folk will sell, store and even teach you about wine.

Cork & Bottle 1158 1st Ave (between 63rd and 64th sts) ⓣ212/838-5300. Excellent selection; deliveries, too.

Garnet Wines & Liquors 929 Lexington Ave (at 68th St) ⓣ212/772-3211. Possibly the city's most inexpensive source for specialty wines.

Morrell & Co 535 Madison Ave (between 54th and 55th sts) ⓣ212/688-9370. One of the best selections of good-value wine in town.

Nancy's Wines For Food 313 Columbus Ave (between 74th and 75th sts) ⓣ212/877-4040. An excellent array of wines to impress at any dinner party.

Schapiro's 126 Rivington St (between Essex and Norfolk sts) ⓣ212/674-4404. Kosher wines made on the premises. Free tours of the cellars, with wine tasting, Sun 11am–4pm on the hour. Closed Sat, and closes two hours before sunset on Fri.

Schumer's Wine & Liquors 59 E 54th St (between Park and Madison aves) ⓣ212/355-0940. Stays open until midnight Fri & Sat, and will also deliver. Extensive range.

Sherry-Lehmann 679 Madison Ave ⓣ212/838-7500. New York's foremost wine merchant.

SoHo Wines and Spirits 461 W Broadway (between Houston and Prince sts) ⓣ212/777-4332. Well-stocked SoHo liquor store, renowned for its selection of Scotch.

Union Square Wines & Spirits 33 Union Square (between 16th and 17th sts) ⓣ212/675-8100. A well-chosen, wide-ranging selection of quality wines.

Warehouse Wines and Spirits 735 Broadway (between 8th and Waverly) ⓣ212/982-7770. The top place to get a buzz for your buck, with a wide selection and frequent reductions on popular lines.

Books

Book lovers bemoan the steady disappearance of New York's independent bookstores, and attribute their loss to the phenomenon of Barnes & Noble superstores, where you can settle in comfortably at the table-filled café and use the place as your personal library-cum-newsstand. But there's still a fantastic selection of **books** in New York, and niches such as mystery or art books are flourishing. New or secondhand, US or foreign, there's little that isn't available somewhere.

Superstores and chains

Barnes & Noble has created book department stores with temptingly comfortable chairs and nice views. Many have *Starbucks* cafés, making them either an all-American fun haven or an atmosphereless exercise in multinational consumerist hell, depending on your politics. But there's no question that their enormous stock makes it likely you'll find what you're looking for and, because Barnes & Noble made its reputation as a discount bookstore, bargains are common. Presentations by authors take place about five evenings a week. Many branches are open from 9am to midnight daily. The store at 105 5th Ave (at E 18th St) ☎212/807-0099 claims to be "The World's Largest Bookstore" and concentrates on college textbooks. There are 12 superstores in Manhattan: **4 Astor Place (at Broadway and Lafayette St) ☎212/420-1322; 385 5th Ave (at 36th St) ☎212/779-7677; 675 6th Ave (at W 22nd St) ☎212/727-1227; 600 5th Ave (at W 48th St) ☎212/765-0592; Citicorp Building at E 54th St and 3rd Ave ☎212/750-8033; 750 3rd Ave (at 47th St) ☎212/697-2251; 2289 Broadway (at W 82nd St) ☎212/362-8835; 240 E 86th St (at 2nd Ave) ☎212/794-1962; 1280 Lexington (at E 86th St) ☎212/423-9900; 1972 Broadway (across from Lincoln Center) ☎212/595-6859; 396 6th Ave (Greenwich Village) ☎212/674-8780 and 33 E 17th St (Union Square) ☎212/253-0810.**

Borders Books and Music **461 Park Ave (at 57th St) ☎212/980-6785 and 550 2nd Ave (at 32nd St) ☎212/685-3938.** This Ann Arbor-based chain rivals Barnes & Noble for selection, if not saturation.

Tower Books **383 Lafayette St (at 4th St) ☎212/228-5100.** The literary arm of Tower Records, next door, focuses on pop culture, music, travel and film. Magazines too.

General interest and new books

Bookberries **983 Lexington Ave (at 71st St) ☎212/794-9400.** Classic uptown New York bookstore with a fine selection of literature.

Coliseum Books **1771 Broadway (at 57th St) ☎212/757-8381.** Very large store, good on paperbacks and academic books.

Corner Bookstore **1313 Madison Ave (at 93rd St) ☎212/831-3554.** Upscale bookstore with an excellent literature selection in a lovely atmosphere.

Gotham Book Mart **41 W 47th St ☎212/719-4448.** In the heart of the Diamond District, this jewel has focused since 1920 on the creative arts, stocking both new publications and out-of-print books – as well as smuggling in banned titles like *Tropic of Cancer* and displaying the artwork of the likes of Edward Gorey. Tennessee Williams, e e cummings, Saul Bellow and Anaïs Nin are among this store's past habitués.

Papyrus **2915 Broadway (at 114th St) ☎212/222-3350.** New and used titles, especially good on literature and textbooks. Many of their film, literature and political philosophy titles have a left-wing slant.

Posman Books **9 Grand Central Terminal at 42nd St ☎212/983-1111.** An excellent selection of books for journeys.

St Mark's Bookshop **31 3rd Ave (between 8th and 9th sts) ☎212/260-7853.** Wonderfully eclectic selection of new titles from mainstream to way alternative; see p.424 for more.

Shakespeare & Co **939 Lexington Ave (at 69th st) ☎212/570-0201; 716 Broadway and Washington Place ☎212/529-1330; 137 E 23rd St ☎212/570-0201 and 1 Whitehall St ☎212/742-7025.** New and used books, paper and hardcover. Great for fiction and psychology. There's also a branch in Brooklyn, at the Brooklyn Academy of Music.

Three Lives & Co **154 W 10th St and Waverly Place ☎212/741-2069.** Excellent literary bookstore that has an especially good selection of books by and for women, as well as general titles. There's an excellent reading series in the fall.

Secondhand books

A neighborhood to browse through for book bargains is centered on Fifth

Avenue and 18th Street; also in the area, the Metropolitan Book Auction sells fine and rare used books – they're on the 4th floor at 123 W 18th St; call ☎212/929-4488 for schedule.

Academy Book Store 10 W 18th St (between 5th and 6th aves) ☎212/242-4848. Small shop carries used, rare and out-of-print books.

Argosy Bookstore 116 E 59th St (between Lexington and Park aves) ☎212/753-4455. Unbeatable for rare books, it also sells clearance books and titles of all kinds, though the shop's reputation means you may find mainstream works cheaper elsewhere.

Gryphon Bookshop 2246 Broadway (between 80th and 81st sts) ☎212/362-0706. Used and out-of-print books, records, CDs and laser discs. Art books, illustrated books and antique children's books. Watch out for overpriced titles, of which there are a good few. There's also the Gryphon Record Shop at 233 W 72nd St, 2nd floor ☎212/874-1588 (see p.425).

Housing Works Used Books Café 126 Crosby St (between Houston and Prince sts) ☎212/334-3324. Very cheap books, comfy and spacious. Proceeds benefit AIDS charity.

Ruby's Book Sale 119 Chambers St ☎212/732-8676. City Hall Park's used bookstore, dealing especially in paperbacks and ancient dog-eared magazines. Excellent value.

Strand Bookstore 828 Broadway (at 12th St) ☎212/473-1452; annex at 95 Fulton St ☎212/732-6070. With about eight miles of books and a stock of 2.5 million+, this is the largest book operation in the city – and one of the few survivors in an area once rife with secondhand book stores. There are recent review copies and new books for half price; older books go for anything from 50¢ up. Also imports British remainders.

Special interest bookstores

New York has many stores specializing in books on a particular area, from travel and art to more arcane subjects. The following is a selective list.

Travel

The Civilized Traveler 2003 Broadway (between 68th and 69th sts) ☎212/875-0306; 864 Lexington Ave (at 65th St) ☎212/288-9190 and 1 E 59th St ☎212/702-9502. Small selection of guidebooks, plus luggage, magazines and other travel accessories.

The Complete Traveler 199 Madison Ave (at 35th St) ☎212/685-9007. Manhattan's premier travel bookshop, excellently stocked, new and secondhand – including a huge collection of Baedekers.

Rand McNally Map and Travel Store 150 E 52nd St (between Lexington and 3rd aves) ☎212/758-7488 and 555 7th Ave ☎212/944-4477. As much a map shop as a place for guidebooks, run by the major map and atlas publisher, with maps of all the world and detailed ones of New York State and City – along with luggage and other travel gear.

Art and architecture

Hacker Art Books 45 W 57th St (between 5th and Madison aves) ☎212/688-7600, ⓦwww.hackerartbooks.com. Rare and out-of-print art books, artists' books and fine bindings line the shelves of this half-century-old New York institution.

Urban Center Books 457 Madison Ave (between 50th and 51st sts) ☎212/935-3592. Architectural book specialists with a very helpful staff.

Photography, cinema, theater and music

Applause Theater & Cinema Books 211 W 71st St (at Broadway) ☎212/496-7511, ⓦwww.applausebooks.com. Theater, film, television, screenplays of films – some books that are unavailable elsewhere. New and used.

Drama Bookshop 723 7th Ave (between 48th and 49th sts), on second floor ☎800-322-0595, ⓦwww.dramabookshop.com. Theater books, scripts and publications on all manner of drama-related subjects.

Juilliard Bookstore 60 Lincoln Center Plaza ☎212/799-5000, ⓦbookstore.juilliard.edu. An absolute must for lovers of classical music and opera.

Richard Stoddard Performing Arts Books 41 Union Square W (at 17th St and Broadway), room 937 ☎212/645-9576. Purchase a playbill from

Broadway's yesteryear hits; they have a good out-of-print theater book selection.

Crime

Black Orchid 303 E 81st St ☎212/734-5980. secondhand and new novels.

Murder Ink 2486 Broadway (between 92nd and 93rd sts) ☎212/362-8905, ⓦwww.murderink.com. The first bookstore to specialize in mystery and detective fiction in the city, and the oldest mystery bookstore in the world. It's still the best, billed as stocking every murder, mystery or suspense title in print, and plenty out.

Mysterious Bookshop 129 W 56th St (between 6th and 7th aves) ☎212/765-0900, ⓦwww.mysteriousbookshop.com. The founder of this store started Mysterious Press (now owned by Warner Books). Signed first editions of new and used titles.

Partners in Crime 44 Greenwich Ave ☎212/243-0440. Crime novels. Also home to the Cranston and Spade Theater Co., which performs classic radio scripts from the 1940s on the first Saturday night of the month.

Sci-fi and comics

Forbidden Planet 840 Broadway (at 13th St) ☎212/473-1576. Science fiction, fantasy and horror fiction, graphic novels and comics. T-shirts and the latest toys and collectibles, including Star Wars and Star Trek paraphernalia.

St Mark's Comics 11 St Mark's Place (between 2nd and 3rd aves) ☎212/598-9439. Tons of comic books, including underground comics; well known for their large stock. Action figures, trading cards and a whole room of back issues.

Village Comics 215 Sullivan St (between Bleecker and W 3rd sts) ☎212/777-2770, ⓦwww.villagecomics.com. Old and new books, limited editions, trading cards, action figures and occasional celebrity appearances. Highly recommended.

Language and foreign

Kinokuniya Bookstore 10 W 49th St (at 5th Ave) ☎212/765-7766. The largest Japanese bookstore in NY, with English books on Japan, too.

Liberation Bookstore 421 Lenox Ave (at 131st St) ☎212/281-4615. Works from Africa and the Caribbean.

Librairie de France/Libreria Hispanica/The Dictionary Store 610 5th Ave (in the Rockefeller Center Promenade) ☎212/581-8810. Small space housing a wealth of French and Spanish books, a dictionary store with 8000 dictionaries of more than 100 languages and a department of teach-yourself language books, records and tapes.

Rizzoli 31 W 57th St (between 5th and 6th aves) ☎212/759-2424 and 434 W Broadway. Manhattan branches of the prestigious Italian bookstore chain and publisher, specializing in European publications, with a selection of foreign newspapers and magazines.

Spirituality

Christian Publications Bookstore 315 W 43rd St (between 8th and 9th aves) ☎212/582-4311. New Christian titles, as well as classics, greeting cards, Christian merchandise; Spanish books as well.

East West Books 78 5th Ave (between 13th and 14th sts) ☎212/243-5994. Bookstore with a mind, body and spirit slant. Eastern religions, New Age and health and healing.

J. Levine Jewish Books and Judaica 5 W 30th St (between 5th and 6th aves) ☎212/695-6888, ⓦwww.levinejudaica.com. The ultimate Jewish bookstore.

Logos Bookstore 1575 York (between 83rd and 84th sts) ☎212/517-7292. Christian books and gifts.

West Side Judaica 2412 Broadway (between 88th and 89th sts) ☎212/362-7846. Books about Judaism, with funky menorahs for sale on the side.

Gay and Lesbian

See "Gay and Lesbian New York," Chapter 34, for more options.

Creative Visions/Gay Pleasures 548 Hudson St (at Perry St) ☎212/645-7573. A community bookstore stocking more than 5000 gay, lesbian, bisexual and transgender titles. There's also a gay and lesbian video rental club.

Oscar Wilde Memorial Bookshop 15 Christopher St (between Gay St and Greenwich Ave) ☎212/255-8097, ⓦwww.oscarwildebooks.com. Aptly situated gay and lesbian bookstore – probably the first in the city – with extensive rare book collection, signed and first editions and framed signed letters from authors, including Edward Albee, Gertrude Stein, and Tennessee Williams.

Radical/Alternative

Bluestockings 172 Allen St (at Stanton St) ☎212/777-6028, ⓦwww.bluestockings.com. New and used titles, authored by or related to women only. Cozy well-stocked collective-style store in what was once a dilapidated crack house; nice café, too.

Ideal Book Store 547 W 110th St, 2nd floor (at Broadway) ☎212/662-1909, ⓦwww.idealbooks.com. Considered by some to have the best philosophy collection in New York. Most books gently used.

Incommunicado/Soft Skull Press 107 Norfolk St (between Delancy and Rivington sts) ☎212/473-9530. Inside *Tonic*, a Lower East Side jazz and electronica venue, this independent bookstore sells books by Incommunicado Press, Soft Skull and 24 other indie presses. Wonderful selection of alternative literature.

Revolution Books 9 W 19th St ☎212/691-3345. New York's major left-wing bookshop and contact point. A wide range of political and cultural books, pamphlets and periodicals. Get their take on current human-rights and globalization controversies.

St Mark's Bookshop 31 3rd Ave (between 8th and 9th sts) ☎212/260-7853. Largest and best-known "alternative" bookstore in the city, with a good array of titles on politics, feminism, the environment and literary criticism, as well as more obscure subjects. Good postcards, too, and one of the best places to buy radical and art magazines. Factory-chic interior. Open until midnight.

Miscellaneous

Audiobook Store 125 Maiden Lane (between Broadway and Church St) ☎212/248-7800. Specializes in fiction and business titles. The biggest books-on-tape selection in New York.

Biography Bookshop 400 Bleecker St (at 11th St) ☎212/807-8655. Letters, diaries, memoirs.

Books of Wonder 16 W 18th St (between 5th and 6th aves) ☎212/989-3270. A heavenly collection of literature for kids.

Cookbooks 488 Greenwich St (between Spring and Houston sts) ☎212/226-5731. Cozy SoHo bookstore that specializes in out-of-print and antiquarian cookbooks.

Center for Book Arts 28 W 27th St (between 5th and 6th aves), 3rd floor ☎212/481-0295. Not so much a bookstore as a space dedicated to the art of bookmaking. Hosts regular readings and workshops – fascinating stuff.

Kitchen Arts & Letters 1435 Lexington Ave (at 94th St) ☎212/876-5550. Cookbooks and books about food, run by a former cookbook editor.

Labyrinth Books 536 W 112th St ☎212/865-1588. Largest scholarly bookstore east of the Mississippi, with an eclectic international fiction section.

Military Bookman 29 E 93rd St (between Madison and 5th aves) ☎212/348-1280, ⓦwww.militarybookman.com. Historical aspects of war, as well as fiction and strategy.

See Hear Fanzines Magazines & Books 59 E 7th St ☎212/505-9781. Great 'zines and small press books, mostly about music and radical culture.

Music

While the top music megastores in New York are the British chain HMV, Tower Records and the Virgin Megastore, specialty pop music stores are clustered in the East and West villages, with particularly cheap used bargains available around St Mark's Place.

Chains

HMV 2081 Broadway ☎212/721-5900. The most pleasant and most fun of the megastores. Also at 86th St and Lexington Ave ☎212/348-0800; 34th and 6th Ave (Herald Square) ☎212/629-0900 and 46th St and 5th Ave ☎212/681-6700.

J&R Music World 23 Park Row (between Beekman and Anne sts) ☎212/238-9000. A large downtown store with a decent selection and good prices. Also at 535 W

116th St near Columbia University ⓣ212/222-3673.

Record Explosion **142 W 34th St (between 6th and 7th aves) ⓣ212/714-0450.** A smaller chain but with more Manhattan locations – check phone book for addresses.

Tower Records **20 E 4th St (at Lafayette St) ⓣ212/505-1500; 692 Broadway (at 4th St) ⓣ212/505-1500; 1961 Broadway (at 66th St) ⓣ212/799-2500 and 725 5th Ave (between 56th and 57th sts in Trump Tower) ⓣ212/838-8110; 383 Lafayette St (ⓣ212/228-1500).**

Virgin Megastore **1540 Broadway (at 45th St) ⓣ212/921-1020 and 52 E 14th St (Union Square) ⓣ212/598-4666.**

Special interest and secondhand

Bleecker Bob's **118 W 3rd St (at McDougal St) ⓣ212/475-9677.** Long-established record store specializing in punk and new wave that is more of a gimmicky, tourist rip-off these days.

Breakbeat Science **181 Orchard St ⓣ212/995-2592, ⓦwww.breakbeatscience.com.** Breakbeat Science was the first drum'n'bass-only store to open in the US.

Dance Trax **91 E 3rd St (at 1st Ave) ⓣ212/260-8729.** Gold mine for techno, house and other forms of electronic music on vinyl.

Etherea **66 Ave A (between 4th and 5th sts) ⓣ212/358-1126.** Specializing in indie rock and electronica; domestic and imports, CDs and vinyl, this is one of the best shops in the city. Good used selection and sweet, obsessive staff.

Fat Beats **406 6th Ave, 2d floor (between 8th and 9th sts) ⓣ212/673-3883.** The name says it all. It's The Source for hip-hop on vinyl in New York City.

Footlight Records **113 E 12th St (between 3rd and 4th aves) ⓣ212/533-1572, ⓦwww.footlight.com.** The place for show music, film soundtracks and jazz. Everything from Broadway to Big Band, Sinatra to Merman. A must for record collectors.

Generation Records **210 Thompson St (between Bleecker and W 3rd sts) ⓣ212/254-1100.** The focus here is on hardcore, metal and punk with some indie. New CDs and vinyl upstairs, used goodies downstairs. It also gets many of the imports the others don't have, plus good bootlegs and a ginger giant masquerading as the store cat.

Gryphon Record Shop **251 W 72nd St (between Broadway and West End Ave), 2nd floor ⓣ212/874-1588.** Specializes in rare LPs.

House of Oldies **35 Carmine St (between Bleecker St and 6th Ave) ⓣ212/243-0500, ⓦwww.houseofoldies.com.** Just what the name says – oldies but goldies of all kinds. Vinyl only.

Kim's **6 St Mark's Place (between 2nd and 3rd aves) ⓣ212/598-9985; 144 Bleecker St (at LaGuardia St) ⓣ212/260-1010 and 350 Bleecker (at 10th St) ⓣ212/675-8996.** Extensive selection of new and used indie obscurities on CD and vinyl, some real cheap. Esoteric videos upstairs. Staff has a serious attitude problem.

Other Music **15 E 4th St (between Broadway and Lafayette St) ⓣ212/477-8150, ⓦwww.othermusic.com.** Around the corner from Tower, this is an excellent spot for "alternative" CDs, both old and new, that can be hard to find. Stocking less indie on vinyl than they once did, and now leaning toward experimental and electronica, they retain the same ever-friendly and knowledgeable staff.

Second Coming **235 Sullivan St (between W 3rd and Bleecker sts) ⓣ212/228-1313.** The place to go for heavy metal and punk.

Shrine **441 E 9th St (between 1st Ave and Ave A) ⓣ212/529-6646.** Collectible rare rock on vinyl. Primarily 1960s and 1970s garage and psychedelic bands you've never heard of.

Sonic Groove **41 Carmine St ⓣ212/675-5284, ⓦwww.sonicgroove.com.** Obscure electronica and underground techno and trance, on vinyl, for all you would-be deejays.

Temple Records **29 Ave B (between 2nd and 3rd sts) ⓣ212/475-7552.** Owned by New York's DJ Khan, this absolute temple to techno spans Detroit to Berlin and is mostly on 12" vinyl. Understandably, then, it's frequented by local DJs who line up at the stack of turntables to pre-hear their wares.

Throb **311 E 14th St (between 2nd and 3rd aves) ⓣ212/533-2328, ⓦwww.throb.com.** Like the name implies, they carry techno, electronica, jungle, hip-hop, etc; they also have a good selection of hardcore records. Turntable is available for previewing selections.

Vinyl Mania **60 Carmine St (between Bleecker St and 6th Ave) ⓣ212/924-7223.** This is where DJs come for the newest, rarest releases, especially of dance music. Hard-to-find imports too, as well as homemade dance tapes.

Musical instruments and accessories

New York's heaviest concentration of **musical instrument stores** is on one block of West 48th Street between Sixth and Seventh avenues. The best are **Manny's** at 156 ⓣ212/819-0576; **Rudy's Music Stop** at 169 ⓣ212/391-1699, ⓦwww.rudysmusic.com; **Alex Musical Instruments** at 165 ⓣ212/819-0070; and **Sam Ash Music** at 160 ⓣ212/719-2299, ⓦwww.samashmusic.com. The five adjacent buildings carry all instruments, recording equipment, music-driven software and sheet music.

A treat for guitar lovers, though harder to get to, is **Mandolin Brothers** at 629 Forest Ave on Staten Island ⓣ718/981-8585, ⓦwww.mandoweb.com, which has one of the world's best collections of vintage guitars. Their stock is half vintage, half new. Easier to reach is **Guitar Salon** 45 Grove St (near 7th Ave and Bleecker St, by appointment only) ⓣ212/675-3236, ⓦwww.theguitarsalon.com. Owner Beverly Maher appraised Segovia's guitars before donating them to the Metropolitan Museum in 1987, and sells handmade classical and flamenco guitars.

Drummer's World, at 151 W 46th St ⓣ212/840-3057, is a drummer's paradise, and carries ethnic instruments as well as drum kits.

Sheet music

Colony Record & Radio Center **1619 Broadway (at 49th St) ⓣ212/265-2050.** Printed sheet music and hard-to-find records.

Sam Ash Music **(see above).**

Art supplies

Lee's Art Shop **220 W 57th St (near Broadway) ⓣ212/247-0110.** A good art supply store, used by students at the Art Students League down the street.

Pearl Paint Company **308 Canal St (between Church St and Broadway) ⓣ212/431-7932.** A likely contender for the title of "World's Largest Art Supply Store." Housed in a jolly old red-and-white warehouse in the heart of Chinatown, Pearl has five floors of competitively-priced artists' supplies, including fabric paint and airbrushing and silkscreening supplies.

Sam Flax **425 Park Ave (at 55th St) ⓣ212/620-3060 and 12 W 20th St ⓣ212/620-3038 or 1-800-628-9512, ⓦwww.samflax.com.** Another well-stocked art store.

Pharmacies and drugstores

There's a **pharmacy** or **drugstore** every few blocks in New York, and during the day it shouldn't be too difficult to find one. If you can't, the *Yellow Pages* has complete listings of places selling medicines and toiletries, listed under "Pharmacies." Most pharmacies are open roughly Monday to Saturday 9am–6pm, though many are also open on Sunday in busy shopping or residential neighborhoods. Corner delis carry some basic necessities; although you will pay more, they are great for late-night needs.

Everywhere

Duane Reade A massive chain of drugstores that has cornered the market on discount medicines, toiletries, cigarettes and basic stationery over much of Manhattan, especially midtown – and absorbed a lot of local pharmacies in the process. There are a good sixty stores and counting, many of them open 24 hours a day. If you need a pharmacy, this is probably where you'll find yourself. Other drugstore chains are **CVS** (the best national chain), **Genovese**, **McKay**, **Rite-Aid** (another extensive one) and **Value Drugs**. Check exact locations in the phone book.

Specialty and independent pharmacies

The following **specialty pharmacies** are worth the visit even if you do not need medical products or cosmetics.

Bigelow Pharmacy **414 6th Ave (between 8th and 9th sts) ☎212/533-2700.** Established in 1882, this is the oldest apothecary in the country – and that's exactly how it looks, with the original Victorian shopfittings still in place. Specializes in homeopathic remedies. Open seven days a week.

Caswell-Massey Ltd **518 Lexington Ave (at 48th St) ☎212/755-2254.** The oldest pharmacy in America, and a national chain, selling a shaving cream created for George Washington and a cologne blended for his wife, as well as more mainstream items.

Kiehl's **109 3rd Ave (between 13th and 14th sts) ☎212/677-3171, ⓦwww.kiehls.com.** An exclusive 150-year-old pharmacy, decorated with the family collection of aviation and motorcycle memorabilia, which sells its own range of natural ingredient-based classic creams, oils, etc. If you're too strapped to buy, try to accumulate some free samples.

L'Occitane **1046 Madison Ave ☎212/639-9185; 198 Columbus Ave ☎212/362-5146; 146 Spring St ☎212/343-0109 and 10 E 39th St (at 5th Ave) ☎212/696-9098.** Call the 39th St HQ for more locations. The perfumes of Provence at more reasonable prices than you'll find in France. Bath and beauty products.

Antiques

New York is the premier antique source in the country, excellent for browsing, with museum-quality pieces available as well as lots of interesting, fairly priced stuff at the junkier end of the market, though top quality articles cost an absolute fortune. Sections of the city with a concentration of antique shops are the East Village and West Village, SoHo, Chelsea, Lower Broadway and the Upper East Side. Lafayette Street, from SoHo to just above Houston Street, has become a prime spot for finding early-twentieth-century American design, and a handful of indoor and outdoor junk shops on East Houston Street (between Lafayette and the Bowery) have eclectic furniture from various funky eras, and even masonry for sale.

The Village and around

Furniture Joint **182 Ave B (between 11th and 12th sts) ☎212/598-4260.** Musty, dingy and totally divine antiques from another era somewhere in deepest Africa.

Susan Parrish **390 Bleecker St (between Perry and W 11th sts) ☎212/645-5020.** Americana and Indian art.

Victor Carl Antiques **74 E 11th St ☎212/673-8740.** This breathtaking shop carries antique lighting, marble fireplaces and more.

White Trash **304 E 5th St (at 2nd Ave) ☎212/598-5956.** A cornucopia of 1950s and 1960s kitsch.

SoHo

Chameleon **231 Lafayette St ☎212/343-9197.** Interesting collection of antique lighting fixtures dating from the nineteenth century to the 1960s. Many from New York residences.

Cobweb Imports **440 Lafayette St (at Cooper Square) ☎212/505-1558.** Tiled tables, iron beds and cabinets from southern Europe, Egypt, Morocco, Indonesia and Argentina.

Elan **345 Lafayette St (between Bleecker and 2nd sts) ☎212/529-2724.** Twentieth-century furniture, specializing in Art Nouveau and Art Deco.

Historical Materialism **125 Crosby St ☎212/431-3424.** Eclectic decorative antiques and unique objects from the 1870s to the 1920s.

Urban Archeology **285 Lafayette St ☎212/431-6969.** Large-scale accessories and furniture, mainly American turn-of-the-century, often rented out for film sets. Great place for browsing.

Chelsea

Annex Antiques Fair and Flea Market **on 6th Ave between 25th and 26th sts.** The biggest antiques fair in the city – with several hundred dealers of furniture, rugs, collectibles, photos and more – is the hub of a major antiques neighborhood. Admission $1. Open every Sat and Sun, year-round. Look one block north, between 26th and 27th sts, for another large weekend flea market, and on Sun you'll find more spillover on 26th St and on 24th St between 6th Ave and Broadway. And in a parking lot on 7th Ave between 25th and 26th sts, there's the junk-sale Chelsea Flea Market, where the pickings aren't quite as good.

Chelsea Antiques Building **110 W 25th St (between 6th and 7th aves) ☎212/929-0909.** Better quality, better condition and higher prices than above listings. 150 dealers on 12 floors offer exceptional estate treasures and collectibles. Open Mon–Fri 10am–6pm, Sat–Sun 8.30am–6pm.

The Garage **112 W 25th St (between 6th and 7th aves).** Just a block away from the Annex Antiques Fair is this market in a parking garage. In the basement level and first floor are 150 dealers – check out the great vintage eyeglass frames.

Metropolitan Arts and Antiques Pavilion **110 W 19th St (between 6th and 7th aves) ☎212/463-0200.** Open a few times a month for special-interest auctions and fairs ranging from vintage fashion to antique toys.

The Showplace **40 W 25th St (between 6th Ave and Broadway) ☎212/741-8520.** Indoor market of more than 100 dealers of antiques and collectibles plus an espresso bar. Mon–Fri 9am–6pm, Sat & Sun 8.30am–5.30pm.

The Upper East Side

56th Street Art & Antiques Center **160 E 56th St ☎212/755-4252, Ⓦwww.artantiques.com.** Three levels of antique furniture, paintings, objets d'art and more.

Christie's **20 Rockefeller Plaza (49th St between 5th and 6th aves) ☎212/636-2000 and Christie's East, 219 E 67th St ☎212/606-0400, Ⓦwww.christies.com.** The premier British auction house. You can attend an auction even if you don't bid, but expect a clipped reception regardless. Busy times are fall and spring. For schedule of auctions or catalogue, call ☎1-800/395-6300. Catalogues $20–75. Seating is first-come, first-served; for evening auctions make reservations.

Manhattan Art and Antiques Center **1050 2nd Ave (at 55th St) ☎212/355-4400.** About 70 dealers, spread over three floors, stocking a vast assortment of goodies – everything from American quilts to Oriental ceramics, with an emphasis on small items. The quality is very good, and the ambience approaches that of a museum.

Newel Art Galleries **425 E 53rd St (east of 1st Ave) ☎212/758-1970.** Dazzle your eyes browsing this six-floor collection of one-of-a-kind big pieces – many for rent.

Sotheby's **1334 York Ave at 72nd St. Mon–Sat 10am–5pm, Sun 1–5pm; closed summer. ☎212/606-7000, Ⓦwww.sothebys.com.** The premier US auction house and rival of Christie's. Come in for a copy of *Preview Magazine*, which gives the auction schedule for 2–3 months – but watch out for snippy staff with a short fuse. Previews are 3–5 days beforehand; reservations are required for some evening auctions. Watch for more affordable Arcade Auctions. Catalogues $15–40.

Electronic and video equipment

The sole reason to buy **electronic and video goods** in New York is if you are visiting from Europe, where such merchandise is more expensive. The place for risky discount shopping is Sixth and Seventh avenues a little north of Times Square in the 50s, where a number of stores sell cameras, stereo equipment, radios and the like. For **cameras**, anywhere in midtown from 30th to 50th streets between Park and Seventh avenues is the patch. You'll be offered different prices depending on whether you buy the equipment with or without a guarantee (ask for the price with guarantee to prevent any misunderstanding), and it's no use going into a shop without an *exact* idea of the model you want. Be on your guard for fake equipment (usually easily spotted) or inferior products that have had the labels of better makes carefully and illegally applied.

Traditional retailers

B&H Photo Video 420 9th Ave (between 33rd and 34th sts) ☎212/444-5041. For films, cameras and specialty equipment; knowledgeable sales help will take the time to guide you through a buying decision. Excellent used goods selection upstairs. Closed Sat.

Bang & Olufsen 952 Madison Ave (at 75th St) ☎212/879-6161. Incredibly good, high-quality audio and some video, in sleek modern Danish design.

CompUSA 420 5th Ave ☎212/627-0222 and 1775 Broadway ☎212/262-9711. This superstore runs a computer camp for kids, offers training for adults, and carries the largest inventory in the city.

DataVision 445 5th Ave ☎212/689-1111. Superstore filled with computer and video equipment.

Grand Central Camera 420 Lexington Ave (at 44th St) ☎212/986-2270. Huge selection, and the staff speak several languages.

Harvey Electronics 2 W 45th St (at 5th Ave) ☎212/575-5000. Top-of-the-line equipment, sold by experts.

J&R Music and Computer World 15–23 Park Row (between Beekman and Ann sts) ☎212/238-9000. In this store down by City Hall, you'll find a good selection with good prices for stereo and computer equipment.

Miscellaneous

The shops below are either offbeat and interesting to visit or sell useful items that are cheaper in New York than elsewhere.

ABC Carpet and Home 888 Broadway (at 19th St) ☎212/473-3000. Six floors of antiques and country furniture, knick-knacks, linens and carpets, of course. The grandiose, museum-like setup is half the fun. Wander to garner decorating ideas.

Body Worship 102 E 7th (between 1st Ave and Ave A) ☎212/614-0124. Fetish fashion and erotica, as attested by the shapely phallic door handle. Get your latex and corsets here. Some of their window displays qualify as art.

Condomania 351 Bleecker St (at W 10th St) ☎212/691-9442. A store for the AIDS-conscious millennium. Condoms in all shapes, sizes, colors and flavors. Some are for jokes but most are to use.

Enchanted Forest 85 Mercer St (between Spring and Broome sts) ☎212/925-6677. Truly lives up to its name: a veritable magic jungle with a plank bridge and a whimsical collection of toys, books, gems and folk art. Perfect for big (and little) kids.

Hammacher Schlemmer 147 E 57th St (between Lexington and 3rd aves) ☎212/421-9000. Established in 1848, and probably New York's longest-running trivia store. Unique items, both practical and whimsical. Claims to be the first store to sell the pop-up toaster.

J&R Tobacco Corp 564 5th Ave ☎212/983-4160 and One Wall St ☎212/233-6620. Self-proclaimed largest cigar store in the world, with an enormous – and affordably priced – range including all the best-known (and some not so known) brands.

Kate's Paperie 561 Broadway (between Prince and Spring sts) ☎212/941-9816; 8 W 13th St (between 5th and 6th aves) ☎212/633-0570 and 1282 3rd Ave ☎212/396-3670. Any kind of paper you could imagine or want. 22,000 square feet of paper in stock from 30 different countries, including great handmade and exotic paper. If you can't find something – ask. They'll even custom-make paper for you.

Little Rickie 49 1/2 1st Ave (at 3rd St) ☎212/505-6467. A selection of kitsch: "Church of Elvis" fridge magnets, plastic nativity scenes for the dashboard, etc.

Maxilla & Mandible 451 Columbus Ave (between 81st and 82nd sts) ☎212/724-6173. Animal and human bones for collectors, scientists or the curious. Worth a visit even if you're not in the market for a perfectly preserved male skeleton.

New York Yankees Clubhouse Shop 8 Fulton St ☎212/514-7182. In case you want that "NY" logo on all your clothing.

Our Name is Mud 1566 2nd Ave (between 81st and 82nd sts) ☎212/570-6868 and 59 Greenwich Ave ☎212/647-7899. You can buy beautiful handmade pottery here, even an unfinished vessel to paint with your own personal design.

Pink Pussycat Boutique 167 W 4th St (between 6th and 7th aves) ☎212/243-0077. All manner of sex toys and paraphernalia. Somewhat of a Village institution.

The Sharper Image inside Pier 17 at South Street Seaport ☎212/693-0477; 900 Madison Ave ☎212/794-4974; 4 W 57th St (between 5th and 6th aves) ☎212/265-2550 and 50 Rockefeller Plaza ☎646/557-0861. Expensive novelty items for yuppies – talking alarm clocks, massage devices and the sort of stuff you find in little catalogues that drop out of Sunday newspaper supplements. Classy meets bratty here, but the latest techno-gizmos always impress.

Tiny Doll House 1179 Lexington Ave (between 80th and 81st sts) ☎212/744-3719. Everything to put in a doll's house – from curtains to teapots to people – plus a variety of houses – and DIY kits. Beautiful.

Village Chess Shop 230 Thompson St (between W 3rd and Bleecker St) ☎212/475-8130. Every kind of chess set for every kind of pocket. Usually packed with people playing. Open until midnight.

Markets

New York's **markets** are a treat – though not as much of an institution or as grand as European outdoor markets. However, they take the cake as far as the rest of the United States is concerned. Produce is always top-quality, there's a lot of organic food available, and bargains are common.

Where to find greenmarkets

Manhattan

Bowling Green at Broadway and Battery Place Thurs 8am–5pm, year-round.
City Hall at Chambers and Centre sts Tues & Fri 8am–3pm, year-round.
Washington Market Park at Greenwich and Reade sts Wed 8am–3pm, year-round.
Federal Plaza at Broadway and Thomas sts Fri 8am–4pm, year-round.
Lafayette Street at Spring St Thurs 8am–5pm, July–Oct.
Tompkins Square at 7th St and Ave A Sun 10am–5pm, year-round.
St Mark's Church at E 10th St and 2nd Ave Tues 8am–7pm, June–Dec.
Abingdon Square at W 12th St and 8th Ave Sat 8am–3pm, May–Dec.
Union Square at E 17th St and Broadway Mon, Wed, Fri & Sat 8am–6pm, year-round.
Sheffield Plaza at W 57th St and 9th Ave Wed & Sat 8am–6pm, year-round.
Verdi Square at 72nd St and Broadway Sat 8am–5pm, June–Dec.
I.S. 44 at W 77th St and Columbus Ave Sun 10am–5pm, Fri 8am–2pm, year-round.
P.S. 234 at Greenwich & Chamber sts, Sat 8am–3pm.
W 97th St between Amsterdam and Columbus aves Fri, June–Dec.
W 144th St and Lenox Ave Tues 8am–3pm, July–Oct.
W 175th St at Broadway Thurs 8am–6pm, July–Dec.

Bronx

Lincoln Hospital at E 149th St and Park Ave Tues & Fri 8am–3pm, July–Oct.
Poe Park E 192nd St and Grand Concourse Tues 8am–2pm, July–Nov.

Brooklyn

Albee Square at Fulton St and DeKalb Ave Wed 8am–3pm, July–Oct.
Bedford-Stuyvesant at Nostrand and DeKalb aves Sat 8am–3pm, July–Oct.
Borough Hall at Court and Remsen sts Tues & Sat 8am–6pm, year-round.
Grand Army Plaza at entrance to Prospect Park Sat 8am–4pm, year-round.
McCarren Park at Lorimer and Driggs aves Sat 8am–3pm, June–Nov.
Williamsburg at Havemeyer St and Broadway Thurs 8am–5pm, July–Oct.
Windsor Terrace at Prospect Park W and 15th St Wed 8am–4pm, year-round.

Queens

Jackson Heights at Junction Blvd and 34th Ave Wed 8am–3pm, July–Oct.

Staten Island

St George at St Mark's and Hyatt sts Sat 8am–2pm, June–Nov.

Greenmarkets

Several days each week, long before sunrise, hundreds of farmers from Long Island, the Hudson Valley and parts of Pennsylvania and New Jersey set out in trucks transporting their fresh-picked bounty to New York City, where they are joined by bakers, cheesemakers and others at **green-markets**. These are run by the city authorities, roughly one to four days a week between June and December. Usually you'll find apple cider, jams and preserves, flowers and plants, maple syrup, fresh meat and fish, pretzels, cakes and breads, herbs, honey – just about anything and everything produced in the rural regions around the city – not to mention occasional live worm composts and baby dairy goats.

To find the greenmarket nearest to you, call ⓣ212/477-3220, or see the box opposite.

Flea markets and craft fairs

New York flea markets are outstanding for funky and old clothes, collectibles, lingerie, jewelry, crafts; there's also any number of odd places – parking lots, playgrounds, or maybe just an extra-wide bit of sidewalk – where people set up to sell their wares. In spring and summer especially you can make a mesmerizing Saturday of neighborhood market strolling.

Below 23rd Street

Avenue A Flea Market **11th St and Ave A.** A random selection of everything under the sun, weekends 10am–6pm.

Essex Street Covered Market **on Essex St between Rivington and Delancey sts. Mon–Fri 9am–6pm.** In an old municipal building you'll find a kosher fish market along with Latino groceries and a Chinese greenmarket, reflecting the diverse neighborhood. Also jewelry and clothes.

SoHo Antiques and Collectibles Fair **Broadway and Grand St. Sat & Sun 9am–5pm.** Collectibles and crafts.

SoHo Flea Market **503 Broadway (between Spring and Broome sts). Sat, Sun & holidays 10am–6pm.** Not as established as Tower Market – in fact, it can be very slow.

Tower Market **Broadway between W 4th and W 3rd sts. Sat & Sun 10am–7pm.** House music, jewelry, clothes, woven goods from South America, New Age paraphernalia and the like.

23rd to 59th streets

Annex Antiques Fair and Flea Market **6th Ave at 26th St. Sat & Sun 10am–6pm.** Surrounded by antique shops, this is the fastest-growing fair in New York with 600 vendors. Four other locations within two blocks. Admission $1. (See p.427 for more detailed information.)

Columbus Circle Market **58th St and 8th Ave. Seven days a week, 11am–7pm.** More than twenty stalls in a convenient location – lots of jewelry and a small homemade food area.

Fifth Avenue Pavilion **5th Ave and 42nd St. Mon–Fri 11am–7pm, Sat & Sun noon–6pm.** Was under a tent, now has a small, crowded building to house 25 vendors – a mix of world crafts and NY souvenirs.

Grand Central Crafts Market **main waiting room, off 42nd St and Park Ave entrance.** Christmas and spring seasons, with the best of New York shops displaying their wares. At other times, check out this beautifully renovated space, often used for offbeat art exhibits.

Above 59th Street

Antique Flea and Farmers Market **PS 183, E 67th St between 1st and York aves. Sat 6am–6pm.** Usually about 150 indoor and outdoor stalls of fresh food, odd antiques and needlework.

Green Flea I.S. 44 Flea Market **Columbus Ave at 77th St. Every Sun 10am–6pm.** One of the best and largest markets in the city; antiques and collectibles, new merchandise and a farmers market.

Malcolm Shabazz Harlem Market **116th St between Lenox and 5th aves. Daily 8am–9pm.** Bazaar-like market, with an entrance marked by colorful fake minarets. A dazzling array of West African cloth, clothes, jewelry, masks, Ashanti dolls and beads. Also sells leather bags, music and Black Pride T-shirts.

37

Sports and outdoor activities

It's no surprise that New York is the number one **sports** city in America. TV stations cover most regular-season games and all post-season games in the big four American team sports – **baseball**, **football**, **basketball** and **ice hockey**. If you want to watch a game, bear in mind that some tickets can be hard to find, some impossible, and most don't come that cheap. Remember, also, that bars – and specifically **sports bars** – are a good alternative to actually being there, especially those with king-sized screens. (See box on p.438 for listings.)

Many **participatory activities** in the city are free or affordable. You can **swim** either at the local pools or the borough beaches, usually for a small fee; **jog**, still one of the city's main obsessions; or join a pick-up **soccer** game on the Great Lawn in Central Park on summer Sundays. However, it is hard to find facilities for some sports, such as tennis, if you are neither a club member nor a city resident. Many New Yorkers spend about $100 a month to be members of private health clubs. For anyone interested, these places fill sizable sections in the city's *Yellow Pages*.

Spectator sports

In this section we've included details on the main **spectator sports** and the teams that represent New York.

Baseball

In the early 1840s, the New York Knickerbocker Club played "base ball" in the northeast part of Madison Square, in Manhattan, before moving to Elysian Fields, across the Hudson River in Hoboken, New Jersey. There, on June 26, 1846, they laid down the basic rules (the Knickerbocker Rules) of the game of **baseball**, as it is played to this day.

For half a century, New York was home to three Major League Baseball (MLB) teams: the New York Giants and Brooklyn Dodgers representing the National League and the **New York Yankees** representing the American League. In addition, in the years before integration, the Negro League had several notable teams based in the Metropolitan area – the New York Lincoln Giants, the Royal Brooklyn Giants, the New York Black Yankees and the Newark Eagles.

The Golden Age of New York baseball was the decade following World War II. Between 1947 and 1956, the Yankees faced the Dodgers six times and the Giants once in the World Series. The city still bears the scars from the Giants' and Dodgers' bolt to California after the 1957 season. New York was bereft of a National League franchise until the **Mets** arrived at the Polo Grounds in 1962, from where they would move, in 1964, to Shea Stadium in Flushing, Queens.

From April to September, each MLB team plays 162 games before two rounds of October playoffs set the stage for the World Series – a best-of-seven series between the champions of the two leagues.

New York Yankees

Reciting the achievements of the **Yankees** (also lovingly called the Bronx Bombers) over the decades can get tedious after a while. They are a team with the most World Series titles (through the year 2000, 26), the most players in the Baseball Hall of Fame, the most Most Valuable Player awards, and the statistics just keep going. The 2000 Yankees were victorious over their city rivals the Mets in a five-game "Subway Series" and, back in 1998, reached a record-breaking 125 victories.

Ticket prices: $8–65; for details on Yankee Stadium and buying tickets, see p.440.

New York Mets

While the 2000 Yankees were lengthening their historical timeline, the **Mets** were there, too – albeit on the losing end of the first "Subway Series" since 1956. The Mets have been on a roller-coaster ride ever since the lovably inept Mets team of 1962 matured into the 1969 World Series champions, and then took a nose dive from their second World Series win in 1986 to the "worst team money can buy" in the early 1990s. Only time and payroll will tell what's in store for the team down the road.

Ticket prices: $12–33; for details on Shea Stadium and buying tickets, see p.440.

Staten Island Yankees

The 1999 season saw the birth of the first new local baseball franchise in several decades: the minor-league **Staten Island Yankees**, who play in the Class A New York–Penn League. They play at the new Richmond County Bank Ballpark at St George, within walking distance of the Staten Island Ferry Terminal, a location providing a great view of Lower Manhattan and the Statue of Liberty.

Yankee Stadium

The home of the New York Yankees, **Yankee Stadium** in the Bronx, has witnessed more than a few awe-inspiring moments since it was consecrated with a home run by Babe Ruth on opening day in 1923. In football, "the greatest game ever played" took place here between the New York Giants and the Baltimore Colts in December 1958 – a televised National Football League championship game that went into a dramatic overtime and helped legitimize and popularize (American) football from that day forth. On June 22, 1938, black heavyweight champion Joe Louis knocked out Hitler's National Socialist hero Max Schmeling in the first round. In baseball alone, certain images from the stadium, recycled over and over, take root in the memories of sports fans nationwide: Babe Ruth tip-toeing daintily around the bases after yet another majestic clout, Joe DiMaggio's phenomenal 56-game hitting streak and his effortless grace in center field, Mickey Mantle's awesome power and the dying Lou Gehrig's July 4, 1939 farewell to the game, in which he declared himself "the luckiest man on the face of the earth."

The season runs from mid-June to early September. It's fun to check out if you're in the area. Call ⓣ718/720-9265 for tickets and information.

Ticket prices: $6–10.

Brooklyn Cyclones

In 2001 baseball returned to Brooklyn after a 43-year absence in the form of the **Brooklyn Cyclones**. The Class A New York–Penn League affiliate of the Mets is sponsored by KeySpan Corporation, which has provided major funding for the new stadium at the former Steeplechase Park. Call ⓣ718/449-8497 for schedule and tickets.

Ticket prices: $6–10.

Football

The **National Football League (NFL) season** stretches from September to the end of December, when the playoffs begin and decide the two teams from the AFC and NFC that will play in the Super Bowl, typically on the fourth Sunday in January. New York's teams are the **Jets** and the **Giants**; both play at **Giants Stadium**, part of the Meadowlands Sports Complex in New Jersey. Although tickets are sold out for both teams well in advance, if you're willing to pay the price you can often buy tickets outside the stadium before the game (from scalpers or extra-ticket holders).

New York Giants

With a 20-year waiting list for season tickets, the franchise that lost the first ever NFL Championship game (to the Chicago Bears) must be doing something right. Since they were founded in 1925, the **Giants** have won four NFL and two Super Bowl championships in 1987 and 1991. They also hold the record for the most championship losses ever (including the loss to the Baltimore Ravens in the 2001 Super Bowl) and are the only team to twice fail to make the playoffs in the season immediately following a Super Bowl victory.

Ticket prices: $45 and $50; for details on Giants Stadium and buying tickets, see p.440.

New York Jets

Founded in 1960 as part of an upstart American Football League, the **Jets**, originally known as the Titans, has yet to find a home of its own. The team shared Shea Stadium in Flushing, Queens, with the Mets for a while (close proximity to La Guardia Airport inspired the nickname) before relocating, in 1984, to the Jersey suburbs as tenants of the New York Giants. The Jets' 16–7 Super Bowl III victory in 1969 (following the 1968 regular season) was particularly significant in that it earned respect for the fledgling AFL and set the stage for the creation of the National Football League as it is today.

Ticket prices: $40 and $50; for details on Giants Stadium and buying tickets, see p.440.

Professional basketball

Basketball is perhaps the most popular American game outside the US. Played over 48 minutes (at the pro level), the game is conducted at a blistering pace. Because the clock runs only when the ball is in play, a game generally lasts about two hours.

The National Basketball Association's regular season begins in November and runs through the end of April. The NBA playoffs begin with the eight best teams in each conference qualifying, and culminate in a best-of-seven finals between the Eastern and Western Conference champions, around the middle of June. The two professional teams in the New York area are the **New York Knicks** (Knickerbockers), who play at Madison Square Garden, and the **New Jersey Nets**, whose venue is the Continental Airlines Arena at the Meadowlands Sports Complex in New Jersey.

New York Knicks

Its not easy being a **Knicks** fan. Madison Square Garden must be one of the ugliest structures in North America (and to build it, one of the city's architectural treasures, Penn Station, was razed); the last championship was way back in 1973 (though the Knicks consistently make the playoffs); and after all that – tickets are expensive and impossible to come by. This in part explains the celebrity quotient: nothing else seems to attract the rich and famous like Knicks basketball, and spectators can usually count on the attendance of Spike Lee, Woody Allen, Sarah Jessica Parker and a contingent of Baldwin brothers. Meanwhile, the vast majority of fiercely loyal and racially diverse fans can only dream of attending a game in person. Still, with such favorites as Latrell Sprewell, Marcus Camby and Allan Houston, it's even harder *not* to be a Knicks fan. Ticket prices constantly vary.

Ticket prices: $10–60 (though actual courtside seats on "celebrity row" run into the thousands); for details on Madison Square Garden and buying tickets, see p.440.

New Jersey Nets

The **Nets** began life, in 1967, as the New Jersey Americans, a founding franchise of the rogue American Basketball Association. At one point in their early history, they decked themselves out in patriotic red, white and blue, to match the ABA's funky, psychedelic ball. Led by the legendary Julius Irving (Dr J), they won two championships (1974 and 1976) before joining the NBA. Since then they've been rather less successful and, of late, appear to be in a perpetual rebuilding mode. In 2001, Nets management swapped Brooklyn playground legend Stephon Marbury, acquired only two years before, for Jason Kidd of the Phoenix Suns. Will the Nets rise again? The city will be watching.

Ticket prices: $30–75; for details on Continental Airlines Arena and buying tickets, see p.440.

New York Liberty

The Women's National Basketball Association season opens when the NBA season ends and runs through the summer to its playoffs in September. The league jumped off in 1997, with the New York team, the **Liberty**, finishing as runners-up for the title. Games are at Madison Square Garden, and prices are a bargain compared with those for the Knicks. Watch for their name players, guard Teresa Weatherspoon and center Tari Phillips. Also, while many games have near sell-out crowds, you can usually get a ticket; call ⓣ1-877/WNBA-TIX or pick some up at MSG.

Ticket prices: $8–58.

College basketball

College basketball is a highly profitable business enterprise, earning millions for its Division I programs and for its star coaches. The season begins in November and ends with "March Madness," in which conference tournaments are followed by a 64-team tournament to select a national champion. The national tournament may be the most exciting, eagerly anticipated sporting event in the US. Madison Square Garden hosts pre-season tournaments and the Big East Conference tournament. ⓣ212/465-6741.

Metropolitan-area colleges pursuing hoop dreams include Long Island, Seton Hall and St John's universities. The last is currently the most successful in the area, and has a huge and loyal fan base; call ⓣ718/990-6211 for game schedule and ticket prices.

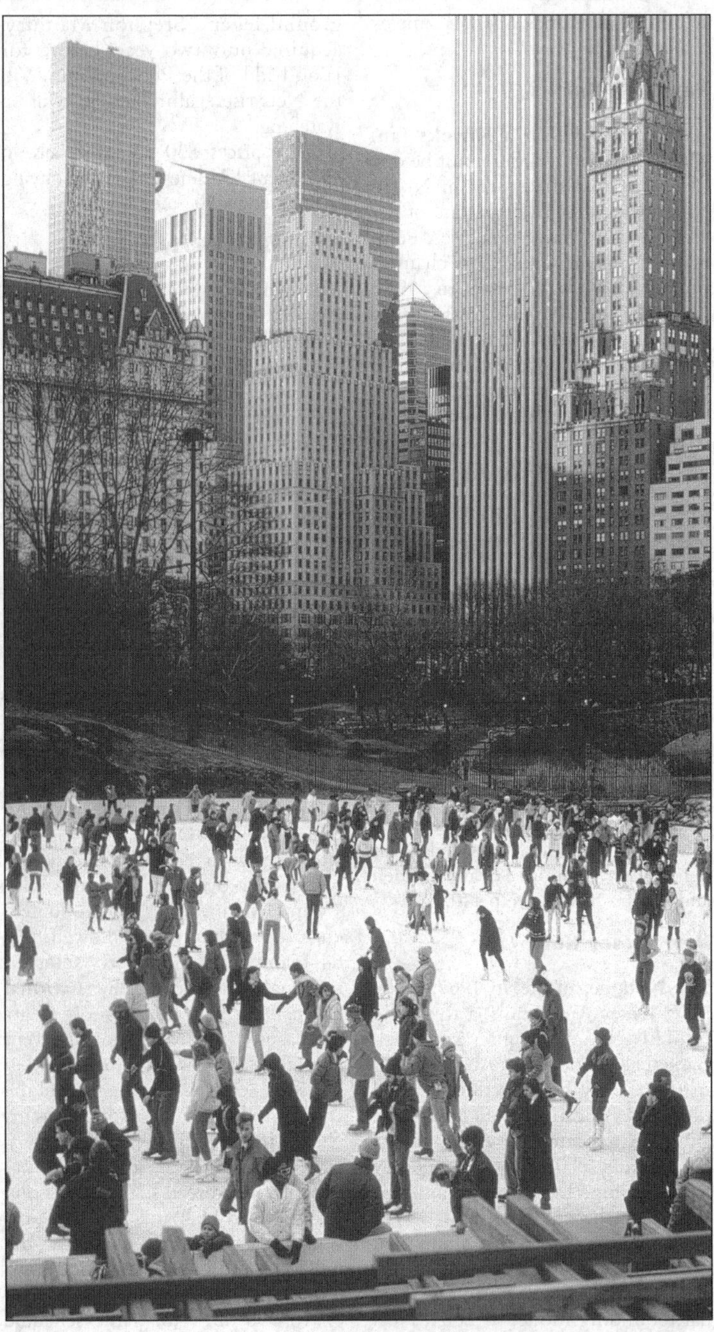

△ Central Park's Wollman Rink has a great view of the midtown skyline

Street basketball

Free of the obsession with image-building, maintenance and marketing that makes the NBA so seductive and so superficial, or the greedy economics that rule in the NCAA, **street basketball** presents the game in its purest and, arguably, most attractive form. New York City is the capital of playground hoops with a host of asphalt legends, past and present: Lew Alcindor (Kareem Abdul-Jabbar), Wilt Chamberlain, Julius Erving and Stephon Marbury are a few who made it to the pros. If you want to play yourself, *Hoops Nation* by Chris Ballard is an invaluable guide to basketball courts in the five boroughs (and across the nation) and a useful primer in the etiquette of pickup ball. Otherwise, the best place to check out the scene is West 4th Street at Sixth Avenue in Manhattan. Scout the next NBA superstar – or look for current ones dropping by for an off-season tune-up.

Ice hockey

To someone unfamiliar with the game, **ice hockey** might seem a very odd excuse for getting a bunch of guys to beat the hell out of each other for the amusement of the paying public. It is a violent sport, certainly, and some players are without doubt chosen in part for their punching ability. But there's a huge amount of skill involved, too. It takes some watching to work out where the puck is – the game moves at phenomenal speed. The two New York pro teams are the **Rangers**, who play at Madison Square Garden, and the **Islanders**, whose venue is the Nassau Coliseum on Long Island. Also, the **New Jersey Devils** play at the Continental Airlines Arena. All three compete in the Atlantic Division of the Eastern Conference of the National Hockey League. The regular season lasts throughout the winter and into early spring, when the playoffs take place.

New York Rangers

One of the six original NHL teams, the **Rangers** were founded in 1926 and won the Stanley Cup – awarded to the winner of the playoffs – three times in the next fifteen years. According to hockey lore, giddy from their 1940 playoff-finals victory over the Toronto Maple Leafs, the Madison Square Garden owners paid off their $3 million mortgage and celebrated by burning the deed in Lord Stanley's cup – an act of desecration that provoked a curse upon the franchise and its fans. When the Rangers finally ended their 54-year drought in 1994, the Stanley Cup accompanied the team on a celebratory tour of the city that included the Howard Stern Show, several bars and at least one strip joint. The team's mediocre performance since then suggests that the hockey gods may be working on another almighty malediction.

Ticket prices: $22–55; for details on Madison Square Garden and buying tickets, see p.440.

New York Islanders

An expansion team, founded in 1972, the **Islanders** were fortunate enough to string together their four Stanley Cups in consecutive years (1980–1983) and thus qualify as a bona fide hockey dynasty. Since then, however, it's been mostly downhill, with the 2000–2001 season especially dismal. They can only get better.

Ticket prices: $14–85; for details on Nassau Coliseum and buying tickets, see p.440.

New Jersey Devils

The franchise was founded in 1974 and moved to New Jersey in 1982. A succession of mediocre seasons was interrupted when the **Devils** beat the heavily favored Detroit Red Wings in four straight games to win the 1995 Stanley Cup. More recently, they regained the Cup in 2000, and the

2001 campaign saw them battle (and lose to) the Colorado Avalanche in the finals.

Ticket prices: $20–74; for details on Continental Airlines Arena and buying tickets, see p.440.

Soccer

Although the game itself continues to grow in popularity, particularly in the city's Latin and Eastern European communities, the **US soccer** team's disappointing performance in the 1998 World Cup was further evidence that the general standard of professional soccer in the US leaves much to be desired.

However, the women's national team won the 1999 Women's World Cup and achieved cult status virtually overnight. Thus, the **Women's United Soccer Association** was born, with eight teams, including the New York Power, vying for supremacy. European soccer turns up fairly regularly on cable TV (though usually delayed by at least a few hours due to the time difference) and some bars show British league games live via satellite (see opposite).

MetroStars

As for the men, the **New York/New Jersey Metrostars**, who play at Giants Stadium, are the metropolitan area's Major League Soccer representatives. They won the Eastern Division title in 2000 and got as far as the playoff semifinals.

Ticket prices: $15–30; for details on Giants Stadium and buying tickets, see p.440.

Horse Racing

The four tracks in the area are the **Aqueduct Race Track**, the **Belmont Race Track**, the **Meadowlands Race Track** and **Yonkers Raceway**. Aqueduct and Belmont have thoroughbred racing. Meadowlands has both thoroughbred and standardbred (harness) racing, and Yonkers has only standardbred.

Aqueduct, in Howard Beach, Queens, has racing from October to May. To get there by subway, take the A train to the Aqueduct station. **Belmont**, in Elmont, Long Island, is home to the Belmont Stakes (June), one of the three races in which three-year-olds compete for the Triple Crown. Belmont is open May–July and September–October. Take the E or F subway train to 169th St and then the #16 bus to the track, or take the Long Island Railroad to the Belmont Race Track stop. For both Belmont and Aqueduct, call ⓣ718/641-4700. Admission at both

Sports bars

ESPN Zone 1540 Broadway (at W 45th St) ⓣ212/921-3776. ABC/Disney-affiliated sports bar/restaurant, where you can catch the action from one of 278 screens (even in the bathroom).

Jimmy's Corner 140 W 44th St (between Broadway and 6th Ave) ⓣ212/221-9510. See p.361.

Kinsdale Tavern 1672 3rd Ave (at 93rd St) ⓣ212/348-4370.

Mickey Mantle's 42 Central Park S (between 5th and 6th aves) ⓣ212/688-7777. Perhaps the city's most famous sports bar, packed with memorabilia; it's hard to tell which is more bland, the food or the decor.

Sporting Club 99 Hudson St (between Franklin and Leonard sts) ⓣ212/219-0900. Rated the no. 1 sports bar in Manhattan by *New York* magazine, it has seven giant screens and a dozen smaller TVs, plus a pool table and other games.

Sushi Generation 1572 2nd Ave (between 81st and 82nd sts) ⓣ212/249-2222. A combination sushi/sports bar. No kidding.

Time Out 349 Amsterdam Ave (between 76th and 77th sts) ⓣ212/362-5400. Upper West Side neighborhood bar.

tracks ranges from $1 to $4 depending on where you park and sit. Valet parking costs $5 at Aqueduct and $6 at Belmont.

Meadowlands, in the Meadowlands Sports Complex in New Jersey, holds harness racing eight months of the year (December–August) and thoroughbred racing September–December (☎201/935-8500). From Manhattan, take NJ Transit bus #164 from the Port Authority. Parking is free, admission is $1 and entry to the Clubhouse is $3. **Yonkers Raceway** holds harness racing only, but operates year-round every night except Sundays (☎914/968-4200). Take subway train #4 to Woodlawn and transfer to the #20 bus. Parking is $2; admission is $3.25.

To **place a bet** anywhere other than the track itself, find an OTB – Off-Track Betting – office. There are plenty around the city; call ☎212/221-5200 for locations (opening hours are Mon–Sat 11.30am–7pm, Sun 11.30am–6.30pm). You need an established account to place a phone bet: to set one up, call ☎800/OTB-8118. To watch racing in comfort, try The Inside Track (run by OTB) at 991 2nd Ave at 53rd St (☎212/752-1940). Open from 11.30am until the last race ends, they offer food, drink and wagering on the premises.

The following bars show regular European soccer games, often with a cover charge.

British Open 320 E 59th St (between 1st and 2nd aves) ☎212/355-8467.

McCormack's 365 3rd Ave (at 27th St) ☎212/683-0911. Irish neighborhood bar.

Nevada Smith's 74 3rd Ave (between 11th and 12th sts) ☎212/982-2591. Jolly East Village dive.

Tennis

The **US Open Championships**, held each September at the National Tennis Center in Flushing Meadows–Corona Park, in Queens, is the top US tennis event of the year. In 1997, the Flushing complex opened a new center court, the Arthur Ashe Stadium. When David Dinkins, an avowed sports fan, was mayor, he ordered the nearby La Guardia Airport planes to be rerouted during the championships, which greatly reduces the volume of noise. Tickets go on sale the first week or two of June at the Tennis Center's box office (☎718/760-6200), open Mon–Fri 9am–5pm and Sat 10am–4pm. To book by phone, call Ticketmaster (☎866/673-6849). Promenade level at the stadium costs $22–69 (better seats can cost several hundred dollars), and seats are more expensive at night and closer to the finals. If they are sold out, keep trying up to the day of the event because corporate tickets are often returned. Tickets for the big matches are incredibly difficult to get – you can either take a chance with scalpers or try your luck at the Will Call window for people who don't show up. The other major tennis option is the Women's Tennis Association Tour Chase Championships, held each year at Madison Square Garden in mid-November (☎212/465-6741). Tickets $10–60.

Track and Field

The **Chase Bank Melrose Games**, at Madison Square Garden each February, feature world-class athletes. The games include almost every track and field event, including sprints, pole vault, high jump, long jump and much more. The event is well attended, but tickets are easier to come by than those for other city sporting events. Call the Garden (☎212/465-6741) for more information.

Wrestling

Held regularly at Madison Square Garden, **wrestling** is perhaps the least "sporting" of all the sports you can watch in New York, more of a theatrical event really, with a patriotically charged, almost salivating crowd cheering on all-American superheroes against evil and distinctly un-American foes. Bouts start with a rendition of The Star-Spangled Banner, after which the staged action takes place against a background of jingoistic roars, with the true-blue US spirit invariably winning the day. Recently, some of the more flamboyant professional athletes from other sports – including basketball's Dennis Rodman and football's Kevin Greene – have tried their hand in the ring. For information, call Madison Square Garden (☎212/465-6741); if wrestling has truly got you in a headlock, visit *WWF NY*, a theme restaurant/bar in Times Square (see p.160).

Tickets and venues

Tickets for most events can be booked ahead with a credit card through Ticketmaster ☎212/307-7171 and collected at the gate, though it's cheaper – and of course riskier for popular events – to try to pick up tickets on the night of the event. You can also call or go to the stadium's box office and buy advance tickets. When the box office has sold out, call a ticketing agency, which buys quantities of tickets for resale. Expect to pay a little bit more to substantially more, depending on the importance of the game and the seats – look in the *Yellow Pages* under tickets, or in the back pages of the free city entertainment papers or the *Village Voice*. Scalping (reselling a ticket, usually on the day of the event outside the arena, at an inflated price) is illegal. If all else fails, simply catch the action on the big screen in a sports bar.

Madison Square Garden Center **7th Ave (between 31st and 33rd sts) ☎212/465-6741.** Subway #1, #2, #3, #9, A, C and E to 34th St–Penn Station. Call box office for hours, which change by season and depend on the calendar of events.

Meadowlands Sports Complex containing both **Giants Stadium** and the **Continental Airlines Arena**, **off routes 3, 17, and Turnpike exit 16W, East Rutherford, New Jersey ☎201/935-3900.** Regular buses from Port Authority Bus Terminal on 42nd St and 8th Ave. Box office open for all arenas Mon–Fri 9am–6pm, Sat 10am–6pm, Sun noon–5pm.

Nassau Coliseum **1255 Hempstead Turnpike, Uniondale, New York ☎516/794-9300.** Long Island Railroad to Hempstead, then bus N70, N71 or N72 from Hempstead bus terminal, one block away. Another option, which may be safer at night, is to take the LIRR to Westbury and take a cab (a 5–10min ride) to the stadium. Box office daily 10.45am–5.45pm.

Shea Stadium **126th St (at Roosevelt Ave), Queens ☎718/507-8499.** Subway #7, direct to Willets Point/Shea Stadium Station. Box office Mon–Fri 9am–6pm, Sat, Sun & holidays 9am–5pm. You can also buy tickets from the Mets Clubhouse Stores in Manhattan, 11 W 42nd St (between 5th and 6th aves), Mon–Sat 9am–7pm, Sun 11am–6pm and at 143 E 54th St (between Lexington and 3rd), Mon–Fri 10am–7pm, Sat 10am–6pm, Sun noon–5pm; www.mets.com. Dress warmly in early spring and autumn: Shea is a windy icebox.

Yankee Stadium **161st St and River Ave, the Bronx ☎718/293-6000.** Subway C, D or #4 direct to 161st St Station. Box office Mon–Sat 9am–5pm, Sun 10am–4pm and until one hour after completion of evening games. You can also buy tickets from these Yankees Clubhouse stores in Manhattan: 110 E 59th St (between Lexington and Park aves) ☎212/758-7844; 393 5th Ave (between 36th and 37th sts) ☎212/685-4693; 245 W 42nd St (between 7th and 8th aves) ☎212/768-9555; 8 Fulton St (South St Seaport) ☎212/514-7182; or on the internet: www.yankees.com. Get to the game early and visit Monument Park, where all the Yankee greats are memorialized.

Participatory activities

Beaches

Few visitors come to New York for the **beaches**, and those New Yorkers with money tend to turn their noses up at the city strands, preferring to move further afield to Long Island, just a couple of hours away and much better. But the city's beaches, though often crowded, are a cool summer escape from Manhattan and most are also just a subway token away.

Brooklyn

Brighton Beach **D train to Brighton Beach.** Technically the same stretch as Coney, but less crowded and given color by the local Russian community. Boardwalk vendors sell ethnic snacks.

Coney Island Beach **at the end of half a dozen subway lines: fastest is the D train to Stillwell Ave.** After Rockaway (see below), NYC's most popular bathing spot, jam-packed on summer weekends. The Atlantic here is only moderately dirty and there's a good, reliable onshore breeze.

Manhattan Beach **D train to Sheepshead Bay Rd, walk to Ocean Ave and cross the bridge.** Small beach much used by locals.

Queens

Jacob Riis Park **#2 train to Flatbush Ave, then Q35 bus.** Good sandy stretches, the western ones used almost exclusively by a gay male crowd.

Rockaway Beach **A and C trains to any stop along the beach.** Forget California: this seven-mile strip is where New Yorkers – up to three-quarters of a million daily in summer – come to get the best surf around, surf so good that the Ramones wrote a song about it. Best beaches are at 9th St, 23rd St and 80–118th sts.

The Bronx

Orchard Beach **subway train #6 local to Pelham Bay Park, then Bx12 bus.** Less easy to get to than the rest.

Staten Island

Great Kills Park **bus #103 from Staten Island Ferry Terminal.** Quiet and used by locals.

South Beach **bus S52.** New ballfields, rollerblading areas and low-key beaches.

Wolfe's Pond Park **bus #103 to Main St in Tottenville, at Hylan and Cornelia.** Regularly packs in the crowds from New Jersey.

Bicycling

There are 100 miles of **cycle paths** in New York; those in Central Park, Riverside Park and the East River Promenade are among the nicest. Two sources have done an excellent job of providing specific cycling routes and maps, laws and regulations, and other relevant info. Transportation Alternatives (115 W 30th St ⓣ212/629-8080, ⓦwww.transalt.org), while concentrating on the environmental aspects, lobbies for funding for bike-related projects, like ramps for bridge access, free bike racks, and additional car-free hours in Central Park. They also sponsor the Century Bike Tour in September (a 35-, 50-, 75-, or 100-mile ride through the boroughs), and have some good maps.

And, surprisingly enough, the New York City Department of City Planning (go to ⓦnycdoitt.ci.nyc.ny.us/html/dcp/html/bikenet.html) has a wealth of information, as part of their BND (Bicycle Network Development) project. You'll find extensive (and downloadable) bike maps for all five boroughs, in addition to information on how to use mass transit in planning your bike ride.

If you want to go further afield, the deal of the century is a MetroNorth Railroads lifetime bike pass for $5, available at the ticket windows in Grand Central Station. These trains will bring you to the scenic small towns of the lower Hudson Valley and coastal Connecticut. When riding on the street, remember that by law you must wear a helmet. It's not enforced, but it's the safe thing to do. Most bike stores rent bicycles by the day or hour (refer to the *Yellow Pages* or call Loeb Boathouse in Central Park).

Here are some clubs and resources for cycling enthusiasts:

Bicycle Habitat **244 Lafayette St ☎212/431-3315.** Known for an excellent repair service, they also offer rentals for $25 a day (plus a deposit equal to the value of the bike) or $7.50 an hour, with a two-hour minimum. You can also have a tune-up (priced at $75 and up). The very knowledgeable staff here help cyclists of all levels of expertise.

Five Borough Bike Club This club organizes rides throughout the year, including the Montauk Century, a hundred-mile ride from New York to Montauk, Long Island. Call ☎212/932-2300 ext 115 for membership details.

New York Cycle Club **☎212/828-5711.** This 1400-member club offers many rides. Visit ⓦwww.nycc.org for registration information.

Times Up **☎212/802-8222.** They do a variety of trips, including Riverside Rides, Moonlight Rides and Cyclone Rides (to Coney Island), along with environment and ecology rides. Call for a schedule.

Boating

Downtown Boathouse **Hudson River, Pier 26** (See Hudson River Park Project, opposite.)

Loeb Boathouse **Central Park ☎212/517-2233.** A new fleet of 100 rowboats for hire between April and Oct, daily 10am–6pm. Rates are $10 an hour plus $30 deposit. Bikes, too.

Bowling

Bowlmor Lanes **110 University Place (between 12th and 13th sts) ☎212/255-8188.** Long-established and large bowling alley with a bar and shop. Open Mon & Fri 10am–4am, Tues & Wed 10am–1am, Thurs 10am–2am, Sat 11am–4am, Sun 11am–1am. $6 per game per person before 5pm, $7 after 5pm. $4 shoe-rent.

Leisure Time Bowling **on 2nd floor of Port Authority, 625 8th Ave, near 40th St ☎212/268-6909.** The nicest place in the city to bowl. $5 per game per person ($6 after 5pm), plus $3.50 shoe-rent.

Golf

Manhattan has no **public golf courses**. Recommended among those in the outer boroughs are:

Dyker Beach Golf Course **86th St and 11th Ave, Dyker Heights, Brooklyn ☎718/836-9722.** Fees around $24.

Split Rock Golf Course & Pelham Golf Course **870 North Shore Rd, Pelham ☎718/885-1258.** *New York* magazine voted Split Rock, in the northwest Bronx, the most challenging course in the city. Pelham, right next door, is somewhat easier. Fees $27–30.

Van Cortlandt Park Golf Course **Van Cortlandt Park S and Bailey Ave, the Bronx ☎718/543-4595.** The oldest 18-hole public golf course in the country. Green fees range from $16 to $27, depending on time of day.

Health and fitness: pools, gyms and baths

You can join one of several newly renovated city **recreation centers** for $25 per year (ages 18–54) or $10 (kids 13–17 and seniors). All have gym facilities and most have an indoor and/or outdoor pool. Call ☎212/447-2020 or look in the *Manhattan Blue Pages* (within the *White Pages*) under NY City Parks; centers are listed under "Recreation" and "Swimming Pools."

East 54th St Pool **348 E 54th St ☎212/397-3154.** Good-sized indoor pool; annual membership just $25. Bring check or money order, no cash. Exercise classes too. Open Mon–Fri 7am–9.30pm, Sat 9am–3pm, closed Sun.

John Jay Pool **E 77th St and Cherokee Place ☎212/794-6566.** Above the FDR Drive, this six-lane, fifty-yard pool is surrounded by playgrounds and park benches. Although it opened in 1940, it is in remarkably great condition. Free to anyone; bring a padlock.

Riverbank State Park **W 145th St and Riverside Drive ☎212/694-3600.** Beautiful new facility built on top of a waste refinery in Harlem. Sounds strange, and it is, but there are great tennis courts, an outdoor track, an ice-skating rink and indoor facilities. Park admission is free; pool is $2, children $1.

Sutton Gymnastics and Fitness Center **20 Cooper Square ☎212/533-9390.** One of the few gyms in New York where you need not be a member to use the facilities. Classes

Central Park, Chelsea Piers and the Hudson River Park Project

Central Park is the focus for almost all forms of recreation – from croquet to chess to soccer to sunning to swimming. Joggers, in-line skaters, walkers and cyclists have the roads to themselves on weekdays 10am–3pm & 7–10pm and all day on weekends. The park is closed each night from 1–6am. To find out what is going on where and when, go to the Arsenal, at 830 5th Ave at 64th St and pick up the following items, or call and ask for them to be mailed to you:

• Green Pages, which tell you about every activity, from archery to wild-food walks. ⓣ212/360-8111 ext 310.

• Special Events Calendar, a day-by-day listing of events in the parks in all the boroughs. There are races, dances, track meets, as well as a lot of concerts and events for children. ⓣ212/360-1492.

Chelsea Piers is located at W 23rd St and the Hudson River (between 17th and 23rd sts) ⓣ212/336-6666 for general info. Take the A, C, E, #1 or #9 trains to 23rd St and walk west; or take the M23 bus, which will drop you off at the front door; or the M14, which terminates at 14th St and the West Side Highway, close to the Piers' south entrance. The complex is the complete renovation of four piers, jutting out into the Hudson River, originally designed in 1912 by Warren & Wetmore, the architects of Grand Central Station.

The **Golf Club** at Pier 59 features Manhattan's only outdoor driving range. The hours are 5am–midnight. For $15, you get a bucket of balls to drive; going during peak hours means fewer balls to knock around. ⓣ212/336-6400.

The **Field House** connects the four piers. This facility houses the largest gymnastics facility in the state. Soccer and lacrosse leagues play here. You can also rock-climb or play basketball without being in a league. ⓣ212/336-6500.

The **Sports Center** at Pier 60 features a quarter-mile running track, the largest rock-climbing wall in the northeast, three basketball/volleyball courts, a boxing ring, a 24-yard swimming pool and whirlpool, indoor sand volleyball courts, exercise studios offering more than 100 classes weekly, a cardiovascular weight-training room, a sundeck right on the Hudson River and spa services.

You must be 16 or older to use the Sports Center. Day passes are available for $50. Mon–Fri 6am–11pm, Sat & Sun 8am–9pm. ⓣ212/336-6000.

The **Roller Rinks** are on Pier 62. They are outdoors and open year-round, weather permitting. Daily session starts at noon, exact times vary. $6.50; children under 12 $5.50. Rentals available. ⓣ212/336-6200.

The **Sky Rink** is on Pier 61. Ice-skate year-round on this indoor rink. Daily sessions start at noon, exact times vary. $11.50; children under 12 $8; seniors $7.50. Rentals $5. ⓣ212/336-6100.

For a peaceful, non-motorized view of Manhattan from the water, join the crew of the *Adirondack,* a beautiful 78-foot wooden schooner, which sails from Pier 62. During the two-hour sail of lower New York harbor, passengers can take the wheel, help hoist the sails, or just enjoy the surroundings. Daily weather permitting 1pm, 3.30pm, 6pm & 9pm; daytime $30, evening $40 includes champagne, $5 extra on weekends. ⓣ1-800/701-7245, ⓦwww.scaranoboat.com/excursions.

The Hudson River Park Project ⓣ212/533-7275, ⓦwww.hudsonriverpark.org

Twenty years in the planning, the Hudson River Project is a much-needed redevelopment of the west side waterfront from Battery Park to 59th St, seeking to transform 550 acres of river and shoreline and repair or reconstruct 13 historic piers for public use. Currently five piers are complete, alongside a continuous esplanade – the close proximity of the path to the West Side Highway striking the only unfortunate note. A few highlights:

Pier 25, Children's Park. Not your average display of prefabricated slides and jungle gyms, the park contains mini-golf, beach volleyball, a water park and an art shack. Free movies at sundown during July and August. (Chambers St subway then walk west.)

Pier 26, Downtown Boathouse. Free kayaks available on weekday nights and weekend days (for opening times ⓣ212/385 2790, ⓦwww.downtownboathouse.org). A second boathouse location at Pier 64, Chelsea Piers.

Pier 40. The picnic house, soccer field, batting cages and climbing wall here are made all the more interesting by the site's location on top of a parking garage. (#1, #9 to Houston St, then walk 4 blocks west.)

for around $25, generally only in summer. Call for hours and class schedule.

Tenth Street Turkish Baths 268 E 10th St ⓣ212/473-8806 or 212/674-9250. An ancient place, something of a neighborhood landmark and still going, with steam baths, sauna and an ice-cold pool, as well as massage and a restaurant. Free lockers, locks, shorts, towel, robe and slippers. Admission $22, extra for massage, etc. Open Mon, Tue, Thur and Fri 11am–10pm, Wed 9am–10pm, Sat–Sun 7.30am–10pm; men only Sun opening until 2pm; women only Wed opening until 2pm; co-ed otherwise.

West 59th St Pool 533 W 59th St (between 10th and 11th aves) ⓣ212/397-3159. Two pools (indoor, outdoor), gym and climbing wall. $25 annual membership (climbing wall extra) paid by money order. The gym is open Mon–Fri 11am–10pm, Sat 10am–6pm; closed Sun. Call for pool hours.

Hiking

For **hikes**, nature walks and other special activities around the city, try the following organizations:

Shorewalkers ⓣ212/330-7686, ⓦwww.shorewalkers.org. This group offers an extensive roster of hikes of different lengths. Contribution $3. The annual Great Saunter ($10) is a 32-mile jaunt around Manhattan.

Urban Park Rangers ⓣ212/360-2774 or 1-800/201-PARK. This arm of the NYC Dept of Recreation conducts wildlife walks, history walks and ecohikes, all free. Their *Redtailer* newsletter details the events.

Appalachian Mountain Club

To get off the beaten track and mix with locals, participate in the New York/New Jersey chapter of the worldwide **Appalachian Mountain Club**.

With friendly people of all ages, you can learn yoga on Fire Island, tour the historic neighborhoods of the five boroughs or hike the scenic Shawangunks.

A four-month guest membership is available. Send $15 to AMC, 5 Tudor City Place, NY, NY 10017 ⓣ212/986-1430.

Horse riding

Claremont Riding Academy 175 W 89th St ⓣ212/724-5100. For riding in Central Park, this place hires out ponies by the hour for $45. Saddles are English-style; lessons $50 per half-hour. You must be an experienced rider.

Jamaica Bay Riding Academy 7000 Shore Parkway, Brooklyn ⓣ212/718/531-8949. Trail riding, with western-style saddles, around the eerie landscape of Jamaica Bay. $23 for a 45min ride; lessons $50 an hour.

Riverdale Equestrian Center in Bronx's Van Cortlandt Park (at W 254th St and Broadway) ⓣ718/548-4848. Lessons only: $36 for 30min, $67 for full hour. Brand-new, beautiful country trails.

Ice-skating . . . and tobogganing

In winter, the freezing weather makes for good **ice-skating**. In milder weather, roller skating is popular, on the paths in Central Park and specifically near the northwest corner of the Sheep Meadow, in Riverside Park and in many smaller open spaces. **Tobogganing** is another popular winter activity, on the slopes of Van Cortlandt Park in the Bronx. Call ⓣ718/549-6494 to see if the snow is deep enough.

Lasker Rink 110th St, Central Park ⓣ212/289-0599. The lesser-known ice rink in Central Park is at the north end of the park. Much cheaper than the Wollman Rink, though less accessible, and the neighborhood isn't great at night. Call for hours and prices.

Rockefeller Center Ice Rink between 49th and 50th sts, off 5th Ave ⓣ212/332-7654. Without doubt the slickest place to skate, though you may have to wait in line and it's pricier than anywhere else. Call for hours and prices.

Sky Rink Chelsea Piers ⓣ212/336-6100. (See box p.443.)

Wollman Rink 62nd St, Central Park ⓣ212/396-1010. Lovely rink, where you can skate to the marvelous, inspiring backdrop of the lower Central Park skyline – incredibly impressive at night. Call for hours and prices.

In-line skating

You'll see commuters to freestylists on **in-line skates** – also known as **rollerblades** – in New York. For the best place to watch freestylists, go to the skate circle near Naumberg Bandshell in Central Park at 72nd St. World-class bladers maneuver between cones with all kinds of fancy footwork just inside Central Park's *Tavern on the Green* entrance, near W 68th St. Other than Central Park, the best places to skate are Battery Park, and Flushing Meadows–Corona Park in Queens, which is forty minutes from midtown on the #7 train. There are free group skates around the city put on by Wednesday Night Skate (Ⓣ212/696-7247), and on Tuesdays, Thursdays and some weekends by Empire Skate (Ⓦwww.empireskate.org). They all require a certain comfort level with the activity, as they are held at night, on regular traffic-strewn streets.

Blades Their several locations make it convenient to rent in-line skates:
128 Chambers St (between W Broadway and Church St) Ⓣ212/964-1944.
120 W 72nd St (between Columbus and Broadway) Ⓣ212/787-3911.
160 E 86th St (between Lexington and 3rd aves) Ⓣ212/996-1644.
$20 for 24 hours.

Jogging and running

Jogging is still very much the number one fitness pursuit in the city, and the number of yearly coronaries in Central Park, the most popular venue, probably runs well into double figures. A favorite circuit in the park is 1.57 miles around the reservoir; just make sure you jog in the right direction – counterclockwise. For company, contact the New York Road Runners Club (9 E 89th St Ⓣ212/860-2280, Ⓦwww.nyrrc.org) to get their schedule for Central Park and elsewhere. They sponsor many races and fun runs per year, including the Frostbite 10 Miler and the Valentine Run. The East River Promenade and almost any other stretch of open space long enough to get up speed are also well jogged. One of the more beautiful routes is through the Bronx Botanical Garden (Ⓣ718/817-8705) – a two-mile loop with eight miles of adjoining trails.

Pool

Along with bars and nightclubs, a good option for an evening in Manhattan is to play **pool**, not in dingy halls but in gleaming bars where well-heeled yuppies mix with the regulars. A number of sports bars and dive bars have pool tables as well, though these are often much smaller than regulation size. Snooker fans will also find a few tables throughout the city.

Amsterdam Billiards 344 Amsterdam Ave at 77th St Ⓣ212/496-8180. Very popular uptown billiards club with 31 tables. They serve liquor and beer along with bar food.

New York City Marathon

If, rather than exhaust yourself, you'd prefer to see thousands of others do so, the **New York City Marathon** takes place on the first Sunday in November. Two million people turn out each year to watch 30,000 runners try to complete the 26.2-mile course, which starts in Staten Island, crosses the Verrazano Narrows Bridge and passes through all the other boroughs before ending at the *Tavern on the Green* in Central Park.

If you are a runner, you can try to take part, but beware, the competition is fierce even before the race starts. Not everyone who submits the necessary entry forms is chosen to participate; preference goes to prior race participants, New York Road Runners Club (NYRRC) members, and those who have applied and been rejected for the last three NYC marathons. Athletes with disabilities (more than 100 participate every year) are guaranteed entry with application by August 1, and a competitive wheelchair racing division has been established. Obtain forms from Ⓦwww.nycmarathon.org or the NYRRC. Applications must be sent before June 1 for that year's race, and you must be at least 18 years old on race day.

The Billiard Club 220 W 19th St (between 7th and 8th aves) ☎212/206-7665. A pool club with a nice, vaguely European atmosphere and a small bar serving beer, liquor and soft drinks.

Chelsea Billiards 54 W 21st St (between 5th and 6th aves) ☎212/989-0096. A casual place with both snooker and pool tables. Bar serves beer and soft drinks.

Le Q Billiards 36 E 12th St (between Broadway and University Place) ☎212/995-8512. Downtown hangout serving soft drinks and snacks only.

Tennis

Court space is at a premium in Manhattan, so finding a court and being able to afford it can be tough, but you can call the following:

New York City Courts ☎212/360-8133 for information on all city courts. Their $50 Permit, which runs from April to November, provides access to all municipal courts in the five boroughs.

Sutton East Tennis Club (mid-Oct–April) York Ave and 59th St ☎212/751-3452. Prices range from $70 an hour on weekdays to $94 an hour on weekends.

Parades and festivals

Major cultural holidays are celebrated with **parades and festivals**. The city takes these, especially the parades, very seriously. Almost every large ethnic group in the city holds an annual get-together, often using Fifth Avenue as the main drag. The events are often political or religious in origin, though now are just as much an excuse for music, food and dance.

Whatever your flavor, chances are your stay will coincide with at least one parade or festival. For more details and exact dates of parades, festivals and the like, phone ⓣ1-800/NYC-VISIT or go to ⓦwww.nycvisit.com. Also, look at listings in *New York* magazine's "CUE" section, the *New Yorker* magazine's "Goings on About Town" section, the *Village Voice*'s "Cheap Thrills" section or the weekly "Obsessive guide to impulsive entertainment," in *Time Out New York* magazine.

Also prominent in New York are summer-long arts festivals, or performance series, often held outdoors – Central Park, Prospect Park and South Street Seaport are all prime locations – and often free. Although there are many summer events like the New York Philharmonic concerts and Celebrate Brooklyn, probably the biggest is SummerStage, held June through August in Central Park's Rumsey Playfield, which hosts events ranging from grand opera to Middle Eastern drumming to the New York Symphony. But to tell the truth, most New Yorkers don't care who is on stage. They often come with blankets, picnic baskets and wine, and catch up with good friends and enjoy summer evenings outside.

January

Chinese New Year and Parade (first full moon between Jan 21 and Feb 19): A noisy, colorful occasion celebrated from noon to sunset around Mott St. And while dragons still dance in the street, firecrackers no longer chase away evil spirits because former Mayor Giuliani banned them for most events. Beware, the chances of getting a meal anywhere in Chinatown at this time is slim. ⓣ212/431-9740.

Lunar New Year (late Jan): Chinese celebration in downtown Flushing, Queens; Main St and 36th St to Roosevelt Ave.

Winter Antiques Show (mid-Jan): Foremost American antiques show in the country, at the Seventh Regiment Armory, Park Ave and 67th St ⓣ212/777-5218.

Juilliard's Focus (call for dates): From the Juilliard School of Music comes an annual

Street Fairs

Street fairs take place all over the city on spring, summer and autumn weekend afternoons. Blocks are closed to traffic, and food vendors offer an enticing selection of food, T-shirts, and other clothing and curios. There's often plenty of fun for the kids, plus music and a generally unvarying array of cold beer and sausage and pepper sandwiches. Street fairs are a good way to get a taste of real neighborhood New York, beyond the sirens and skyscrapers. The website ⓦwww.nyctourist.com has an extensive summer street-fair schedule. Smaller versions, and an even better way to witness real New York City living, are known as **block parties**. Many blocks reserve a day or two a year when the city closes their street to car traffic. Kids put on puppet shows, parents catch up on local gossip, politicos pop in to shake hands and everyone takes part in a huge pot-luck meal.

festival with six contemporary music concerts at Lincoln Center's Juilliard Theater. ⓣ212/769-7406, ⓦwww.juilliard.edu.

Outsider Art Fair (late Jan): Leading dealers for self-taught artists exhibit their collections at the Puck Building. ⓣ212/777-5218, ⓦwww.sanfordsmith.com/out/out.

February

New York Yankees Fan Festival (early Feb): Meet current and former players. ⓣ718/293-4300.

Twenty-four-Hour Marriage Marathon (Valentine's Day): Get hitched or watch while more than 50 couples take the plunge 110 stories and 1377 ft above Manhattan on the Observation Deck of the Empire State Building. ⓣ212/323-2340.

Empire State Building Run Up Foot Race (mid-Feb): Sponsored by the New York Road Runners Club, contenders race up the 1575 steps of this New York City landmark. ⓣ212/423-2229, ⓦwww.nyrrc.org.

Manhattan Antiques and Collectibles (usually last two weekends): Triple Pier Expo at the Passenger Ship Terminal (Piers 88, 90 and 92) ⓣ212/255-0020, ⓦwww.stellashows.com.

Presidents' Day Parade (first or third Mon): for Abe and George, on 5th Ave from 35-50th sts. Check newspapers and TV news for parade route.

Westminster Kennel Club Dog Show (late Feb): Second only to the Kentucky Derby as the oldest continuous sporting event in the country, the show welcomes 2500 dogs competing for best in breed ⓣ1-800/455-3647, ⓦwww.westminsterkennelclub.org.

March

New York Underground Film Festival (mid-March): A bit out of the mainstream – but usually showing very interesting films. Locations vary – call or check out their site ⓣ212/925-3440, ⓦwww.nyuff.com.

St Patrick's Day Parade (March 17): Celebrating an impromptu march through the streets by Irish militiamen on St Patrick's Day in 1762, it has become a draw for every Irish band and organization in the US and Ireland. Usually starting just before noon, it heads up 5th Ave between 44th and 86th sts. ⓣ212/484-1222.

Brooklyn Irish-American Parade (March 18): Travels up Prospect Park West from 15th St to 17th Ave. ⓣ212/788-2958.

Greek Independence Day Parade (late March): Not as long or as boozy as St Pat's, more a patriotic nod to the old country from floats of pseudo-classically dressed Hellenes. When Independence Day falls in the Orthodox Lent, the parade is shifted to April or May. It usually kicks off from 62nd St and 5th Ave to 79th St. ⓣ718/204-6500.

International Asian Art Fair (late March): More than 50 dealers from around the world showcase painting, sculpture, furniture, jewelry, carpets and more. ⓣ212/642-8572.

The Circus Animal Walk (late March to early April): At midnight the animals from Ringling Brothers' Barnum & Bailey Circus march from their point of arrival to Madison Square Garden prior to opening of circus. ⓣ212/465-6741 for tickets or 212/302-1700 for information.

April

International Vintage Poster Fair (first weekend): A tradition for more than 15 years at the Metropolitan Pavilion at 110 W 19th St. ⓣ212/206-0499, ⓦwww.posterfair.com.

Macy's Flower Show (usually the week before Easter): Fragrant flowers, plants and trees, lush landscapes and global gardens fill up Macy's main floor and Rockefeller Center. ⓣ212/494-2922.

Easter Parade (Easter Sun): From Central Park down to Rockefeller Center on 50th St, New Yorkers dress up in outrageous Easter bonnets. 10am–5pm. There's also an Eggstravaganza, a children's festival including an egg-rolling contest in Central Park, on the Great Lawn.

Bang on a Can Festival (late March–early May): A major "new music" festival featuring musicians from all over the world. ⓣ212/777-8442, ⓦwww.bangonacan.org.

New Directors, New Films (early April): Lincoln Center and MoMA have presented this popular two-week film festival for more than 25 years, showcasing films of overlooked or emerging filmmakers. ⓣ212/875-5638, ⓦwww.filmlinc.com.

International African Dance/Drum Conference and Festival (mid-April): five days of African dance and drum lectures and classes. Benefit performance held at Symphony Space. ⓣ718/455-7136, ⓦwww.angelfire.com/ny/africandance/.

Annual Antiquarian Book Fair (late April): Collection of rare books, letters, drawings, etc, held at the Seventh Regiment Armory, Park Ave and 67th St. ⓣ212/944-8291, ⓦwww.aba.org.

May

Sakura Matsuri Cherry Blossom Festival (early May): Music, art, dance and food celebrate Japanese culture and the blossoming of the Brooklyn Botanic Garden's 200 cherry trees. Free with garden admission. ⓣ718/622-4433.

The Great Five Boro Bike Tour (early May): A 42-mile ride without NYC traffic through all five boroughs; 30,000 cyclists. ⓣ212/932-2453, ⓦwww.bikenewyork.org.

Ukrainian Festival (mid-May): This fills a weekend on E 7th St between 2nd and 3rd aves with marvelous Ukrainian costumes, folk music and dance, plus authentic foods. At the Ukrainian Museum (12th St and 2nd Ave) there's a special exhibition of *pysanky* – traditional hand-painted eggs. ⓣ212/674-1615.

Summer Outdoor Fun

Midsummer Night Swing (late June–late July): At Lincoln Center's Fountain Plaza, 65th St at Columbus Ave every Wed through Sat evening; learn a different dance en masse each night to the rhythm of live swing, mambo, merengue, samba, country and other styles. ⓣ212/875-5766.

Music at Castle Clinton (July–Aug): Free waterside music performances by top performers in Battery Park. ⓣ212/835-2789.

Bryant Park Film Festival (June–Aug): Every summer Mon night picnickers watch classic films on the lush lawn of Bryant Park. ⓣ212/922-9393 or 212/512-5700.

SummerStage (June–Aug): free music, opera and readings in Central Park's SummerStage Amphitheater. ⓣ212/360-2777, ⓦwww.summerstage.org.

Shakespeare in the Park (June–Aug): Stars perform in the Bard's plays at Central Park's Delacorte Theater. ⓣ212/539-8750.

Celebrate Brooklyn (June–Aug): New York's longest-running free music and theater series, at the bandshell in Prospect Park; great Latin performances. ⓣ718/855-7882.

The New York Philharmonic (June–Aug): Free summer events at the Great Lawn in Central Park; bring a picnic basket, a blanket and wine. ⓣ212/875-5656.

Opera in the Parks (June–July): The Metropolitan Opera performs free in parks. ⓣ212/362-6000 or ⓦwww.metopera.org/news.

Sounds at Sunset (June–Aug): Free at the Battery Park Esplanade at 6.30pm. ⓣ212/416-5300.

Martin Luther King Jr Parade (mid-May): Celebrating Dr King's contribution to civil rights, the parade covers 5th Ave from 66th to 86th sts. It also pays tribute to African-Americans who have served in the US military. ⓣ212/374-5176.

Ninth Avenue International Food Festival (mid-May): It closes down 9th Ave between 37th and 57th sts for the weekend and offers tantalizing food, delicious scents, colorful crafts and great deals. ⓣ212/484-1222.

Crafts on Columbus (first 3 weekends): Columbus Ave between 77th and 81st sts. ⓣ212/866-2239.

Salute to Israel Parade (call for date): On 5th Ave, between 52nd and 79th sts, then east to 3rd Ave. ⓣ212/245-8200 ext 106 or 255.

Fleet Week (end of May): The annual welcome of sailors from the US, Canada, Mexico and the UK, among others, held at the Intrepid Sea-Air-Space Museum. Activities and events ⓣ212/245-0072.

Irish American Festival (last weekend): At Gateway National Recreation Area in Brooklyn. ⓣ718/338-3687.

Washington Square Outdoor Art Exhibit (late May–early June): It's free, held for more than 65 years and featuring more than 200 artists. ⓣ212/982-6255.

June

Museum Mile Festival (first Tues evening): On 5th Ave from 82nd St to 105th St. Museums, including the Museum of the City of New York, Jewish Museum, the Guggenheim, the Met and others are open free 6–9pm. ⓣ212-606-2296, ⓦwww.museummile.org.

The Belmont Stakes (early June): New York's jewel in horse racing's Triple Crown at Belmont Park in Long Island, just east of Queens. ⓣ718/641-4700, ⓦwww.nyra.com.

Philippine Independence Day Parade (early June): Usually on Madison Ave from midtown down, but call for exact route ⓣ212/683-2990 or 212/741-6806.

American Crafts Festival (early June): At Lincoln Center, you'll also see demonstrations, puppets, clowns and singing. ⓣ212/875-5593, ⓦwww.craftsatlincoln.com.

Puerto Rican Day Parade (second Sun): The largest of several Puerto Rican celebrations in the city, seven hours of bands and baton-twirling from 44th to 86th sts on 5th Ave, then east to 3rd Ave. ⓣ718/401-0404, ⓦwww.nationalpuertoricanparade.org.

Lower East Side Jewish Spring Festival (check Jewish Weekly for date and location): Kosher foods, Yiddish and Hebrew folk singing and guided tours of the Jewish Lower East Side.

The Festival of St Anthony (begins the first Thurs): A ten-day Italian celebration on Sullivan St from Spring to Houston sts, culminating in a procession of Italian bands, led by a life-size statue of the saint carried on the shoulders of four men. ⓣ212/777-2755.

Mermaid Parade (first Sat after June 21): At this hilarious event, participants dress like mermaids and King Neptune and saunter down the Coney Island boardwalk, after which everyone throws fruit into the sea. If you're around, don't miss it. ⓣ718/392-1267, ⓦwww.coneyislandusa.com.

Lesbian and Gay Pride Week (late June): The world's biggest Pride event kicks off with a rally and ends with a parade, street fair and dance. ⓣ212/807-7433, ⓦwww.nycpride.org.

JVC Jazz Festival (late June): The jazz world's top names appear at large venues such as Carnegie Hall, Lincoln Center and Beacon Theater, and at other smaller clubs around the city. ⓣ212/787-2020.

Washington Square Music Festival (late June–early July): A series of free Tuesday night classical, jazz and big-band concerts at this outdoor venue. ⓣ212/431-1088.

July

Mostly Mozart (July–Aug): At Lincoln Center's Avery Fisher Hall and Alice Tully Hall at 8pm. Distinguished guests join the orchestra. ⓣ212/875-5103.

International African Arts Festival (first week): World-class music and dance, a parade, talent contest, children and family programs, all sorts of fun. 10am–midnight at 1700 Fulton St in Brooklyn. ⓣ718/638-6700, ⓦwww.iaafestival.com.

Independence Day (July 4): The fireworks from Macy's, South Street Seaport and the display over the East River are visible all over Manhattan, but the best place to view them is either from the Seaport, Battery Park, the Esplanade at Brooklyn Heights or from atop almost any building at about 9pm. ⓣ212/484-1222 or 212/560-4060.

Bastille Day (Sun closest to July 14): Celebrate with the Alliance Française on 60th St between Lexington and 5th Ave. ⓣ212/355-6100.

Japanese Obon Festival (Sat nearest July 15): Slow and simple dancing in lantern-hung Bryant Park, and a service the following Sun. ⓣ212/678-0305.

New York City Tap Festival (mid-July): This week-long festival features hundreds of tap dancers who perform and give workshops. ⓣ646/230-9564, ⓦwww.nyctapfestival.com.

August

Harlem Month (culminates with Harlem Day on the third Sun): The month-long celebration of African, Caribbean and Latin cultures includes a children's festival, a dance show, a fashion parade, talent contest and other festivities, such as the Black Film Festival and the Taste of Harlem. ⓣ212/862-7200.

Dance Theater of Harlem Street Festival (usually the second week): A variety of dance performances plus events for children, on 152nd St between Amsterdam and Convent aves. ⓣ212/690-2800.

Macy's Tap A Mania (mid-Aug): It starts at noon, and there is a rain date. There have often been more than 3500 dancers, and Guinness lists this as the "record for the largest line of dancers ever to tap in unison." 34th St and 7th Ave, near Broadway ⓣ212/494-5247.

New York International Fringe Festival (usually mid-Aug): Cutting-edge performance art, theater, dance, puppetry, etc, at many different venues on the Lower East Side. ⓣ212-420-8877, ⓦwww.fringeny.com.

Brooklyn's County Fair (late Aug): Just like you might find in the Midwest – pony rides, watermelon-seed spitting contests and all sorts of knick-knacks for sale. ⓣ718/689-8600.

U.S. Open Tennis Tournament (late Aug–early Sept): Top-seeded pros battle for the cup in Flushing Meadows–Corona Park, Queens. ⓣ800/524-8440, ⓦwww.usopen.com.

September

Tugboat Challenge (Sun before Labor Day): Pier 86 is the finish line for this kid-pleasing annual race between NY's working tugboats. It concludes Seafest, when ships visit and pier events are held at the Intrepid Sea-Air-Space Museum. ⓣ212/245-0072, ⓦwww.seafest.com.

West Indian Day Parade and Carnival (Labor Day): Brooklyn's largest parade, modeled after the carnivals of Trinidad and Tobago, features music, food and dance (see description on p.250). ⓣ718/774-8807 or 212/484-1222.

Labor Day Parade and Street Fair (Labor Day). Check newspapers and local TV news for parade route and related events.

Caribbean American Family Day Festival (Labor Day): Exotic music, foods, arts and crafts. Webster Ave between 233rd St and East Gun Hill Road in the Bronx ⓣ718/653–2808, ⓦwww.caribbeanfestival.org.

Broadway on Broadway (Sun after Labor Day): Free performances feature songs by casts of virtually every Broadway musical, culminating in a shower of confetti; held in Times Square. ⓣ212/768-1560 or 212/563-BWAY.

Festival of the Feast of San Gennaro (ten days in mid-Sept): For more than 70 years, the festival has celebrated the patron saint of Naples along Mulberry St and its environs in Little Italy, with wonderful food, great people-watching and fun things to buy. The saint's statue is carried through the streets with donations of dollar bills pinned to his cloak. ⓣ212/764-6330.

New York is Book Country (usually third Sunday): 11am–5pm on 5th Ave between 48th and 57th sts, and from Madison to 6th Ave on 52nd and 53rd sts. Just about every local bookstore and publisher has a display of new and recent books. ⓣ212/207-7242, ⓦwww.nybookcountry.com.

African-American Day Parade (late Sept): Runs from 111th St and Adam Clayton Powell Blvd to 142nd St, then east toward 5th Ave, Harlem. ⓣ212/862-7200.

Korean-American Parade (late Sept): From 42nd St and Broadway to 23rd St. ⓣ212/255-6969.

Steuben Day Parade (third Sat in Sept): The biggest German-American event. Baron von Steuben was a Prussian general who was with Washington at Valley Forge – as good an excuse as any for a costumed parade in his honor from 63rd to 86th sts and 5th Ave. ⓣ516/239-0741.

Gracie Square Art Show (call for date): 11am–dusk, at Carl Shurz Park, on East End Ave from 84th to 87th sts. ⓣ212/535-9132.

New York Film Festival (2 weeks late Sept–mid-Oct): One of the world's leading film festivals unreels at Lincoln Center. ⓣ212/875-5610, ⓦwww.filmlinc.com/nyff/nyff.

October

Next Wave Festival (Oct–Nov): Experimental arts festival conceived by Roy Lichtenstein, held at the Brooklyn Academy of Arts, featuring regulars like Lou Reed and dance troupe Pina Bausch. ⓣ718/636-4111.

Promenade Art Show (call for dates): On Brooklyn Promenade, the historic walkway that provides a great view of downtown Manhattan. ⓣ718/625-0080.

Lexington Avenue Oktoberfest (usually the first weekend): München-style sudsflood with bratwurst and beer on Lexington Ave from 42nd to 57th sts. ⓣ212/808-4900.

Pulaski Day Parade (call for exact date): On 5th Ave for the celebration of Polish heritage ⓣ212/374-5176.

Hispanic Day Parade (on or around Oct 8): On 5th Ave between 44th and 72nd sts ⓣ212/242-2360.

Columbus Day Parade (on or around Oct 12): One of the city's largest binges commemorates the day America was put on the map. 5th Ave from 44th to 79th sts ⓣ212/249-2360.

DUMBO Art Under the Bridge Festival (mid-Oct): More than 700 emerging and professional artists show their work in 250 open galleries. The Parade of Concept (robots, remote-controlled vehicles and floats) kicks off the show in the neighborhood of DUMBO (Down Under the Manhattan Bridge Overpass) – in Brooklyn between the Manhattan and Brooklyn bridges. ⓣ718/624-3772, ⓦwww.dumboartscenter.org.

Children's Halloween Carnival (around Halloween, usually a few days before Oct 31): At Chelsea Piers ⓣ212/336-6666.

Greenwich Village Halloween Parade (Oct 31): In the 7pm procession on 6th Ave from Spring to 23rd sts you'll see spectacular costumes, wigs and make-up. The music is great and the spirit is wild and gay. Get there early for a good viewing spot. ⓣ212/475-3333 x4044, ⓦwww.halloween-nyc.com. (A tamer children's parade takes place earlier that day in Washington Square Park.)

Antique and craft fairs include **Crafts on Columbus** on the first three weekends behind the American Museum of Natural History (ⓣ212/866-2239) and the **St Ignatius Loyola Antiques Show** at Park Ave and 84th St, a small and intimate show in a unique setting with quality antiques at affordable prices. ⓣ212/288-3588.

November

Radio City Christmas Spectacular (Nov–Jan): See the Rockettes rocking. ⓣ212/247-4777.

New York City Marathon (first Sun): Some 30,000 runners from all over the world assemble for this 26.2-mile run on city pavement through the five boroughs. One of the best places to watch is Central Park S, almost at the finish line. ⓣ212/860-4455, ⓦwww.nyrrc.org.

Macy's Parade Inflation Eve

See Mickey Mouse and the other balloons being inflated the night before Macy's Thanksgiving Day Parade. It's not as crowded, and you can experience something not televised to every home in America. They're blown up on W 77th and W 81st streets between Central Park W and Columbus Ave at the American Museum of Natural History. Wander around these huge objects and watch their shapes appear. It starts at dusk and can go past midnight.

Shorts International Film Fest (early Nov): Animation, comedy, documentary, drama and experimental films of 40 minutes or less at Cineplex Odeon Worldwide Cinemas, 50th St between 8th and 9th aves. ⓣ212/907-1288, ⓦwww.shorts.org.
Veteran's Day Parade (Nov 11): The United War Veterans sponsor this annual event on 5th Ave from 39th to 23rd sts. ⓣ212/693-1475.
Fall Antiques Show (mid-Nov): Foremost American antiques show in the country, at the Seventh Regiment Armory, Park Ave and 67th St. ⓣ212/777-5218.
Triple Pier Expo (two weekends, mid-Nov): Largest metropolitan antiques fair, on piers 88, 90 and 92. ⓣ212/255-0020.
Macy's Thanksgiving Day Parade (Thanksgiving Day): New York's most televised parade, with floats, dozens of marching bands from around the country, the Rockettes, and Santa Claus's first appearance of the season. More than two million spectators watch it from 77th St down Central Park W to Columbus Circle, then down Broadway to Herald Square, 9am–noon. ⓣ212-494-4495, ⓦwww.macysparade.com.
Thanksgiving Weekend Annual Uptown/Downtown Thanksgiving Crafts Fair (Fri–Sun after Thanksgiving): For a more sedate scene, start your holiday shopping here. At Wallace Hall at 84th St and Park Ave ⓣ212/866-2239.

December

Out of the Darkness (Dec 1): Candle-lit march to City Hall observes World AIDS Day, coinciding with the 24-hour reading of the names of the deceased. ⓣ212/580-7668.
Miracle on Madison Avenue Festival (first Sun): Covers 15 blocks, between 57th and 72nd sts, with a variety of things to do and buy. Proceeds go to benefit needy children. ⓣ212/988-4001.
Rockefeller Center Christmas Tree Lighting (early Dec): The lighting of the tree begins the festivities. ⓣ212/632-3975.
Chanukah Celebrations: During the eight nights of this holiday, usually in mid-December, a menorah-lighting ceremony takes place at Brooklyn's Grand Army Plaza. ⓣ718/778-6000.
Holiday Windows (beginning Dec 1): The windows on 5th Ave, especially those of Lord & Taylor and Saks Fifth Avenue, are well worth waiting on their long lines for.
Kwanzaa Fest (early Dec): The world's largest celebration of African-American Arts and Culture at the Jacob K. Javits Convention Center features entertainment, a children's pavilion and much more. ⓣ718/585-3530, ⓦwww.tike.com/kwanzaa.
New Year's Eve in Times Square (Dec 31): Some 200,000-plus revelers party in the cold streets. ⓣ212/768-1560, ⓦwww.timessquarebid.org. There are also fireworks at the South Street Seaport and in Central Park and Brooklyn's Prospect Park. More family-oriented, alcohol-free First Nights with dancing, music and food take place throughout the city. ⓣ212/818-1777.

39

Kids' New York

New York can be a wonderful city to visit with **children**. Obvious attractions include museums, skyscrapers and ferry rides, as well as the simple pleasures of just walking the streets, seeing the street entertainers and taking in the shopping scene. Free events, especially common in the summer, range from puppet shows and nature programs in the city's parks to storytelling hours at local libraries and bookstores. In addition, many museums and theaters have specific children's programs. Following are details on some attractions especially appealing to kids. Be sure to phone ahead for specific times, programs and availability to avoid any disappointment.

General advice

For a further **listing** of what is available when you're in town, see Friday's *Daily News* or *New York Times*, and "Activities for Children" in the weekly *New York* magazine, as well as *Time Out* and the *Village Voice*. An excellent automated directory of family-oriented current events all around the city is available through the New York Convention and Visitors Bureau, 810 7th Ave (between 52nd and 53rd sts) NY 10019 ⓣ212/484-1222 Mon–Fri 8.30am–6pm, Sat & Sun 9am–5pm; ⓦwww.nycvisit.com. They also have a free seasonal booklet, "The Big Apple Visitor's Guide," with a good map, directions and coupons. Also, check the family activity listings on the New York City website: ⓦwww.citysearchnyc.com.

Your main problem won't be finding stuff to do with your kids, but perhaps how to transport the younger ones around: though many natives navigate the streets and subways with a stroller, some prefer to keep infants and even toddlers conveniently contained in a backpack or front carrier. Indeed, most attractions listed here do not allow strollers, though most will store yours for you while you visit – call ahead for details. Most sights, restaurants and stores, however, are quite tolerant of children, if not actually child-friendly.

Subways are the fastest way to get around and are perfectly safe – don't worry about taking your kids on them, in fact they will probably get quite a kick out of them, crowds, noise and all. Buses are slower, but antsy or bored kids can stare through the large windows and watch the hustle and bustle outside. Also, remember that children under 44 inches (112cm) tall ride free on the subway and buses when accompanied by an adult.

Don't hesitate to ask a stranger for help getting a stroller up (or down) steps to the subway – it can be a hassle on your own – or directions to a sight or the nearest bathroom (large hotels and chain bookstores are great for this). Contrary to their reputation, most New Yorkers like kids and are quite willing to help.

Museums

One could spend an entire holiday just checking out the city's many museums, which almost always contain something of interest for the kids. The following is a brief overview of the ones that should evoke more than just the usual enthusiasm. See the appropriate chapters for more details on these and other museums.

American Museum of Natural History and the Rose Center for Earth and Space

Central Park W (at 79th St) ⓣ212/769-5100, ⓦwww.amnh.org. Sun–Thurs 10am–5.45pm, Fri & Sat 10am–8.45pm. IMAX shows 10.30am–4.30pm, every hour on the half-hour. Suggested donation $10, children $6, students/seniors $7.50 (includes the Rose Center). Special exhibits and IMAX additional charge, combination packages available.

One of the best museums of its kind, this enormous complex of buildings is filled with fossils, gems, meteorites and other natural artifacts (34 million in all). The recently renovated Dinosaur Halls offer enormous, creative displays and interactive computer stations that are sure to please all ages and are a good first stop. Extensive dioramas of animals from around the world allow children an up-close look at wildlife, and the new Hall of Biodiversity offers video presentations about the world's environment and a multimedia re-creation of a Central African rainforest. Several interactive children's programs are held the last weekend of each month, Oct–May; call for the schedule.

Just across from the Hall of Biodiversity lies the first installation of **the Rose Center for Earth and Space** – the state-of-the-art Hall of Planet Earth. The Rose Center features the Space Theater, the Big Bang Theater and the Hayden Planetarium, among other spanking new attractions that appeal to kids and adults.

American Museum of the Moving Image

35th Ave at 36th St, Astoria, Queens ⓣ718/784-0077. Tues–Fri noon–5pm, Sat & Sun 11am–6pm; $8.50, students/seniors $5.50, 5–12 $4.50, under 5 free (museum admission includes film screening).

This museum, in an old movie lot, is dedicated to all aspects of film, video and TV. Its exhibit halls are filled with historic costumes, cameras and props, as well as the entire *Seinfeld* set. Interactive displays, movie special effects demonstrations, and an exhibit of classic video games (that you can actually play) are just some of the things kids will love. Free film screenings are held in a lovely old movie palace on the premises. Definitely worth a visit, especially for kids 6 and older.

Brooklyn Children's Museum

145 Brooklyn Ave (on the corner of St Mark's Ave) ⓣ718/735-4400. Wed–Fri 2–5pm, Sat & Sun 10am–5pm; suggested contribution $4.

Founded in 1899, this is the world's first museum for children. A participatory, hands-on museum full of authentic ethnological, natural history and technological artifacts with which to play.

Children's Museum of the Arts

182 Lafayette St (between Broome and Grand sts) ⓣ212/274-0986. Wed noon–7pm, Thurs–Sun noon–5pm; $5, under 1 year free.

Art gallery of works by or for children. Children are encouraged to look at different types of art and then create their own, with paints, clay, plaster of Paris and any other simple medium. There are even projects for small toddlers.

Children's Museum of Manhattan

212 W 83rd St (between Broadway and Amsterdam Ave) ⓣ212/721-1234, ⓦwww.cmom.org. Tues–Sun 10am–5pm; $6, under age 1 free.

A terrific participatory museum founded in 1973 to "inspire learning through interactive exhibits and educational programs." The exhibit space covers five floors, with imaginative displays; not to be missed is "Seuss!" – a whimsical area with decor inspired by the Dr. Seuss books, where kids can (literally) cook up some green eggs and ham. As if that's not enough, children can produce their own television shows in the Media Center. For ages 1–12, and highly recommended.

Ellis Island Immigration Museum

Ellis Island ☎212/363-3200, access by the Circle Line Statue of Liberty Ferry (212/269-5755) from Battery Park, ⓦwww.ellisisland.org or ⓦwww.wallofhonor.com (a searchable database of the names of the people who came through the immigration center). Daily 9.30am–5pm; free. Ferries run every hour from 9.30am–3.30pm (though you need to be on the 3pm ferry at the latest to see the museum); $8 round-trip, 3–17 $3.

This is one of the least expensive ways to spend a day in New York, and also one of the best; you can combine a fun trip on a ferry with visits to this and the Statue of Liberty. Ellis Island became an immigration processing station in 1894, and in 1990 the main buildings were renovated and reopened as the Immigration Museum. Special features include the "Ellis Island Stories," a dramatic re-enactment of the immigrant experience based on oral histories (April–Sept only; $3, children $2.50; call ahead for schedule); and "Treasures From Home," a collection of family heirlooms, photos and other artifacts donated by descendants of the immigrants. Take your break at a lovely restaurant with a terrace and great views.

Fire Museum

278 Spring St (between Hudson and Varick sts) ☎212/691-1303. Tues–Sun 10am–4pm; $4, students $2, under 12 $1.

A sure hit with the pre-school crowd, it's an unspectacular but pleasing homage to New York City's firefighters, and indeed firepeople everywhere. On display are fire engines from yesteryear (hand-drawn, horse-drawn and steam-powered), helmets, dog-eared photos and a host of motley objects on three floors of a former fire station. A neat and appealing display.

Intrepid Sea-Air-Space Museum

W 46th St and 12th Ave at Pier 86 ☎212/245-0072. Summer hours: April 1–Sept 30 Mon–Sat 10am–5pm, Sun 10am–6pm; winter hours: Oct 1–March 31 Wed–Sun 10am–5pm; closed Jan for repair and cleaning; last admission 1 hour prior to closing; $10, 12–17 $7.50, 6–11 $5, 3–5 $1, under 2 free.

This old aircraft carrier has a distinguished history. Today it holds the world's fastest spy plane, a guided missile submarine, and other modern and vintage air and sea craft, as well as interactive CD-ROM exhibits and a restaurant. Not especially recommended for kids under 5 years.

Museum of the City of New York

1220 5th Ave (at 103rd St). Wed–Sat 10am–5pm, Sun noon–5pm, Tues 10am–2pm for pre-registered tour groups only; suggested donation $7, students $4, families $12. ☎212/534-1672 for exhibit information.

The permanent collection of this museum provides several opportunities to engage children. New York Toy Stories is a super way to bring young ones back to simpler times, before video games, when wooden toys, rubber balls and board games were just about the only options in the late 1800s. For girls (and grownups) there is a worthwhile and surprising group of doll houses. The painted New York landmarks in the picture gallery are easily recognizable, and kids can talk about what they've seen of the city, and what they'd like to see.

National Museum of the American Indian (Smithsonian Institution)

1 Bowling Green (at Battery Park) ☎212/514-3700, ⓦwww.si.edu/nmai. Daily 10am–5pm, Thurs until 8pm; free.

A beautiful museum housing the largest collection in the world devoted to North, Central and South American Indian cultures. Though much of the exhibit is behind glass, the layout makes it very accessible and the background sound and music set the mood. Kids will enjoy looking at the ancient dolls and feathered headdresses, and the replicas of a reservation home and schoolroom. Programs often include theater troupes, performance artists, dancers and films.

New York Hall of Science

47-01 111th St (at 46th Ave), Flushing Meadows, Corona, Queens ☎718/699-0005. Mon–Wed 9.30am–2pm, Thurs–Sun 9.30am–5pm; in July & Aug Tues & Wed also 9.30am–5pm; $7.50, children $5.

Built for the 1964–65 World's Fair, this museum (ranked one of the top ten science museums in the country) continues to add the latest in scientific and technological displays; hands-on exhibits make it really fun for kids. A highlight is the outdoor Science Playground (open May–Oct), for ages 6 and older. Though not worth a special trip in itself, it certainly merits a visit on the way out to nearby Shea Stadium, the Queens Zoo, Queens Art Museum or the World's Fair grounds in Flushing Meadows Park.

New York Transit Museum

Old subway entrance (at Schermerhorn St and Boerum Place), Brooklyn ⓣ718/243-3060, ⓦwww.mta.nyc.ny.us. Tues–Fri 10am–4pm, Sat & Sun noon–5pm; $3, children $1.50. Also: Transit Museum Gallery and Store at Grand Central Terminal, open daily, free admission.

Housed in an abandoned 1930s subway station, this museum offers more than 100 years' worth of transportation history and memorabilia, including old subway cars and buses dating back to the turn of the last century (including, amazingly, a wooden train car from 1914). Frequent activities for children include underground tours, workshops and an annual bus festival – all best for younger school kids. The NY Transit Museum Gallery and Store opened in 1999 and has changing exhibits about public transit; a gift shop sells transit-related items.

Queens County Farm Museum

73-50 Little Neck Parkway, Queens. Subway E, F to Kew Gardens-Union Turnpike, transfer to Q46 bus to Little Neck Parkway. Museum open April–Dec Sat & Sun 10am–5pm; farm grounds open year-round Mon–Fri, 9am–5pm, April–Dec also Sat & Sun 10am–5pm. ⓣ718/347-3276.

Yes, there really is a working farm in Queens, with cows, sheep, geese, ducks and other farm animals, and a large orchard. Built in 1772, this 47-acre farm was continuously worked for more than 200 years, and has a lovely farmhouse with wooden-beamed ceilings and Dutch detail. Special events include apple festivals in the fall, craft shows, weekend hayrides and other regular activities for kids.

South Street Seaport Center and Museum

207 Front St (at the east end of Fulton St at the East River) ⓣ212/748-8600, ⓦwww.southstseaport.org. April–Sept daily 10am–6pm; Oct–March 10am–5pm; $5.

Eighteenth- and nineteenth-century buildings house three galleries, a children's center, a maritime craft center and a library, and the adjacent dock is home to a small fleet of historic ships. New York Unearthed is a site the museum has devoted to archeological work currently being done in the city. Children can watch archeologists work, learn how dug-up artifacts tell us about New York's history, and ride an elevator into a simulated "dig" site. Kids will enjoy the free Saturday-evening concerts in July and August and the street entertainers who perform around the Seaport in warm weather.

Staten Island Children's Museum

Snug Harbor Cultural Center, 1000 Richmond Terrace, Staten Island ⓣ718/273-2060. Tues–Sun noon–5pm; $4, children under 2 free.

This is a good way to round off a trip on the Staten Island ferry; it's reachable on a trolleybus from the ferry terminal. The many hands-on exhibits cover subjects like the environment and technology, puppets and toys. In the summer the downstairs gallery hosts many special exhibits and events that are free with admission, but the space is often full. Call for reservations.

Sights and entertainment

Again, this is just a small selection of the top attractions children will enjoy:

Bronx Zoo (formally, the International Wildlife Conservation Park)

Bronx River Parkway at Fordham Rd ⓣ718/367-1010, ⓦwww.wcs.org. Mar–Oct Mon–Fri 10am–5pm, Sat & Sun 10am–5.30pm; Nov–Feb daily 10am–4.30pm; $9, kids $5, free to all on Wed, rides and some exhibits are an additional charge. Parking $7.

The largest urban zoo in America has more than 4000 species of animals, reptiles

Babysitting

The Babysitters' Guild 60 E 42nd St (☎212/682-0227) offers babysitting services with approved sitters; 16 foreign languages are spoken. Fees are $15 an hour, depending on the age and how many children there are, plus a flat fee of $4.50 to cover transportation – after midnight the fee for transportation is $7. Most sitters have teaching and nursing backgrounds, and are fully licensed and bonded. As always, call for the full picture. Be sure to book as far in advance as you can – at the latest the day before you need the sitter, if possible.

Also, the **Avalon Nurse Registry and Child Service** 162 W 56th St (☎212/245-0250) provides full- or part-time nannies and babysitters at a reasonable $16 per hour (in a hotel) plus transportation costs, and $2 extra for each additional child, with a 4-hour minimum. English and Spanish are spoken.

and birds on display, many in huge simulated natural habitats such as Wild Asia, where tigers, elephants and other large animals roam (almost) free. A children's section allows kids to climb around on large exhibits, including a giant spider web, and pet some of the tamer animals. Come to visit the new animal babies in the summer. Highly recommended for an all-day excursion.

Central Park

Year-round, Central Park provides sure-fire entertainment for children. In the summer it becomes one giant playground, with activities ranging from storytelling to rollerblading to rowboating. The following are merely a few of the highlights – for much more detailed information on these and other sights, see Chapter 18, "Central Park."

Belvedere Castle 79th St mid-park. Kids will enjoy scrambling up the narrow spiral staircase to the lookout. Nature center has turtles, other crawly things.

The Carousel 64th St mid-park. For just $1, children can take a spin on the country's largest hand-carved horses.

Central Park Wildlife Conservation Center (Zoo), 5th Ave at 64th St. A small but enjoyable zoo, with sea lions, polar bears, monkeys and the Tisch Children's Zoo.

Hans Christian Andersen statue 72nd St on the East Side (next to the Boat Pond). A forty-or-so-year tradition of storytelling sessions; Wed & Sat 11am–noon, June to Sept.

Loeb Boathouse 72nd St mid-park. Rent a rowboat on the Central Park lake and enjoy the views or take a gondola ride in the evening. Bike rentals available too.

Wollman Rink 62nd St mid-park ☎212/396-1010. Roller/in-line skating during the summer and ice-skating during the winter. Skate rental and instruction available.

Chelsea Piers Sports & Entertainment Complex

Piers 59–62 at W 23rd St and the Hudson River ☎212/336-6666 (general info) or 336-6500 (fieldhouse, soccer, basketball, etc). Each activity priced separately. This huge, wildly popular sports center has 2 indoor ice-skating rinks, an outdoor rollerblading rink, basketball courts, a rock-climbing wall for kids, 2 indoor astro-turf soccer fields, batting cages, gymnastics facilities and much more.

New York Aquarium

W 8th St and Surf Ave, Coney Island, Brooklyn ☎718/265-3474. Daily 10am–6pm; $9.75, 2–12 $6, under 2 free.

First opened in 1896, the aquarium is a division of the Wildlife Conservation Society. Mostly it's a series of darkened halls containing creatures from the deep, but open-air shows of whales and dolphins are held several times daily, as are the shark, sea otter and walrus feedings. Call for daily show/program info. This is also the site of the famous Coney Island boardwalk and amusement park – older children and teens will find it a good spot to people-watch. Note that no pets, bikes, radios, skates or skateboards are allowed.

New York Botanical Garden

200th St and Southern Blvd (Kazimiroff Blvd), the Bronx (across from the Bronx Zoo) ☎718/817-8777, Ⓦwww.nybg.org. Tues–Sun

Times Square

Just north of 42nd St, where Broadway and 7th Ave converge in midtown Manhattan, is the heart of the new **Times Square**, which has been transformed from an infamous den of iniquity into a family-oriented entertainment zone. Much of this has to do with Disney's new and very obvious presence in the area. For more on the neighborhood, see p.160. Below are some of the more kid-oriented options in the district.

Bar Code 1540 Broadway (near 46th St) ⓣ212/869-9397, ⓦwww.barcodeentertainment.com. This is a must-stop for the age 8 and over crowd. Upon entering this very dark and very loud futuristic world all senses go into overdrive, which is exactly the idea. There are tons of games to try, from high-tech interactive video and virtual reality games to hoop shoot and air hockey. The *Bar Code* itself is for adults 21 and over at night (and features a full bar), but Galactic Circus, on the second level up, has more of a family, Coney Island atmosphere, with carnival games and tickets that can be redeemed for prizes. Both set-ups have a full snack menu. Another alternative is Broadway City, at 241 W 42nd St between 8th Ave and Broadway ⓣ212/997-9797.

The Disney Store 210 W 42nd St at Broadway ⓣ212/302-0595. This retail outlet is found in many American malls, though this one is considerably larger than the standard. The giant movie screen runs ads for DisneyWorld in Orlando, Florida, and of course segments of the many Disney movies.

New Victory Theater 209 W 42nd St ⓣ646/223-3020. See p.160.

10am–6pm; grounds only $3, students, 2–12 $1, free admission on Wed.

One of America's foremost public gardens, with 250 acres of flowers, trees and park. The Enid A. Haupt Conservatory (known as the crystal palace) has been magnificently restored and is currently housing a rainforest containing several thousand medicinal herbs. The Everett Adventure Garden is a 12-acre kids' discovery center, with more than 40 hands-on activities, including plant and rock mazes, as well as storytelling, music, puppet shows and other special events (summer: Tues–Fri 1–6pm, Sat & Sun 10am–6pm; $3, 2–12 $1; call for events info). Otherwise, a beautiful, tranquil spot, perfect if you've got a baby or toddler in need of a nap (especially good for the adults).

Skyride

350 5th Ave (at 34th St) in the Empire State Building ⓣ212/279-9777. Daily 10am–10pm; $13.50, 4–12 $10.50. Combination ticket to skyride and observatory $17 and $10.

The Skyride, in the Empire State Building, is a big-screen thrill ride through the most well-known sights in the city, complete with tilting seats and surround sound. Bring a strong stomach; it may be too much for small children. Don't miss the observatory at the top of the Empire State Building, offering spectacular day and nighttime views 1050 feet above Manhattan.

Sony Imax Theater

1998 Broadway and 68th St, info at ⓣ212/336-5000, ⓦwww.sony.com. $10, 12 and under $6.50.

See the city past and present in 3-D. Also housed in the Lincoln Square Entertainment Complex is a Sony twelve-screen movie theater and the *Real Java Café*. Show times vary.

Sony Wonder Technology Lab

550 Madison Ave (at 56th St) ⓣ212/833-8100. Tues–Sat 10am–6pm, Thurs until 8pm, Sun noon–6pm; free.

The lab offers amazing hands-on experience with communication technology. Try your hand at editing rock videos or editing or producing TV programs. You can even participate in directing an action movie while sitting in the audience. Very futuristic; every person receives a card-key that imprints his or her photo image, name and a voice sample, and a completion certificate is issued at the end. This is a hugely popular attraction, so get here early.

Shops: toys, books and clothes

Bank Street Bookstore 610 W 112th St (between Broadway and Riverside Drive) ☎212/678-1654. The store is affiliated with Bank Street College of Education. The first floor is filled with children's books and games, while the second floor is devoted to educational material for parents and teachers. Their knowledgeable and helpful staff will recommend the perfect book for your child. Frequent special events.

Big City Kites 1210 Lexington Ave (at 82nd St) ☎212/472-2623. Manhattan's largest and best kite store, with a huge range to choose from.

Books of Wonder 16 W 18th St (between 5th and 6th aves) ☎212/989-3270. Excellent kids' bookstore, with a great story-hour on Sun at 11.45am, and author appearances Sat in the spring and fall.

Cozy's Cuts for Kids 1125 Madison Ave (at 84th St) ☎212/744-1716; also 448 Amsterdam Ave (between 81st and 82nd sts) ☎212/579-2600. For the first haircut through 12 years old, kids can get their hair cut while sitting in a play jeep and watching videos. Little ones receive an honorary diploma for their first haircut.

Enchanted Forest 85 Mercer St (between Spring and Broome sts) ☎212/925-6677. A marvelous shop that hides its unique merchandise – stuffed animals, puppets, masks and the like – partly in the branches of its mock forest.

F.A.O. Schwarz 767 5th Ave (at 58th St) ☎212/644-9400. Showpiece of a nationwide chain sporting three huge floors of everything a child could want. Fans of Barbie will want to check out the Barbie store, in the back of F.A.O. Schwarz, with its own Madison Ave entrance. Not to be missed.

Gymboree 2015 Broadway (at 69th St) ☎212/595-7662; also 1049 3rd Ave (at 62nd St) ☎212/688-4044, and other locations in the city. Welcoming stores offering brightly colored kids' clothes for newborns through seven years old. Very reasonable prices and great sales.

Little Eric 1331 3rd Ave (between 76th and 77th sts) ☎212/288-8987; also 1118 Madison (between 83rd and 84th sts) ☎212/717-1513. Large selection of shoes, mostly imported from Italy (and expensive), for children. Kids won't mind shopping here because they

New York for teens

Manhattan itself should be enough to excite and enrapture **teenagers**, but if you're searching for additional entertainment, there are a number of options. For high-tech thrills, check the **Sony Wonder Technology Lab** (p.459), **Broadway City** or **Bar Code** (see the "Times Square" box above). Or you could hit one of the city's many music stores. **Manny's Music**, 156 W 48th St, has walls covered with hundreds of autographed photographs of music's biggest stars, past and present, in addition to musical instruments and recording gear. See p.424 for a list of best record shops.

For a backstage look at real television production, take the **NBC Studio Tour** (30 Rockefeller Plaza–50th St, between 5th and 6th aves ☎212/664-4000; Mon–Sat 9.30am–4.30pm, about every 15min; $10 per person; children under 6 not admitted). The hour-long tour takes in the studios of *NFL Today*, *Dateline* and *Saturday Night Live*, as well as general production facilities. It also includes a mock radio show with audience participation. The **Kramer Reality Tour** (P.O. Box 391, NY 10036 ☎212/268-5525 or 1-800/KRAMERS; Sat & Sun tours at noon; $37.50) is a tour of New York spots highlighted in the popular *Seinfeld* sitcom, led by the person who inspired the character of Cosmo Kramer.

For the sports enthusiast the **Madison Square Garden Tour** (7th Ave between 31st and 33rd sts ☎212/465-5800) offers a 1-hour behind-the-scenes look at the arena, theater, and the Knick and Ranger locker rooms; **Chelsea Piers** for participatory sports ☎212/336-6000 (see p.443); or ESPN Zone ☎212/921-3776 or WWF NY ☎212/398-2563 for a loud audiovisual assault with your dinner.

For a rockin' eating experience, there are the established favorites: **Hard Rock Café** (221 W 57th St ☎212/489-6565); **Planet Hollywood** (1540 Broadway ☎212/333-7827); and **the Harley Davidson Café** (1370 6th Ave ☎212/245-6000), which also has a cool retail shop. For that **clothes-shopping** spree, head to the East Village and SoHo for all the funky stores and "in" fashions – see Chapter 36, "Shops and markets." And of course, a simple walk through some neighborhoods, like the streets of the West Village, can be entertaining on its own.

play videos and cartoons all day.

Penny Whistle Toys 1283 Madison Ave (at 91st St) ⓣ212/369-3868; also 448 Columbus Ave (at 81st St) ⓣ212/873-9090. Wonderful shop selling a fun, imaginative range of toys that deliberately eschews guns and war accessories, including replicas of old-fashioned toys rarely seen these days. Highly recommended.

Red Caboose 23 W 45th St (between 5th and 6th aves); lower level – follow the flashing railroad sign in back of lobby ⓣ212/575-0155. A unique shop specializing in models, particularly trains and train sets.

Second Childhood 283 Bleecker St (between 6th and 7th aves) ⓣ212/989-6140. Toys dating back to 1850, with a wide assortment of miniatures, soldiers and lead animals.

Space Kiddets 46 E 21st St (between Park Ave and Broadway) ⓣ212/420-9878. Eclectic mix of unusual, funky clothes from newborn to size twelve. They also have shoes and toys.

Tannen's Magic Studio 24 W 25th St (between Broadway and 6th Ave) ⓣ212/929-4500. Your kids will never forget a visit to the largest magic shop in the world, with nearly 8000 props, tricks and magic sets. The staff is made up of magicians who perform free magic shows throughout the day.

Zany Brainy 112 E 86th St (between Lexington and Park aves) ⓣ212/427-6611; also Broadway and 88th St ⓣ917/441-2066. Well-stocked educational toy shop.

Theater, puppet shows, circuses and others

The following is a highly selective roundup of other activities, particularly cultural ones that might be of interest to young children. Bear in mind that you can – as always – find out more by checking the listings in local newspapers and magazines. Note too that stores like Macy's and F.A.O. Schwarz often have events for children – puppet shows, story-hours and the like – as do the children's bookstores (see above).

Barnum & Bailey Circus Madison Square Garden ⓣ212/465-6741. This large touring circus is usually in New York between the end of March and the beginning of May.

Big Apple Circus Lincoln Center ⓣ212/546-2656. Small circus that performs in a tent in Damrosch Park next to the Met, from late Oct to early Jan. Tickets $10–45.

Miss Majesty's Lollipop Playhouse Children's theater company with performances at the Grove St Playhouse, 39 Grove St ⓣ212/741-6436, Sat & Sun at 1.30pm & 3.30pm, closed in the summer; and at the Gene Frankel Theater, 24 Bond St off Lafayette ⓣ212/777-1767, Sat & Sun at 1pm and 3pm, open year-round; tickets at both locations are $8.50. Mostly comedies based on fairy tales, with audience participation, for kids 2–10. Well-done and quite popular – reserve your seats in advance.

New Victory Theater 209 W 42nd St ⓣ646/223-3020. The city's first theater for families. There is always a rich mix of theater, music, dance, storytelling, film and puppetry, in addition to pre-performance workshops and post-performance participation. The interior has been beautifully restored, the seats are plush but small. Everything about this theater is child-oriented from the affordable cost (most shows $10–25) to the duration of performances (60–90 minutes). Strangely enough, the theater is dark (no performances) during the summer.

Puppet Playhouse 555 E 90th St (at York Ave, within Asphalt Green) ⓣ212/369-8890 (ext 159). Puppet theater that stages shows on weekends. $7, groups of 10 or more, $6 each. Season runs Sept to early May – call for a schedule and reservations.

Thirteenth Street Repertory Company 50 W 13th St (between 5th and 6th aves) ⓣ212/675-6677. Sat & Sun 1pm and 3pm, year-round; $7. 45-minute original musicals – such as "Rumplewho?" – specifically created for "little humans." Reservations needed, as these are very popular shows.

40 Directory

Airlines Toll-free phone numbers of foreign airlines include: Air India ☎1-800/223-7776; Air New Zealand ☎1-800/262-1234; British Airways ☎1-800/247-9297; El Al ☎1-800/223-6700; Japan Air Lines ☎1-800/525-3663; Korean Airlines ☎1-800/438-5000; Kuwait Airways ☎1-800/458-9248; Qantas Airways ☎1-800/227-4500; Virgin Atlantic Airways ☎1-800/862-8621. For the toll-free numbers of the major US and Canadian airlines, see p.12.

Bring . . . your credit cards – you'll be considered barely human without them.

Buy . . . Good things to take home include all American-style gear (such as baseball caps, basketball shoes and Levis). CDs are significantly cheaper than in many parts of the US and Europe; the same is true of almost any photographic or electronic equipment (foreign visitors, read our warning below about electric current).

Consulates Australia, 150 E 42nd St (☎212/351-6500); Canada, 1251 6th Ave at 50th St (☎212/596-1628); Denmark, 1 Dag Hammarskjöld Plaza (☎212/223-4545); France, 934 Fifth Ave (☎212/606-3600); Germany, 871 UN Plaza (☎212/610-9700); Ireland, 345 Park Ave at 51st St (☎212/319-2555); Italy, 690 Park Ave (☎212/737-9100); Netherlands, 1 Rockefeller Plaza (entrance at 14 W 49th St between 5th and 6th aves) (☎212/246-1429); New Zealand, 780 3rd Ave (☎212/832-4038); Spain, 150 E 58th St (☎212/355-4080); Sweden, 1 Dag Hammarskjöld Plaza (☎212/583-2550); UK, 845 3rd Ave between 51st and 52nd sts (☎212/745-0200).

Contraception Condoms are available in all pharmacies and delis. If you're on the pill it's obviously best to bring a supply with you; should you run out, or need advice on other aspects of contraception, abortion or related matters, contact Planned Parenthood, Margaret Sanger Center, 26 Bleecker St at Mott (☎212/274-7200) or the Women's Healthline (☎212/230-1111).

Drugs See the Basics section, "Crime and personal safety."

Electric current 110V AC with two-pronged plugs. Unless they're dual voltage, all British appliances will need a voltage converter as well as a plug adapter. Be warned, some converters may not be able to handle certain high-wattage items, especially those with heated elements.

Emergencies For Police, Fire or Ambulance dial ☎911.

Getting married If it's a quick holiday wedding you're after (but Vegas doesn't suit you), consider New York. Bring two money orders made out to the City Clerk of New York – one for the marriage license ($30) and one for the ceremony itself ($25). You'll both need passports and, if applicable, details concerning the dissolution of any previous marriages. Licenses may be purchased and ceremonies performed at any of the five borough halls (Manhattan's is listed below). After obtaining the license, a 24-hour gap is required before you can be married, giving you ample time to find a witness (one is required at City Hall, two in a church). City Hall, 2nd floor, Municipal Building South Side, 1 Centre St, Mon–Fri 8.30am–4pm ☎212/669-2400.

ID Carry some at all times, as there are any number of occasions on which you may be asked to show it. Two pieces of ID are preferable and one should have a photo –

passport and credit card are the best bets. Almost every bar and restaurant (serving alcohol) in New York will ask for proof of age (21 and over).

Jaywalking This is how New Yorkers cross the streets – when they can, regardless of what the light, if any, might say. However, be aware that from time to time the city announces a "get tough" policy on jaywalking.

Laundry Hotels do it but charge a lot. You're much better off going to an ordinary laundromat or dry cleaners, both of which you'll find plenty of in the *Yellow Pages* under "Laundries." Some budget hotels, YMCAs and hostels also have coin-operated washers and dryers.

Left luggage The most likely place to dump your stuff is Grand Central Station (42nd St and Park Ave ⓣ212/340-2555), where the luggage/lost and found department is by Track 100, on the lower level, open Mon–Fri 7am–11pm, Sat & Sun 10am–11pm, and charges $2 per item per calendar day. Photo ID required.

Libraries The real heavyweight is the central reference section of the New York Public Library, 5th Ave at 42nd St (see p.136). However, although this library is a great place to work and its stock of books one of the best in the world, you can't check out books. To do this, go to a branch (for a full list ask in the reference library) and produce proof of residence in the city. (The closest, with acres of open shelves, is the Mid-Manhattan Library, just down 5th Ave at 40th St.) Across the board, library hours have been cut drastically due to budget cuts. Not a problem for the visitor, but for the city's 9-to-5ers it's a definite bone of contention.

Lost property Things lost on buses or on the subway: NYC Transit Authority, at the 34th St/8th Ave Station at the north end on the lower level subway mezzanine (Mon–Wed & Fri 8am–noon, Thurs 11am–6.30pm ⓣ212/712-4500). Things lost on Amtrak: Penn Station (Mon–Fri 7.30am–4pm ⓣ212/630-7389). Things lost in a cab: Taxi & Limousine Commission Lost Property Information Dept, 40 Rector St between Washington St and the West Side Highway (Mon–Fri 9am–5pm except national holidays ⓣ212/302-8294).

Measurements and sizes The US has yet to go metric, and measurements of length are in inches, feet, yards and miles, with weight measured in ounces, pounds and tons. Liquid measures are slightly more confusing in that an imperial pint is roughly equivalent to 1.25 American pints, and an American gallon thus only equal to about four-fifths of an imperial one. Add to this the fact that milk and orange juice are sold in quarts, while soft drinks are sold in liters. Clothing and shoe sizes are easier: women's garment sizes are always two figures less than they would be in Britain. Thus, a British size 12 will be a size 8 in the States, a size 14 a size 10. To calculate shoe sizes in America, simply add 2 to your British size – thus, if you're normally size 8 you'll need a size 10 shoe in New York. See p.408 for more.

Notice boards For contacts, casual work, articles for sale, etc, it's hard to beat the notice board just inside the doorway of the *Village Voice* office at 36 Cooper Square (just south of the Astor Place subway stop). Otherwise there are numerous notice boards up at Columbia University, in the Loeb Student Center of NYU on Washington Square, and in the groovier coffee shops, health food stores and restaurants in the East Village.

Public holidays You'll find all banks, most offices, some stores and certain museums closed on the following days: January 1; Martin Luther King's Birthday (third Mon in Jan); Presidents' Day (third Mon in Feb); Memorial Day (last Mon in May); Independence Day (July 4 or, if it falls on a weekend, the following Mon); Labor Day (first Mon in Sept); Columbus Day (second Mon in Oct); Veterans Day (Nov 11); Thanksgiving (the third or last Thurs in Nov); Christmas Day (Dec 25). Also, New York's numerous parades mean that on certain days – St Patrick's Day, Gay Pride Day, Easter Sunday and Columbus Day, to name a few – much of Fifth Avenue is closed to traffic altogether.

Street names/street signs New York likes to honor its favorite sons – or daughters – by renaming thoroughfares after them. Just recently the West Side Highway was rechristened the Joe Di Maggio Highway in honor of the late Yankee Clipper. So don't panic when you're strolling up Sixth Avenue only to find yourself on the Avenue of the Americas.

Tax Within New York City you'll pay an 8.25 percent sales tax on top of marked prices on just about everything but the very barest of essentials, a measure brought in to help alleviate the city's 1975 economic crisis, and one that stuck. To prevent the masses from crossing the George Washington Bridge to buy their clothes tax-free in New Jersey, clothing (excluding shoes) was exempted in 2001; now items up to $100 are without tax.

Terminals and transit information Grand Central Terminal, 42nd St and Park Ave (Metro-North commuter trains ☎212/532-4900); Pennsylvania Station, 33rd St and 8th Ave (Amtrak ☎1-800/USA-RAIL or 582-6875); New Jersey Transit (☎973/762-5100); Long Island Railroad (LIRR ☎718/217-5477); PATH trains (☎1-800/234-7284); Port Authority Bus Terminal, 41st St and 8th Ave and George Washington Bridge Bus Terminal, W 178th St (between Broadway and Fort Washington) both ☎212/564-8484; Greyhound (☎1-800/231-2222); Peter Pan Trailways (☎1-800/343-9999); Bonanza (☎1-800/556-3815).

Time Three hours ahead of West Coast North America, five hours behind Britain and Ireland, fourteen to sixteen hours behind East Coast Australia (variations for Daylight Savings Time), sixteen to eighteen hours behind New Zealand (variations for Daylight Savings Time).

Tipping Tipping, in a restaurant, bar, taxi cab, hotel lobby and even in some posh washrooms, is a part of life in the States – in restaurants in particular, it's unthinkable not to leave the minimum (15 percent of the bill or double the tax) even if you hated the service.

Toilets The only public pay toilet in existence (remaining from a previous failed experiment) is in City Hall park across from the Municipal Building, and it's such an unusual sight that you may see people taking each other's picture going in and out. If you're anywhere else in the city, however, you must resort to bravely flouting signs like "Restrooms for patrons only." Otherwise check out the lobbies of any of the swanky hotels in midtown; the Trump Tower, where there are public loos on the Garden level; the New York Public Library at 42nd St and 5th Ave; and the Lincoln Center's Avery Fisher Hall and Library, both of which have several bathrooms. *Starbucks*, Barnes & Noble Superstores, and Macy's and Bloomingdale's department stores also have accessible and clean restrooms.

Worship There are regular services and masses at the following churches and synagogues. Anglican (Episcopal): Cathedral of St John the Divine, 1047 Amsterdam Ave at 112th St (☎212/316-7400); St Bartholomew's, 109 E 50th St (☎212/751-1616); Trinity Church, Broadway and Wall St (☎212/602-0800). Catholic: St Patrick's Cathedral, 5th Ave between 50th and 51st sts (☎212/753-2261). Jewish (Reform): Temple Emanu-el, 5th Ave at 65th St (☎212/744-1400); Central Synagogue, Lexington Ave at 55th St (☎212/838-5122). Jewish (Conservative): Park Avenue Synagogue, 87th St at Madison Ave (☎212/369-2600). Unitarian: Church of All Souls, Lexington Ave at 80th St (☎212/535-5530).

contexts

contexts

The historical framework

To Europe she was America, to America she was the gateway of the earth. But to tell the story of New York would be to write a social history of the world.

—H.G. Wells

Early days and colonial rule

In the earliest times, the area that today is New York City was populated by Native Americans. Each tribe had its own territory and lived a settled existence in villages of bark huts, gaining a livelihood from crop planting, hunting, trapping and fishing. In the New York area, the Algonquin tribe was the most populous. Survivors of this and other tribes still live on Long Island's **Shinnecock reservation** and remnants of their native cultures can be seen at the upstate Turtle Center for the Native American Indian. Native American life, as it had existed for several thousand years, sadly ended with the arrival of European explorers.

In 1524 **Giovanni da Verrazano**, an Italian in the service of the French King Francis I, arrived, following in the footsteps of Christopher Columbus 32 years earlier. On his ship, the *Dauphane*, Verrazano had set out to find the legendary Northwest Passage to the Pacific and, much like Columbus' fortunate folly, he instead he discovered Manhattan:

We found a very agreeable situation located within two small prominent hills, in the midst of which flowed to the sea a very great river, which was deep within the mouth; and from the sea to the hills, with the rising of the tide, which we found at eight feet, any laden ship might have passed.

Verrazano returned, "leaving the said land with much regret because of its commodiousness and beauty, thinking it was not without some properties of value" to woo the court with tales of fertile lands and friendly natives. But oddly enough, it was nearly a century before the powers of Europe were tempted to follow him.

In 1609 **Henry Hudson**, an Englishman employed by the **Dutch East India Company**, landed at Manhattan and sailed his ship, the *Half-Moone*, upriver as far as Albany. Hudson found that the route did not lead to the Northwest Passage he had been commissioned to discover – but in charting its course for the first time he gave his name to the mighty river. "This is a very good land to fall with," noted the ship's mate, "and a pleasant land to see." In a series of skirmishes, Hudson's men gave the native people a taste of what to expect from future adventurers. Chastised by the British for exploring new territory for the Dutch, Hudson embarked on another expedition, this time under the British flag. He arrived in Hudson Bay, the temperature falling and the mutinous crew doubting his ability as a navigator; he, his son and several others were set adrift in a small boat on the icy waters where, presumably, they froze to death.

British fears that the Dutch had gained the upper hand in the newly discovered land proved justified, for they had the commercial advantage and wasted no time in making the most of it. In the next few years the Dutch established a trading post at the most northerly point Hudson had reached, **Fort Nassau**.

In 1624, four years after the Pilgrim Fathers had sailed to Massachusetts, thirty families left Holland to become New York's first European settlers, most sailing up to Fort Nassau. But a handful – eight families in all – stayed behind on a small island they called Nut Island because of the many walnut trees there: today's Governor's Island. Slowly the community grew as more settlers arrived, and the little island became crowded; the decision was made to move to the limitless spaces across the water, and **the settlement of Manhattan**, taken from the Algonquin Indian word *Manna-Hata* meaning "Island of the Hills," began.

The Dutch gave their new outpost the name **New Amsterdam**, and in 1626 **Peter Minuit** was sent out to govern the small community of just over three hundred. Among his first, and certainly more politically adroit moves was to buy the whole of Manhattan Island from the Indians for trinkets worth 60 guilders (about $25 today); of course the other side of the anecdote is that the Indians Minuit dealt with didn't even come from Manhattan, let alone own it. As the colony slowly grew, a string of governors succeeded Minuit, the most famous of them **Peter Stuyvesant** – "Peg Leg Pete," a seasoned colonialist from the Dutch West Indies who'd lost his leg in a scrap with the Portuguese. Under his leadership New Amsterdam doubled in size and population, protected from British settlers to the north by an encircling wall (**Wall Street** today follows its course) and defended by a rough-hewn fort on what is now the site of the Customs House. Stuyvesant also built himself a farm (a *bouwerij* in Dutch) nearby, that gave its name to Manhattan's **Bowery** district.

Meanwhile the **British** were steadily and stealthily building up their presence to the north. Though initially preoccupied by civil war at home, they maintained their claim that all of America's East Coast, from New England to Virginia, was theirs, and in 1664 sent Colonel Richard Nicholls to claim the lands around the Hudson that King Charles II had granted to his brother, the Duke of York. To reinforce his sovereignty Charles sent along four warships and landed troops on Nut Island and Long Island. The Dutch settlers had by then had enough of Stuyvesant's increasingly dictatorial rule, especially the high taxation demanded by the nominal owners of the colony, the Dutch West India Company, and so refused to defend Dutch rule against the British. Captain Nicholls' men took New Amsterdam, renamed it **New York** in honor of the duke and settled down to a hundred-odd years of British rule, interrupted only briefly in 1673 when the Dutch once more managed to gain the upper hand.

During this period not all was smooth sailing. When King James II was forced to abdicate and flee Britain in 1689, a German merchant called **James Leisler** led a revolt against British rule. Unfortunately for Leisler, it mustered little sympathy, and he was hanged for treason. Also, by now black slaves constituted a major part of New York's population, and though laws denied them weapons and the right of assembly, in 1712 a number of slaves set fire to a building near Maiden Lane and killed nine people who attempted to stop the blaze. When soldiers arrived, six of the incendiaries committed suicide and twenty-one others were captured and executed. In other areas primitive civil rights were slowly being established: in 1734 **John Peter Zenger**, publisher of the *New York Weekly Journal*, was tried and acquitted of libeling the British government, establishing freedom for the press that would later result in the First Amendment to the Constitution.

Revolution

By the 1750s the city had reached a population of 16,000, spread roughly as far north as Chambers Street. As the new community became more confident, it realized that it could exist independently of the government in Britain. But in 1763 the **Treaty of Paris** concluded the Seven Years' War with France, and sovereignty over most of explored North America was conceded to England. British rule was thus consolidated and the government decided to try throwing its weight about. Within a year, discontent over British rule escalated with the passage of the punitive **Sugar**, **Stamp** and **Colonial Currency acts**, which allowed the British to collect taxes to pay for their local army. Further resentment erupted over the **Quartering Act**, which permitted British troops to requisition private dwellings and inns, their rent to be paid by the colonies themselves. Ill feeling steadily mounted, and skirmishes between soldiers and the insurrectionist **Sons of Liberty** culminated in January 1770 with the killing of a colonist and the wounding of several others. **The Boston Massacre**, in which British troops fired upon taunting protestors, occurred a few weeks later and helped foster revolutionary sentiment.

In a way, New York's role during the **War of Independence** was not crucial, for all the battles fought in and around the city were generally won by the side that lost the war. But New York – the borough of Brooklyn to be exact – was the site of the first military engagements between the British and American forces after the **Declaration of Independence** was proclaimed to cheering crowds outside the site of today's **City Hall Park**. These crowds then went off to tear down the statue of George III that stood on the Bowling Green. The British, driven from Boston the previous winter, resolved that New York should be the place where they would reassert their authority over the rebels, and in June and July of 1776 some two hundred ships under the command of **Lord Howe** arrived in New York Harbor. The troops made camp on Staten Island while the commander of the American forces, **George Washington**, consolidated his men, in the hope that the mouth of the harbor was sufficiently well defended to stop British ships from entering it and encircling his troops. But Howe decided to make his assault on the city by land: on August 22, 1776 he landed 15,000 men, mainly Hessian mercenaries, on the southwest corner of Brooklyn. His plan was to occupy Brooklyn and launch an attack on Manhattan from there. In the **Battle of Long Island**, Howe's men penetrated the American forward lines at a number of points, the most important engagement taking place at what is today Prospect Park.

The Americans fell back to their positions and as the British made preparations to attack, Washington could see that his garrison would be easily defeated. On the night of August 29, under cover of rain and fog, he evacuated his men safely to Manhattan from the ferry slip beneath where the Brooklyn Bridge now stands, preserving the bulk of his forces. A few days later Howe's army set out in boats from Green Point and Newtown Creek in Brooklyn to land at what is now the 34th Street heliport site. The defenders of the city retreated north to make a stand at Harlem Heights, but were pushed back again to eventual defeat at the **Battle of White Plains** in Westchester County (the Bronx), where Washington lost 1400 of his 4000 men. More tragic still was the defense of **Fort Washington**, perched on a rocky cliff 230 feet above the Hudson, near today's George Washington Bridge. Here, rather than evacuate the troops, the local commander made a decision to stand and fight. It was a fatal mistake: they were trapped by the Hudson to the west, and upwards of 3000 men were killed or taken prisoner. Gathering more forces, Washington retreated, and for the next seven years New York was occupied by the British as a garrison town. During this period many of the remaining inhabitants and most of the prisoners taken by the British slowly starved to death.

Lord Cornwallis' **surrender** to the Americans in October 1783 marked the end of the War of Independence, and a month later New York was finally freed. Washington, the man who had held the American army together by sheer willpower, was there to celebrate, riding in triumphal procession down Canal Street and saying farewell to his officers at **Fraunces Tavern**, a building that still stands at the end of Pearl Street. It was a tearful occasion for men who had fought through the worst of the war years together: "I am not only retiring from all public employments," Washington declared, "but am retiring within myself." But that was not to be. New York was now the fledgling nation's **capital** and, as Benjamin Franklin et al framed the Constitution and the role of president of the United States, it became increasingly clear that there was only one candidate for the position. On April 30, 1789, Washington took the oath of President at the site of the **Federal Hall National Memorial** on Wall Street. The federal government was transferred to the District of Columbia a year later.

Immigration and civil war

In 1790 the first official census of Manhattan put the population at around 33,000: business and trade were on the increase, with the market under a buttonwood tree on Wall Street being a forerunner to the New York Stock Exchange. A few years later, in 1807, **Robert Fulton** launched the *Clermont*, a steamboat that managed to splutter its way up the Hudson River from New York to Albany, pioneering trade with upstate areas. A year before his death in 1814, Fulton also started a ferry service between Manhattan and Brooklyn, and the dock at which it moored became a focus of trade and eventually a maritime center, taking its name from the inventor.

But it was the opening of the **Erie Canal** in 1825 that really allowed New York to develop as a port. The Great Lakes were suddenly opened to New York, and with them the rest of the country; goods manufactured in the city could be sent easily and cheaply to the American heartland. It was because of this transportation network, and the mass of **cheap labor** that flooded in throughout the nineteenth and early twentieth centuries, that New York – and to an extent the nation – became wealthy. The first waves of **immigrants**, mainly **German** and **Irish**, began to arrive in the mid-nineteenth century, the latter forced out by the potato famine of 1846, the former by the failed revolution of 1848–49, which had left many German liberals, laborers, intellectuals and businessmen dispossessed. The city could not handle people arriving in such great numbers and epidemics of yellow fever and cholera were common, exacerbated by poor water supplies, unsanitary conditions and the poverty of most of the newcomers. Despite this, in the 1880s large-scale **Italian** immigration began, mainly of laborers and peasants from southern Italy and Sicily, while at the same time refugees from **eastern Europe** started to arrive – many of them Jewish. The two communities shared a home on the **Lower East Side**, which became one of the worst slum areas of its day. On the eve of the

Civil War the majority of New York's population of 750,000 were immigrants; in 1890 one in four of the city's inhabitants was Irish.

During this period life for the well-off was fairly pleasant and development in the city proceeded apace. Despite a great fire in 1835 that destroyed most of the business district downtown, trade boomed and was celebrated in the opening of the **World's Fair** of 1835 at the Crystal Palace on the site of Bryant Park – an iron and glass building that fared no better than its London namesake, burning down in 1858. In the same year work began on clearing the shantytowns in the center of the island to make way for a new, landscaped open space – a marvelous design by Frederick Law Olmsted and Calvert Vaux that became **Central Park**.

Two years later the **Civil War** broke out, caused by growing differences between the northern and southern states, notably on the issues of slavery and trade. New York sided with the Union (north) against the Confederates (south), but had few experiences of the hand-to-hand fighting that ravaged the rest of the country. It did, however, form a focus for much of the radical thinking behind the war, particularly with **Abraham Lincoln**'s influential "Might makes Right" speech from the **Cooper Union Building** in 1860. In 1863 a **conscription law** was passed that allowed the rich to buy themselves out of military service. Not surprisingly this was deeply unpopular, and New Yorkers rioted, burning buildings and looting shops: more than a thousand people were killed in these **Draft Riots**. A sad addendum to the war was the assassination of Lincoln in 1865: when his body lay in state in New York's City Hall, 120,000 people filed past to pay last respects.

The late nineteenth century

The end of the Civil War saw much of the country devastated but New York intact, and it was fairly predictable that the city would soon become the wealthiest and most influential in the nation. Broadway developed into the main thoroughfare, with grand hotels, restaurants and shops catering to the rich; newspaper editors **William Cullen Bryant** and **Horace Greeley** respectively founded the *Evening Post* and the *Tribune*; and the city became a magnet for writers and intellectuals, with **Washington Irving** and **James Fenimore Cooper** among notable residents. By dint of its skilled immigrant workers, its facilities for marketing goods and the wealth to build factories, New York was also the greatest business, commercial and manufacturing center in the country. **Cornelius Vanderbilt** controlled a vast shipping and railroad empire, and **J.P. Morgan**, the banking and investment wizard, was instrumental in organizing financial mergers that led to the formation of a prototype corporate business.

But even bigger in a way was a character who was not a businessman but a politician: **William Marcy "Boss" Tweed**. From lowly origins Tweed worked his way up the Democratic Party ladder to the position of alderman at the age of 21, eventually becoming chairman of the party's State Committee. Surrounded by his own men – the **Tweed Ring** – and aided by a paid-off mayor, "Boss" Tweed took total control of the city's government and finances. Anyone in a position to challenge his money-making schemes was bought off with cash extorted from contractors eager to carry out municipal services; in this way $160 million found its way into Tweed's and his friends' pockets.

Tweed stayed in power by organizing the speedy naturalization of immigrant aliens, who, in repayment, were expected to vote Tweed's way. For his part, Tweed gave generously to the poor, who knew he was swindling the rich but saw him as a Robin Hood figure. As a contemporary observer remarked, "The government of the rich by the manipulation of the poor is a new phenomenon in the world." Tweed's swindles grew in audacity and greed until a determined campaign by **George Jones**, editor of the *New York Times*, and **Thomas Nast**, whose vicious portrayals of Tweed and his henchmen appeared in *Harper's Weekly*, brought him down. The people who kept Tweed in power may not have been able to read or write, but they could understand a cartoon – and Tweed's heyday was finally over. A committee was established to investigate corruption in City Hall and Tweed found himself in court. Despite a temporary escape to Spain he was returned to the US, and died in Ludlow Street jail – ironically a building he had commissioned as Chief of Works.

The latter part of the nineteenth century was in many ways the city's golden age: elevated railways (the **Els**) sprang up to transport people quickly and cheaply around the city; **Thomas Edison** lit the streets with his new electric light bulb, powered by the first electricity plant on Pearl Street; and in 1883, to the wonderment of New Yorkers, the **Brooklyn Bridge** was unveiled. Brooklyn, Staten Island, Queens and the part of Westchester known as the Bronx, along with Manhattan, were officially **incorporated** into New York City in 1898. All this commercial expansion stimulated the city's cultural growth; **Walt Whitman** eulogized the city in his poems and **Henry James** recorded its manners and mores in novels like *Washington Square*. **Richard Morris Hunt** built palaces for the wealthy robber barons along Fifth Avenue, who plundered Europe to assemble art collections to furnish them – collections that would eventually find their way into the newly opened **Metropolitan Museum**. For the "Four Hundred," the wealthy elite that reveled in and owned the city, New York in the "gay nineties" was a constant string of lavish balls and dinners that vied with each other until opulence became obscenity. At one banquet the millionaire guests arrived on horseback and ate their meals in the saddle; afterwards the horses were fed gourmet-prepared fodder.

Turn-of-the-century development

At the same time, the emigration of Europe's impoverished peoples continued unabated, and in 1884 new immigrants from the Orient settled in what became known as **Chinatown**; the following year saw a huge influx of southern Italians to the city. As the Vanderbilts, Astors and Rockefellers lorded in their uptown mansions, overcrowded tenements downtown led to terrible living standards for the poor. Working conditions were little better, and were compassionately described by police reporter and photographer **Jacob Riis**, whose book *How the Other Half Lives* detailed the long working hours, exploitation and child labor that allowed the rich to get richer.

More Jewish immigrants arrived to cram the Lower East Side, and in 1898 the population of New York amounted to more than three million – the largest city in the world. Twelve years earlier Augustus Bartholdi's **Statue of Liberty** was completed, holding a symbolic torch to guide the huddled masses; now pressure grew to limit immigration, but still people flooded in. **Ellis Island**, the depot that processed arrivals, was handling two thousand people a day, leading to a total of ten million by 1929, when laws were passed to curtail immigration. By the turn of the century, around half of the city's people were foreign-born, and a quarter of the population was made up of German and Irish migrants, most of them living in slums. The section of Manhattan bounded by the East River, East 14th Street and Third Avenue, the Bowery and Catherine Street was probably the most densely populated area on earth, inhabited by an "underclass" who lived under worse conditions and paid more rent than the inhabitants of any other big city in the world. By stark contrast, in 1900, J.P. Morgan's United States Steel Company became the first billion-dollar corporation.

The early 1900s saw some of this wealth going into adventurous new architecture. SoHo had already utilized the **cast-iron building** to mass-produce classical facades, and the **Flatiron Building** of 1902 announced the arrival of what was to become the city's trademark – the skyscraper. On the arts front **Stephen Crane**, **Theodore Dreiser** and **Edith Wharton** used New York as the subject for their writing, **George M. Cohan** was the Bright Young Man of Broadway, and in 1913 the **Armory Exhibition** of modernist painting by Picasso, Duchamp and others caused a sensation. Skyscrapers pushed ever higher, and in 1913 a building that many consider the *ne plus ultra* of the genre, the **Woolworth Building**, was completed. Also that year, **Grand Central Terminal** opened, celebrating New York as the gateway to the continent.

The first two decades of the century saw a further wave of immigration. In that period one-third of all the Jews in Eastern Europe arrived in New York, and upwards of 1.5 million of them settled in New York City, primarily in the Lower East Side. Despite advances in public building, caused by the outcry that followed Jacob Riis' reports, the area could not cope with a population density of 640,000 per square mile, and the poverty and inhuman conditions continued to worsen. Many people worked for the growing garment industry in sweatshops in the Hester Street area, which were notoriously exploitive. Most of the garment manufacturers, for example, charged women workers for their needles and the hire of lockers, and handed out stiff fines for spoilage of fabrics. Workers began to strike to demand better wages and working conditions, but the strikes of 1910–11 achieved only limited success, and it took disaster to rouse public and civic conscience. On March 25, 1911, just before the **Triangle Shirtwaist Factory** at Washington Place was about to finish work for the day, a fire broke out. The workers were trapped on the tenth floor and 146 of them died (125 were women), many by leaping from the blazing building. Within months the state had passed 56 factory reform measures, and unionization spread through the city.

The war years and the Depression: 1914–45

With America's entry into World War I in 1917, New York benefited from wartime trade and commerce. Perhaps surprisingly, there was little conflict between the various European communities crammed into the city. Although

Germans comprised roughly one-fifth of the city's population, there were few of the attacks on their lives or property that occurred elsewhere in the country.

The postwar years saw one law and one character dominating the New York scene: the law was **Prohibition**, passed in 1920 in an attempt to sober up the nation; the character was **Jimmy Walker**, elected mayor in 1925. Walker led a far from sober lifestyle: "No civilized man," he said, "goes to bed the same day he wakes up," and it was during his flamboyant career that the Jazz Age came to the city. In speakeasies all over town the bootleg liquor flowed and writers as diverse as **Damon Runyon**, **F. Scott Fitzgerald** and **Ernest Hemingway** portrayed the excitement of the times. Musicians such as **George Gershwin** and **Benny Goodman** packed nightclubs with their new sound, and the **Harlem Renaissance** soared to prominence with writers like **Langston Hughes** and **Zora Neale Hurston**, and music from **Duke Ellington**, **Billie Holiday** and the **Apollo Theatre**.

With the **Wall Street** crash of 1929 (see Chapter 2, "The Financial District"), however, the party came to an abrupt end. The Depression began and Mayor Walker was sent packing, along with the torrent of civic corruption and malpractice that the changing times had uncovered. By 1932 approximately one in four New Yorkers was unemployed, and shantytowns, known as "Hoovervilles" (after then President Hoover who was widely blamed for the Depression), had sprung up in Central Park to house the jobless and homeless. Yet during this period three of New York's most opulent – and most beautiful – skyscrapers were built: the **Chrysler Building** in 1930, the **Empire State** in 1931 (though it was to stand near-empty for years) and in 1932 **Rockefeller Center** – all very impressive, but of little immediate help to those in Hooverville, Harlem or other depressed parts of the city.

The job fell to **Fiorello LaGuardia**, Jimmy Walker's successor as mayor, to take over the running of the crisis-strewn city. He did so with stringent taxation and anti-corruption programs, along with social spending, that won him the approval of the people in the street: Walker's good living had gotten the city into trouble, reasoned voters; hard-headed, straight-talking LaGuardia would undo the damage. Moreover President Roosevelt's **New Deal** supplied funds for roads, housing and parks, the latter undertaken by the controversial Parks Commissioner **Robert Moses**. Under LaGuardia and Moses, the most extensive public housing program in the country was undertaken; the Triborough, Whitestone and Henry Hudson bridges were completed; fifty miles of new expressway and five thousand acres of new parks were opened; and, in 1939, Mayor LaGuardia opened the airport that still carries his name.

LaGuardia was in office for three terms (twelve years), taking the city into the **war years**. The country's entry into World War II in 1941 had few direct effects on New York City: lights were blacked out at night in case of bomb attacks, two hundred Japanese were interned on Ellis Island and guards were placed on bridges and tunnels. But, more importantly, behind the scenes experiments taking place at Columbia University split the uranium atom, giving a name to the **Manhattan Project** – the creation of the first atomic weapon.

The postwar years

The city maintained its pre-eminent position in the fields of finance, art and communications, both in America and the world, its intellectual and creative community swollen by refugees escaping the Nazi threat to Europe. When the **United Nations Organization** was seeking a permanent home, New York was the obvious choice: lured by Rockefeller-donated land, the UN began the building of the Secretariat in 1947. The building of the UN complex, along with the boost in the economy that followed the war, brought about the development of midtown Manhattan. First off in the race to fill the once-residential Park Avenue with offices was the **Lever House** of 1952, quickly followed by skyscrapers like the **Seagram Building** that give the area its distinctive look. Downtown, the **Stuyvesant Town** and **Peter Cooper Village** housing projects went ahead, along with many others all over the city. As ever, there were plentiful scandals over the financing of the construction, most famously concerning the **Manhattan Urban Renewal Project** on the Upper East Side.

A further scandal, this time concerning organized crime, ousted Mayor **William O'Dwyer** in 1950: he was replaced by a series of uneventful characters who did little to stop the gradual **decline** that had begun in the early 1950s as the growth of suburbs led to a general stagnation among the country's urban centers. New York was one of the hardest hit: immigration from Puerto Rico and elsewhere in Latin America once more crammed East Harlem and the Lower East Side, and the nationwide trend of black migration from poorer rural areas was also magnified here. Both groups were forced into the ghetto area of Harlem, unable to get a slice of the city's wealth. Racial disturbances and riots occurred in what had for two hundred years been one of the more liberal of American cities. One response to the problem was a general exodus of the white middle classes – the **Great White Flight** as the media gleefully labeled it – out of New York. Between 1950 and 1970 more than a million families left the city. Things went from bad to worse during the 1960s with **race riots** in Harlem, Bedford-Stuyvesant and East Harlem.

The **World's Fair** of 1964 was a white elephant to boost the city's international profile, but on the streets the call for civil liberties for blacks and protest against US involvement in Vietnam were, if anything, stronger than in the rest of the country. What few new buildings went up during this period seemed willfully to destroy much of the best of earlier traditions: a new, uninspired **Madison Square Garden** was built on the site of the old grandly Neoclassical **Pennsylvania Station**, and the **Singer Building** in the Financial District was demolished for an ugly skyscraper. In Harlem municipal investment stopped altogether and the community stagnated.

The 1970s and 1980s

Manhattan reached **crisis point** in 1975. By now the city was spending billions more than it received in taxes. In part, this could be attributed to the effects of the White Flight: companies closed their headquarters in the city when offered lucrative relocation deals elsewhere, and their white-collar employees were usually glad to go with them, thus doubly eroding the city's tax base. Even after municipal securities were sold, New York ran up a debt of millions of dollars. Essential services, long shaky due to underfunding, were ready to collapse. Ironically, the mayor who oversaw this fiasco, **Abraham Beame**, was an accountant.

Three things saved the city: the **Municipal Assistance Corporation** (aka the **Big Mac**), which was formed to borrow the money the city could no longer get its hands on and save it from bankruptcy; the election of **Edward I. Koch** as mayor in 1978; and, in a roundabout way, the plummeting of the dollar on the world currency market following the oil price rises of the 1970s. This last effect, combined with cheap transatlantic airfares, brought European tourists into the city en masse for the first time, and with them came money for the city's hotels and service industries. Tough-talking Koch helped reassure jumpy corporations that staying in New York was all right for business, and gained the reluctant appreciation of New Yorkers for his pugnacious defense of the city. His brash opinions and indifferent swagger managed to offend liberal groups, but win the critical electoral support of wealthy Upper East Siders, and the more conservative outer borough ethnic groups.

The slow reversal of fortunes coincided with the completion of two face-saving building projects: though, like the Empire State Building, it long remained half empty, the former **World Trade Center** was a gesture of confidence by the Port Authority of New York and New Jersey which financed it; and in 1977 the **Citicorp Center** added modernity and prestige to its environs on Lexington Avenue. Despite the fact that the city was no longer facing bankruptcy, it was still suffering from a massive nationwide recession, and the city turned to its nightlife for relief. Starting in the mid-1970s, singles bars sprang up all over the city, gay bars proliferated in the Village, and Disco was king. **Studio 54** was an internationally known hotspot, where drugs and illicit sex were the main events off the dance floor.

In the 1980s the real estate and stock markets boomed and another era of Big Money was ushered in; fortunes were made and lost overnight and big Wall Street names, like **Michael Milken**, were thrown in jail for insider trading. A spate of building gave the city yet more fabulous architecture, notably **Battery Park City**, and master builder **Donald Trump** provided glitzy housing for the super-wealthy (and plastered his name on everything he could get his hands on). Nevertheless, the welfare rolls in the city, and throughout the country, swelled and the number of homeless people was staggering.

The stock market crash in 1987 started yet another downturn, and Koch's popularity waned. Many middle-class constituents considered Koch to have only rich property-owners' and developers' interests at heart; he also alienated a number of minorities – particularly blacks – with ill-advised off-the-cuff statements. And although he was not directly implicated, the scandals in his administration took their political toll, beginning with the suicide of his friend and supporter Queens borough president **Donald Manes** (after an investigation into the city's various debt-collecting agencies was announced), and continuing with the indictment for bribery (though she was acquitted) of another prominent friend, former Arts Commissioner, **Bess Myerson**.

In 1989, Koch lost the Democratic nomination for the mayoral elections to **David Dinkins**, a 61-year-old, black ex-Marine and borough president of Manhattan. In a toughly fought general election, Dinkins beat Republican Rudolph Giuliani, a hard-nosed US attorney (whose role as leader of the prosecution in a police corruption case was made into the film *Prince of the City*). But even before the votes were counted, pundits were forecasting that the condition of the city was beyond any mayoral healing.

New York was slipping hard and fast into a **massive recession**: in 1989 the city's budget deficit ran at $500 million; of the 92 companies that had made the city their base in 1980, only 53 were left, the others having moved to cheaper pastures; and one in four New Yorkers was officially classed as poor – a figure unequaled since the Depression. Dinkins oversaw his first year as mayor reasonably well, quelling racial unrest and skillfully passing a complex budget through the Council.

Dinkins' – and to some extent the city's – downward slide can be traced to events during the first week of the US Open tennis tournament in summer 1990. On his way to the match, Brian Watkins, a tennis fan from Utah, was stabbed to death in a subway station by a group of muggers while trying to protect his mother. Instead of holding a Koch-style "What is this city coming to?" press conference, Dinkins issued a statement saying that the media were exaggerating the importance of the murder – and then boarded a police helicopter to fly to the tennis event. He fell swiftly from popular favor, becoming known as the man "to whom everything sticks but praise."

The city's fortunes also went into free fall. The unions went on the offensive when it was learned the city intended to lay off 15,000 workers; crime – especially related to the sale of crack cocaine – escalated; businesses failed. By the end of the year the city's budget deficit had reached $1.5 billion; creditors were less than amused.

The 1990s: the Giuliani years

Throughout 1991 the effects of these financial problems on the city's ordinary people became more and more apparent: homelessness increased as city aid was cut back; some public schools became no-go zones with armed police and metal detectors at the gates (fewer than half of high school kids in the city graduated, a far smaller proportion than elsewhere in the United States); and a garbage workers' strike in May left piles of rubbish rotting on the streets. Once again, New York seemed to have hit rock bottom, and this time there was no obvious solution. Unlike in 1976, the state government refused to bail the city out with aid or loans; and, as far as the federal government was concerned, the coffers ran out for New York long ago.

Worse yet, a number of serious racial incidents and riots throughout his term contradicted Dinkins' coining of the phrase "gorgeous mosaic" for the city's multicultural make-up, and seemed to prove that the mayor's race alone was not enough to diffuse tensions. In the 1993 mayoral elections, Dinkins narrowly lost a rematch with **Rudolph Giuliani**. New York, traditionally a Democratic city, wanted a change and with Giuliani – the city's first Republican mayor in 28 years – they got it.

Though it might have been coincidental, Giuliani's first term helped usher in a dramatic upswing in New York's prosperity. A *New York Times* article described 1995 as "the best year in recent memory for New York City." Even the pope came to town and called New York "the capital of the world." The city's reputation flourished, with remarkable decreases in crime statistics and a revitalized economy that helped spur the tourism industry to some of its best years ever.

Giuliani emerged as a very proactive mayor, and one quite happy to take credit for reducing crime – making the city streets and its subways safe – and the bloated city bureaucracy. Giuliani made political friends and enemies in equal measure – and with equal energy. One famous faux pas came when he actively supported long-time Democratic New York State governor Mario Cuomo over his own party's eventual winner **George Pataki** in the 1994 gubernatorial elections, a move calculated to appease his more liberal city constituents. A red-faced Giuliani had to kowtow to Republicans so that New York City did not get its snout pushed out of the trough by State spending authorities. In 1996, Giuliani's constant battles with Police Commissioner

William Bratton, whose policies of community policing and crackdowns on petty as well as major crime were widely considered responsible for the lower crime rates, forced the popular "Top Cop" into resigning. Many said that the notoriously egotistical Giuliani simply didn't like Bratton sharing the spotlight.

A bitter fight over **rent control** (it was salvaged, but with vacancy clauses that allow for rent increases) in 1997, along with continued concern about serious overcrowding in the public school system and cutbacks in health and welfare programs seemed to turn the tide against the mayor. However, Giuliani won re-election easily in fall 1997 to a second term, with barely a challenge mounted by his Democratic opponent, Ruth Messinger. More quality-of-life laws followed; growth of the city's economy continued, at least until the general downturn in 2001 spurred on by the bursting of the dot-com bubble; and civic "improvements" such as the cleaning up of Times Square, the renovation of Grand Central Terminal, and the influx of chain stores into Harlem, ensued. Tourism, and the city's coffers, felt the positive effects – if sometimes seemingly at the expense of local business and local workers.

Several high profile incidents, such as the Abner Louima torture case, involving shocking allegations of **police brutality**, marred Giuliani's second term and led to charges of indifference at the top and a disregard for minority rights. Giuliani's once astounding popularity began to diminish – though it was never that high anyway with blacks and Hispanics – as reports on the practice of racial profiling and other "wide net" techniques used in catching criminals were published. These became major issues in the mayoral campaign in 2001, though they would all be superseded by events that would shock the city – and cause the locals to lean on Giuliani once more.

September 11, 2001 – and beyond

Nothing could prepare New York, or the world really, for the tragic events of **September 11, 2001**. Two hijacked planes crashed into the Twin Towers of the World Trade Center (a third struck the Pentagon in Washington, DC, and a fourth crashed in a field south of Pittsburgh); soon after, each tower collapsed, and the fallout and debris resulted in the destruction of a number of other nearby buildings. More than 5000 people were killed in the attack; smoking rubble was piled tens of feet high; New York's signature skyline was no more.

New Yorkers, and many others from states near and far, rallied to the rescue and rebuilding cause, under the compassionate yet firm leadership of Giuliani. Suddenly no one wanted to see him go; in fact, the attacks occurred the same day as the primary elections for city mayor, which were immediately postponed. Giuliani even seemed to be charting a course to try to stay on past the end of his term – for the sake of the city.

Certainly the city needed help. Beyond the staggering number of lives lost, the billions in assets wiped out, the wreckage of subway lines and so on, there were other holes to deal with: entire firefighting crews, and quite a few at or near the top of the ranks in the fire and police departments died in the collapse.

After the US responded to the attacks in early October, fear gripped the city as reports of anthrax being found in various offices – mostly those of major media operations – circulated; suddenly New Yorkers had to wonder about being attacked in a much less visible manner.

New York's new mayor, Michael Bloomberg, has a yeoman's task ahead. Rebuilding the city will take a long while; restoring shaken faith and economic fortune will take more than just time – and it's not as if the city's other problems have gone away, just taken a back seat and been put in slightly different perspective. Still, if any city is resilient enough to weather the damage and bounce back, clearly it's this one.

Architectural chronology

1625 ▶ First permanent **Dutch settlement** on Manhattan. No buildings remain of the period. **Wall Street** marks the settlement's defensive northern boundary in 1653.

Late 18th c. ▶ New York under **British colonial rule**. **St Paul's Chapel** (1766) built in Georgian style.

1812 ▶ British blockade of Manhattan. **City Hall** built.

1825 ▶ Opening of **Erie Canal** increases New York's wealth. **Fulton Street** dock and market area built. Greek Revival rowhouses popular – eg **Schermerhorn Row**, **Colonnade Row**, **St Mark's Place**, **Chelsea**. Of much Federal-style building, few examples remain: The **Abigail Adams Smith House**, the **Morris–Jumel Mansion** and **Gracie Mansion** the most notable.

1830–50 ▶ First wave of **immigration**, principally German and Irish. The **Lower East Side** developed. **Trinity Church** built (1846) in English Gothic style, **Federal Hall** (1842) in Greek Revival.

1850–1900 ▶ **More immigrants** (mostly Irish and Germans, later Italians and East European Jews) settle in Manhattan. **Industrial development** brings extreme wealth to individuals. The **Civil War** (1861–65) has little effect on the city. Cast-iron architecture enables buildings to mimic grand classical designs cheaply. Highly popular in SoHo, eg the **Haughwout Building** (1859). Large, elaborate mansions built along Fifth Avenue for America's new millionaires. **Central Park** opens (1876). The **Brooklyn Bridge** (1883) links Gothic with industrial strength; **St Patrick's Cathedral** (1879) and **Grace Church** (1846) show it at its most delicate. **Statue of Liberty** is unveiled (1886).

Early 20th c. ▶ The **Flatiron Building** (1902) is the first skyscraper. Much civic architecture in the Beaux Arts Neoclassical style: **Grand Central Terminal** (1919), **New York Public Library** (1911), **US Customs House** (1907), **General Post Office** (1913) and the **Municipal Building** (1914) are the finest examples. The **Woolworth Building** (1913) becomes Manhattan's "Cathedral of Commerce."

1915 ▶ The **Equitable Building** fills every square inch of its site on Broadway, causing the first zoning ordinances to ensure a degree of setback and allow light to reach the streets.

1920 ▶ **Prohibition** law passed. Economic confidence of the 1920s brings the **Jazz Age**. Art Deco influences show in the **American Standard Building** (1927) and the **Fuller Building** (1929).

1929 ▶ **Wall Street Crash**. America enters the **Great Depression**. Many of the lavish buildings commissioned and begun in the 1920s reach completion. Skyscrapers combine the monumental with the decorative: **Chrysler Building** (1930), **Empire State Building** (1930), **Waldorf Astoria Hotel** (1931) and the **General Electric Building** (1931). **Rockefeller Center**, the first exponent of the idea of a city-within-a-city, is built throughout the decade. The

McGraw-Hill Building (1931) is self-consciously modern.

1930s ▸ The **New Deal** and **WPA** schemes attempt to reduce unemployment. Little new building other than housing projects. WPA murals decorate buildings around town, notably in the **New York Public Library** and **County Courthouse**.

1941 ▸ America enters **World War II**. New zoning regulations encourage the development of the setback skyscraper: but little is built during the war years.

1950s ▸ **United Nations Organization** established. The **UN Secretariat** (1950) introduces the glass curtain wall to Manhattan. Similar Corbusier-influenced buildings include the **Lever House** (1952) and, most impressively, the **Seagram Building** (1958), whose plaza causes the zoning regulations to be changed in an attempt to encourage similar public spaces. The **Guggenheim Museum** (1959) opens.

1960s ▸ **Protest movement** stages demonstrations against US involvement in Vietnam. Much early-1960s building pallidly imitates the glass box skyscraper. The **Pan Am Building** (1963) attempts something different, but more successful is the **Ford Foundation** (1967). In the hands of lesser architects, the plaza becomes a liability. New **Madison Square Garden** (1968) is built on the site of the old Penn Station. The minimalist **Verrazano-Narrows Bridge** (1964) links Brooklyn to Staten Island.

1970s ▸ Mayor Abraham Beame presides over **New York's decline**. City financing reaches **crisis point** as businesses leave Manhattan. The **World Trade Center Towers** (1970) add a soaring landmark to the lower Manhattan skyline. **The Rockefeller Center Extensions** (1973–74) clone the glass-box skyscraper. Virtually no new corporate development until the **Citicorp Center** (1977) adds new textures and profile to the city's skyline. Its popular atrium is adopted by later buildings.

Late 1970s ▸ Investment in the city increases. **Ed Koch elected mayor** (1978). **One UN Plaza** adapts the glass curtain wall to skilled ends (1975).

1980s ▸ **Corporate wealth returns** to Manhattan. The **IBM Building** (1982) shows the conservative side of modern architecture; postmodernist designs like the **AT&T Building** (1983) and **Federal Reserve Plaza** (1985) mix historical styles in the same building. **Statue of Liberty** restoration completed. The mixed-use **Battery Park City** opens to wide acclaim.

1986 ▸ Wall Street **crashes**; Dow Jones index plunges 500 points in a day. Real estate market takes a dive. Philip Johnson's **Lipstick Building** at 885 Third Ave and the **Equitable Building** on Seventh Avenue opens.

1989 ▸ **Ed Koch** loses Democratic nomination to **David Dinkins**, who goes on to become NYC's first black mayor. **Rockefeller Center** sold to international conglomerate partially owned by Japanese. **RCA Building** renamed **General Electric Building**.

1990 ▸ Major **recession** hits New York. **Ellis Island Museum of Immigration** opens to public.

1991 ▸ NYC's **budget deficit** reaches record proportions. **Guggenheim Museum** reopens with new extension.

1993 ▸ A car bomb explodes at the **World Trade Center**, killing five people and wounding many more. Republican **Rudolph Giuliani** beats Dinkins in mayoral race. Famed **Ed Sullivan Theater** is given complete overhaul and turned into David Letterman Show studio.

1996 ▶ **NY Yankees** win first World Series in almost twenty years. **SoHo Grand** opens – the first Downtown hotel to be built for decades.

1997 ▶ **Murder rates** drop for fourth consecutive year. **Rent Control/Rent Stabilization** laws amended; **Giuliani re-elected** to second term. **MetroCard** introduced on subways and buses. Redevelopment of **Times Square**; **New Victory Theater** opens on 42nd Street; opening of Battery Park City's **Museum of Jewish Heritage**.

1998 ▶ **100th anniversary** of the incorporation of New York City. **NY Yankees** win the World Series again. Due to **unlimited-ride Metropasses**, ridership on subways is at all time high of eight million people a day. Legislation is passed to create **waterfront park** along the Hudson River from Battery Park City to 72nd Street. The grandly renovated **Grand Central Terminal** opens, dedicated by John Kennedy Jr. in honor of his mother, Jacqueline Kennedy Onassis, who helped raise money for the restoration. A new **stadium** is unveiled in Flushing Meadow for US Open tennis tournament.

1999 ▶ 30th running of New York Marathon. The new **Conde Nast** skyscraper is completed in Times Square. Upscale shops and restaurants open in the renovated **Grand Central Terminal**. Looking like a perfume bottle, the **LVMH (Louis Vuitton Moet Hennessey) Tower** opens on 57th Street.

2000 ▶ NY Yankees beat the NY Mets in the **Subway Series**. The new **Hayden Planetarium** opens in early spring at the American Museum of Natural History.

2001 ▶ **Bill Clinton** takes up office space in Harlem. Some changes in **subway** routes; the **W train** is introduced. **World Trade Center**'s Twin Towers destroyed in terrorist attacks.

Modern American art

This is no more than a brief introduction to a handful of American painters; for more detailed appraisals, both of the century's major movements and specific painters, see "Books."

Twentieth-century American art begins with **The Eight**, otherwise known as the **Ashcan School**, a group of artists who were painting in New York in the first decade of this century. Led by Robert Henri, many of them worked as illustrators for city newspapers, and they tried to depict modern American urban life – principally in New York City – as honestly and realistically as possible, in much the same way as earlier painters had depicted nature. Their exhibitions, in 1908 and 1910, were, however, badly received, and most of their work was scorned for representing subjects not seen as fit for painting. Paralleling the work of the Ashcan School was that of the group that met at the **Photo-Secession Gallery** of the photographer Alfred Stieglitz on Fifth Avenue. They were more individual, less concerned with social themes than expressing their own individual styles, but were equally unappreciated. Art, for Americans, even for American critics, was something that came from Europe, and in the early years of the twentieth century, attempts to Americanize it were regarded with suspicion.

Change came with the **Armory Show** of 1913: an exhibition, set up by the remaining Ashcan artists (members of the new Association of American Painters and Sculptors), to bring more than 1800 European works together and show them to the American public for the first time. The whole of the French nineteenth century was represented at the show, together with Cubist and Expressionist painters, and, from New York, the work of the Ashcan painters and the Stieglitz circle. It was visited by over 85,000 people in its month-long run in New York, and plenty more caught it as it toured America. The immediate effect was uproar. Americans panned the European paintings, partly because they resented their influence but also since they weren't quite sure how to react; the indigenous American artists were criticized for being afraid to adopt a native style; and the press fanned the flames by playing up to public anxieties about the subversive nature of modern art. But there was a positive effect: the modern art of both Europe and America became known all over the continent, particularly abstract painting. From now on American artists were free to develop their own approach.

The paintings that followed were, however, far from abstract in style. The Great Crash of 1929 and subsequent Depression led to the school of **Social Realism** and paintings like **Thomas Hart Benton**'s *America Today* sequence (now in the Equitable Center at 757 7th Ave): a vast mural that covered, in realistic style, every aspect of contemporary American life. The New Deal and the resultant **Federal Art Project** of the WPA supported many artists through the lean years of the 1930s by commissioning them to decorate public buildings, and it became widely acknowledged that not only were work, workers and public life fit subjects for art, but also that artists had some responsibility to push for social change. Artists like **Edward Hopper** and **Charles Burchfield** sought to re-create, in as precise a way as possible, American contemporary life, making the particular (in Hopper's case empty streets, lone buildings, solitary figures in diners) "epic and universal." Yet while Hopper and Burchfield can be called great artists in their own right, much of the work of the time, particularly that commissioned as public works, was inevitably dull and conformist, and it wasn't long before movements were afoot to inject new life into American painting. It was the beginning of abstraction.

With these ideas so, the center of the visual art world gradually began to shift. The founding of the **Museum of Modern Art**, and also of the **Guggenheim Museum** some years later, combined with the arrival of many European artists throughout the 1930s (Gropius, Hans Hofmann, the Surrealists) to make New York a serious rival to Paris in terms of influence. **Hans Hofmann** in particular was to have considerable influence on New York painters, both through his art school and his own boldly Expressionistic works. Also, the many American artists who had lived abroad came back armed with a set of European experiences which they could couple with their native spirit to produce a new, indigenous and wholly original style. First and most prominent of these was **Arshile Gorky**, a European-born painter who had imbibed the influences of Cézanne and Picasso – and, more so, the Surrealists. His technique, however, was different: not cold and dispassionate like the Europeans but expressive, his paintings textured and more vital. **Stuart Davis**, too, once a prominent member of the Ashcan School, was an important figure, his paintings using everyday objects as subject matter but jumbling them into abstract form – as in works like *Lucky Strike*, which hangs in the Museum of Modern Art. Another artist experimenting with abstract forms was **Georgia O'Keeffe** – who was married to the early twentieth-century photographer Alfred Stieglitz – is best known for her lonely Southwestern landscapes, stark death-white cattle skulls and depictions of blossoming flowers. These she magnified so they became no more than unidentified shapes, in their curves and ovular forms curiously erotic and suggestive of fertility and growth. The Whitney Museum holds a good stock of her work.

The **Abstract Expressionists** – or the **New York School** as they came to be known – were a fairly loose movement, and one that splits broadly into two groups: the first created abstractions with increasing gusto and seemingly endless supplies of paint, while the rest employed a more ordered approach to their work. Best known among the first group is **Jackson Pollock**, a farmer's son from Wyoming who had studied under Thomas Hart Benton in New York and in the 1930s was painting Cubist works reminiscent of Picasso. Pollock considered the American art scene to be still under the thumb of Europe, and he deliberately set about creating canvases that bore little relation to anything that had gone before. For a start his paintings were huge, and it was difficult to tell where they ended; in fact Pollock would simply determine the edge of a composition by cutting the canvas wherever he happened to feel was appropriate at the time – a large-scale approach that was much imitated and in part determined by the large factory spaces and lofts where American artists worked. Also, it was a reaction against bourgeois (and therefore essentially European) notions of what a painting should be: the average Abstract Expressionist painting simply couldn't be contained in the normal collector's home, and as such was at the time impossible to classify. Often Pollock would paint on the floor, adding layers of paint apparently at random, building up a dense composition that said more about the action of painting than any specific subject matter: hence the term "action painting," which is invariably used to describe this technique. As a contemporary critic said: with Pollock the canvas became "an arena in which to act – rather than as a space in which to reproduce..."

Similar to Pollock in technique, but less abstract in subject matter, was the Dutch-born artist **Willem de Kooning**, whose *Women* series clearly attempts to be figurative – as do a number of his other paintings, especially the earlier ones, many of which are in the Museum of Modern Art. Where he and Pollock are alike is in their exuberant use of paint and color, painted, splashed, dripped or scraped on to the canvas with a palette knife. **Franz Kline** was also of this "gestural" school, though he cut down on color and instead covered his canvas with giant black shapes against a stark white background: bold images reminiscent of Chinese ideograms and Oriental calligraphy. **Robert Motherwell**, who some have called the leading light of the Abstract Expressionist movement (in so far as it had one), created a similar effect in his *Elegies to the Spanish Republic*, only here his symbols are drawn from Europe and not the East – and unlike Abstract Expressionist paintings they gain their inspiration from actual events. Again, for his work the Whitney and MoMA are good sources.

Foremost among the second group of Abstract Expressionists was **Mark Rothko**, a Russian-born artist whose work is easy to recognize by its broad rectangles of color against a single-hued background. Rothko's paintings are more controlled than Pollock's, less concerned with exuding their own painterliness than with expressing, as Rothko put it, "a single tragic idea." Some have called his work mystic, religious even, and his paintings are imbued with a deep melancholy, their fuzzy-edged blocks of color radiating light and, in spite of an increasingly lightened palette, a potent sense of despair. Rothko, a deeply unhappy man, committed suicide in 1970, and it was left to one of his closest friends, **Adolf Gottlieb**, to carry on where he left off. With his "pictographs" Gottlieb spontaneously explored deep psychological states, covering his canvases with "Native" American signs. He also used a unique set of symbols of cosmos and chaos – disks of color above a blotchy earth – as in his *Frozen Sounds* series of the early 1950s, currently in the Whitney collection.

The Abstract Expressionists gave Native American art stature worldwide and helped consolidate New York's position as center of the art world. But other painters weren't content to follow the emotional painting of Pollock and Rothko et al, and toned down the technique of excessive and frenzied brushwork into impersonal representations of shapes within clearly defined borders – **Kenneth Noland**'s *Target* and the geometric (and later three-dimensional) shapes of **Frank Stella** being good examples. **Ad Reinhardt**, too, honed down his style until he was using only different shades of the same color, taking this to its logical extreme by ultimately covering canvases with differing densities of black.

Barnett Newman is harder to classify, though he is usually associated with the Abstract Expressionists, not least because of the similarities to Rothko of his bold "fields" of color. But his controlled use of one striking tone, painted with only tiny variations in shade, and cut (horizontally or vertically) by only a single contrasting strip, give him more in common with the trends in art that followed. **Helen Frankenthaler** (and later **Morris Louis**) took this one stage further with pictures like *Mountains and Sea*, which by staining the canvas rather than painting it lends blank areas the same importance as colored ones, making the painting seem as if it were created by a single stroke. With these two artists, color was the most important aspect of painting, and the canvas and the color were absorbed as one. In his mature period Louis began – in the words of a contemporary critic – "to think, feel and conceive almost exclusively in terms of open color." And as if in rejection of any other method, he destroyed most of his work of the previous two decades.

With the 1960s came **minimalism** and **Pop Art**. The former produced works composed of industrial materials and fabricated for urban and site-specific landscapes, the medium's physical properties emphasized above all else, including the oeuvre of **Richard Serra**. **Louise Nevelson**, born in Kiev in 1899 and raised in Maine, had come to the Art Students League in Manhattan in 1929 and over a number of decades gained recognition for her grid-and-pillar installations, many of them stark black aluminum sculptures, some now on permanent display along upper Park Avenue and at Louise Nevelson Plaza in the Financial District. Pop Art turned to America's popular media for subject – its films, TV, advertisements and magazines – and depicted it in heightened tones and colors. **Jasper Johns**' *Flag* bridges the gap, cunningly transforming the Stars and Stripes into little more than a collection of painted shapes, but most Pop Art was more concerned with monumentalizing the tackier side of American culture: **Andy Warhol** did it with Marilyn Monroe and Campbell's Soup; **Claes Oldenburg** by re-creating everyday objects (notably food) in soft fabrics and blowing them up to giant size; **Robert Rauschenberg** by making collages or "assemblages" of ordinary objects; **Roy Lichtenstein** by imitating the screen process of newspapers and cartoon strips; and **Ed Kienholz** through realistic tableaux of the sad, shabby or just plain weird aspects of modern life. But what Pop Art really did was to make art accessible and fun. With it the commonplace became acceptable material for the twentieth-century artist, and as such paved the way for what was to follow. **Graffiti** has since been elevated to the status of art form, and New York painters like **Keith Haring** (who died of AIDS in 1990) and **Kenny Scharf** were celebrities in their own right, regularly called in to decorate Manhattan nightclubs. Haring's last finished work was an altar – complete with his trademark cartoonish stick figures – installed in the Cathedral of St John the Divine.

In the Eighties and Nineties, there has been a return to straight figurative depictions, either supra-realistically as in the poignant acetate figures of **Duane Hanson**, or in the more conventional nude studies of **Philip Pearlstein**. The expansive re-creations of Polaroid close-ups by **Chuck Close** took realism to a fantastic level as he replicated the photos segment by segment at enormous scale. After a collapsed spinal artery left him paralyzed from the shoulders down in 1988, his artistry took on a new level as he explored more impressionistic interpretations of his old technique – astonishing the art world once more with his inventive methods. In the 1970s and 1980s, **Cindy Sherman** and **Nan Goldin** took photographic portraiture and atmospheric documentary photography into new territory – the former with her sexually provocative, chameleon-like self-representations in the guises of B-movie characters, the latter in a poignant record of her friends-cum-adoptive family, many of them transvestites now dead from AIDS. **Susan Rothenberg**, a conceptual and atmospheric Impressionist artist with her roots in 1960s New York, is well regarded for her canvases of Southwestern desert landscapes.

One of the best-known artists of the last three decades has been **Jean-Michel Basquiat**, who began his career in the mid-Eighties as part of a two-man graffiti team called SAMO ("Same Old Shit"). He was marketed by the city's art dealers as a wild street kid – even though his family background was in fact comfortably middle class. Sadly, their prophecy turned out to be a self-fulfilling one: Basquiat was a confirmed heroin user and died in 1989. The 1990s failed to generate a New York artist as famous internationally as Basquiat or his mixed-media artist colleague **Julian Schnabel**, who directed a 1996 movie about Basquiat's life. Perhaps fortunately, the city's artistic scene in the 1990s was significantly less trend-obsessed than it had been during the previous decade.

With the advent of the new millennium, New York offers a vibrant art scene while courting the occasional controversy. In the winter of 1999–2000, the Brooklyn Museum of Art presented **Sensation**, an exhibit of works from the C & M Saatchi art collection that drew the wrath of conservative and Catholic groups, as well as then-Mayor Rudy Giuliani. Inspiring particular fury was the critically acclaimed *Virgin Mary* by the Nigerian painter **Chris Ofili**, who applied cow dung to the canvas to employ what the artist considered to be the dung's regenerative powers. Some found the display blasphemous, however, and demonstrated vociferously outside the museum. As the controversy over the exhibit's merits and values became a hot-button issue in New York politics and the American art world, Giuliani tried to punish the museum by withholding city funding, only to be overruled by a federal judge. While the Sensation show won't be regarded by posterity on the same plateau as the Armory Show of 1913 (see above), the widespread response to the exhibit attests to the immediacy of the art world in contemporary New York City.

Books

Since the number of books about or set in New York is so vast, what follows is necessarily selective – use it as a launchpad for further sleuthing.

Essays, memoirs and narrative nonfiction

Ron Alexander *Metropolitan Diary: The Best Selections from the* New York Times *Column.* Indulge your eavesdropping fantasies with these observations, anecdotes and quotes from ordinary New Yorkers overheard on movie lines and in buses, restaurants, bars and elevators, to name just a few of the places where New Yorkers listen to each other's conversations.

Djuna Barnes *New York.* This collection of newspaper stories – from 1913 to 1919 – looks mostly at out-of-the-way characters and places. Highly evocative of the times – a period in New York, and the world over, of great flux. See especially the piece on the "floating hotel for girls."

Anatole Broyard *Kafka Was the Rage: A Greenwich Village Memoir.* Readable, if somewhat slight account of "bohemian" 1940s Greenwich Village life; occasionally misogynistic and somewhat self-congratulatory, but Broyard's style and his descriptions of City College's radical/intellectual scene are gripping.

Jerome Charyn *Metropolis.* A native of the Bronx, Charyn dives into the New York of the 1980s from every angle and comes up with a book that still reads as sharp, sensitive and refreshingly real.

Josh Alan Friedman *Tales of Times Square.* Chronicles activities on and around the square between 1978 and 1984, pornography's golden age. Its no-nonsense style of narration documents a culture under siege of impresarios, pimps and 25-cent thrills.

Federico García Lorca *Poet in New York.* The Andalusian poet and dramatist spent nine months in the city around the time of the Wall Street Crash. This collection of over thirty poems reveals his feelings on loneliness, greed, corruption, racism and mistreatment of the poor.

Phillip Lopate (ed) *Writing New York.* A massive literary anthology taking in both fiction and nonfiction writings on the city, and with selections from everyone from Washington Irving to Tom Wolfe.

Frank McCourt *'Tis.* In the follow-up memoir to the phenomenon *Angela's Ashes*, McCourt relates life in NYC – concentrating on his time teaching in the public school system – once he's left Ireland behind.

★ **Joseph Mitchell** *Up in the Old Hotel.* Mitchell's collected essays (he calls them stories), all of which appeared in the *New Yorker*, are works of a sober if manipulative genius. Mitchell depicts characters and situations with a reporter's precision and near-perfect style – he is the definitive chronicler of NYC street life.

Jan Morris *Manhattan '45.* Morris's best piece of writing on Manhattan, reconstructing New York as it greeted returning GIs in 1945. Effortlessly written, fascinatingly anecdotal, marvelously warm about the city.

Willie Morris *New York Days.* The literary socialite and great editor of *Harper's* magazine tells his story of moving from Mississippi to NYC – and his rise through the new journalism ranks.

Georges Perec and Robert Bober *Ellis Island.* A brilliant, moving, original account of the "island of tears": part history, meditation and interviews. Some of the stories are heartbreaking (between 1892 and

1924 there were 3000 suicides on the island), and the pictures are even more so.

Guy Trebay *In the Place to Be: Guy Trebay's New York*. Collected columns by one of the more notable *Village Voice* writers. They celebrate populations on the margins which, as the warm columns show, are the very fabric and spirit of the city – and hence not "marginal" at all.

History, politics and society

Herbert Asbury *The Gangs of New York*. First published in 1928, this fascinating account of the seamier side of New York is essential reading. Full of historical detail, anecdotes and character sketches of crooks, the book describes New York mischief in all its incarnations and locales.

Edwin G. Burrows and Mike Wallace *Gotham: A History of New York City to 1898*. Enormous and encyclopedic in its detail, this is a serious history of the development of New York, with chapters on everything from its role in the Revolution to reform movements to its racial make-up in the 1820s.

Vincent Cannato *The Ungovernable City: John Lindsay and His Struggle to Save New York*. A not overly sympathetic portrait of New York's mayor during the volatile late 1960s and early 1970s, revealing for its depth on issues and city politics.

Robert A. Caro *The Power Broker: Robert Moses and the Fall of New York*. Despite its imposing length, this brilliant and searing critique of New York City's most powerful twentieth-century figure is one of the most important books ever written about the city and its environs. Caro's book brings to light the megalomania and manipulation responsible for the creation of the nation's largest urban infrastructure.

George Chauncey *Gay New York: The Making of the Gay Male World 1890–1940*. Definitive, revealing account of the city's gay subculture, superbly researched.

Robert Daley *Prince of the City*. A blow-by-blow account of Detective Bob Leuci's decision to testify against the New York criminal justice system and the hellish aftermath.

Anne Douglas *Terrible Honesty: Mongrel Manhattan in the 1920s*. The media and artistic culture of the Roaring Twenties, a fluke that was a casualty of the Depression.

Mitchell Duneier *Sidewalk*. Sociological study of New York City's ubiquitous street vendors, specifically those who make a living selling yesterday's bestsellers and last month's magazines.

Sanna Feirstein *Naming New York*. Look here and you'll never have to wonder any more about how the city streets, neighborhoods and parks got their names.

Peter Golenbock *Bums: An Oral History of the Brooklyn Dodgers*. If you're nostalgic for the good old days of baseball in Brooklyn, this is an absorbing read; he also wrote *Dynasty*, on the Yankees of the 1950s and 1960s.

Kenneth T. Jackson (ed) *The Enyclopedia of New York*. Massive, engrossing and utterly comprehensive guide to just about everything in the city. Much dry detail, but packed with incidental wonders: did you know, for example, that there are more (dead) people in Calvary Cemetery, Queens, than there are (living) people in the whole borough? Or that Truman Capote's real name was Streckford Persons? Jackson also recently published *The Neighborhoods of Brooklyn*, which in photographs and text offers insight into this borough.

Roger Kahn *The Boys of Summer*. Perhaps better than Golenbock's

Bums (see above), this account of the 1950s Brooklyn Dodgers by a beat writer who covered them, is considered one of the classic baseball reads.

John A. Kouwenhoven *Columbia Historical Portrait of New York.* Interpreting the evolution of the city in visual terms (with illuminating captions accompanying the illustrations), this opus is monumental, fascinating and definitive.

George J. Lankevich *American Metropolis.* Written in a direct, readable style, this is the concise alternative to *Gotham* (see above).

David Levering Lewis *When Harlem was in Vogue.* Much-needed account of the Harlem Renaissance, a brief flowering of the arts in the 1920s and 1930s that was suffocated by the dual forces of Depression and racism. Lewis also edited the anthology *Portable Harlem Renaissance Reader.*

Legs McNeil and Gillian McCain *Please Kill Me.* An oral history of punk music in New York, artfully constructed by juxtaposing snippets of interviews as if the various protagonists (artists, financiers, impresarios) were in a conversation. Sometimes hilarious, often quite bleak.

Luc Sante *Low Life: Lures and Snares of Old New York.* This chronicle of the seamy side between 1840 and 1919 is a pioneering work. Full of outrageous details usually left out of conventional history, it reconstructs the day-to-day life of the urban poor, criminals and prostitutes with a shocking clarity. Sante's prose is poetic and nuanced, his evocations of the seedier neighborhoods, their dives and pleasure-palaces, quite vivid.

James B. Stewart *Den of Thieves.* An account by this *Wall Street Journal* reporter about the wheeler-dealers of the takeover 1980s that gave Wall Street such a bad name, focusing on four major culprits – Ivan Boesky, Dennis Levine, Michael Milken and Martin Siegel.

Gay Talese *Fame and Obscurity.* Talese deftly presents interviews with New York City's famous (Sinatra, DiMaggio, etc) and its obscure (bums, chauffeurs, etc) offering not only a window into the heart of NYC, but that of human existence.

Jennifer Toth *Mole People.* A creepy sociological study of the people who live below NYC streets, in the dark reaches of the subway tunnel system. You'll never again ride the subway without your face plastered to the window looking for signs of human life.

Lloyd Ultan and Barbara Unger *Bronx Accent: A Literary and Pictorial History of the Borough.* The authors, two local university professors, use historical and contemporary personalities to tell the Bronx's past in text and photos. A must read if you plan on spending time in the city's northernmost borough.

Art, architecture and photography

Lorraine Diehl *The Late Great Pennsylvania Station.* The anatomy of a travesty. How could a railroad palace, modeled after the Baths of Caracalla in Rome, stand for only fifty years before being destroyed? The pictures alone warrant the price.

Horst Hamann *New York Vertical.* This beautiful book pays homage to the New York skyscraper, and is filled with dazzling black-and-white vertical shots of Manhattan, accompanied by witty quotes from famous and obscure folk.

H. Klotz (ed) *New York Architecture 1970–1990.* Extremely well-illustrated account of the shift from modernism to postmodernism and beyond.

David McCullough *Great Bridge: The Epic Story of the Building of the Brooklyn Bridge.* The story of the father and son Roebling team who fought the laws of gravity, sharp-toothed competitors and corrupt politicians to build a bridge that has withstood the test of time and has become one of NYC's most noted landmarks.

Francis Morrone *An Architectural Guidebook to Brooklyn.* More so than the *AIA Guide*, this goes more deeply into the various architectural styles and standouts of this huge and historic borough.

Museum of the City of New York *Our Town: Images and Stories from the Museum of the City of New York.* A lovely collection of paintings, photographs, artifacts and prints from the Museum's collection, reproduced here to commemorate its 75th anniversary in 1997. New York is explored from early days to contemporary times, with informative captions that place the images in context and essays by Oscar Hijuelos and Louis Auchincloss, among others.

Jacob Riis *How the Other Half Lives.* Republished photojournalism reporting on life in the Lower East Side at the end of the nineteenth century. Its original publication awakened many to the plight of New York's poor.

Stern, Gilmartin, Mellins/Stern, Gilmartin, Massengale/Stern, Mellins, Fishman *New York 1900/1930/1960.* These three exhaustive tomes, subtitled "Metropolitan Architecture and Urbanism," contain all you'd ever want or need to know about architecture and the organization of the city. The facts are dazzling and numbing, the photos nostalgia-inducing.

★ **N. White and E. Willensky** (eds) *AIA Guide to New York.* Perhaps even more than the above, the definitive contemporary guide to the city's architecture, far more interesting than it sounds, and useful as an on-site reference.

Gerard R. Wolfe *New York: A Guide to the Metropolis.* Set up as a walking tour, this is a little more academic – and less opinionated – than others, but it does include some good stuff on the outer boroughs. Also informed historical background.

Other guides

Richard Alleman *The Movie Lover's Guide to New York.* More than two hundred listings of corners of the city with cinematic associations. Interestingly written, painstakingly researched and indispensable to anyone with even a remote interest in either New York or film history.

Joann Biondi and James Kaskins *Hippocrene USA Guide to Black New York.* Borough-by-borough gazetteer of historic sites, cultural spots, music and food of special African-American interest. Somewhat out-of-date but the only one of its kind.

William Corbett *New York Literary Lights.* An informative introduction to New York's literary history, with thumbnail profiles of writers, publishers and other figures of the literary scene, along with descriptions of their hangouts, neighborhoods and favorite publications.

Judi Culbertson and Tom Randall *Permanent New Yorkers.* This unique guide to the cemeteries of New York includes the final resting-places of such notables as Herman Melville, Duke Ellington, Billie Holiday, Horace Greeley, Mae West, Judy Garland and 350 others.

★ **Federal Writers' Project** *The WPA Guide to New York City.* Originally written in 1939 and recently reissued, this detailed guide offers a fascinating look at life in New York City when the Dodgers played at Ebbetts Field, a trolley ride cost five cents and a room at the Plaza was $7.50. Nevertheless, a surprising amount of description remains apt.

Alfred Gingold and Helen Rogan *The Cool Parents Guide to All of New York.* A terrific resource for people traveling with kids, it covers everything from museums and kid-oriented theater to parks, sports, festivals and other special events, all in a down-to-earth conversational style (it's obviously written by cool parents).

Marina Harrison and Lucy D. Rosenfeld *Artwalks in New York.* This is a great guide that will help locate smaller public art venues and gardens around the city.

Robert Heide and John Gilman *Greenwich Village: A Primo Guide to Shopping, Eating and Making Merry in True Bohemia.* Written by two local eccentrics, this guide tells anything and everything about this historic hipster, musical, cultural, gay and lesbian, literate and gastronomic hotspot.

Daniel Hurewitz *Stepping Out: 9 Walks through New York City's Gay and Lesbian Past.* An inspiring book, full of fascinating tidbits of gay lore and avowedly trashy. The book takes you on walking tours through every corner of the city, pointing out the signs and highlights of gay life and gay culture in a conversational, anecdotal style.

Jim Leff *The Eclectic Gourmet Guide to Greater New York City.* An offbeat guide to the smaller, lesser known, foreign food vendors in all five boroughs. The decor may not be something to savor, but the flavors are straight from their home countries.

Ed Levine *New York Eats.* Covering all five boroughs – with a small section on that trendiest of Manhattan "suburbs," the Hamptons – each chapter covers a different type of food, from smoked fish to spices, from pizza to pastries, and Levine tells you where to find the best of each, arranged by neighborhood. He rates and reviews the best butchers, bakeries, gourmet takeout, greengrocers, delis and ethnic restaurants, and includes fascinating behind-the-scenes notes on each place.

Andrew Roth *Infamous Manhattan.* A vivid and engrossing history of New York crime, revealing the sites of Mafia hits, celebrity murders, nineteenth-century brothels and other wicked spots, including a particularly fascinating guide to restaurants with dubious, infamous or gory pasts.

Fiction

Julia Alvarez *How the Garcia Girls Lost Their Accents.* Four Latina sisters are uprooted from a privileged life in the Dominican Republic to the Bronx, in this compelling look at the modern immigrant experience.

★ **Martin Amis** *Money.* Following the wayward movements of degenerate film director John Self between London and New York, a weirdly scatological novel that's a striking evocation of 1980s excess.

Paul Auster *The New York Trilogy: City of Glass, Ghosts and The Locked Room.* Three Borgesian investigations into the mystery, madness and murders of contemporary NYC. Using the conventions of the crime thriller, Auster unfolds a disturbed and disturbing picture of the city.

James Baldwin *Another Country.* Baldwin's best-known novel, tracking the feverish search for meaningful relationships among a group of 1960s New York bohemians. The so-called liberated era in the city has never been more vividly documented.

Jennifer Belle *Going Down*. First novel that chronicles the "descent" of an NYU student into working as a call girl. Full of surprising turns of phrase and some deadpan black humor.

Lawrence Block *When the Sacred Ginmill Closes*. Tough to choose between Block's hard-hitting Matthew Scudder suspense novels, all set in the city; this might be the most compelling, with Hell's Kitchen, downtown Manhattan and far-flung parts of Brooklyn expertly woven into a dark mystery.

Claude Brown *Manchild in the Promised Land*. Gripping autobiographical fiction set on the hard streets of Harlem and published in the mid-1960s; not as famous as *Invisible Man*, but still worth the trip.

Truman Capote *Breakfast at Tiffany's*. Far sadder and racier than the movie, this novel is a rhapsody to New York in the early 1940s, tracking the dissolute youthful residents of an Uptown apartment building and their movements about town.

Caleb Carr *The Alienist*. This thriller, set in 1896, evokes Old New York to perfection. The heavy-handed psychobabble grates at times, but the story line (the pursuit of one of the first serial killers) is worth it. Best for its descriptions of New York's "in places," as well as saliva-inducing details of meals at long-gone restaurants.

Jerome Charyn *War Cries over Avenue C*. Alphabet City is the derelict backdrop for this novel of gang warfare among the Vietnam-crazed coke barons of New York City. An offbeat tale of conspiracy and suspense. A later work, *Paradise Man*, is the violent story of a New York hit man.

Don DeLillo *Underworld*. Following the fate of the baseball that Bobby Thomson hit out of the park to win the 1951 pennant for the New York Giants, DeLillo's sprawling novel seeks to make grand statements about twentieth-century America. Occasionally slow, but worthwhile.

E.L. Doctorow *Ragtime*. Doctorow cleverly weaves together fact and fiction in WWI-era New York to create a biting indictment of racism. See also *World's Fair*, a beautiful evocation of a Bronx boyhood in the 1930s.

Dominick Dunne *People Like Us*. In typical Dunne fashion, here we witness the three pillars of high New York culture: money, society and scandal.

Ralph Ellison *Invisible Man*. The definitive if sometimes long-winded novel of what it's like to be black and American, using Harlem and the 1950s race riots as a backdrop.

Jack Finney *Time and Again*. Equal parts love story, mystery and fantasy, this is really a glowing tribute to the city itself. Part of a secret government experiment in time travel, Simon Morley is transported back to 1880s New York and finds himself falling in love and being torn between his past and present lives. Richly detailed on old New York.

Oscar Hijuelos *Our House in the Last World*. A warmly evocative novel of immigrant Cuban life in New York from before the war to the present day.

★ **Chester Himes** *The Crazy Kill*. Himes wrote violent, fast-moving and funny thrillers set in Harlem; this and *Cotton Goes to Harlem* are among the best.

Andrew Holleran *Dancer from the Dance*. Enjoyable account of the embryonic gay disco scene of the early 1970s. Interesting location detail of Manhattan haunts and Fire Island, but suffers from over-exaltation of the central character.

Henry James *Washington Square*. Skillful and engrossing examination of the mores and strict social expectations of New York genteel society in the late nineteenth century.

★ **Joyce Johnson** *Minor Characters*. Women were never a

prominent feature of the Beat generation; its literature examined a male world through strictly male eyes. This book, written by the woman who lived for a short time with Jack Kerouac, redresses the balance superbly; there's no better novel on the Beats in New York.

Joseph Koenig *Little Odessa*. An ingenious, twisting thriller set in Manhattan and Brooklyn's Russian community in Brighton Beach. A readable, exciting novel and a good contemporary view of New York City.

Jonathan Lethem *Motherless Brooklyn*. Brooklyn author sets this quirky suspense novel in Cobble Hill and its environs, where a detective who suffers from Tourette's tries to track down his boss's killer. A terrific read and great guide to local haunts.

Mary McCarthy *The Group*. Eight Vassar graduates making their way in the New York of the Thirties. Sad, funny and satirical.

Alice McDermott *Charming Billy*. Billy is a poetry-loving drunkard from Queens, looking to bring his Irish love over to New York City. National Book Award winner.

Jay McInerney *Bright Lights, Big City*. A trendy, "voice of a generation" book when it came out in the Eighties, it made first-time novelist McInerney a mint. It follows a struggling New York writer in his job as a fact-checker at an important literary magazine (a thinly disguised *New Yorker*), and from one cocaine-sozzled nightclub to another. Amusing now, as it vividly captures the times.

Henry Miller *Crazy Cock*. Semiautobiographical work of love, sex and angst in Greenwich Village in the 1920s. The more easily available trilogy of *Sexus*, *Plexus* and *Nexus* and the famous *Tropics* duo (*...of Cancer*, *...of Capricorn*) contain generous slices of 1920s Manhattan sandwiched between the bohemian life in 1930s Paris.

Dorothy Parker *Complete Stories*. Parker's stories are, at times, surprisingly moving. She depicts New York in all its glories, excesses and pretensions with perfect, searing wit. "The Lovely Leave" and "The Game," which focus, as many of the stories do, on the lives of women, are especially worthwhile.

Ann Petry *The Street*. The story of a black woman's struggle to rise from the slums of Harlem in the 1940s. Convincingly bleak.

Judith Rossner *Looking for Mr Goodbar*. A disquieting book, tracing the life – and eventual demise – of a female teacher in search of love in volatile and permissive 1970s New York. Good on evoking the feel of the city, but on the whole a depressing read.

Henry Roth *Call It Sleep*. Roth's novel traces – presumably autobiographically – the awakening of a small immigrant child to the realities of life among the slums of the Jewish Lower East Side. Read more for the evocations of childhood than the social comment.

Paul Rudnick *Social Disease*. Hilarious, often incredible send-up of Manhattan night owls. Very New York, very funny.

Damon Runyon *First to Last* and *On Broadway*; also *Guys and Dolls*. Collections of short stories drawn from the chatter of Lindy's Bar on Broadway and since made into the successful musical *Guys and Dolls*.

J.D. Salinger *The Catcher in the Rye*. Salinger's gripping novel of adolescence, following Holden Caulfield's sardonic journey of discovery through the streets of New York. A classic.

Sarah Schulman *The Sophie Horowitz Story*; *After Delores*. Lesbian detective stories: dry, downbeat and very funny. See also *Girls, Visions and Everything*, a stylish and humorous study of the lives of Lower East Side lesbians.

Hubert Selby Jr. *Last Exit to Brooklyn*. When first published in

Britain in 1966, this novel was tried on charges of obscenity and even now it's a disturbing read, evoking the sex, the immorality, the drugs and the violence of downtown Brooklyn in the 1960s with fearsome clarity.

Betty Smith *A Tree Grows in Brooklyn*. Something of a classic, and rightly so, in which a courageous Irish girl learns about family, life and sex against a vivid prewar Brooklyn backdrop. Totally absorbing.

Rex Stout *The Doorbell Rang*. Stout's Nero Wolfe is perhaps the most intrinsically "New York" of all the literary detectives based in the city, a larger-than-life character who, with the help of his dashing assistant, Archie Goodwin, solves crimes from the comfort of his sumptuous midtown Manhattan brownstone. Compulsive reading and wonderfully evocative of the city in the 1940s and 1950s.

Kay Thompson *Eloise*. Renowned children's book that works just as well for adults. It details a day in the life of our heroine Eloise, who lives at the *Plaza Hotel* with her nanny.

Edith Wharton *Old New York*. A collection of short novels on the manners and mores of New York in the mid-nineteenth century, written with Jamesian clarity and precision. See also her *Hudson River Bracketed* and *The Mother's Recompense*, both of which center around the lives of women in nineteenth-century New York.

Tom Wolfe *Bonfire of the Vanities*. Set all around New York City, this sprawling novel skewers Eighties status mongers to great effect.

New York on film

With its skyline and its rugged facades, its mean streets and its swanky avenues, its electric energy and its no-quarter attitude, New York City is a natural-born **movie star**. From the silent era's cautionary tales of young lovers ground down by the metropolis, through the smoky location-shot noirs of the 1940s, right through to the Lower East Side indies of the past twenty years, New York has probably been the most filmed city on earth. The city's visual pizzazz is matched by the vitality of its filmmaking, fostered by a tough, eccentric and independent spirit that has created mavericks like John Cassavetes, Jim Jarmusch, Shirley Clarke, Spike Lee and Martin Scorsese, as well as directors like Woody Allen and Sidney Lumet who hate to film anywhere else.

What follows is a selection not just of the best New York movies but the most *New York* of New York movies – movies that capture the city's atmosphere, its pulse and its style; movies that celebrate its diversity or revel in its misfortunes; and movies that, if nothing else, give you a pretty good idea of what you're going to get before you get there.

Ten great New York movies

Breakfast at Tiffany's *(Blake Edwards, 1961)*. This most charming and cherished of New York movie romances stars Audrey Hepburn as party girl Holly Golightly flitting through the glittering playground of the Upper East Side. Hepburn and George Peppard run up and down each other's fire escapes and skip down Fifth Avenue taking in the New York Public Library and that jewelry store.

Do the Right Thing *(Spike Lee, 1989)*. Set over 24 hours on the hottest day of the year in Brooklyn's Bed-Stuy section – a day on which the melting pot is reaching boiling point – Spike Lee's colorful, stylish masterpiece moves from comedy to tragedy to compose an epic song of New York that just looks better every time you see it.

King Kong *(Merian C. Cooper and Ernest B. Schoedsack, 1933)*. Though half of it takes place on the tropical island from which the eponymous thirty-foot ape is kidnapped, *King Kong* paints a vivid picture of Depression-era Manhattan upon which Kong wreaks havoc, and gives us the city's most indelible movie image: King Kong straddling the Empire State Building and swatting at passing planes.

Manhattan *(Woody Allen, 1979)*. A black-and-white masterpiece of middle-class intellectuals' self-absorptions, lifestyles and romances, cued by a Gershwin soundtrack in what is probably the greatest eulogy to the city ever made.

On the Town *(Gene Kelly and Stanley Donen, 1949)*. Three sailors get 24 hours' shore leave in NYC and fight over whether to do the sights or chase the girls. This exhilarating, landmark musical with Gene Kelly, Frank Sinatra, and Ann Miller flashing her gams in the Museum of Natural History was the first to take the musical out of the studios and onto the streets. Contrast with the directors' *It's Always Fair Weather* (1955), where a trio of wartime buddies vow to reunite in the Apple ten years hence, only to discover that they loathe one other and their own lives. Smart, cynical, satirical musical with a bunch of terrific numbers, including a back-alley trash-can dance.

On the Waterfront *(Elia Kazan, 1954)*. Few images of New York are as indelible as Marlon Brando's rooftop pigeon coop at dawn and those misty views of the New York harbor (actually shot just over the river in Hoboken), in this unforgettable story of long-suffering longshoremen and union racketeering.

Shadows *(John Cassavetes, 1960).* Cassavetes later headed West, but his debut is a New York movie par excellence: a New Wave melody about jazz musicians, young love and racial prejudice, shot with a bebop verve and a jazzy passion in Central Park, Greenwich Village and even the MoMA sculpture garden.

The Sweet Smell of Success *(Alexander Mackendrick, 1957).* Broadway as a nest of vipers. Gossip columnist Burt Lancaster and sleazy press agent Tony Curtis eat each other's tails in this jazzy, cynical study of showbiz corruption. Shot on location and mostly at night, in steely black and white, Times Square and the Great White Way never looked so alluring.

Taxi Driver *(Martin Scorsese, 1976).* A long night's journey into day by the great chronicler of the dark side of the city – and New York's greatest filmmaker. Scorsese's New York is hallucinatorily seductive and thoroughly repellent in this superbly unsettling study of obsessive outsider Travis Bickle (Robert De Niro).

West Side Story *(Robert Wise and Jerome Robbins, 1961).* Sex, singing and Shakespeare in a hyper-cinematic Oscar-winning musical (via Broadway) about rival street gangs. Lincoln Center now stands where the Sharks and the Jets once rumbled and interracial romance ended in tragedy.

Modern New York

All Over Me *(Alex Sichel, 1997).* A beautifully acted coming-of-age tale about a heavyset teenager who is patently but unspokenly in love with her baby-doll best friend. Set during a humid Hell's Kitchen summer, this doomed romance is played out in cramped tenement bedrooms and sweltering neighborhood bars and set to a pounding riot grrrl score.

Bad Lieutenant *(Abel Ferrara, 1992).* Nearly every movie by Ferrara from *Driller Killer* to *The Funeral* deserves a place in a list of great New York movies, but this, above all, seems his own personal *Manhattan*: a journey through the circles of Hell with Harvey Keitel as a depraved Dante.

The Cruise *(Bennett Miller, 1998).* A documentary portrait of a true New York eccentric, Timothy "Speed" Levitch, a Dostoyevskian character with a baroque flair for language and an encyclopedic knowledge of local history, who takes puzzled tourists on guided "cruises" around the city on which he rails against the tyranny of the grid plan and rhapsodizes about "the lascivious voyeurism of the tour bus."

The Daytrippers *(Greg Mottola, 1996).* This sleeper hit follows a hilariously dysfunctional Long Island family on a Manhattan odyssey in search of their eldest daughter's errant husband, taking them from Park Avenue publishing houses to a startling denouement at a rooftop SoHo party.

Eyes Wide Shut *(Stanley Kubrick, 1999).* Kubrick's much-hyped priapic folly plays out in a New York netherworld of the rich and decadent. Upscale doctor Tom Cruise prowls Greenwich Village – strangely but stunningly re-created on a Pinewood set by its reclusive director – and finds himself an unwelcome guest at a masked orgy in a Long Island mansion.

Kids *(Larry Clark, 1995).* The best New York summer movie since *Do* *the Right Thing*, and just as controversial. An overhyped but affecting portrait of a group of amoral, though supposedly typical, teenagers hanging out on the Upper East Side, in Washington Square Park and in the Carmine Street swimming pool on one muggy, mad day.

Little Odessa *(James Gray, 1995)*. Tim Roth plays the prodigal son returning to Brooklyn in this somber, beautifully shot story of the Russian Mafia in Brighton Beach and Coney Island. One of a spate of New York ethnic gangster films made in the 1990s which, among others, portrayed Irish mobsters (*State of Grace*), Jewish hoodlums (*Amongst Friends*) and African-American gang-bangers (*New Jack City*).

Metropolitan *(Whit Stillman, 1990)*. Away from all the racism, the crime and the homelessness, a group of debutantes and rich young men socialize on the Upper East Side one Christmas, tackling head-on such pressing issues as where to buy a good tuxedo, and behaving as if the 1980s, or the 1880s for that matter, had never ended.

Night Falls on Manhattan *(Sidney Lumet, 1996)*. Gotham's great cinematic chronicler of police corruption delivers another swinging blow in the Giuliani era in this underrated drama about Harlem drug dealers, bent cops and the District Attorney's office. Stars Andy Garcia as an idealistic D.A. and Ian Holm as his veteran cop pop.

A Price Above Rubies *(Boaz Yakin, 1998)*. Set among the ultra-orthodox Hasidic community of Borough Park in Brooklyn, this film offers tantalizing glimpses of a little-seen world, but its risible story of the rebellion of one young wife (Renée Zellweger) against patriarchal oppression offers little in the way of enlightenment.

Ransom *(Ron Howard, 1996)*. The haves and the have-nots battle it out on the Upper East Side in this ludicrous Mel Gibson thriller about a millionaire airline magnate whose son is kidnapped by underworld thugs at the Bethesda Fountain in Central Park.

The Saint of Fort Washington *(Tim Hunter, 1992)*. Nearly invisible on film, the plight of the city's homeless is portrayed in this heartfelt and sentimental tale of a schizophrenic (Matt Dillon) and a Vietnam vet (Danny Glover) who meet at the Fort Washington shelter in Washington Heights.

Six Degrees of Separation *(Fred Schepisi, 1993)*. Brilliant, enthralling adaptation of John Guare's acclaimed play uses the story of a young black man (Will Smith) who turns up at a rich Upper East Side apartment claiming to be the son of Sidney Poitier as a springboard for an examination of the great social and racial divides of the city.

Smoke *(Wayne Wang, 1995)*. A clever, beguiling film scripted by novelist Paul Auster, which connects a handful of stories revolving around Harvey Keitel's Brooklyn cigar store. Deals with the "beautiful mosaic" in a somewhat self-satisfied way, but, as a fairy tale about how we might all be able to get along, it's just fine.

Thomas Crown Affair *(John McTiernan, 1999)*. Remake of the 1968 caper film, this time with Pierce Brosnan as the wealthy Mr. Crown, Rene Russo as the insurance investigator, and the Metropolitan Museum of Art playing host to a daring heist and its bookend scene.

Unmade Beds *(Nicholas Barker, 1998)*. This poignant, occasionally hilarious and beautifully stylized documentary about four single New Yorkers looking for love in the personal columns, visualizes the city as one endless Edward Hopper painting, full of lonely souls biding time in rented rooms.

New York past

The Age of Innocence *(Martin Scorsese, 1993)*. The upper echelons of New York society in the 1870s brought gloriously to life. Though Scorsese, by necessity, restricts most of the action to drawing rooms and ballrooms, look out for the breathtaking matte-shot of a then undeveloped Upper East Side.

Basquiat *(Julian Schnabel, 1996)*. Haunting portrait of the artist as a young (doomed) man, rising from spray-painting graffiti and living in a box in a Lower East Side park to taking the New York art world by storm in the early 1980s. David Bowie plays a sensitive Andy Warhol.

A Bronx Tale *(Robert De Niro, 1993)*. An overlooked film with depth and heart. In a 1960s Bronx, Calogero witnesses a traffic accident and its aftermath at the hands of a local gangster, Sonny (Chazz Palminteri). Over the next several years, his loyalties to his bus driver father (De Niro) are tested as he is seduced by Sonny's glamorous world. Great soundtrack.

The Crowd *(King Vidor, 1928)*. "You've got to be good in that town if you want to beat the crowd." A young couple try to make it in the big city but are swallowed up and spat out by the capitalist machine. A bleak vision of New York in the 1920s, and one of the great silent films.

The Docks of New York *(Josef von Sternberg, 1928)*. Opening with dramatic shots of New York's shoreline during its heyday as a great port, this story of a couple of sailors' shore leave in waterfront flophouses and gin-soaked bars is a far cry from *On the Town*; an ugly world beautifully filmed.

The Godfather Part II *(Francis Ford Coppola, 1974)*. Flashing back to the early life of Vito Corleone, Coppola's great sequel re-created the Italian immigrant experience at the turn of the century, portraying Corleone quarantined at Ellis Island and growing up tough on the meticulously re-created streets of Little Italy.

Hallelujah, I'm a Bum *(Lewis Milestone, 1933)*. Set during the Depression, this eccentric musical comedy (written in rhyming dialogue) imagines Central Park as a benign haven for the homeless. Diehard hobo Al Jolson travels north to spend the summer *en plein air* in New York, but when he falls in love with a girl he meets in the park, he has to take a job on Wall Street.

Hester Street *(Joan Micklin Silver, 1975)*. Young, tradition-bound Russian-Jewish immigrant joins her husband in turn-of-the-century Lower East Side to find he's cast off old world ways. Simple but appealing tale with splendid period feeling. The tenements and markets of 1896 Hester Street were convincingly re-created on the quaint backstreets of the West Village.

The Last Days of Disco *(Whit Stillman, 1998)*. About the most unlikely setting for Stillman's brand of square WASPy talkfests would be the bombastic glittery bacchanals that were *Studio 54* in its late-1970s heydey, which is what makes this far more enjoyable than the same season's overly literal and melodramatic *54* (Mark Christopher, 1998).

Little Fugitive *(Morris Engel and Ruth Orkin, 1953)*. A Brooklyn seven-year-old, tricked into believing he has killed his older brother, takes flight to Coney Island where he spends a day and a night indulging in all its previously forbidden pleasures. This beautifully photographed time capsule of 1950s Brooklyn influenced both the American indie scene and the French New Wave.

Lonesome *(Paul Fejos, 1928)*. This recently rediscovered silent classic follows two lonely working-class New Yorkers through one eventful summer Saturday, culminating in an ebullient afternoon at a breathtakingly crowded Coney Island.

Pollock *(Ed Harris, 2000).* From a cramped Manhattan apartment to the barren nature of the Hamptons, abstract artist Jackson Pollock drips on canvases and battles his wife (Oscar winner Marcia Gay Harden), fame and drink. Powerful Harris in title role.

Radio Days *(Woody Allen, 1987).* Woody contrasts reminiscences of his loud, vulgar family in 1940s Rockaway with reveries of the golden days of radio and the glamour of Times Square. He used the same kind of cynical nostalgia in *Bullets Over Broadway* (1994), a yarn about gangsters and theater folk in the 1920s, and in the trials of showbiz manager/former comic *Broadway Danny Rose* (1984), which begins and ends at the Carnegie Deli.

Speedy *(Ted Wilde, 1928).* This silent Harold Lloyd comedy shot on location in the city is a priceless time capsule of New York in the 1920s, featuring a horse-drawn trolley chase through the Lower East Side, a visit to Yankee Stadium and an unforgettably exuberant trip to Coney Island.

Summer of Sam *(Spike Lee, 1999).* The dark summer of 1977 – the summer of the "Son of Sam" killings, a blistering heatwave, power blackouts, looting, arson and the birth of punk – provides the perfect backdrop for Lee's sprawling tale of paranoia and betrayal in an Italian-American enclave of the Bronx.

Yankee Doodle Dandy *(Michael Curtiz, 1932).* James Cagney's Oscar-winning performance as showbiz renaissance man George M. Cohan is a big-spirited biopic with music. Of its kind, probably the best ever.

New York comedy and romance

An Affair to Remember *(Leo McCarey, 1957).* After a romance at sea, Cary Grant and Deborah Kerr dock in New York and plan to meet six months hence at the top of the Empire State Building if they can free themselves from prior engagements, and if playboy Grant can make it as a painter in Greenwich Village. A weepy romance canonized by *Sleepless in Seattle*, whose romantic denouement also hinged on an Empire State Building meeting.

Annie Hall *(Woody Allen, 1977).* Oscar-winning autobiographical comic romance, which flits from reminiscences of Alvy Singer's childhood living beneath the Coney Island Cyclone, to life and love in uptown Manhattan (enlivened by endless cocktail parties and trips to see *The Sorrow and the Pity* at the Thalia), is a valentine both to ex-lover co-star Diane Keaton and to the city. Simultaneously clever, bourgeois and very winning.

Big *(Penny Marshall, 1988).* Tom Hanks grows up far too soon and has to move from New Jersey to the Big City while still at Junior High. A natural at a Madison Avenue toy firm where he finds work as a computer clerk, he impresses his boss with his unbridled enthusiasm for the F.A.O. Schwarz toy store, and relocates from a hellish Times Square dive to a to-die-for SoHo loft while trying to find a cure for the secret of his precocious yuppie success.

Crossing Delancey *(Joan Micklin Silver, 1989).* Lovely story of a Jewish woman (Amy Irving) who lives Uptown but visits her grandmother south of Delancey each week. The grandmother and the local yenta hitch her up with a nice young pickle vendor when all she wants is a nasty famous novelist. An engaging view of contemporary life in the Jewish Lower East Side and the yuppie Upper West.

Desperately Seeking Susan *(Susan Seidelman, 1985)*. Bored New Jersey housewife Rosanna Arquette arrives in Manhattan on a mission: to find Madonna, or rather Susan, the mysterious subject of a number of cryptic personal ads. Infected with East Village élan, Arquette is transformed into a grungy Madonna clone and finds happiness in this charming paean to the joys of Downtown.

Living Out Loud *(Richard LaGravenese, 1998)*. A lovely, quirky portrait of loneliness in New York. Holly Hunter stars as a rich divorcee suddenly alone in a fabulous Fifth Avenue apartment who finds unlikely companionship with Danny DeVito, her elevator operator, and Queen Latifah, a singer in an Uptown jazz club.

Men in Black *(Barry Sonnenfeld, 1997)*. One of the most wittily imaginative Manhattan movies in years portrays the city as a haven for a brave new wave of immigration, with Tommy Lee Jones and Will Smith keeping watch for extraterrestrials and the future of the universe hanging in the balance in a MacDougal Street jewelry store.

Miracle on 34th Street *(George Seaton, 1947)*. The perfect antidote to all the nightmares and mean streets of New York films, *Miracle* opens during Macy's annual Christmas parade, where a kindly old gentleman with a white beard offers to replace the store's inebriated Santa.

Moonstruck *(Norman Jewison, 1988)*. Plenty of nostalgic New York backdrops in this middling romance, in which an Italian woman with "no luck" (an Oscar-winning role for Cher) reluctantly falls for her fiance's estranged brother (Nicolas Cage). Heavy on the tomato sauce, opera and accents.

Quick Change *(Howard Franklin and Bill Murray, 1990)*. The "change" is cash stolen from a bank. The "quick" of the title is ironic: though the robbery was easy, it's fleeing the city that proves difficult, as Bill Murray and his cohorts are delayed by cops, other crooks and regular, eccentric New Yorkers. One of Murray's best overall efforts.

The Seven Year Itch *(Billy Wilder, 1955)*. When his wife and kid vacate humid Manhattan, Mitty-like pulp editor Tom Ewell is left guiltily leching over the innocent TV-toothpaste temptress upstairs – Marilyn Monroe, at her most wistfully comic. The sight of her pushing down her billowing skirt as she stands on a subway grating (at Lexington Ave and 52nd St) is one of the era's and the city's most resonant movie images.

Stranger than Paradise *(Jim Jarmusch, 1984)*. Only the first third of this, the original slacker indie, is set in New York, but its portrayal of Lower East Side lethargy is hilariously spot-on and permeates the rest of the film in which a couple of hipster fish venture out of water in Ohio and Florida. The film's Downtown credentials – John Lurie is a jazz saxophonist with the Lounge Lizards, Richard Edson used to drum for Sonic Youth, and Jarmusch himself is an East Village celebrity – are impeccable.

Tootsie *(Sidney Pollack, 1982)*. Tired of being rejected in audition after audition, a struggling actor (comic turn for Dustin Hoffman) dons a wig and woman's attire to win a prize role on an afternoon soap. Great script, with a memorable scene set in the *Russian Tea Room* (see p.337).

Working Girl *(Mike Nichols, 1988)*. Fun fluff about a secretary (Melanie Griffith) who dreams of breaking away from her drab Staten Island existence. Her chance comes when her boss (Sigourney Weaver) breaks a leg on a ski trip, and Tess discovers Katherine was planning to steal one of her ideas; comedy and romance (with Harrison Ford) ensue.

New York nightmares

The Addiction *(Abel Ferrara, 1995).* A simple trip home from the college library turns into a living nightmare for Lili Taylor when she is bitten by a vampiric streetwalker on Bleecker Street and transformed into a blood junkie cruising the East Village for fresh kill.

After Hours *(Martin Scorsese, 1985).* Yuppie computer programmer Griffin Dunne inadvertently ends up on a nightlong odyssey into the Hades of downtown New York, a journey that goes from bad to worse to awful as he encounters every kook south of 14th Street.

American Psycho *(Mary Harron, 2000).* This stylized adaptation of the Bret Easton Ellis novel succeeds largely due to Christian Bale, pulling off some blacker-than-black comedy in his role as a securities trader consumed by designer labels, the ladder of success, and Huey Lewis lyrics.

Escape from New York *(John Carpenter, 1981).* In the not too distant future (1997, in fact), society has given up trying to solve the problems of Manhattan and has walled it up as a lawless maximum-security prison from which Kurt Russell has to rescue the hijacked US president.

Gravesend *(Salvatore Stabile, 1996).* Low-rent literally (shot for $5000) and figuratively, this wannabe gangster movie relates one crazy, violent night in the lives of its do-nothing protagonists in deepest Brooklyn.

Jacob's Ladder *(Adrian Lyne, 1990).* Tim Robbins gets off the subway in Brooklyn but discovers himself locked inside a deserted station . . . and then his troubles really begin as his Vietnam-induced hallucinations turn Manhattan into one hell of a house of horrors.

The Lost Weekend *(Billy Wilder, 1945).* Alcoholic Ray Milland is left alone in the city with no money and a desperate thirst. The film's most famous scene is his long trek up Third Avenue (shot on location) trying to hawk his typewriter to buy booze, only to find all the pawn shops closed for Yom Kippur.

Marathon Man *(John Schlesinger, 1976).* Innocent, bookish Dustin Hoffman runs for his life all over Manhattan after he's dragged into a conspiracy involving old Nazis and tortured with dental instruments.("Is it safe?"). Shot memorably around the Central Park Reservoir and Zoo, Columbia University, the Diamond District and Spanish Harlem.

The Out-of-Towners *(Arthur Hiller, 1969).* If you have any problems getting into town from the airport take solace from the fact that they can be nothing compared to those endured by Jack Lemmon and Sandy Dennis – for whom everything that can go wrong does go wrong – in Neil Simon's frantic comedy. Recently remade with Steve Martin and Goldie Hawn (but stick with the original).

Rosemary's Baby *(Roman Polanski, 1968).* Mia Farrow and John Cassavetes move into their dream New York apartment in the Dakota Building (72nd and Central Park West, where John Lennon lived and died) and think their problems stop with nosy neighbors and thin walls until Farrow gets pregnant and hell, literally, breaks loose. Arguably the most terrifying film ever set in the city.

The Siege *(Edward Zwick, 1998).* Zwick's controversial film speculates on what would happen if a series of major terrorist attacks by Arab militants in New York City were to lead to the declaration of martial law and the sealing off of Brooklyn. The results are muddle-headed but the images of troops marching over the Brooklyn Bridge are indelible.

The Taking of Pelham One Two Three *(Joseph Sargent, 1974).* Just when you thought it was safe to get back on the subway. A gang of mercenary hoods hijacks a train on its way through Midtown and threatens to start killing the passengers at the rate of one a minute if their million-dollar ransom is not paid within the hour.

The Warriors *(Walter Hill, 1979).* The Coney Island Warriors ride to the Bronx for a meeting with all of New York's gangs; when the organizer is killed, the Warriors are unjustly blamed and have to navigate their way back to their home turf. Old-school subway grafitti, distinctive gang costumes, and a pervading sense of nighttime paranoia all contribute to this dark and original cult film.

Wolfen *(Michael Wadleigh, 1981).* The sins of New York's founding fathers and venal property developers return to haunt the city in the form of vicious wolves in this beautiful and serious horror movie from the director of *Woodstock*(!), one of the very few films that touch on the city's Native American history and one of the first to use the Steadicam to intelligent effect.

The mean streets

The Cool World *(Shirley Clarke, 1964).* A 1960s *Boyz'n'the Hood*, this radical, documentary-type study of a Harlem teenager who longs to be a gun-toting gang member proved Clarke to be the political conscience of New York's streets, as had *The Connection* (1962), her portrait of a group of addicts awaiting their pusher, and *Portrait of Jason* (1967), her record of the monologue of an aging black hustler.

Cruising *(William Friedkin, 1980).* The Greenwich Village scene of the late 1970s plays a supporting character in this crime pic, in which cop Al Pacino delves into the underworld of gay S&M clubs to nab a serial killer. As one might expect, it was loudly protested by just about everyone on its release.

Dead End *(William Wyler, 1937).* Highly entertaining, stage-derived tragedy of the Lower East Side's teeming poor, starring Humphrey Bogart as a mother-obsessed small-time gangster, and a pack of lippy adolescents who earned their own movie series as The Dead End Kids.

Fort Apache, The Bronx *(Daniel Petrie, 1981).* A film to confirm people's worst fears about the Bronx. Paul Newman stars as veteran cop based in the city's most crime-infested and corrupt precinct. Tense, entertaining and totally unbelievable.

The French Connection *(William Friedkin, 1971).* Plenty of heady Brooklyn atmosphere in this sensational Oscar-winning cop thriller starring Gene Hackman, whose classic car-and-subway chase takes place under the Bensonhurst Elevated Railroad.

Goodfellas *(Martin Scorsese, 1990).* Vibrant and nuanced tale, based on a true story of a mob turncoat; another in a fine series of Scorcese New York stories. Seduced by the allure of the Mafia from a young age, Brooklyn native Henry Hill (a fine Ray Liotta) recounts 25 years of crime, his rise through the ranks, and decision to turn on his brethren.

Kiss of Death *(Henry Hathaway, 1947; Barbet Schroeder, 1995).* The 1947 *Kiss*, with squealing ex-con Victor Mature battling giggling psycho Richard Widmark, was one of the very first films to be shot entirely on real New York locations. Schroeder's remake retells the story in the brighter, tackier Queens of the 1990s, with squealing ex-con David Caruso battling dumb ox Nicolas Cage.

Madigan *(Don Siegel, 1968).* Opens with a jazzy montage of Manhattan skyscrapers and affluent avenues, then plunges rogue cop Richard Widmark into the mean streets of

Spanish Harlem. *Madigan* is a vivid study of the inevitability of police corruption with Henry Fonda as the police commissioner struggling to live within the law.

Mean Streets *(Martin Scorsese, 1973).* Scorsese's brilliant breakthrough film breathlessly follows small-time hood Harvey Keitel and his volatile, harum-scarum buddy Robert De Niro around a vividly portrayed Little Italy before reaching its violent climax.

Midnight Cowboy *(John Schlesinger, 1969).* The odd love story between Jon Voight's bumpkin hustler and Dustin Hoffman's touching urban creep Ratso Rizzo plays out against both the seediest and swankiest of New York locations. The only X-rated film to receive an Oscar for Best Picture (it also won for Director and Adapted Screenplay), it looks considerably tamer today.

Naked City *(Jules Dassin, 1948).* A crime story that views the city with a documentarist's eye. Shot on actual locations, it follows a police manhunt for a ruthless killer all over town toward an unforgettable chase through the Lower East Side and a shoot-out on the Williamsburg Bridge.

Prince of the City *(Sidney Lumet, 1981).* Lumet is a die-hard New York director, and his crime films, including *Serpico, Dog Day Afternoon, Q&A* and *Twelve Angry Men* are all superb New York movies, but this is his New York epic. A corrupt narcotics detective turns federal informer to assuage his guilt, and Lumet takes us from drug busts in Harlem to the cops' suburban homes on Long Island to federal agents' swanky pads overlooking Central Park.

State of Grace *(Phil Joanou, 1990).* Terry Noonan (Sean Penn) returns to Hell's Kitchen after ten years and promptly falls in with the same thugs he outgrew (Gary Oldman, Ed Harris), while falling for their sister. The pull of the neighborhood is everywhere, from the shadow of the *Intrepid* to the slo-mo St Patrick's Day Parade footage intercut with the bloody finale.

Superfly *(Gordon Parks Jr, 1972).* Propelled by its ecstatic Curtis Mayfield score, this Blaxploitation classic about one smooth-looking drug dealer's ultimate score is best seen today for its mind-boggling fashion excess and its almost documentary-like look at the Harlem bars, streets, clubs and diners of thirty years ago.

New York song and dance

42nd Street *(Lloyd Bacon, 1933).* One of the best films ever made about Broadway – though the film rarely ventures outside the theater. Starring Ruby Keeler as the young chorus girl who has to replace the ailing leading lady: she goes on stage an unknown and, well, you know the rest.

Fame *(Alan Parker, 1980).* Set in Manhattan's High School for the Performing Arts, the film may be a gawky musical, but in its haphazard, sentimental, ungainly way it still manages to capture some of the city's agony and ecstasy.

A Great Day in Harlem *(Jean Bach, 1994).* A unique jazz documentary that spins many tales around the famous Art Kane photograph for which the cream of New York's jazz world assemble on the steps of a Harlem brownstone one August morning in 1958. Using home-movie footage of the event and present-day interviews, Bach creates a wonderful portrait of a golden age.

Guys and Dolls *(Joseph L. Mankiewicz, 1955).* The great Broadway musical shot entirely on soundstages and giving as unlikely a picture of Times Square hoodlums (all colorfully suited sweetie-pies) as was ever seen. And a singing and dancing Marlon Brando to boot!

Hair *(Milos Forman, 1979)*. Film version of the counterculture musical turns Central Park into a hippie paradise for the hirsute, charismatic (and very young) Treat Williams and his fellow Aquarians. Laced with humor, it's got a spectacular opening sequence, with choreography (including dancing police horses) by Twyla Tharp.

New York, New York *(Martin Scorsese, 1977)*. Scorsese's homage to the grand musicals of postwar Hollywood, reimagined for the post-Vietnam era. His grand folly opens on V-J Day in Times Square with sax player Robert De Niro picking up Liza Minnelli in a dance hall, and follows their career and romance together through the Big Band era. Unusually for Scorsese, but befitting the film, the eponymous city was stylishly re-created on studio soundstages.

Saturday Night Fever *(John Badham, 1977)*. What everybody remembers is the tacky glamour of flared white pantsuits and mirror-balled discos, but *Saturday Night Fever* is actually a touching and believable portrayal of working-class youth in the 1970s (Travolta works in a paint store when he's not strutting the dance floor), Italian-American Brooklyn, and the road to Manhattan.

Sweet Charity *(Bob Fosse, 1969)*. Shirley MacLaine's lovable prostitute Charity hoofs around Manhattan getting the short end of the stick at every turn. Mugged in Central Park *by her boyfriend*, Charity blithely wanders the city dancing on rooftops and in swank Uptown clubs, and ends up back in the Park rescued by a merry band of escapees from *Hair*.

Glossaries

Terms and acronyms

Art Deco Style of decoration popular in the 1930s, characterized by geometrical shapes and patterns.

Art Nouveau Art, architecture and design of the 1890s, typified by stylized flower and plant forms.

Beaux Arts Style of Neoclassical architecture taught at the Ecole des Beaux Arts in Paris at the end of the last century and widely adopted in New York City.

Bridge and tunnel A derogatory term used by Manhattanites for people from the Outer Boroughs, Long Island or New Jersey – who have to take bridges or tunnels to get to Manhattan.

Brownstone Originally a nineteenth-century terraced house with a facade of brownstone (a kind of sandstone); now often any townhouse.

Condo An individually owned apartment within a building.

Colonial Style of Neoclassical architecture popular in the eighteenth century.

Co-op The most popular form of apartment ownership in the city. A co-op differs from a condo in that you buy shares in the building in which the apartment is sited, rather than the apartment itself.

CUNY City University of New York.

DUMBO Local shorthand for the area Down Under the Manhattan Bridge Overpass.

Federal Hybrid of French and Roman domestic architecture common in the late eighteenth century and early nineteenth century.

Greek Revival Style of architecture that mimicked that of classical Greece. Highly popular for major banks and larger houses in the early nineteenth century.

Gridlock Traffic freeze – when cars get trapped in intersections, preventing traffic on the cross streets from passing through.

MTA (Metropolitan Transit Authority) Runs the city's buses and subway lines; the IND (Independent), BMT (Brooklyn-Manhattan Transit) and IRT (Interborough Rapid Transit).

NoLiTa *No*rth of *Li*ttle *Ita*ly; trendy area along Mulberry, Mott and Elizabeth streets.

On line Unlike people in the rest of the country, New Yorkers wait on line, not in line (for movies, etc).

Outer Boroughs Local term for the boroughs of New York City other than Manhattan (in other words, the Bronx, Brooklyn, Queens or Staten Island).

PATH (Port Authority Trans Hudson) The agency that operates the commuter train, also known as the PATH, between Manhattan and New Jersey.

Robber barons Late-nineteenth-century magnates who made their vast fortunes in banking, railroads and steel, among other things, often at the expense of their workers.

Skyscraper The word comes from the highest sail on a sailing ship, and hence refers to any high building.

SRO Single-room occupancy hotel – most often seedy spaces lived in long-term by those on welfare.

Stoop Open platform, with steps leading up to it, at the entrance to an apartment house.

SUNY State University of New York.

Tenement Large, often slummy building divided into small apartments.

WPA (Works Project Administration) Agency begun by President Roosevelt in 1935 to create employment. In addition to construction work, the

WPA art projects produced many murals in public buildings and a renowned set of guidebooks to the country.

Zoning ordinances Series of building regulations. The first, passed in 1915, stated that the floor space of a building could not be more than twelve times the area of its site, discouraging giant monoliths and leading to the setback or wedding cake style of skyscraper. A later ordinance allowed developers to build higher provided they supplied a public space at the foot of the building.

People

ABZUG Bella (1920–98) Congresswoman and liberal crusader, easily recognizable by the large hats she was fond of wearing. Outspoken and insistent on issues ranging from women's rights to civil liberties to the war in Vietnam, she was a groundbreaking female politician with a loyal (mostly female) following. Several high-profile runs for the Senate and New York mayor in the 1970s resulted in severe financial debt and a loss of political influence.

ALLEN Woody Writer, director, comedian. Many people's clichéd idea of the neurotic Jewish Manhattanite. His clever, crafted films, particularly *Annie Hall*, *Manhattan*, *Hannah and Her Sisters*, and *Crimes and Misdemeanors*, comment on, and have become part of, the New York myth. Suffered a major fall from grace in 1993, when he was accused of child abuse by Mia Farrow after he left her for her adopted daughter.

ASTOR John Jacob (1822–90) Robber baron, slum landlord and, when he died, the richest man in the world. Astor made his packet from exacting exorbitant rents from those living in abject squalor in his many tenement buildings. By all accounts, a real bastard.

BEECHER Henry Ward (1813–87) Revivalist preacher famed for his support of women's suffrage, the abolition of slavery – and as the victim of a scandalous accusation of adultery that rocked nineteenth-century New York. His sister, Harriet Beecher Stowe, wrote the best-selling novel *Uncle Tom's Cabin*, which contributed greatly to the anti-slavery cause.

BRESLIN Jimmy Bitter, often brilliant columnist for *New York Newsday*. Once ran for mayor on a Secessionist ticket (declaring New York City independent from the State) with Norman Mailer as running mate.

BRYANT William Cullen (1794–1878) Poet, newspaper editor and main proponent of Central Park and the Metropolitan Museum. The small park that bears his name at 42nd Street and Fifth Avenue has been expertly cleaned up and is now a fitting memorial to this nineteenth-century hero.

BURR Aaron (1756–1836) Fascinating politician whose action-packed career included a stint as vice-president, a trial and acquittal for treason and, most famously, the murder of Alexander Hamilton (q.v.) in a duel. His house, the Morris-Jumel Mansion, still stands.

CARNEGIE Andrew (1835–1919) Émigré Scottish industrialist who spent most of his life amassing a vast fortune and his final years giving it all away. Unlike most of his wealthy contemporaries he was not an ostentatious man, as his house, now the Cooper-Hewitt Museum, shows.

CHISHOLM Shirley In 1968 she became the first black woman elected to Congress, from her home district in Brooklyn.

DINKINS David First black mayor of New York City, elected in 1989 after a hard, mud-slinging mayoral battle against Republican Rudolph Giuliani.

His term in office left him seeming ineffectual and weak: "Everything sticks to him but praise," said a pundit.

FRICK Henry Clay (1849–1919) One of the robber barons, Frick's single contribution to civilization was to use his inestimable wealth to collect some of the finest art treasures of Europe, now on show at his home on Fifth Avenue.

GARVEY Marcus (1887–1940) Activist who did much to raise the consciousness of blacks in the early part of the century (and is now a Rasta myth). When he started to become a political threat to the white government he was thrown in prison for fraud; pardoned but deported, he spent his last years in London.

GINSBERG Allen (1926–97) Revered beatnik poet, activist and hero of the Lower East Side.

GIULIANI Rudolph Former US district attorney who carried his bulldog ways of prosecuting crimes to the mayor's office. He presided over two terms of relative prosperity and reduced crime, though was occasionally criticized for his arrogant tactics and for giving too much power to the police.

GOULD Jay (1836–92) Robber baron extraordinaire. Gould made his fortune with a telegraph network during the Civil War, and went on to manipulate the stock market and make millions more. His most spectacular swindle cornered the gold market, netted him $11 million in a fortnight and provoked the "Black Friday" crash of 1869.

GREELEY Horace (1811–72) Campaigning founder-editor of the *New Yorker* magazine and *Tribune* newspaper who coined the phrase, "Go West, young man!," but never did himself. An advocate of women's rights, union rights, the abolition of slavery and other worthy, liberal matters.

HAMILL Pete Newspaper editor, writer, broadcaster and expert on Manhattan and – especially – the Outer Boroughs. One of the best no-bullshit commentators around.

HAMILTON Alexander (1755–1804) Brilliant Revolutionary propagandist, soldier, political thinker (drafted sections of the Constitution) and statesman (first Secretary to the Treasury). Shot and killed in a duel by Aaron Burr (q.v.). His house, Hamilton Grange, is preserved at the edge of Harlem.

HARING Keith (1958–90) Big-name artist who used crude animal forms for decoration and art. His early death of AIDS prematurely removed one of America's most promising artists and designers.

HELMSLEY Harry (1904–97) Property-owning tycoon who, like Donald Trump (q.v.), had a penchant for slapping his name on all that fell into his grasp. Hence many old hotels are now Helmsley Hotels.

IRVING Washington (1783–1859) Satirist, biographer, short story writer (*The Legend of Sleepy Hollow*, *Rip Van Winkle*) and diplomat. His house, just outside the city near Tarrytown, is worth a visit.

JOHNSON Philip Architect. Disciple of Ludwig Mies Van der Rohe, high priest of the International Style glass-box skyscraper, he designed the Seagram Building on Park Avenue, the AT&T Building on Third Avenue and the Federal Reserve Plaza on Liberty Street, among others.

KOCH Ed Still-popular former mayor, elected by a slender majority in 1978, who won New Yorkers over with his straight-talking approach. After three terms in office, he lost the Democratic nomination in 1989 to David Dinkins (q.v.) following scandals involving other city officials and his insensitive handling of black issues.

LAGUARDIA Fiorello (1882–1947) NYC mayor who replaced Jimmy Walker and who gained great popularity with his honest and down-to-earth administration, focusing on anti-corruption programs and social spending for the poor.

MORGAN J. Pierpont (1837–1913) Top industrialist and financier who used a little of his spare cash to build the Morgan Library on Third Avenue. He created a financial empire that was bigger than the Gettys' and that enabled him to buy out both Andrew Carnegie and Henry Frick.

MOSES Robert (1889–1981) Moses is perhaps more than anyone else responsible for the way the city looks today. Holder of all the key planning and building posts from the 1930s to the 1960s, his philosophy of urban development was to tear down whatever was old, build anew and create ordered public spaces with a lot of concrete.

OLMSTED Frederick Law (1822–1903) Landscape designer and writer. Central Park, Riverside Park and many others were the fruits of his partnership with architect Calvert Vaux.

ONASSIS Jacqueline Kennedy (1929–94). The former First Lady spent most of her later years in the city, working as an editor for Doubleday. Long a byword in style and grace, by the time of her death she had regained much of the public favor lost after her unpopular marriage to a Greek shipping magnate.

O'NEILL Eugene (1888–1953) NYC's (and America's) most influential playwright. Many of the characters from plays like *Mourning Becomes Electra*, *The Iceman Cometh* and *Long Day's Journey into Night* are based on his drinking companions in *The Golden Swan* bar.

PARKER Dorothy (1893–1967) Playwright, essayist and acid wit. A founding member of the Round Table group at the *Algonquin Hotel*, she was one of the few respected women in the New York literary world.

REED Lou In many ways the pre-eminent NYC poet, musician Reed has written numerous song cycles both condemning and celebrating life on the city streets. His early career was closely tied to Andy Warhol (q.v.), as Reed was frontman for the Velvet Underground.

ROCKEFELLER JR John D. (1874–1960) Unlike his tightfisted dad (founder of the fortune), Rockefeller Junior gave away tidy sums for philanthropic ventures in New York. The Cloisters Museum, The Museum of Modern Art, Lincoln Center, Riverside Church and, most famously, Rockefeller Center were mostly his doing.

ROCKEFELLER Nelson (1908–79) Politician son of John D. Jr. Elected governor of New York State in 1958, he held on to the post until 1974, when he turned to greater things and sought the Republican Party presidential nomination. He didn't get it, but before his death served briefly as vice-president under Gerald Ford.

SHARPTON JR Al (The Reverend) Ordained minister, political activist and perennial candidate for office, Sharpton is known for always putting himself in the center of a publicity storm, particularly if it involves police corruption or racial incidents.

STEINBRENNER George Controversial baseball team owner/entrepreneur. Known as "The Boss," Steinbrenner runs the beloved NY Yankees, often with an iron fist, though generous pockets.

STEINEM Gloria Feminist/activist and writer. From early feminist consciousness-raising to the founding of *Ms* magazine and the publication of numerous influential essays and books (such as *Outrageous Acts and Everyday Rebellions*), Steinem has been a steady, vocal crusader for women's rights in New York and elsewhere.

TRUMP Donald Property tycoon whose creations include the glammed-out Trump Tower on Fifth Avenue and Trump Plaza near Bloomingdale's. Much despised by New Yorkers for embodying nouveau riche excess and greed.

TWEED William Marcy "Boss" (1823–78) Head of the NY Democratic Party machine whose corrupt practices netted him city funds to the tune of $200 million and gave Democratic Party headquarters Tammany Hall its bad name.

WARHOL Andy (1926–87) Artist and media hound. Instigator of Pop Art, the Velvet Underground, The Factory, *Interview* magazine and *Empire* – a 24-hour movie of the Empire State Building (no commentary, no gorillas, nothing but the building). Died, oddly enough, after a routine gallstone operation.

WHITE Stanford (1853–1906) Partner of the architectural firm McKim, Mead and White, which designed such Neoclassical landmarks as the General Post Office, Washington Square Arch, the Municipal Building and parts of Columbia University.

index

and small print

Index

Map entries are in color

I INDEX

C

D

E

F

G

H

I

V

W

Y

Z

INDEX

Twenty Years of Rough Guides

In the summer of 1981, Mark Ellingham, Rough Guides' founder, knocked out the first guide on a typewriter, with a group of friends. Mark had been travelling in Greece after university, and couldn't find a guidebook that really answered his needs.There were heavyweight cultural guides on the one hand – good on museums and classical sites but not on beaches and tavernas – and on the other hand student manuals that were so caught up with how to save money that they lost sight of the country's significance beyond its role as a place for a cool vacation. None of the guides began to address Greece as a country, with its natural and human environment, its politics and its contemporary life.

Having no urgent reason to return home, Mark decided to write his own guide. It was a guide to Greece that tried to combine some erudition and insight with a thoroughly practical approach to travelers' needs. Scrupulously researched listings of places to stay, eat and drink were matched by careful attention to detail on everything from Homer to Greek music, from classical sites to national parks and from nude beaches to monasteries. Back in London, Mark and his friends got their Rough Guide accepted by a farsighted commissioning editor at the publisher Routledge and it came out in 1982.

The Rough Guide to Greece was a student scheme that became a publishing phenomenon. The immediate success of the book – shortlisted for the Thomas Cook award – spawned a series that rapidly covered dozens of countries. The Rough Guides found a ready market among backpackers and budget travelers, but soon acquired a much broader readership that included older and less impecunious visitors. Readers relished the guides' wit and inquisitiveness as much as the enthusiastic, critical approach that acknowledges that everyone wants value for money – but not at any price.

Rough Guides soon began supplementing the "rougher" information – the hostel and low-budget listings – with the kind of detail that independent-minded travelers on any budget might expect. These days, the guides – distributed worldwide by the Penguin group – include recommendations spanning the range from shoestring to luxury, and cover more than 200 destinations around the globe. Our growing team of authors, many of whom come to Rough Guides initially as outstandingly good letter-writers telling us about their travels, are spread all over the world, particularly in Europe, the USA and Australia. As well as the travel guides, Rough Guides publishes a series of dictionary phrasebooks covering two dozen major languages, an acclaimed series of music guides running the gamut from Classical to World Music, a series of music CDs in association with World Music Network, and a range of reference books on topics as diverse as the Internet, Pregnancy and Unexplained Phenomena. Visit **www.roughguides.com** to see what's cooking.

Rough Guide credits

Text editor: Richard Koss
Series editor: Mark Ellingham
Editorial: Martin Dunford, Jonathan Buckley, Jo Mead, Kate Berens, Ann-Marie Shaw, Helena Smith, Judith Bamber, Orla Duane, Olivia Eccleshall, Ruth Blackmore, Geoff Howard, Claire Saunders, Gavin Thomas, Alexander Mark Rogers, Polly Thomas, Joe Staines, Richard Lim, Duncan Clark, Peter Buckley, Lucy Ratcliffe, Clifton Wilkinson, Alison Murchie, Matthew Teller, Fran Sandham (UK); Andrew Rosenberg, Stephen Timblin, Yuki Takagaki, Hunter Slaton, Julie Feiner (US)
Production: Susanne Hillen, Andy Hilliard, Link Hall, Helen Prior, Julia Bovis, Michelle Draycott, Katie Pringle, Mike Hancock, Zoë Nobes, Rachel Holmes, Andy Turner
Cartography: Melissa Baker, Maxine Repath, Ed Wright, Katie Lloyd-Jones
Picture research: Louise Boulton, Sharon Martins, Mark Thomas
Online: Kelly Cross, Anja Mutić-Blessing, Jennifer Gold, Audra Epstein, Suzanne Welles, Cree Lawson (US)
Finance: John Fisher, Gary Singh, Edward Downey, Mark Hall, Tim Bill
Marketing & Publicity: Richard Trillo, Niki Smith, David Wearn, Chloë Roberts, Claire Southern, Demelza Dallow, (UK); Simon Carloss, David Wechsler, Kathleen Rushforth (US)
Administration: Tania Hummel, Julie Sanderson

Publishing information

This eighth edition published February 2002 by **Rough Guides Ltd**,
62–70 Shorts Gardens, London WC2H 9AH.
Penguin Putnam, Inc. 345 Hudson Street, NY 10014, USA.
Distributed by the Penguin Group
Penguin Books Ltd,
80 Strand, London WC2R ORL
Penguin Putnam, Inc.
345 Hudson Street, NY 10014, USA
Penguin Books Australia Ltd,
487 Maroondah Highway, PO Box 257, Ringwood, Victoria 3134, Australia
Penguin Books Canada Ltd,
10 Alcorn Avenue, Toronto, Ontario, Canada M4V 1E4
Penguin Books (NZ) Ltd,
182–190 Wairau Road, Auckland 10, New Zealand
Typeset in Bembo and Helvetica to an original design by Henry Iles.
Printed in Italy by LegoPrint S.p.A

544pp includes index
A catalogue record for this book is available from the British Library
ISBN 1-85828-716-2

Help us update

We've gone to a lot of effort to ensure that the eighth edition of **The Rough Guide to New York City** is accurate and up-to-date. However, things change – places get "discovered", opening hours are notoriously fickle, restaurants and rooms raise prices or lower standards. If you feel we've got it wrong or left something out, we'd like to know, and if you can remember the address, the price, the time, the phone number, so much the better.

We'll credit all contributions, and send a copy of the next edition (or any other Rough Guide if you prefer) for the best letters. Everyone who writes to us and isn't already a subscriber will receive a copy of our full-colour thrice-yearly newsletter. Please mark letters: "**Rough Guide New York City Update**" and send to: Rough Guides, 62–70 Shorts Gardens, London WC2H 9AH, or Rough Guides, 4th Floor, 345 Hudson St, New York, NY 10014. Or send an email to: **mail@roughguides.co.uk** or **mail@roughguides.com**

Acknowledgements

Nicky Agate offers praise to Kate and Damaris for the love (and phone line), Maguire for the lunchtime counseling, Jenny and Nick for support, and Spigot for barking when it hurt. Thanks also to everyone at Rough Guides.

Todd Obolsky would like to thank Mom, Dad, Suzanne and Billy Fishkin; Donna Metz, Elyse Topalian, Adele Gutman, Harold Anderson of the Schomburg Center and Victoria Barr; and Martin Dunford, Andrew Rosenberg and Richard Koss at Rough Guides.

Nelson Taylor would like to thank cheap eats pal Jeffrey Yamaguchi; his wife, Kelly Taylor; Joe Veltre and Neal Bascomb, who unknowingly helped in food and drink research; and to the editors of Rough Guides for giving an excuse to get to know the great city of New York so much better.

Heartfelt thanks go to Donald Young for his editorial assistance, Melissa Baker for her mapmaking expertise, Nicky Agate for the fine index, Diane Margolis for her diligent proofreading, Andrew Rosenberg and Martin Dunford for their astute guidance, Katie Pringle for her flawless production work and Zoë Nobes for the impeccable photo research. Thanks are due also to Darren Colby and Theresa Swink who together make New York feel so much like home.

Readers' letters

We'd like to thank all the readers who wrote in with comments and updates to the eighth edition: Julie Baker, John Bax, Teresa Deacon, Jennifer Estes, Will Fairclough, David Griffin, Edward Henry, Socrates Jimeñez, Russell Jones, Martin Lievers and Nerina Gnesutta, Nicholas Mace, Edward McLoughlin, P. Pozzi, Clive Roberts, Laura Rosenfield, June Sappe, Adam Schaye, Delia Secker-Walker, Jeanne Shubazz, Paul Smyth, Andel Singh, Lyn Stephens, Ian Turner and all the folks who contacted us via email but preferred to remain anonymous.

Photo Credits

Cover

Front (small top image) Chrysler Building © Robert Harding

Front (small bottom image) Brooklyn Bridge © Pictures Colour Library

Back (top) taxi © Robert Harding

Back (lower) Rockefeller Centre © Robert Harding

Color introduction

View of Central Park across lake © Gereint Tellem/Travel Ink

Waldorf Astoria hotel entrance © Lynn McDonnell/Travel Ink

Fast food stands © Abbie Enock/Travel Ink

Subway platform, NYC, Images Copyright © 1999 Photodisc.inc

Manhattan from Empire State Building © Jerry Dennis

Liberty Island, Statue of Liberty © E. Simanor/Axiom

Lobster Salad © Bob Krist/CORBIS

Bagels © Trevor Wood/Robert Harding

Things not to miss

Interior of Grand Central Station © Simon Harris/Robert Harding

Gotham Bar and Grill Interior © Kevin Fleming/CORBIS

The Unicorn Tapestries: Seventh Tapestry – The Unicorn in Captivity © Francis G. Mayer/CORBIS

Nathan's Hot Dogs, Coney Island © Peter Foley

Chrysler Building from the Empire State Building © Jerry Dennis

Brooklyn Bridge with sailing ship © Jerry Dennis

Cathedral of St John the Divine, Main Doorway © M. Barlow/Trip

Katz's Deli, New York © Jenny Acheson/Axiom

Radio City Music Hall © Jerry Dennis

New York Stock Exchange © Robert Harding

Jazz Band at the Knitting Factory © Kevin Fleming/CORBIS

Central Park looking south © Robert Harding

Chinatown © Abbie Enock/Travel Ink

New York Public Library, Lion at entrance © Lynn McDonnell/Travel Ink

Interior View of the Living Hall at the Frick Collection © The Frick Collection, New York. Photo: John Bigelow Taylor

Cheeses at Zabar's Deli/Grocery © Kevin Fleming/CORBIS

Rockefeller Center skating rink © NYC & Company

Yankee Stadium © Chris Bradley/Axiom

Macy's department store © David Cohen/Travel Ink

Ellis Island Immigration Museum © Jeremy Richards/Travel Ink

Metropolitan Museum of Art © Jerry Dennis

Fulton Fish Market © Peter Foley

"Mice" © 1988, Mariette Pathy Allen, used with permission of the Village Halloween Parade

The Bronx Zoo © Andrew Cowin/Travel Ink

Sylvia's Restaurant © Kevin Fleming/CORBIS

Empire State Building © Joe Beynon/Axiom

Strand Bookstore © Brendan Impson

Brooklyn Heights, The Promenade © Jerry Dennis

Poetry Reading at the Nuyorican Poets Café © Kevin Fleming/CORBIS

Lower East Side Tenement Museum Room © Kevin Fleming/CORBIS

Metropolitan Opera at the Lincoln Center © NYC & Company

Black and white Photos

Wall Street, Street Sign © TH-FOTO Werbung/Trip

Grace Church © M. Lee/Trip

Radio City Music Hall © Abbie Enock/Travel Ink

Ornate iron fire escapes on Upper West side building under archway © Abbie Enock/Travel Ink

Cyclone Rollercoaster, Coney Island © Peter Foley

Pretzels © Peter Foley

Martini Glass and Shaker © David Paler Photography

Cartier Building at Christmas © Viesti Associates/Trip

Wollman Rink, Central Park © NYC & Company

roughnews
WINTER 2001 · ISSUE 17 · Published by Rough Guides
Outback
David Leffman
India
Agra-phobia
Wired World
Rough Guide e-books
Letter from Nigeria
What corruption?
On the rails
Trains are special
ROUGH GUIDES

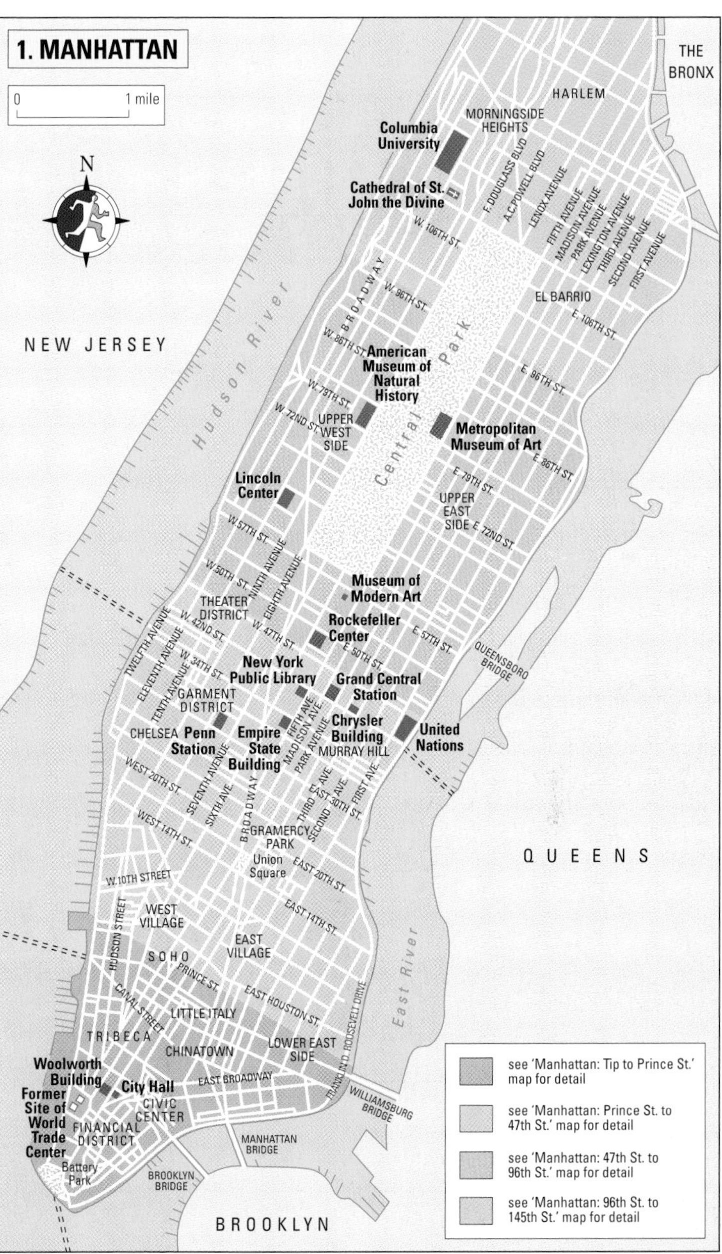
1. MANHATTAN
0
1 mile
N
NEW JERSEY
Hudson River
THE BRONX
HARLEM
MORNINGSIDE HEIGHTS
Columbia University
Cathedral of St. John the Divine
F. DOUGLASS BLVD
A.C.POWELL BLVD
LENOX AVENUE
FIFTH AVENUE
MADISON AVENUE
PARK AVENUE
LEXINGTON AVENUE
THIRD AVENUE
SECOND AVENUE
FIRST AVENUE
W. 106TH ST.
BROADWAY
W. 96TH ST.
EL BARRIO
E. 106TH ST.
W. 86TH ST.
American Museum of Natural History
Central Park
E. 96TH ST.
W. 79TH ST.
W. 72ND ST.
UPPER WEST SIDE
Metropolitan Museum of Art
E. 86TH ST.
Lincoln Center
E. 79TH ST.
UPPER EAST SIDE
E. 72ND ST.
W. 57TH ST.
NINTH AVENUE
EIGHTH AVENUE
W. 50TH ST.
Museum of Modern Art
THEATER DISTRICT
W. 47TH ST.
Rockefeller Center
E. 57TH ST.
TWELFTH AVENUE
W. 42ND ST.
E. 50TH ST.
QUEENSBORO BRIDGE
ELEVENTH AVENUE
W. 34TH ST.
New York Public Library
Grand Central Station
TENTH AVENUE
GARMENT DISTRICT
FIFTH AVE.
MADISON AVE.
Chrysler Building
United Nations
CHELSEA
Penn Station
Empire State Building
PARK AVENUE
MURRAY HILL
WEST 20TH ST.
SEVENTH AVENUE
THIRD AVE.
SECOND AVE.
FIRST AVE.
EAST 30TH ST.
SIXTH AVE.
WEST 14TH ST.
GRAMERCY PARK
Union Square
EAST 20TH ST.
QUEENS
W. 10TH STREET
WEST VILLAGE
HUDSON STREET
EAST 14TH ST.
EAST VILLAGE
East River
SOHO
PRINCE ST.
EAST HOUSTON ST.
CANAL STREET
LITTLE ITALY
FRANKLIN D. ROOSEVELT DRIVE
TRIBECA
CHINATOWN
LOWER EAST SIDE
Woolworth Building
City Hall
EAST BROADWAY
Former Site of World Trade Center
CIVIC CENTER
WILLIAMSBURG BRIDGE
FINANCIAL DISTRICT
MANHATTAN BRIDGE
Battery Park
BROOKLYN BRIDGE
BROOKLYN
see 'Manhattan: Tip to Prince St.' map for detail
see 'Manhattan: Prince St. to 47th St.' map for detail
see 'Manhattan: 47th St. to 96th St.' map for detail
see 'Manhattan: 96th St. to 145th St.' map for detail

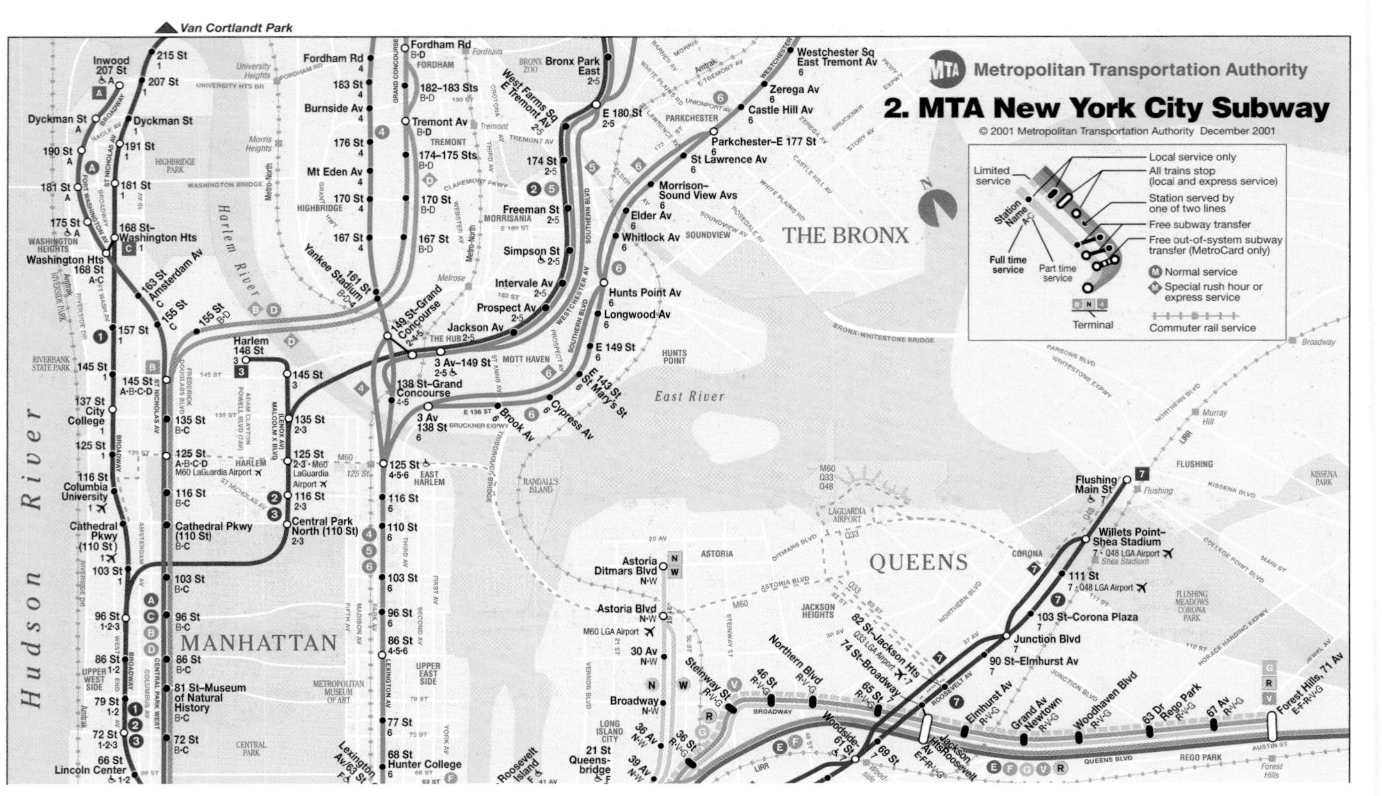

Metropolitan Transportation Authority
2. MTA New York City Subway
© 2001 Metropolitan Transportation Authority December 2001
Local service only
All trains stop (local and express service)
Station served by one of two lines
Free subway transfer
Free out-of-system subway transfer (MetroCard only)
Limited service
Station Name
Full time service
Part time service
Normal service
Special rush hour or express service
Terminal
Commuter rail service
Van Cortlandt Park
THE BRONX
QUEENS
MANHATTAN
Hudson River
Harlem River
East River
Inwood 207 St
215 St
207 St
Dyckman St
190 St
191 St
181 St
175 St
168 St–Washington Hts
Washington Hts 168 St
163 St Amsterdam Av
155 St
157 St
145 St
137 St City College
125 St
116 St Columbia University
Cathedral Pkwy (110 St)
103 St
96 St
86 St
81 St–Museum of Natural History
79 St
72 St
66 St Lincoln Center
Harlem 148 St
135 St
116 St
Central Park North (110 St)
Fordham Rd
183 St
Burnside Av
176 St
Mt Eden Av
170 St
167 St
161 St Yankee Stadium
182–183 Sts
Tremont Av
174–175 Sts
149 St–Grand Concourse
138 St–Grand Concourse
Bronx Park East
West Farms Sq E Tremont Av
E 180 St
174 St
Freeman St
Simpson St
Intervale Av
Prospect Av
Jackson Av
3 Av–149 St
3 Av 138 St
Brook Av
Cypress Av
E 143 St St Mary's St
E 149 St
Longwood Av
Hunts Point Av
Whitlock Av
Elder Av
Morrison–Sound View Avs
St Lawrence Av
Parkchester–E 177 St
Castle Hill Av
Zerega Av
Westchester Sq East Tremont Av
125 St
110 St
103 St
96 St
86 St
77 St
68 St Hunter College
Lexington Av/63 St
Roosevelt Island
21 St Queensbridge
Astoria Ditmars Blvd
Astoria Blvd
30 Av
Broadway
36 Av
39 Av
36 St
Steinway St
46 St
Northern Blvd
65 St
Woodside–61 St
69 St
74 St–Broadway
82 St–Jackson Hts
Jackson Hts Roosevelt Av
90 St–Elmhurst Av
Elmhurst Av
Grand Av Newtown
Junction Blvd
103 St–Corona Plaza
111 St
Willets Point–Shea Stadium
Flushing Main St
Woodhaven Blvd
63 Dr Rego Park
67 Av
Forest Hills, 71 Av
LAGUARDIA AIRPORT
RANDALL'S ISLAND

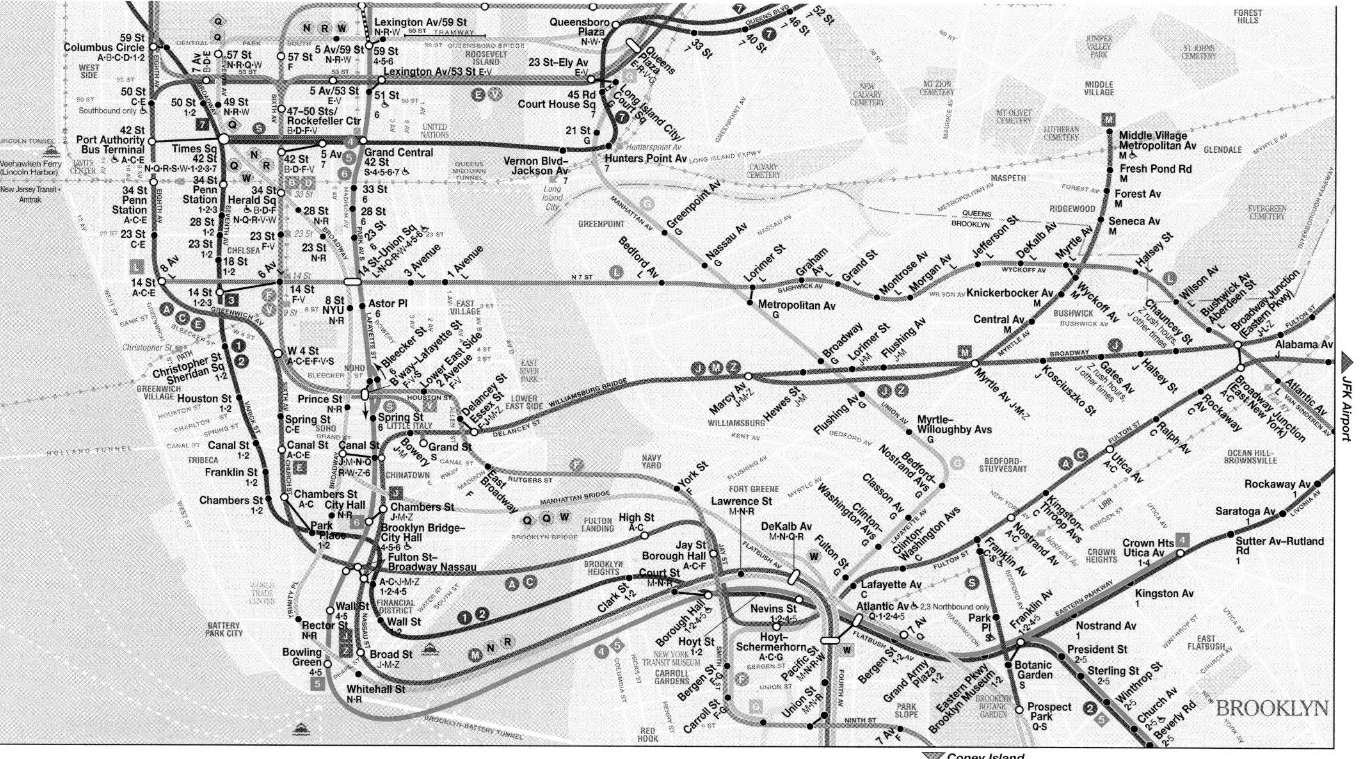

JFK Airport
Coney Island
BROOKLYN
59 St Columbus Circle A·B·C·D·1·2
50 St C·E Southbound only
42 St Port Authority Bus Terminal A·C·E
34 St Penn Station A·C·E
23 St C·E
14 St A·C·E
8 Av L
7 Av B·D·E
57 St N·R·Q·W
50 St 1·2
49 St N·R·W
Times Sq 42 St N·Q·R·S·W·1·2·3·7
34 St Penn Station 1·2·3
28 St 1·2
23 St 1·2
18 St 1·2
14 St 1·2·3
Christopher St Sheridan Sq 1·2
Houston St 1·2
Canal St 1·2
Franklin St 1·2
Chambers St 1·2
57 St F
47–50 Sts/Rockefeller Ctr B·D·F·V
42 St B·D·F·V
34 St Herald Sq B·D·F N·Q·R·V·W
23 St F·V
14 St F·V
6 Av L
W 4 St A·C·E·F·V·S
Spring St C·E
Canal St A·C·E
Chambers St A·C
Park Place 1·2
Rector St N·R
Bowling Green 4·5
Whitehall St N·R
Wall St 4·5
Wall St 1·2
Broad St J·M·Z
Fulton St–Broadway Nassau A·C·J·M·Z 1·2·4·5
Chambers St J·M·Z
Brooklyn Bridge–City Hall 4·5·6
City Hall N·R
Canal St J·M·N·Q R·W·Z·6
Prince St N·R
Spring St 6
Bleecker St 6
B'way–Lafayette St F·V·S
8 St NYU N·R
Astor Pl 6
14 St–Union Sq L·N·Q·R·W·4·5·6
23 St 6
28 St 6
33 St 6
23 St N·R
28 St N·R
5 Av 7
5 Av/53 St E·V
5 Av/59 St N·R·W
Lexington Av/59 St N·R·W
59 St 4·5·6
Lexington Av/53 St E·V
51 St 6
Grand Central 42 St S·4·5·6·7
3 Avenue L
1 Avenue L
Lower East Side 2 Avenue F·V
Delancey St Essex St F·J·M·Z
Grand St S
Bowery J·M
East Broadway F
Queensboro Plaza N·W·7
Queens Plaza E·R·V·G
Long Island City/Court Sq G·7
45 Rd Court House Sq 7
21 St G
23 St–Ely Av E·V
Vernon Blvd–Jackson Av 7
Hunters Point Av 7
33 St 7
40 St 7
46 St 7
52 St 7
Greenpoint Av G
Nassau Av G
Metropolitan Av G
Bedford Av L
Lorimer St L
Graham Av L
Grand St L
Montrose Av L
Morgan Av L
Jefferson St L
DeKalb Av L
Myrtle Av L
Halsey St L
Wilson Av L
Bushwick Av Aberdeen St L
Broadway Junction (Eastern Pkwy) J·L·Z
Atlantic Av L
Alabama Av J
Middle Village Metropolitan Av M
Fresh Pond Rd M
Forest Av M
Seneca Av M
Knickerbocker Av M
Central Av M
Wyckoff Av M
Myrtle Av J·M·Z
Chauncey St Z rush hours, J other times
Halsey St J
Gates Av Z rush hours, J other times
Kosciuszko St J
Flushing Av J·M
Lorimer St J·M
Hewes St J·M
Marcy Av J·M·Z
Broadway G
Flushing Av G
Myrtle–Willoughby Avs G
Bedford–Nostrand Avs G
Classon Av G
Clinton–Washington Avs G
Fulton St G
Broadway Junction (East New York) A·C
Rockaway Av C
Ralph Av C
Utica Av A·C
Kingston–Throop Avs C
Nostrand Av A·C
Franklin Av C·S
Clinton–Washington Avs C
Lafayette Av C
Atlantic Av Q·1·2·4·5 2,3 Northbound only
DeKalb Av M·N·Q·R
Lawrence St M·N·R
York St F
Jay St Borough Hall A·C·F
High St A·C
Court St M·N·R
Borough Hall 1·2·4·5
Clark St 1·2
Hoyt St 1·2
Nevins St 1·2·4·5
Hoyt–Schermerhorn A·C·G
Bergen St F·G
Carroll St F·G
Pacific St M·N·R·W
Union St M·N·R
7 Av Q
7 Av F
Bergen St 1·2
Grand Army Plaza 1·2
Eastern Pkwy Brooklyn Museum 1·2
Botanic Garden S
Park Pl S
Prospect Park Q·S
Franklin Av 1·2·4·5
Nostrand Av 1
Kingston Av 1
Crown Hts Utica Av 1·4
President St 2·5
Sterling St 2·5
Winthrop St 2·5
Church Av 2·5
Beverly Rd 2·5
Sutter Av–Rutland Rd 1
Saratoga Av 1
Rockaway Av 1
Weehawken Ferry (Lincoln Harbor)
New Jersey Transit · Amtrak

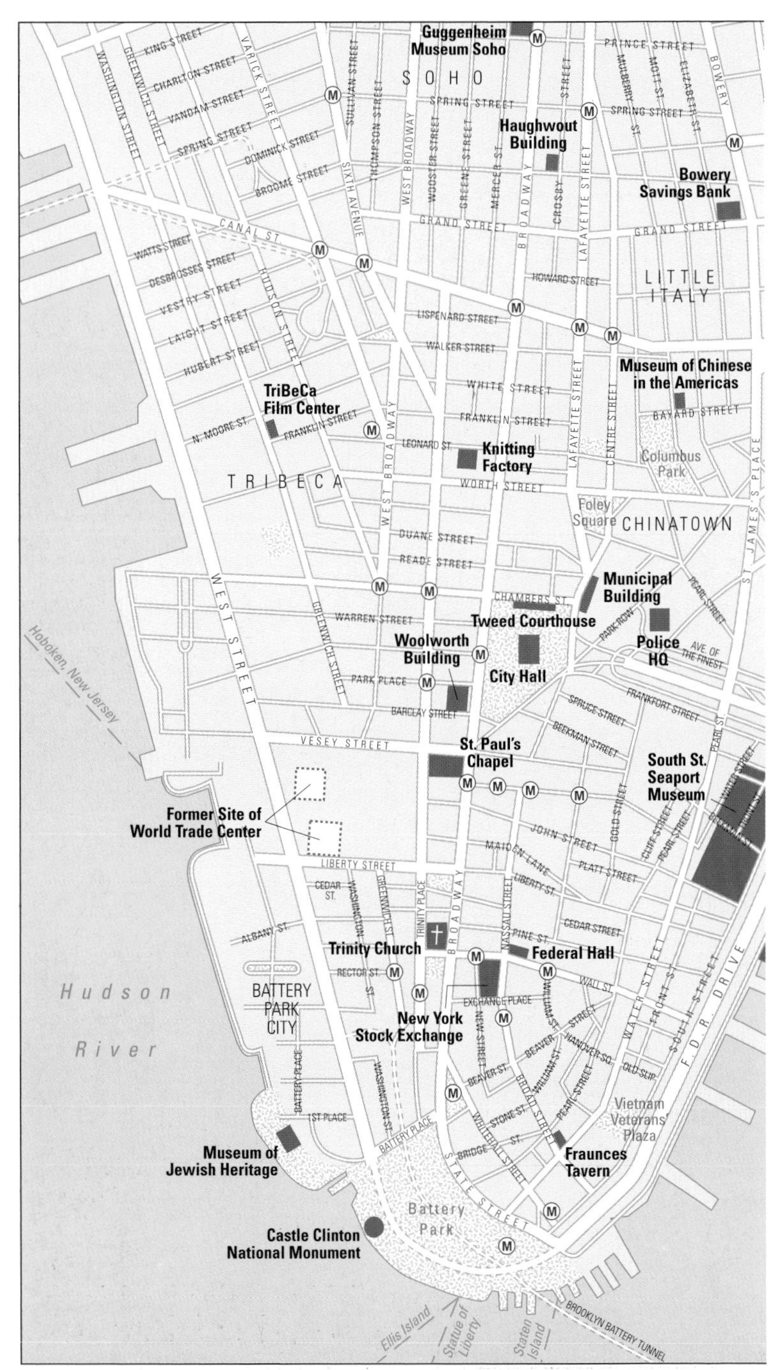
Guggenheim Museum Soho
SOHO
Haughwout Building
Bowery Savings Bank
LITTLE ITALY
Museum of Chinese in the Americas
TriBeCa Film Center
Knitting Factory
TRIBECA
Foley Square
CHINATOWN
Columbus Park
Municipal Building
Tweed Courthouse
Police HQ
Woolworth Building
City Hall
St. Paul's Chapel
South St. Seaport Museum
Former Site of World Trade Center
Trinity Church
Federal Hall
New York Stock Exchange
Hudson River
BATTERY PARK CITY
Vietnam Veterans' Plaza
Fraunces Tavern
Museum of Jewish Heritage
Battery Park
Castle Clinton National Monument
Hoboken, New Jersey
Ellis Island
Statue of Liberty
Staten Island
BROOKLYN BATTERY TUNNEL
KING STREET
CHARLTON STREET
VANDAM STREET
SPRING STREET
DOMINICK STREET
BROOME STREET
CANAL ST.
WATTS STREET
DESBROSSES STREET
VESTRY STREET
LAIGHT STREET
HUBERT STREET
N. MOORE ST.
FRANKLIN STREET
WASHINGTON STREET
GREENWICH STREET
VARICK STREET
HUDSON STREET
SULLIVAN STREET
THOMPSON STREET
SIXTH AVENUE
WEST BROADWAY
WOOSTER STREET
GREENE STREET
MERCER ST.
BROADWAY
CROSBY
LAFAYETTE STREET
PRINCE STREET
MULBERRY ST
MOTT ST
ELIZABETH ST
BOWERY
GRAND STREET
HOWARD STREET
LISPENARD STREET
WALKER STREET
WHITE STREET
LEONARD ST.
WORTH STREET
CENTRE STREET
BAYARD STREET
ST. JAMES'S PLACE
DUANE STREET
READE STREET
CHAMBERS ST.
WARREN STREET
PARK ROW
PEARL STREET
AVE OF THE FINEST
PARK PLACE
BARCLAY STREET
FRANKFORT STREET
SPRUCE STREET
BEEKMAN STREET
VESEY STREET
WEST STREET
JOHN STREET
MAIDEN LANE
GOLD STREET
CLIFF STREET
PLATT STREET
LIBERTY STREET
CEDAR ST.
CEDAR STREET
TRINITY PLACE
NASSAU STREET
PINE ST.
ALBANY ST.
RECTOR ST.
WALL ST.
EXCHANGE PLACE
WILLIAM ST.
NEW STREET
BEAVER ST.
HANOVER SQ.
OLD SLIP
WATER STREET
FRONT ST.
SOUTH STREET
F.D.R. DRIVE
BATTERY PLACE
1ST PLACE
STONE ST.
BROAD STREET
BRIDGE ST.
WHITEHALL STREET
STATE STREET

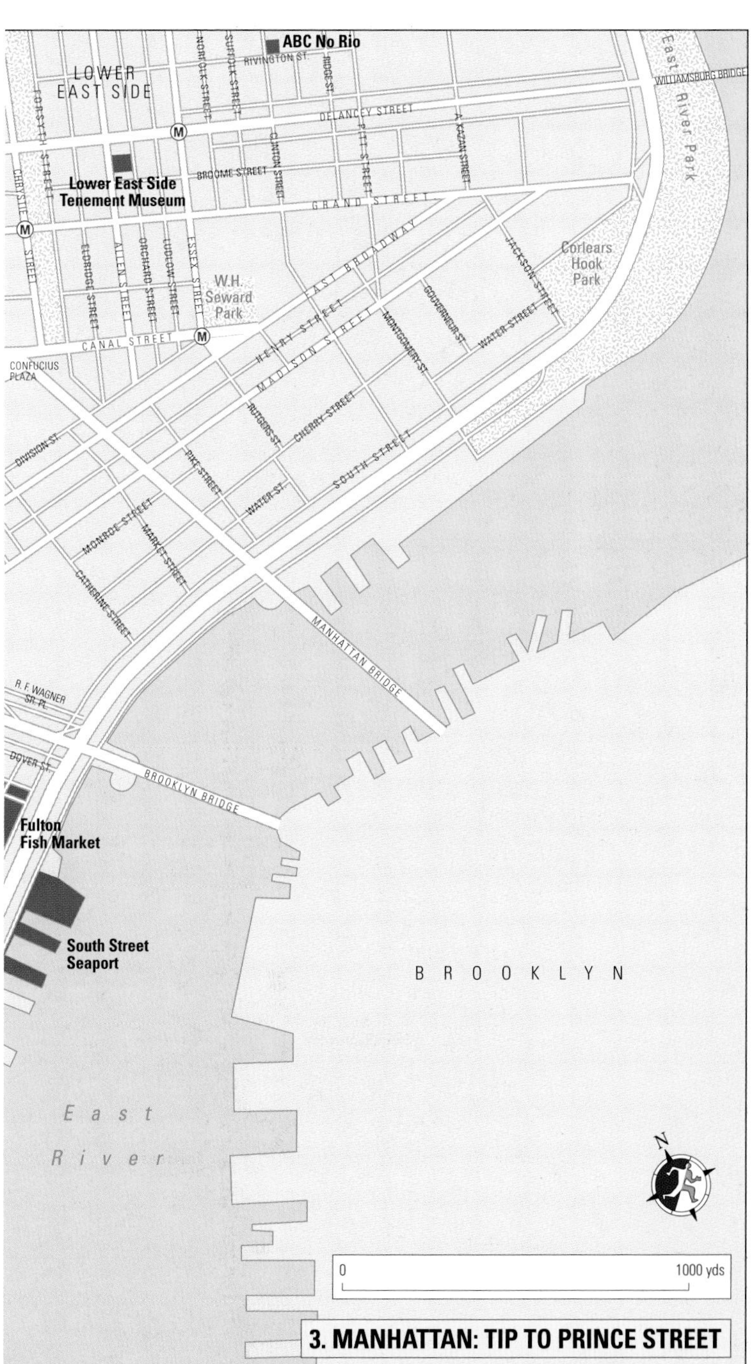

3. MANHATTAN: TIP TO PRINCE STREET

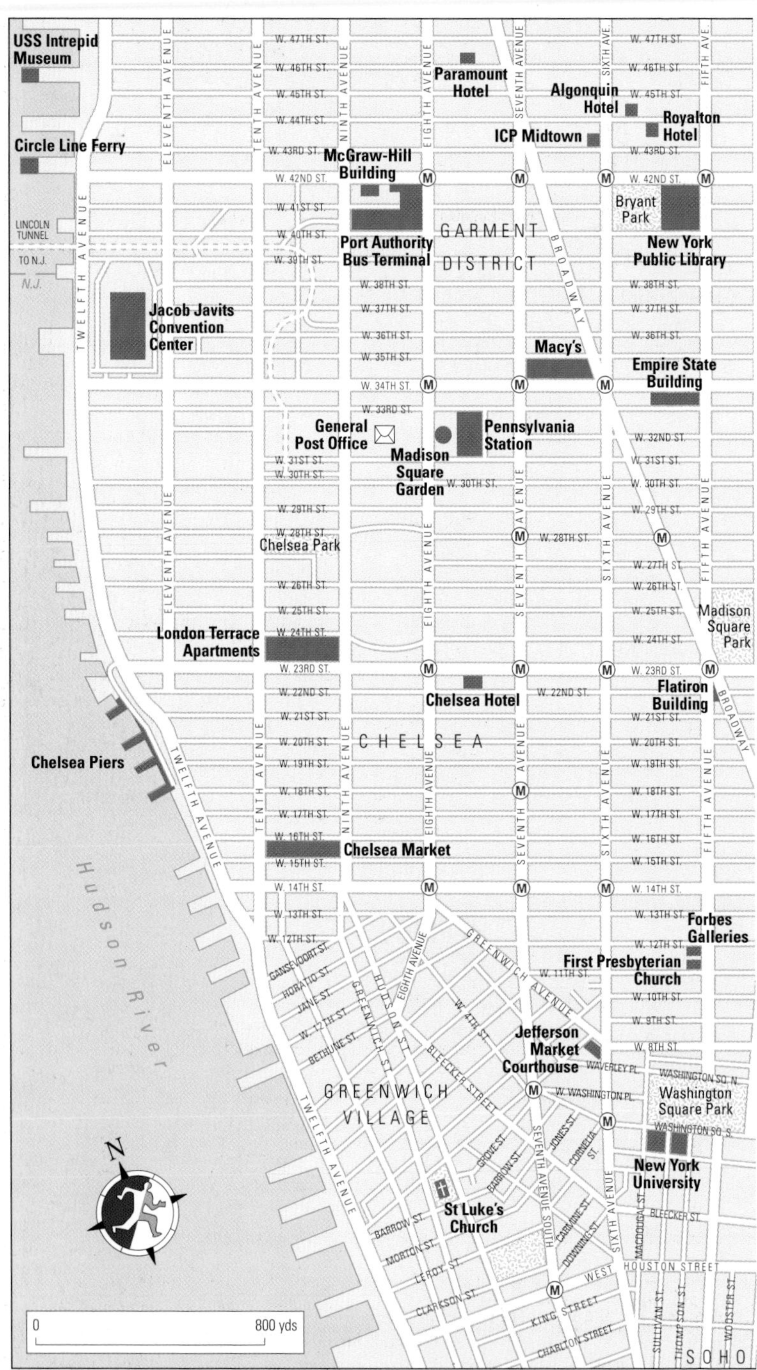

USS Intrepid Museum
Circle Line Ferry
Paramount Hotel
Algonquin Hotel
Royalton Hotel
ICP Midtown
McGraw-Hill Building
Bryant Park
New York Public Library
Port Authority Bus Terminal
GARMENT DISTRICT
LINCOLN TUNNEL
TO N.J.
N.J.
Jacob Javits Convention Center
Macy's
Empire State Building
General Post Office
Pennsylvania Station
Madison Square Garden
Chelsea Park
Madison Square Park
London Terrace Apartments
Flatiron Building
Chelsea Hotel
CHELSEA
Chelsea Piers
Chelsea Market
Hudson River
Forbes Galleries
First Presbyterian Church
Jefferson Market Courthouse
Washington Square Park
GREENWICH VILLAGE
New York University
St Luke's Church
SOHO
N
0
800 yds

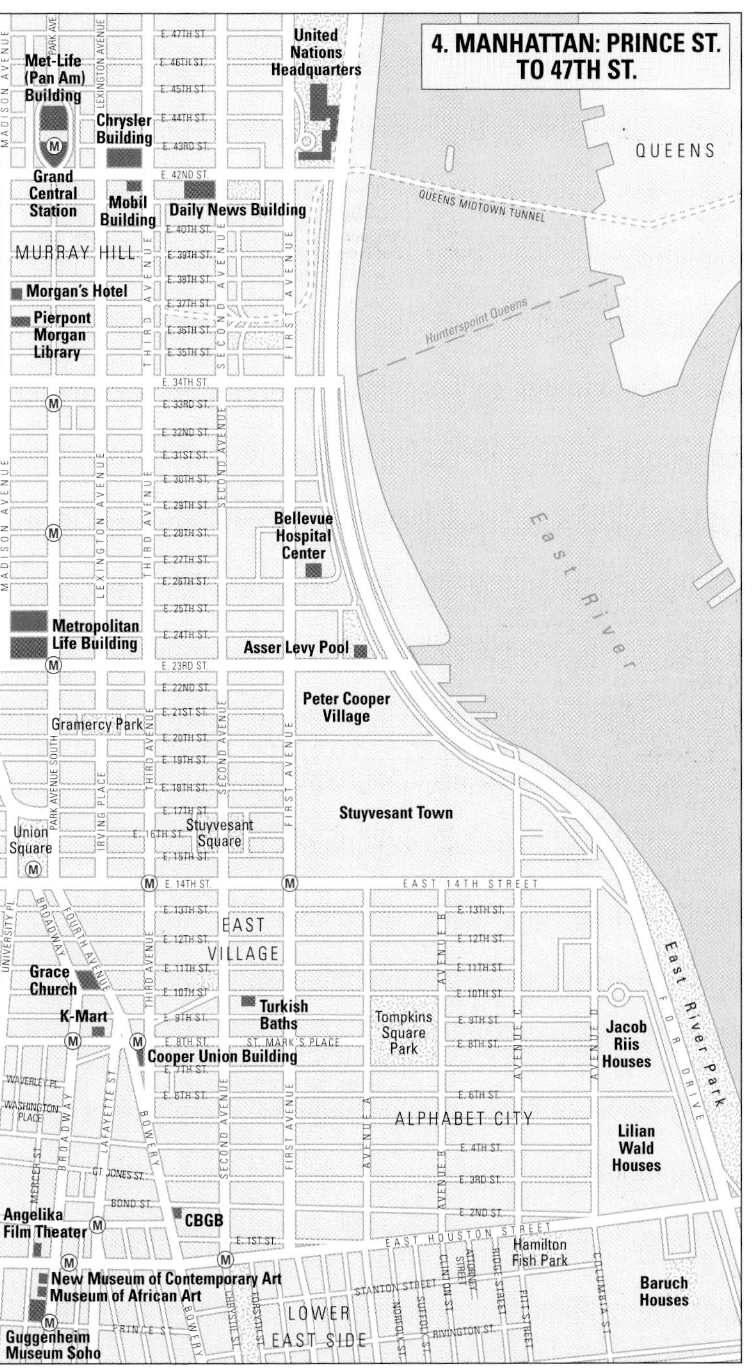
4. MANHATTAN: PRINCE ST. TO 47TH ST.
QUEENS
QUEENS MIDTOWN TUNNEL
Hunterspoint Queens
East River
United Nations Headquarters
Met-Life (Pan Am) Building
Chrysler Building
Grand Central Station
Mobil Building
Daily News Building
MURRAY HILL
Morgan's Hotel
Pierpont Morgan Library
Bellevue Hospital Center
Metropolitan Life Building
Asser Levy Pool
Peter Cooper Village
Gramercy Park
Stuyvesant Town
Union Square
Stuyvesant Square
EAST VILLAGE
Grace Church
K-Mart
Turkish Baths
Tompkins Square Park
Cooper Union Building
Jacob Riis Houses
East River Park
F.D.R. DRIVE
ALPHABET CITY
Lilian Wald Houses
Angelika Film Theater
CBGB
Hamilton Fish Park
New Museum of Contemporary Art
Museum of African Art
Baruch Houses
LOWER EAST SIDE
Guggenheim Museum Soho
MADISON AVENUE
PARK AVE
LEXINGTON AVENUE
THIRD AVENUE
SECOND AVENUE
FIRST AVENUE
PARK AVENUE SOUTH
IRVING PLACE
UNIVERSITY PL.
BROADWAY
FOURTH AVENUE
LAFAYETTE ST.
BOWERY
MERCER ST.
AVENUE A
AVENUE B
AVENUE C
AVENUE D
E. 47TH ST.
E. 46TH ST.
E. 45TH ST.
E. 44TH ST.
E. 43RD ST.
E. 42ND ST.
E. 40TH ST.
E. 39TH ST.
E. 38TH ST.
E. 37TH ST.
E. 36TH ST.
E. 35TH ST.
E. 34TH ST.
E. 33RD ST.
E. 32ND ST.
E. 31ST ST.
E. 30TH ST.
E. 29TH ST.
E. 28TH ST.
E. 27TH ST.
E. 26TH ST.
E. 25TH ST.
E. 24TH ST.
E. 23RD ST.
E. 22ND ST.
E. 21ST ST.
E. 20TH ST.
E. 19TH ST.
E. 18TH ST.
E. 17TH ST.
E. 16TH ST.
E. 15TH ST.
E. 14TH ST.
EAST 14TH STREET
E. 13TH ST.
E. 12TH ST.
E. 11TH ST.
E. 10TH ST.
E. 9TH ST.
E. 8TH ST.
ST. MARK'S PLACE
E. 7TH ST.
E. 6TH ST.
E. 4TH ST.
E. 3RD ST.
E. 2ND ST.
E. 1ST ST.
EAST HOUSTON STREET
WAVERLEY PL.
WASHINGTON PLACE
GT. JONES ST.
BOND ST.
PRINCE ST.
CHRYSTIE ST.
FORSYTH ST.
STANTON STREET
NORFOLK ST.
SUFFOLK ST.
CLINTON ST.
ATTORNEY STREET
RIDGE STREET
PITT STREET
COLUMBIA ST.
RIVINGTON ST.

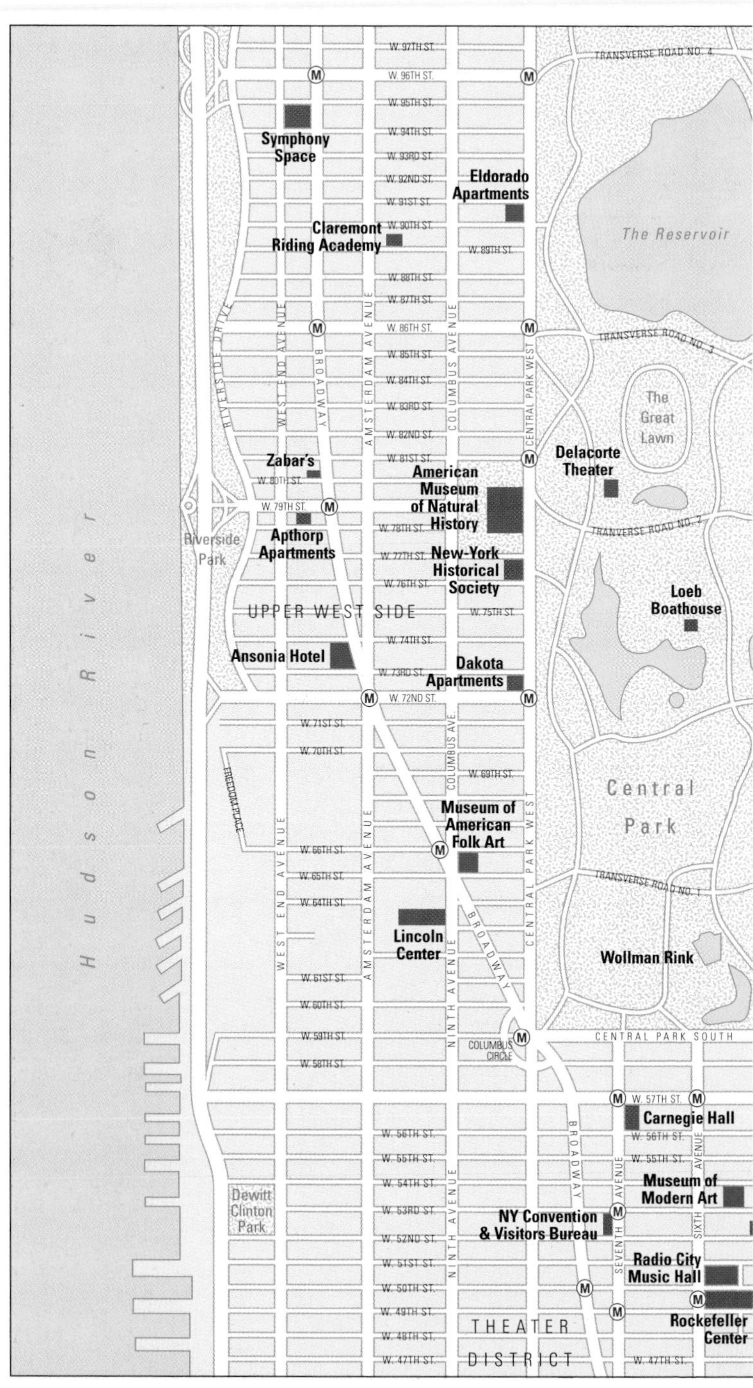
Symphony Space
Eldorado Apartments
Claremont Riding Academy
The Reservoir
The Great Lawn
Delacorte Theater
Zabar's
American Museum of Natural History
Apthorp Apartments
Riverside Park
New-York Historical Society
Loeb Boathouse
UPPER WEST SIDE
Ansonia Hotel
Dakota Apartments
Central Park
Museum of American Folk Art
Lincoln Center
Wollman Rink
Hudson River
Carnegie Hall
Museum of Modern Art
Dewitt Clinton Park
NY Convention & Visitors Bureau
Radio City Music Hall
Rockefeller Center
THEATER DISTRICT
COLUMBUS CIRCLE
CENTRAL PARK SOUTH
TRANSVERSE ROAD NO. 4
TRANSVERSE ROAD NO. 3
TRANVERSE ROAD NO. 2
TRANSVERSE ROAD NO. 1
RIVERSIDE DRIVE
WEST END AVENUE
BROADWAY
AMSTERDAM AVENUE
COLUMBUS AVENUE
COLUMBUS AVE.
CENTRAL PARK WEST
NINTH AVENUE
SEVENTH AVENUE
SIXTH AVENUE
FREEDOM PLACE
W. 97TH ST.
W. 96TH ST.
W. 95TH ST.
W. 94TH ST.
W. 93RD ST.
W. 92ND ST.
W. 91ST ST.
W. 90TH ST.
W. 89TH ST.
W. 88TH ST.
W. 87TH ST.
W. 86TH ST.
W. 85TH ST.
W. 84TH ST.
W. 83RD ST.
W. 82ND ST.
W. 81ST ST.
W. 80TH ST.
W. 79TH ST.
W. 78TH ST.
W. 77TH ST.
W. 76TH ST.
W. 75TH ST.
W. 74TH ST.
W. 73RD ST.
W. 72ND ST.
W. 71ST ST.
W. 70TH ST.
W. 69TH ST.
W. 66TH ST.
W. 65TH ST.
W. 64TH ST.
W. 61ST ST.
W. 60TH ST.
W. 59TH ST.
W. 58TH ST.
W. 57TH ST.
W. 56TH ST.
W. 55TH ST.
W. 54TH ST.
W. 53RD ST.
W. 52ND ST.
W. 51ST ST.
W. 50TH ST.
W. 49TH ST.
W. 48TH ST.
W. 47TH ST.

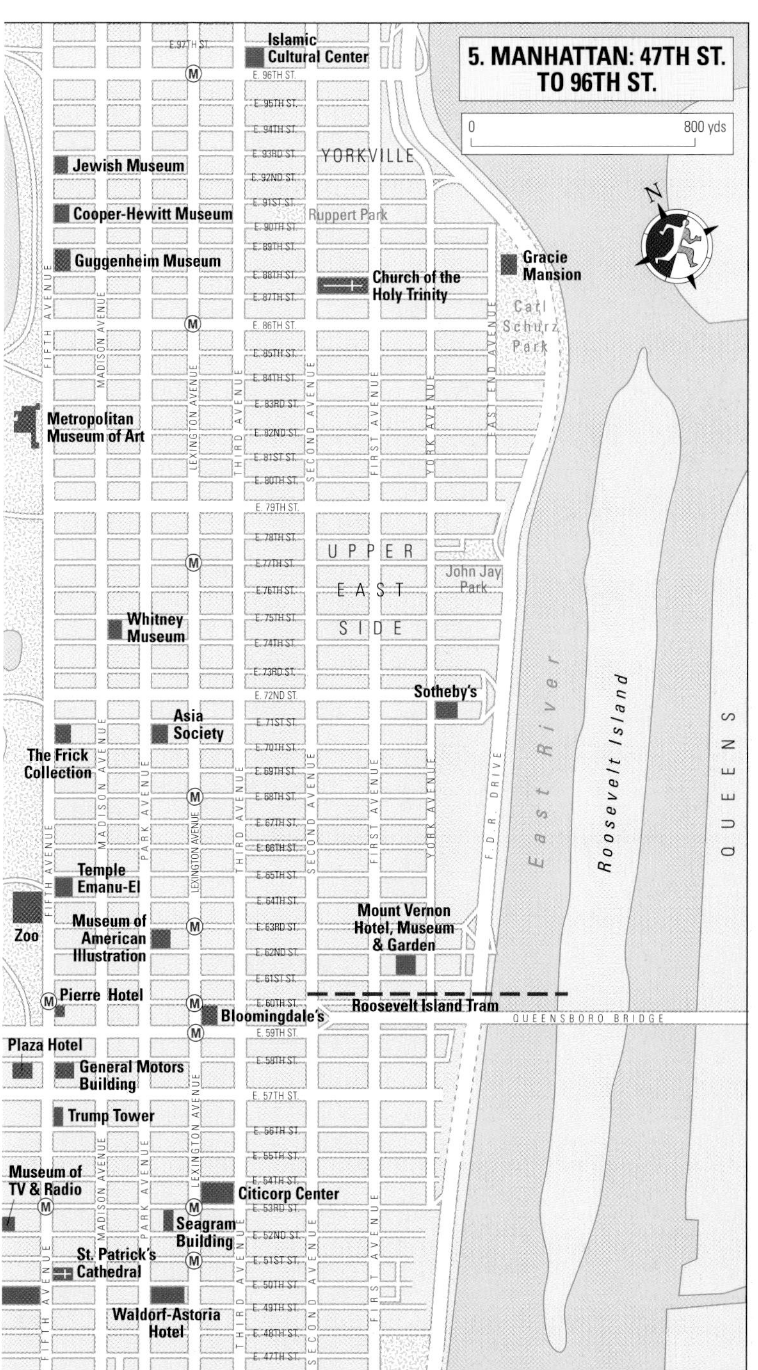

5. MANHATTAN: 47TH ST. TO 96TH ST.
0
800 yds
N
Islamic Cultural Center
Jewish Museum
Cooper-Hewitt Museum
Guggenheim Museum
YORKVILLE
Ruppert Park
Church of the Holy Trinity
Gracie Mansion
Carl Schurz Park
Metropolitan Museum of Art
UPPER EAST SIDE
John Jay Park
Whitney Museum
Sotheby's
Asia Society
The Frick Collection
Temple Emanu-El
Zoo
Museum of American Illustration
Mount Vernon Hotel, Museum & Garden
Pierre Hotel
Bloomingdale's
Roosevelt Island Tram
QUEENSBORO BRIDGE
Plaza Hotel
General Motors Building
Trump Tower
Museum of TV & Radio
Citicorp Center
Seagram Building
St. Patrick's Cathedral
Waldorf-Astoria Hotel
East River
Roosevelt Island
QUEENS
FIFTH AVENUE
MADISON AVENUE
PARK AVENUE
LEXINGTON AVENUE
THIRD AVENUE
SECOND AVENUE
FIRST AVENUE
YORK AVENUE
EAST END AVENUE
F. D. R. DRIVE
E. 97TH ST.
E. 96TH ST.
E. 95TH ST.
E. 94TH ST.
E. 93RD ST.
E. 92ND ST.
E. 91ST ST.
E. 90TH ST.
E. 89TH ST.
E. 88TH ST.
E. 87TH ST.
E. 86TH ST.
E. 85TH ST.
E. 84TH ST.
E. 83RD ST.
E. 82ND ST.
E. 81ST ST.
E. 80TH ST.
E. 79TH ST.
E. 78TH ST.
E. 77TH ST.
E. 76TH ST.
E. 75TH ST.
E. 74TH ST.
E. 73RD ST.
E. 72ND ST.
E. 71ST ST.
E. 70TH ST.
E. 69TH ST.
E. 68TH ST.
E. 67TH ST.
E. 66TH ST.
E. 65TH ST.
E. 64TH ST.
E. 63RD ST.
E. 62ND ST.
E. 61ST ST.
E. 60TH ST.
E. 59TH ST.
E. 58TH ST.
E. 57TH ST.
E. 56TH ST.
E. 55TH ST.
E. 54TH ST.
E. 53RD ST.
E. 52ND ST.
E. 51ST ST.
E. 50TH ST.
E. 49TH ST.
E. 48TH ST.
E. 47TH ST.

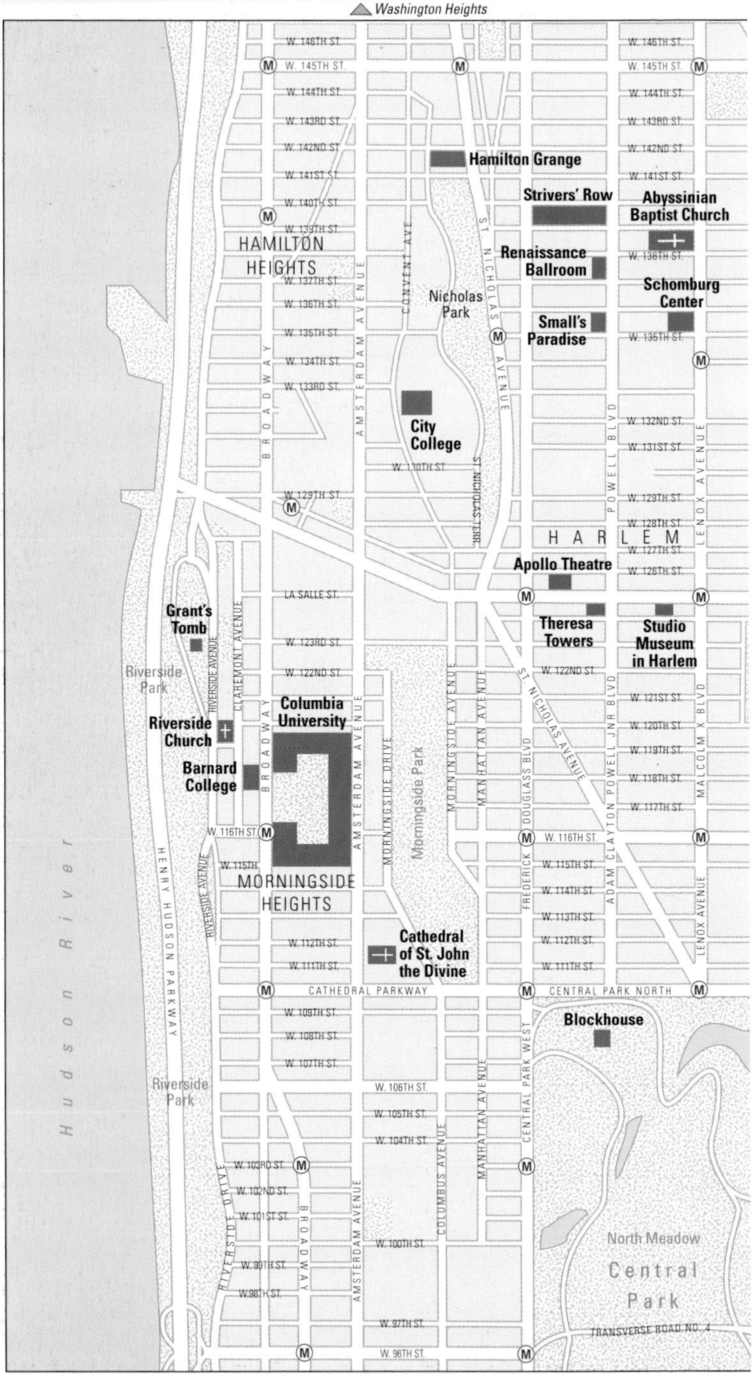

Washington Heights

W. 146TH ST.
W. 145TH ST.
W. 144TH ST.
W. 143RD ST.
W. 142ND ST.
W. 141ST ST.
W. 140TH ST.
W. 139TH ST.
W. 138TH ST.
W. 137TH ST.
W. 136TH ST.
W. 135TH ST.
W. 134TH ST.
W. 133RD ST.
W. 132ND ST.
W. 131ST ST.
W. 130TH ST.
W. 129TH ST.
W. 128TH ST.
W. 127TH ST.
W. 126TH ST.
LA SALLE ST.
W. 123RD ST.
W. 122ND ST.
W. 121ST ST.
W. 120TH ST.
W. 119TH ST.
W. 118TH ST.
W. 117TH ST.
W. 116TH ST.
W. 115TH ST.
W. 114TH ST.
W. 113TH ST.
W. 112TH ST.
W. 111TH ST.
CATHEDRAL PARKWAY
CENTRAL PARK NORTH
W. 109TH ST.
W. 108TH ST.
W. 107TH ST.
W. 106TH ST.
W. 105TH ST.
W. 104TH ST.
W. 103RD ST.
W. 102ND ST.
W. 101ST ST.
W. 100TH ST.
W. 99TH ST.
W. 98TH ST.
W. 97TH ST.
W. 96TH ST.
TRANSVERSE ROAD NO. 4

HAMILTON HEIGHTS
MORNINGSIDE HEIGHTS
HARLEM

Hamilton Grange
Strivers' Row
Abyssinian Baptist Church
Renaissance Ballroom
Schomburg Center
Nicholas Park
Small's Paradise
City College
Apollo Theatre
Theresa Towers
Studio Museum in Harlem
Grant's Tomb
Riverside Park
Riverside Church
Columbia University
Barnard College
Morningside Park
Cathedral of St. John the Divine
Blockhouse
North Meadow
Central Park
Hudson River

BROADWAY
AMSTERDAM AVENUE
CONVENT AVE.
ST. NICHOLAS AVENUE
ST. NICHOLAS TERR.
POWELL BLVD
LENOX AVENUE
RIVERSIDE AVENUE
CLAREMONT AVENUE
MORNINGSIDE DRIVE
MORNINGSIDE AVENUE
MANHATTAN AVENUE
FREDERICK DOUGLASS BLVD
ADAM CLAYTON POWELL JNR BLVD
MALCOLM X BLVD
HENRY HUDSON PARKWAY
RIVERSIDE DRIVE
COLUMBUS AVENUE
CENTRAL PARK WEST

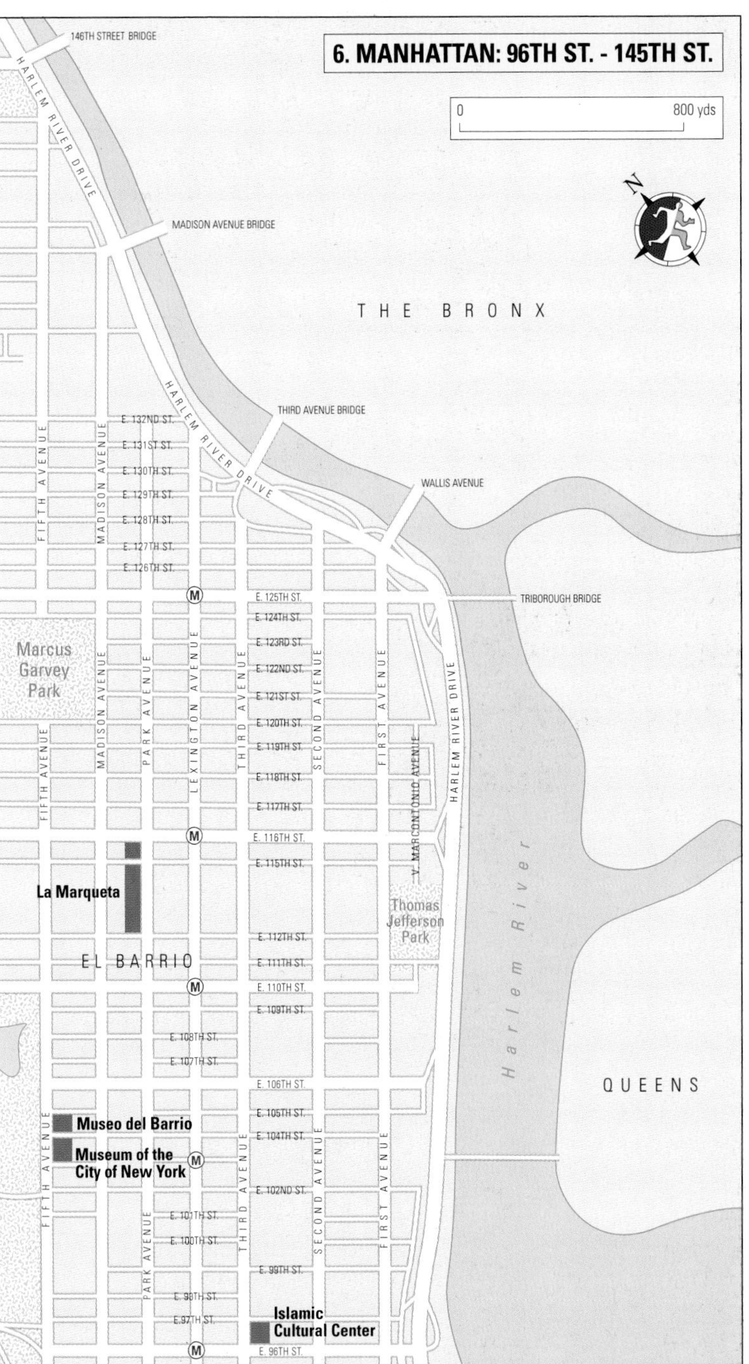
6. MANHATTAN: 96TH ST. - 145TH ST.
0
800 yds
146TH STREET BRIDGE
HARLEM RIVER DRIVE
MADISON AVENUE BRIDGE
THE BRONX
THIRD AVENUE BRIDGE
WALLIS AVENUE
TRIBOROUGH BRIDGE
E. 132ND ST.
E. 131ST ST.
E. 130TH ST.
E. 129TH ST.
E. 128TH ST.
E. 127TH ST.
E. 126TH ST.
E. 125TH ST.
E. 124TH ST.
E. 123RD ST.
E. 122ND ST.
E. 121ST ST.
E. 120TH ST.
E. 119TH ST.
E. 118TH ST.
E. 117TH ST.
E. 116TH ST.
E. 115TH ST.
E. 112TH ST.
E. 111TH ST.
E. 110TH ST.
E. 109TH ST.
E. 108TH ST.
E. 107TH ST.
E. 106TH ST.
E. 105TH ST.
E. 104TH ST.
E. 102ND ST.
E. 101TH ST.
E. 100TH ST.
E. 99TH ST.
E. 98TH ST.
E. 97TH ST.
E. 96TH ST.
FIFTH AVENUE
MADISON AVENUE
PARK AVENUE
LEXINGTON AVENUE
THIRD AVENUE
SECOND AVENUE
FIRST AVENUE
V. MARCONTONIO AVENUE
Marcus Garvey Park
La Marqueta
EL BARRIO
Thomas Jefferson Park
Harlem River
QUEENS
Museo del Barrio
Museum of the City of New York
Islamic Cultural Center

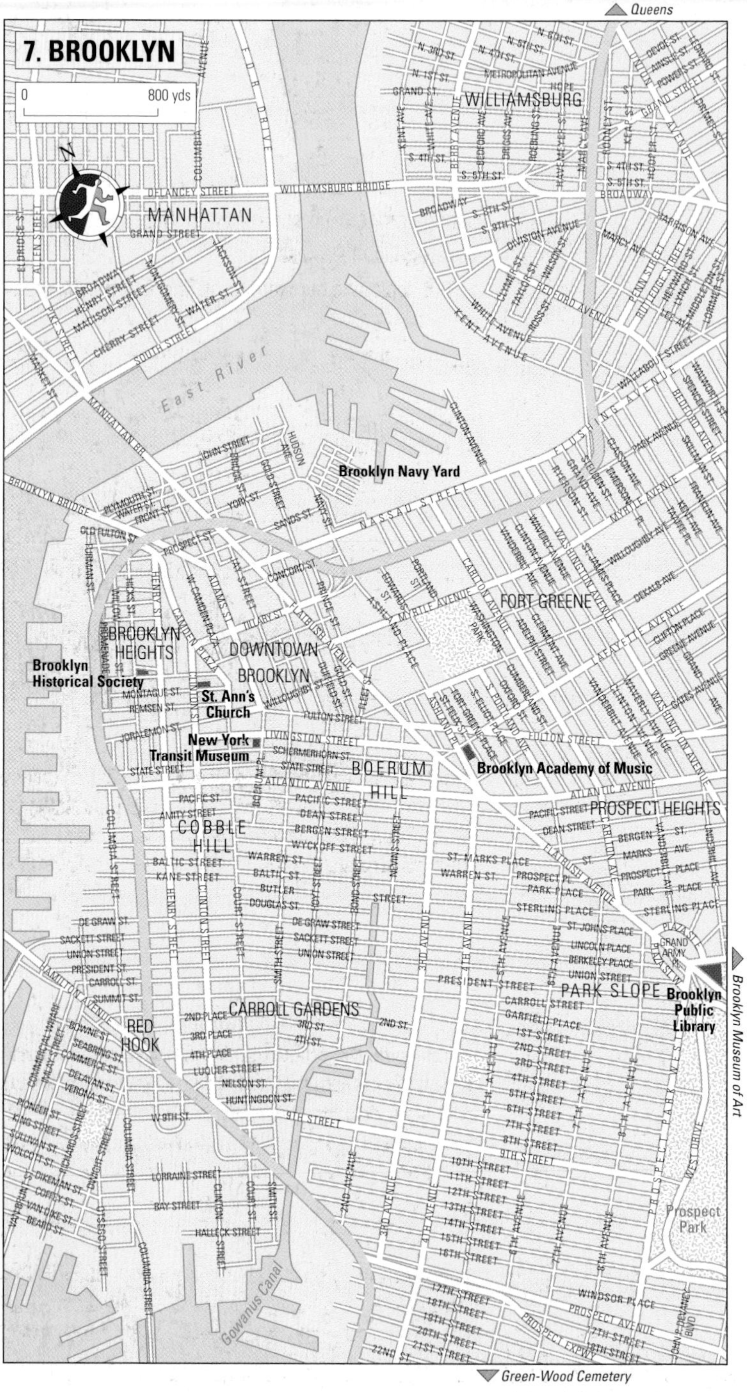
7. BROOKLYN
0
800 yds
N
Queens
MANHATTAN
WILLIAMSBURG
East River
Brooklyn Navy Yard
FORT GREENE
BROOKLYN HEIGHTS
DOWNTOWN BROOKLYN
Brooklyn Historical Society
St. Ann's Church
New York Transit Museum
BOERUM HILL
Brooklyn Academy of Music
PROSPECT HEIGHTS
COBBLE HILL
CARROLL GARDENS
PARK SLOPE
Brooklyn Public Library
Brooklyn Museum of Art
RED HOOK
Prospect Park
Gowanus Canal
WILLIAMSBURG BRIDGE
MANHATTAN BR.
BROOKLYN BRIDGE
FLATBUSH AVENUE
ATLANTIC AVENUE
FULTON STREET
PROSPECT EXPWY
Green-Wood Cemetery